C000255450

PHILIP'S

STREET ATLAS

Norfolk

First published in 2003 by

Philip's, a division of
Octopus Publishing Group Ltd
2-4 Heron Quays, London E14 4JP

Second edition 2006
First impression 2006
NORBA

ISBN-10   0-540-08958-3 (spiral)
ISBN-13   978-0-540-08958-1 (spiral)

© Philip's 2006

OS Ordnance Survey®

This product includes mapping data licensed
from Ordnance Survey® with the permission of
the Controller of Her Majesty's Stationery Office.
© Crown copyright 2006. All rights reserved.
Licence number 100011710.

Contents

III   **Key to map symbols**

IV   **Key to map pages**

VI   **Route planning**

X   **Administrative and Postcode boundaries**

1   **Street maps** at 1¾ inches to 1 mile

132   **Street maps** at 3½ inches to 1 mile

178   **Street map of Norwich city centre** at 7 inches to 1 mile

179   **Index** of towns and villages

182   **Index** of streets, hospitals, industrial estates, railway stations, schools, shopping centres, universities and places of interest

Digital Data

The exceptionally high-quality mapping found in this atlas is available as digital data in TIFF format, which is easily convertible to other bitmapped (raster) image formats.

The index is also available in digital form as a standard database table. It contains all the details found in the printed index together with the National Grid reference for the map square in which each entry is named.

For further information and to discuss your requirements, please contact Philip's on 020 7644 6932 or james.mann@philips-maps.co.uk

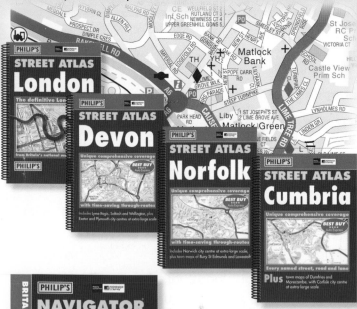

Symbol	Description
	Motorway with junction number
	Primary route – dual/single carriageway
	A road – dual/single carriageway
	B road – dual/single carriageway
	Minor road – dual/single carriageway
	Other minor road – dual/single carriageway
	Road under construction
	Tunnel, covered road
	Rural track, private road or narrow road in urban area
	Gate or obstruction to traffic (restrictions may not apply at all times or to all vehicles)
	Path, bridleway, byway open to all traffic, road used as a public path
	Pedestrianised area
DY7	**Postcode boundaries**
	County and unitary authority boundaries
	Railway, tunnel, railway under construction
	Tramway, tramway under construction
	Miniature railway
Walsall	**Railway station**
	Private railway station
South Shields	**Metro station**
	Tram stop, tram stop under construction
	Bus, coach station

Symbol	Description
	Ambulance station
	Coastguard station
	Fire station
	Police station
	Accident and Emergency entrance to hospital
H	**Hospital**
	Place of worship
i	**Information Centre** (open all year)
	Shopping Centre
P P&R	**Parking, Park and Ride**
PO	**Post Office**
	Camping site, caravan site
	Golf course
	Picnic site
Prim Sch	**Important buildings, schools, colleges, universities and hospitals**
	Built up area
	Woods
River Ouse	**Tidal water, water name**
	Non-tidal water – lake, river, canal or stream
	Lock, weir, tunnel
Church	**Non-Roman antiquity**
ROMAN FORT	**Roman antiquity**
87	**Adjoining page indicators and overlap bands** The colour of the arrow and the band indicates the scale of the adjoining or overlapping page (see scales below)
246	

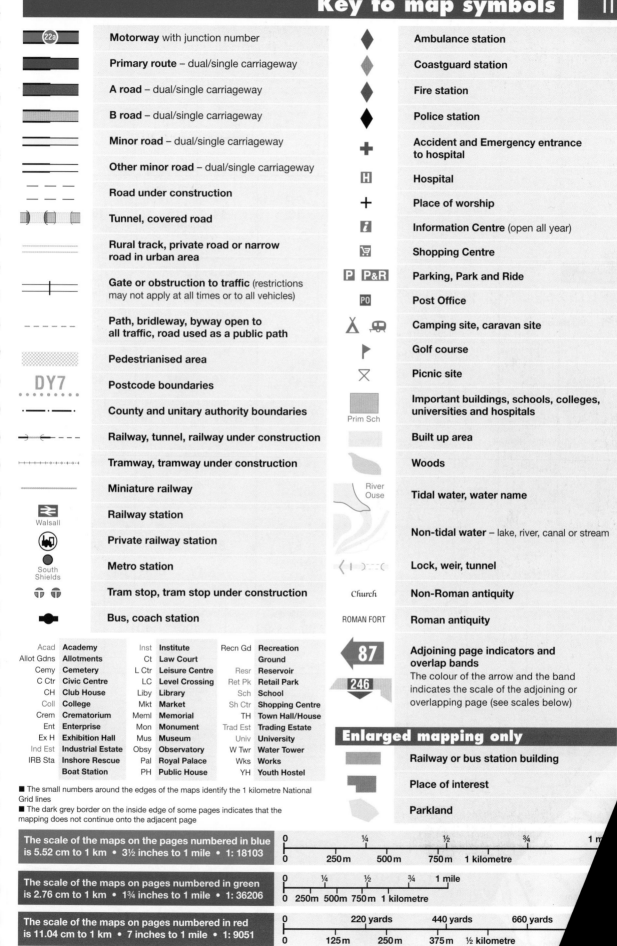

Enlarged mapping only

Symbol	Description
	Railway or bus station building
	Place of interest
	Parkland

Acad	**Academy**	Inst	**Institute**	Recn Gd	**Recreation Ground**
Allot Gdns	**Allotments**	Ct	**Law Court**		
Cemy	**Cemetery**	L Ctr	**Leisure Centre**	Resr	**Reservoir**
C Ctr	**Civic Centre**	LC	**Level Crossing**	Ret Pk	**Retail Park**
CH	**Club House**	Liby	**Library**	Sch	**School**
Coll	**College**	Mkt	**Market**	Sh Ctr	**Shopping Centre**
Crem	**Crematorium**	Meml	**Memorial**	TH	**Town Hall/House**
Ent	**Enterprise**	Mon	**Monument**	Trad Est	**Trading Estate**
Ex H	**Exhibition Hall**	Mus	**Museum**	Univ	**University**
Ind Est	**Industrial Estate**	Obsy	**Observatory**	W Twr	**Water Tower**
IRB Sta	**Inshore Rescue Boat Station**	Pal	**Royal Palace**	Wks	**Works**
		PH	**Public House**	YH	**Youth Hostel**

■ The small numbers around the edges of the maps identify the 1 kilometre National Grid lines
■ The dark grey border on the inside edge of some pages indicates that the mapping does not continue onto the adjacent page

The scale of the maps on the pages numbered in blue is 5.52 cm to 1 km • 3½ inches to 1 mile • 1: 18103

0	¼	½	¾	1 m
0	250 m	500 m	750 m	1 kilometre

The scale of the maps on pages numbered in green is 2.76 cm to 1 km • 1¾ inches to 1 mile • 1: 36206

0	¼	½	¾	1 mile
0	250m 500m 750m	1 kilometre		

The scale of the maps on pages numbered in red is 11.04 cm to 1 km • 7 inches to 1 mile • 1: 9051

0	220 yards	440 yards	660 yards
0	125m	250m 375m	½ kilometre

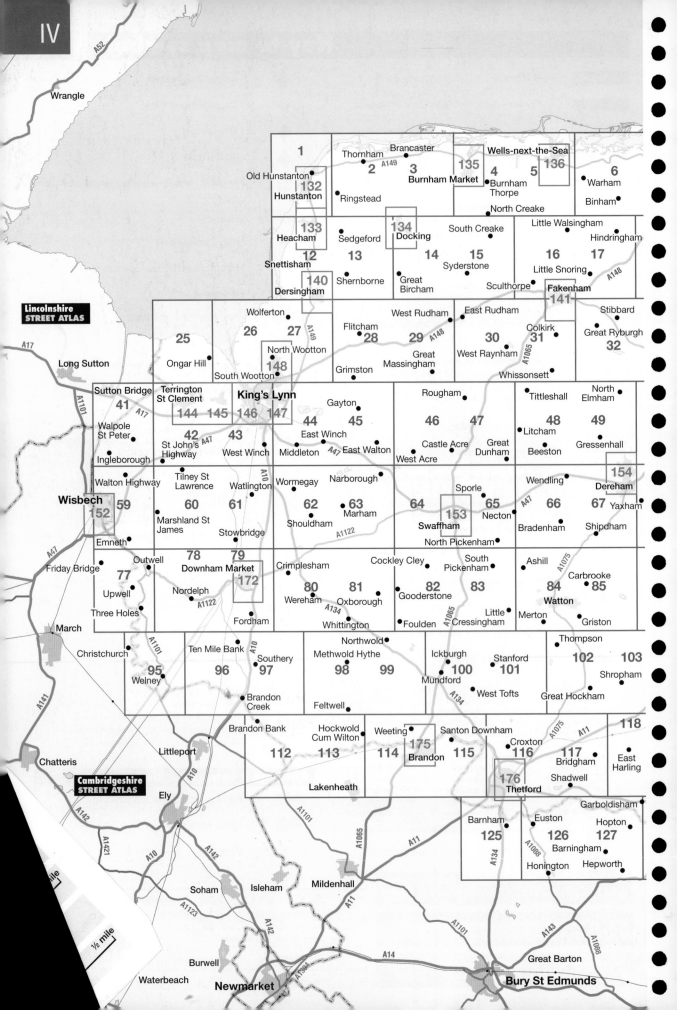

Key to map pages

178 — Map pages at 7 inches to 1 mile

139 — Map pages at 3½ inches to 1 mile

41 — Map pages at 1¾ inches to 1 mile

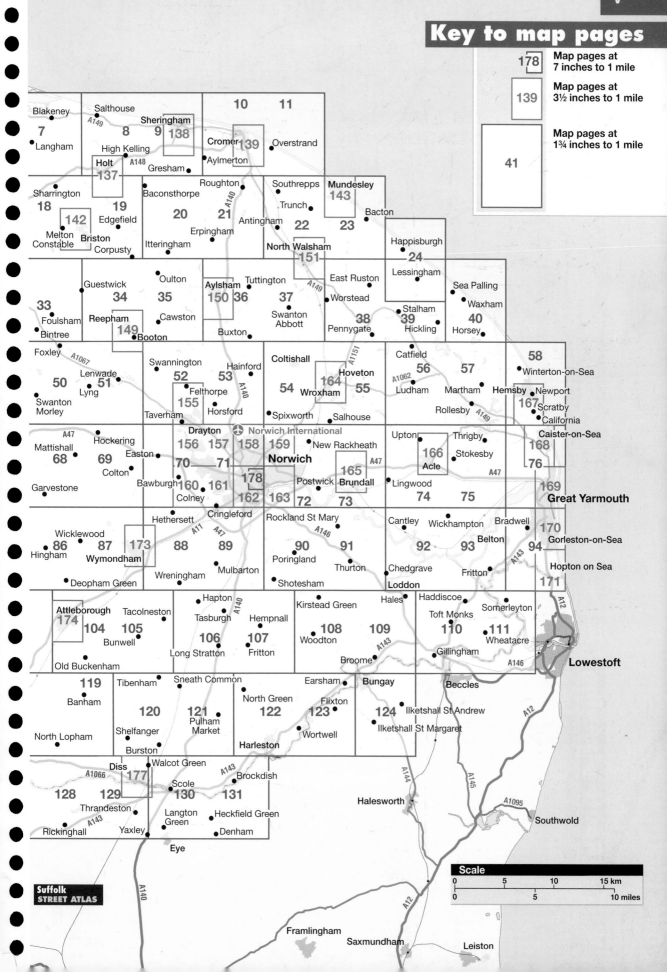

Blakeney
7
Langham
Salthouse A149
8 Sheringham **9** 138
High Kelling
Holt A148 Gresham
137
10 **11**
Cromer **139** Overstrand
Aylmerton

Sharrington
18
142
Melton Constable
Briston
Corpusty
Edgefield
19
20
Baconsthorpe
Itteringham
Roughton A140
21
Erpingham
Antingham
Southrepps
143 Mundesley
Trunch
22 **23** Bacton
Happisburgh
North Walsham
151
24 Lessingham

Guestwick
33
Foulsham
Bintree
34
Reepham
149 Booton
Oulton
35
Cawston
Aylsham
150 **36**
Buxton
Tuttington
37
Swanton Abbott
East Ruston
Worstead
38
Pennygate
Stalham
39
Hickling
Sea Palling
Waxham
40
Horsey

Foxley
A1067
50
Swanton Morley
Lenwade
51
Lyng
Swannington
52
Felthorpe
155
Taverham
Hainford
53
Horsford
Coltishall
54 Wroxham
164 Hoveton
55
Spixworth
Salhouse
Catfield
A1062 **56**
Ludham
57
Martham
Rollesby
58
Winterton-on-Sea
Hemsby
167 Newport
Scratby
California

Mattishall
A47
68
Hockering
Easton
69
Colton
Drayton
156 **157**
70 **71**
Bawburgh
Colney
Norwich International
158 **159**
New Rackheath
Norwich
160 **161**
178
162 **163**
Postwick
72
Upton
166 Thrigby
Acle Stokesby
Lingwood
74
Brundall
165
73
A47
75
Caister-on-Sea
168
76
169
Great Yarmouth

Garvestone
Wicklewood
86
Hingham
87
Wymondham
173
Hethersett
A11 A47
88
Wreningham
Mulbarton
89
Cringleford
Rockland St Mary
A146
90
Poringland
Shotesham
91
Thurton
Cantley
Wickhampton
Chedgrave
Loddon
92
Bradwell
Belton
93
Fritton
A143
94
Gorleston-on-Sea
Hopton on Sea
170
171
Lowestoft

Attleborough
174
104 **105**
Bunwell
Old Buckenham
Hapton A140
Tacolneston
Tasburgh
Hempnall
106 **107**
Long Stratton Fritton
Kirstead Green
108 **109**
Woodton
Broome A143
Hales
Haddiscoe
Toft Monks
110 **111**
Wheatacre
Somerleyton
A12

119
Banham
North Lopham
Tibenham
120
Shelfanger
Burston
Sneath Common
121
Pulham Market
North Green
122
Harleston
Wortwell
Earsham
123
Flixton
Bungay
124
Ilketshall St Andrew
Ilketshall St Margaret
Beccles
A144
A145
A146

Diss
A1066
177
128 **129**
Thrandeston
Rickinghall A143
Yaxley
Eye
Walcot Green
A143
Scole
130
Langton Green
Denham
131
Heckfield Green
Brockdish
A140
Halesworth
A1095
Southwold

Scale
0 5 10 15 km
0 5 10 miles

Framlingham
Saxmundham
Leiston

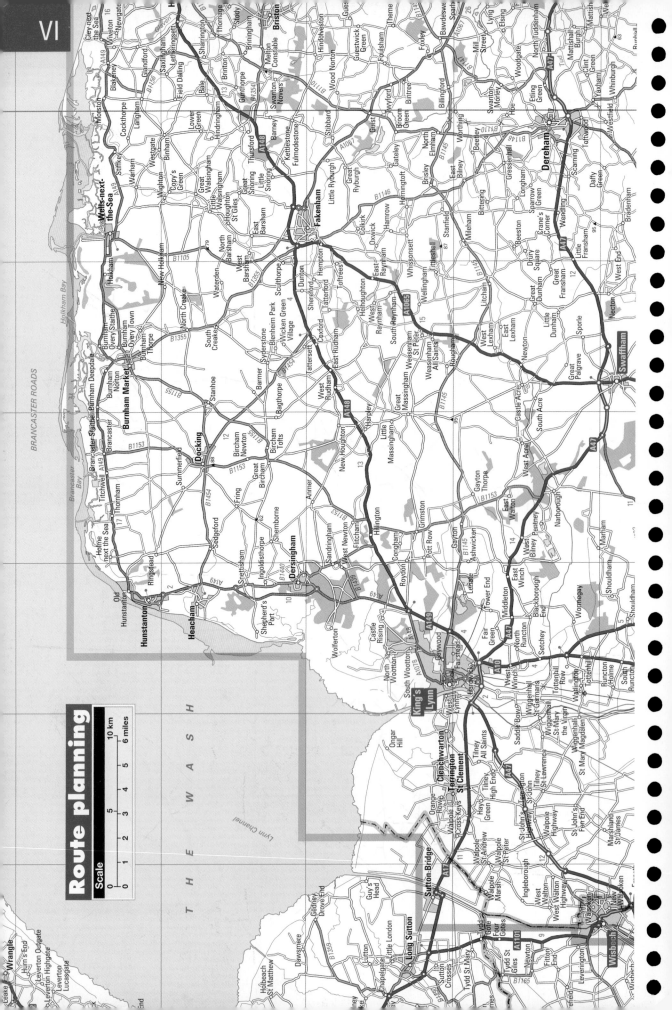

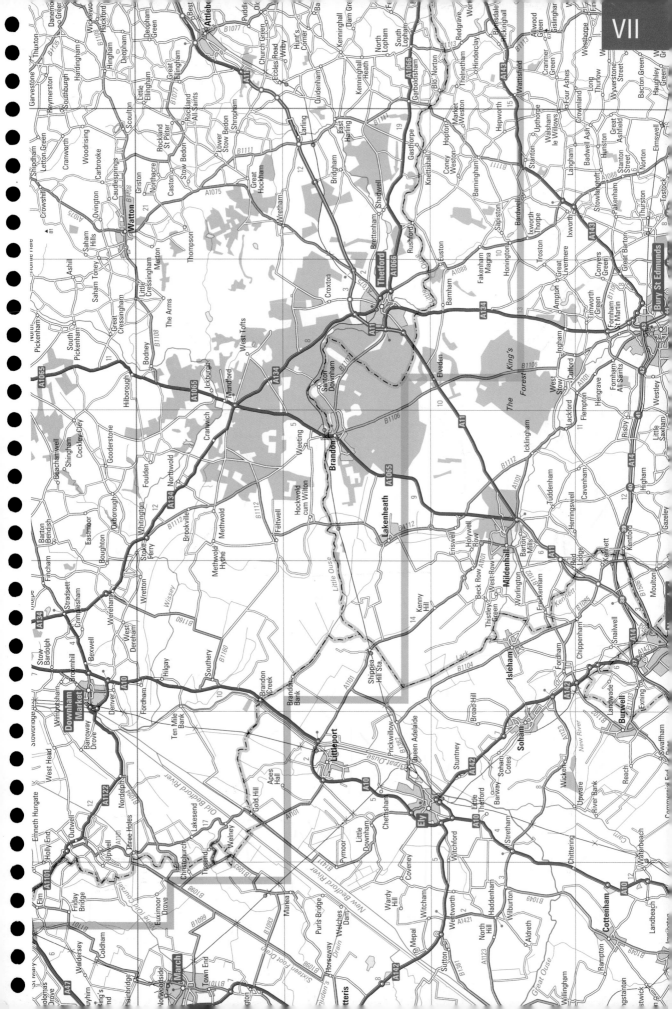

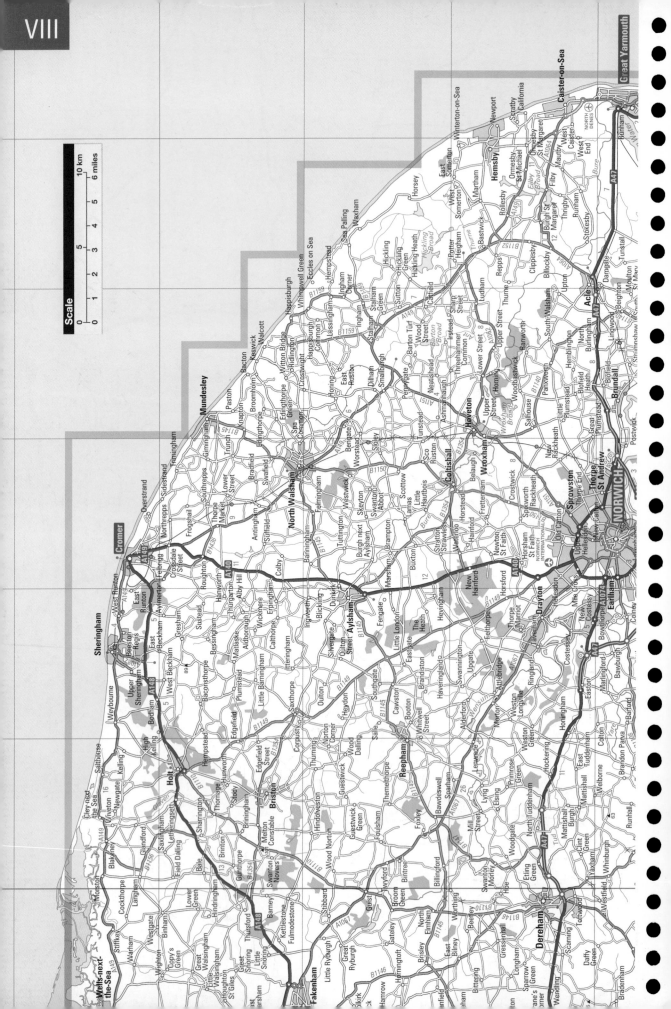

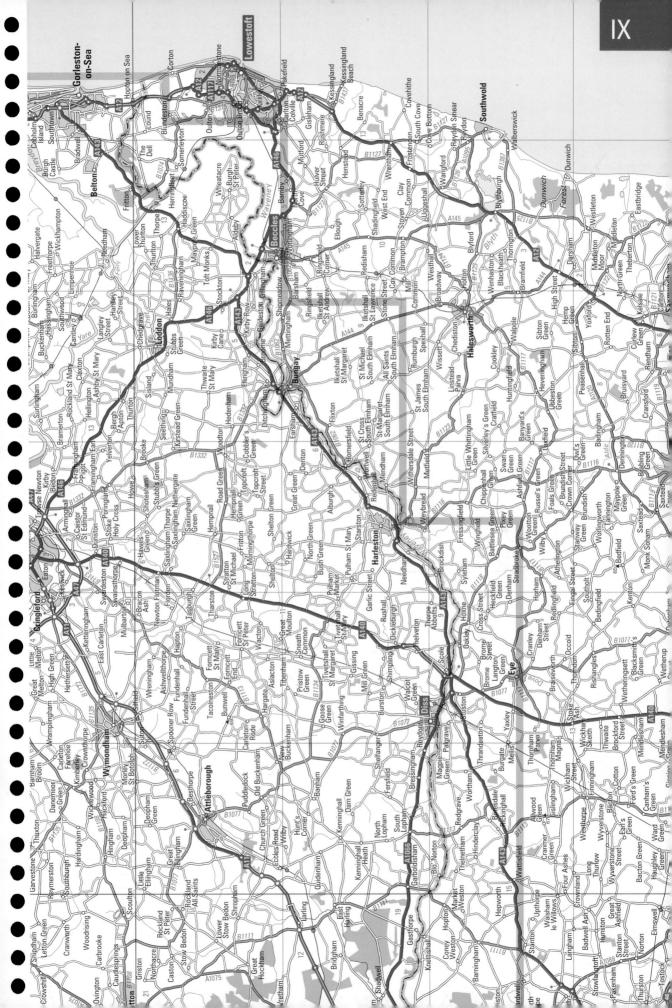

Administrative and Postcode boundaries

Legend:
- County and unitary authority boundaries
- District boundaries
- Postcode boundaries
- Area covered by this atlas

Scale
0 5 10 15 20 25 30km
0 5 10 15 20 miles

Lincolnshire

Cambridgeshire

Suffolk

North Norfolk

Broadland

Norfolk

Brecklands

King's Lynn and West Norfolk

Great Yarmouth

South Norfolk

Norwich

TF | TG
TL | TM

Hunstanton, Heacham, Wells-next-the-Sea, Blakeney, Weybourne, Sheringham, Cromer, Overstrand, Mundesley, Bacton, Winterton-on-Sea, Hemsby, Caister-on-Sea, Great Yarmouth, Somerleyton, Belton, Lound, Beccles, Wheatacre, Kirby Row, Bungay, Harleston, Hoxne, Eye, Diss, Scole, Dickleburgh, Shelfanger, Denton, Hempnall, Long Stratton, Pulham Market, Brooke, Seething, Loddon, Hales, Thurton, Poringland, Woodton, Reedham, Cantley, Brundall, Acle, Upton, Freethorpe, Stokesby, Martham, Cattfield, Stalham, North Walsham, Swanton Abbott, Coltishall, Hoveton, Wroxham, Spixworth, Norwich, Drayton, Horsford, Aylsham, Reepham, Saxthorpe, Southrepps, Holt, Briston, Foulsham, Lyng, Swanton Morley, Mattishall, Garveston, Cringleford, Hethersett, Barford, Wymondham, Spooner Row, Ashwellthorpe, Bunwell, Great Ellingham, Attleborough, Banham, North Lopham, Rickinghall, Coney Weston, Barnham, Thetford, Honington, Lakenheath, Brandon Bank, Brandon, Feltwell, Methwold, Southery, Hilgay, Downham Market, Welney, Upwell, Outwell, Emneth, Wisbech, Walpole St Peter, Terrington St Clement, Clenchwarton, Sutton Bridge, Friday Bridge, King's Lynn, Gayton, Narborough, Watlington, Marham, Stoke Ferry, Gooderstone, Northwold, Mundford, Great Hockham, Wretham, East Harling, Caston, Thompson, Great Cressingham, Cockley Cley, Ashill, Watton, Shipdham, Necton, Litcham, Castle Acre, Swaffham, Great Massingham, West Rudham, South Creake, Docking, Snettisham, Dersingham, Sandringham, Burnham Market, Little Walsingham, Great Snoring, Fakenham, Colkirk, Stibbard, North Elmham, Dereham, Shelfanger, Hingham

Postcode areas: NR1–NR35, PE12–PE38, IP19–IP31, CB6, CB7, PE13, PE14, PE15, IP15, IP28

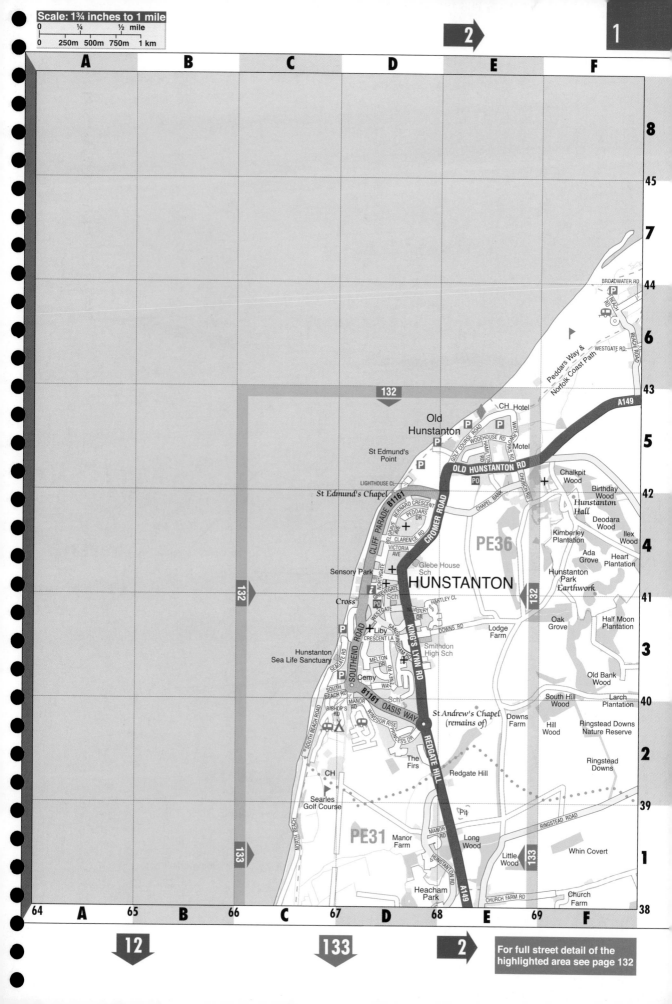

A B C D E F

8
45
7
44
BROADWATER RD

P

BEACH RD

BEACH ROAD

6
Peddars Way &
Norfolk Coast Path

WESTGATE RD.

132

43
A149

CH Hotel

Old
Hunstanton

P
P
P

GOLF COURSE ROAD

WODEHOUSE RD
HAMILTON RD
DOWNS RD

Motel

OLD HUNSTANTON RD

5
St Edmund's
Point

P

CHURCH RD

PO

Chalkpit
Wood

Birthday
Wood

LIGHTHOUSE CL.

St Edmund's Chapel

42

CHAPEL BANK

Hunstanton
Hall

B1161

BERNARD CRESCENT

PEDDARS
DR

CROMER ROAD

Deodara
Wood

Kimberley
Plantation

Ilex
Wood

CLIFF PARADE

BELGRAVE AVE

CLARENCE RD

VICTORIA
AVE

PE36

Ada
Grove

Heart
Plantation

4
Glebe House
Sch

HUNSTANTON

Hunstanton
Park
Earthwork

Sensory Park

NORTHGATE
GREEVEGATE

Sch

132

41
Cross

PO

WESTGATE

NURSERY
DR

HARTLEY CL.

DOWNS RD

Oak
Grove

Half Moon
Plantation

P

Liby

CRESCENT LA

SANDRINGHAM RD

KING'S LYNN RD

Smithdon
High Sch

Lodge
Farm

3
Hunstanton
Sea Life Sanctuary

SEAGATE RD

P

SOUTHEND ROAD

MELTON
DR

FINLEY WAY

Cemy

Old Bank
Wood

South Hill
Wood

Larch
Plantation

40
SOUTH BEACH ROAD

B1161

OASIS WAY

Sch

BISHOP'S
RD

MANOR
RD

WINDSOR RISE

PRINCESS DR

St Andrew's Chapel
(remains of)

Downs
Farm

Hill
Wood

Ringstead Downs
Nature Reserve

REDGATE HILL

Ringstead
Downs

2
NORTH BEACH

The
Firs

Redgate Hill

CH

Searles
Golf Course

39
Pit

RINGSTEAD ROAD

PE31

Manor
Farm

MANOR
RD

Long
Wood

Little
Wood

133

Whin Covert

1
HUNSTANTON RD

A149

Heacham
Park

CHURCH FARM RD

Church
Farm

38

64 A 65 B 66 C 67 D 68 E 69 F

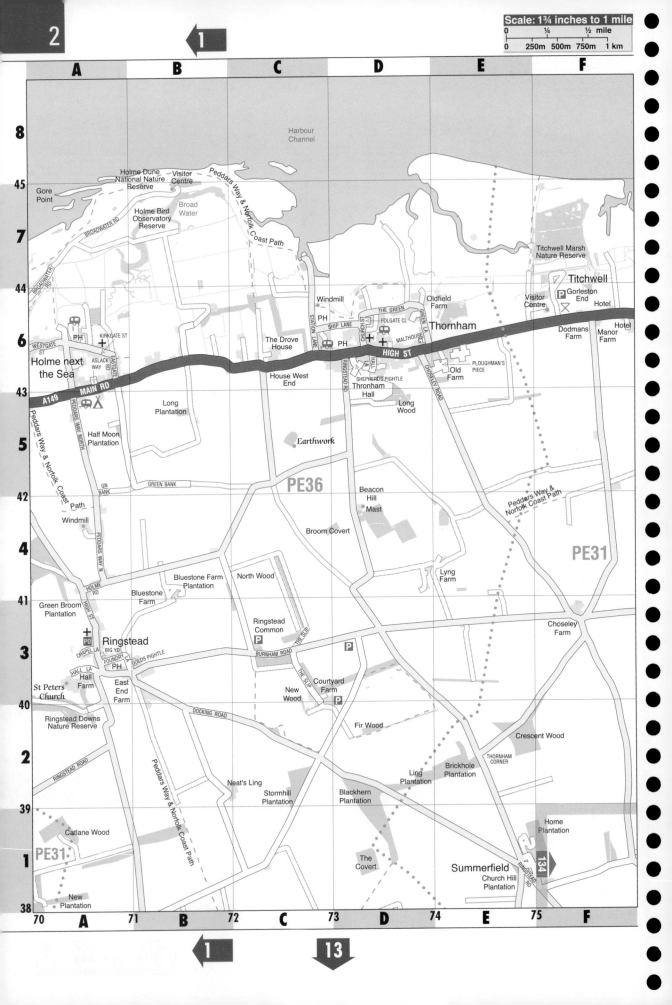

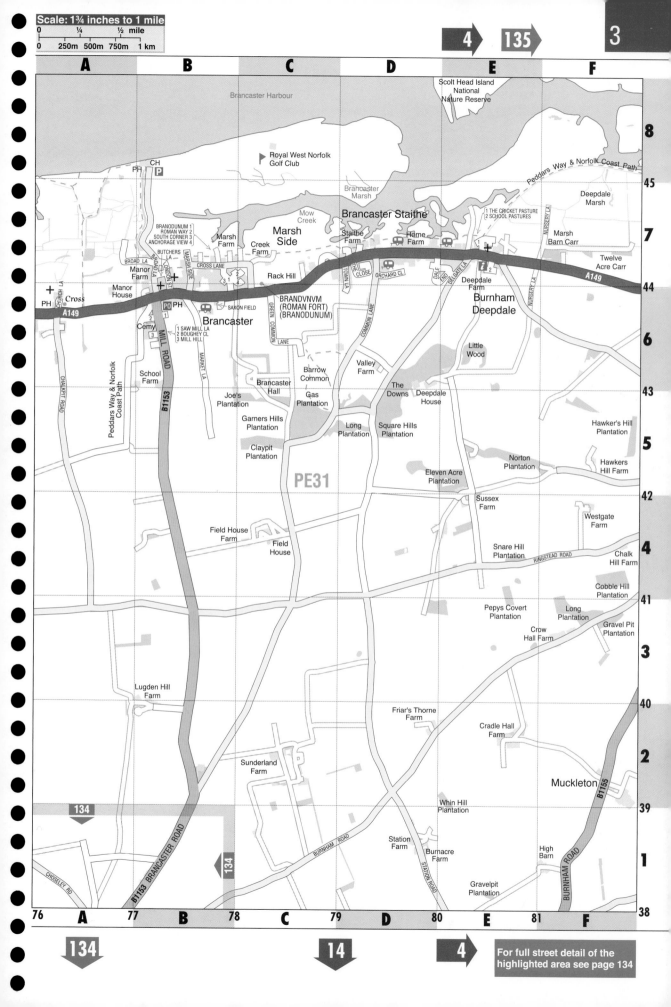

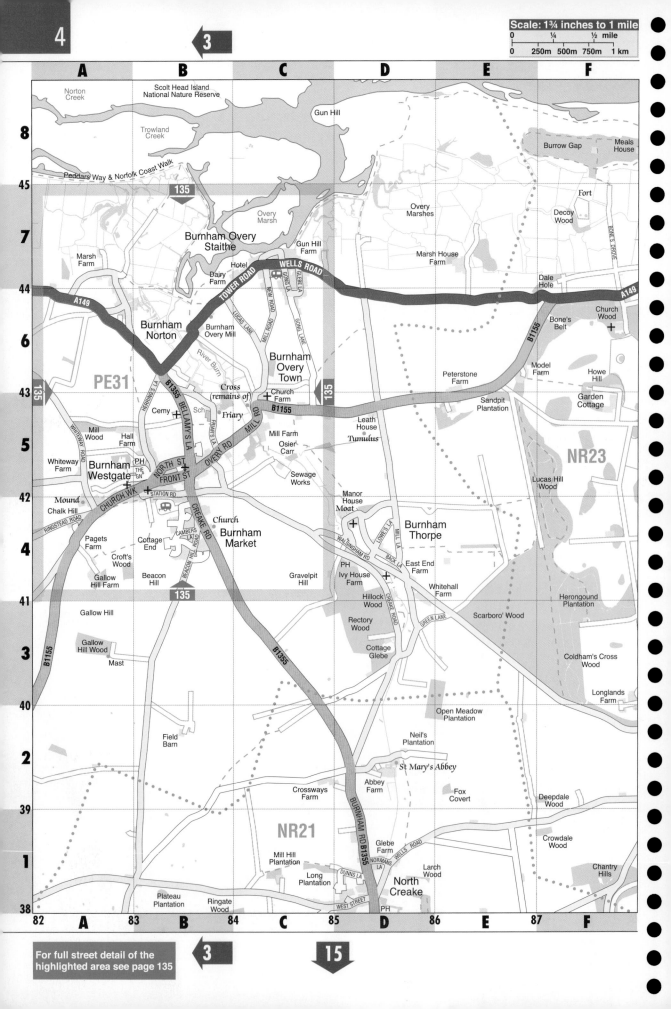

A B C D E F

Norton
Creek

Scolt Head Island
National Nature Reserve

Gun Hill

8

Trowland
Creek

Burrow Gap

Meals
House

45

Peddars Way & Norfolk Coast Walk

135

Overy
Marsh

Overy
Marshes

Fort

Decoy
Wood

7

Marsh
Farm

Burnham Overy
Staithe

Gun Hill
Farm

Marsh House
Farm

Dale
Hole

44

A149

Hotel

Dairy
Farm

WELLS ROAD

TOWER ROAD

GONG LA

GLEBE LA

NEW ROAD

LUCAS LANE

A149

BONE'S DROVE

B1155

Bone's
Belt

Church
Wood

6

Burnham
Norton

Burnham
Overy Mill

GONG LANE

NEW ROAD TWR

Peterstone
Farm

Model
Farm

Howe
Hill

Garden
Cottage

PE31

B1355

HERRING'S LA

BELLAMY'S LA

River Burn

Burnham
Overy
Town

Cross
(remains of)

Church
Farm

B1155

Sandpit
Plantation

43

135

135

Cemy

Sch

Friary

FRIAR'S LA

MILL RD

Leath
House

Tumulus

NR23

5

Mill
Wood

Hall
Farm

OVERY ROAD

Mill Farm

Osier
Carr

Lucas Hill
Wood

Whiteway
Farm

PH
THE
GN

NORTH ST

FRONT ST

Sewage
Works

42

Whiteway Road

Burnham
Westgate

CHURCH WK

STATION RD

Manor
House
Moat

Burnham
Thorpe

Mound

Chalk Hill

CREAKE RD

CAMBERS LA

THE BEACON

Church

Burnham
Market

WALSINGHAM RD

LOWE'S LA

BACK LA

East End
Farm

Ringstead Road

Pagets
Farm

Croft's
Wood

Cottage
End

PH
Ivy House
Farm

Whitehall
Farm

4

Gallow
Hill Farm

Beacon
Hill

135

Gravelpit
Hill

Hillock
Wood

CREAKE ROAD

Herongound
Plantation

41

B1155

Gallow Hill

Rectory
Wood

GREEN LANE

Scarboro' Wood

Coldham's Cross
Wood

3

Gallow
Hill Wood

Mast

B1355

Cottage
Glebe

Longlands
Farm

40

Field
Barn

Open Meadow
Plantation

2

Neil's
Plantation

St Mary's Abbey

Fox
Covert

Deepdale
Wood

39

Crossways
Farm

NR21

Abbey
Farm

BURNHAM RD B1355

WELLS ROAD

Crowdale
Wood

1

Mill Hill
Plantation

Long
Plantation

DUNNS LA

NORMANS LA

Glebe
Farm

Larch
Wood

North
Creake

Chantry
Hills

38

Plateau
Plantation

Ringate
Wood

WEST STREET

PH

82 A 83 B 84 C 85 D 86 E 87 F

For full street detail of the
highlighted area see page 135

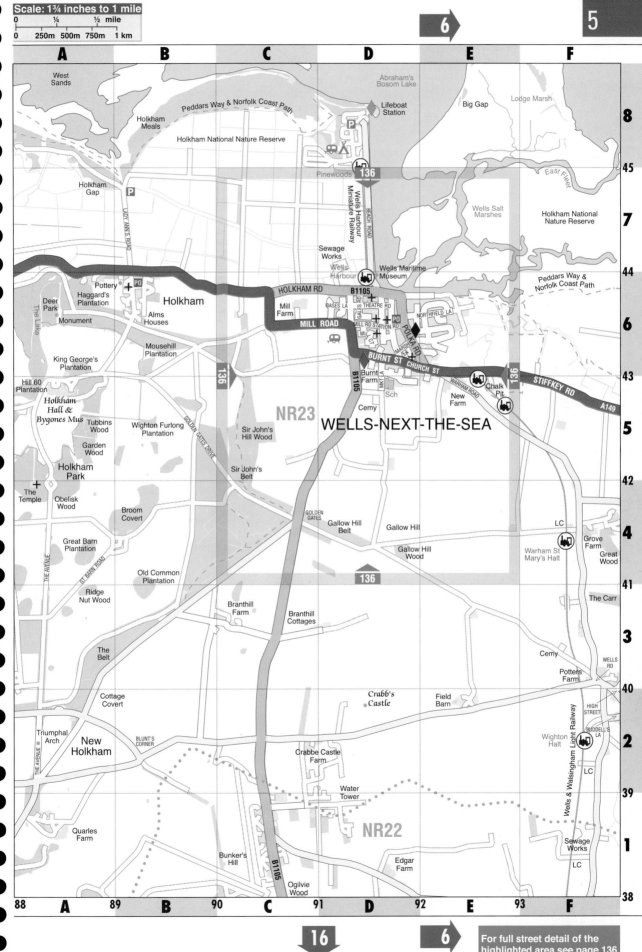

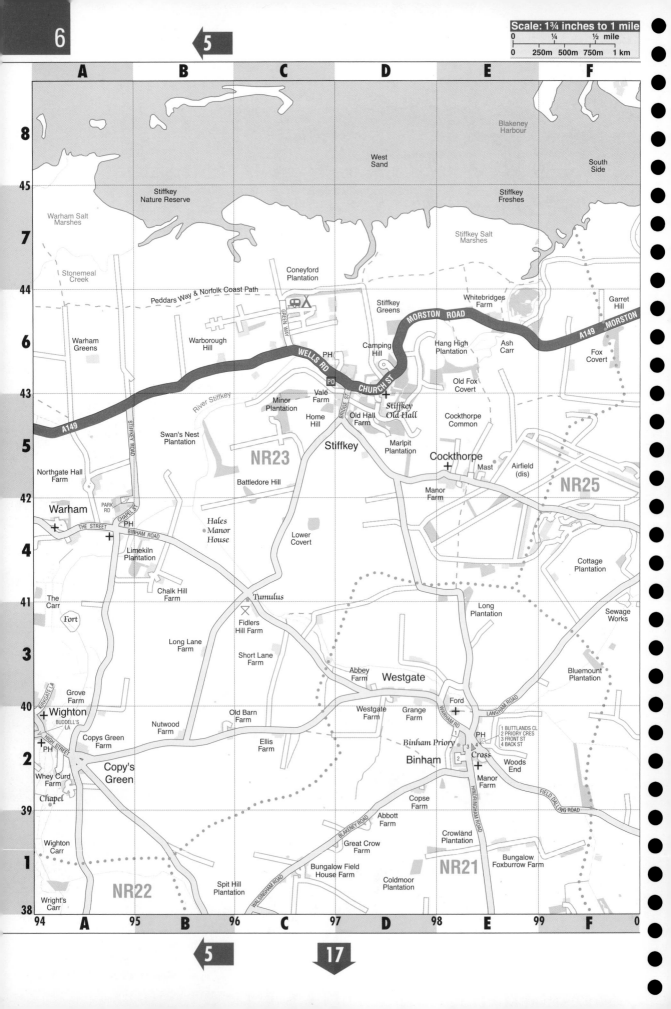

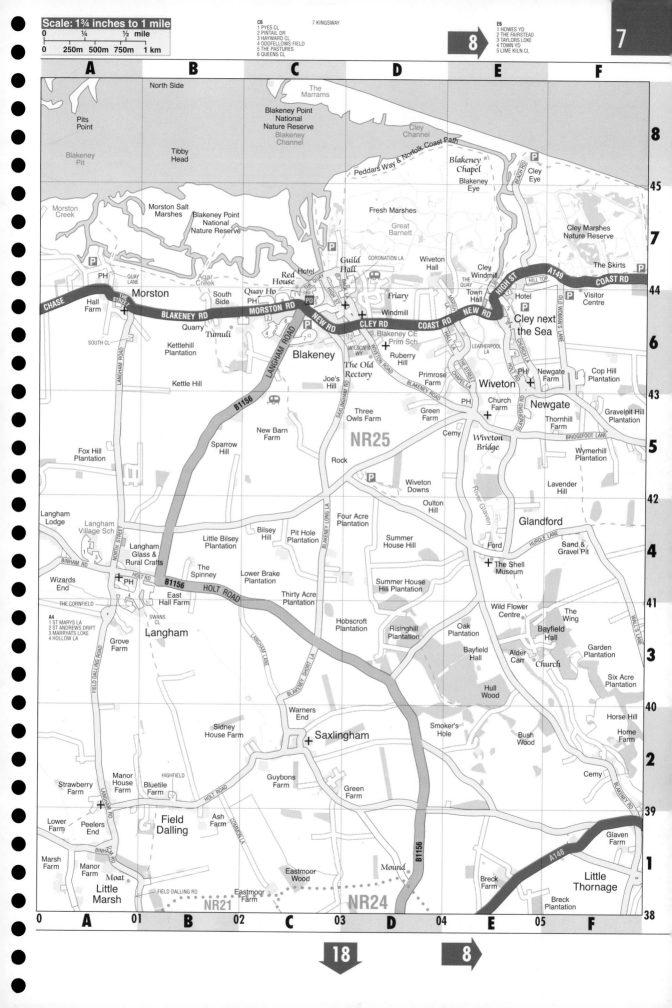

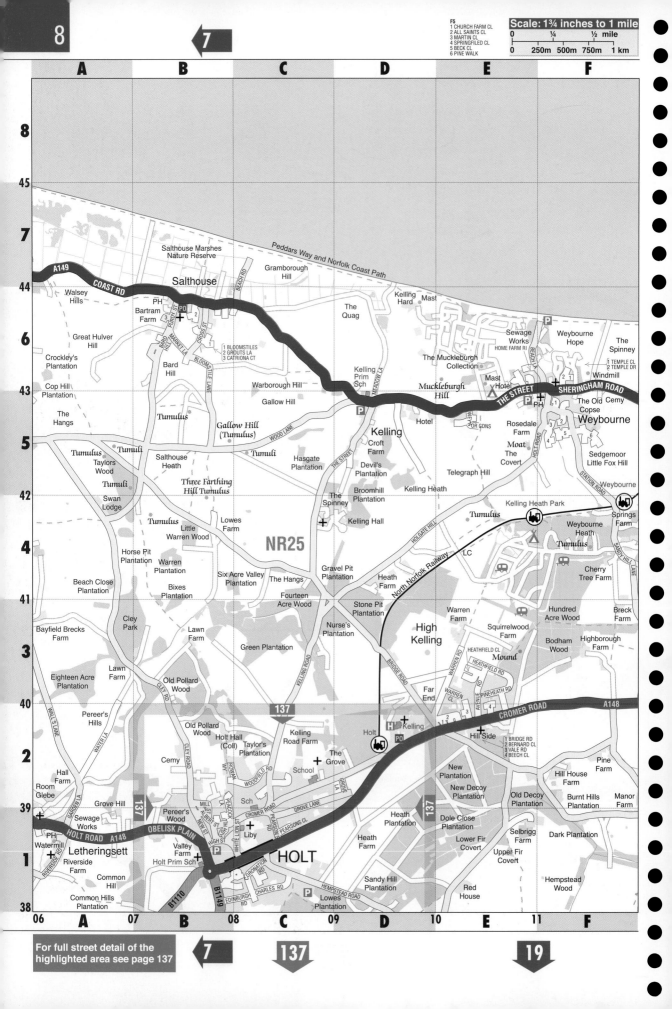

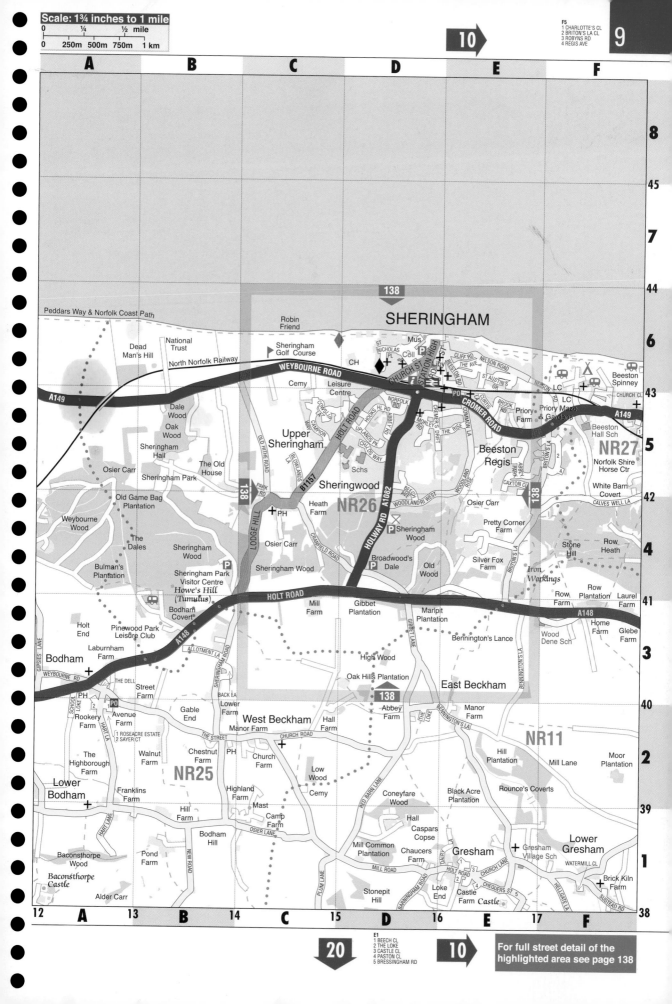

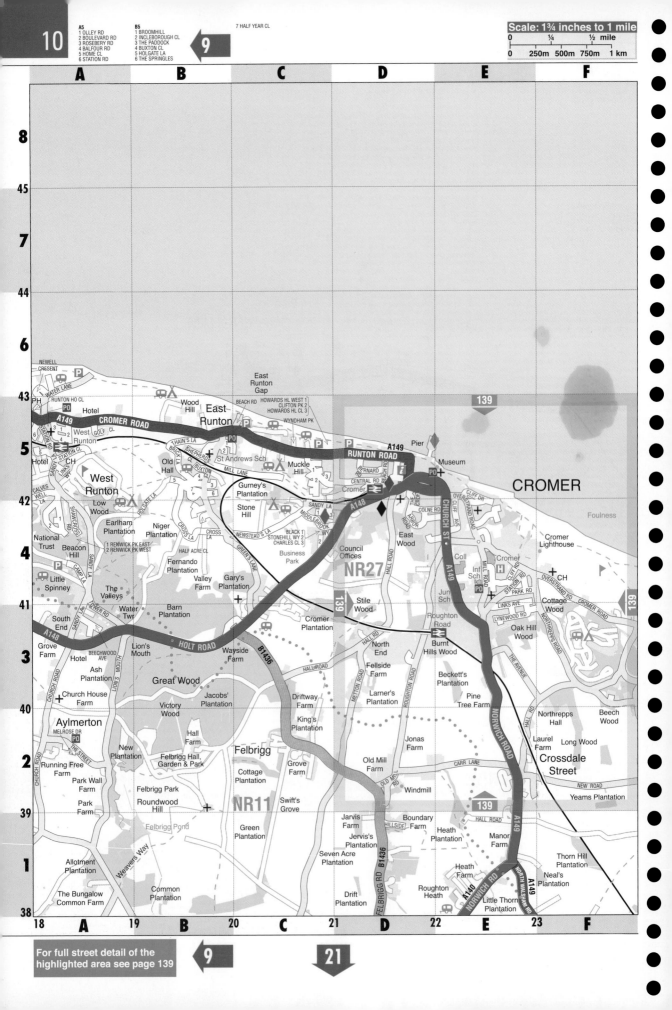

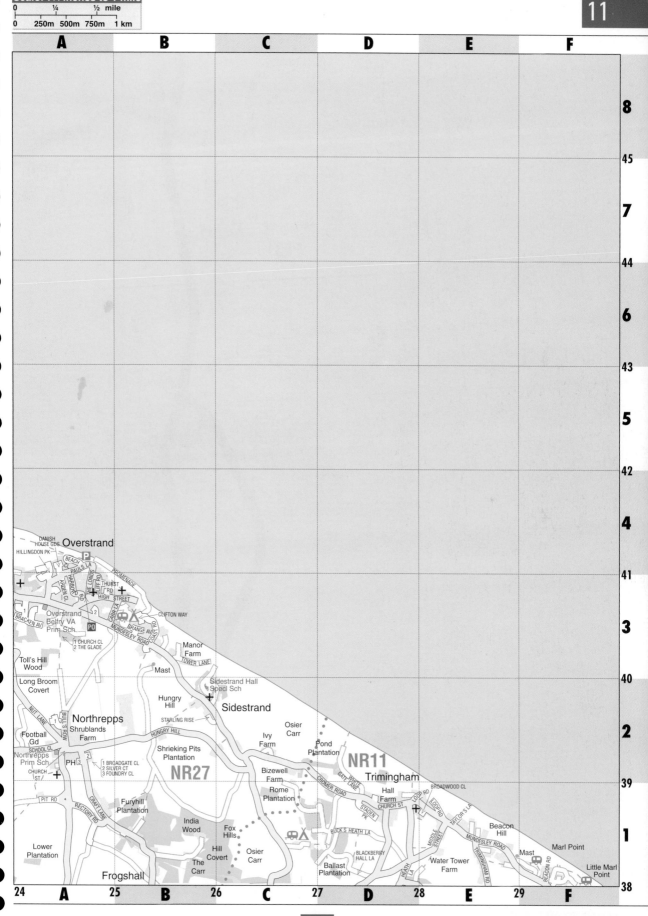

A   B   C   D   E   F

8

45

7

44

6

43

5

42

4

DANISH
HOUSE GDS   **Overstrand**
HILLINGDON PK

41

Overstrand
Belfry VA
Prim Sch

1 CHURCH CL
2 THE GLADE

Toll's Hill
Wood

Manor
Farm

TOWER LANE

Mast

Long Broom
Covert

Sidestrand Hall
Specl Sch

40

Hungry
Hill

Sidestrand

STARLING RISE

Northrepps

Shrublands
Farm

HUNGRY HILL

Ivy
Farm

Osier
Carr

2

Football
Gd

SCHOOL CL

Shrieking Pits
Plantation

Pond
Plantation

NR11

Northrepps
Prim Sch

PH

1 BROADGATE CL
2 SILVER CT
3 FOUNDRY CL

NR27

Bizewell
Farm

CROMER ROAD

Trimingham

BROADWOOD CL

CHURCH
ST

Rome
Plantation

Hall
Farm
CHURCH ST

39

PIT RD

CRAFT LANE

Furyhill
Plantation

India
Wood

Fox
Hills

BUCK'S HEATH LA

Water Tower
Farm

Beacon
Hill

Marl Point

1

Lower
Plantation

The
Carr

Hill
Covert

Osier
Carr

Ballast
Plantation

BLACKBERRY
HALL LA

Mast

Little Marl
Point

Frogshall

24   A   25   B   26   C   27   D   28   E   29   F   38

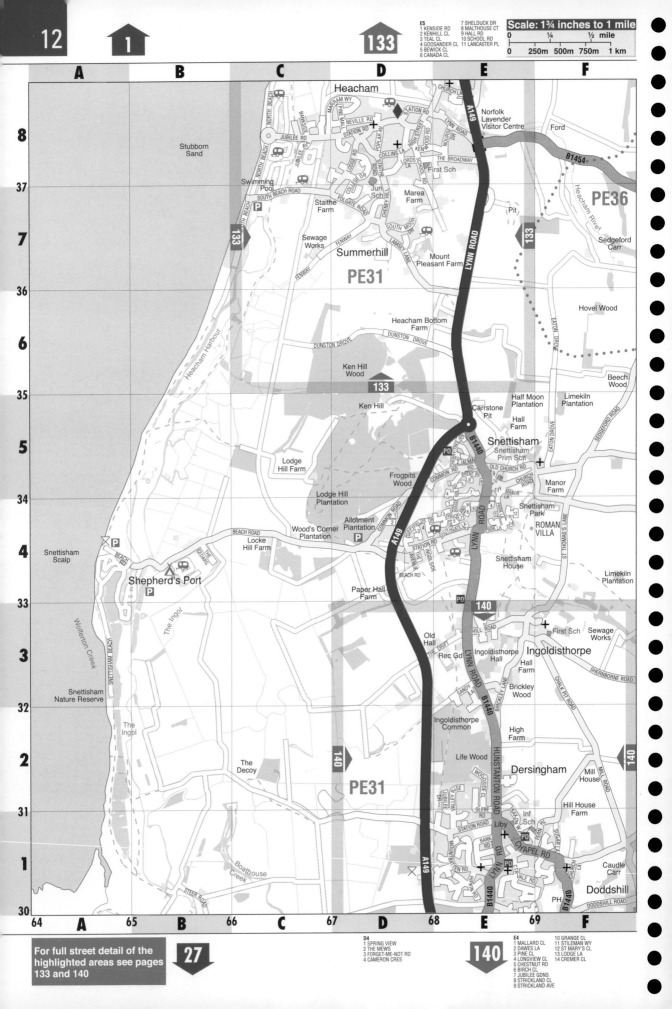

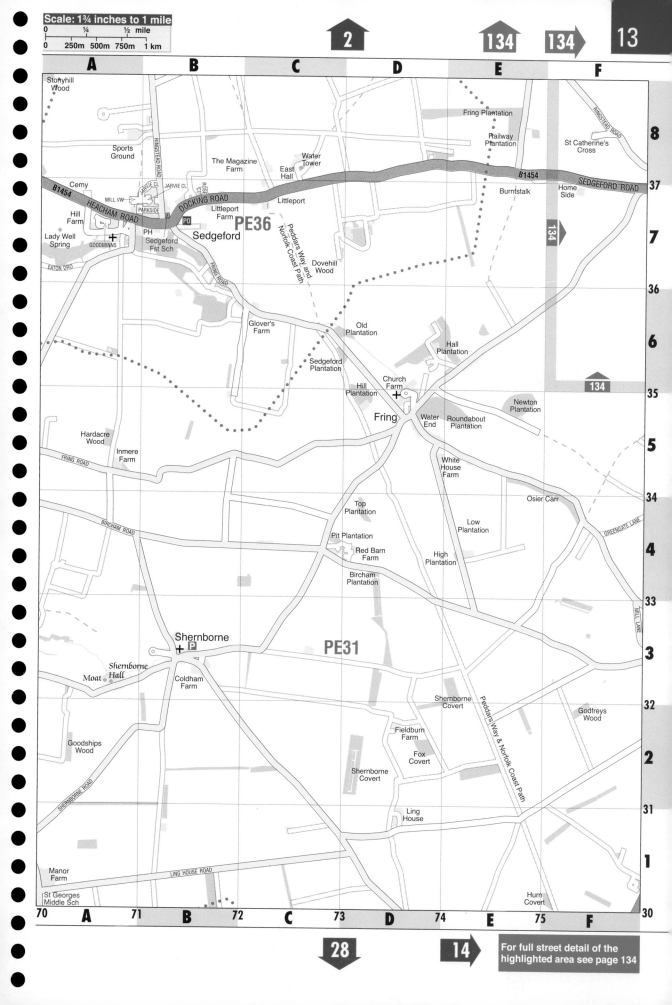

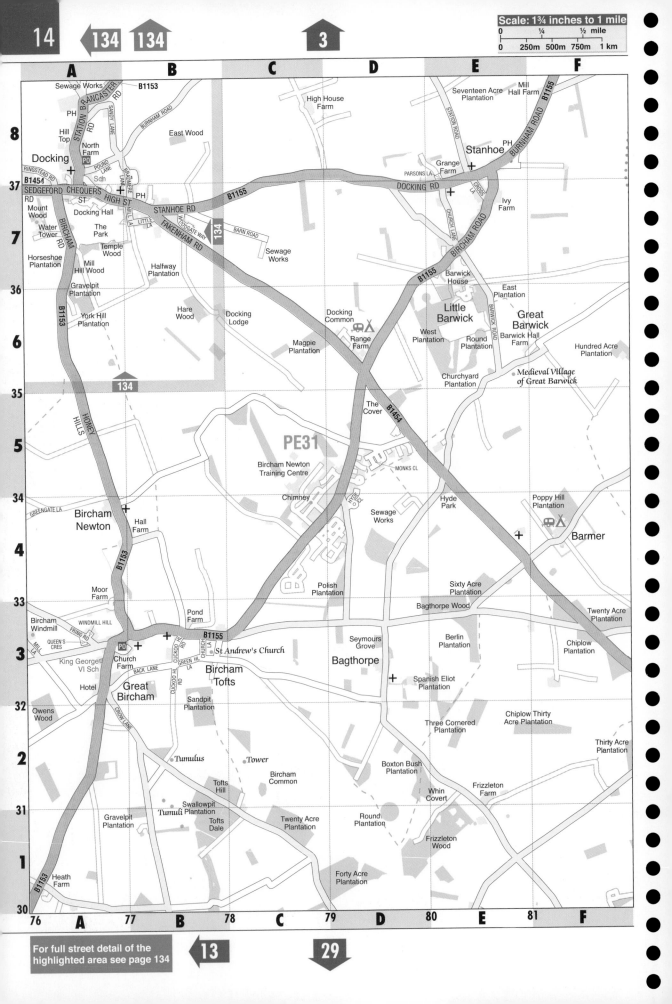

Scale: 1¾ inches to 1 mile

Docking

Stanhoe

Little Barwick

Great Barwick

Medieval Village of Great Barwick

PE31

Bircham Newton

Bircham Newton Training Centre

Barmer

Bircham Tofts

Bagthorpe

St Andrew's Church

Great Bircham

Bircham Windmill

King George VI Sch

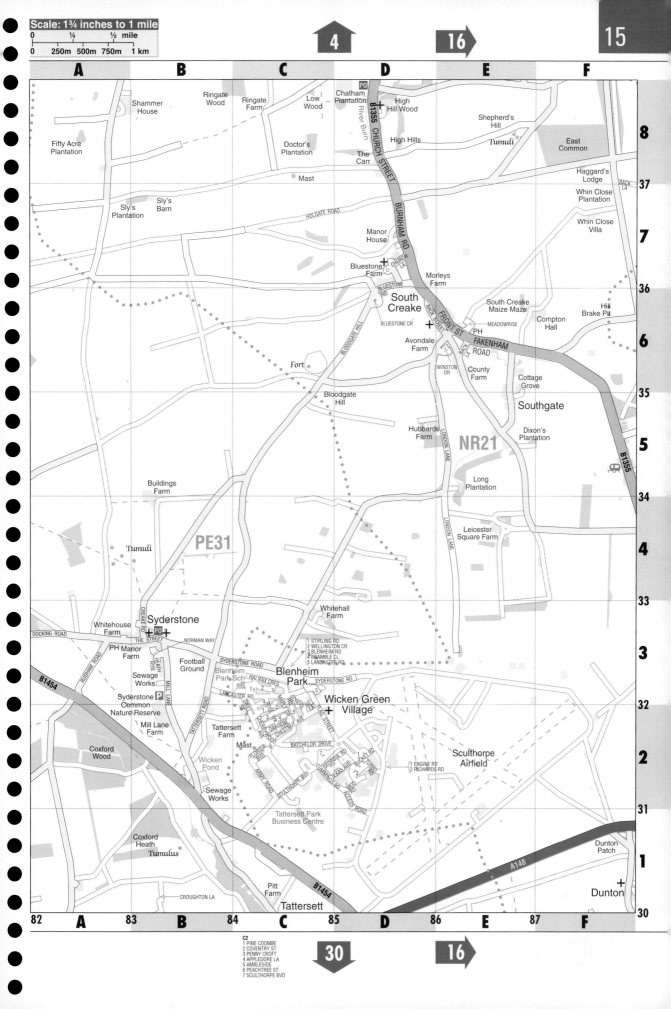

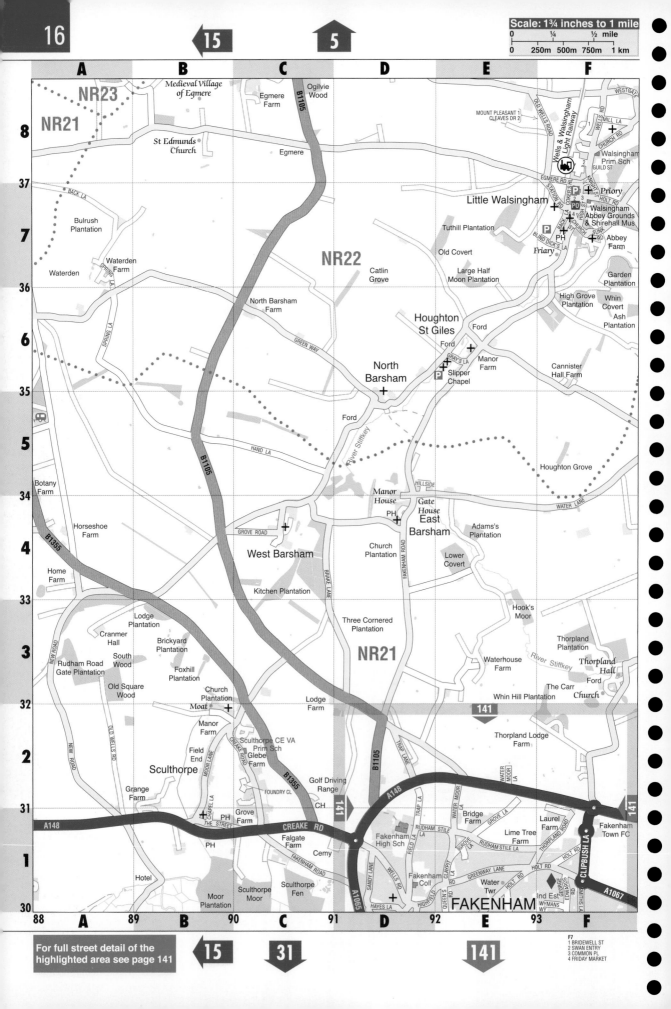

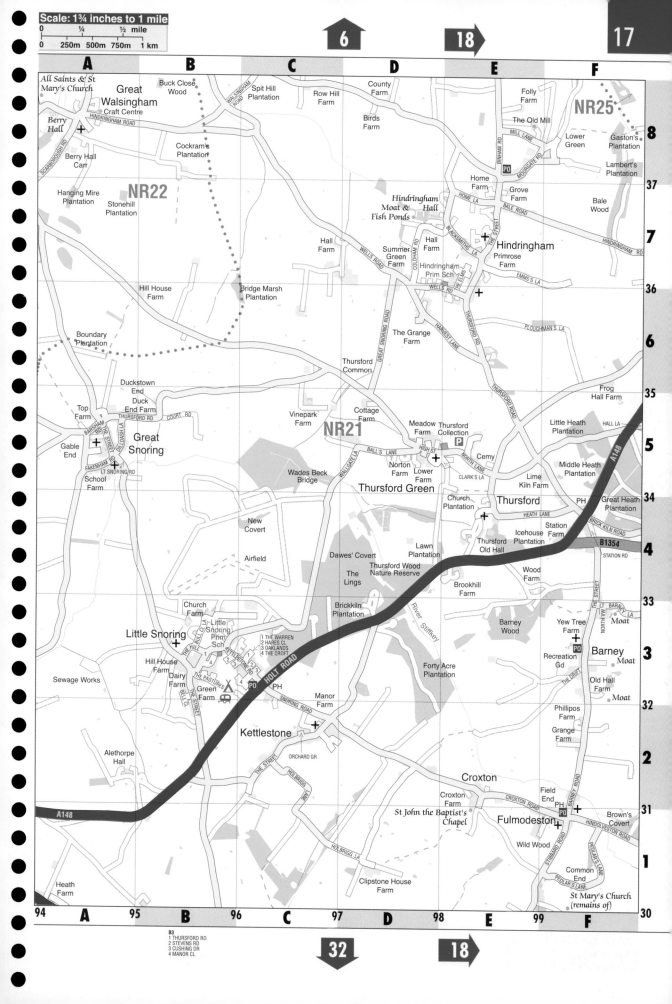

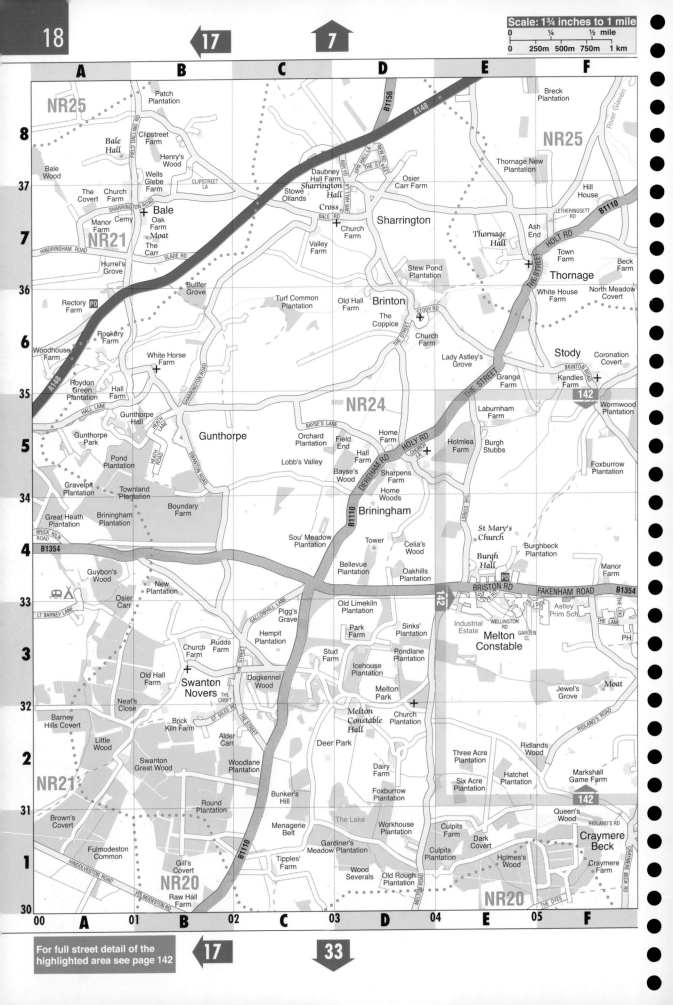

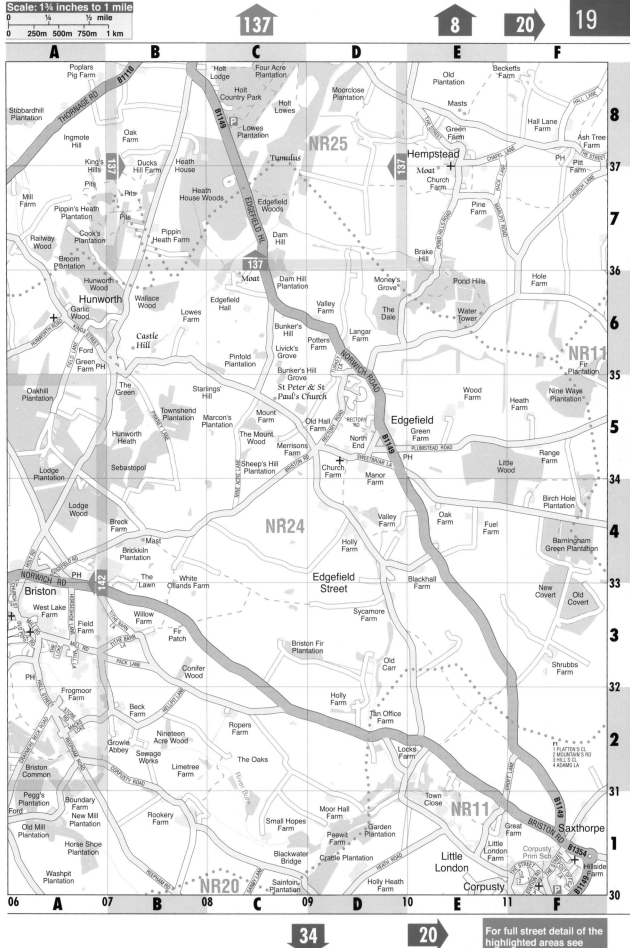

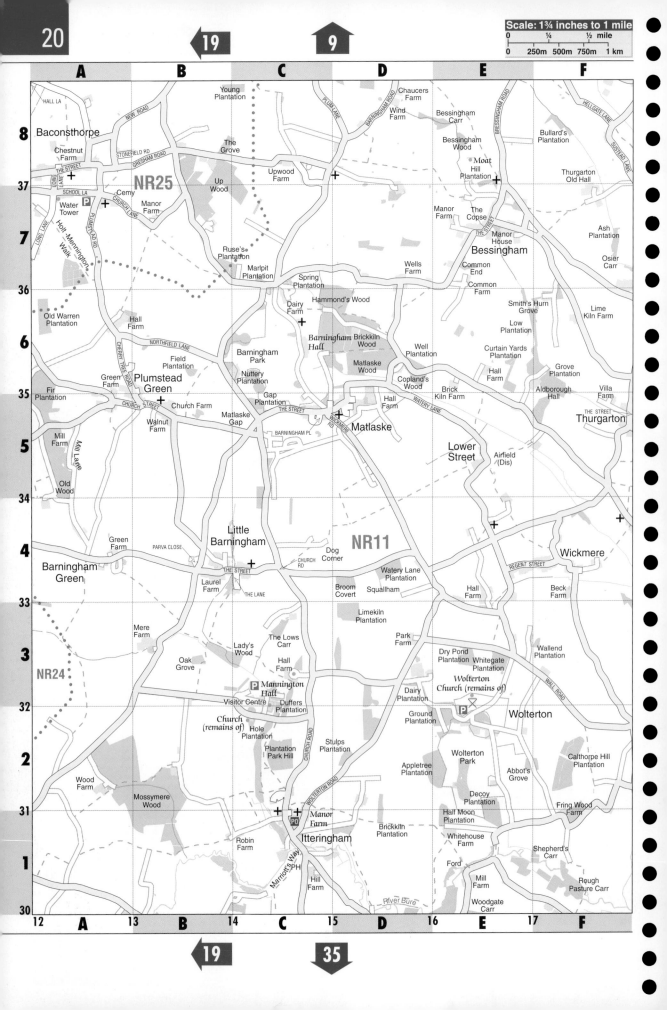

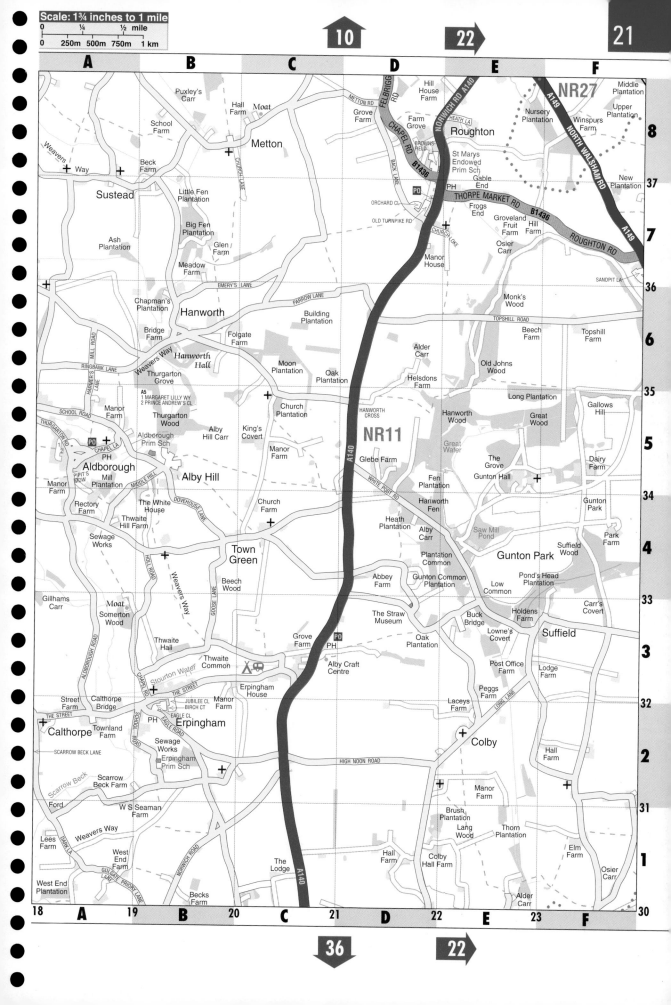

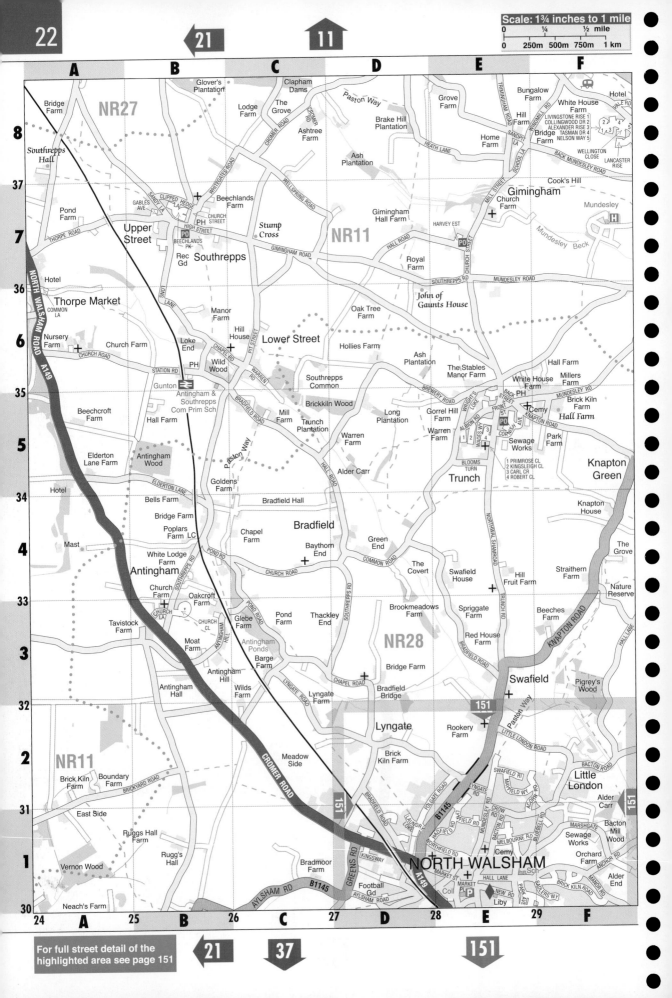

Scale: 1¾ inches to 1 mile

0   ¼   ½   mile
0   250m   500m   750m   1 km

A   **B**   **C**   **D**   **E**   **F**

NR27

Glover's Plantation
Clapham Dams
Paston Way
Grove Farm
Bungalow Farm
Hotel
Lodge Farm
The Grove
Brake Hill Plantation
White House Farm
Hill Farm
Southrepps Hall
Ashtree Farm
Ash Plantation
Home Farm
LIVINGSTONE RISE 1
COLLINGWOOD DR 2
ALEXANDER RISE 3
TASMAN DR 4
NELSON WAY 5
Bridge Farm
WELLINGTON CLOSE
LANCASTER RISE
Bridge Farm

8

Pond Farm

37

Beechlands Farm
GABLES AVE
CLIPPED HEDGE LA
CHURCH STREET
PH
Gimingham Hall Farm
NR11
HARVEY EST
Gimingham Church Farm
Mundesley
H
Cook's Hill
Mundesley Beck

7

Upper Street
PO
BEECHLANDS PK
Rec Gd
Southrepps
Stump Cross
GIMINGHAM ROAD
Royal Farm
HALL ROAD
SCHOOL LA
MILL STREET

36

Hotel
Thorpe Market
COMMON LA
Manor Farm
Hill House
Lower Street
Oak Tree Farm
SOUTHREPPS RD
John of Gaunts House
MUNDESLEY ROAD

6

Nursery Farm
Church Farm
CHURCH ROAD
Loke End
CHAPEL RD
PIT STREET
PH
Wild Wood
WARREN RD
Hollies Farm
Ash Plantation
The Stables Manor Farm
White House Farm
Hall Farm
Millers Farm
BACK STREET
Brick Kiln Farm

35

STATION RD
Gunton
Antingham & Southrepps Com Prim Sch
BRADFIELD ROAD
Mill Farm
Southrepps Common
Brickkiln Wood
BREWERY ROAD
Gorrel Hill Farm
WRIGHTS LOKE
ALBION RD
FRONT ST
PO
CORNER
Cemy
PH
Hall Farm
Park Farm

Beechcroft Farm
Hall Farm
Trunch Plantation
Long Plantation
Warren Farm
Warren Farm
WADES RD
BLOOMS TURN
1 PRIMROSE CL
2 KINGSLEIGH CL
3 CARL CR
4 ROBERT CL
Sewage Works

5

Elderton Lane Farm
Antingham Wood
ELDERTON LANE
Goldens Farm
Paston Way
Alder Carr
HALL ROAD
Trunch
Knapton Green

34

Hotel
Bells Farm
Bridge Farm
Poplars Farm LC
SOUTHREPPS RD
Bradfield Hall
Chapel Farm
Bradfield
Green End
Knapton House

4

Mast
White Lodge Farm
Antingham
POND RD
Baythorn End
COMMON ROAD
The Covert
Swafield House
NORTHWAL SHAMROAD
Hill Fruit Farm
Straithern Farm
The Grove
Nature Reserve

33

Church Farm
CHURCH LA
Oakcroft Farm
CHURCH CL
Glebe Farm
Pond Farm
Thackley End
Brookmeadows Farm
Spriggate Farm
TRUNCH RD
Beeches Farm
KNAPTON ROAD

Tavistock Farm
ANTINGHAM HILL
Moat Farm
Antingham Ponds
Barge Farm
NR28
Bridge Farm
Red House Farm
BRADFIELD ROAD
Swafield
Pigrey's Wood
HALL LANE

3

Antingham Hall
Wilds Farm
LYNGATE ROAD
Lyngate Farm
CHAPEL ROAD
Bradfield Bridge
151
Paston Way

32

CROMER ROAD
Meadow Side
Lyngate
Rookery Farm
LITTLE LONDON ROAD
BACTON ROAD
151

NR11
Meadow Side
Brick Kiln Farm
FOLGATE ROAD
SWAFIELD RI
MAYFIELD WY
Little London

2

Brick Kiln Farm
Boundary Farm
BRICKYARD ROAD
B1145
LAUNDRY LOKE
MADFIELD LOKE
LYNGATE RD
CROW RD
MELBOURNE RD
BLUEBELL RD
MARSHGATE
Sewage Works
ANCHOR RD
Bacton Mill Wood
Alder Carr
151

31

East Side
Ruggs Hall Farm
B1145
GREENS RD
NORTHFIELD RD
MARKET ST
MAYFIELD WY
BACTON RD
Cemy
Orchard Farm
MANOR RD
BRICK KILN ROAD
Alder End

Vernon Wood
Rugg's Hall
Bradmoor Farm
KINGSWAY
Football Gd
A149
NORTH WALSHAM
Sch
MARKET PL
HALL LANE
NEW RD
PARK AVE
SADLERS WY
Coll
Liby

1

Neach's Farm
AYLSHAM RD
B1145
AYLSHAM ROAD

30

24   **A**   **25**   **B**   **26**   **C**   **27**   **D**   **28**   **E**   **29**   **F**

NORTH WALSHAM ROAD A149

THORPE ROAD
LONG LANE
HIGH STREET
WHITEGATES ROAD
CROMER RD
WELLSPRING ROAD
HEATH LANE
THIRLMBAND ROAD
WINDMILL LANE
SANDPIT LA
BACK MUNDESLEY ROAD
WALFIELD RD

Scale: 1¾ inches to 1 mile

0   ¼   ½   mile
0   250m 500m 750m 1 km

A **B** **C** **D** **E** **F**

143

8

Cliftonville

Liby

Mundesley Maritime Museum

Mundesley

37

SEA VW RD

CROMER ROAD

CHURCH LA

BEACH RD

HIGH ST

PO

Water Tower

PASTON RD

MEADOW WAY

Hotel

7

LINKS ROAD

WARREN DR

HEATH RD

HEATH LANE

BECKMEAD WAY

Sch

Water Lane

143

TRUNCH ROAD

Stow Mill

Stow Farm

Stow Hill

Holiday Centre

143

36

NR11

B1145 KNAPTON RD

MUNDESLEY ROAD

Stow Hill

Paston Way

6

The Spinney

Paston

POND LANE

BEARS CHAPEL RD

VICARAGE RD

Great Barn

Hall Farm

Gas Distribution Station

Mast

Mast

35

Knapton

Church Farm

BACTON RD

Rookery Plantation

Bacton Road

COAST ROAD

BEACH RD

PH

Bacton

Watch House Gap

5

Water Tower

Sewage Works

143

Paston Green

Lowlands Farm

Church Farm

WODEHOUSE RD

PO

PH

MILL LANE

Bromholm Field End

Keswick

ANNE STANNARD WAY

KESWICK RD

34

Old Hall Street

Paston Way

P

Croft Farm

SCHOOL ROAD

CHURCH LANE

Church Farm

RECTORY ROAD

NR12

Hall Farm

SANDY LANE

BEACH RD

THE PADDOCKS

BLOODSLAT LANE

Bacton-on-Sea First Sch

P

WALCOTT RD (COAST RD)

ABBEY STREET

PH

Rudram's Gap

4

Parrs Farm

Hill Farm

The Grove

Church Farm

Edingthorpe

Pollard Street

Grange Farm

Broomholm

Stories Farm

Abbey Farm

PRIORY RD

Gap End

ST HELENS RD

HELENA RD

THE CEDARS

POPLAR DR

33

Dead Man's Grave

BOUNDARY LANE

Honeytop Farm

Clay Farm

THE STREET

CLAY LANE

NORTH WALSHAM ROAD

NR28

Park Farm

WELL STREET

Ash Tree Farm

The Grange

Mill Common

Rookery Farm

COAST RD

3

Barchams Farm

Heath Farm

HENNESSEY'S LOKE

North Plantation

Odessa Farm

ROOKERY FARM ROAD

Barrington Farm

BACK LANE

PH

32

Edingthorpe Green

Cooper's Covert

Green Farm

Witton Hall

Church Plantation

Common Farm

Stonebridge Cottage Selfs Carr

MILL COMMON ROAD

BACHELOR'S LANE

NORTH WALSHAM RD

2

Edingthorpe Heath

MILL ROAD

Bacton Wood

Philip's Grove

Road Plantation

BACTON ROAD

Manor Farm

STONEBRIDGE ROAD

Witton Bridge

HAPPISBURGH ROAD

Ridlington

NR12

31

Spa Common

Muckle Hill Farm

Witton Heath

Verona Plantation

OLD HALL RD

Old Hall

NORTH WALSHAM ROAD

HALL ROAD

Ivy Farm

MARSH LOKE

Hoole House

Primrose Farm

Church Farm

South Side

THE STREET

Ridlington Street

Bransmeadow Carr

HEATH RD

Heath Farm

NASH'S LANE

Nashs Farm

Ridlington Plantation

OLD LANE

1

Tumulus

30

A 31 **B** 32 **C** 33 **D** 34 **E** 35 **F** 30

38

24

For full street detail of the highlighted area see page 143

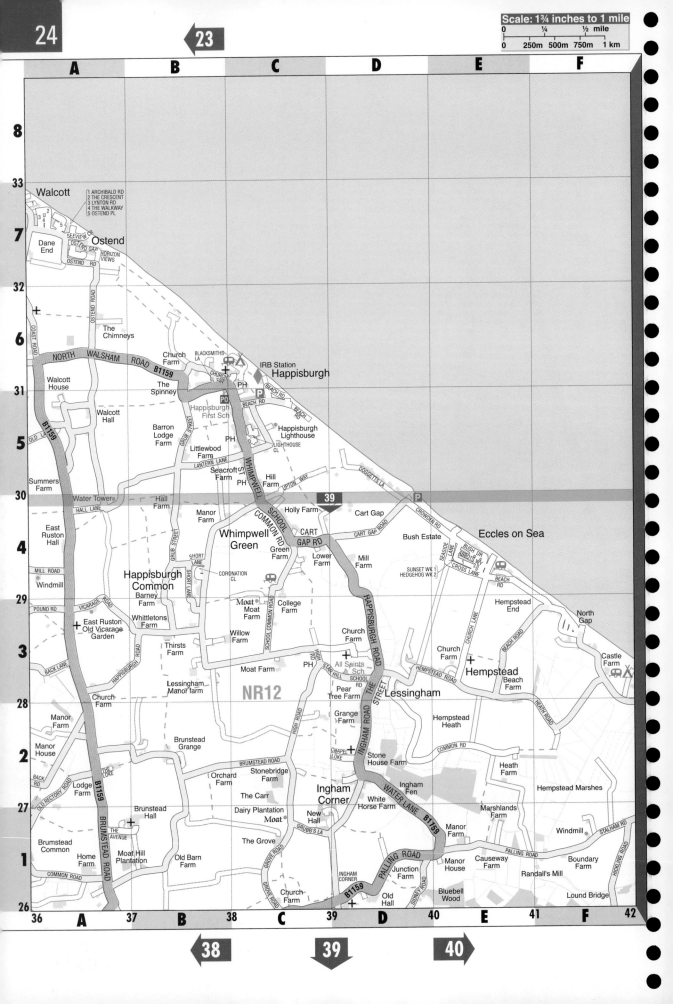

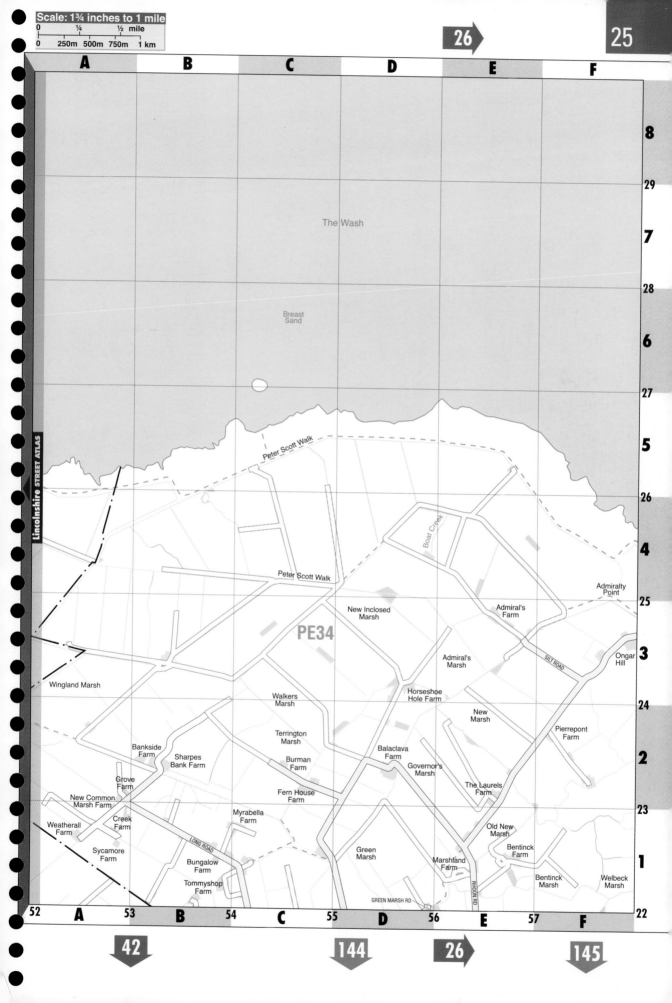

Lincolnshire STREET ATLAS

A   B   C   D   E   F

The Wash

Breast Sand

Peter Scott Walk

Peter Scott Walk

Boat Creek

New Inclosed Marsh

PE34

Admiral's Farm

Admiralty Point

Admiral's Marsh

SILT ROAD

Ongar Hill

Wingland Marsh

Walkers Marsh

Horseshoe Hole Farm

New Marsh

Terrington Marsh

Pierrepont Farm

Bankside Farm

Sharpes Bank Farm

Burman Farm

Balaclava Farm

Governor's Marsh

The Laurels Farm

Grove Farm

Fern House Farm

New Common Marsh Farm

Myrabella Farm

Old New Marsh

Bentinck Farm

Weatherall Farm

Creek Farm

LONG ROAD

Green Marsh

Marshland Farm

RHOON RD

Bentinck Marsh

Welbeck Marsh

Sycamore Farm

Bungalow Farm

Tommyshop Farm

GREEN MARSH RD

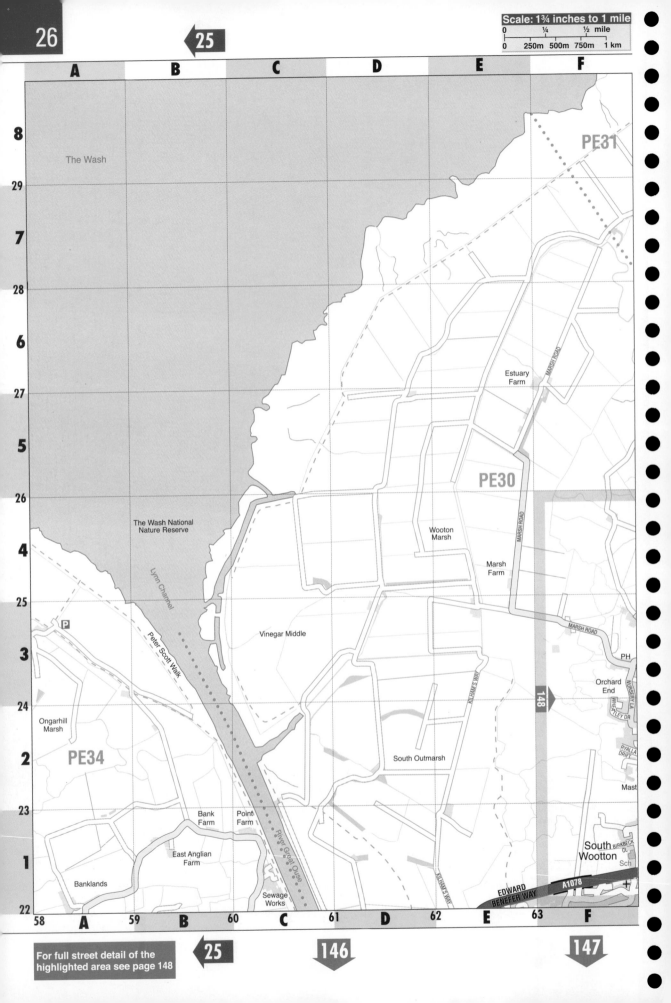

Scale: 1¾ inches to 1 mile

0   ¼   ½ mile
0 250m 500m 750m 1 km

A **B** **C** **D** **E** **F**

8

29

The Wash

7

28

PE31

6

27

Estuary
Farm

MARSH ROAD

5

PE30

26

The Wash National
Nature Reserve

Wooton
Marsh

MARSH ROAD

Marsh
Farm

4

Lynn Channel

25

Vinegar Middle

MARSH ROAD

P

Peter Scott Walk

PH

Orchard
End

NURSERY LA

WHERTLEY DR

148

3

24

Ongarhill
Marsh

KILHAM'S WAY

RYALLA
DRIFT

2

PE34

South Outmarsh

Mast

23

Bank
Farm

Point
Farm

River Great Ouse

1

East Anglian
Farm

South
Wootton

BIRKBECK
CL

Sch

Banklands

KILHAM'S WAY

EDWARD
BENEFER WAY

A1078

22

58 **A** 59 **B** 60 **C** 61 **D** 62 **E** 63 **F**

Sewage
Works

25

For full street detail of the
highlighted area see page 148

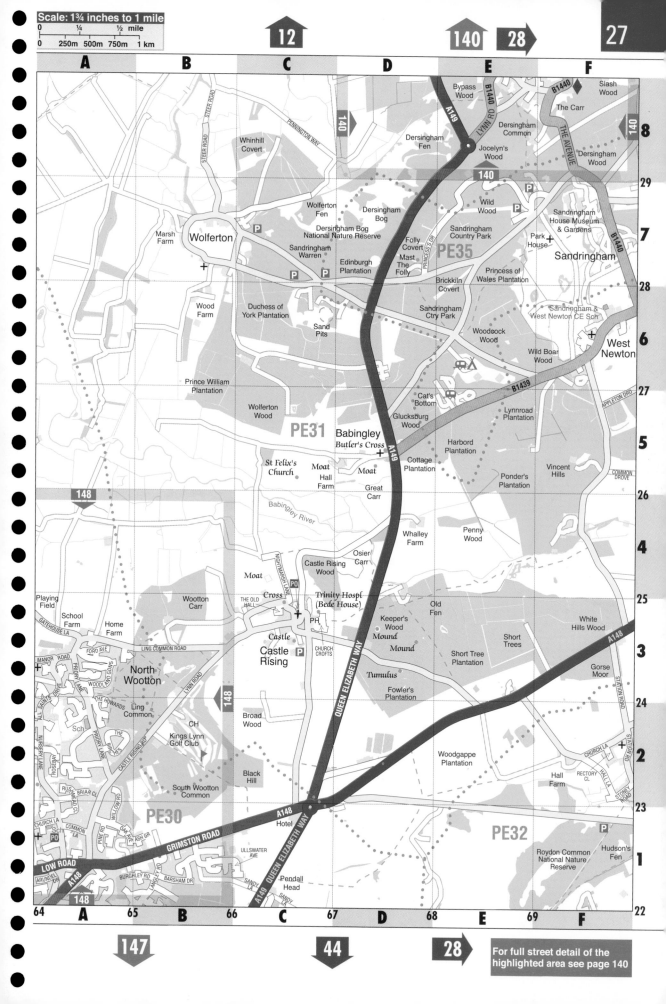

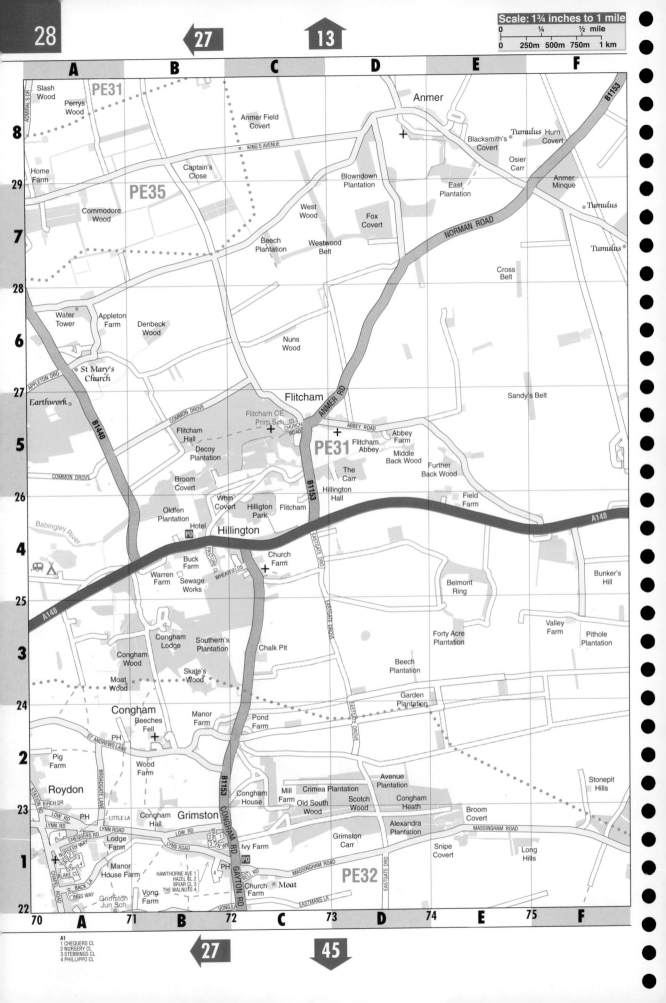

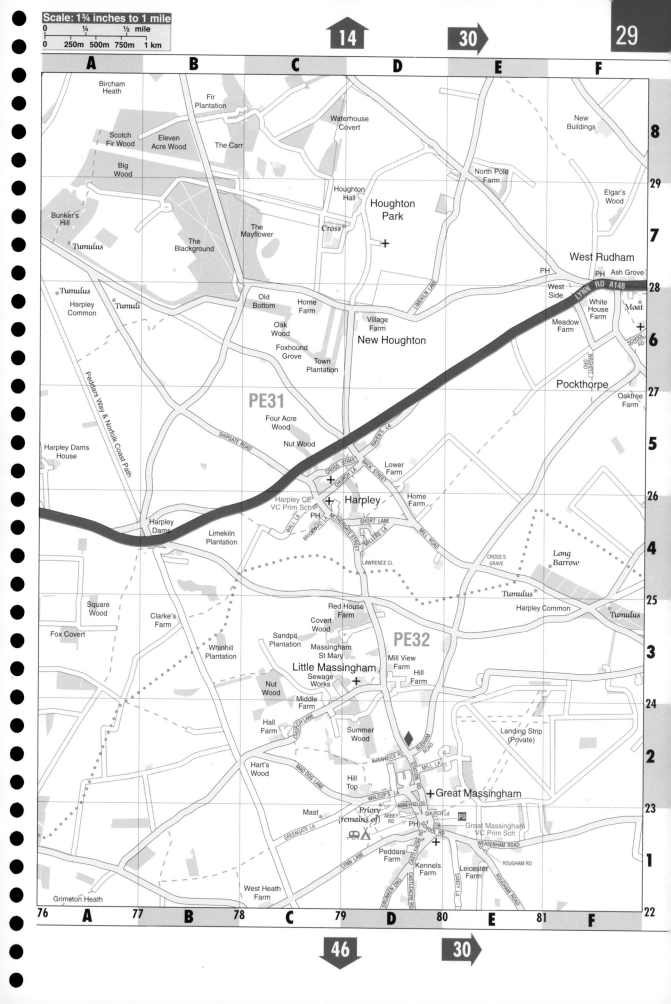

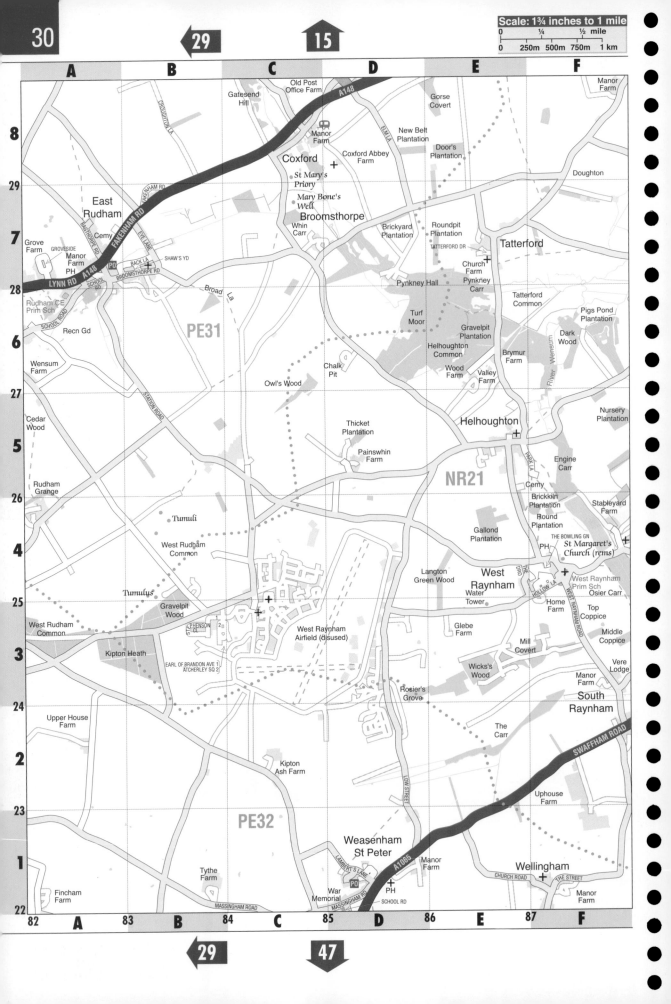

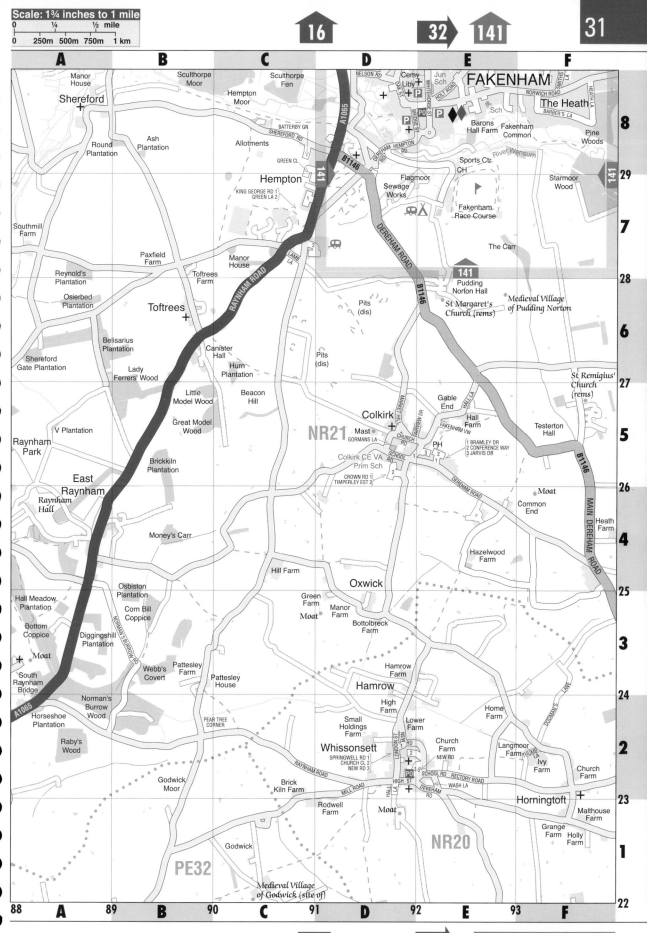

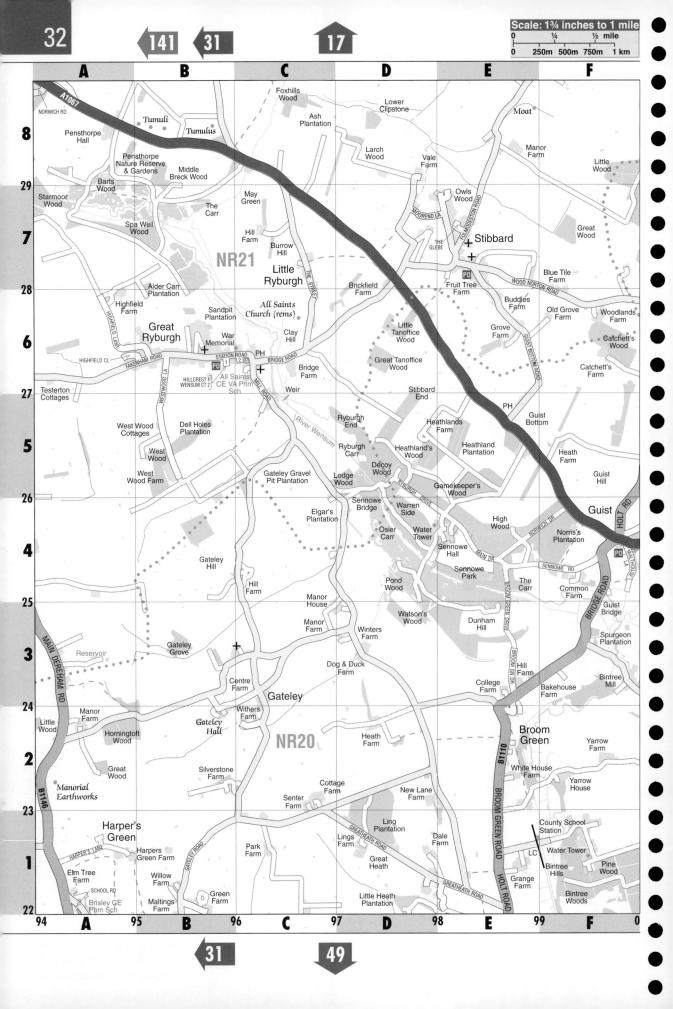

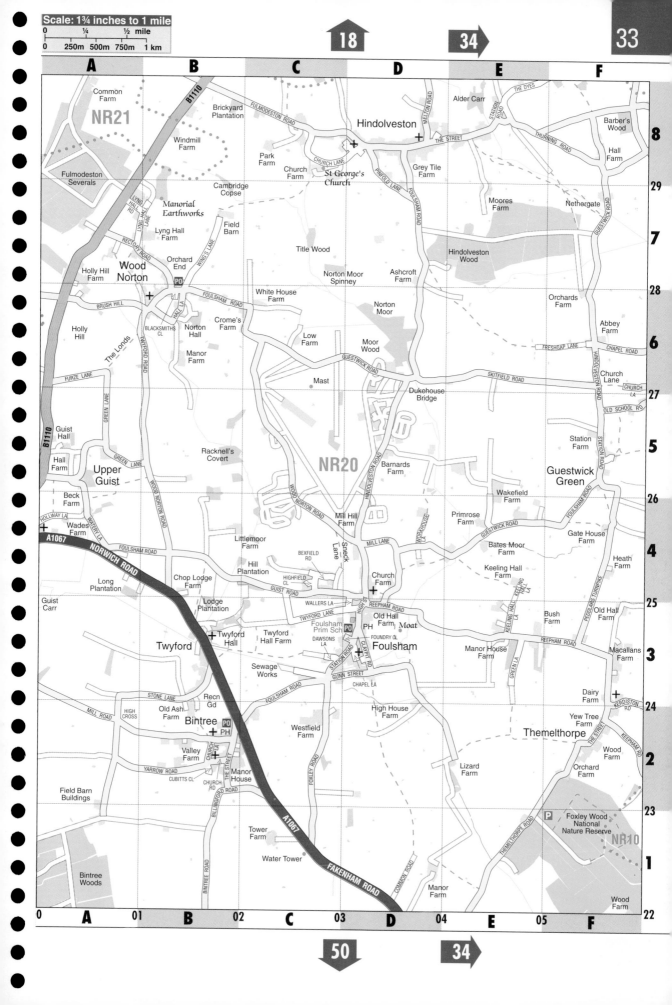

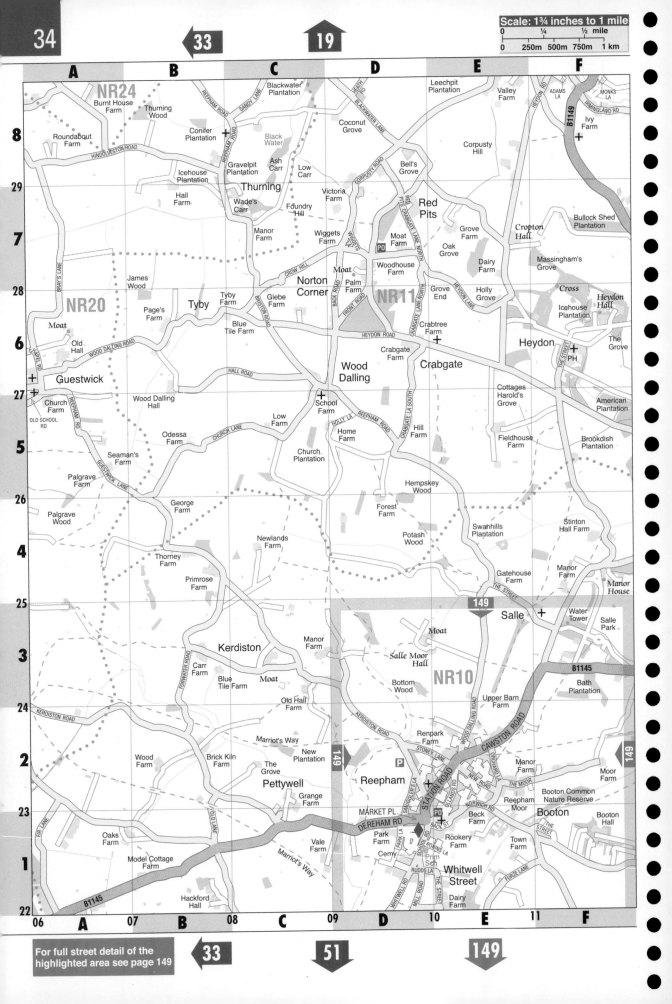

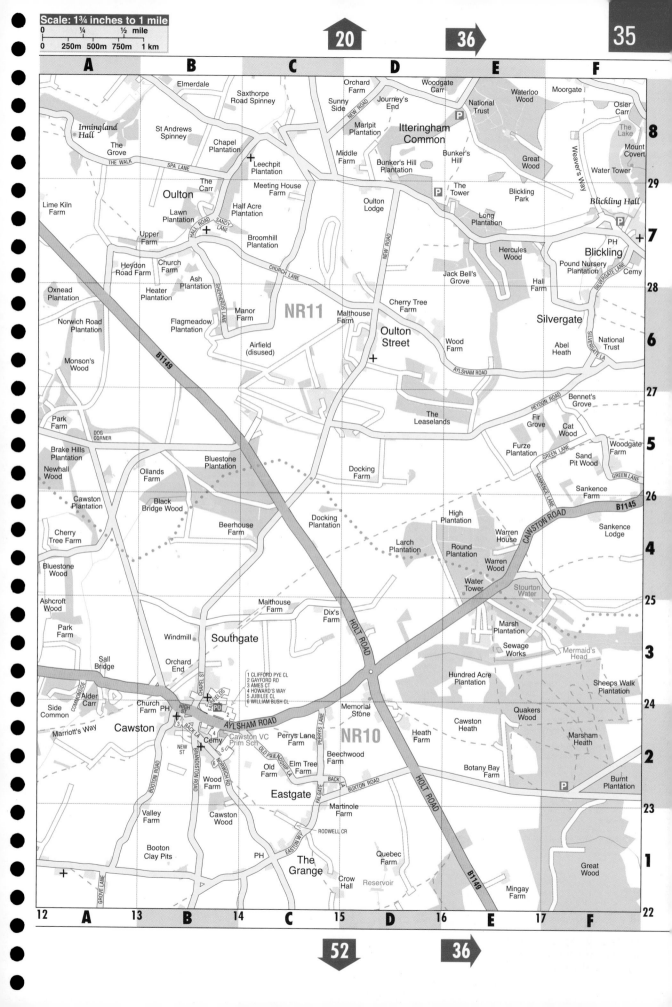

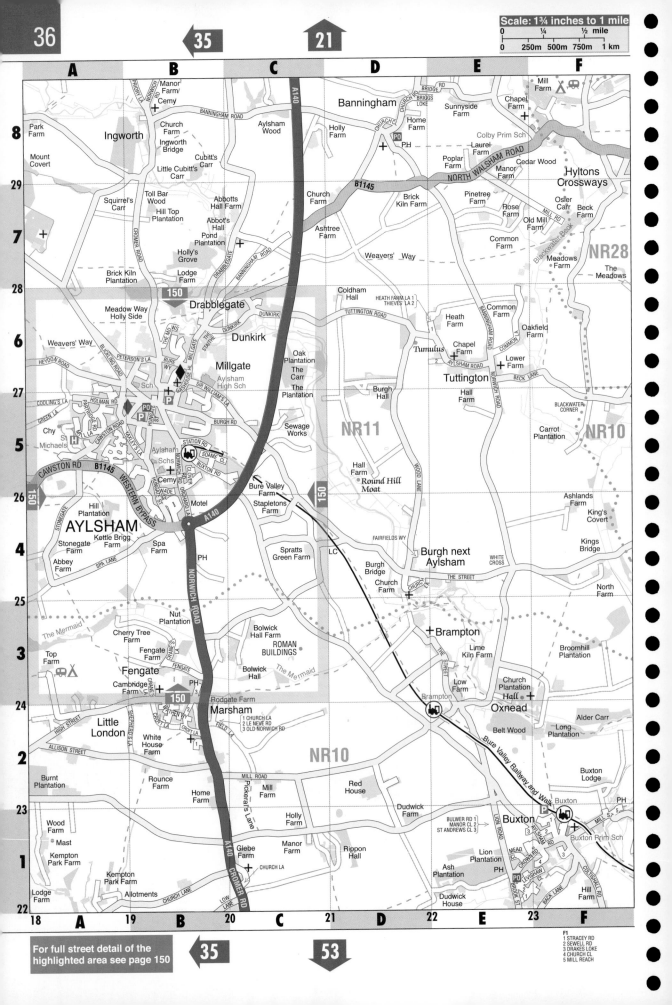

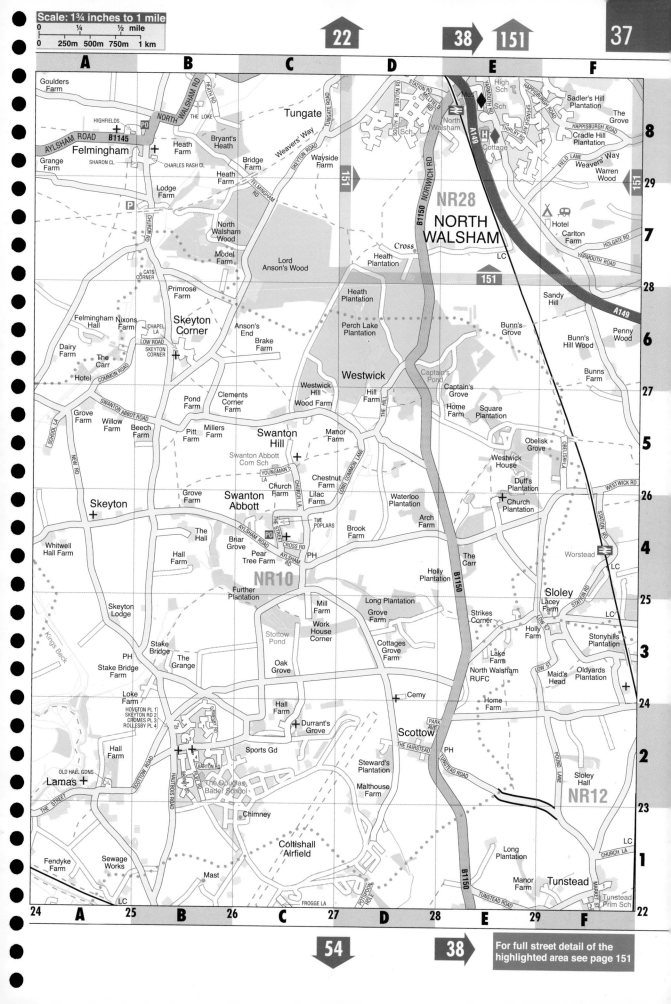

A   B   C   D   E   F

Goulders Farm

HIGHFIELDS

North Walsham Rd
Heath Rd
The Loke

Tungate

Station Rd
South Rd
Buxton Rd
Millfield Rd
Yarmouth Rd
High Sch
Happisburgh Road
Spenser Av
Thirlby Rd
Field Lane
Sadler's Hill Plantation
The Grove

PO

B1145

Aylsham Road

Felmingham

Grange Farm
Sharon Cl
Charles Rash Cl
Heath Farm
Bryant's Heath
Heath Farm
Bridge Farm
Wayside Farm
Weavers' Way

Lodge Farm

P

North Walsham Wood

Model Farm

Lord Anson's Wood

Felmingham Rd
Skeyton Rd

151

Norwich Rd
B1150
A149

North Walsham

Mus
H
Cottage
Sch
Happisburgh Road
Cradle Hill Plantation
Weavers Way
Warren Wood

151

NR28

NORTH WALSHAM

Hotel
Carlton Farm
Holgate Rd
Yarmouth Road

A149

151

29

8

7

28

Cross
Heath Plantation
Heath Plantation

LC

Sandy Hill

Bunn's Grove
Bunn's Hill Wood
Penny Wood

6

Felmingham Hall
Nixons Farm
Chapel La
Low Road
Skeyton Corner

Skeyton Corner

Anson's End
Brake Farm

Perch Lake Plantation

Westwick

Captain's Pond
Captain's Grove

Bunns Farm

27

Dairy Farm
The Carr
Hotel
Common Road

Grove Farm
Willow Farm
Swanton Abbot Road
Beech Farm
Pitt Farm
Millers Farm
Pond Farm
Clements Corner Farm

Westwick Hill
Wood Farm

Hill Farm
The Hill

Home Farm
Square Plantation
Obelisk Grove
Obelisk La

Westwick Rd

5

School La
New Rd

Swanton Hill
Swanton Abbott Com Sch
Youngman's La
Church Farm
Chestnut Farm
Manor Farm
Lilac Farm
Long Common Lane

Waterloo Plantation

Westwick House
Duff's Plantation
Church Plantation
Station Rd

26

Skeyton

Grove Farm
Swanton Abbott
Church La
Church La
The Poplars
Cross Rd

Aylsham Rd
PH
Brook Farm
Arch Farm

Holly Plantation

B1150
The Carr
Worstead
LC

Sloley
Lacey Farm
LC

4

Whitwell Hall Farm
The Hall
Hall Farm
Briar Grove
Pear Tree Farm

NR10

Further Plantation

Mill Farm
Work House Corner

Long Plantation
Grove Farm

Strikes Corner

Holly Farm
Stonyhills Plantation

25

Skeyton Lodge

Stake Bridge
The Grange
PH
Stake Bridge Farm

Stottow Pond

Oak Grove
Cottages Grove Farm

North Walsham RUFC
Lake Farm
Low St
Maid's Head
Oldyards Plantation

3

Loke Farm
HOVETON PL 1
SKEYTON RD 2
CROMES PL 3
ROLLESBY PL 4

Hall Farm
Durrant's Grove
Sports Gd
Chrisby Rd
Barton Rd

Hall Farm

Steward's Plantation

Cemy

Scottow
Home Farm

Park Ave
PH
The Fairstead

Sloley Hall

2

Hall Farm
OLD HALL GDNS

Lamas
The Street

Scottow Rd
Haubois Rd
Bangy Rd
The Douglas Bader School

Chimney

Coltishall Airfield

Malthouse Farm

Tunstead Road
B1150
Pound Lane

NR12

23

Fendyke Farm
Sewage Works
Mast
LC
Frogge La
Potspoon Hole

Tunstead Road
B1150

Long Plantation
Manor Farm

Tunstead
LC
Church La
Market St
Tunstead Prim Sch

1

24   A   25   B   26   C   27   D   28   E   29   F   22

Kings Beck

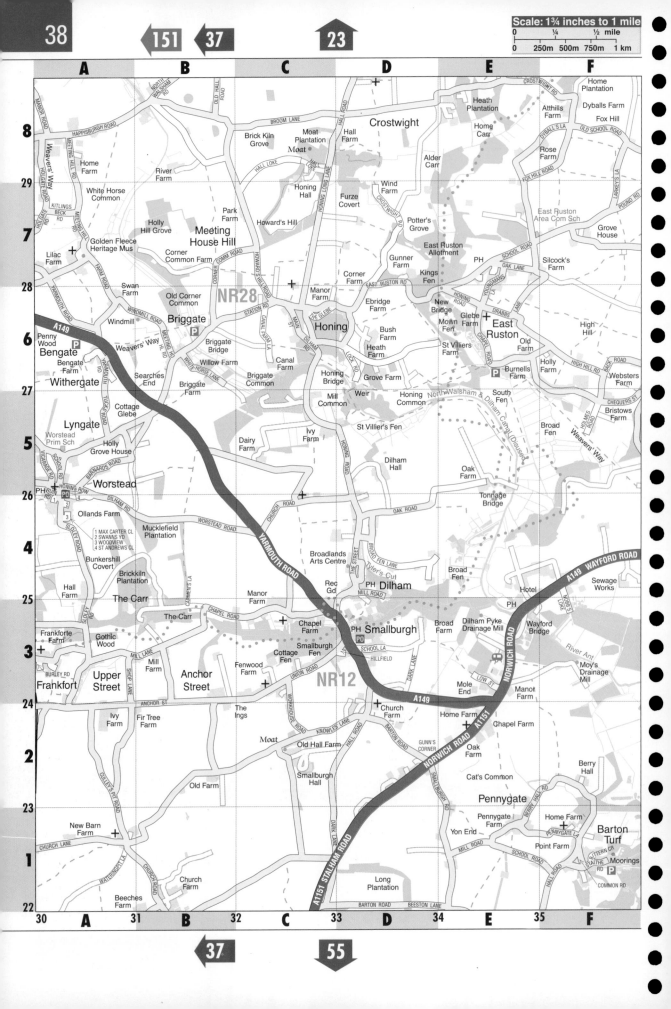

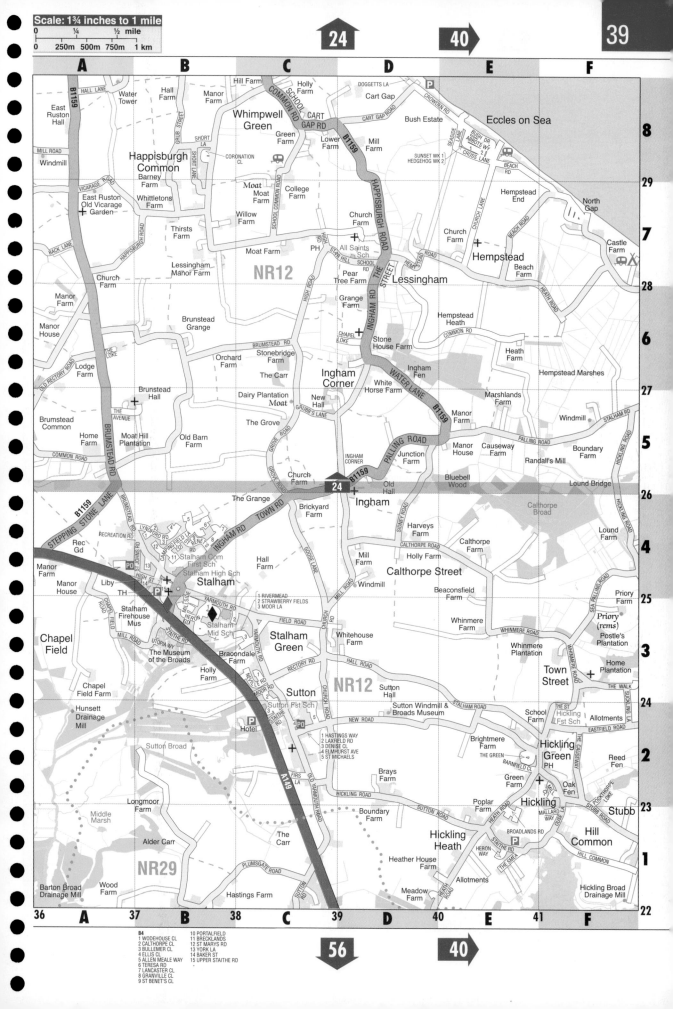

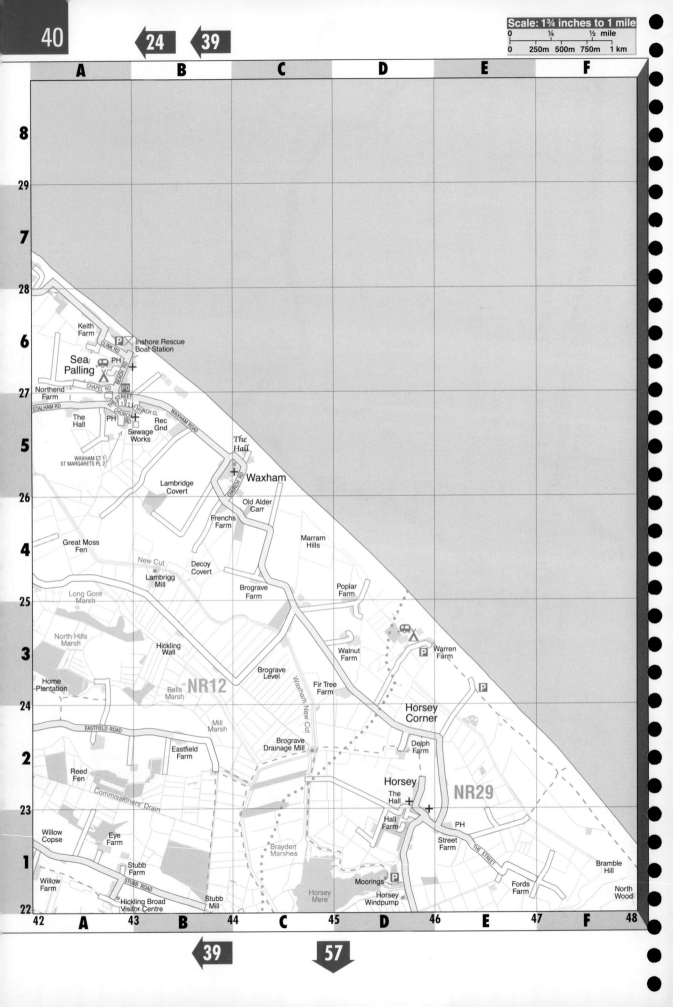

Scale: 1¾ inches to 1 mile

0 ¼ ½ mile
0 250m 500m 750m 1 km

A B C D E F

8
29
7
28
6
27
5
26
4
25
3
24
2
23
1
22

Keith Farm
Inshore Rescue Boat Station
CLINK RD
P
PH
Sea Palling
CHAPEL RD
PO
Northend Farm
STALHAM RD
THE STREET
CHURCH CL
CHURCH RD
WAXHAM ROAD
BEACH RD
The Hall
PH
Rec Gnd
Sewage Works
WAXHAM CT 1
ST MARGARETS PL 2
The Hall
Waxham
Lambridge Covert
Old Alder Carr
Frenchs Farm
Great Moss Fen
Marram Hills
New Cut
Decoy Covert
Lambrigg Mill
Brograve Farm
Poplar Farm
Long Gore Marsh
North Hills Marsh
Hickling Wall
Walnut Farm
Warren Farm
P
P
Home Plantation
NR12
Bells Marsh
Brograve Level
Waxham New Cut
Fir Tree Farm
Horsey Corner
EASTFIELD ROAD
Mill Marsh
Eastfield Farm
Brograve Drainage Mill
Delph Farm
Reed Fen
Horsey
NR29
Commissioners' Drain
The Hall
Hall Farm
PH
Willow Copse
Eye Farm
Brayden Marshes
Street Farm
THE STREET
Bramble Hill
Stubb Farm
Willow Farm
STUBB ROAD
Moorings
P
Fords Farm
North Wood
Hickling Broad Visitor Centre
Stubb Mill
Horsey Mere
Horsey Windpump

42 A 43 B 44 C 45 D 46 E 47 F 48

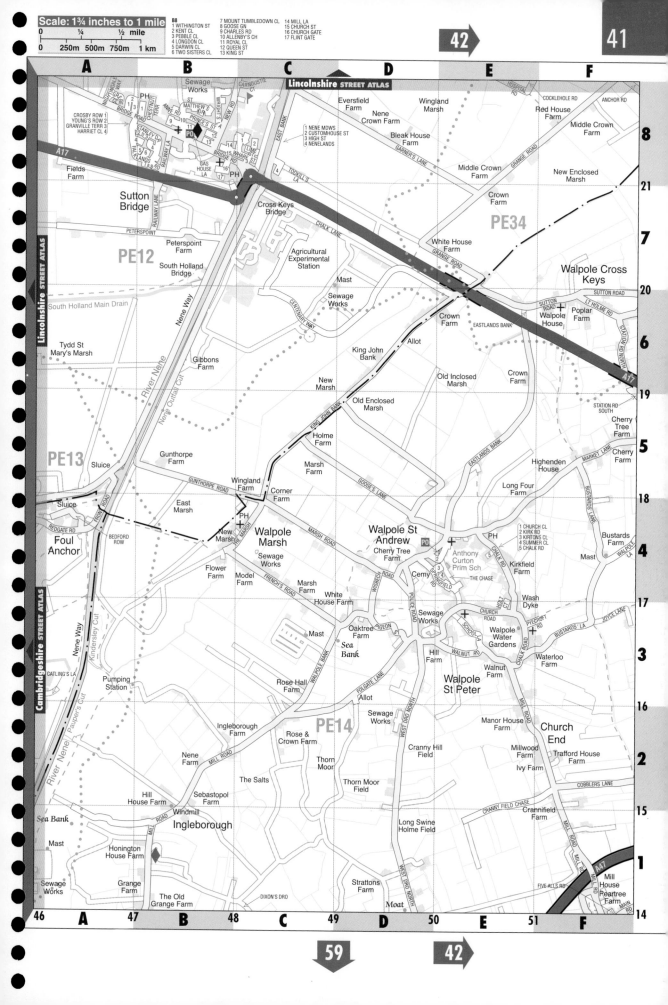

B8
1 WITHINGTON ST
2 KENT CL
3 PEBBLE CL
4 LONGDON CL
5 DARWIN CL
6 TWO SISTERS CL
7 MOUNT TUMBLEDOWN CL
8 GOOSE GN
9 CHARLES RD
10 ALLENBY'S CH
11 ROYAL CL
12 QUEEN ST
13 KING ST
14 MILL LA
15 CHURCH ST
16 CHURCH GATE
17 FLINT GATE

Lincolnshire STREET ATLAS

Lincolnshire STREET ATLAS

Cambridgeshire STREET ATLAS

Eversfield
Farm

Wingland
Marsh

Cocklehole Rd   Anchor Rd

Red House
Farm

Middle Crown
Farm

8

Nene
Crown Farm

Bleak House
Farm

Middle Crown
Farm

New Enclosed
Marsh

21

1 NENE MDWS
2 CUSTOMHOUSE ST
3 HIGH ST
4 NENELANDS

Garner's Lane

Crown
Farm

PE34

Sutton
Bridge

Cross Keys
Bridge

White House
Farm

Walpole Cross
Keys

7

Peterspoint

PE12

Peterspoint
Farm

South Holland
Bridge

Agricultural
Experimental
Station

Sutton Road

Sutton
Road

Walpole
House

Poplar
Farm

20

South Holland Main Drain

Mast

Sewage
Works

Crown
Farm

Eastlands Bank

6

Tydd St
Mary's Marsh

Gibbons
Farm

King John
Bank

Allot

Old Inclosed
Marsh

Crown
Farm

Station Rd
South

19

PE13

Sluice

Gunthorpe
Farm

New
Marsh

Old Enclosed
Marsh

Eastlands Bank

Highenden
House

Cherry
Tree
Farm

Cherry
Tree
Farm

5

Sluice

East
Marsh

Wingland
Farm

Holme
Farm

Long Four
Farm

Market Lane

18

Foul
Anchor

Bedford
Row

New
Marsh

Corner
Farm

Marsh
Farm

Goose's Lane

Walpole St
Andrew

1 CHURCH CL
2 KIRK RD
3 KIRTONS CL
4 SUMMER CL
5 CHALK RD

Bustards
Farm

4

Flower
Farm

Walpole
Marsh

Model
Farm

Marsh
Farm

Cherry Tree
Farm

Anthony
Curton
Prim Sch

Kirkfield
Farm

Mast

Sewage
Works

White
House Farm

Cemy

The Chase

Wash
Dyke

17

Nene Way

Kindersley Cut

Mast

Oaktree
Farm

Sewage
Works

Walpole
Water
Gardens

Waterloo
Farm

3

Pumping
Station

Sea
Bank

Hill
Farm

Walnut
Farm

Rose Hall
Farm

Walpole
St Peter

16

River Nene

Pauper's Cut

Ingleborough
Farm

Rose &
Crown Farm

PE14

Allot

Sewage
Works

Manor House
Farm

Church
End

Nene
Farm

Cranny Hill
Field

Millwood
Farm

Trafford House
Farm

2

The Salts

Thorn
Moor

Thorn Moor
Field

Ivy Farm

Cobblers Lane

Sea Bank

Hill
House Farm

Sebastopol
Farm

Crannifield
Farm

15

Mast

Windmill

Ingleborough

Long Swine
Holme Field

Cranny Field Chase

Sewage
Works

Honington
House Farm

Mill
House
Peartree
Farm

1

Grange
Farm

The Old
Grange Farm

Dixon's Dro

Strattons
Farm

Moat

Five-Alls Rd

A47

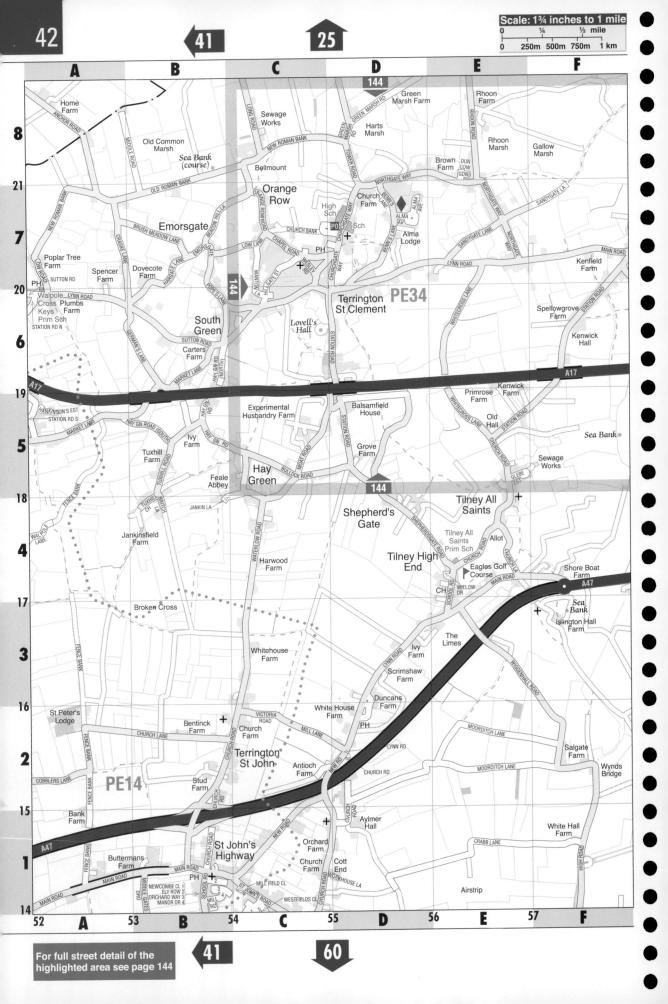

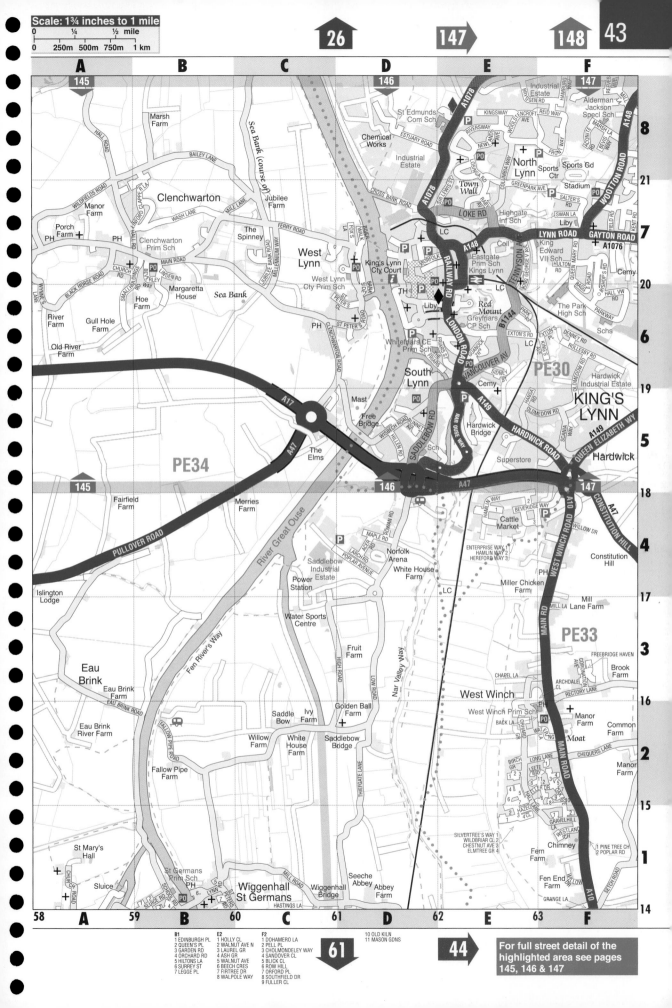

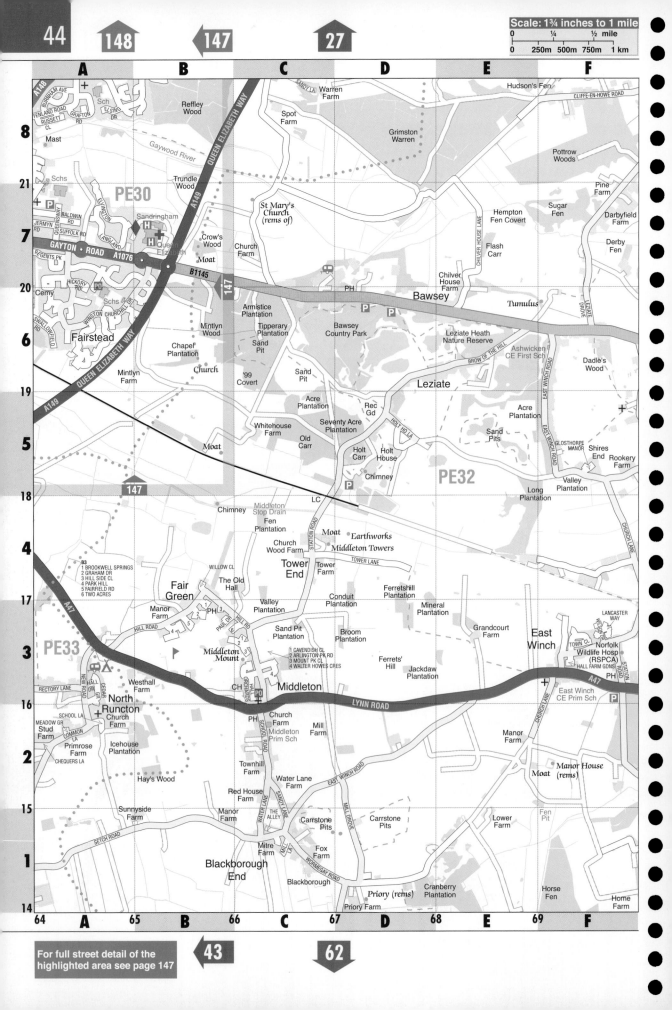

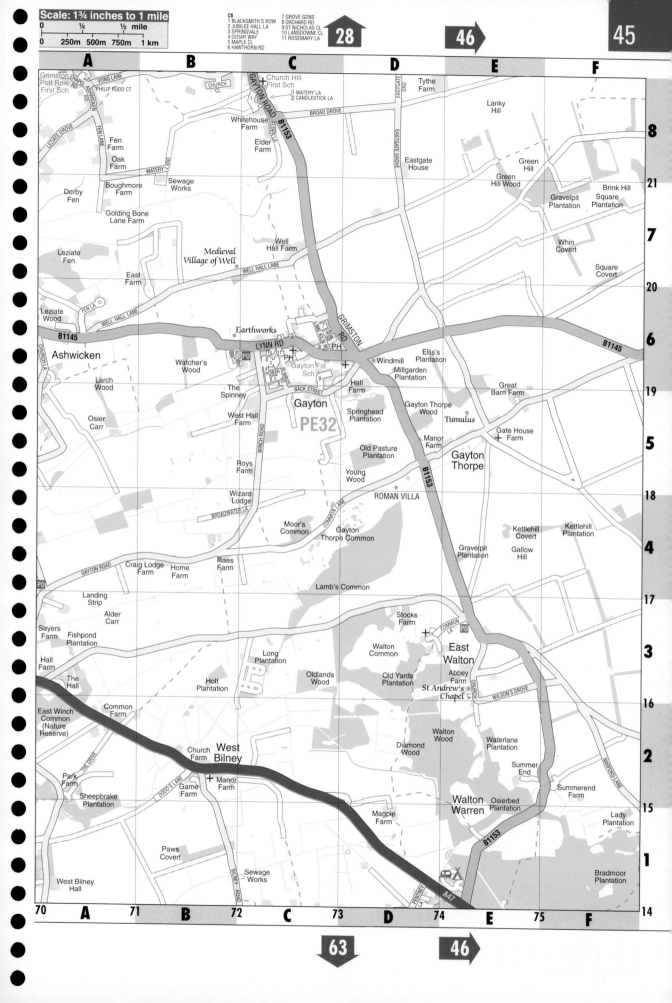

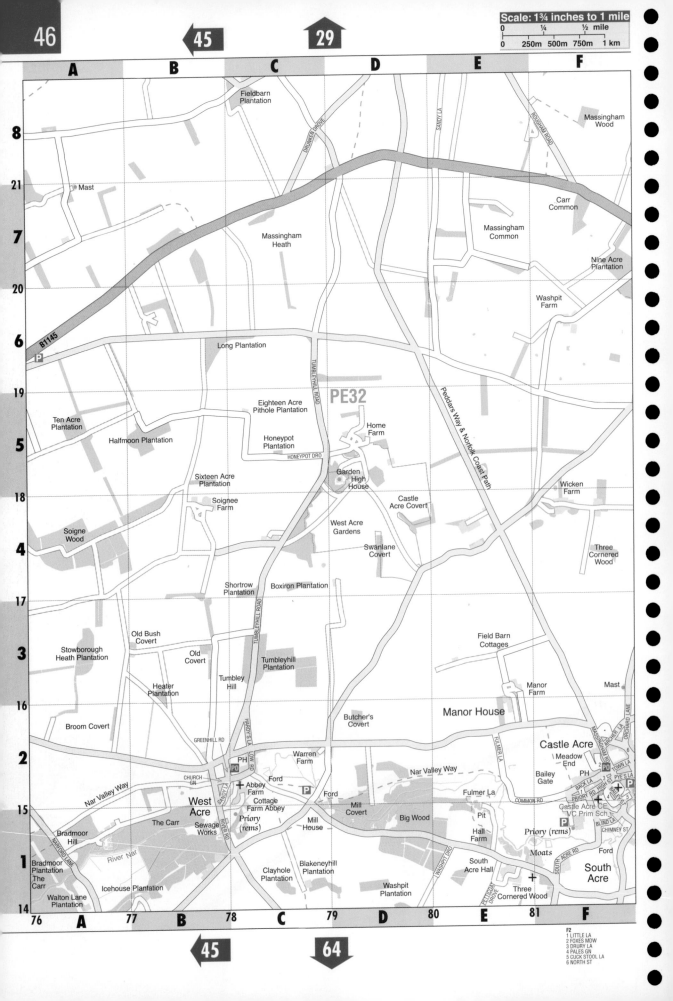

45

29

Scale: 1¾ inches to 1 mile
0   ¼   ½ mile
0   250m   500m   750m   1 km

A   B   C   D   E   F

8

21

7

20

6

19

5

18

4

17

3

16

2

15

1

14

76   A   77   B   78   C   79   D   80   E   81   F

Fieldbarn Plantation

SANDY LA

ROUGHAM ROAD

Massingham Wood

Mast

Carr Common

Massingham Heath

Massingham Common

Nine Acre Plantation

Washpit Farm

B1145

Long Plantation

PE32

DRUNKEN DROVE

TUMBLEYHILL ROAD

Eighteen Acre Pithole Plantation

Ten Acre Plantation

Halfmoon Plantation

Honeypot Plantation

HONEYPOT DRO

Home Farm

Peddars Way & Norfolk Coast Path

Sixteen Acre Plantation

Garden High House

Wicken Farm

Soignee Farm

Castle Acre Covert

West Acre Gardens

Soigne Wood

Swanlane Covert

Three Cornered Wood

Shortrow Plantation

Boxiron Plantation

TUMBLEYHILL ROAD

Field Barn Cottages

Old Bush Covert

Stowborough Heath Plantation

Old Covert

Tumbleyhill Plantation

Manor Farm

Mast

Heater Plantation

Tumbley Hill

Butcher's Covert

Manor House

Broom Covert

GREENHILL RD

HARDY'S LA

LOW RD

Castle Acre

Meadow End

MASSINGHAM RD

ARCHER LA

ORCHARD LANE

FULMER LA

Warren Farm

Nar Valley Way

Bailey Gate

PH

PO

TOWN LA

PYE'S LA

PH

PO

CHURCH GN

SANDY LA

Abbey Farm

Ford

Ford

Nar Valley Way

BACK LA

PRIORY RD

HIGH ST

Nar Valley Way

West Acre

P

Cottage Farm Abbey

Mill Covert

Big Wood

Fulmer La

COMMON RD

Castle Acre CE VC Prim Sch

BLIND LA

CHIMNEY ST

The Carr

Sewage Works

Priory (rems)

Mill House

Pit

Hall Farm

P

Priory (rems)

Ford

Bradmoor Hill

MARGROF LANE

River Nar

Clayhole Plantation

Blakeneyhill Plantation

WASHPIT DRO

South Acre Hall

Moats

South Acre

Bradmoor Plantation The Carr

Icehouse Plantation

Washpit Plantation

PETTICOAT DROVE

Three Cornered Wood

SOUTH ACRE RD

Walton Lane Plantation

45

64

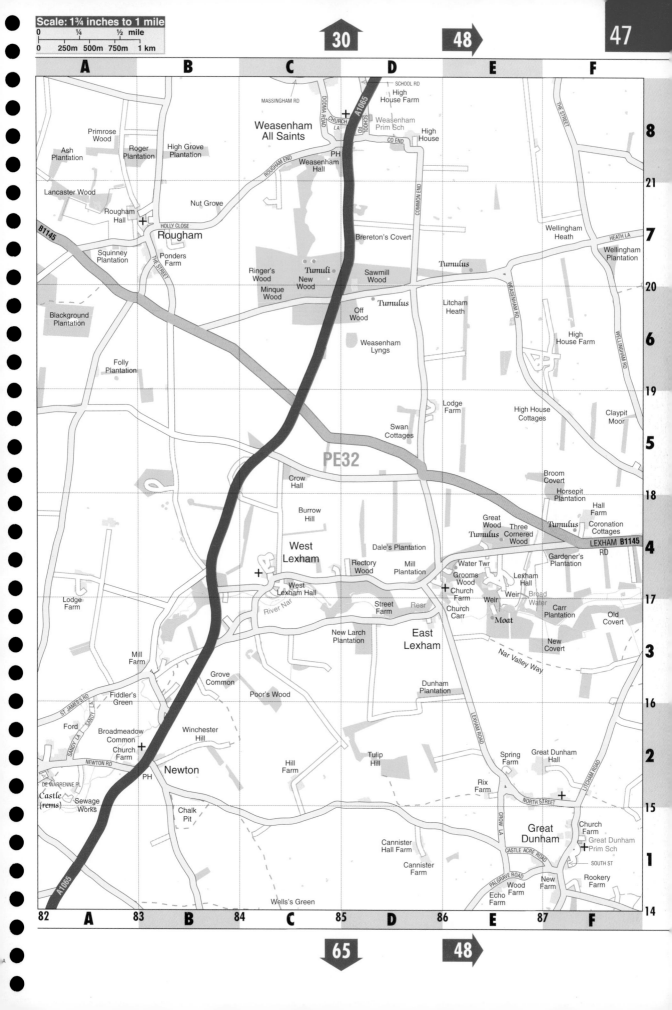

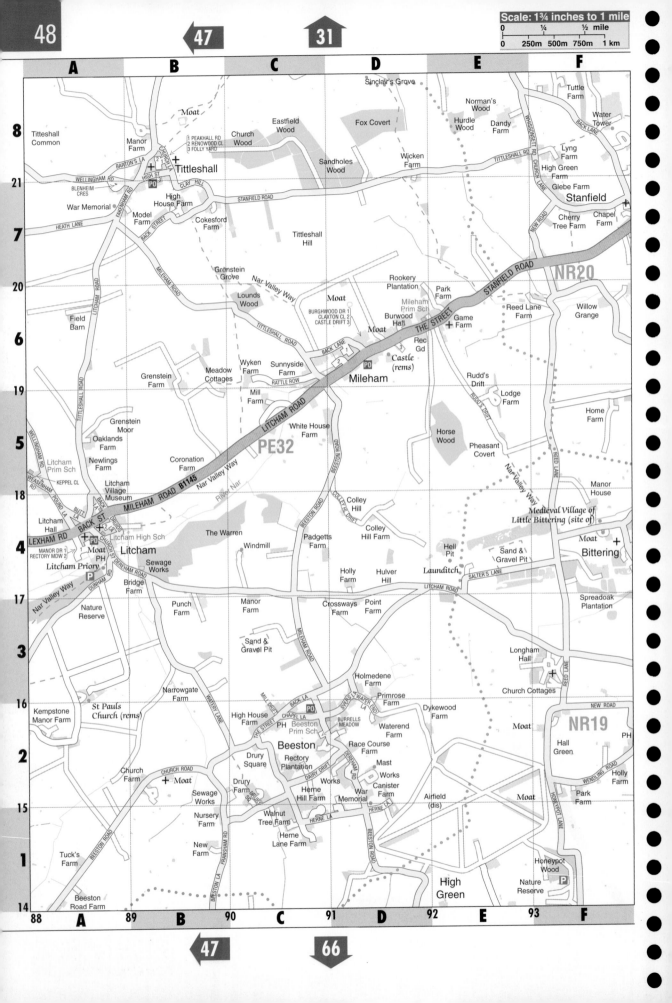

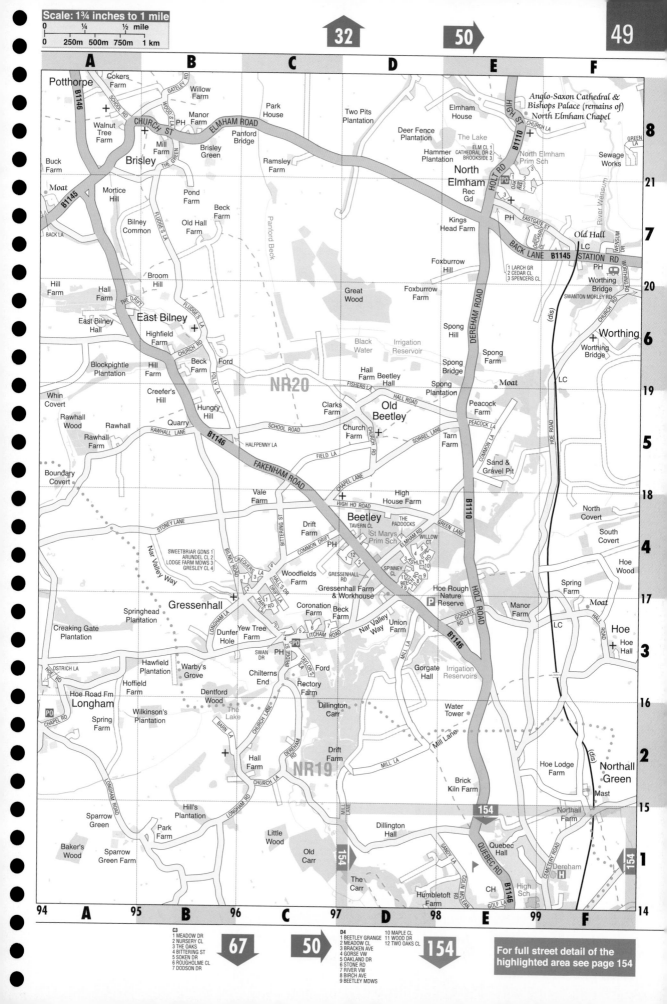

67   50   154

For full street detail of the highlighted area see page 154

C3
1 MEADOW DR
2 NURSERY CL
3 THE OAKS
4 BITTERING ST
5 SOKEN DR
6 ROUGHOLME CL
7 DODSON DR

D4
1 BEETLEY GRANGE
2 MEADOW CL
3 BRACKEN AVE
4 GORSE VW
5 OAKLAND DR
6 STONE RD
7 RIVER VW
8 BIRCH AVE
9 BEETLEY MDWS
10 MAPLE CL
11 WOOD DR
12 TWO OAKS CL

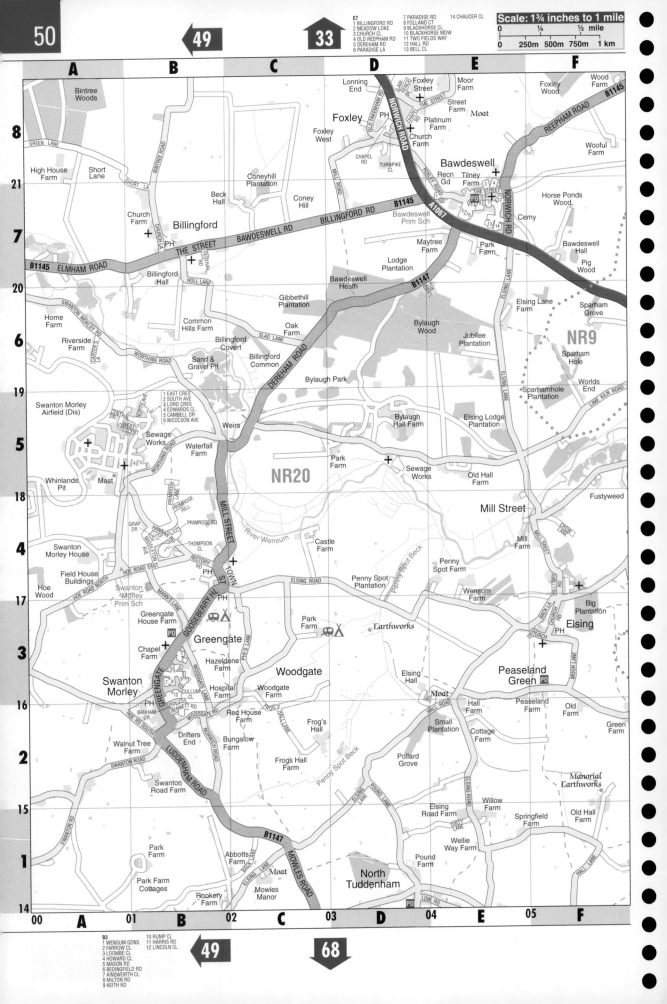

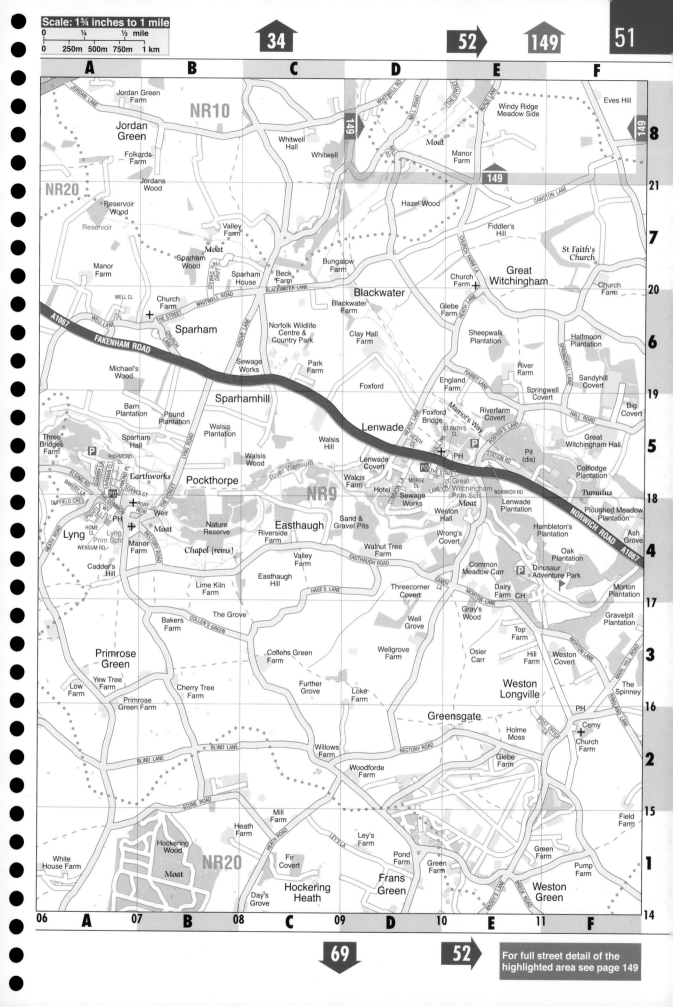

A   B   C   D   E   F

8
Jordan Lane
Jordan Green Farm
NR10
Whitwell Hall
Whitwell
Whitwell Rd
Mill Road
Moat
The Street
Rupe Lane
Windy Ridge Meadow Side
Eves Hill
149
Jordan Green
Folkards Farm
Jordans Wood
Manor Farm
149

21

7
NR20
Reservoir Wood
Reservoir
Valley Farm
Moat
Sparham Wood
Beck Farm
Bungalow Farm
Hazel Wood
Cawston Lane
Fiddler's Hill
St Faith's Church
Manor Farm
Sparham House

20
Church Farm
Well Cl
Well La
The Street
Whitwell Road
Blackwater Lane
Blackwater
Heath Lane
Church Farm
Great Witchingham
Church Lane
Church Farm
Grone La
Blackwater Farm
Glebe Farm
Church Lane

6
A1067
Fakenham Road
Michael's Wood
Sparham
Clay Hall Farm
Sheepwalk Plantation
Halfmoon Plantation
Norfolk Wildlife Centre & Country Park
Park Farm
Foxford
England Farm
River Farm
Springhill Lane
Sandyhill Covert
Big Covert

19
Barn Plantation
Pound Plantation
Sparhamhill
Sewage Works
Walsis Plantation
Foxford Bridge
Marriot's Way
Springwell Covert
Hall Road

5
Three Bridges Farm
Sparham Hall
Walsis Wood
Walsis Hill
River Wensum
Lenwade
St Faith's Cl
Heath Cl
Riverfarm Covert
Porter's Lane
Pit (dis)
Great Witchingham Hall
Coltlodge Plantation
Richmond Cl
Quarry La
Farman Cl
Richmond Pl
Soanes Ct
Earthworks
Pockthorpe
Walcis Wood
Lenwade Covert
Hotel
Morse Cl
The Street
P
PH
Station Rd
Norwich Rd
Tumulus
Bakery La
Duffield Cres
Weir
Nature Reserve
NR9
Walcis Farm
Lake Cl
PO
Great Witchingham Prim Sch
Sewage Works
Moat
Lenwade Plantation
Norwich Road
Ploughed Meadow Plantation

18
Lyng
Port Row
Moat
Chapel (rems)
Easthaugh
Riverside Farm
Sand & Gravel Pits
Weston Hall
Wrong's Covert
Hambleton's Plantation
Oak Plantation
Ash Grove
A1067

4
Home Cl
Lyng Prim Sch
Wensum Rd
Manor Farm
Cadder's Hill
Lime Kiln Farm
Valley Farm
Easthaugh Hill
Easthaugh Road
Hase's Lane
Walnut Tree Farm
Threecorner Covert
Sandy La
Morton Lane
Common Meadow Carr
Gray's Wood
Dairy Farm
CH
P
Dinosaur Adventure Park
Morton Plantation

17
The Grove
Bakers Farm
Collen's Green
Well Grove
Wellgrove Farm
Osier Carr
Top Farm
Hill Farm
Weston Covert
Morton Lane
Gravelpit Plantation

3
Primrose Green
Yew Tree Farm
Cherry Tree Farm
Collens Green Farm
Further Grove
Loke Farm
Weston Longville
Post Office La
PH
Marl Hill Road
England Lane
The Spinney

16
Low Farm
Primrose Green Farm
Greensgate
Cemy
Church Farm

2
Blind Lane
Blind Lane
Willows Farm
Rectory Road
Holme Moss
Glebe Farm

15
Stone Road
Mill Farm
Heath Farm
Field Farm

1
White House Farm
Hockering Wood
Moat
NR20
Heath Road
Fir Covert
Day's Grove
Hockering Heath
Ley's La
Ley's Farm
Frans Green
Pond Farm
Green Farm
Paddy's Lane
Breck Road
Weston Green
Green Farm
Pump Farm

14

06   A   07   B   08   C   09   D   10   E   11   F

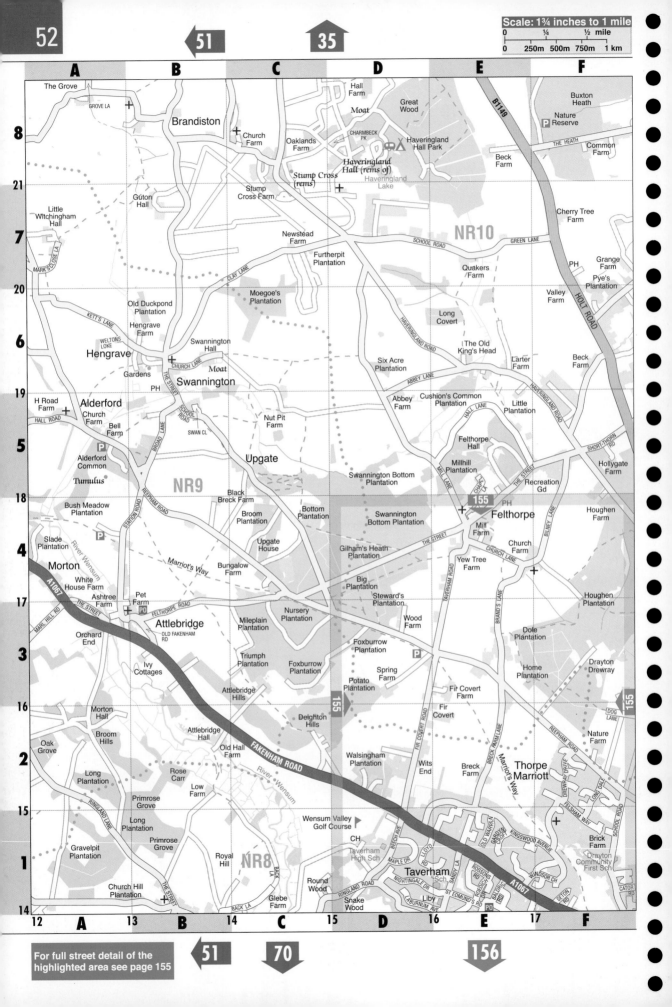

51 35

The Grove
GROVE LA
Brandiston
Church Farm
Hall Farm
Moat
Great Wood
Buxton Heath
Nature Reserve
B1149
Oaklands Farm
CHARMBECK PK
Haveringland Hall Park
Beck Farm
Common Farm
THE HEATH

8

Stump Cross (rems)
Haveringland Hall (rems of)
Haveringland Lake
NR10

21

Little Witchingham Hall
Gúton Hall
Stump Cross Farm
Newstead Farm
SCHOOL ROAD
GREEN LANE
Cherry Tree Farm

MARK'S CLOSE LA

7

CLAY LANE
Furtherpit Plantation
Quakers Farm
Grange Farm
Pye's Plantation
PH

20

KETT'S LANE
Old Duckpond Plantation
Moegoe's Plantation
Long Covert
Valley Farm
HOLT ROAD

WELTONS LOKE
Hengrave Farm
Swannington Hall
HAVERINGLAND ROAD
Six Acre Plantation
The Old King's Head
Larter Farm
Beck Farm

6

Hengrave
CHURCH LANE
Moat
Swannington
THE STREET
Gardens
PH
ABBEY LANE
Abbey Farm
Cushion's Common Plantation
HAVERINGLAND ROAD

19

H Road Farm
Church Farm
Bell Farm
BROAD LANE
SCHOOL ROAD
SWAN CL
Nut Pit Farm
HALL LANE
Felthorpe Hall
Little Plantation
SHORT-THORN RD

HALL ROAD

5

Alderford
P
Alderford Common
Upgate
Swannington Bottom Plantation
CHAPEL LA
Millhill Plantation
THE STREET
Recreation Gd
Hollygate Farm

Tumulus

NR9
Black Breck Farm
Broom Plantation
Bottom Plantation
Swannington Bottom Plantation
155
PH
Felthorpe
Houghen Farm

18

Bush Meadow Plantation
REEPHAM ROAD
STATION ROAD
Upgate House
Gilham's Heath Plantation
THE STREET
Mill Farm
MILL LANE
BILNEY LA
Church Farm

4

Slade Plantation
P
Marriot's Way
Bungalow Farm
Big Plantation
Yew Tree Farm
CHURCH LANE
Houghen Plantation

Morton
River Wensum
White House Farm
Steward's Plantation
TAVERHAM ROAD
Dole Plantation

A1067
Ashtree Farm
Pet Farm
PO
Nursery Plantation
Wood Farm
BRAND'S LANE
Drayton Drewray

17

THE STREET
MARL HILL RD
FELTHORPE ROAD
Attlebridge
OLD FAKENHAM RD
Mileplain Plantation
Foxburrow Plantation
P
Home Plantation

Orchard End
Triumph Plantation
Foxburrow Plantation
Spring Farm
DOG LANE

3

Ivy Cottages
Attlebridge Hills
Potato Plantation
Fir Covert Farm
REEPHAM ROAD
Nature Farm
155

16

Morton Hall
Attlebridge Hall
Deighton Hills
155
Fir Covert
FIR COVERT ROAD
BRECK FARM LANE

Broom Hills
Old Hall Farm
FAKENHAM ROAD
Walsingham Plantation
Wits End
Breck Farm
Marriot's Way
Thorpe Marriott
DREWRAY DRIVE

2

Oak Grove
Rose Carr
River Wensum
TOMS DALE
FELSHAM WAY
SCHOOL ROAD

Long Plantation
Low Farm
Wensum Valley Golf Course
KINGSWOOD AVENUE

15

Primrose Grove
CH
OLD WARREN
GARDYN CROFT
Brick Farm

RINGLAND LANE
Long Plantation
Primrose Grove
Taverham High Sch
BEECH AVE
MAPLE DR
Drayton Community First Sch

1

Gravelpit Plantation
Royal Hill
NR8
Round Wood
RINGLAND ROAD
Taverham
Sch
ROSSONS RD
CATOR RD

Church Hill Plantation
THE STREET
BACK LA
Glebe Farm
Snake Wood
NIGHTINGALE DR
LLOYD RD
SAINT LA
ST EDMUND'S LA
LABURNUM AVE
Liby
A1067
PO
WINDSOR CH
SETON RD
BALDING RD
RIVERDENE

14

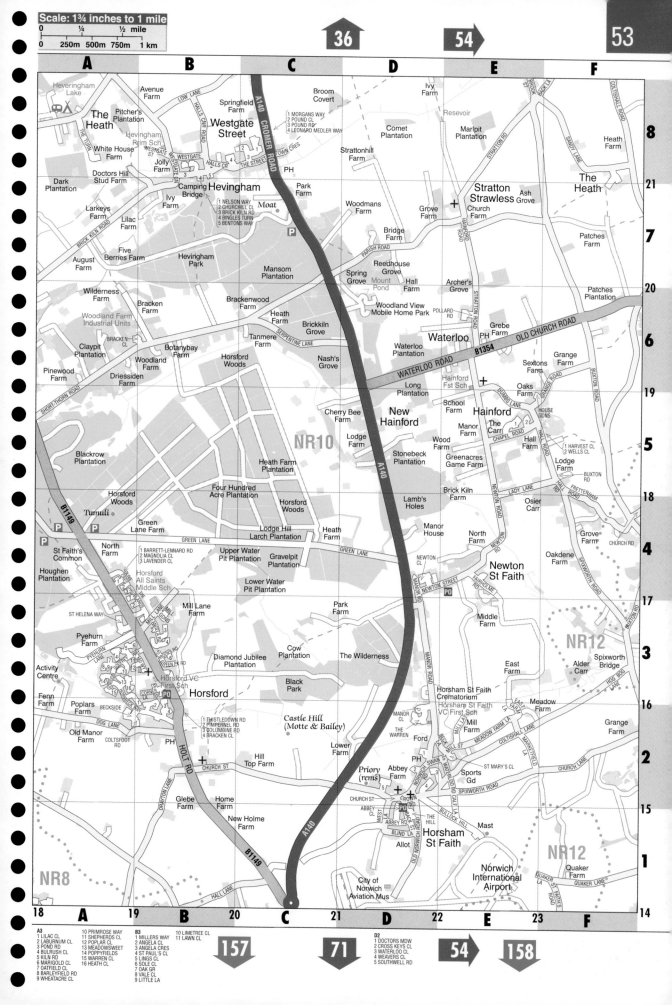

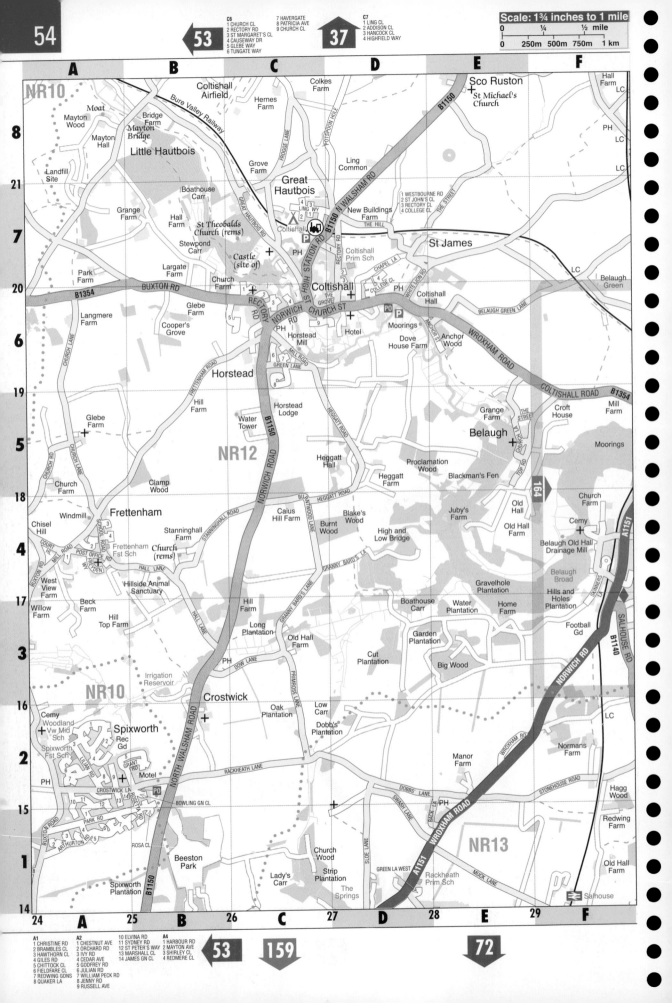

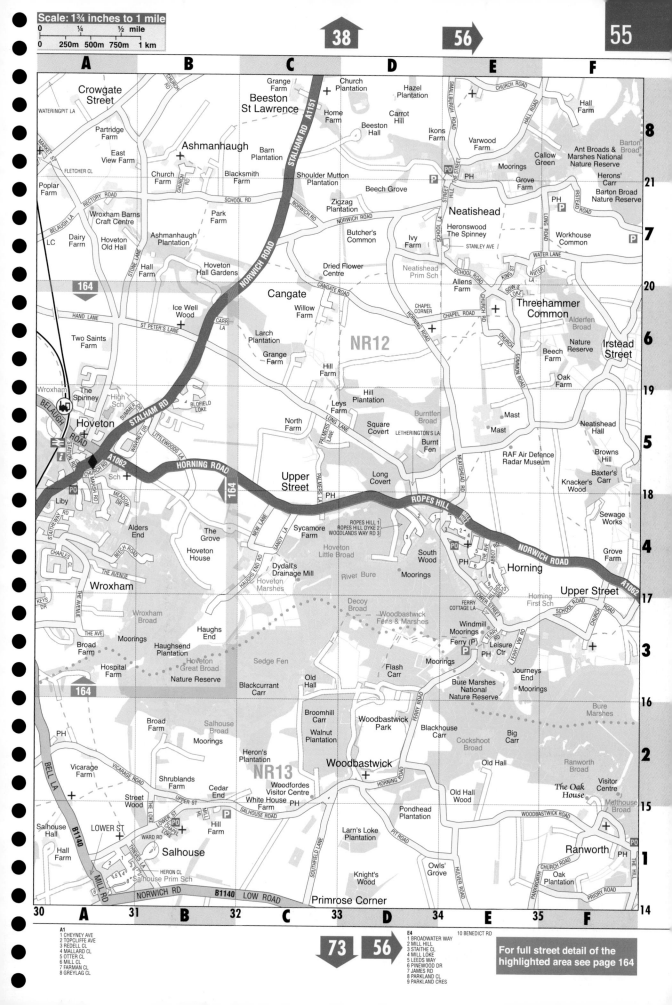

73   56

A1
1 CHEYNEY AVE
2 TOPCLIFFE AVE
3 REDELL CL
4 MALLARD CL
5 OTTER CL
6 MILL CL
7 FARMAN CL
8 GREYLAG CL

E4
1 BROADWATER WAY
2 MILL HILL
3 STAITHE CL
4 MILL LOKE
5 LEEDS WAY
6 PINEWOOD DR
7 JAMES RD
8 PARKLAND CL
9 PARKLAND CRES

10 BENEDICT RD

For full street detail of the
highlighted area see page 164

C5
1 LAURELS CRES
2 WILLOW WAY
3 SCHOOL CL
4 PIKES NURSERY

C8
1 CHAPELFIELD CL
2 LEA RD
3 LIMES RD
4 CANON WAKE CT
5 ST CATHERINE'S AVE

F6
1 VICARAGE CL
2 GLEBE CL
3 ORCHARD DR
4 DOVE HOUSE LA
5 STATION RD

Scale: 1¾ inches to 1 mile
0   ¼   ½ mile
0   250m 500m 750m 1 km

Catfield
Alder Carr
Catfield Common
Hickling Broad
Barton Broad Nature Reserve
Fenside
Staithe Farm
Heath Farm
Weavers Way
Swim Cootts Drainage Mill
Swim Coots
Barton Broad
Middle Marsh Drainage Mill
Catfield Hall
Catfield CE Fst Sch
Oak Farm
Little Fen
Irstead
Church Wood
Hurst Wood
Sharp Street
Laurels Farm
High House Farm
Coll's Plantation
Deek Side
Little Fen
Elderbush Lane
Rose Farm
Old Carr
Moorings
Cobbs Farm
Summer House Farm
Furrows End
Rookery Farm
Falgate Carr
Hall Fen
Jock's Wood
Cottage Grove Farm
Water Tower
Walton Hall
Potter Heigham
NR12
How Hill Nature Reserve
Broad Fen
Summer House Wood
Sewage Works
Ludham Airstrip
Allot
Post Office Farm
Pigeon Wood
Toad Hole Wood
Cromes Farm
How Hill
Ludham Rd
A1062
Clay Rack Drainage Mill
Boardman's Drainage Mill
Toad Hole Cottage Mus
How Hill Farm
Pages Farm
NR29
Fritton
Red Roofs Farm
Reedham Marsh
Turf Fen Drainage Mill
Turf Fen
Moorings
Rec Gd
Ludham Fst Sch
High Mill Hill
High House Farm
Lower Farm
Potter Heigham New Bridge
Broad Mead Farm
Norwich Road
Yarmouth Road
Ludham
Green Farm
Horse Fen
Repps Level
The Limes Farm
Rec Gd
Journey's End
Weavers Way
White House Farm
Hall Common
Manor Farm
Horse Fen
Womack Water Drainage Mill
Repps
Elm Tree Farm
Moorings
Willow Fen
Fen Hill
Ludham Hall
Moorings
River Thurne
Hall Farm
Neaves Mill
Johnson Street
Bridge Farm
Cold Harbour Farm
Lilac Farm
Ludham Bridge Drainage Mill
A1062
Ludham Bridge
Wind Farm
Hundred Dike
Woodside Farm
Shallam Dike
Abbey Farm
Repps Road
NR12
Horning Hall
Thurne
St Benet's Abbey Drainage Mill
St Benet's Abbey
Thurne Dyke Drainage Mill
St Benet's Level Drainage Mill
Home Farm
School Farm
Ashby Hall
Ward Marsh
River Bure
Manor Farm
Boundary Rd
Glebe Farm
Ranworth Marshes
Thurne Mouth
Boundary House
Cross Road
New House Farm
Harrisons Farm
Dairy Farm
Reed Side
Moorings
NR13
Tall Mill Drainage Mill
Manor Farm
Dovehouse Plantation
South Walsham Broad

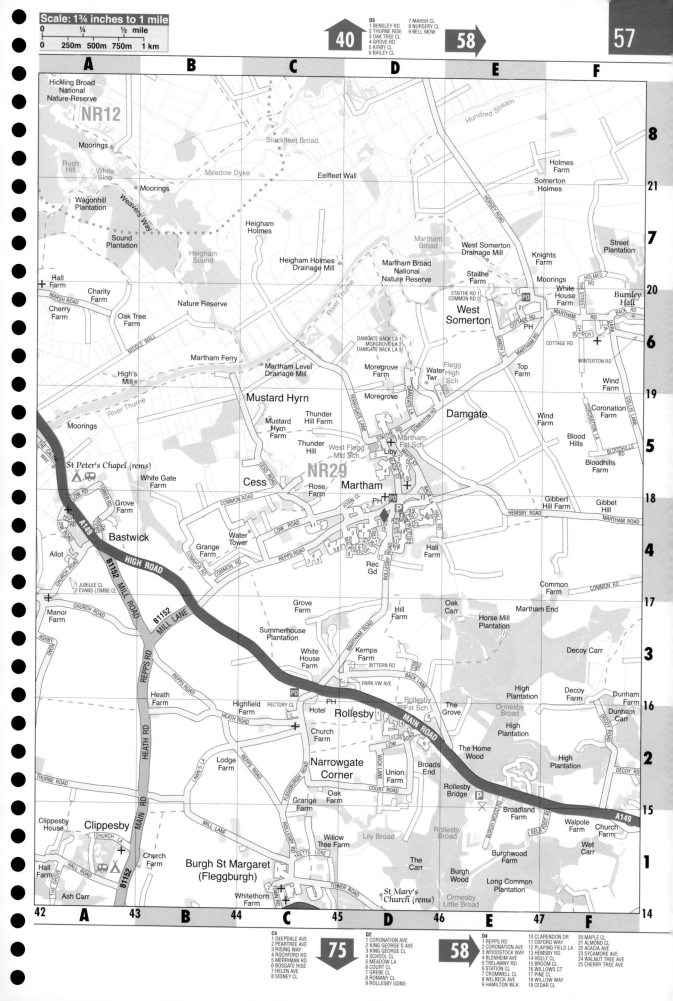

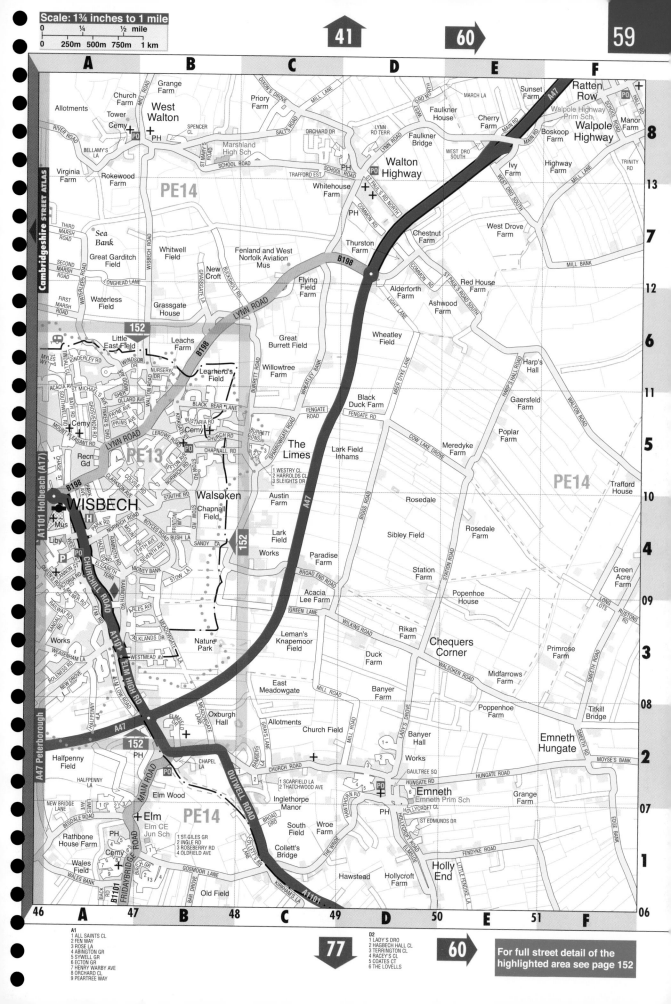

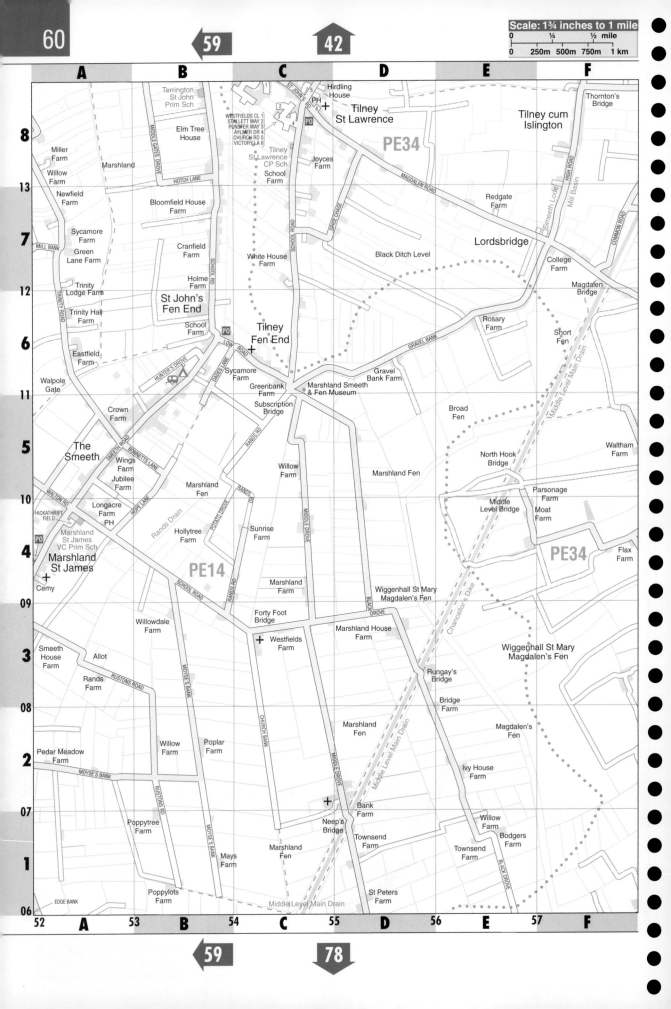

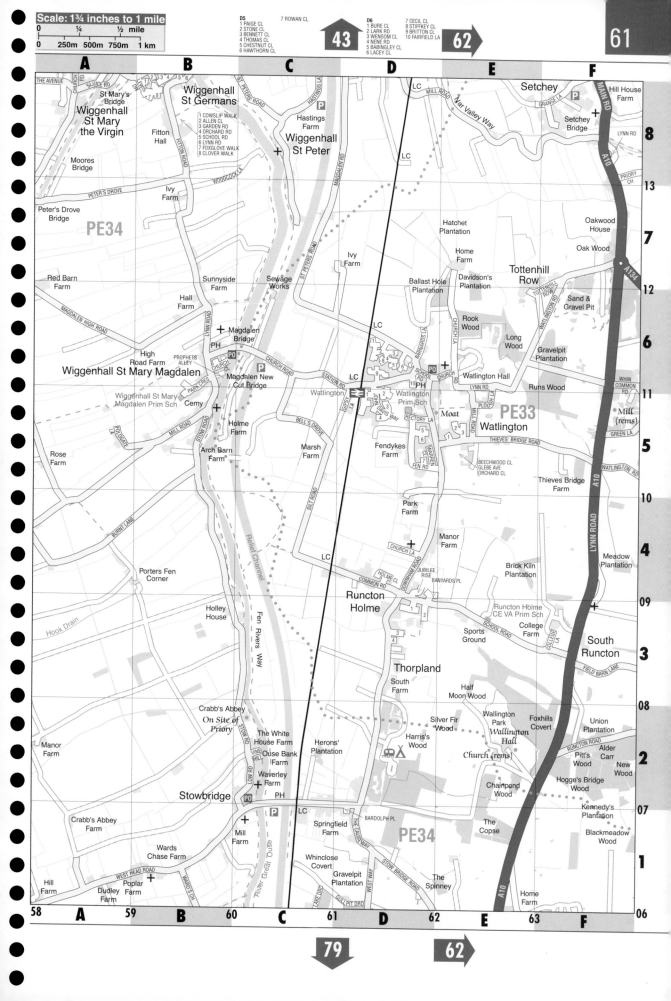

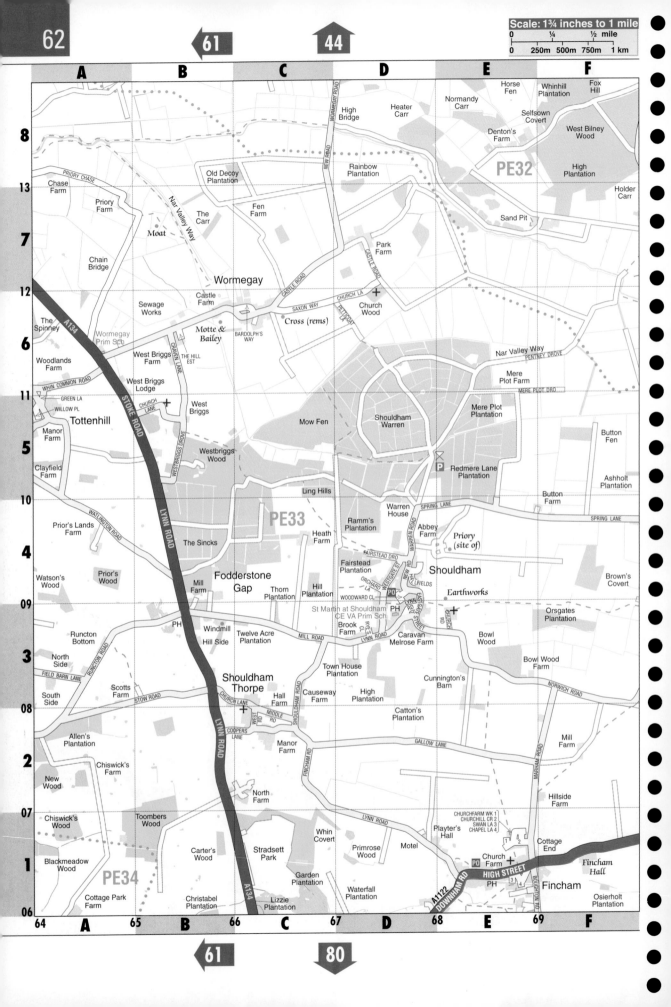

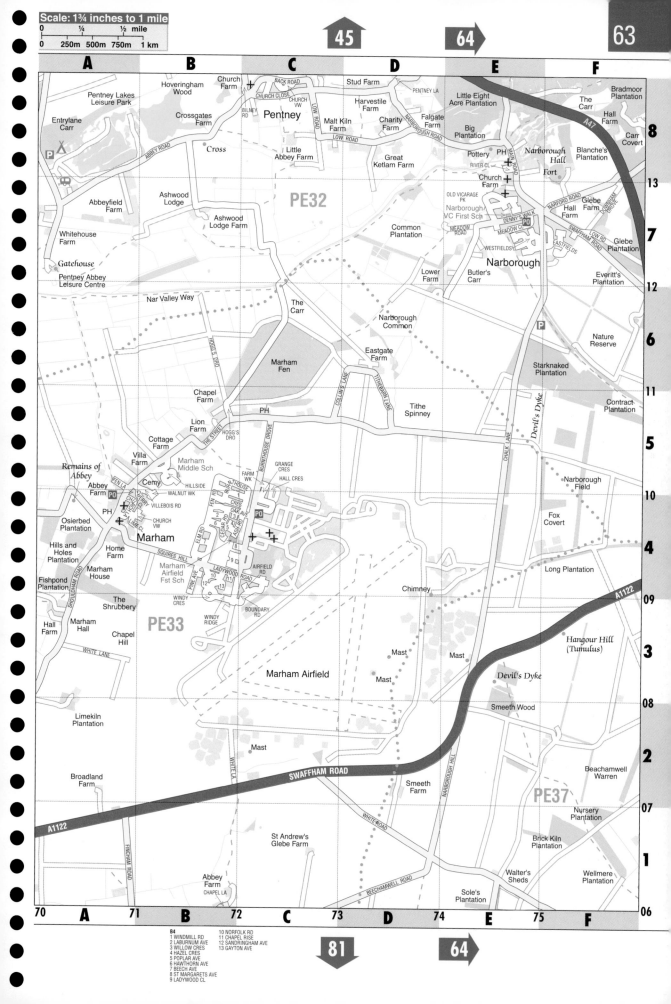

A **B** **C** **D** **E** **F**

Pentney Lakes Leisure Park

Entrylane Carr

Hoveringham Wood

Crossgates Farm

Church Farm

Church Close

Back Road

Stud Farm

PENTNEY LA

Little Eight Acre Plantation

The Carr

Bradmoor Plantation

Hall Farm

A47

8

Whitehouse Farm

Abbeyfield Farm

Ashwood Lodge

Cross

BILNEY RD

Pentney

Little Abbey Farm

Malt Kiln Farm

Charity Farm

Harvestile Farm

Falgate Farm

Big Plantation

Pottery

PH

Narborough Hall

Fort

Blanche's Plantation

Carr Covert

13

Gatehouse

Pentney Abbey Leisure Centre

Ashwood Lodge Farm

PE32

Great Ketlam Farm

Common Plantation

OLD VICARAGE PK
Narborough VC First Sch

Church Farm

MEADOW ROAD

DENNY'S WALK
PO

Narborough

Hall Farm

NARFORD ROAD

Glebe Farm

Hall Farm

LOW RD

Glebe Plantation

7

Nar Valley Way

The Carr

Narborough Common

Lower Farm

Butler's Carr

WESTFIELDS

MEADOW CL

EASTFIELDS

SWAFFHAM ROAD

Everitt's Plantation

12

Eastgate Farm

Marham Fen

Narborough Common

COLLIN'S LANE

TITHEBARN LANE

Tithe Spinney

Starknaked Plantation

Devil's Dyke

Nature Reserve

6

Chapel Farm

PH

Lion Farm

THE STREET

HOGG'S DRO

BURNTHOUSE DROVE

Contract Plantation

11

Cottage Farm

Villa Farm

Marham Middle Sch

FARM WK

GRANGE CRES

HALL CRES

CHALK LANE

Narborough Field

5

Remains of Abbey

Abbey Farm
PO

Cemy

HILLSIDE

WALNUT WK

VILLEBOIS RD

FEN RD

OAK AVE

PO

Fox Covert

10

PH

Marham

CHURCH VW

ELM RD

CEDAR

ASH

LADYWOOD ROAD

AIRFIELD RD

Long Plantation

4

Osierbed Plantation

Hills and Holes Plantation

Home Farm

Marham House

SQUIRES HILL

PINE AVE

Marham Airfield Fst Sch

WINDY CRES

Chimney

A1122

09

Fishpond Plantation

Hall Farm

Marham Hall

The Shrubbery

Chapel Hill

WHITE LANE

PE33

WINDY RIDGE

BOUNDARY RD

Marham Airfield

Mast

Mast

Mast

Devil's Dyke

Hangour Hill (Tumulus)

3

Smeeth Wood

08

Limekiln Plantation

Mast

Mast

NARBOROUGH HILL

Beachamwell Warren

PE37

2

Broadland Farm

FINCHAM ROAD

WHITE CL

SWAFFHAM ROAD

Smeeth Farm

Nursery Plantation

07

A1122

WHITE ROAD

Brick Kiln Plantation

St Andrew's Glebe Farm

Abbey Farm

CHAPEL LA

BEACHAMWELL ROAD

Sole's Plantation

Walter's Sheds

Wellmere Plantation

1

06

70 **A** **71** **B** **72** **C** **73** **D** **74** **E** **75** **F**

B4
1 WINDMILL RD
2 LABURNUM AVE
3 WILLOW CRES
4 HAZEL CRES
5 POPLAR AVE
6 HAWTHORN AVE
7 BEECH AVE
8 ST MARGARETS AVE
9 LADYWOOD CL
10 NORFOLK RD
11 CHAPEL RISE
12 SANDRINGHAM AVE
13 GAYTON AVE

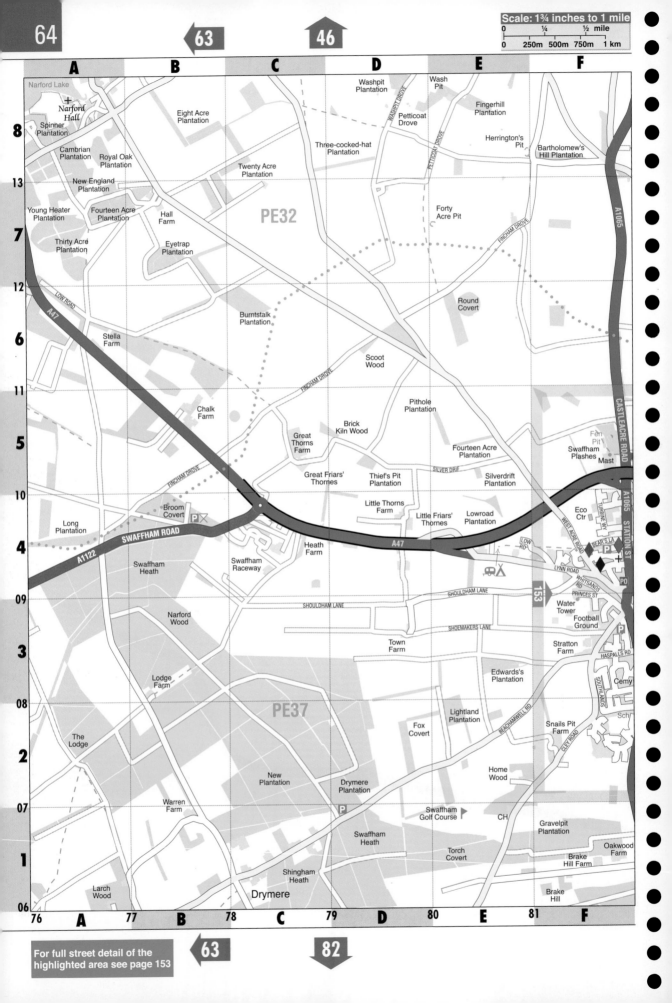

Scale: 1¾ inches to 1 mile

0 ¼ ½ mile

0 250m 500m 750m 1 km

Narford Lake

Narford Hall

Spinner Plantation

Cambrian Plantation

Royal Oak Plantation

Eight Acre Plantation

Washpit Plantation

Wash Pit

Fingerhill Plantation

Herrington's Pit

Bartholomew's Hill Plantation

Three-cocked-hat Plantation

Petticoat Drove

New England Plantation

Twenty Acre Plantation

PE32

Forty Acre Pit

Young Heater Plantation

Fourteen Acre Plantation

Hall Farm

Thirty Acre Plantation

Eyetrap Plantation

LOW ROAD

A47

Burntstalk Plantation

Round Covert

Stella Farm

FINCHAM DROVE

Scoot Wood

Chalk Farm

Pithole Plantation

Fen Pit

Swaffham Plashes

Mast

Great Thorns Farm

Brick Kiln Wood

Fourteen Acre Plantation

SILVER DRIF

Long Plantation

Broom Covert

Great Friars' Thornes

Thief's Pit Plantation

Silverdrift Plantation

Little Thorns Farm

Little Friars' Thornes

Lowroad Plantation

Eco Ctr

A1065

TURBINE WY

SWAFFHAM ROAD

A1122

FINCHAM DROVE

A47

LOW RD.

WEST ACRE ROAD

BEAR'S LA.

Swaffham Heath

Heath Farm

WHITSANDS RD.

LYNN ROAD

PO

Swaffham Raceway

PRINCES ST

153

Water Tower

Football Ground

Narford Wood

SHOULDHAM LANE

SHOEMAKERS LANE

Stratton Farm

HASPALLS RD.

Lodge Farm

Town Farm

Edwards's Plantation

Cemy

SOUTHLANDS

Sch

PE37

Lightland Plantation

Fox Covert

Snails Pit Farm

GLEB ROAD

The Lodge

Home Wood

BEACHAMWELL RD.

New Plantation

Drymere Plantation

Swaffham Golf Course

CH

Gravelpit Plantation

Warren Farm

Oakwood Farm

Torch Covert

Brake Hill Farm

Larch Wood

Shingham Heath

Swaffham Heath

Drymere

Brake Hill

For full street detail of the highlighted area see page 153

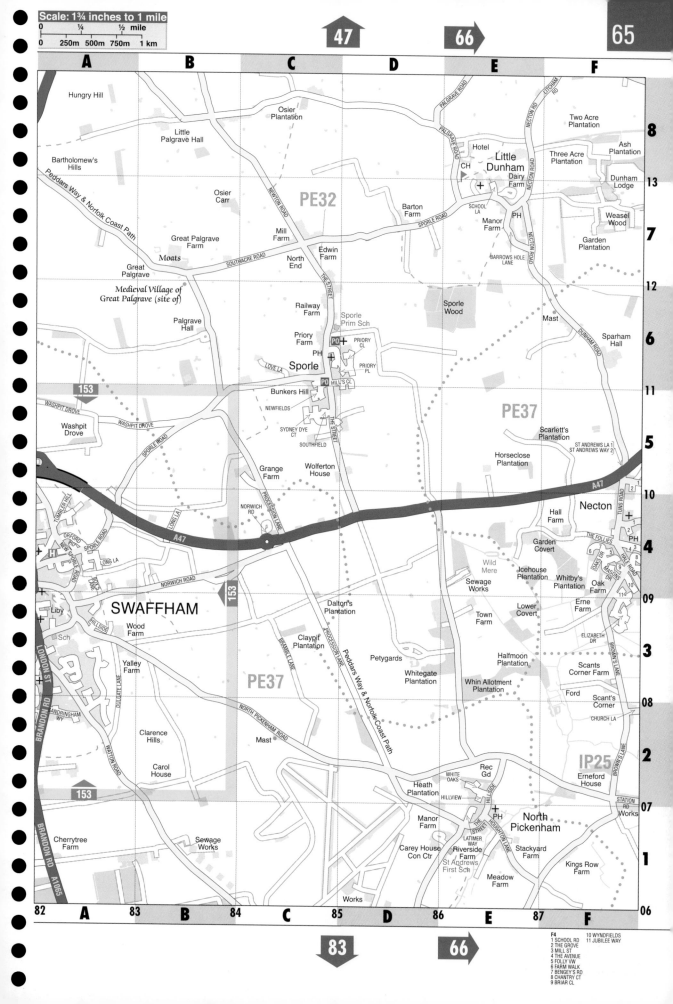

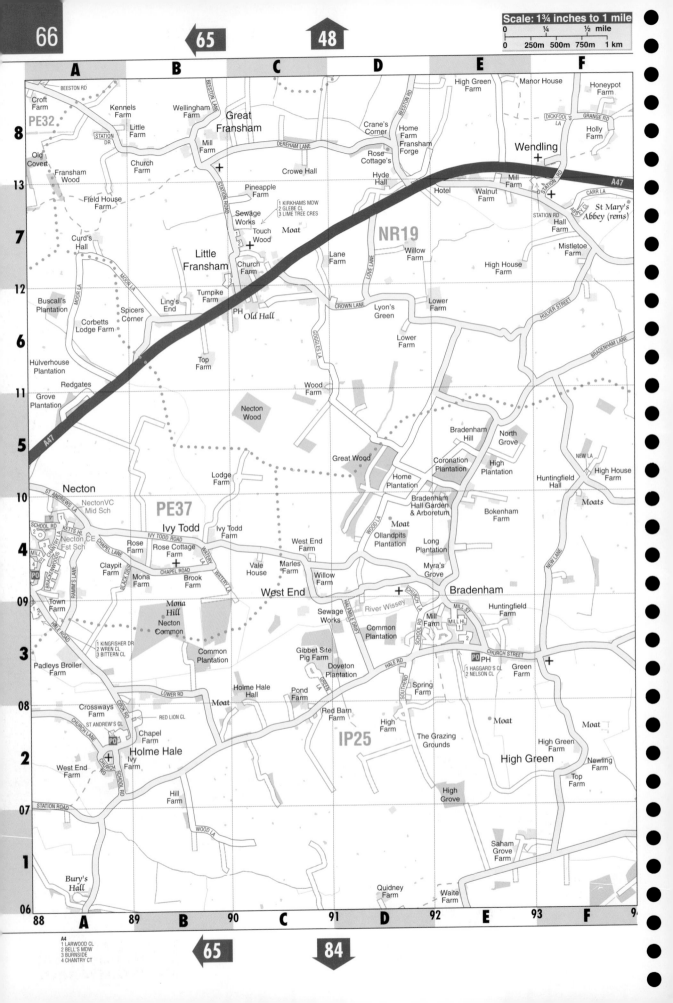

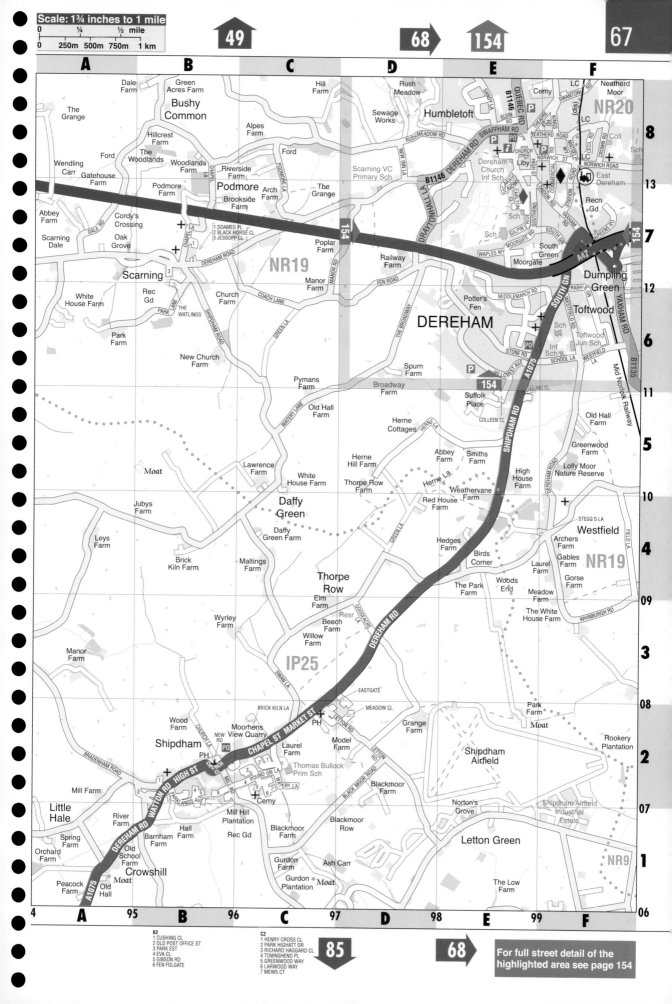

A   B   C   D   E   F

8
13
7
12
6
11
5
10
4
09
3
08
2
07
1
06

Dale Farm
Green Acres Farm
Bushy Common
Hill Farm
Rush Meadow
Sewage Works
Humbletoft
NR20
Cemy
Neatherd Moor
SWANTON
LC
QUEBEC RD
B1146
The Grange
Hillcrest Farm
The Woodlands
Alpes Farm
Ford
DEREHAM RD
SWAFFHAM RD
ELVIN RD
Church
Norwich
Liby
Coll
Sch
Wendling Carr
Ford
Gatehouse Farm
Woodlands Farm
Riverside Farm
RUSTYMEADOW RD
Scarning VC Primary Sch
B1146
Dereham Church Inf Sch
East Dereham
Norwich Road
Abbey Farm
Podmore Farm
Brookside Farm
Arch Farm
The Grange
DRAYTONHALL LA
Sch
Recn Gd
Scarning Dale
Cordy's Crossing
1 SOAMES PL
2 BLACK HORSE CL
3 JESSOPP CL
Poplar Farm
154
Railway Farm
FEN ROAD
Sch
South Green
A47
154
Scarning
Oak Grove
DEREHAM ROAD
NR19
Manor Farm
Moorgate
WAPLES WY
Moorgate
Dumpling Green
White House Farm
Rec Gd
Church Farm
Coach Lane
GREEN LA
Potter's Fen
MIDDLEMARCH RD
SOUTH GN
Toftwood
YAXHAM RD
Park Farm
PARK LANE
The Watlings
SHIPDHAM ROAD
DEREHAM
Spurn Farm
Sch
Inf Sch
Toftwood Jun Sch
SCHOOL LA
WESTFIELD RD
B1135
New Church Farm
Pymans Farm
Broadway Farm
154
Suffolk Place
Mid Norfolk Railway
HILLCREST AVE
A1075
DOWLING CL
COLLEEN CL
Old Hall Farm
WATERY LANE
Old Hall Farm
Herne Cottages
HERNE LA
Abbey Farm
Smiths Farm
High House Farm
Greenwood Farm
Lolly Moor Nature Reserve
Moat
Lawrence Farm
White House Farm
Herne Hill Farm
Thorpe Row Farm
HERNE LA
Weathervane Farm
STEGG'S LA
Westfield
Jubys Farm
Daffy Green
GREEN LA
Red House Farm
Archers Farm
Gables Farm
NR19
Leys Farm
Daffy Green Farm
Hedges Farm
Birds Corner
Laurel Farm
Gorse Farm
FIELD LA
Brick Kiln Farm
Maltings Farm
Thorpe Row
Woods End
The Park Farm
Meadow Farm
WHINBURGH RD
Wyrley Farm
Elm Farm
Resr
GOSSACRE LA
Beech Farm
The White House Farm
Manor Farm
IP25
Willow Farm
DEREHAM RD
Park Farm
Moat
SWAN LA
EASTGATE
MEADOW CL
Rookery Plantation
Wood Farm
BRICK KILN LA
Moorhens View Quarry
CHAPEL ST
MARKET ST
PH
LETTON RD
Grange Farm
Shipdham Airfield
Shipdham
PH
CHURCH LA
NEW RD
PO
Laurel Farm
Model Farm
LETTON RD
Shipdham Airfield Industrial Estate
Bradenham Road
DEREHAM RD
WATTON RD
HIGH ST
Thomas Bullock Prim Sch
WATERY LA
Blackmoor Farm
Norton's Grove
Mill Farm
POUND GN LA
Cemy
Blackmoor Row
NR9
Little Hale
River Farm
Barnham Farm
MILL RD
Mill Hill Plantation
Rec Gd
Blackmoor Farm
Blackmoor Row
Letton Green
Spring Farm
Hall Farm
Gurdon Farm
Ash Carr
The Low Farm
Orchard Farm
Crowshill
A1075
Old Hall
Moat
Gurdon Plantation
Moat
Peacock Farm

4   95   96   97   98   99   06

B2
1 CUSHING CL
2 OLD POST OFFICE ST
3 PARK EST
4 EVA CL
5 GIBSON RD
6 FEN FOLGATE

C2
1 HENRY CROSS CL
2 PARK HIGHATT DR
3 RICHARD HAGGARD CL
4 TOWNSHEND PL
5 GREENWOOD WAY
6 LARWOOD WAY
7 MEWS CT

85

68

For full street detail of the highlighted area see page 154

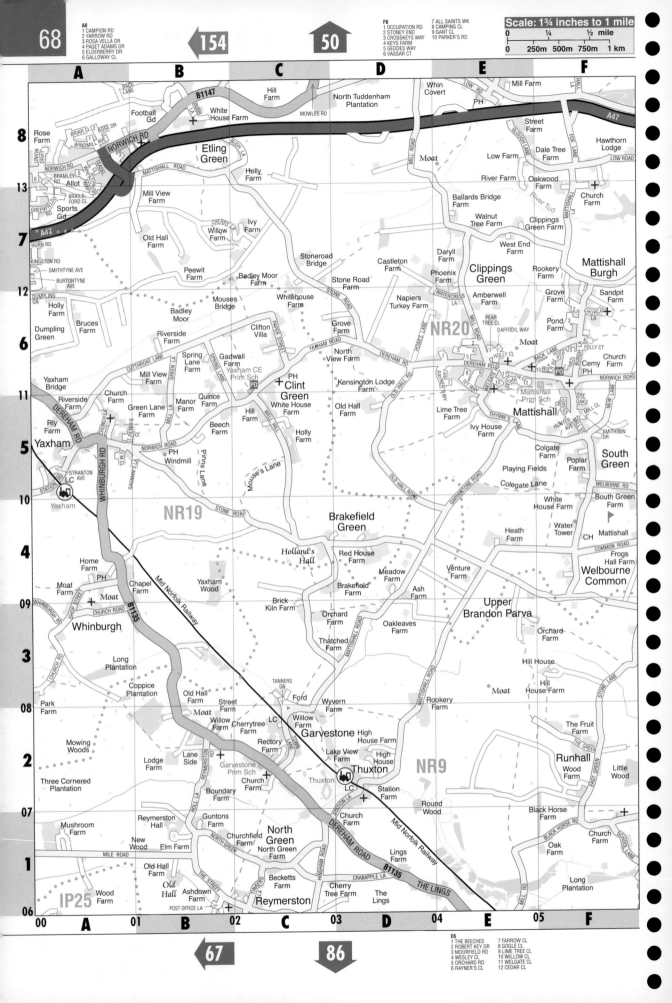

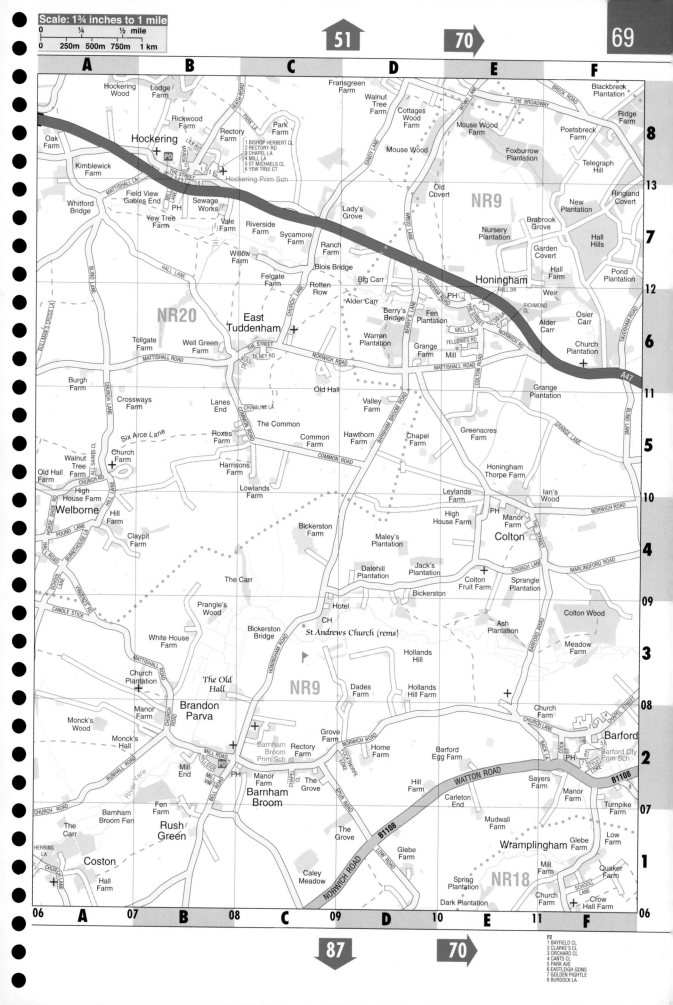

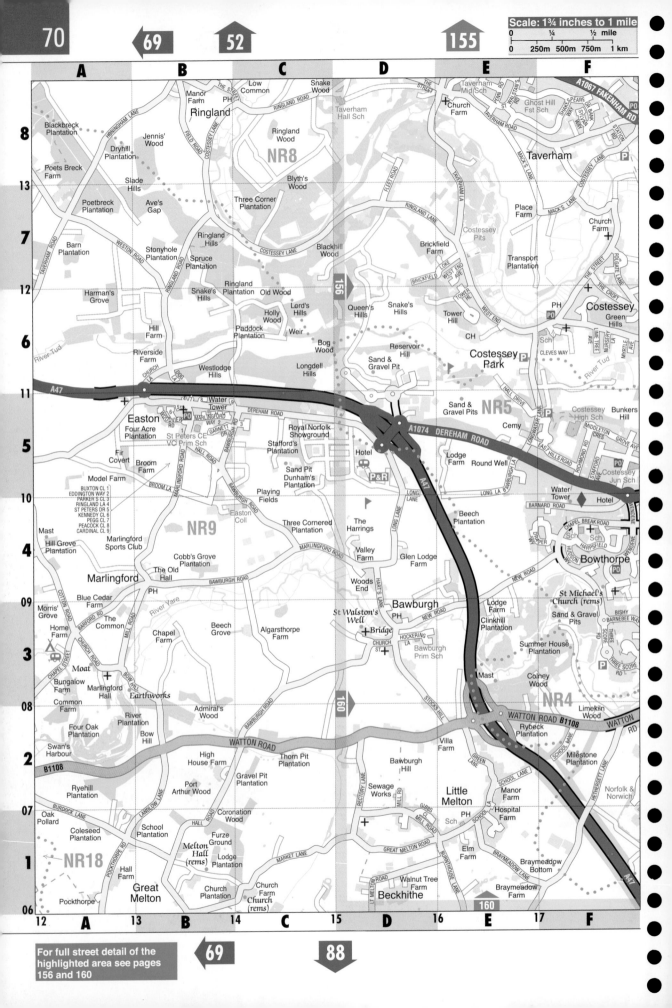

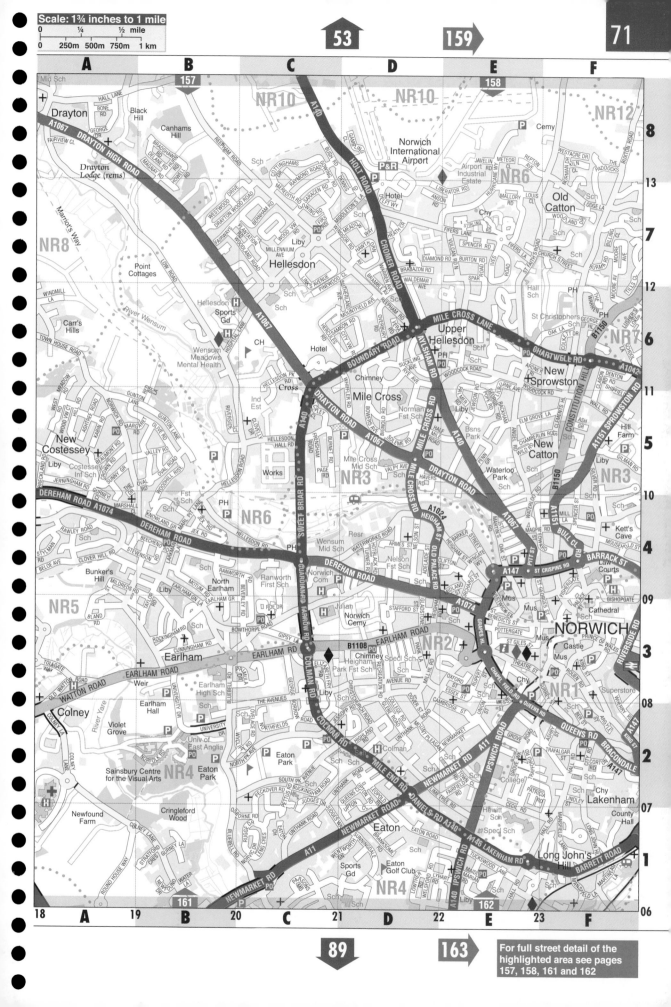

158   54

D6
1 ALTONGATE
2 HALLGATE
3 NORTHGATE
4 BROAD VW
5 BARKER WAY
6 BEECHBANK DR

7 HEATHERWOOD CL
8 ST DAVIDS DR
9 HEATH RD

D5
1 WOODLANDS CRES
2 LUCAS CT
3 GUNNER CL
4 FIENNES RD
5 DOWSING CT
6 FAIRFAX DR

7 LYNN CL
8 LEVEN CL
9 JOYCE WAY
10 MARVELL GN

Scale: 1¾ inches to 1 mile

0 ¼ ½ mile
0 250m 500m 750m 1 km

E7
1 WILDE RD
2 FULLER CL
3 TAGG WAY
4 WEBB DR
5 WILLOUGHBY WAY
6 LUSCOMBE WAY
7 CANFOR RD
8 PALMER RD
9 BURTON DR
10 VERA CL
11 BERNARD CL
12 CORNWALL CL

1 SEPPINGS WAY
2 BROADMEAD GN
3 PLUMSTEAD RD
4 THE BOULEVARD
5 SOUTH WK
6 LAWN CRES

1 PIKEMAN PL
2 PYM CL
3 HYDE CT
4 CORNET CL

E4
1 MAIDENS CL
2 DALBIER CL
3 BUNYAN CL
4 EDGEHILL
5 PEACHMAN WAY

D3
1 HIGHFIELD CL
2 PRIMROSE CRES
3 PRIMROSE CT
4 BIRCHWOOD
5 ST ANDREWS AVE

Map area codes: NR12, NR6, NR7, NR1, NR13, NR14

Place names: Beeston Park, Sprowston Wood, Tollshill Wood, Lower Blacksmith's Wood, Rackheath, Salhouse, Oak Tree Business Park, Mousehold Farm, Sprowston, New Rackheath, March Farm, Hall Farm, March Covert, Newman's Farm, Thorpe End, Racecourse Plantation, Oaks Farm, Hall Farm, Great Plumstead, Smee Farm, Apple Tree Farm, Thorpe St Andrew, Dussindale Park, Cicero Cottage, Heath Farm, The Grange, Field House Heath Farm, Thorpe Hamlet, Postwick, Sports Ground, Carrow Abbey, County H, Trowse Newton, Whitlingham Marsh, Postwick Grove, Nature Reserve, River Yare, Kirby Marsh, Hall Farm, Postwick Marsh, Long Plantation, Cottages Wood's End, Boer Plantation, Jubilee Plantation, Oaks Farm, New Wood, Big Wood, Sarah's Carr, Barn Wood, Beech Plantation, Old Wood, New Plantation, Trowse Newton Hall (rems), St Andrew's Church (rems), The Carr, Moorings, NR14

For full street detail of the highlighted area see pages 159 and 163

162   90

D4
1 MONTROSE CT
2 ASSOCIATION WAY
3 NEWCASTLE CL
4 FLEETWOOD DR
5 PARLIAMENT CT
6 HOPTON CL
7 MARSTON MOOR
8 MINION CL
9 CULVERIN CL
10 TURNHAM GN
11 SAKER CL
12 COMMONWEALTH WAY
13 DUSSINDALE DR
14 INDEPENDENT WAY
15 WINCENY CL
16 ROWTON HEATH
17 ROUNDWAY DOWN
18 LENTHALL WAY
19 HAMPDEN DR
20 NEWBURY WAY
21 WINSTANLEY RD
22 NEWARK CL
23 NASEBY WAY
24 LAUD CL
25 IRETON CL
26 ROUNDHEAD CT
27 DRAGOON CL
28 ROYALIST DR
29 MUSKETEER WAY
30 CAVALIER CL
31 MARY CHAPMAN CL
32 EASTERN CL

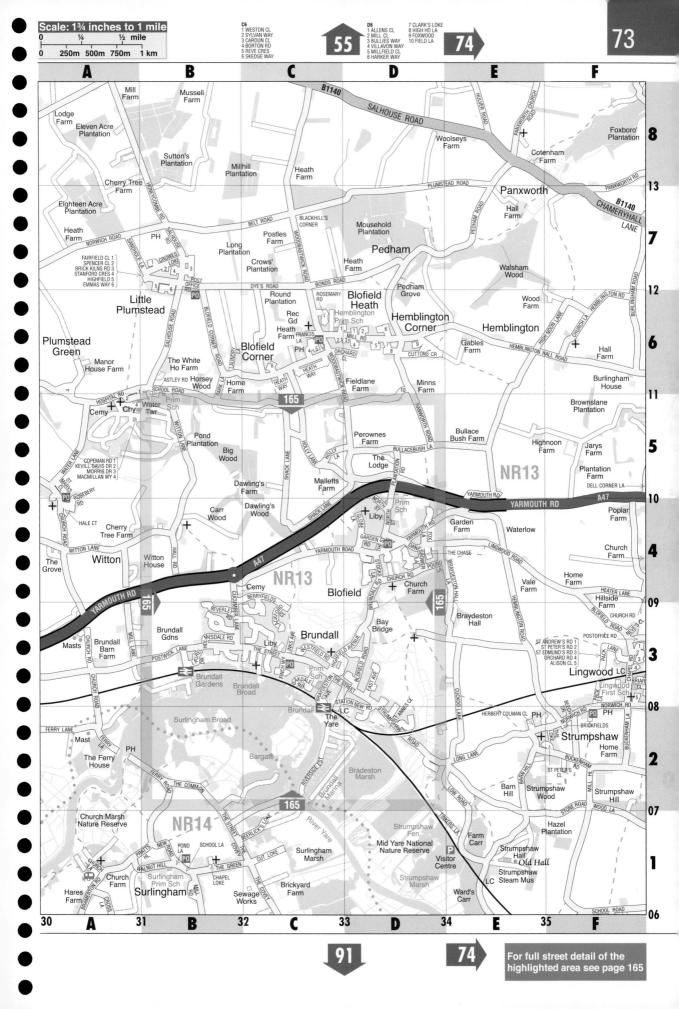

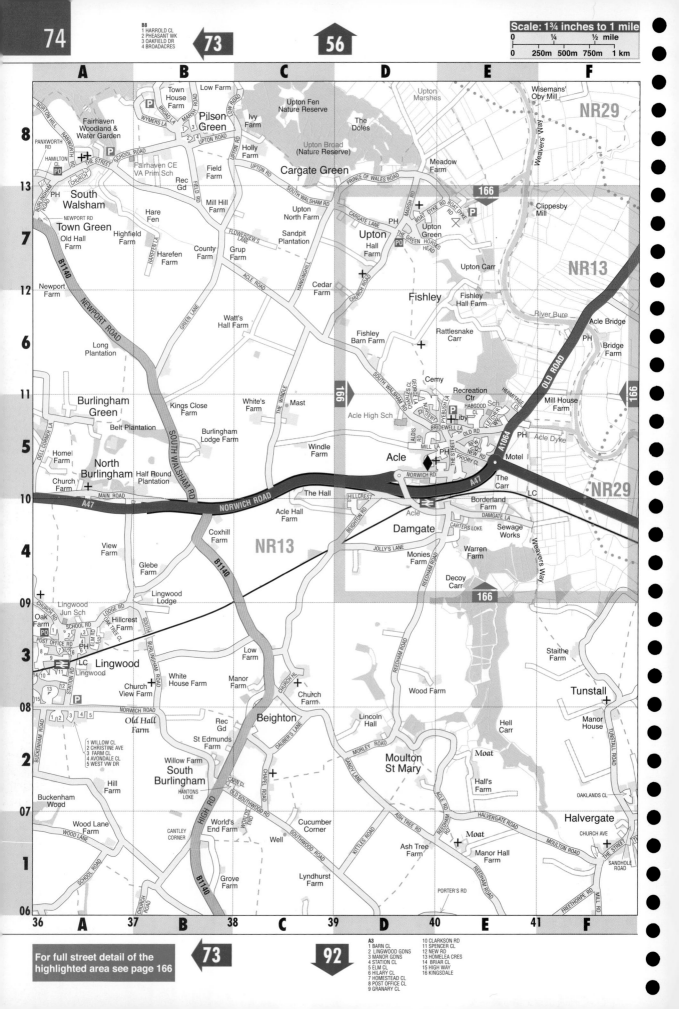

NR29

NR13

NR29

NR13

Upton Fen
Nature Reserve

Upton
Marshes

Wisemans'
Oby Mill

Clippesby
Mill

Town
House
Farm

Low Farm

Pilson
Green

Ivy
Farm

The
Doles

Meadow
Farm

Fairhaven
Woodland &
Water Garden

Holly
Farm

Upton Broad
(Nature Reserve)

Cargate Green

Field
Farm

Mill Hill
Farm

Upton
North Farm

Cargate Lane

Upton
Hall
Farm

Upton
Green

Upton Carr

Fishley
Hall Farm

Acle Bridge

Bridge
Farm

South
Walsham

Town Green

Hare Fen

Sandpit
Plantation

Fishley

Rattlesnake
Carr

River Bure

Old Hall
Farm

Highfield
Farm

Harefen
Farm

County
Farm

Grup
Farm

Cedar
Farm

Fishley
Barn Farm

Cemy

Recreation
Ctr

Mill House
Farm

Newport
Farm

Long
Plantation

Watt's
Hall Farm

Acle High Sch

Acle

Acle
Dyke

Mill House
Farm

Burlingham
Green

Kings Close
Farm

White's
Farm

Mast

The Windle

Windle
Farm

Motel

Belt Plantation

Burlingham
Lodge Farm

The Carr

Homel
Farm

North
Burlingham

Half Round
Plantation

Church
Farm

View
Farm

Main Road

A47

Norwich Road

The Hall

Acle Hall
Farm

Hillcrest

Acle

Damgate

Borderland
Farm

Sewage
Works

Coxhill
Farm

Glebe
Farm

Lingwood
Lodge

Monies
Farm

Warren
Farm

Staithe
Farm

Lingwood
Jun Sch

Oak
Farm

Hillcrest
Farm

Low
Farm

Decoy
Carr

Tunstall

Lingwood

White
House Farm

Manor
Farm

Church
Farm

Wood Farm

Manor
House

Church
View Farm

Old Hall
Farm

Rec
Gd

St Edmunds
Farm

Beighton

Lincoln
Hall

Hell
Carr

Moat

Buckenham
Wood

Hill
Farm

Willow Farm

South
Burlingham

Hantons
Loke

Moulton
St Mary

Moat

Hall's
Farm

Halvergate

Wood Lane
Farm

Cantley
Corner

World's
End Farm

Cucumber
Corner

Well

Sandhole
Road

Grove
Farm

Lyndhurst
Farm

Ash Tree
Farm

Manor Hall
Farm

Moat

Porter's Rd

A3
1 BARN CL
2 LINGWOOD GDNS
3 MANOR GDNS
4 STATION CL
5 ELM CL
6 HILARY CL
7 HOMESTEAD CL
8 POST OFFICE CL
9 GRANARY CL
10 CLARKSON RD
11 SPENCER CL
12 NEW RD
13 HOMELEA CRES
14 BRIAR CL
15 HIGH WAY
16 KINGSDALE

A2
1 WILLOW CL
2 CHRISTINE AVE
3 FARM CL
4 AVONDALE CL
5 WEST VW DR

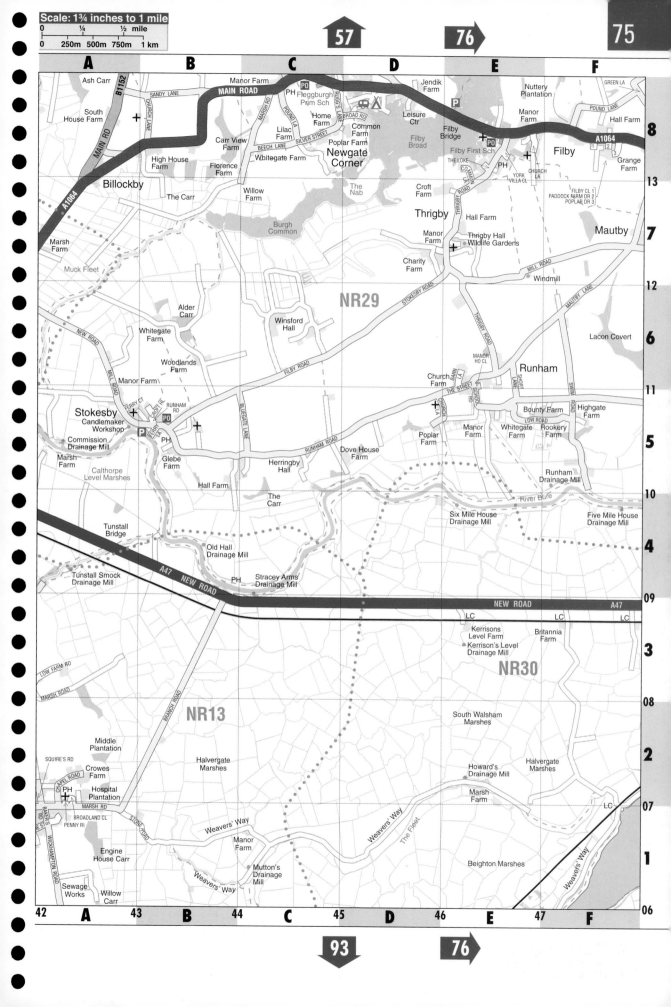

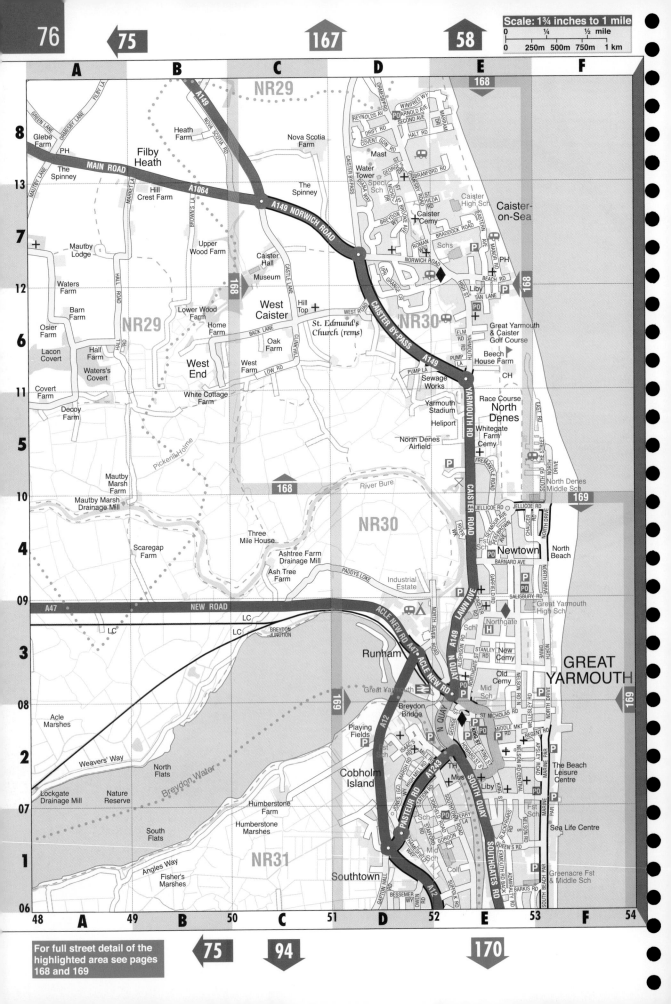

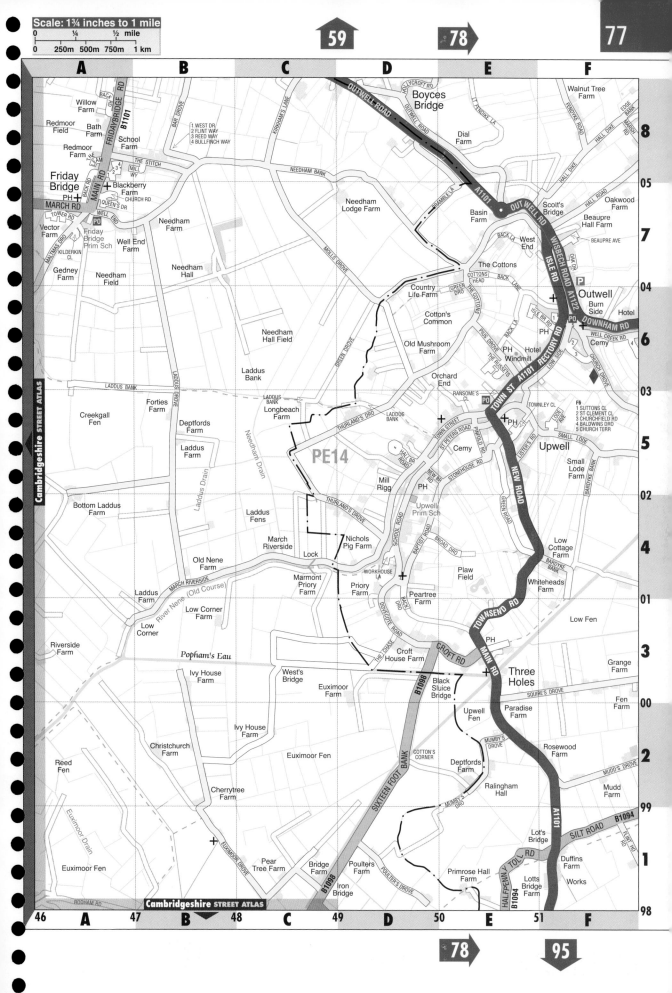

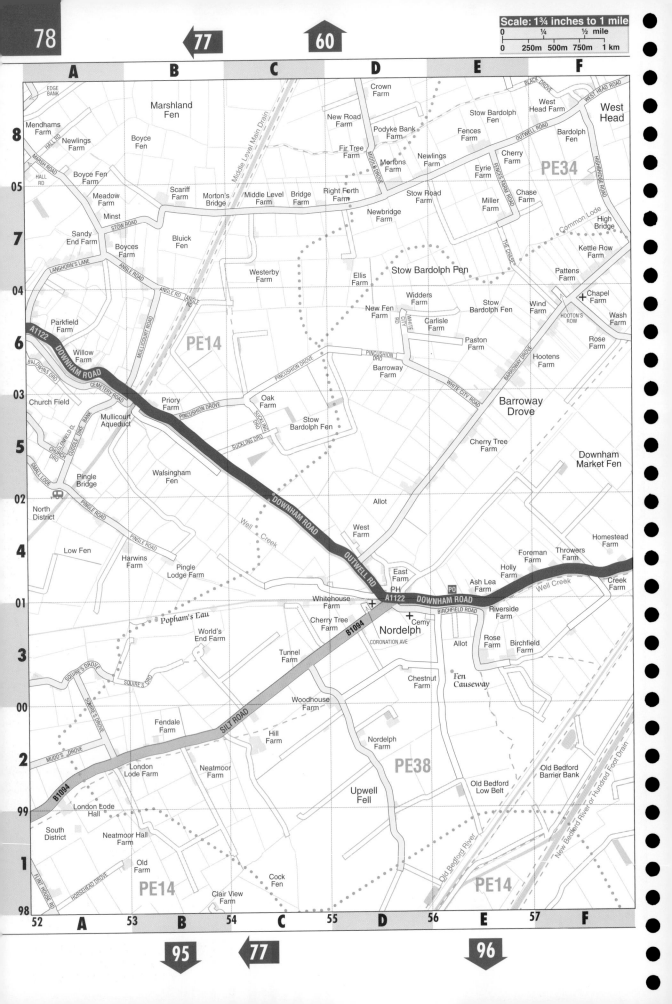

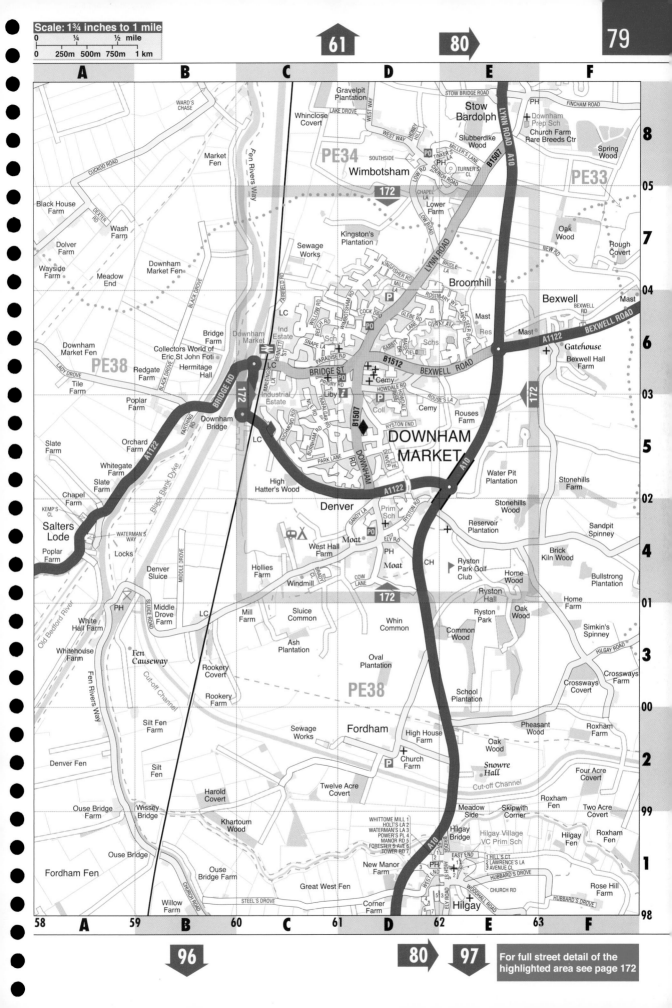

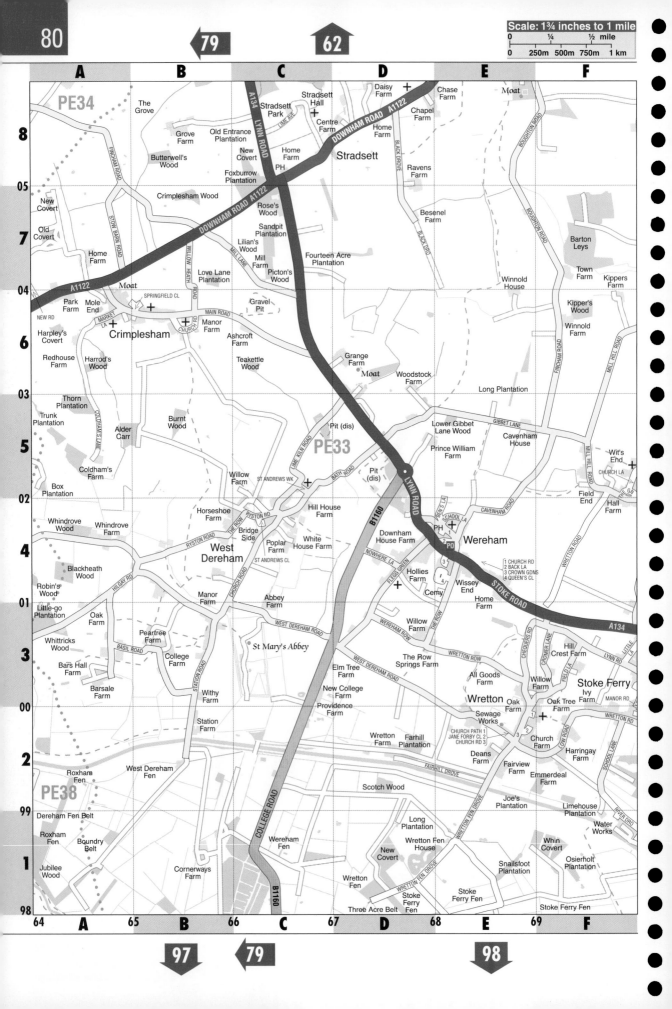

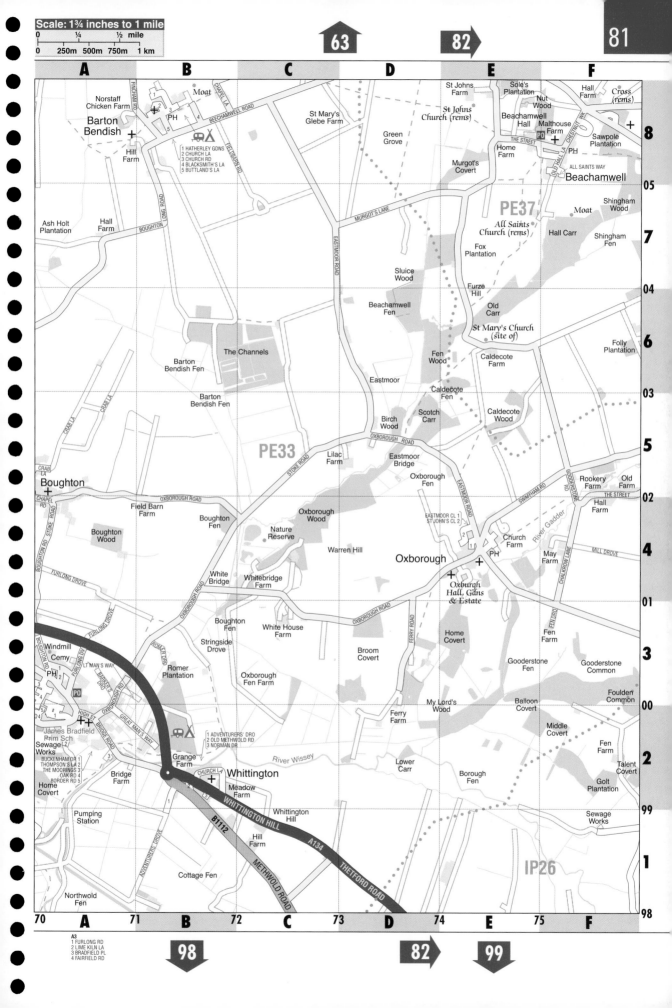

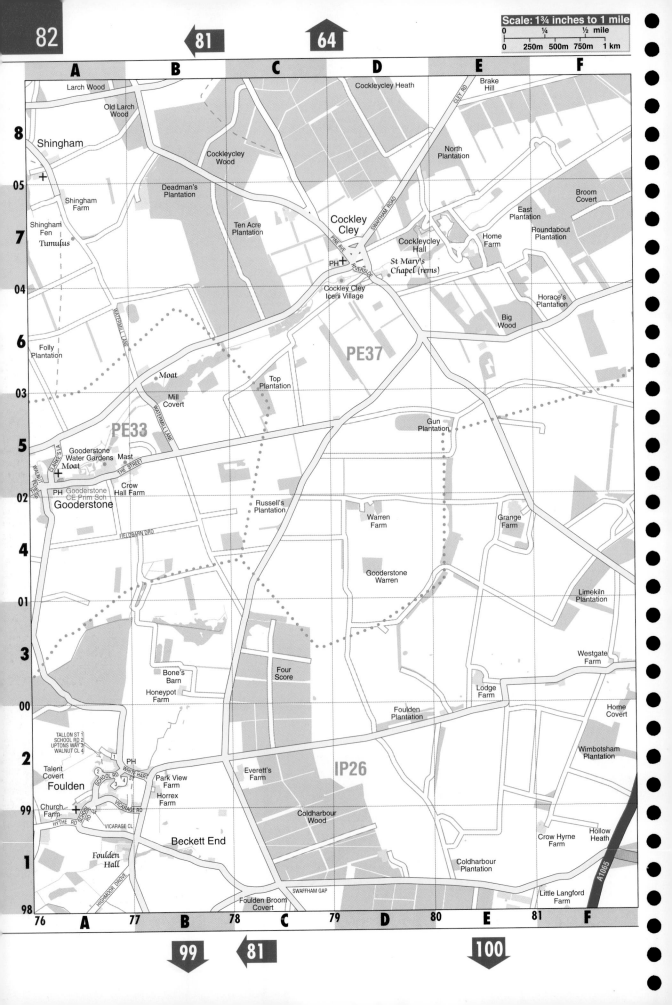

Scale: 1¾ inches to 1 mile

0   ¼   ½ mile
0   250m   500m   750m   1 km

A **B** **C** **D** **E** **F**

Larch Wood

Old Larch Wood

Cockleycley Heath

CLEY RD

Brake Hill

8

Shingham

Cockleycley Wood

North Plantation

Broom Covert

05

+

Shingham Farm

Deadman's Plantation

East Plantation

Roundabout Plantation

Home Farm

7

Shingham Fen
Tumulus

Ten Acre Plantation

Cockley Cley

SWAFFHAM ROAD

Cockleycley Hall

St Mary's Chapel (rems)

04

PINE AVE

PH +

RIVERSIDE

Cockley Cley Iceni Village

Horace's Plantation

Big Wood

6

Folly Plantation

PE37

WATERMILL LANE

Moat

Top Plantation

03

Mill Covert

Gun Plantation

PE33

5

Gooderstone Water Gardens

CLARKE'S LA

Mast

Moat

THE STREET

WATERMILL LANE

THE STREET

02

PH

WALNUT... PE

Gooderstone CE Prim Sch

Crow Hall Farm

Russell's Plantation

Warren Farm

Grange Farm

Gooderstone

FIELDBARN DRO

4

Gooderstone Warren

Limekiln Plantation

01

3

Bone's Barn

Four Score

Westgate Farm

Honeypot Farm

Lodge Farm

Home Covert

00

Foulden Plantation

TALLON ST 1
SCHOOL RD 2
UPTONS WAY 3
WALNUT CL 4

Wimbotsham Plantation

2

Talent Covert

SCHOOL RD

PH
WHITE HART ST

Park View Farm

Everett's Farm

IP26

Foulden

Horrex Farm

VICARAGE RD

99

Church Farm

+

HYTHE RD

SCHOOL RD

VICARAGE CL

Coldharbour Wood

Crow Hyrne Farm

Hollow Heath

Beckett End

A1065

1

Foulden Hall

HIGHMOOR DRIVE

Coldharbour Plantation

98

Foulden Broom Covert

SWAFFHAM GAP

Little Langford Farm

76 **A** **77** **B** **78** **C** **79** **D** **80** **E** **81** **F**

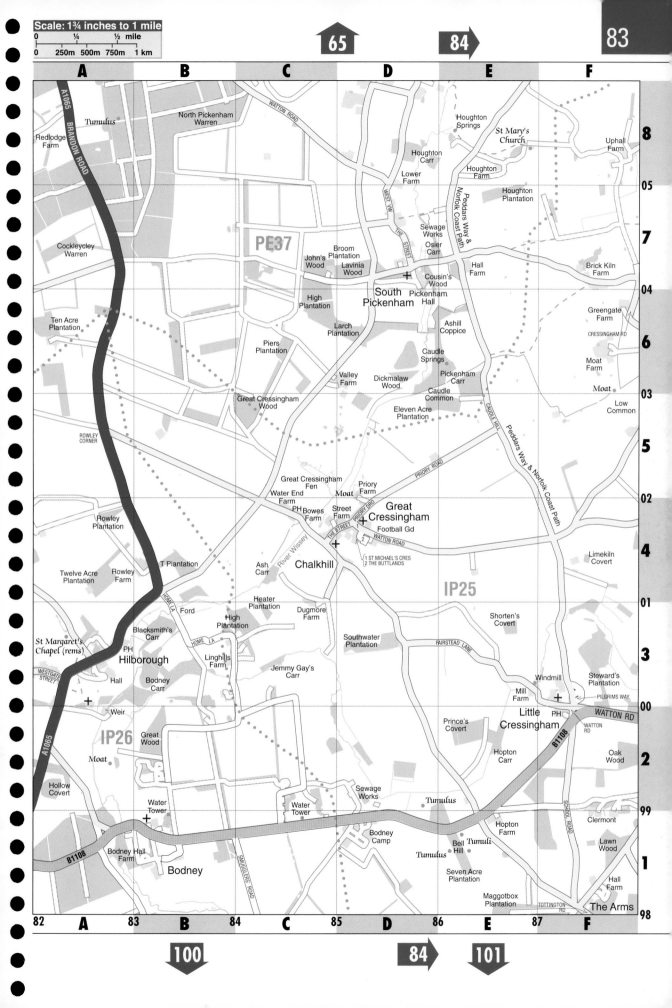

F3
1 HENRY'S CT
2 SLESSOR CL
3 DOWDING RD
4 TRENCHARD CRES
5 CHANGI RD
6 HASTINGS RD
7 COMET RD
8 HALTON RD
9 FARNBOROUGH RD
10 CRANWELL RD
11 SALMOND RD
12 HARRIS RD
13 HENDON AVE

Grid columns (top): A B C D E F
Grid rows: 8 05 7 04 6 03 5 02 4 01 3 00 2 99 1 98

IP25

Map labels

Hannover Farm, Cutbush Farm, ROMAN EARTHWORK (SITE OF), Fisher's Plantation, Peter's Plantation, Corner Farm, Reeves Farm, Ashill Common, Devils Dyke, Coe Farm, Dye Farm, LONG ROAD, Pear Tree Farm, Uphall Grange, Homestead Farm, Panworth Farm, Park Farm, Willow Bushes Plantation, Otterwood Farm, Mill Farm, Green Farm, Panworth Hall, Woodbottom Farm, Ashill, Chapel Yd, Ashill VC Prim Sch, PH, The Woodlands, White House Farm, HILLS ROAD, Saham Wood, Saham Park, Highfield Farm, College Farm, SWAFFHAM RD, Old Hall Farm, Ashill Fruit Farm, Lower Homestead Farm, Field Farm, Saham Hills, Earthworks, Alston Farm, Daisy Farm, The Limes, Crossways Farm, Hunts Farm, High House Farm, Rose Farm, Lodge Farm, Water End Farm, The Lodge, Waterend Farm, Low Common Farm, Page's Place, Ovington, Bleak House Farm, Grape Farm, Bush Farm, Grange Farm, Saham Toney, Wood Farm, Church Farm, Stanway Farm, Mill View, Brick Kiln Farm, Dairy Farm, Saham RD, Ovington Cross, Parkers Prim Sch, Windmill, Neaton, Dorrs Farm, Redhill, Moat, Watton Green, Saham Hall, Hall Farm, Sandpit Plantation, The Grove, Richmond Park Golf Course, Sports Centre, Redhill Farm, Rokeles Hall, Breckland Business Park, Church Farm, Sewage Works, Brandon Rd, High St, NORWICH ROAD, B1108, Threxton Hill, Watton Plantation, Watton Junior Sch, Westfield Inf Sch, Wayland Com High Sch, WATTON, Water Twrs, WATTON ROAD B1108, Peddars Way & Norfolk Coast Path, Merton Common, Wick Farm, New Plantation, Rabbit Plantation, Wayland Wood Nature Reserve, Oak Wood, Grove Farm, Milestone Grove, Broom Hill Farm, Hall Farm House, HM Prison, Threxton House, Hawthorne Farm, Old Farm, Merton, Home Farm, Moat, Wood Farm, Cottage Farm, Blackhill Plantation, Slate Plantation, North West Covert, Broadflash Farm, Victoria Plantation, Deal Wood, DEREHAM ROAD, A1075, CHURCH RD, CROWN CR, MILL LA, THE STREET, GRISTON ROAD, SLEIGH LANE

C3
1 LANGMERE RD
2 RINGMERE CL
3 RINGMERE RD
4 WAYLAND AVE
5 THREE POST RD
6 WEST END CT
7 CURLEW CL
8 WOODPECKER DR
9 TERN CL
10 MALLARD RD
11 KINGFISHER WAY
12 HERON WAY
13 GOLDFINCH WAY

THE OVAL 1
NEVILLE CL 2
OLD HALL CL 3
ST GEORGE'S CL 4

BELLMERE WAY 1
MERE CL 2
WOODVIEW CL 3
AMYS CL 4

Grid columns (bottom): A B C D E F
Grid numbers: 88 89 90 91 92 93

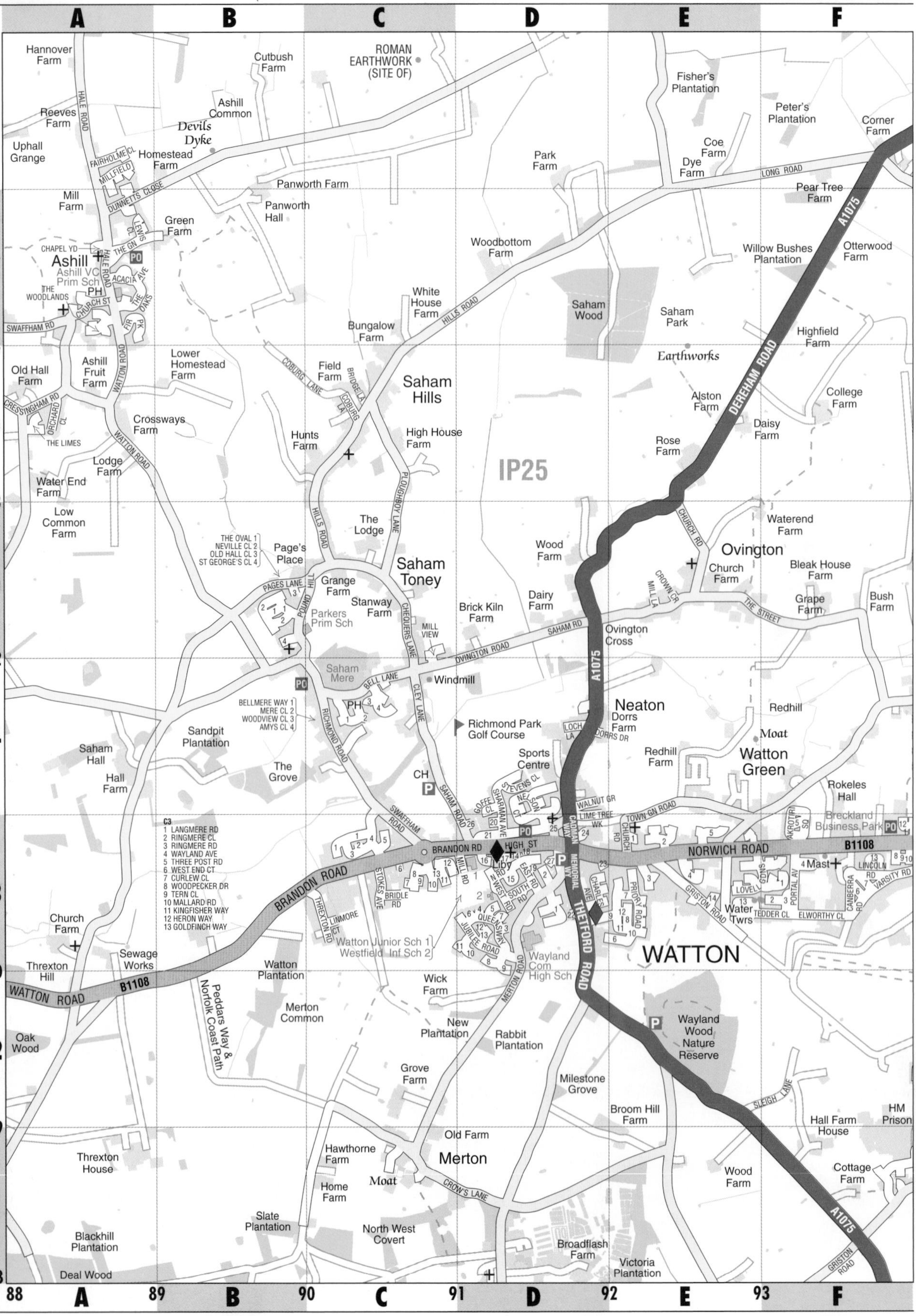

D3
1 CHURCHILL CL
2 GREEN OAK RD
3 WICK FARM CL
4 WINDSOR CT
5 WILLIAM CL
6 SANDRINGHAM CT
7 PRINCESS CL
8 FLEMING CT
9 MALTHOUSE CL
10 COBURG CL
11 WODEHOUSE CT
12 SPENCER CT
13 EDINBURGH CL
14 GODDARDS CT
15 GEORGE TROLLOPE RD
16 VINCENT PL
17 CLARENCE CT
18 BEECHWOOD AVE
19 ORCHARD CL
19 ORCHARD CL
20 FROST CL
21 HARVEY ST
22 VICTORIA CT
23 REGAL CT
24 KITTEL CL
25 DEREHAM RD
26 MEADOW GR
27 GREGOR SHANKS WAY

E3
1 ST MARY'S CL
2 HUNTERS OAK
3 LINMORE CRES
4 GARDEN CL
5 BLENHEIM WAY
6 CANON CL
7 GLEBE RD
8 CHESTNUT RD
9 MONKHAMS DR
10 ABBEY RD
11 VICARAGE WK
12 ASHTREE RD
13 TEDDER CL
14 BURR CL

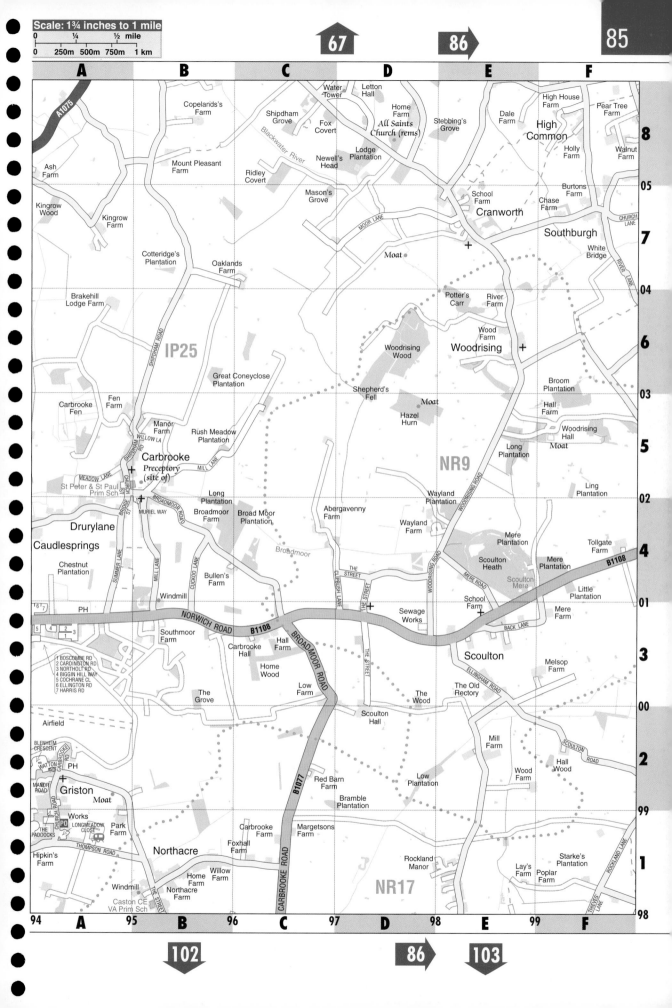

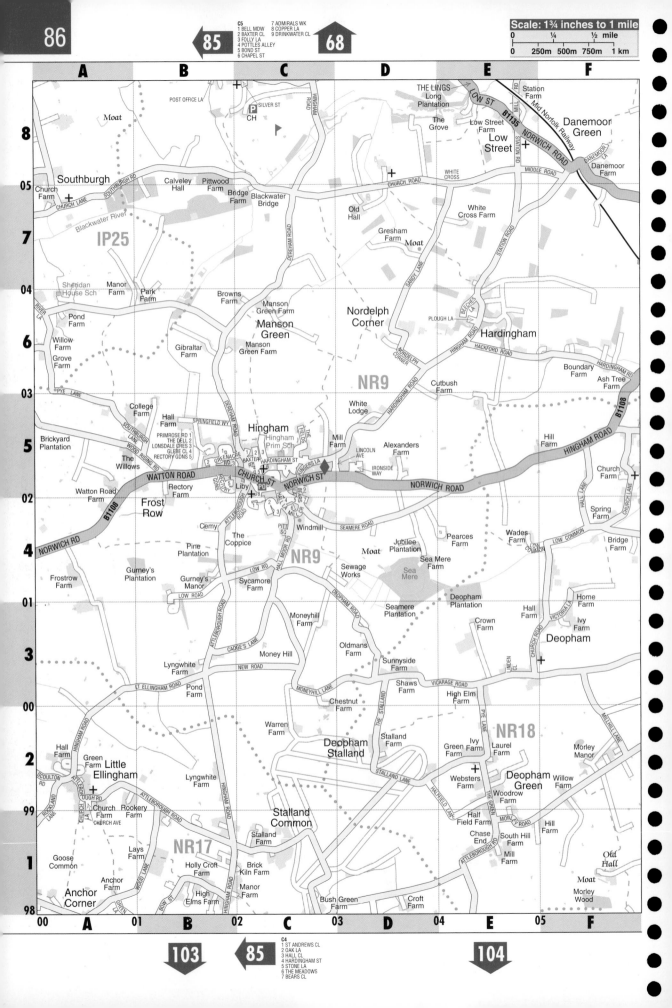

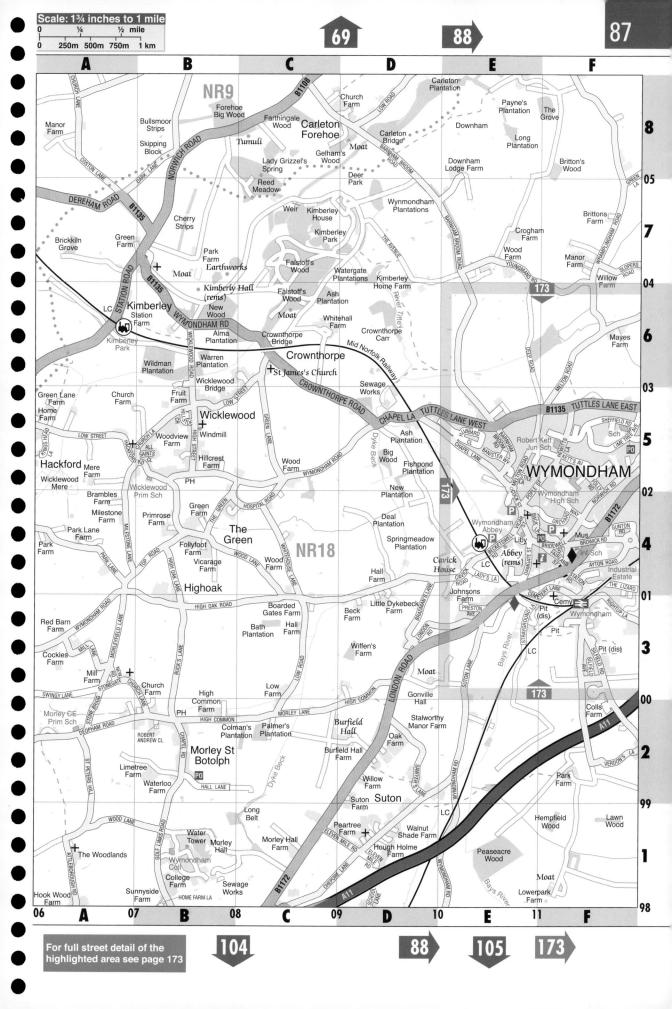

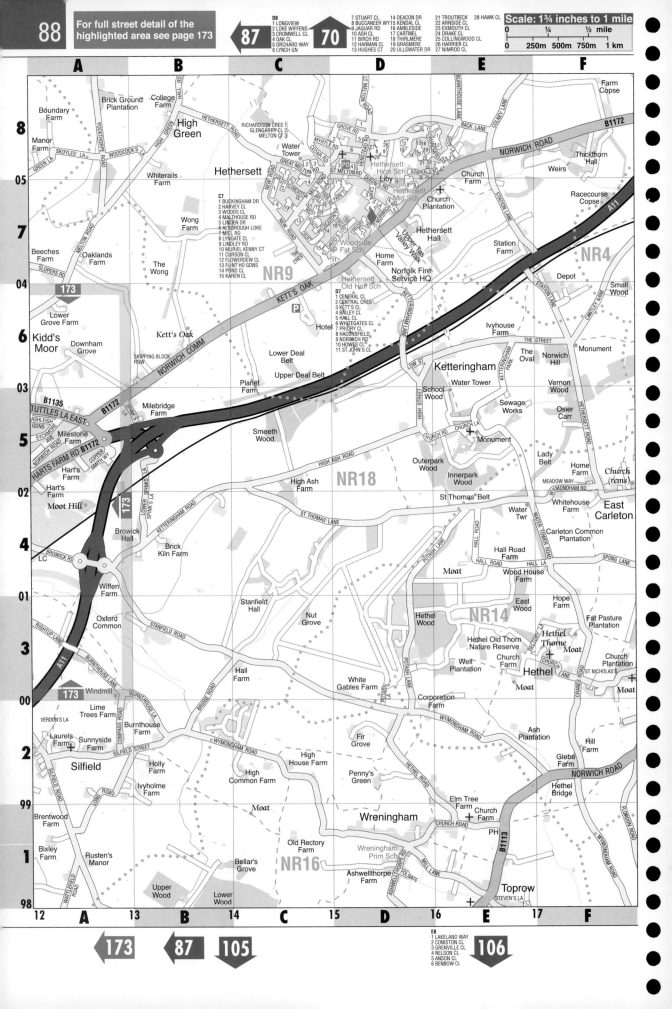

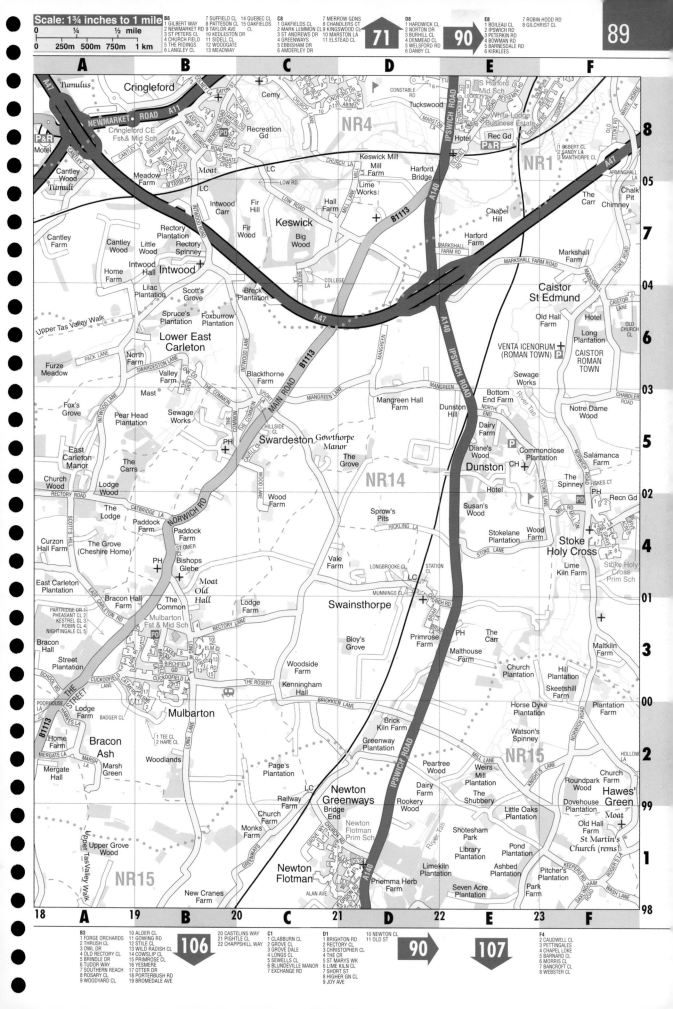

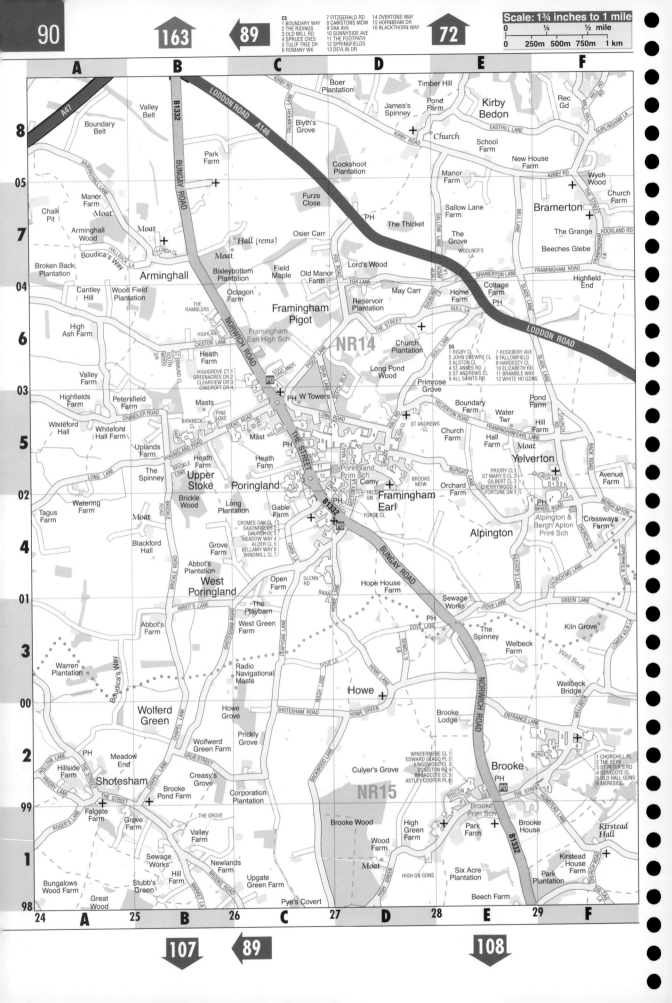

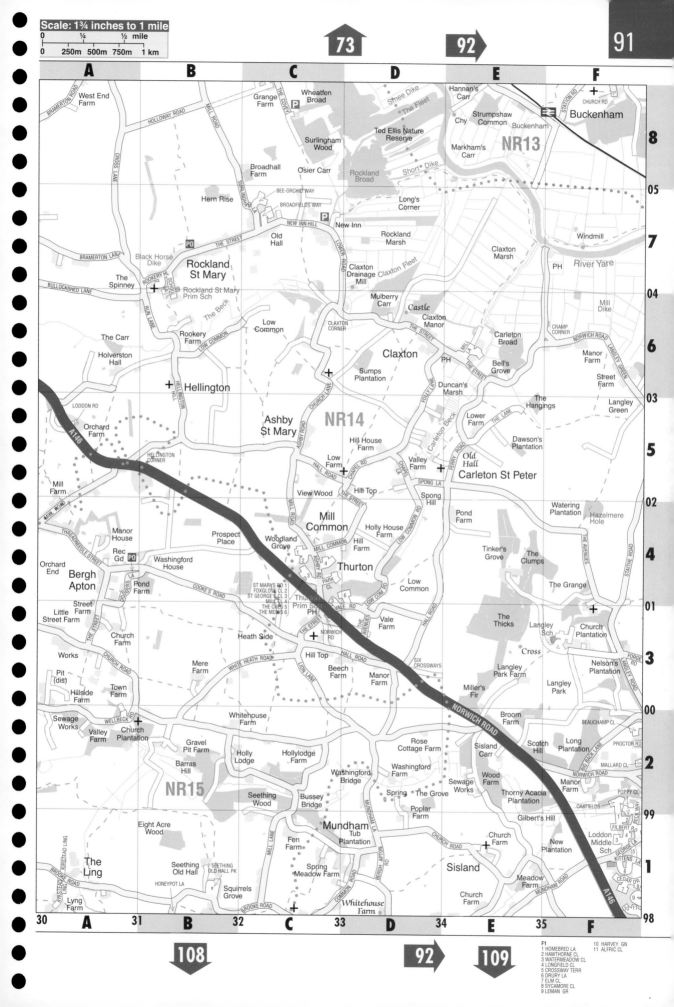

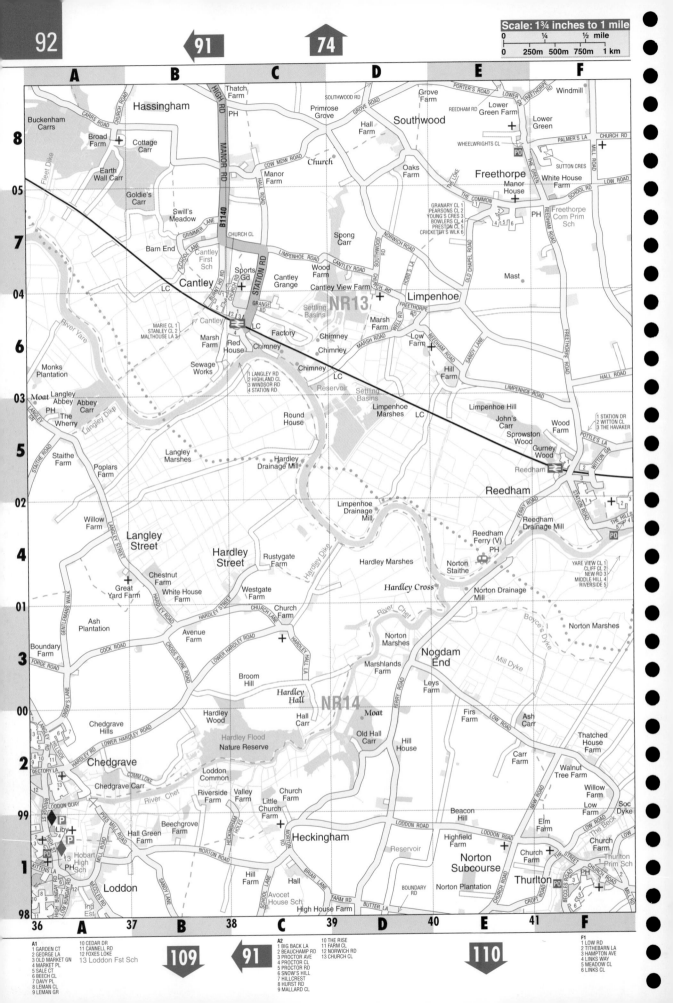

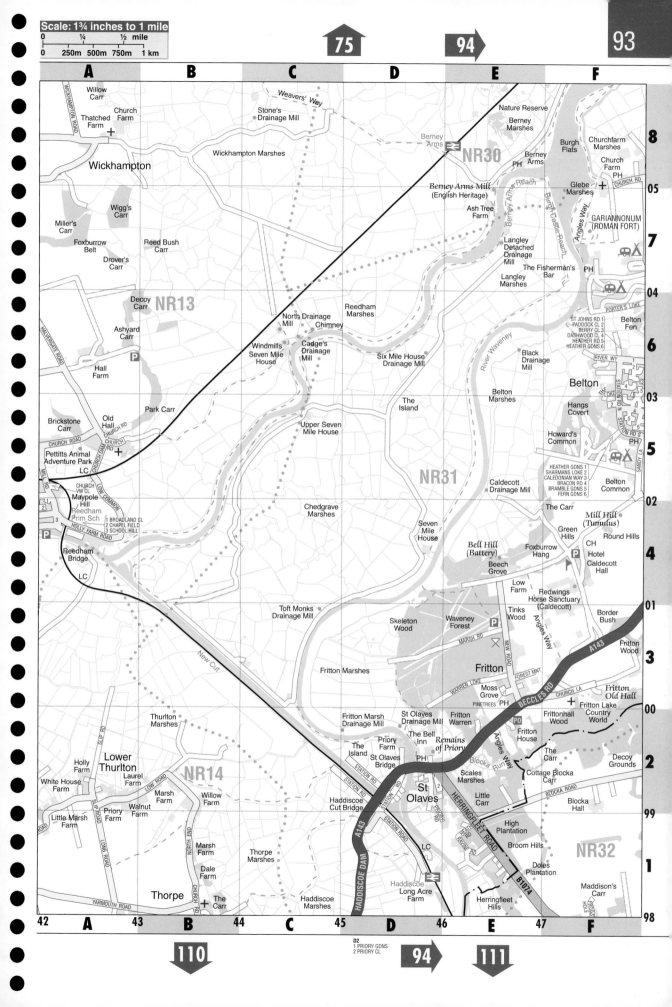

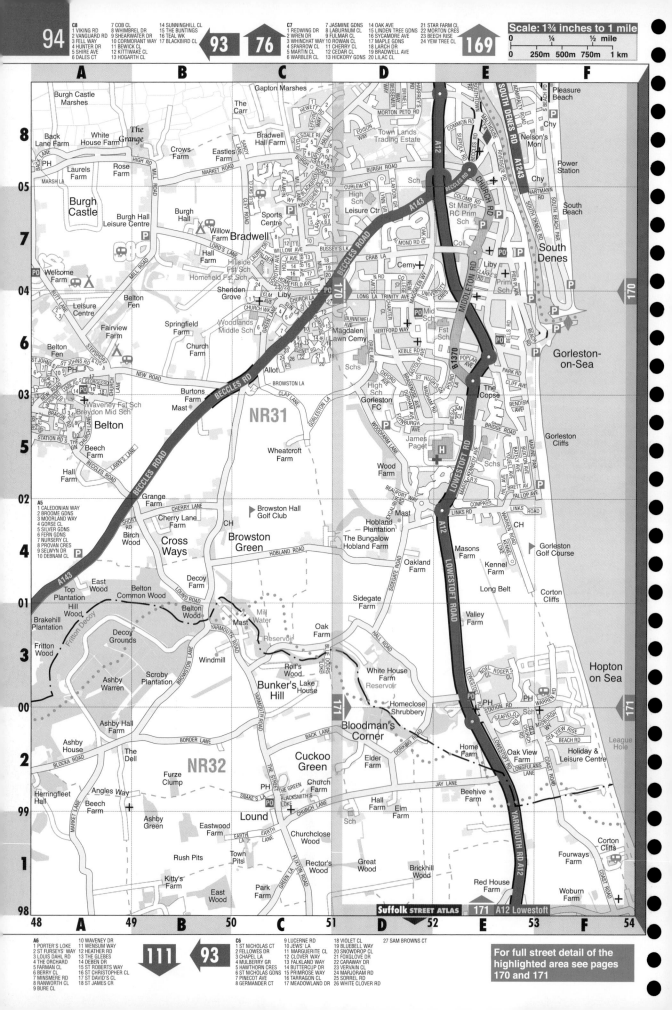

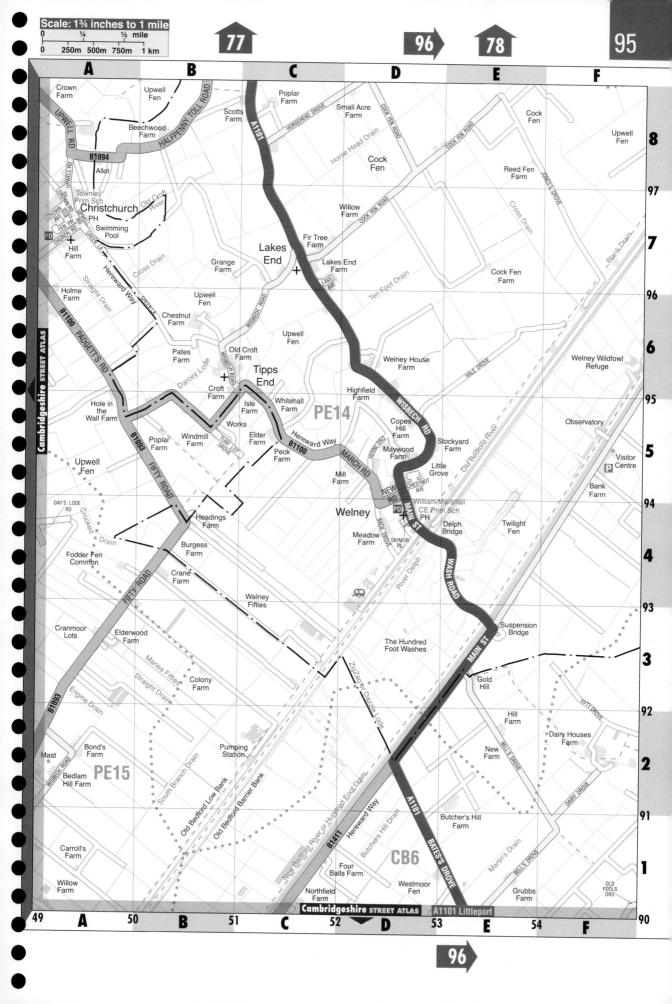

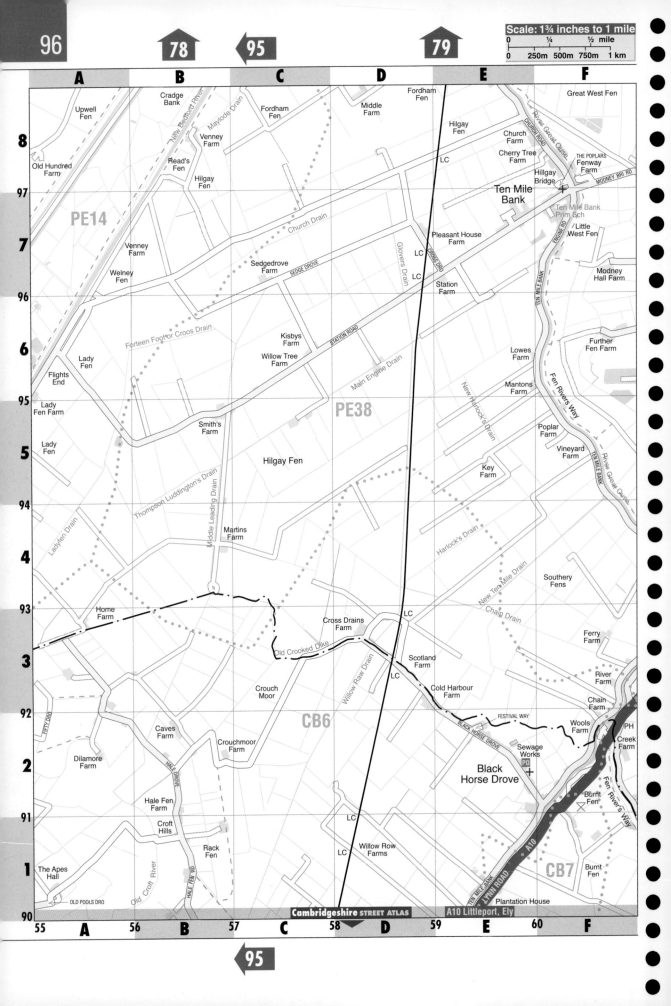

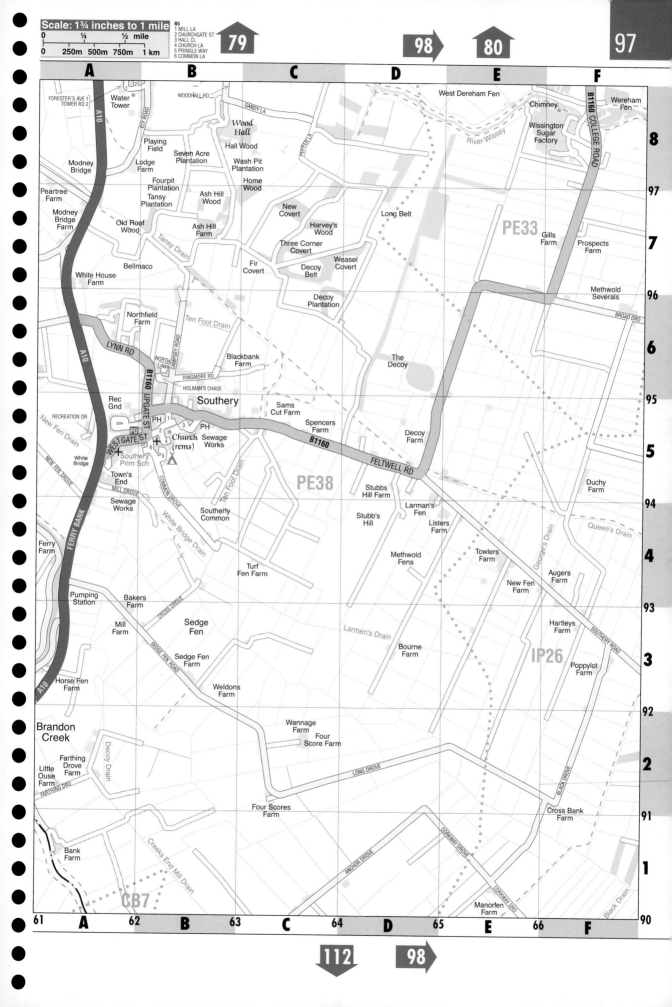

Scale: 1¾ inches to 1 mile
0   ¼   ½ mile
0 250m 500m 750m 1 km

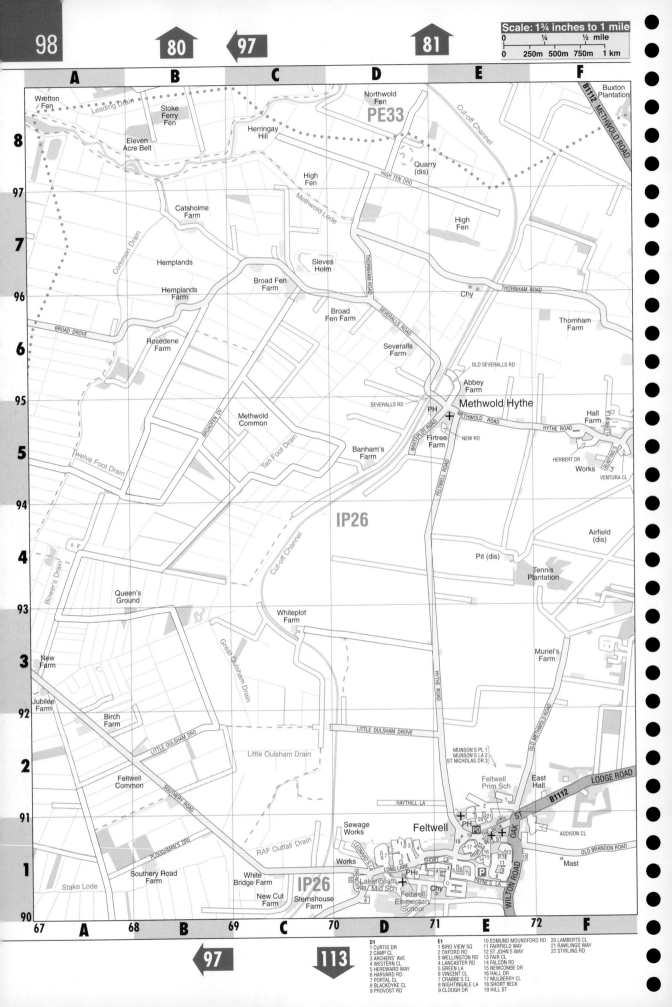

A   B   C   D   E   F

Buxton
Plantation
B1112 METHWOLD ROAD

Wretton
Fen
Leading Drain
Stoke
Ferry Fen
Northwold
Fen
PE33

8

Eleven
Acre Belt
Herringay
Hill
Cut-off Channel

97

High
Fen
Quarry
(dis)
HIGH FEN DRO

Catsholme
Farm
Methwold Lode
High
Fen

7

Hemplands
Sleves
Holm
THORNHAM ROAD
Chy
THORNHAM ROAD

Broad Fen
Farm
Thornham
Farm

96

Hemplands
Farm
Broad
Fen Farm
SEVERALLS ROAD

6

BROAD DROVE
Rosedene
Farm
Severalls
Farm
OLD SEVERALLS RD

Abbey
Farm
Hall
Farm
ELDENS LA

95

Twelve Foot Drain
BROADFEN DV
Methwold
Common
SEVERALLS RD
PH
Methwold Hythe
METHWOLD ROAD
HYTHE ROAD
BUNTINGS

5

Ten Foot Drain
Banham's
Farm
WHITEPLOT ROAD
Firtree
Farm
NEW RD
HERBERT DR
Works
VENTURA CL

94

FELTWELL ROAD
IP26
Airfield
(dis)

4

Bower's Drain
Cut-off Channel
Pit (dis)
Tennis
Plantation

93

Queen's
Ground
Great Oulsham Drain
Whiteplot
Farm

3

New
Farm
HYTHE ROAD
Muriel's
Farm

92

Jubilee
Farm
Birch
Farm
LITTLE OULSHAM DRO
Little Oulsham Drain
LITTLE OULSHAM DROVE
MUNSON'S PL 1
MUNSON'S LA 2
ST NICHOLAS DR 3
East
Hall
LODGE ROAD
OLD METHWOLD ROAD

2

Feltwell
Common
SOUTHERY ROAD
Feltwell
Prim Sch
HAYTHILL LA
B1112
ADDISON CL

91

PLOUGHMAN'S DRO
RAF Outfall Drain
Sewage
Works
Feltwell
PH
THE BECK
OAK ST
Mast
OLD BRANDON ROAD

1

Stake Lode
Southery Road
Farm
White
Bridge Farm
Works
LONG LANE
LEONARD'S ST
FRENCH'S RD
SHORT LA
HIGH ST
PAYNE'S LA
WILTON ROAD
Lakenheath
Mid Sch
Feltwell
Elementary
School
Chy
New Cut
Farm
Sternshouse
Farm
IP26

90

67   A   68   B   69   C   70   D   71   E   72   F

D1
1 CURTIS DR
2 CAMP CL
3 ARCHERS' AVE
4 WESTERN CL
5 HEREWARD WAY
6 HARVARD RD
7 PORTAL CL
8 BLACKDYKE CL
9 PROVOST RD

E1
1 BIRD VIEW SQ
2 OXFORD RD
3 WELLINGTON RD
4 LANCASTER RD
5 GREEN LA
6 VINCENT CL
7 CRABBE'S CL
8 NIGHTINGALE LA
9 CLOUGH DR

10 EDMUND MOUNDFORD RD
11 FAIRFIELD WAY
12 ST JOHN'S WAY
13 FAIR CL
14 FALCON RD
15 NEWCOMBE DR
16 HALL DR
17 MULBERRY CL
18 SHORT BECK
19 HILL ST

20 LAMBERTS CL
21 RAWLINGS WAY
22 STIRLING RD

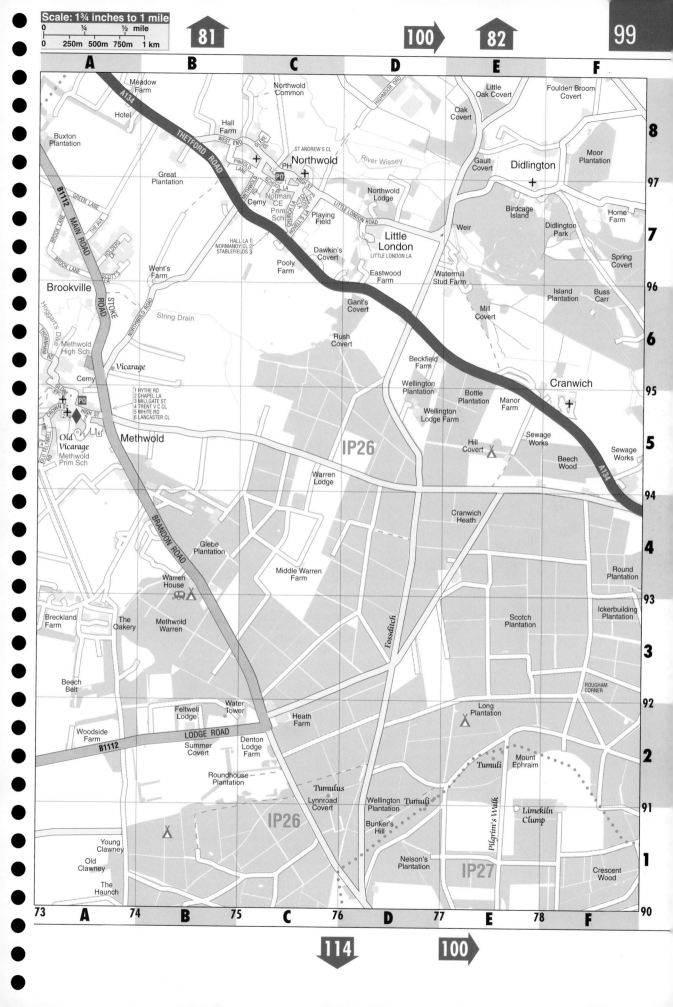

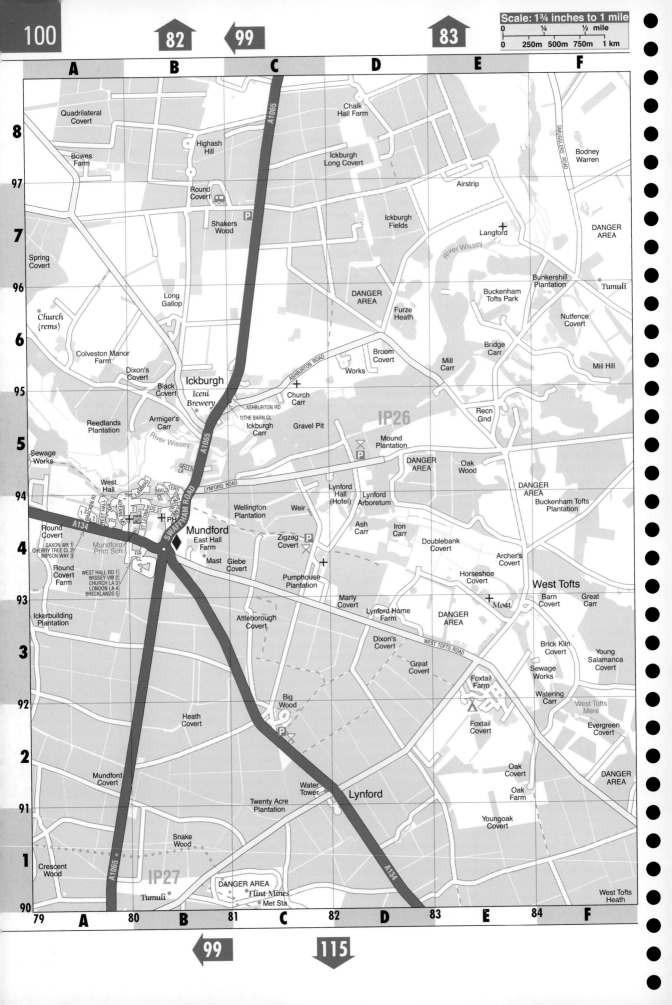

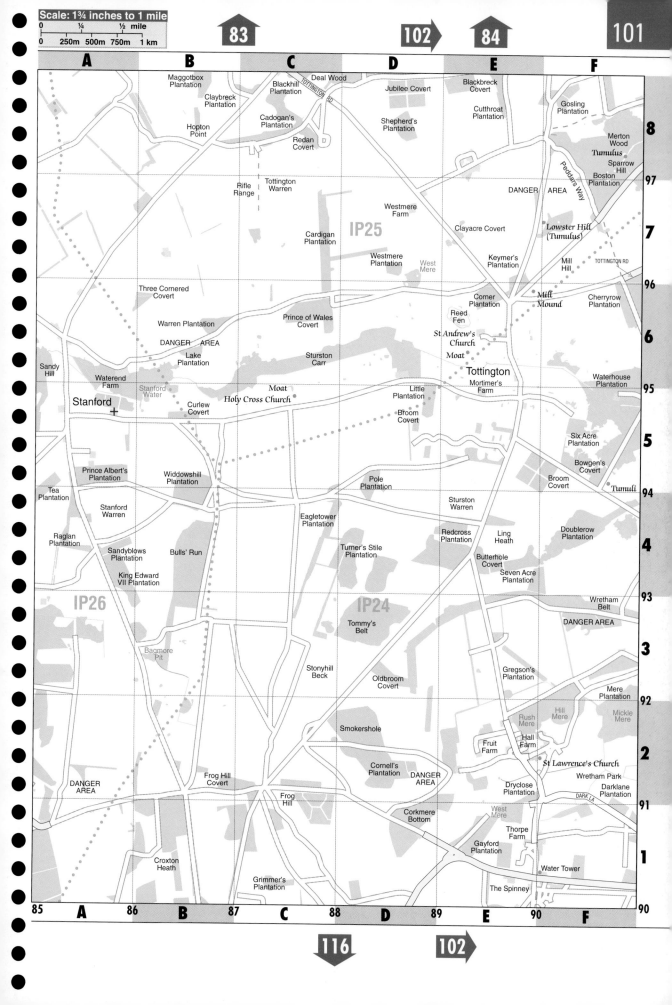

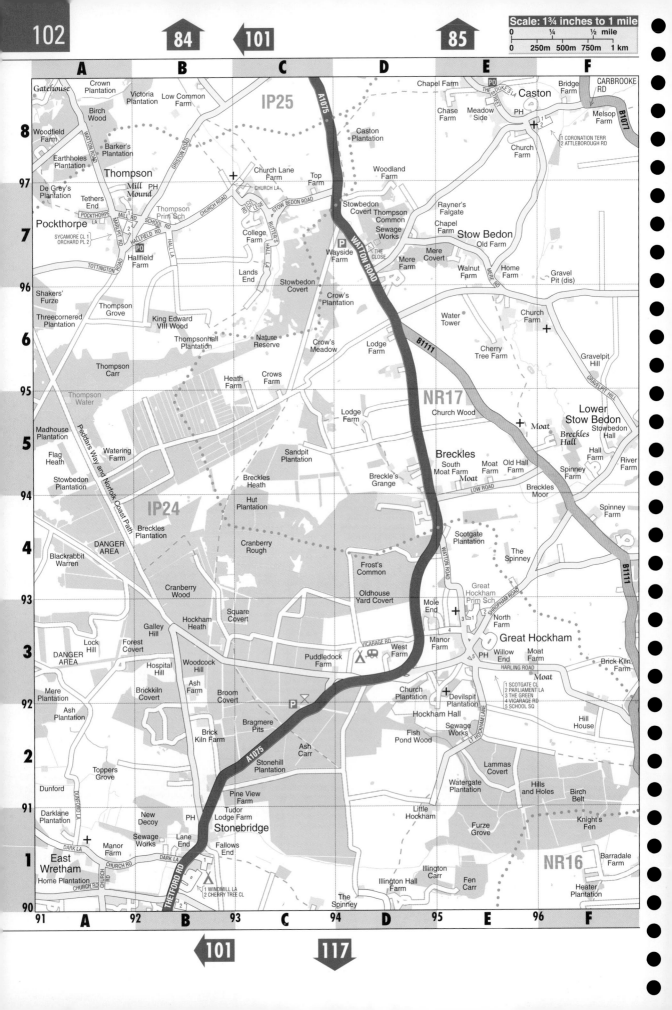

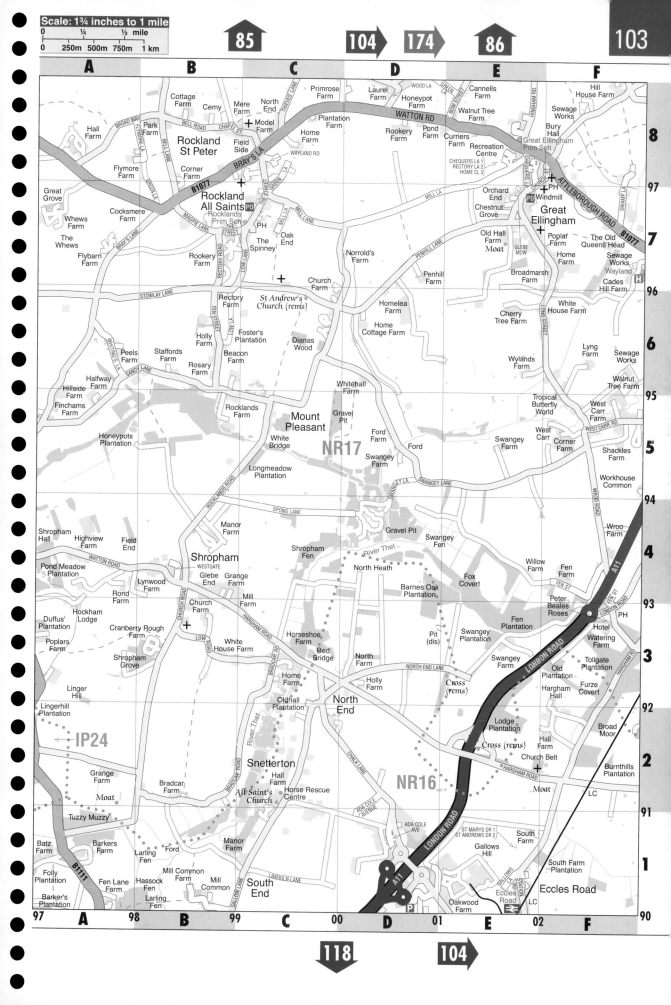

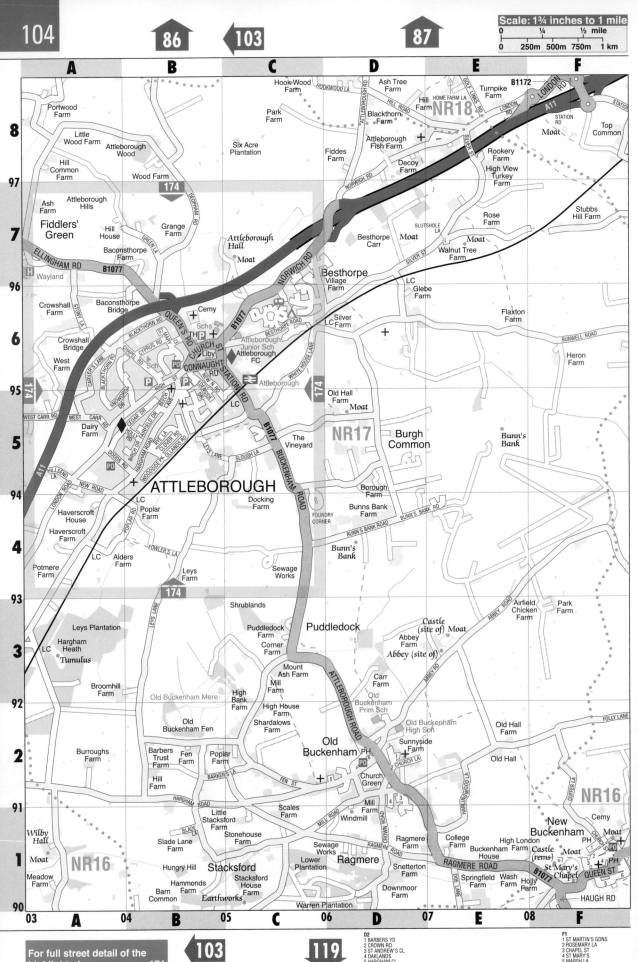

Scale: 1¾ inches to 1 mile

0 ¼ ½ mile

0 250m 500m 750m 1 km

For full street detail of the highlighted area see page 174

103

D2
1 BARBERS YD
2 CROWN RD
3 ST ANDREW'S CL
4 OAKLANDS
5 HARGHAM CL
6 FORGE CL

F1
1 ST MARTIN'S GDNS
2 ROSEMARY LA
3 CHAPEL ST
4 ST MARY'S
5 MARSH LA
6 BOOSEY'S WALK
7 TANNING LA

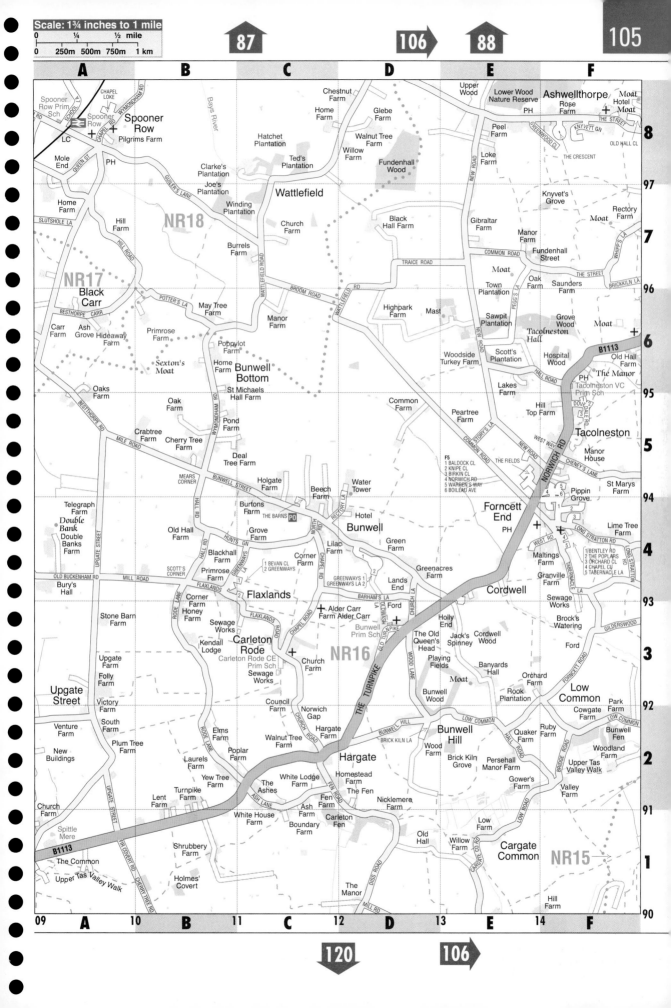

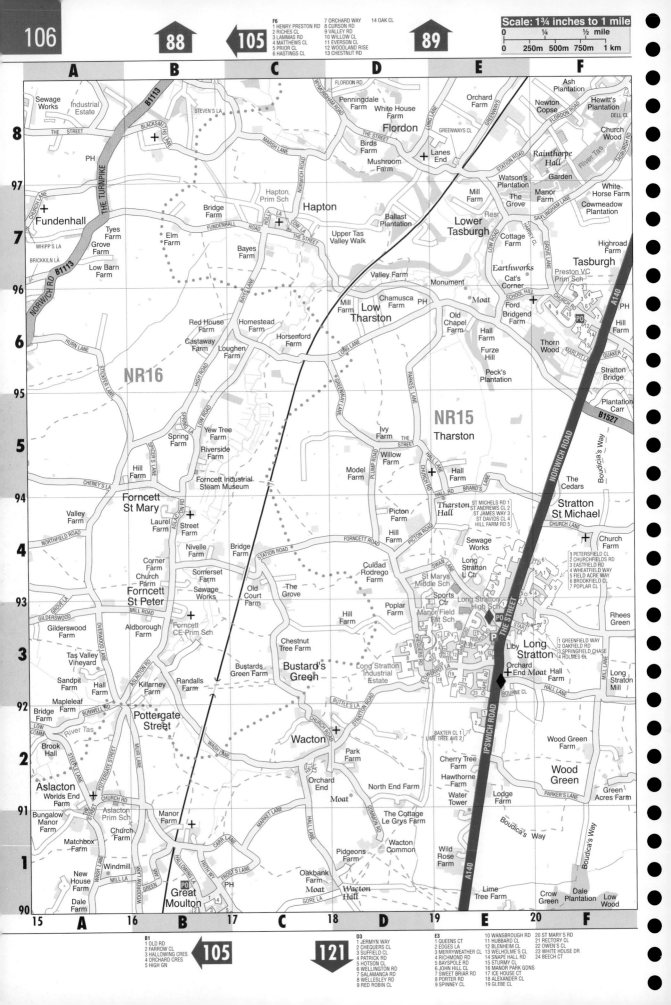

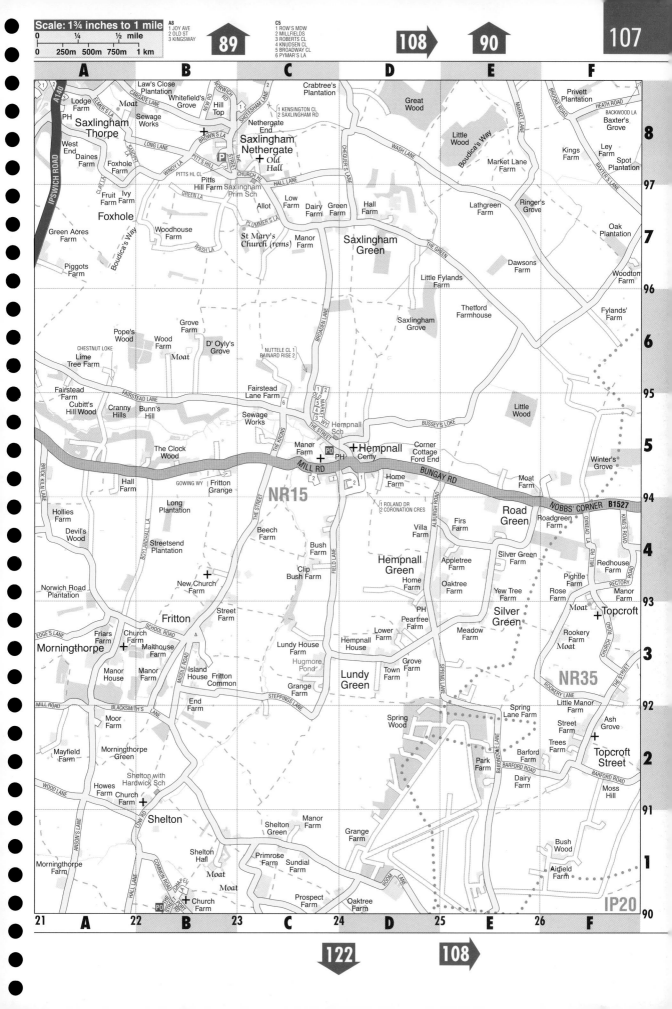

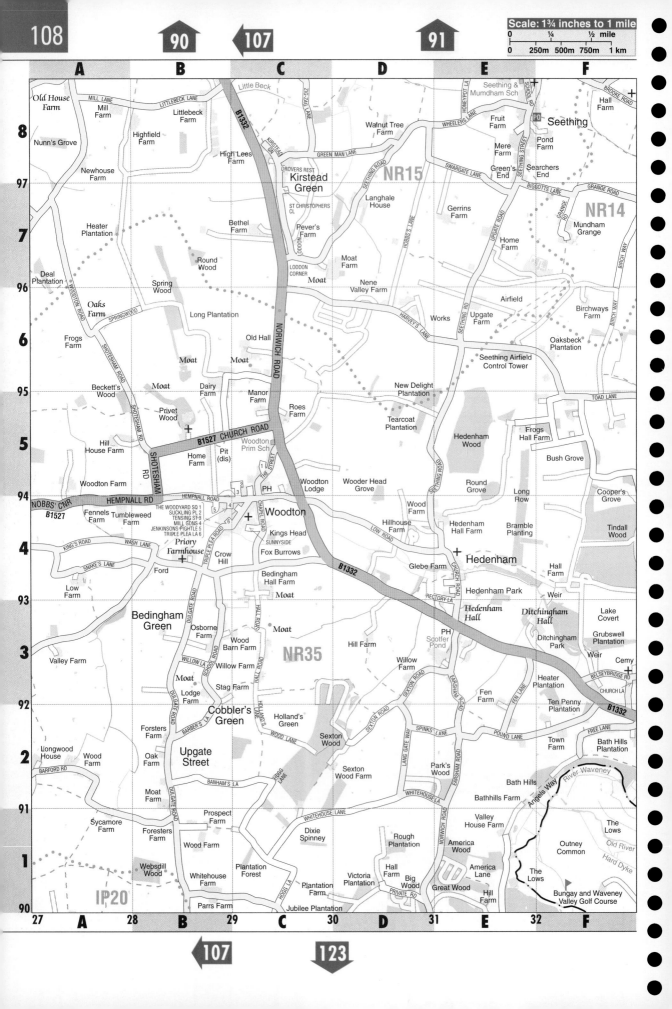

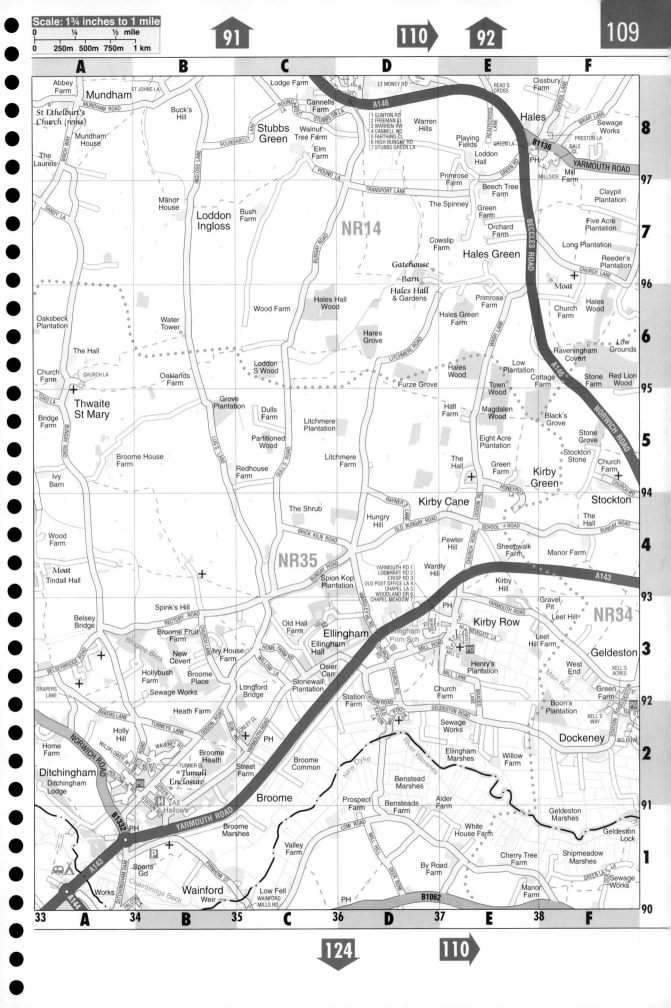

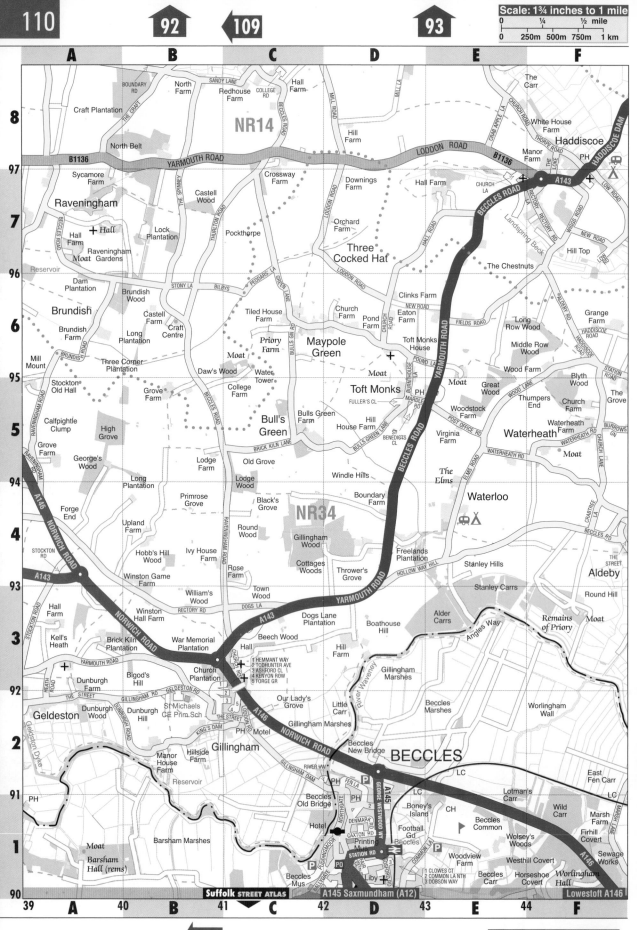

A   B   C   D   E   F

8

97

7

96

6

95

5

94

4

93

3

92

91

1

90

39   A   40   B   41   C   42   D   43   E   44   F

NR14

The Carr

White House Farm

Haddiscoe

Craft Plantation

BOUNDARY RD

North Farm

Redhouse Farm

College RD

Hall Farm

MILL ROAD

MILLA

CHURCH ROAD

CRAB APPLE LA

THORPE ROAD

Manor Farm

PH

HADDISCOE DAM

LOW ROAD

North Belt

SANDY LANE

BECCLES ROAD

Hill Farm

LODDON ROAD

B1136

THE LOKE

A143

B1136

YARMOUTH ROAD

Sycamore Farm

Crossway Farm

Downings Farm

Hall Farm

CHURCH LA

RECTORY ROAD

WIGGS ROAD

NEW ROAD

Hill Top

Raveningham

THE SPINNEY

Castell Wood

LODDON ROAD

Orchard Farm

Three Cocked Hat

BECCLES ROAD

Landspring Beck

The Chestnuts

Hall Farm

THURLTON ROAD

Lock Plantation

Pockthorpe

Church Farm

Clinks Farm

NEW ROAD

Long Row Wood

Grange Farm

BECCLES ROAD

Reservoir

Dam Plantation

STONY LA

BILBYS

PEDDARS LA

GREEN LANE

Tiled House Farm

Pond Farm

Eaton Farm

FIELDS ROAD

HADDISCOE ROAD

Middle Row Wood

STATION ROAD

Brundish

Brundish Wood

Craft Centre

Priory Farm

Maypole Green

Toft Monks House

Wood Farm

Blyth Wood

The Grove

Brundish Farm

Castell Farm

Long Plantation

Moat

Moat

YARMOUTH ROAD

POUND LA

Great Wood

WOOD LANE

Thumpers End

Church Farm

Mill Mount

BRUNDISH ROAD

Three Corner Plantation

Grove Farm

Daw's Wood

College Farm

Water Tower

Toft Monks

BURNTHOUSE LA

MARDLE RD

PH

FULLER'S CL

Woodstock Farm

Waterheath Farm

WATERHEATH RD

Waterheath

Moat

CHURCH LANE

BURROWS GN

Stockton Old Hall

Calfpightle Clump

High Grove

Bull's Green

St BENEDICTS CL

Hill House Farm

Bulls Green Farm

BULLS GREEN LANE

BECCLES ROAD

Virginia Farm

POST OFFICE RD

ELMS ROAD

The Grove

Grove Farm

George's Wood

Lodge Farm

BRICK KILN LANE

Old Grove

Windle Hills

The Elms

Waterloo

CRABTREE LA

BECCLES RD

RAVENINGHAM ROAD

Long Plantation

Primrose Grove

Lodge Wood

Black's Grove

NR34

Boundary Farm

A146

A143

Forge End

Upland Farm

RAVENINGHAM ROAD

Hobb's Hill Wood

Ivy House Farm

Round Wood

Gillingham Wood

Freelands Plantation

HOLLOW WAY HILL

Stanley Hills

THE STREET

Aldeby

STOCKTON RD

STOCKTON RD

Winston Game Farm

William's Wood

RECTORY RD

Town Wood

DOGS LA

Cottages Woods

Thrower's Grove

YARMOUTH ROAD

Stanley Carrs

Round Hill

Moat

Hall Farm

Kell's Heath

Brick Kiln Plantation

Winston Hall Farm

War Memorial Plantation

A143

Rose Farm

Dogs Lane Plantation

Boathouse Hill

Hill Farm

Alder Carrs

Angles Way

Remains of Priory

YARMOUTH ROAD

HEATH ROAD

Dunburgh Farm

Bigod's Hill

CHURCH LANE

Church Plantation

1 HEMMANT WAY
2 TODHUNTER AVE
3 ASHFORD CL
4 KENYON ROW
5 FORGE GR

Beech Wood

Gillingham Marshes

Beccles Marshes

Worlingham Wall

Geldeston

THE STREET

GILLINGHAM RD

GELDESTON RD

St Michaels CE Prim.Sch

Our Lady's Grove

Little Carr

River Waveney

Worlingham Wall

Geldeston Dyke

Dunburgh Wood

Dunburgh Hill

Dunburgh Hill

KING'S DAM

PH

Motel

LODDON RD

Gillingham Marshes

Beccles Marshes

MARSH LANE

PH

Manor House Farm

Hillside Farm

Gillingham

A146

NORWICH ROAD

GILLINGHAM DAM

RIVER VW

Beccles New Bridge

BECCLES

LC

East Fen Carr

Reservoir

FEN LANE

P

PH

GEORGE WESTWOOD WY

A145

LC

Lotman's Carr

LC

PH

Beccles Old Bridge

NORTHGATE

Boney's Island

CH

Wild Carr

Marsh Farm

Moat

Barsham Hall (rems)

Barsham Marshes

Beccles Old Bridge

Hotel

CAXTON RD

DENMARK RD

PIDDINGMOOR

Football Gd Beccles

Beccles Common

P

Wolsey's Woods

Westhill Covert

Firhill Covert

A146

Printing Mus

P

STATION RD

PO

COMMON LA

COMMON LA

Woodview Farm

Beccles Carr

Horseshoe Covert

Sewage Works

Beccles Mus

BELLGATE

Liby

1 CLOWES CT
2 COMMON LA NTH
3 DOBSON WAY

Worlingham Hall

Suffolk STREET ATLAS

A145 Saxmundham (A12)

Lowestoft A146

109

For full street detail of Beccles see
Philip's STREET ATLAS of Suffolk

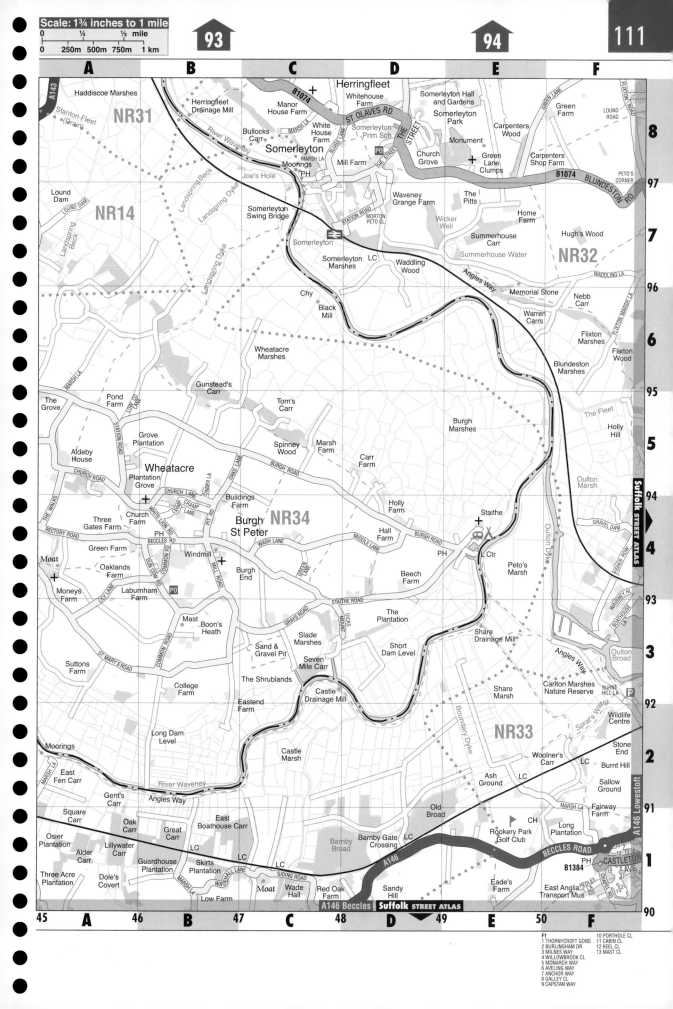

97

Scale: 1¾ inches to 1 mile
0   ¼   ½   mile
0   250m   500m 750m 1 km

A   B   C   D   E   F

8

89

7

88

6

87

5

86

4

85

3

84

2

83

1

82

Cambridgeshire STREET ATLAS

Little
Ouse

Church
Farm

Stokes
Farm

ANCHOR DROVE

School
Farm

SMITHS DROVE

Anchor
End Farm

Brandon
Bank

Orchard
House

Little Ouse River

WHITE HOUSE ROAD

Feltwell
Anchor

CORKWAY DROVE

Black Drain

IP26

SEDGEFEN DROVE

PE38

Shrubhill
Farm

SHRUB DROVE

Black Drain

SHRUB DROVE

Sallowrow Drain

Osier
Holt

Pumping
Station

Temple
Farm

REDMERE DROVE

REDMERE DRO

Redmere
Fen

BLACKDIKE DROVE

Crossbank
Farm

CB7

Letter F
Farm

Flanders
Farm

Plantation
Farm

Decoy
Farm

Decoy
Fen

DECOY RD

IP27

LC

Lodge
Farm

STATION RD

SEDGEFEN ROAD

A1101 Littleport

B1382 MILE END RD

Hereward Way

MILDENHALL ROAD

Peacock's
Farm

Burnt
Fen

Bulldog
Bridge

Herward Way

STATION ROAD

Sedge
Fen

Stonehorse
Plantation

Shippea
Hill Farm

LC

Shippea
Hill

LC

Sparrow
Hall Farm

Willow
Farm

FARTHING DROVE

DUCK DROVE

Engine Drain

Lark Engine
Farm

BURNT FEN TURNPIKE

Grosvenor
House Farm

Elderberry
Farm

River Lark

Spooner's
Farm

Friesland
Farm

WHISTLE DROVE

Whistle
Farm

IP28

Mildenhall Drain

A1101

Harris Farms

61   A   62   B   63   C   64   D   65   E   66   F

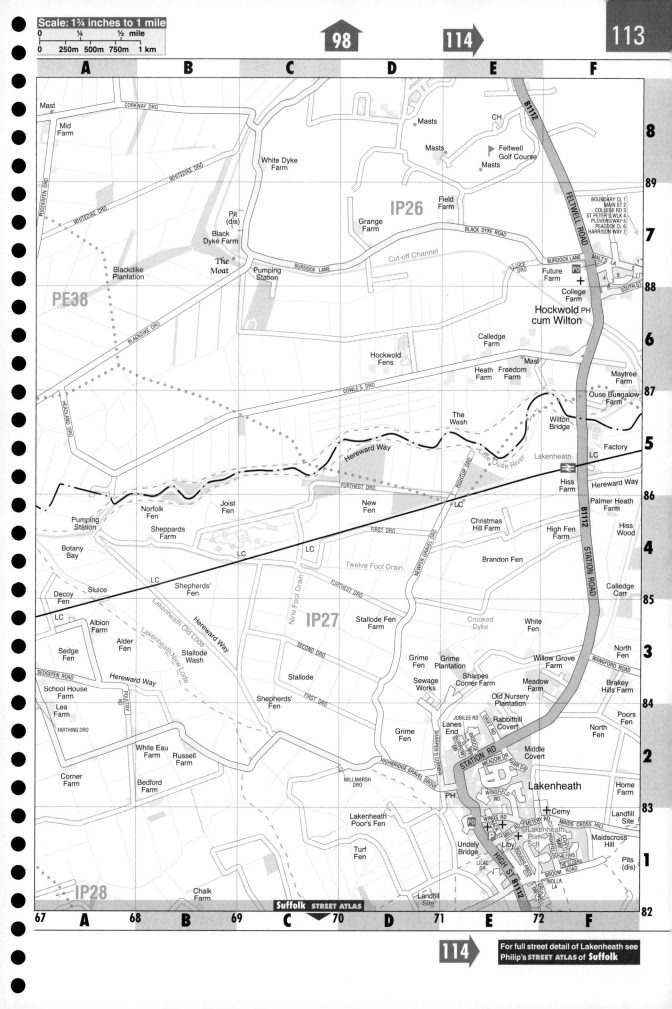

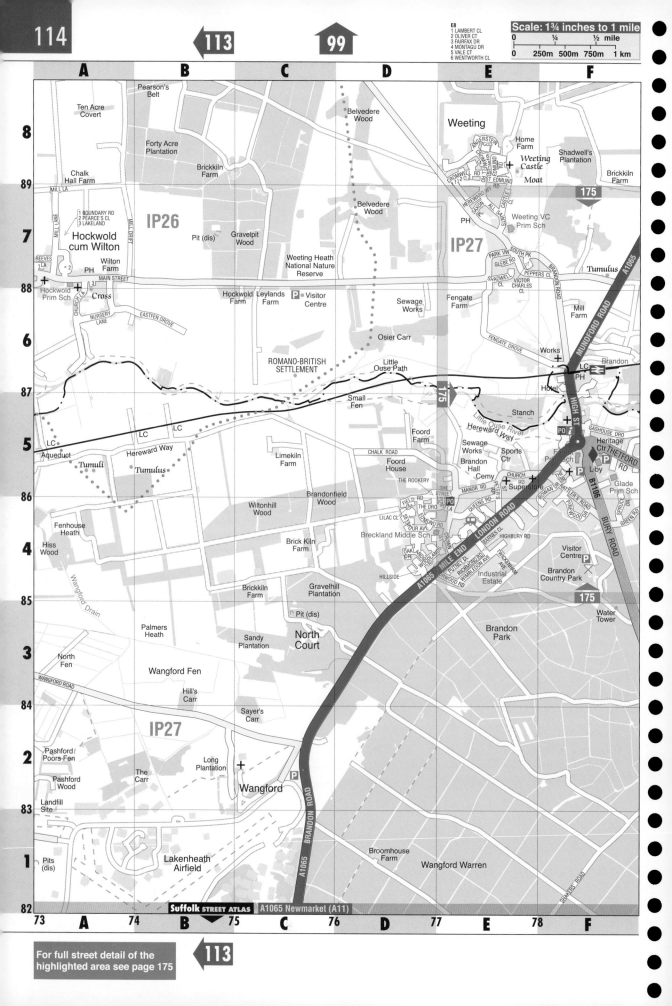

114

113

99

Scale: 1¾ inches to 1 mile
0   ¼   ½   mile
0 250m 500m 750m 1 km

E8
1 LAMBERT CL
2 OLIVER CT
3 FAIRFAX DR
4 MONTAGU DR
5 VALE CT
6 WENTWORTH CL

A   B   C   D   E   F

8

Ten Acre Covert

Pearson's Belt

Belvedere Wood

Weeting

Angerstein Cl

Home Farm

Weeting Castle Moat

Shadwell's Plantation

Brickkiln Farm

89

Chalk Hall Farm

Forty Acre Plantation

Brickkiln Farm

Cromwell

St Edmund Rd

175

Brickkiln Farm

MILL LA

IP26

1 BOUNDARY RD
2 PEARCE'S CL
3 LAKELAND

Pit (dis)

Gravelpit Wood

Belvedere Wood

Hereward Wy

Saxon

All Saints

Weeting VC Prim Sch

IP27

7

Hockwold cum Wilton

Wilton Farm

PH

Weeting Heath National Nature Reserve

PH

Park Vw

South Pk

Glebe Rd

Brandon Rd

Tumulus

A1065

REEVES LA

2

Main Street

Shadwell Cl

Victor Charles Cl

Peppers Cl

88

Hockwold Prim Sch

Cross

PH

3

Hockwold Farm

Leylands Farm

P Visitor Centre

Sewage Works

Fengate Farm

Mill Farm

CHURCH LA

Nursery Lane

Eastfen Drove

Fengate Drove

Works

LC

Brandon

6

Osier Carr

M

PH

Romano-British Settlement

Little Ouse Path

Hotel

87

Small Fen

Stanch

Little Ouse River

Hereward Way

175

PO

Gashouse Dro

Heritage Ctr Thetford

Aqueduct

LC   LC

Hereward Way

LC

Foord Farm

Sewage Works

Sports Ctr

Foord Prim Sch

P Liby

RD

5

Tumuli

Tumulus

Limekiln Farm

Chalk Road

Foord House

Brandon Hall

Cemy

The Rookery

Church Rd

Superstore

Roman Dr

Battler's Ch

Pinewood

B1106

Glade Prim Sch

Green Rd

Spruce Rd

86

Wiltonhill Wood

Brandonfield Wood

Manor Rd

The Street

Field Rd

PO

Queens Rd

London Road

4

Fenhouse Heath

Brick Kiln Farm

Lilac Cl

Breckland Middle Sch

Seymour Ave

Edmund Rd

Highbury Rd

Barnes Cl

Hiss Wood

Oaklands Dr

Woodlands Rd

Crown

Putney El

Richmond Rd

Wimbledon Ave

Twickenham Ave

Industrial Estate

Visitor Centre P

Brandon Country Park

85

Wangford Drain

Brickkiln Farm

Gravelhill Plantation

Hillside

A1065 Mile End

Norwood Rd

175

Water Tower

3

North Fen

Palmers Heath

Pit (dis)

Sandy Plantation

North Court

Brandon Park

Wangford Road

Wangford Fen

Hill's Carr

84

IP27

Sayer's Carr

2

Pashford Poors Fen

The Carr

Long Plantation

P

Brandon Road

Pashford Wood

Wangford

83

Landfill Site

A1065

Broomhouse Farm

1

Pits (dis)

Lakenheath Airfield

Wangford Warren

Shakers Road

82

For full street detail of the highlighted area see page 175

113

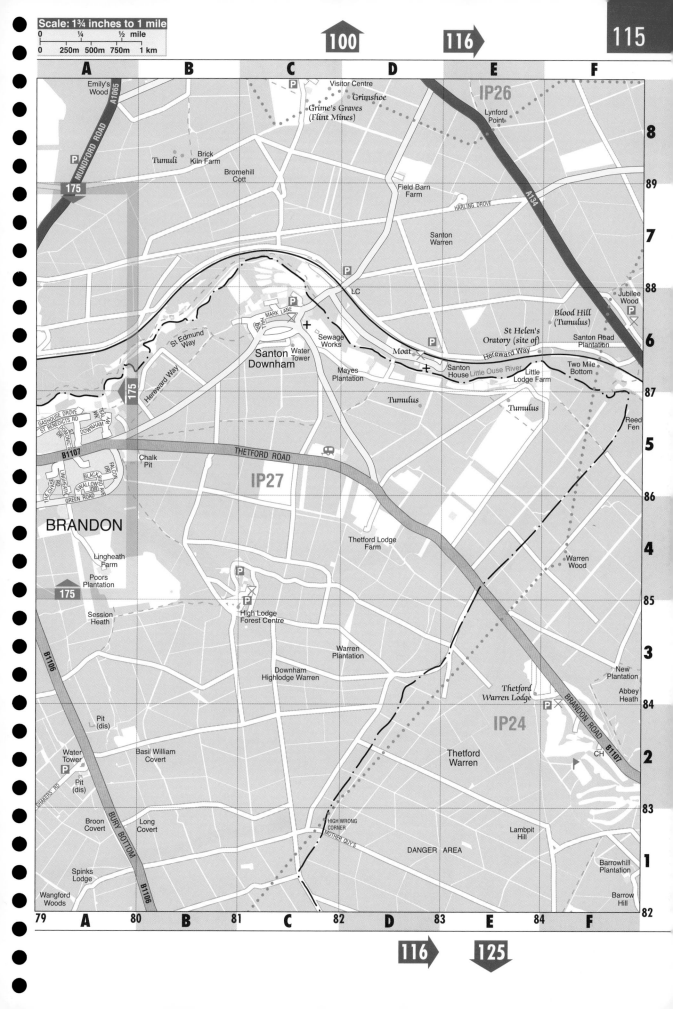

A   B   C   D   E   F

IP26

Emily's Wood

Visitor Centre
Grimshoe
Grime's Graves
(Flint Mines)

Lynford Point

Tumuli
Brick Kiln Farm
Bromehill Cott

Field Barn Farm

HARLING DROVE

A134

Santon Warren

Jubilee Wood

LC

Blood Hill
(Tumulus)

Santon Road Plantation

St Edmund Way

Santon Downham

Water Tower

Sewage Works

Moat

St Helen's Oratory (site of)

Hereward Way

Two Mile Bottom

HILL MARK LANE

Mayes Plantation

Santon House   Little Ouse River

Little Lodge Farm

Reed Fen

Hereward Way

175

Tumulus

Tumulus

GASHOUSE DROVE
ST BENEDICTS RD
DOMINIC ST
DOWNHAM

B1107

Chalk Pit

THETFORD ROAD

IP27

FALCON DR
BLACK
LINGHEATH RD
SWALLOW DR
GREEN ROAD
THE CHASE

BRANDON

Thetford Lodge Farm

Warren Wood

Lingheath Farm

Poors Plantation

175

Session Heath

High Lodge Forest Centre

Warren Plantation

New Plantation

Abbey Heath

Downham Highlodge Warren

Thetford Warren Lodge

BRANDON ROAD
B1107

IP24

CH

B1106

Pit (dis)

Basil William Covert

Thetford Warren

Water Tower

Pit (dis)

SHAKERS RD

DANGER   AREA

Lambpit Hill

Barrowhill Plantation

Broon Covert

Long Covert

HIGH WRONG CORNER

MOTHER QUY'S

BURY BOTTOM

Spinks Lodge

Barrow Hill

Wangford Woods

B1106

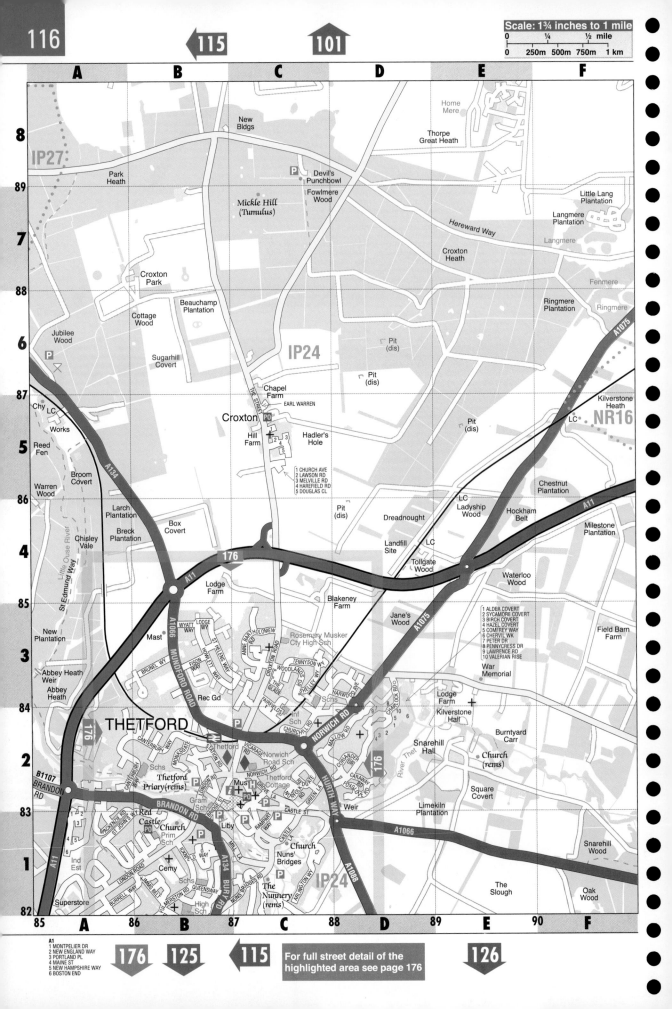

IP27

8

89

Park
Heath

New
Bldgs

Devil's
Punchbowl

Fowlmere
Wood

Thorpe
Great Heath

Home
Mere

Little Lang
Plantation

7

Mickle Hill
(Tumulus)

Hereward Way

Croxton
Heath

Langmere
Plantation

Langmere

88

Croxton
Park

Beauchamp
Plantation

IP24

Pit
(dis)

Fenmere

Ringmere
Plantation

Ringmere

6

Jubilee
Wood

Cottage
Wood

Sugarhill
Covert

Pit
(dis)

A1075

87

Chy LC
Works

Chapel
Farm

EARL WARREN

Croxton PO

Pit
(dis)

LC

Kilverstone
Heath

LC

NR16

5

Reed
Fen

Warren
Wood

Hill
Farm

Hadler's
Hole

1 CHURCH AVE
2 LAWSON RD
3 MELVILLE RD
4 HAREFIELD RD
5 DOUGLAS CL

LC
Ladyship
Wood

Chestnut
Plantation

A11

86

Larch
Plantation

Broom
Covert

Chisley
Vale

Breck
Plantation

Box
Covert

Pit
(dis)

Dreadnought

Hockham
Belt

Milestone
Plantation

4

A134

176

A11

Landfill
Site

LC

Waterloo
Wood

A1075

New
Plantation

A1066

Lodge
Farm

Blakeney
Farm

Jane's
Wood

Tollgate
Wood

1 ALDER COVERT
2 SYCAMORE COVERT
3 BIRCH COVERT
4 HAZEL COVERT
5 COMFREY WAY
6 CHERVIL WK
7 PETER DR
8 PENNYCRESS DR
9 LAWRENCE RD
10 VALERIAN RISE

Field Barn
Farm

85

Abbey Heath
Weir

Abbey Heath

Mast

LODGE
WY

WYATT
WAY

ST HELENS WAY

FISON
WAY

HOWLETT WAY

BRUNEL WY

Rec Gd

ANNE BARTHOLOMEW

CROXTON ROAD

Rosemary Musker
Cty High Sch

WOODLANDS RD

THE
GLADE

TENNYSON WY

SHELLEY WY

HARWOOD LANE

Schs

Inf
Sch

CASTOR RD

River Thet

War
Memorial

Lodge
Farm

Kilverstone
Hall

Burntyard
Carr

3

176

THETFORD

P

Thetford

Schs

Thetford
Priory (rems)

CANTERBURY WAY

NUNNSGATE

STATION RD

LONDON RD

Gram
Sch

CHURCHILL RD

Thetford
Cottage

Norwich
Road Sch

VICARAGE
RD

NORWICH
RD

GROVE LA

BRIDGATE

NORFOLK RD

NORWICH RD

MARLOW DR

GREEN LA

CARAWAY RD

FOXGLOVE RD

Snarehill
Hall

Church
(rems)

2

B1107
BRANDON
RD

CANTERBURY
WAY

Mus H

Liby

PO

BRANDON RD

Red
Castle
PO

Church
Prim
Sch

MACKENZIE RD

ST JOHN'S WY

LONDON ROAD

ICKNIELD WAY

Cemy

P

BRIDGES

BURRELL WAY

Ind
Est

RAMPART
WAY

MILL LA

CASTLE ST

CASTLE LA

Church

Nuns'
Bridges

Weir

A1066

Square
Covert

Limekiln
Plantation

Snarehill
Wood

1

A11

Superstore

BURRELL WAY

PALMERSTON RD

JAMES BELT

A134
BURY RD

NUNS BRIDGES RD

QUEENSWAY

Schs

High
Sch

BOWLING GREEN

The
Nunnery
(rems)

ARLINGTON WAY

IP24

A1088

The
Slough

Oak
Wood

82

85   A   86   B   87   C   88   D   89   E   90   F

A1
1 MONTPELIER DR
2 NEW ENGLAND WAY
3 PORTLAND PL
4 MAINE ST
5 NEW HAMPSHIRE WAY
6 BOSTON END

▼ **176** ▼ **125** ← **115**

For full street detail of the
highlighted area see page 176

▼ **126**

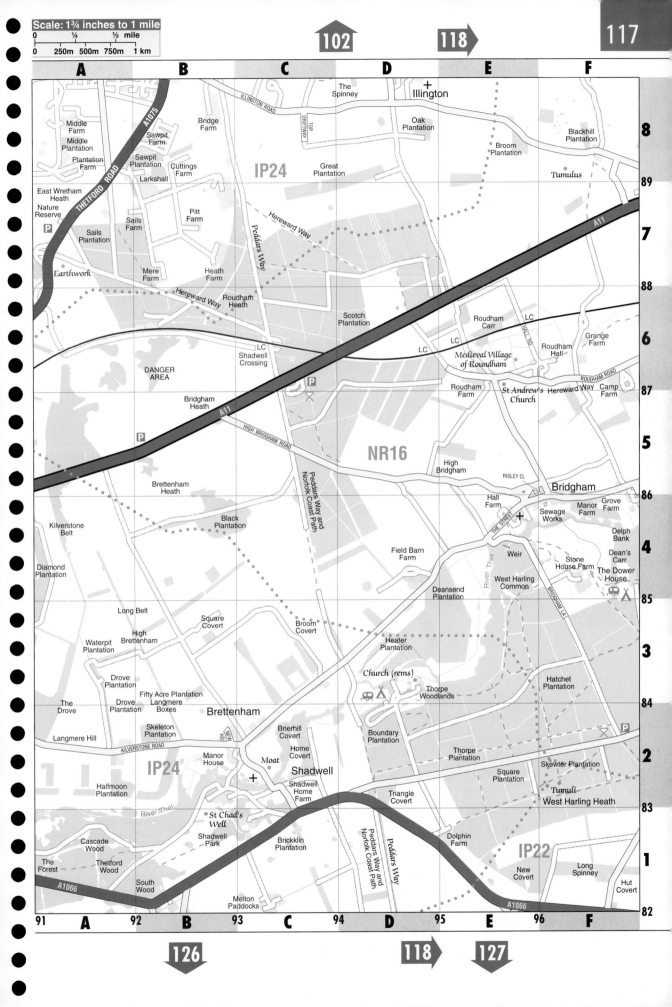

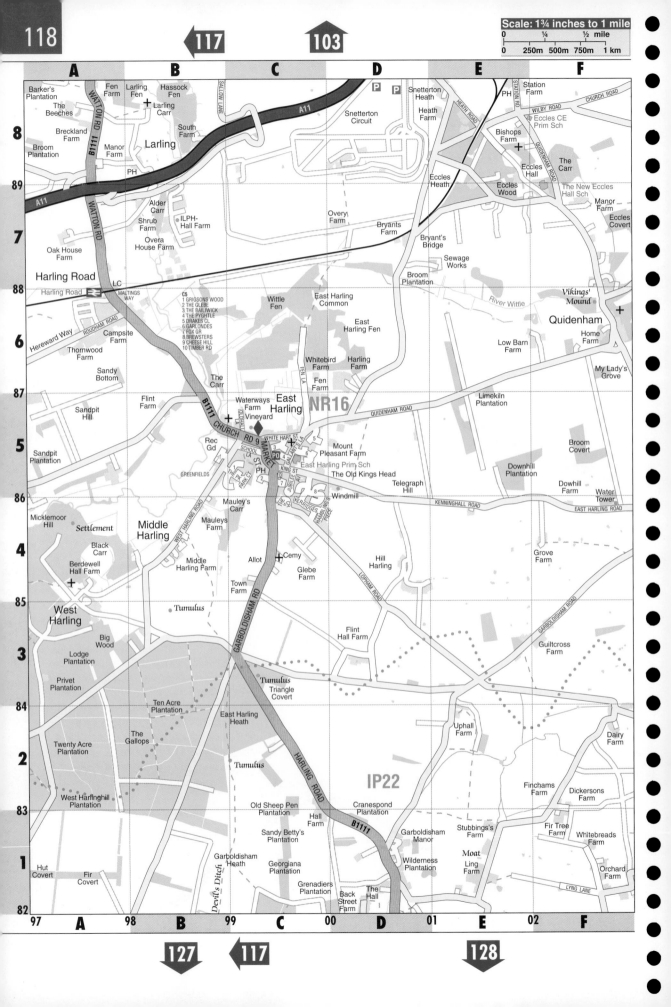

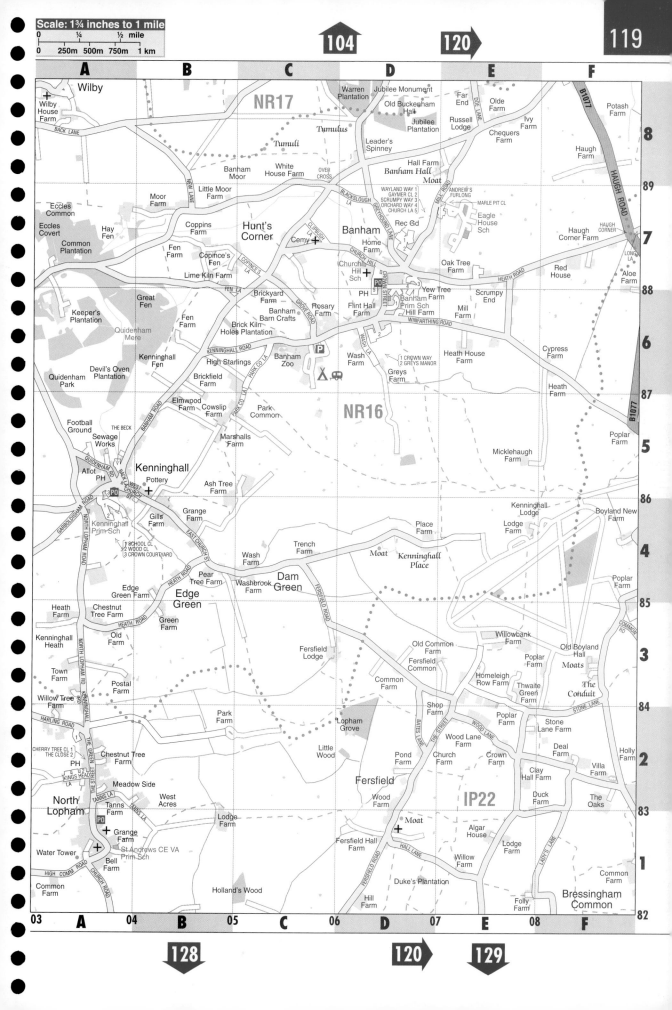

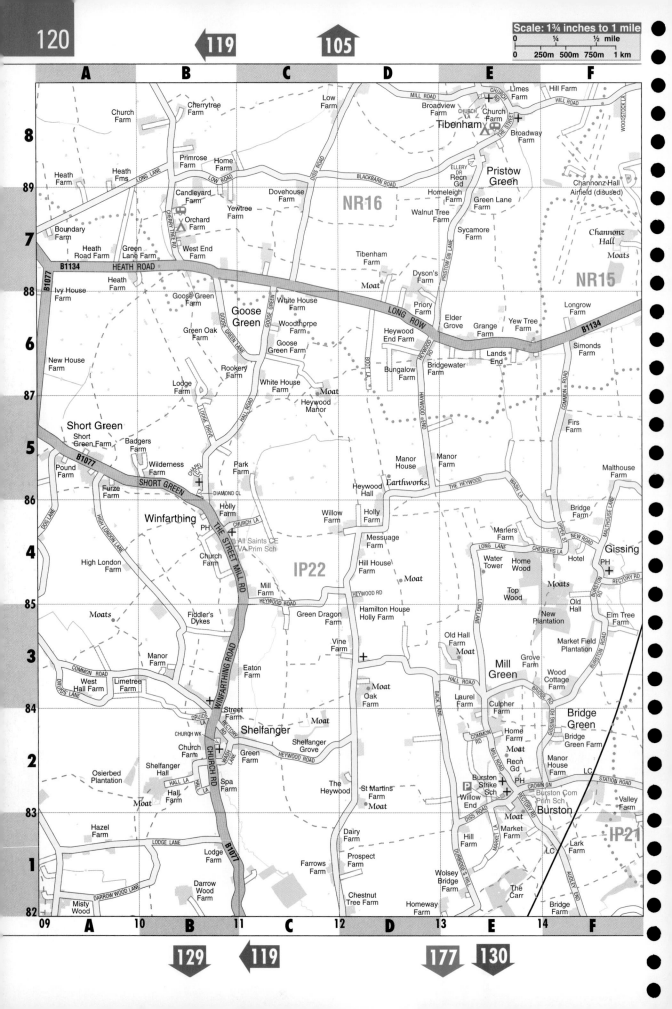

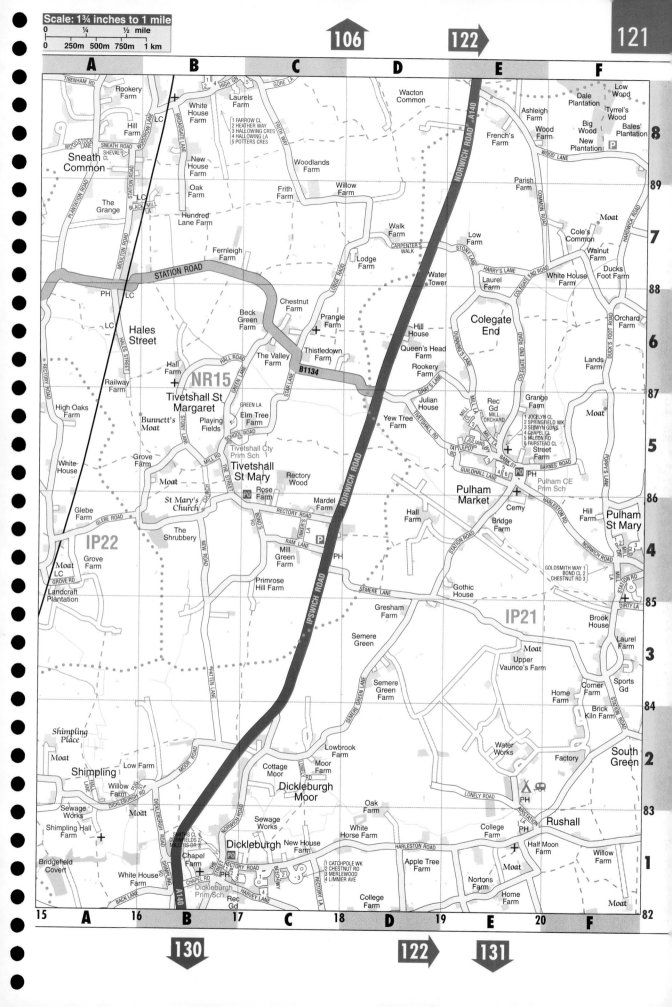

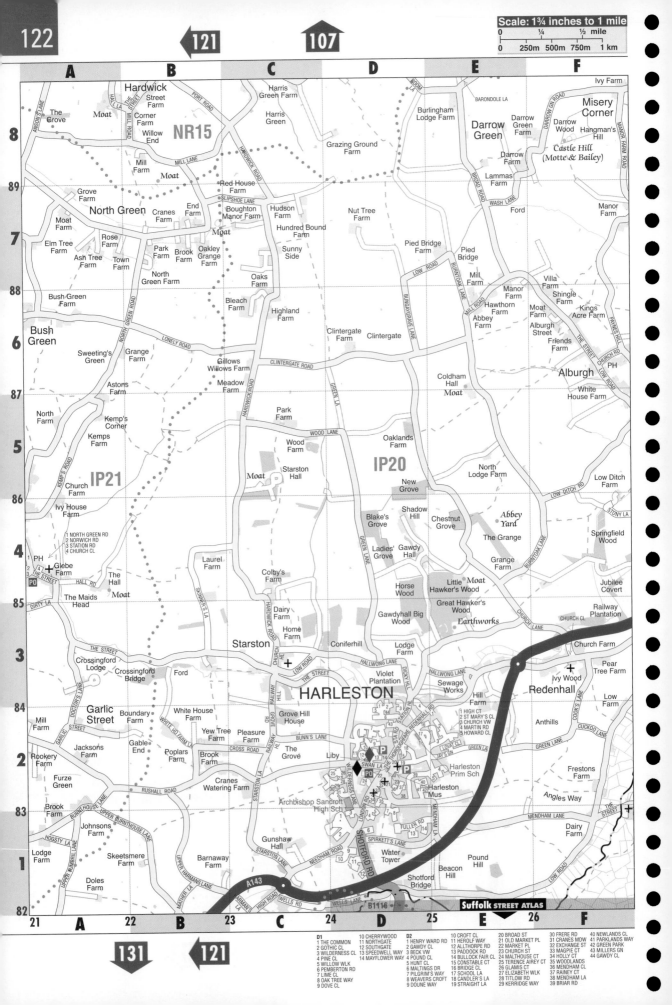

Scale: 1¾ inches to 1 mile
0   ¼   ½   mile
0   250m   500m   750m   1 km

Ivy Farm

Hardwick
Street Farm
Harris Green Farm
Harris Green
Burlingham Lodge Farm
Darrow Green
Darrow Green Farm
Darrow Wood
Misery Corner
Hangman's Hill

The Grove
Moat
Corner Farm
Willow End
NR15
BARONDOLE LA
Darrow Farm
Castle Hill (Motte & Bailey)

Mill Farm
Moat
Grazing Ground Farm
Lammas Farm
Ford
Manor Farm

Grove Farm
Red House Farm
Manor Farm

North Green
Cranes Farm
End Farm
Boughton Manor Farm
Hudson Farm
Nut Tree Farm
Pied Bridge Farm
Pied Bridge
Villa Farm
Shingle Farm
Kings Acre Farm

Moat Farm
Rose Farm
Park Farm
Brook Farm
Moat
Hundred Bound Farm
Mill Farm
Manor Farm
Hawthorn Abbey Farm
Moat Farm
Friends Farm

Elm Tree Farm
Ash Tree Farm
Town Farm
Oakley Grange Farm
Sunny Side
Alburgh Street
PH

North Green Farm
Oaks Farm
Clintergate Farm
Clintergate
Alburgh
White House Farm

Bush Green Farm
Bleach Farm
Highland Farm

Bush Green
Sweeting's Green
Grange Farm
Gillows Willows Farm
Meadow Farm
CLINTERGATE ROAD
Coldham Hall Moat

Astons Farm
Park Farm
Oaklands Farm
North Lodge Farm
Low Ditch Farm

North Farm
Kemp's Corner
Kemps Farm
Wood Farm
Starston Hall
IP20
New Grove
Abbey Yard
Stony La

Church Farm
IP21
Moat
Shadow Hill
Chestnut Grove
The Grange
Springfield Wood

Ivy House Farm
1 NORTH GREEN RD
2 NORWICH RD
3 STATION RD
4 CHURCH CL
Laurel Farm
Blake's Grove
Ladies' Grove
Gawdy Hall
Grange Farm
Jubilee Covert

PH
Glebe Farm
Colby's Farm
Horse Wood
Little Moat
Hawker's Wood
Great Hawker's Wood

THE STREET
PO
The Hall
Moat
Dairy Farm
Gawdyhall Big Wood
Earthworks
Railway Plantation

DIRTY LA
The Maids Head
Home Farm
Coniferhill
Lodge Farm
Church Farm

Crossingford Lodge
Starston
Hallwong Lane
Pear Tree Farm

The Street
Crossingford Bridge
Ford
HARLESTON
Violet Plantation
Sewage Works
Redenhall
Ivy Wood
Low Farm

Garlic Street
Boundary Farm
White House Farm
Grove Hill House
Hill Farm
Anthills

Mill Farm
Jacksons Farm
Gable End
Yew Tree Farm
Pleasure Farm
1 HIGH CT
2 ST MARY'S CL
3 ALLTHORPE RD
4 MARTIN RD
5 HOWARD CL
Harleston Prim Sch
Frestons Farm

Rookery Farm
Poplars Farm
Brook Farm
The Grove
Liby
Harleston Mus
Angles Way

Furze Green
Cranes Watering Farm
Archbishop Sancroft High Sch
Mendham Lane
Dairy Farm

Brook Farm
Johnsons Farm
FULLER RD
MENDHAM LANE

Lodge Farm
Skeetsmere Farm
Gunshaw Hall
Barnaway Farm
Water Tower
Shotford Bridge
Beacon Hill
Pound Hill

Doles Farm
A143
WELLS RD
B1116
Suffolk STREET ATLAS

D1		D2					
1 THE COMMON	10 CHERRYWOOD	1 HENRY WARD RD	10 CROFT CL	20 BROAD ST	30 FRERE RD	40 NEWLANDS CL
2 GOTHIC CL	11 NORTHGATE	2 GAWDY CL	11 HEROLF WAY	21 OLD MARKET PL	31 CRANES MDW	41 PARKLANDS WAY
3 WILDERNESS CL	12 SOUTHGATE	3 BECK VW	12 ALLTHORPE RD	22 MARKET PL	32 MAGPIE CT	42 GREEN PARK
4 PINE CL	13 SPEEDWELL WAY	4 POUND CL	13 PADDOCK RD	23 CHURCH ST	33 MAGPIE CT	43 MILLERS GN
5 WILLOW WLK	14 MAYFLOWER WAY	5 HUNT CL	14 BULLOCK FAIR CL	24 MALTHOUSE CT	34 HOLLY CT	44 GAWDY CL
6 PEMBERTON RD		6 MALTINGS DR	15 CONSTABLE CT	25 TERENCE AIREY CT	35 WOODLANDS	
7 LIME CL		7 PILGRIM'S WAY	16 BRIDGE CL	26 GLAMIS CT	36 MENDHAM CT	
8 OAK TREE WAY		8 WEAVERS CROFT	17 SCHOOL LA	27 ELIZABETH WLK	37 RAINEY CT	
9 DOVE CL		9 DOUNE WAY	18 CANDLER'S LA	28 TITLOW RD	38 MENDHAM LA	
			19 STRAIGHT LA	29 KERRIDGE WAY	39 BRIAR RD	

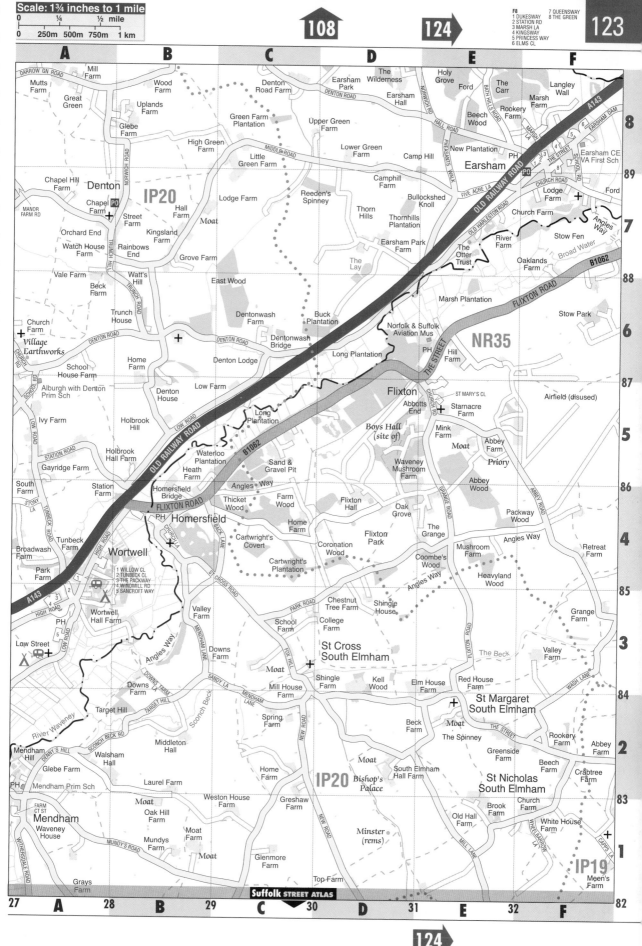

Scale: 1¾ inches to 1 mile

0   ¼   ½   mile
0   250m   500m   750m   1 km

108

124

F8
1 DUKESWAY
2 STATION RD
3 MARSH LA
4 KINGSWAY
5 PRINCESS WAY
6 ELMS CL
7 QUEENSWAY
8 THE GREEN

123

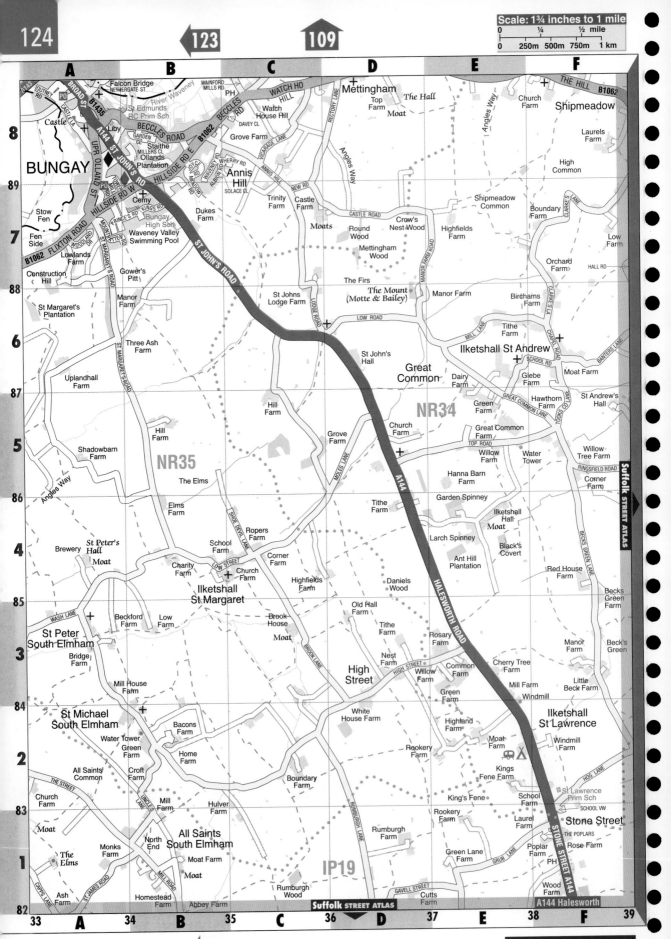

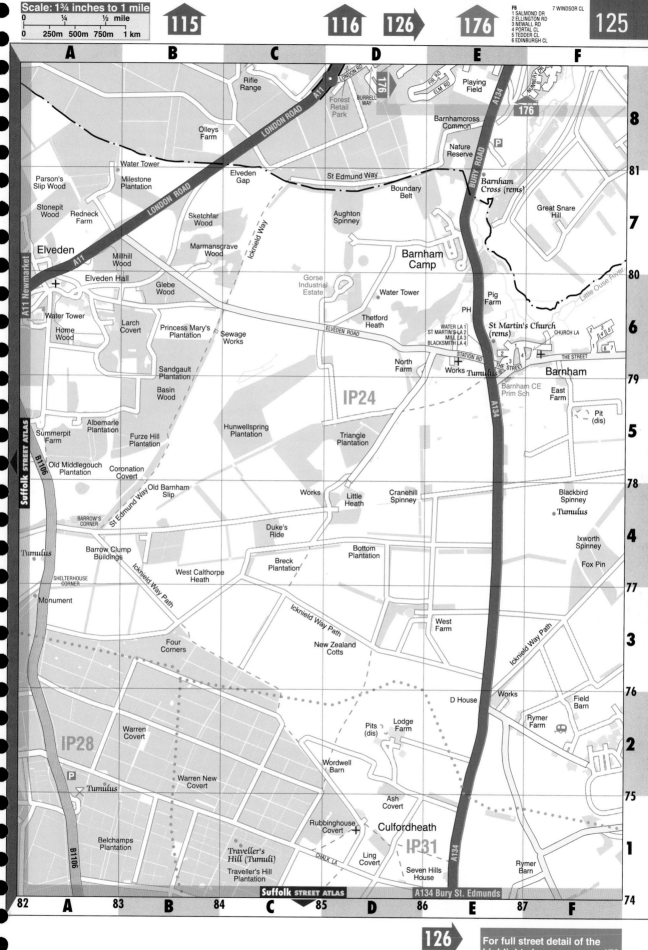

Scale: 1¾ inches to 1 mile

0 ¼ ½ mile
0 250m 500m 750m 1 km

115 116 126 176

125

F6
1 SALMOND DR
2 ELLINGTON RD
3 NEWALL RD
4 PORTAL CL
5 TEDDER CL
6 EDINBURGH CL

7 WINDSOR CL

Rifle Range
LONDON ROAD
A11
176
Forest Retail Park
BURRELL WAY
FIR RD ELM RD
Playing Field
A134
176
TURNER DR

Olleys Farm
Barnhamcross Common
8

Water Tower
LONDON ROAD
Elveden Gap
St Edmund Way
Boundary Belt
Nature Reserve
BURY ROAD
P
Barnham Cross (rems)
81

Parson's Slip Wood
Milestone Plantation
Sketchfar Wood
Aughton Spinney
Great Snare Hill
7

Stonepit Wood
Redneck Farm
Marmansgrave Wood
Icknield Way
Barnham Camp
80

Elveden
A11
Millhill Wood

Elveden Hall
Glebe Wood
Water Tower
Pig Farm
Little Ouse River

A11 Newmarket
Water Tower
Home Wood
Larch Covert
Princess Mary's Plantation
Sewage Works
ELVEDEN ROAD
Thetford Heath
Gorse Industrial Estate
Water Tower
PH
St Martin's Church (rems)
CHURCH LA
6

WATER LA 1
ST MARTIN S LA 2
MILL LA 3
BLACKSMITH LA 4
1 2
3 4 5
1
6

Sandgault Plantation
North Farm
Works
Tumulus
STATION RD
THE STREET
Barnham
THE STREET

Basin Wood
IP24
Barnham CE Prim Sch
East Farm
79

Suffolk STREET ATLAS
B1106
Summerpit Farm
Albemarle Plantation
Furze Hill Plantation
Hunwellspring Plantation
Triangle Plantation
Pit (dis)
5

Old Middlegouch Plantation
Coronation Covert
St Edmund Way
Old Barnham Slip
Works
Little Heath
Cranehill Spinney
Blackbird Spinney
Tumulus
78

BARROW'S CORNER
Tumulus
Barrow Clump Buildings
Icknield Way
West Calthorpe Heath
Duke's Ride
Bottom Plantation
Ixworth Spinney
Fox Pin
4

SHELTERHOUSE CORNER
Monument
Breck Plantation
Icknield Way Path
77

Icknield Way Path
West Farm
Icknield Way Path
3

Four Corners
New Zealand Cotts
76

IP28
Warren Covert
D House
Works
Field Barn
Rymer Farm

P
Tumulus
Pits (dis)
Lodge Farm
2

Warren New Covert
Wordwell Barn
75

Belchamps Plantation
B1106
Ash Covert
Rubbinghouse Covert
Culfordheath
IP31
A134

Traveller's Hill (Tumuli)
CHALK LA
Ling Covert
Seven Hills House
Rymer Barn
1

Traveller's Hill Plantation

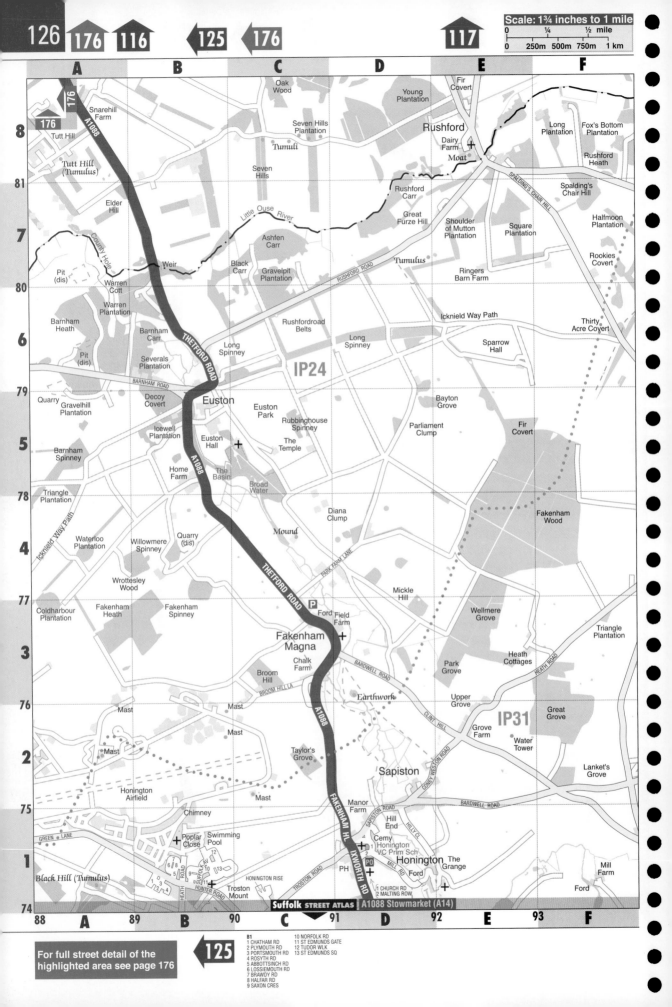

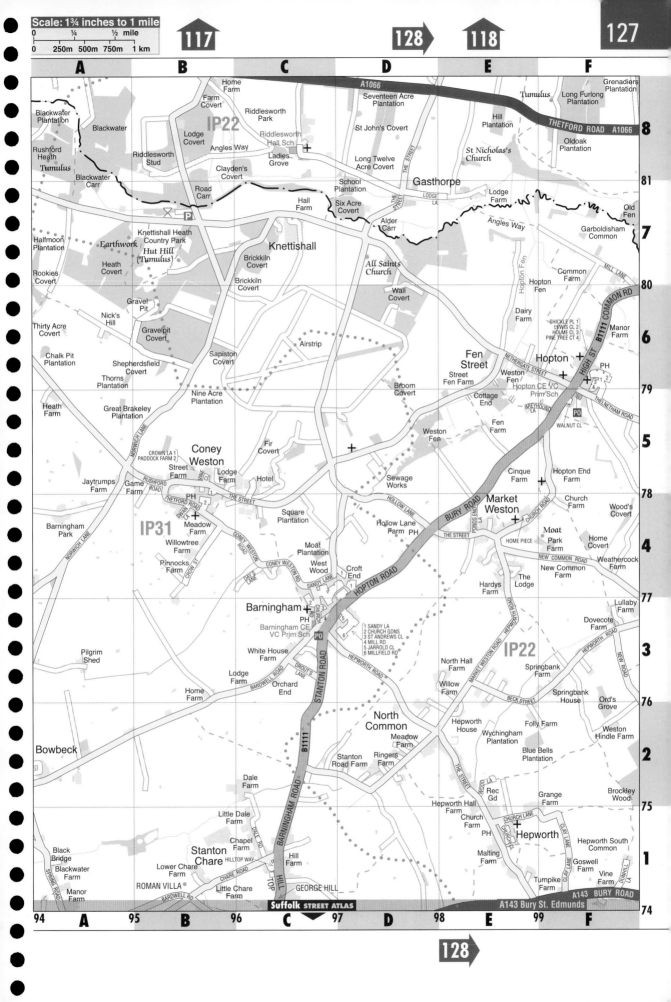

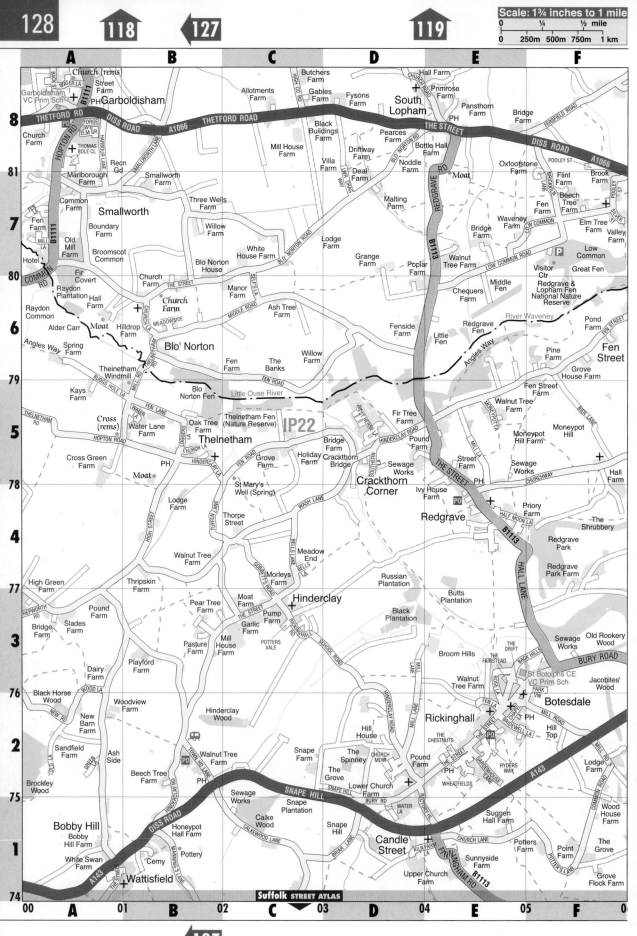

Scale: 1¾ inches to 1 mile
0   ¼   ½ mile
0   250m 500m 750m 1 km

A   B   C   D   E   F

8
Church (rems)
Garboldisham VC Prim Sch
Street Farm
PH Garboldisham
Church Farm
THETFORD RD
DISS ROAD A1066 THETFORD ROAD
Butchers Farm
Allotments Farm
Gables Farm
Fysons Farm
South Lopham
Hall Farm
Primrose Farm
THE STREET
Pansthorn Farm
Bridge Farm
DISS ROAD A1066

81
HOPTON RD
FORGE
IVY
ELM GR
THOMAS BOLE CL
Recn Gd
Marlborough Farm
Smallworth Farm
Mill House Farm
Black Buildings Farm
Villa Farm
Driftway Farm
Deal Farm
Pearces Farm
Noddle Farm
Bottle Hall Farm
Moat
Oxfootstone Farm
Pooley St
Flint Farm
Brook Farm
BRICKKILN
SILVER ST
Beech Tree Farm

7
FEN LA
Fen Farm
Common Farm
Smallworth
Boundary Farm
Three Wells Farm
Willow Farm
B1111
Lower Drag Way
Bdlo Norton Rd
Lodge Farm
Malting Farm
BLO NORTON ROAD
Grange Farm
Poplar Farm
Redgrave Rd
B1113
Walnut Tree Farm
Bridge Farm
Waveney Farm
Low Common
Elm Tree Farm
Valley Farm
Low Common

80
Hotel
MILL LA
Old Mill Farm
Broomscot Common
COMMON RD
Fir Covert
Raydon Plantation
Hall Farm
Church Farm
THE STREET
White House Farm
Blo Norton House
SELF ST LA
Manor Farm
Self St La
Chequers Farm
Middle Fen
Visitor Ctr
P
Redgrave & Lopham Fen National Nature Reserve
Great Fen
Low Common

6
Raydon Common
Alder Carr
Spring Farm
Moat
Hilldrop Farm
Church Farm
MEADOWSIDE
MIDDLE ROAD
Ash Tree Farm
Blo' Norton
Fenside Farm
Little Fen
Redgrave Fen
River Waveney
Pond Farm
Pine Farm
Grove House Farm
Fen Street

79
Angles Way
Theinetham Windmill
BURGS HOLE LA
MILL LA
Fen Farm
The Banks
Willow Farm
FEN ROAD
Blo Norton Fen
Little Ouse River
Angles Way
Fen Street Farm
Walnut Tree Farm
BIER LANE

5
THELNETHAM RD
Kays Farm
Cross (rems)
WATER LA
Water Lane Farm
LOGGERS LA
Oak Tree Farm
Thelnetham Fen (Nature Reserve)
IP22
WEST HERNE LA
Fir Tree Farm
Pound Farm
MONEYPOT LA
Street Farm
MILL LA
Moneypot Hill Farm
Moneypot Hill
HOPTON ROAD
Thelnetham
CHURCH LA
HINDERCLAY LA
Grove Farm
Bridge Farm
Holiday Farm
Crackthorn Bridge
SOUTHERN
Sewage Works
THE STREET
PH
Sewage Works
CHURCHWAY
Hall Farm

78
Cross Green Farm
Moat
PH
Lodge Farm
St Mary's Well (Spring)
WASH LANE
Crackthorn Corner
Ivy House Farm
PO
Redgrave
Priory Farm
Half Moon La
The Shrubbery

4
High Green Farm
High Street
Thorpe Street
TUFFEN LANE
Walnut Tree Farm
BELLS LANE
GOBGET'S ROAD
Meadow End
BELLS
Russian Plantation
Butts Plantation
B1113
HALL LANE
Redgrave Park
Redgrave Park Farm

77
HEPWORTH RD
Bridge Farm
Slades Farm
Thripskin Farm
Pound Farm
Pear Tree Farm
Moat Farm
THE STREET
Pump Farm
Garlic Farm
RICKINGHALL RD
Hinderclay
SCHOOL ROAD
Black Plantation
Broom Hills
THE DRIFT
THE FAIRSTEAD
BACK HILLS
Sewage Works
Old Rookery Wood
BURY ROAD

3
Dairy Farm
Playford Farm
Pasture Farm
Mill House Farm
POTTERS VALE
HINDERCLAY ROAD
MILL LANE
Walnut Tree Farm
PARK
St Botolphs CE VC Prim Sch
VW
Jacobites' Wood

76
Black Horse Wood
WOOD LA
NEW RD
New Barn Farm
Woodview Farm
Hinderclay Wood
Hill House
RIDGE LA
FEN LA
CHAPEL LA
Botesdale
Rickinghall
THE CHESTNUTS
THE STREET
PO
CHAPEL LA
PH
BRIDEWELL LA
Hill Top
MILL ROAD

2
Sandfield Farm
GREEN
Ash Side
TOWN HO LANE
Beech Tree Farm
PO
Walnut Tree Farm
PH
Snape Farm
The Spinney
The Grove
CHURCH MDW
Pound Farm
PH
GARDENHOUSE LANE
RYDERS WAY
WHEATFIELDS
Lodge Farm
A143
COMMON ROAD
MILL RD S

75
Brockley Wood
BRIAR LANE
DISS ROAD
Honeypot Hall Farm
Sewage Works
Snape Plantation
SNAPE HILL
Lower Church Farm
BURY RD
WATER LA
RECTORY RL
Suggen Hall Farm
Wood House Farm
CALKEWOOD LANE
Snape Hill
Candle Street
CHURCH LANE
Potters Farm
The Grove

1
Bobby Hill
Bobby Hill Farm
White Swan Farm
Cemy
Pottery
MANNINGS LANE
Calke Wood
Upper Church Farm
KILN FARM LA
FINNINGHAM RD
B1113
Sunnyside Farm
Point Farm
POTTER'S LANE
Grove Flock Farm

74
A143
THE STREET
Wattisfield
Suffolk STREET ATLAS

00   A   01   B   02   C   03   D   04   E   05   F   0

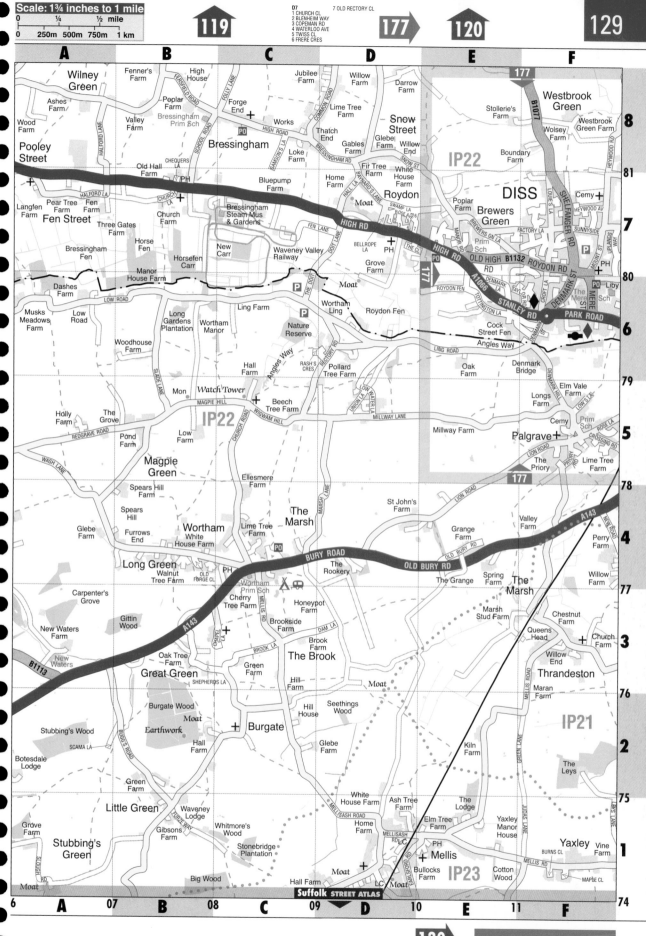

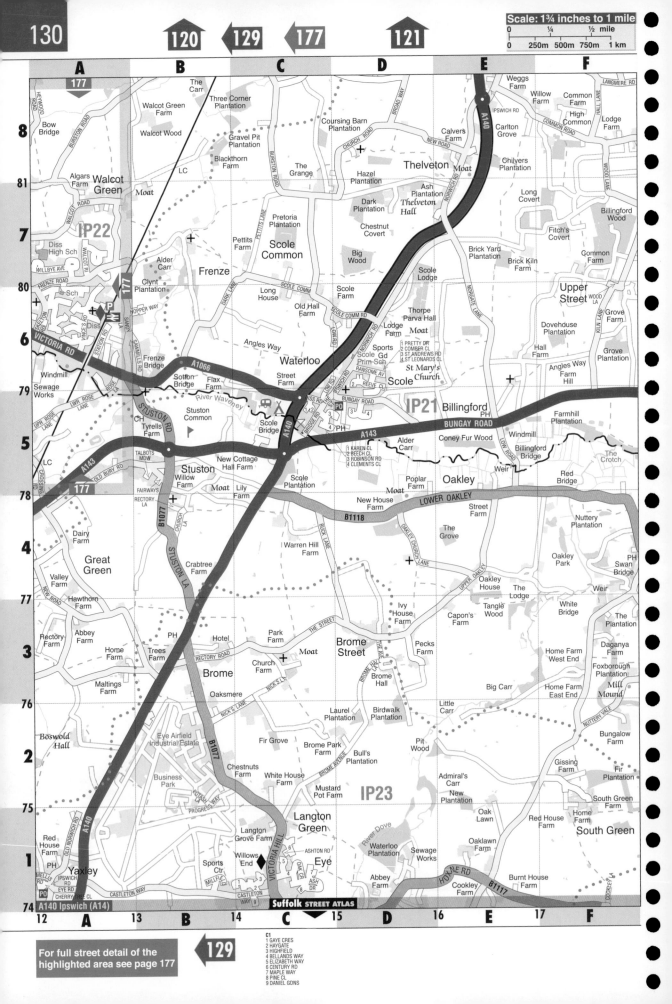

A B C D E F

8 81 7 80 6 79 5 78 4 77 3 76 2 75 1 74

HEYWOOD ROAD
BURSTON ROAD
Bow Bridge
177
The Carr
Walcot Green Farm
Three Corner Plantation
Walcot Wood
Gravel Pit Plantation
Blackthorn Farm
LC
Coursing Barn Plantation
BROAD WAY
CHURCH ROAD
NEW ROAD
Calvers Farm
IPSWICH RD
A140
Weggs Farm
Willow Farm
Common Farm
High Common
LANGMERE RD
HALL LANE
COMMON ROAD
Lodge Farm

Algars Farm
Walcot Green
Moat
The Grange
Hazel Plantation
Thelveton
Ash Plantation
Moat
Carlton Grove
Chilvers Plantation
Long Covert
Billingford Wood

WALCOT ROAD
IP22
Diss High Sch
Pretoria Plantation
Pettits Lane
Pettits Farm
Scole Common
Dark Plantation
Chestnut Covert
Thelveton Hall
NORWICH ROAD
Brick Yard Plantation
Brick Kiln Farm
Fitch's Covert
Common Farm

WILLBYE AVE
Sch
Alder Carr
Frenze
BURSTON ROAD
Big Wood
Scole Lodge
NORGATE LANE
Upper Street
WOOD LA
Grove Farm

FRENZE ROAD
WALCOT RD
Clynt Plantation
HOPPER WAY
Long House
SCOLE COMM RD
Scole Farm
Thorpe Parva Hall
Moat
Lodge Farm
Hall Farm
Dovehouse Plantation
KILN LANE
Grove Plantation

Windmill
VICTORIA RD
STATION RD
SANDY LA
Frenze Bridge
A1066
Sotton Bridge
Flax Farm
Old Hall Farm
Street Farm
Waterloo
Sports Gd
Scole Prim Sch
1 PRETTY DR
2 COMBER CL
3 ST ANDREWS RD
4 ST LEONARDS CL
Angles Way Farm Hill
Angles Way

Sewage Works
LWR ROSE LANE
ROSE LA
STUSTON RD
River Waveney
Scole Bridge
DISS RD
BRIDGE RD
NORWICH RD
IPSWICH RD
RANSOME AV
REEVE CL
St Mary's Church
Scole
IP21
Billingford
PH
Farmhill Plantation

UPR ROSE LANE
CH
Tyrells Farm
Stuston Common
A140
PO
PH
BUNGAY ROAD
Alder Carr
Coney Fur Wood
Windmill
Billingford Bridge
LOW ROAD
The Crotch

LC
A143
OLD BURY RD
TALBOTS MDW
Stuston
New Cottage Hall Farm
1 KAREN CL
2 BEECH CL
3 ROBINSON RD
4 CLEMENTS CL
Weir
Red Bridge

CROSSING
177
FAIRWAYS
RECTORY LA
Willow Farm
Moat
Lily Farm
Scole Plantation
Moat
New House Farm
Poplar Farm
Oakley
LOWER OAKLEY
Street Farm
Nuttery Plantation

Dairy Farm
STUSTON LA
CHURCH LA
B1077
Crabtree Farm
B1118
Warren Hill Farm
BUCK LANE
The Grove
OAKLEY CHURCH LANE
PH Swan Bridge

Great Green
Valley Farm
Hawthorn Farm
Oakley Park
Oakley House
The Lodge
Weir
White Bridge
The Plantation

Rectory Farm
Abbey Farm
Home Farm
Trees Farm
PH
RECTORY ROAD
Hotel
Park Farm
THE STREET
Moat
Brome Street
Ivy House Farm
Capon's Farm
Tangle Wood
UPPER OAKLEY
Daganya Farm
Foxborough Plantation

Maltings Farm
Brome
Oaksmere
Church Farm
NICK'S LA
Pecks Farm
Brome Hall
BROME HALL LA
THE AVE
Home Farm West End
Home Farm East End
Mill Mound

Boswold Hall
NICK'S LANE
B1077
Chestnuts Farm
Laurel Plantation
Birdwalk Plantation
Little Carr
Big Carr
NUTTERY VALE
Bungalow Farm

Eye Airfield Industrial Estate
COTTAGE WAY
Fir Grove
White House Farm
Brome Park Farm
Bull's Plantation
BROME AVENUE
Pit Wood
Admiral's Carr
New Plantation
Gissing Farm
Fir Plantation

Business Park
PROGRESS WAY
Mustard Pot Farm
IP23
South Green Farm

Red House Farm
PH
MELLIS RD
IPSWICH RD
EYE RD
CHERRY TREE CL
PO
Yaxley
A140
VICTORIA HILL
Langton Grove Farm
Langton Green
Sports Ctr
MILLFIELD
Willows End
ASHTON RD
Eye
ASH DR
River Dove
Waterloo Plantation
Sewage Works
Oak Lawn
Oaklawn Farm
HORNE RD
B1117
Red House Farm
Home Farm
South Green

Castleton Way
CASTLETON WAY
Abbey Farm
Cookley Farm
Burnt House Farm
COOKLEY LA

A140 Ipswich (A14)
Suffolk STREET ATLAS

12 A 13 B 14 C 15 D 16 E 17 F

For full street detail of the highlighted area see page 177

← 129

C1
1 GAYE CRES
2 HAYGATE
3 HIGHFIELD
4 BELLANDS WAY
5 ELIZABETH WAY
6 CENTURY RD
7 MAPLE WAY
8 PINE CL
9 DANIEL GDNS

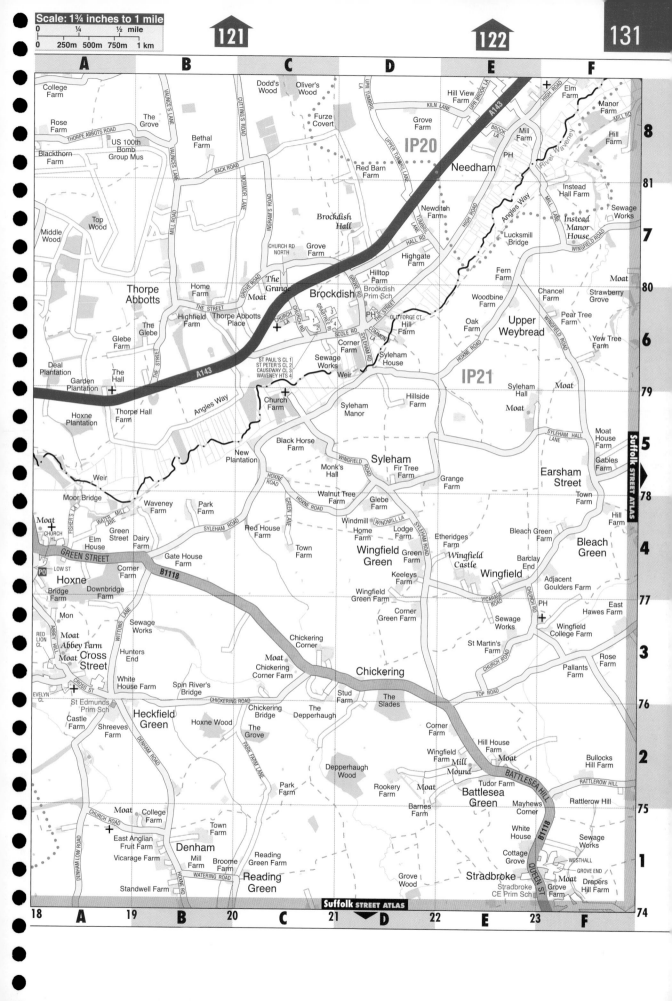

A B C D E F

8

Old
Hunstanton

GOLF COURSE RD
SANDY LA
ASHDALE PK
SMUGGLERS CL
Hotel

IRB
Station

WODEHOUSE RD
HAMILTON RD
HAMILTON RD WEST
WATERWORKS ROAD
Motel

7

KELSEY CL
HAMILTON RD WEST
ERPINGHAM CT
THE BIG YARD
OLD HUNSTANTON RD A149
CHURCH ROAD
A149

St Edmund's
Point

HOWARDS CL
PO

42

St Edmund's Chapel
LIGHTHOUSE LANE
BERNARD CRESCENT
KING'S RD
PEDDARS DR
OLD TOWN WY
CHAPEL BANK

Lighthouse (dis)

LIGHTHOUSE CL

6

B1161
BERNARD CRESCENT
QUEENS DRIVE
BEGRAVE AVE
ASTLEY CRESCENT
HASTINGS
PEDDARS DR
KINGS RD
QUEENS GDNS
CROMER ROAD

CLIFF PARADE
CLARENCE CT
VICTORIA AVE
CLARENCE RD

BUCKINGHAM CT
YORK AVE
ST EDMUNDS
GLEBE AVE
Glebe
House Sch
PE36

LINCOLN SQ N
NORTHGATE
LINCOLN ST

5

LINCOLN SQUARE S
Boston Sq
Sensory Park
BOSTON SQ
LINCOLN STREET
1 LOWER LINCOLN ST
2 AUSTIN ST
3 NORTHGATE PREC
4 THE GREEN

HUNSTANTON

CLIFF CT
CLIFF TR
TH
GREEVEGATE
VALENTINE COURT
Hunstanton Infant Sch
The Coll of West Anglia
(Hunstanton Learning Ctr)

41

Cross
Princess Theatre
ST EDMUND'S TERR
GREEVEGATE
CHURCH ST
ST JAMES ST
HIGH ST
Rec Gd
CYPRESS PL
C&M HARTLEY CL
Beech
Wood

Liby
WESTGATE
VALENTINE RD
NURSERY DR
Downs

4

SIR DOUGLAS
BADER
ESPLANADE
BEACH TERR RD
LESTRANGE
SOUTHEND RD
AVENUE RD
HOMEFIELDS RD
SEAFIELD GDNS
DOWNS CL
DOWNS RD
DOWNS ROAD
Lodge
Farm

YH
PARK RD
Smithdon
High Sch
Chimney

Oasis Leisure Centre
CLK RD
NENE ST
HILL STREET
SANDRINGHAM ROAD
HOMEFIELDS RD

Coach Park
LYNDHURST CT

Hunstanton
Sea Life Sanctuary
CHILTERN CR 1
PRINCE WILLIAM CL 2
MELTON DR
WILLOW
WAVENEY RD
HANOVER GDNS
RAMSAY GDNS
FRISBEE RD
KING'S LYNN ROAD
Hunstanton
Commercial
Park

3

SEAGATE ROAD
ALEXANDRA RD
CHATSWORTH RD
LINGWOOD RD
EVANS GDNS
NELSON RD

Superstore
Cemy

SOUTH BEACH RD
B1161
ELIZABETH CL
JUBILEE CL
ELIZABETH CL
COLLINGWOOD RD

40

BISHOPS
MANOR RD
OASIS WAY
Redgate
Jun Sch
MERCEDES AVE
St Andrew's Chapel
(remains of)
Cottages
Downs Farm

WINDSOR RI
CHARLES RD
ENFIELD CL
REDGATE HILL
Hill
Wood
Downs
Farm

2

PRINCESS DR
ANDREWS PL
1 TUDOR CRES
2 MARGARETS CL

DIANAS DRO
SARAHS CL
AGNES DR
PHILIPS CL
REDGATE HL

HARRY WAY

A149

CH

Redgate
Hill
PE31

1

Searles
Golf Course
NORTH BEACH
SOUTH BEACH ROAD
HUNSTANTON RD

39

66 A B 67 C D 68 E F

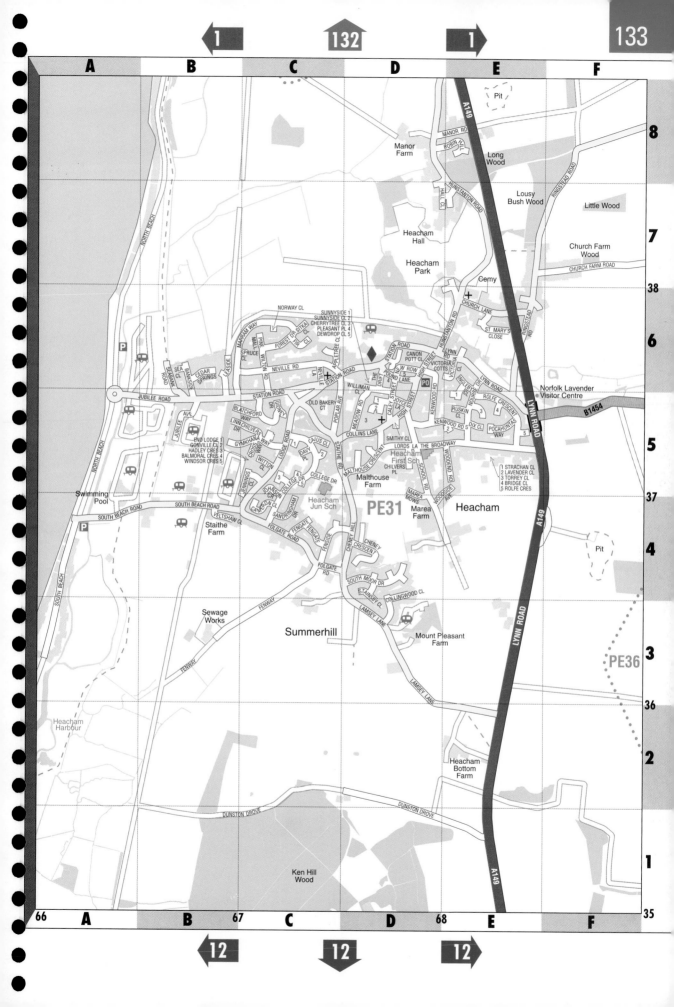

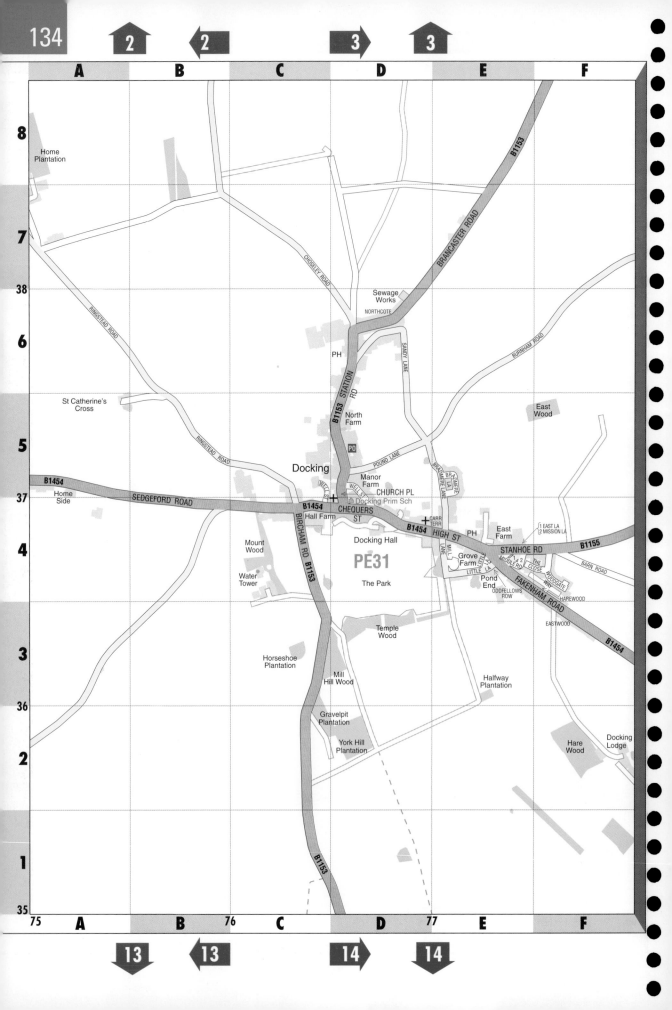

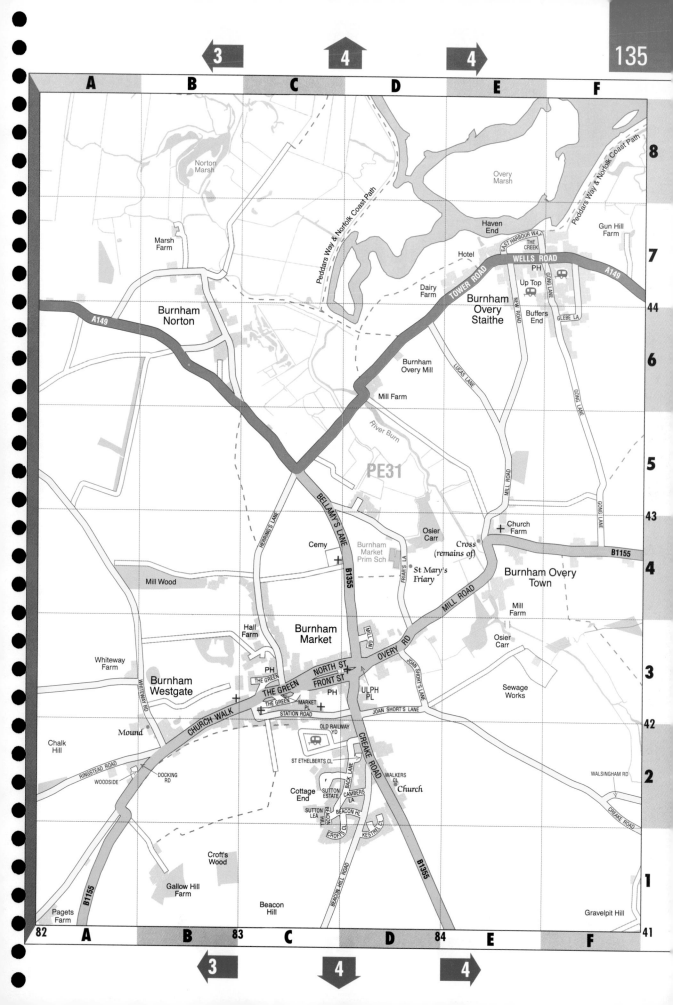

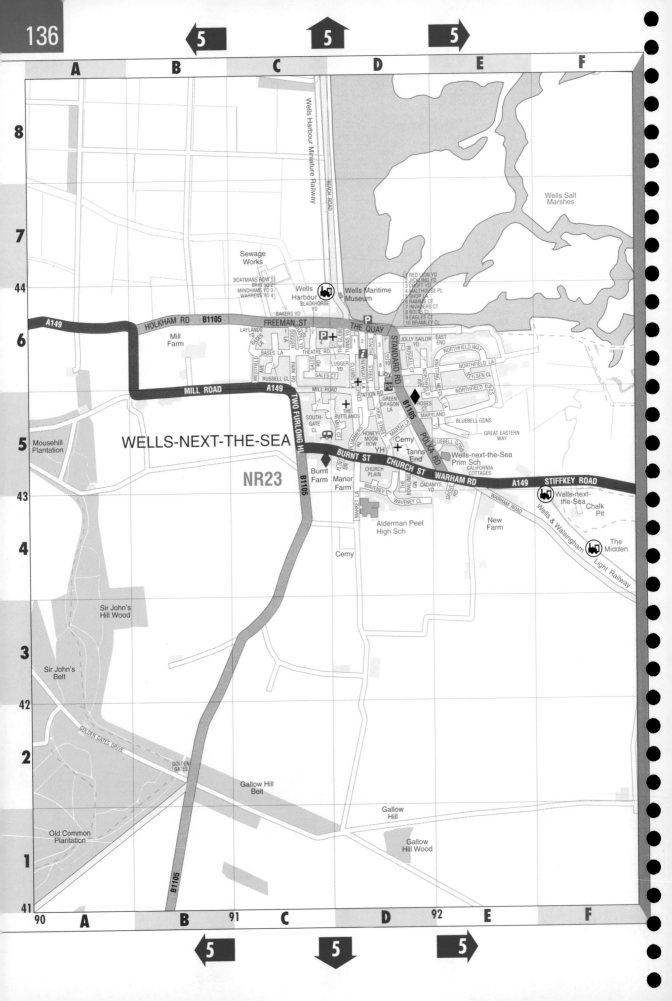

8

44

Wells Harbour Miniature Railway

BEACH ROAD

Wells Salt Marshes

7

Sewage Works

BOATMANS ROW 1
BRIB SQ 2
MINDHAMS YD 3
WARRENS YD 4

Wells Harbour
BLACKHORSE YD

BAKERS YD

Wells Maritime Museum

1 RED LION YD
2 JICKLING YD
3 CROFT YD
4 MALTHOUSE PL
5 SHOP LA
6 RAMNS CT
7 INVADERS CT
8 BOLTS CL
9 EAGLES CT
10 BRAMLEY CL

A149

HOLKHAM RD   B1105

FREEMAN ST

THE QUAY

6

Mill Farm

LAYLANDS YD

WESTFIELD AVE

BASES LA

CHAPEL LA

DOGGER

PARK RD

RUSSELL CL

THEATRE RD

OLD STH YD

THE GLEBE

TUNNS YD

NEWGATE

STAITHE STREET

CLUBBS YD

1
2
6
8
10

STANDARD RD

RUSSELL CT

JOLLY SAILOR YD

EAST END

NORTHFIELD WAY

KNITTING NEEDLE

NORTHFIELD LA

FILSEN CL

NORTHFIELD C&S

Liby

MILL ROAD   A149

MILL ROAD

GALES CT

STATION RD

PO

NORTHFIELD

B1105

ROSES CT

MARYLAND

BLUEBELL GDNS

GREAT EASTERN WAY

5

WELLS-NEXT-THE-SEA

TWO FURLONG HL

SOUTH-GATE CL

THE BUTTLANDS

HIGH STREET

GREEN DRAGON LA

HONEY MOON ROW

YH

MARSH LA

Cemy

Tanns End

POLKA RD

BLUEBELL GDNS

Wells-next-the-Sea Prim Sch

CALIFORNIA COTTAGES

GREAT EASTERN WAY

NR23

Burnt Farm

FLINT DRE

BURNT ST

PLUMMERS HL

Manor Farm

CHURCH PLAIN

CHURCH ST

WAVENEY CL

WARHAM RD

A149

STIFFKEY ROAD

Wells-next-the-Sea Chalk Pit

43

MARKET LA

WAVENEY C

THE BOWLING

GROVE RD

CADAMYS YD

New Farm

WARHAM ROAD

Wells & Walsingham Light Railway

The Midden

4

Cemy

Alderman Peel High Sch

New Farm

Mousehill Plantation

3

Sir John's Hill Wood

Sir John's Belt

42

GOLDEN GATES DRIVE

2

GOLDEN GATES

Gallow Hill Belt

1

B1105

Old Common Plantation

Gallow Hill

Gallow Hill Wood

41

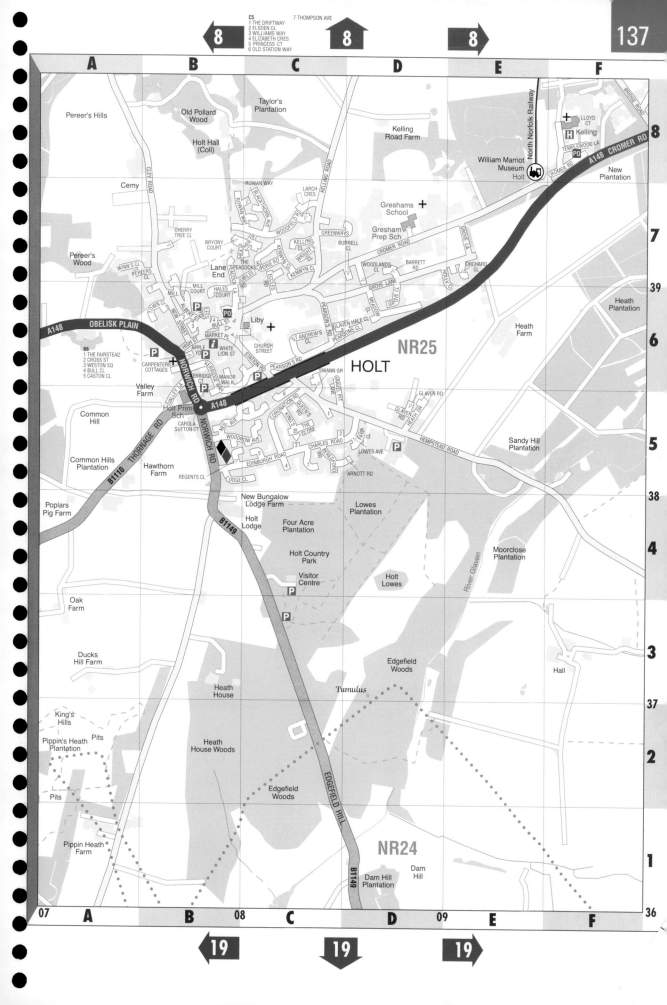

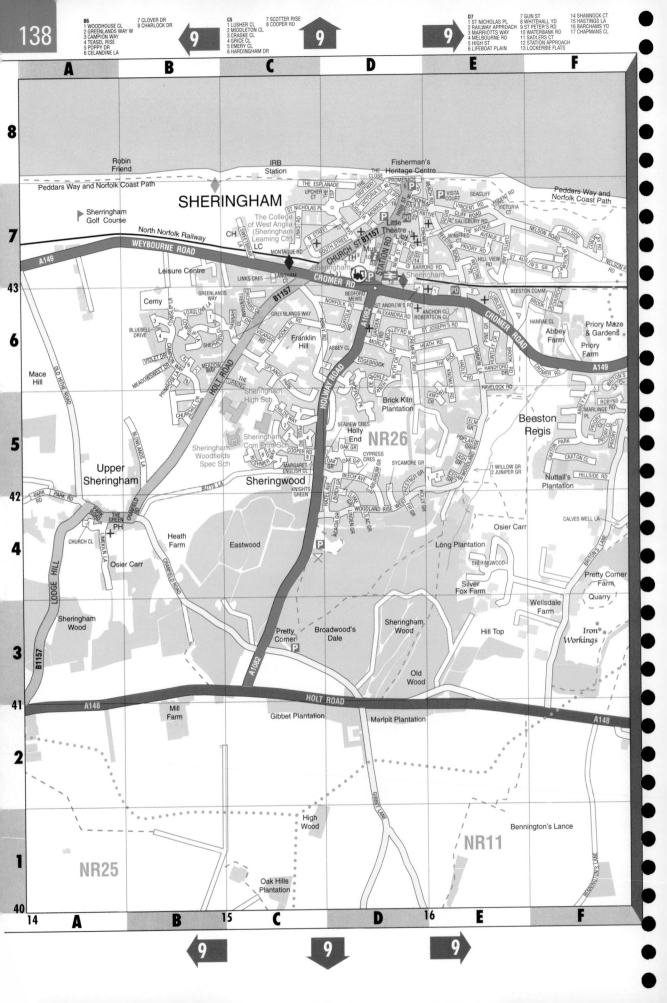

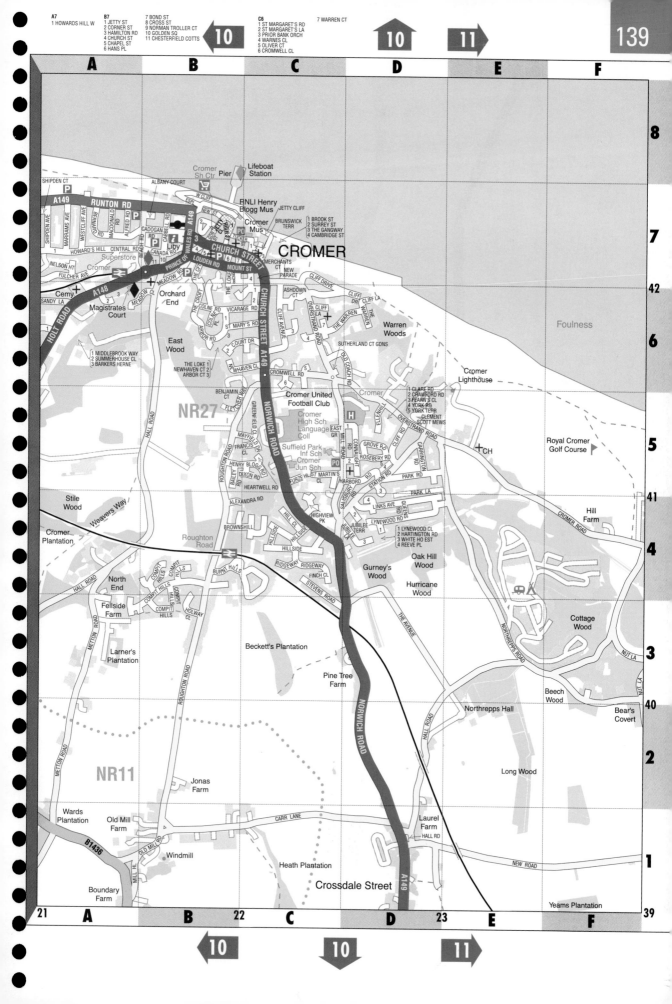

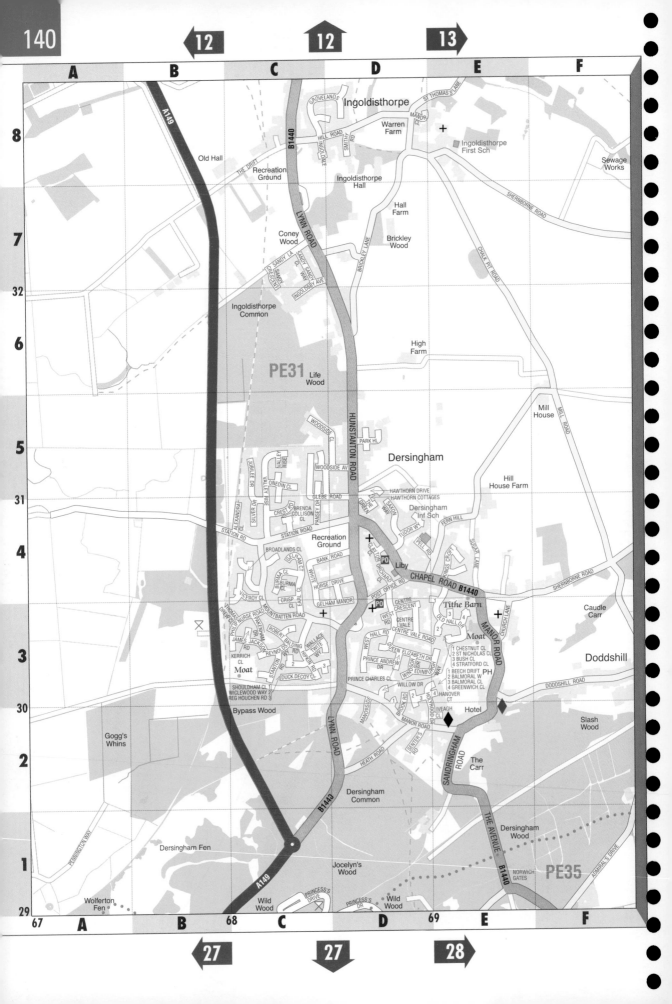

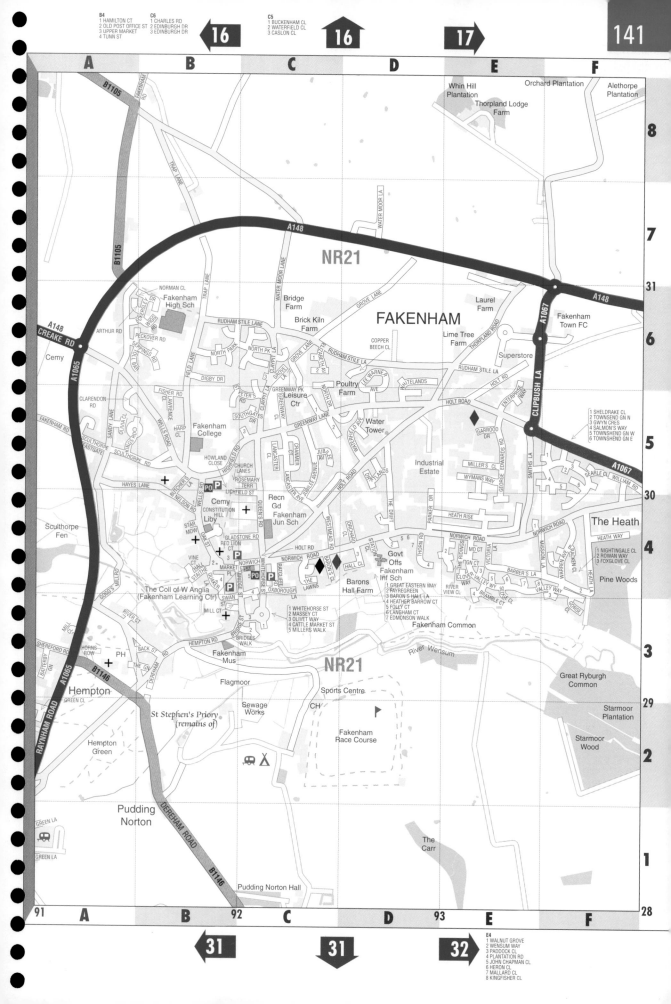

B4
1 HAMILTON CT
2 OLD POST OFFICE ST
3 UPPER MARKET
4 TUNN ST

C6
1 CHARLES RD
2 EDINBURGH DR
3 EDINBURGH DR

C5
1 BUCKENHAM CL
2 WATERFIELD CL
3 CASLON CL

16   16   17

A   B   C   D   E   F

8

7

31

Whin Hill Plantation
Thorpland Lodge Farm
Orchard Plantation
Alethorpe Plantation

B1105

A148

NR21

A148

A148

Creake Rd
A1065

Cemy

B1105

Norman Cl

Fakenham High Sch

Arthur Rd

Peckover Rd

Trap Lane

Water Moor Lane

Water Moor La

Bridge Farm

Brick Kiln Farm

Grove Lane

Grove Lane

FAKENHAM

Laurel Farm

Lime Tree Farm

Thorpland Road

Fakenham Town FC

A1067

Clipbush La

Superstore

6

Rudham Stile Lane

North Park

North Pk La

Clapyit St

Grove Lane

Rudham Stile La

Copper Beech Cl

Holt Rd

Rudham Stile La

Enterprise Way

1 SHELDRAKE CL
2 TOWNSEND GN N
3 GWYN CRES
4 SALMON'S WAY
5 TOWNSHEND GN W
6 TOWNSHEND GN E

Clarendon Rd

Fisher Rd

Lawrence Cl

Harp Cl

St Peter's Rd

Southgates Dr

Greenway Pk
Leisure Ctr

Greenway Lane

Poultry Farm

Lee Warner Av

Whitelands

Holt Road

Garrood Dr

A1067

5

Fakenham Rd

Sandy Lane

Olivia Cl

Kings Rd

Wells Road

Fakenham College

Howland Close

Church Lanes

Rosemary Terr

Lancaster Cl

Cramer

Jub Av

Jubilee Avenue

Waterfield Av

Water Tower

Industrial Estate

Miller's Cl

George Edwards Rd

Wymans Way

Smiths La

Searle Cl

William Rd

30

Sculthorpe Fen

Hayes Lane

Sculthorpe

Eastgate

Butcher's

Nelson Rd

Cemy
Constitution Hill
Liby

Lancaster Ave

Lichfield St

Queen's Rd

Recn Gd
Fakenham Jun Sch

Holt Rd

Westmead Rd

Orchard Cl

The Drift

Parker Dr

Heath Rise

Norwich Road

The Ridings

MD Ct

Norwich Road

Mission La

The Heath

HEATH WAY

1 NIGHTINGALE CL
2 ROWAN WAY
3 FOXGLOVE CL

Pine Woods

4

Vine Ct
Hall

Staithe

Star Mdw

Gladstone Rd

Red Lion Ct

Market St

Quaker La

Whitehouse St

Bridges St

Oxborough La

Norwich Road

Hall Cl

Station Rd

Govt Offs
Fakenham Inf Sch

Thorn Rd

Victoria Ct

Clover Way

Valley Wy

Barber's La

Warren Ave

Chicken Cl

Sedge Cl

Valley Way

Gorse Cl

Mill Ct

Gogg's Mill

The Coll of W Anglia
(Fakenham Learning Ctr)

Swan St

Mill Ct

1 WHITEHORSE ST
2 MASSEY CT
3 OLIVET WAY
4 CATTLE MARKET ST
5 MILLERS WALK

Barons Hall Farm

Barons Cl

The Lawns

1 GREAT EASTERN WAY
2 FAYREGREEN
3 BARON'S HALL LA
4 HEATHER BARROW CT
5 FOLLY CT
6 LANGHAM CT
7 EDMONSON WALK

River View Cl

Bramble Ct

Fakenham Common

River Ct

Shereford Rd

A1065

Mill Ct

Battery Rd

Horns Row

PH

Back St

Dereham

The Gn

Hempton Rd

Bridges Walk

Fakenham Mus

Hempton

Green Cl

Flagmoor

NR21

River Wensum

Great Ryburgh Common

3

Hempton Green

St Stephen's Priory
(remains of)

Sewage Works

Sports Centre

CH

Fakenham Race Course

Starmoor Plantation

29

Green La

Raynham Road

A1065

Dereham Road

B1146

Pudding Norton

Starmoor Wood

2

Green La

The Carr

1

Pudding Norton Hall

B1146

E4
1 WALNUT GROVE
2 WENSUM WAY
3 PADDOCK CL
4 PLANTATION RD
5 JOHN CHAPMAN CL
6 HERON CL
7 MALLARD CL
8 KINGFISHER CL

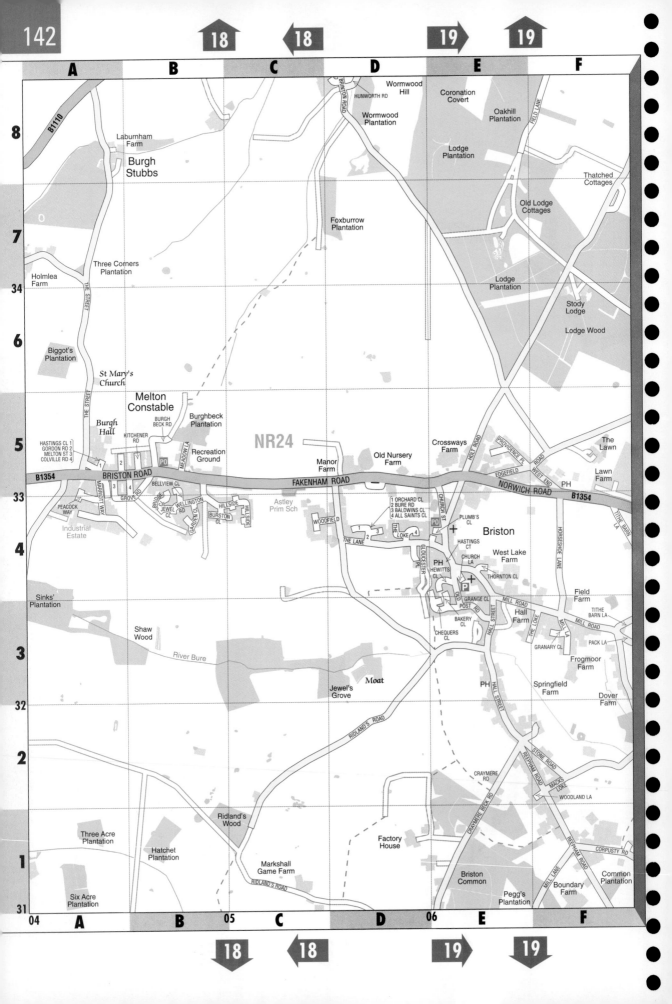

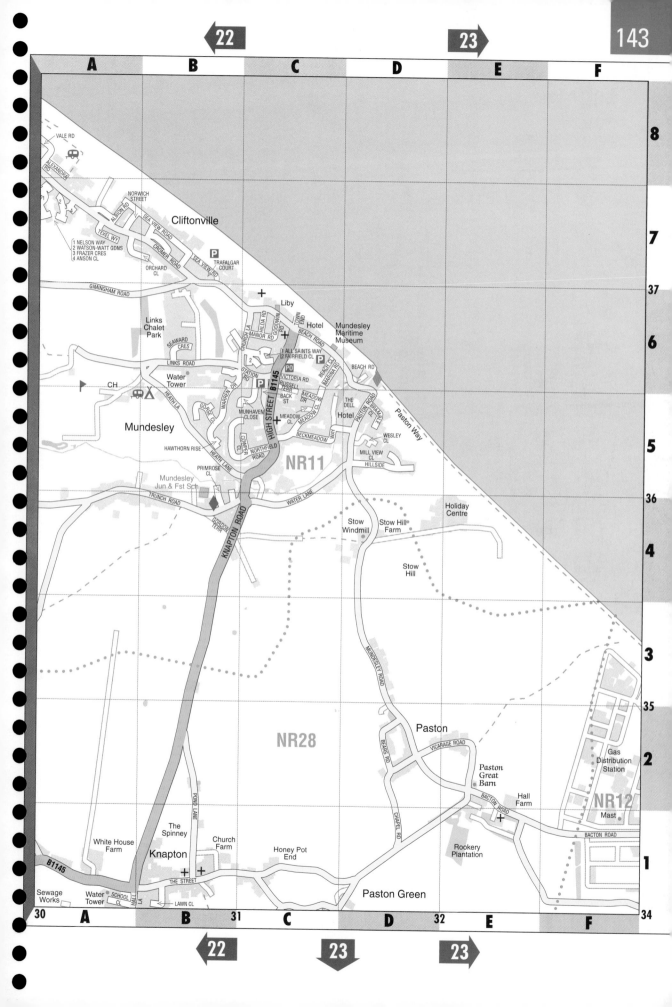

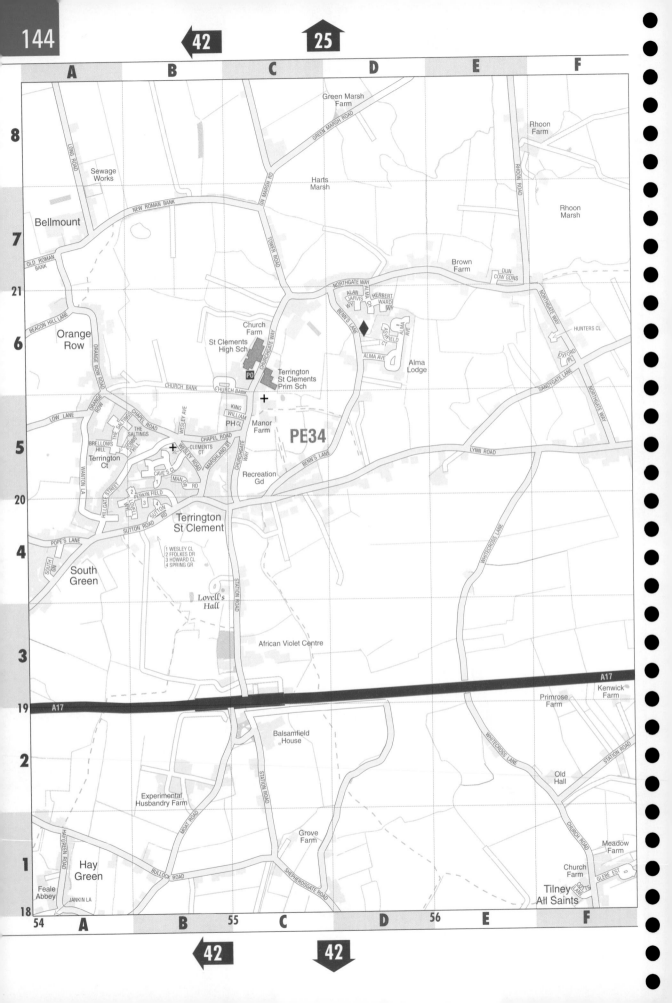

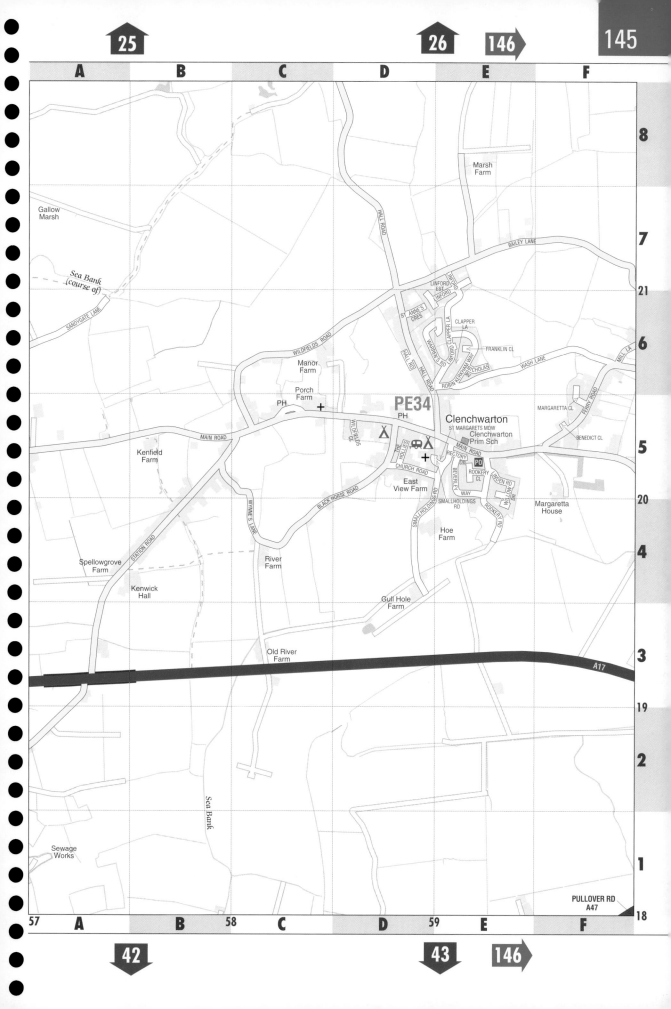

D5
1 ST NICHOLAS CL
2 PILOT ST
3 ST NICHOLAS ST
4 WATER LA
5 TUESDAY MKT PL
6 SURREY ST
7 PARADISE LA
8 ST DOMINIC SQ
9 PARADISE RD
10 PARADISE PAR
11 PURFLEET ST
12 PURFLEET PL
13 TRENOWATHS PL

E6
1 WALKER ST
2 TOWNSHEND TERR
3 WOODWARK AVE
4 LANSDOWNE ST
5 BIRCHWOOD ST
6 GEORGE ST
7 HARECROFT PAR
8 HAREWOOD PAR
9 HAREWOOD DR
10 HOMELAND RD

E5
1 KETTLEWELL LA
2 EASTGATE ST
3 ARCHDALE ST
4 NORFOLK ST
5 MARSHALL ST
6 ENMMERICH CT
7 EDINBURGH CT
8 LITTLEPORT TERR
9 COBURG ST
10 STANLEY ST
11 WELLESLEY ST
12 PORTLAND ST
13 WATERLOO ST
14 OLD MKT ST
15 MARKET ST

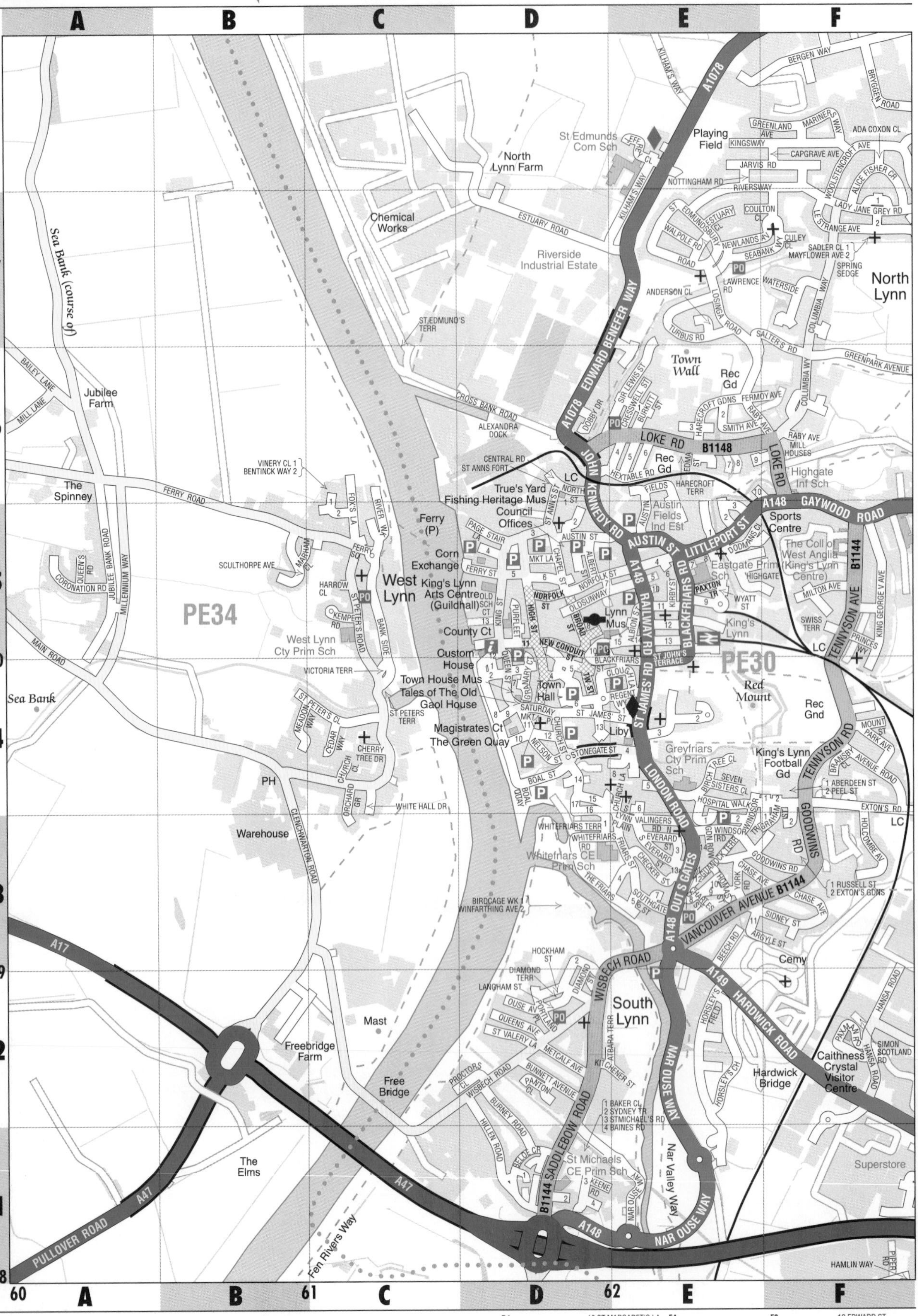
A
B
C
D
E
F
8
7
21
6
5
20
4
3
19
2
1
18
60
61
62
North Lynn Farm
Chemical Works
Riverside Industrial Estate
St Edmunds Com Sch
Playing Field
North Lynn
Sea Bank (course of)
Jubilee Farm
The Spinney
PE34
West Lynn
West Lynn Cty Prim Sch
Sea Bank
Warehouse
PH
Town Wall
Rec Gd
Highgate Inf Sch
Sports Centre
The Coll of West Anglia (King's Lynn Centre)
Eastgate Prim Sch
PE30
King's Lynn
Red Mount
Rec Gnd
King's Lynn Football Gd
Greyfriars Cty Prim Sch
Whitefriars CE Prim Sch
True's Yard Fishing Heritage Mus
Council Offices
Ferry (P)
Corn Exchange
King's Lynn Arts Centre (Guildhall)
County Ct
Custom House
Town House Mus
Tales of The Old Gaol House
Magistrates Ct
The Green Quay
Town Hall
Lynn Mus
Liby
Austin Fields Ind Est
South Lynn
Mast
Freebridge Farm
Free Bridge
The Elms
St Michaels CE Prim Sch
Nar Valley Way
Hardwick Bridge
Caithness Crystal Visitor Centre
Superstore
Cemy
A17
A47
A148
A149
A1078
B1144
B1148
PULLOVER ROAD
Fen Rivers Way
EDWARD BENEFER WAY
JOHN KENNEDY RD
LOKE RD
GAYWOOD ROAD
TENNYSON AVE
TENNYSON RD
GOODWINS RD
VANCOUVER AVENUE
HARDWICK ROAD
LONDON ROAD
WISBECH ROAD
SADDLEBOW ROAD
NAR OUSE WAY
FERRY ROAD
CLENCHWARTON ROAD
ESTUARY ROAD
CROSS BANK ROAD
MAIN ROAD
HAMLIN WAY

D4
1 KING'S STAITHE SQ
2 KING'S STAITHE LA
3 BAKER LA
4 UNION LA
5 SEDGEFORD LA
6 REGENT WAY
7 JUBILEE CT
8 SOUTH QUAY
9 COLLEGE LA
10 ST MARGARET'S LA
11 ST MARGARET'S PL
12 PRIORY LA
13 TOWER PL
14 BRIDGE ST
15 ALL SAINTS' ST
16 CARMELITE TERR
17 THE FRIARS

E4
1 REGENT PL
2 SOUTH ST
3 COUNTY CT RD
4 MILLFLEET
5 PROVIDENCE ST
6 VALINGER'S PL
7 FREESTONE CT
8 HILLINGTON SQ

E3
1 PLEASANT CT
2 WINDSOR PK
3 JOHN ST
4 GLADSTONE RD
5 ETHEL TERR
6 CROMWELL TERR
7 HORSLEY'S CT
8 ROBERT ST
9 WILLIAM ST
10 EDWARD ST
11 SOMERVILLE RD
12 GUANOCK PL
13 LYNWOOD TERR
14 OLD BREWERY CT

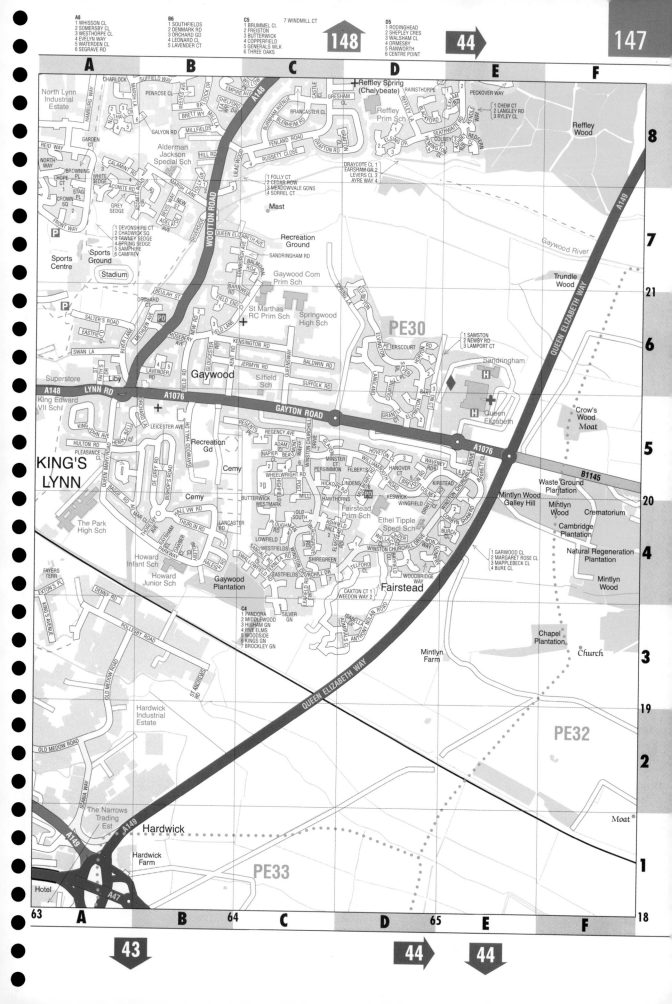

A   B   C   D   E   F

8

7

PE30

PE31

25

6

MARSH ROAD

Playing Field

Wootton Carr

C5
1 GREGORY CL
2 WILTON CRES
3 MEADOW CL
4 CUTHBERT CL

GATEHOUSE LANE

School Farm
THE GREEN

Wootton Carr

LING COMMON ROAD

North Wootton

FREDERICK

OLD RECTORY

LING COMMON ROAD

PH

STATION ROAD

FORD AVE

CARLTON DRIVE

LT CARR RD

HEATHER CL

Church Farm

MANOR ROAD

PRIORY LANE

BUCKINGHAM CL

1 SANDRINGHAM CRES
2 CAMBRIDGE RD
3 EXETER CRES
4 DEVON CRES

5

Orchard End

JULIAN RD

HOLT RD

PRIORY ROAD

WOODLAND GDNS

Ling Common

NURSERY LANE

DALE

ST ALBAN RD

WOOD AND GDNS

WESLEY RD

ALL SAINTS DRIVE

CRANMER AVE

PINGLES RD

THE HOWARDS

24

WHEATLEY DR

KEBLE

HAYFIELD RD

1 RYELANDS RD

CH

4

RILL CL

BECK RD

North Wootton Prim Sch

FOUNTAINE

THE BIRCHES

Kings Lynn Golf Club

WALTON

PRIORY LANE

THE BIRCHES

C4
1 STOCK LEA RD
2 RYELAND RD
3 ST AUGUSTINES WAY
4 TINTERN GR
5 FINCHDALE CL
6 BECKETT CL

CHINNEY

RYALLA DRIFT

BLACK HORN ROAD

CLARE RD

ST AUGUSTINES WAY

CASTLE RISING ROAD

3

C3
1 ROSEBAY
2 CASTLE ACRE CL
3 ST BOTOLPH'S CL
4 BINHAM RD
5 HAZEL CL

Mast

BRYONY CT

WALSINGHAM

THETFORD WY

MALVERN

South Wootton Common

NURSERY LANE

RUSHMEAD CL

BRIAR CL

MAPLE DR

PE30

WINDERMERE RD

GRIMSTON RD

23

BRACKEN ROAD

MEADOW

AVON RD

BOURNE

AVON ROAD

PEBBLE

South Wootton

HOLLY CL

WILLOW RD

1 SYCAMORE CL
2 LARCH CL

A148

2

GREENACRE

CHURCH LA

COMMON LA

NURSERY LA

BRAMBLE CL

OAK AVENUE

BEECH AVE

PINE RD

POPLAR DR

ELM CL

ASH GR

GRIMSTON ROAD

GREEN LA

SANDY LA

DERWENT AVE

ENNERDALE AVE

THE MDWS

ST MARY'S CL

South Wootton Fst Sch

APPLECROFT RD

THE GREEN

Superstore

MELFORD

DADBOROUGH DR

FELBRIGG

ENNERDALE DRIVE

ULLSWATER AVE

CONISTON CLOSE

FURNESS

BIRKBECK CL

ELMHURST DR

OLD MANOR CL

BARSHAM DR

SANDY LANE

Carter's Cl 1
Festival Cl 2
Baldock Dr 3
Willow Pk 5
Monkshood 6
Tamarisk 7

South Wootton Junior Sch

CHAPEL TERR

HALL LANE

THE BOLTONS

PO

BURGHLEY RD

WHOLE ST

LANGLEY RD

1 ICKWORTH CL
2 HINCHINGBROOK CL

1

A1078   EDWARD BENEFER WAY

LOW ROAD   A1078

LOW ROAD

Spring Wood

EUSTON WAY

BECKOVER WAY

MANNINGTON PL

Reffley Wood

HAMBURG WAY

CLIFFORD

BURMAN

DASELEY DR

BEDFORD DR

JAMES

SPENSER RD

MARSH LA

KINGCUP

SUFFIELD WAY

PEPPERS

WILLOW PK

DAWNAY AVE

FFOLKES

SOUTH WOOTTON LA

DRIFTWAY

A148   WOOTTON ROAD

SPRING CL

GASKELL WY

JAMES

GOLF RD

TEMPLE RD

GASKELL WY

HOUGHTON AVE

RAILSTHORPE

1

BERGEN WAY

HALL RD

ARUNDEL DR

REFFLEY LA

F1
1 BLICKLING CL
2 KIRKSTONE GR

22

63   A   B   64   C   D   65   E   F

PE30
PE31
Church Farm

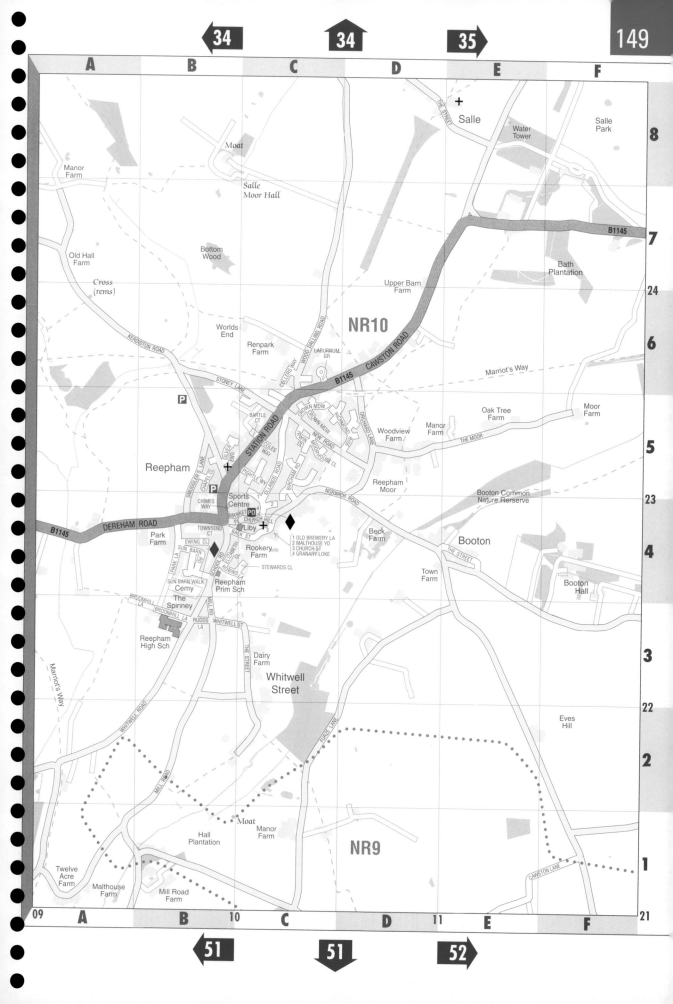

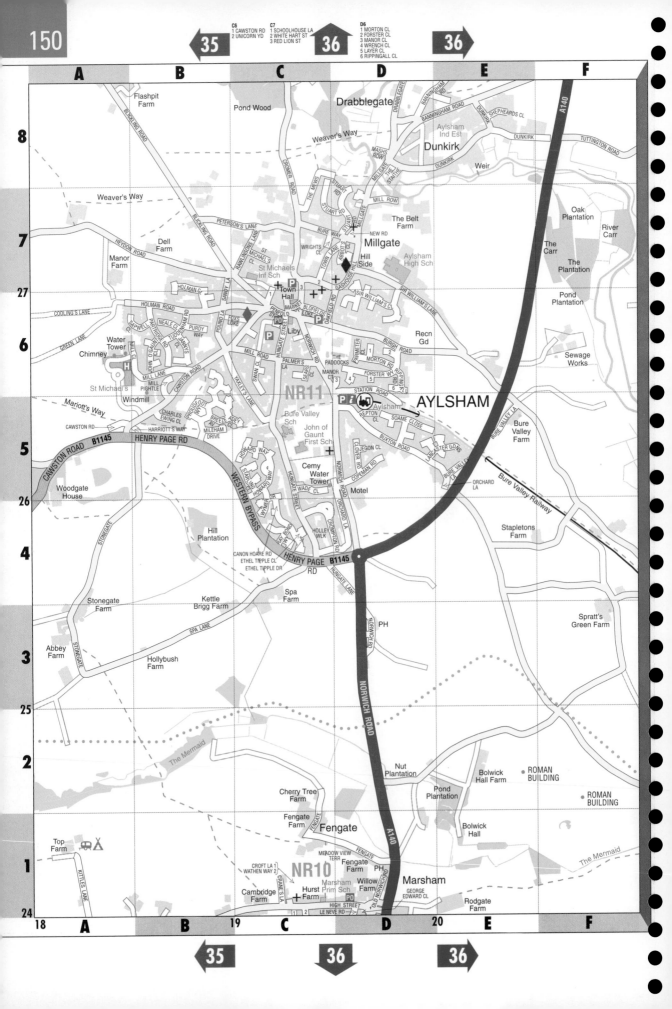

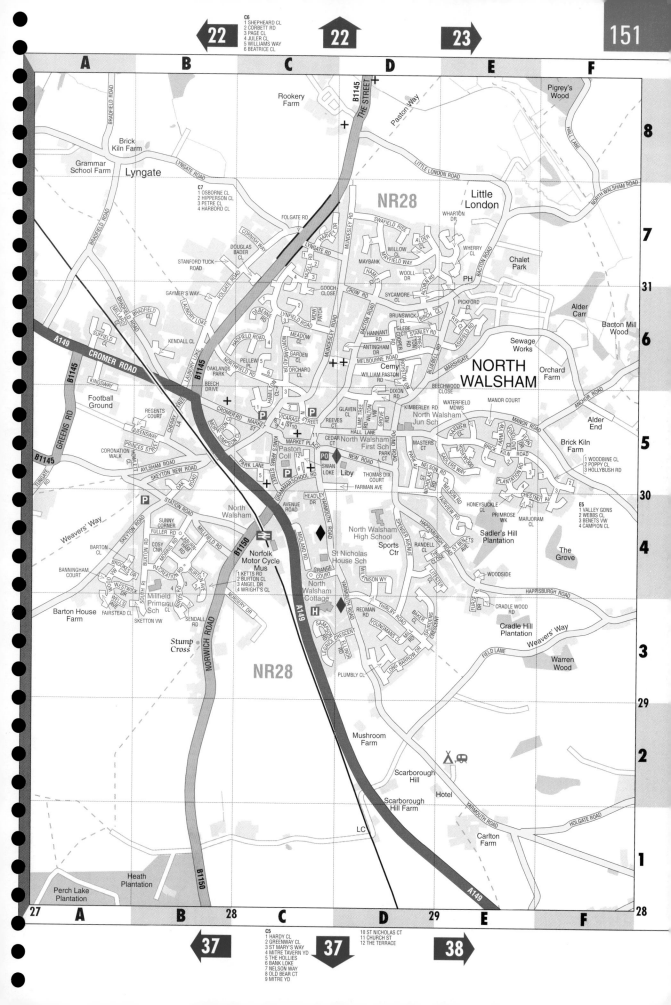

59 **59**

A1101 Holbeach (A17)

Little East Field

PE14

Leahard's Field

Cambridgeshire STREET ATLAS

PE13

WISBECH

Walsoken

Osborne Park

Orchards Prim Sch

Gordon Fendick Sch

Cemy

Weston Miller Dr

Mount Pleasant Road

Football Ground / Sports Ground

The Clarkson Inf Sch

St Peters CE Jun Sch

Peckover Cty Prim Sch

Yacht Harbour

Windmill

North Cambs

Horse Fair Shop Cen

Park

Hudson Leisure Centre

Peckover House

Octavia Hill Birthplace Mus

Wisbech Gram Sch

Castle

The Angles Theatre

The Castle Mus

Liby

The Nene Sch

Elgood's Brewery & Gdn

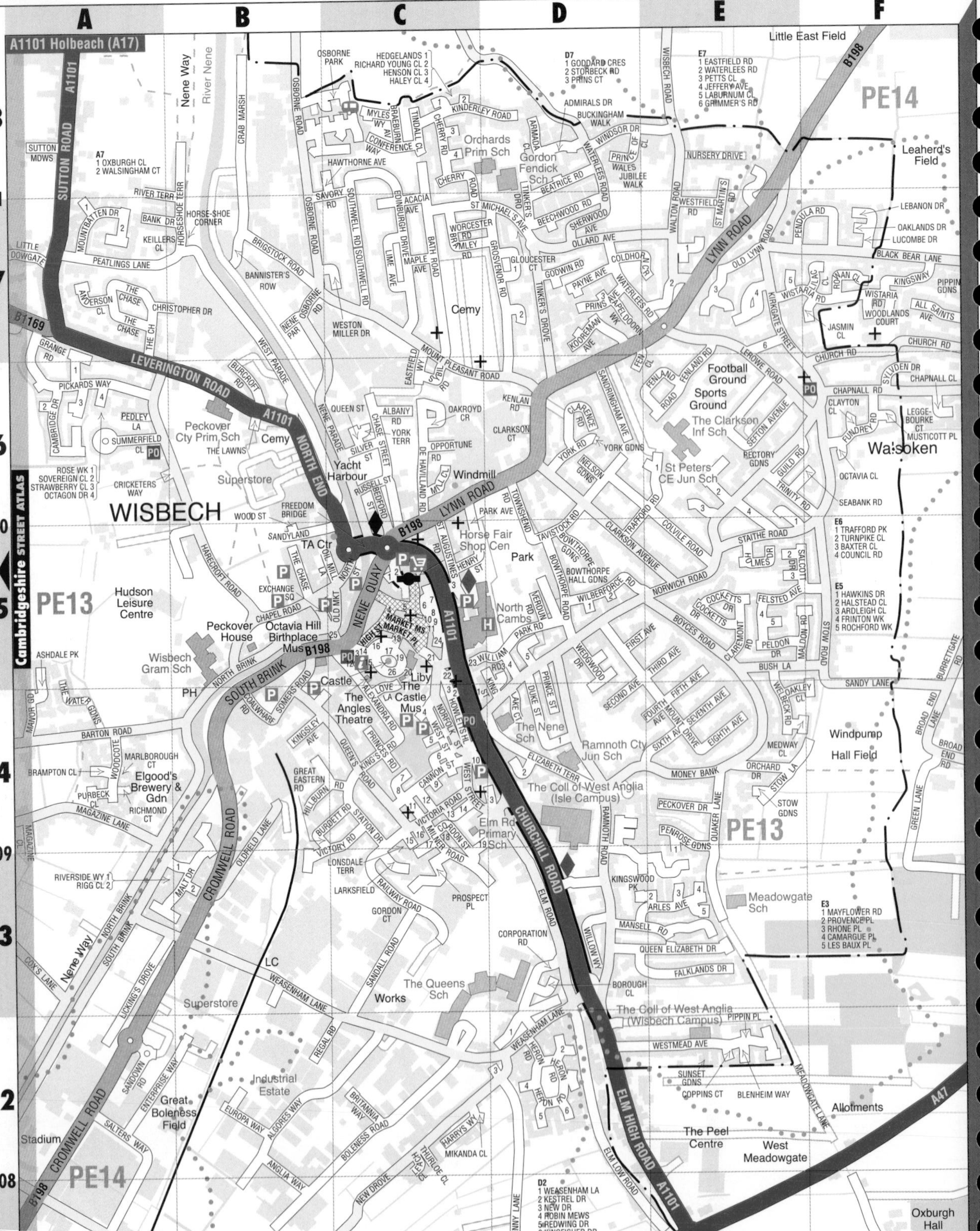

Great Eastern

Ramnoth Cty Jun Sch

The Coll of West Anglia (Isle Campus)

PE13

Windpump Hall Field

Elm Rd Primary

Meadowgate Sch

Corporation Rd

The Queens Sch

Works

Industrial Estate

Great Boleness Field

The Coll of West Anglia (Wisbech Campus)

West Meadowgate

The Peel Centre

Stadium

PE14

New Bridge LC

New Bridge Farm

Town Field

Oxburgh Hall

PE14

A1122

A47

59 **59**

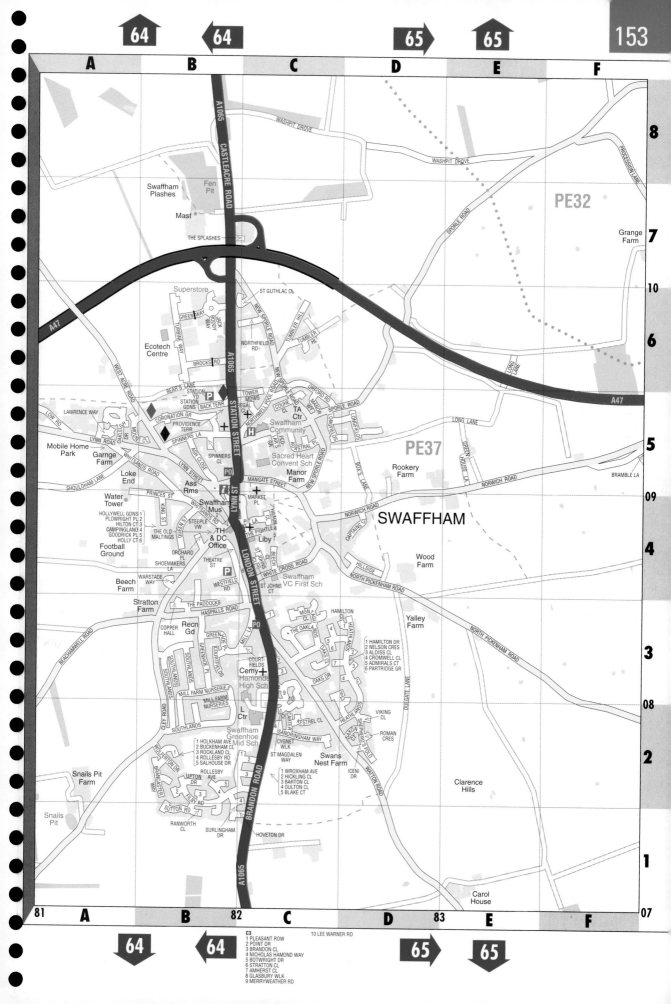

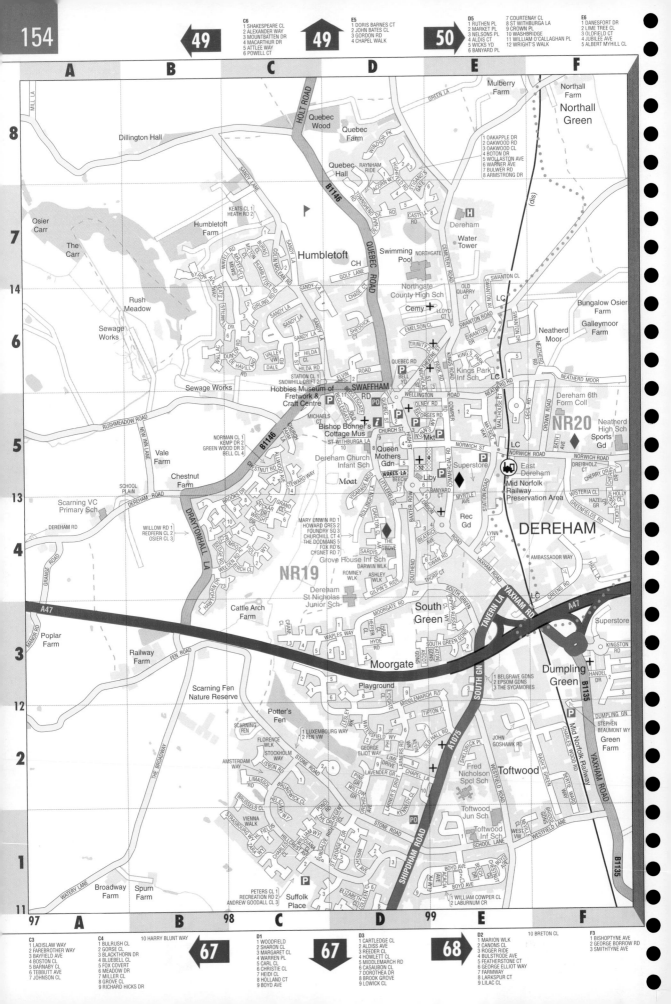

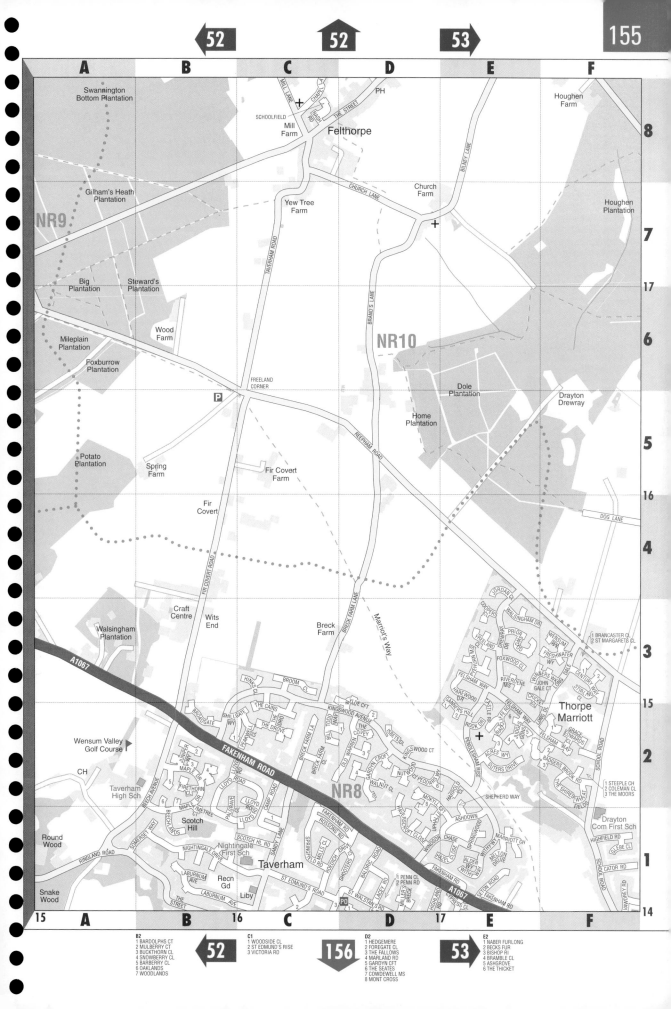

B2
1 BARDOLPHS CT
2 MULBERRY CT
3 BUCKTHORN CL
4 SNOWBERRY CL
5 BARBERRY CL
6 OAKLANDS
7 WOODLANDS

C1
1 WOODSIDE CL
2 ST EDMUND'S RISE
3 VICTORIA RD

D2
1 HEDGEMERE
2 FOREGATE CL
3 THE FALLOWS
4 MARLAND RD
5 GARDYN CFT
6 THE SEATES
7 COWDEWELL MS
8 MONT CROSS

E2
1 NABER FURLONG
2 BECKS FUR
3 BISHOP RI
4 BRAMBLE CL
5 ASHGROVE
6 THE THICKET

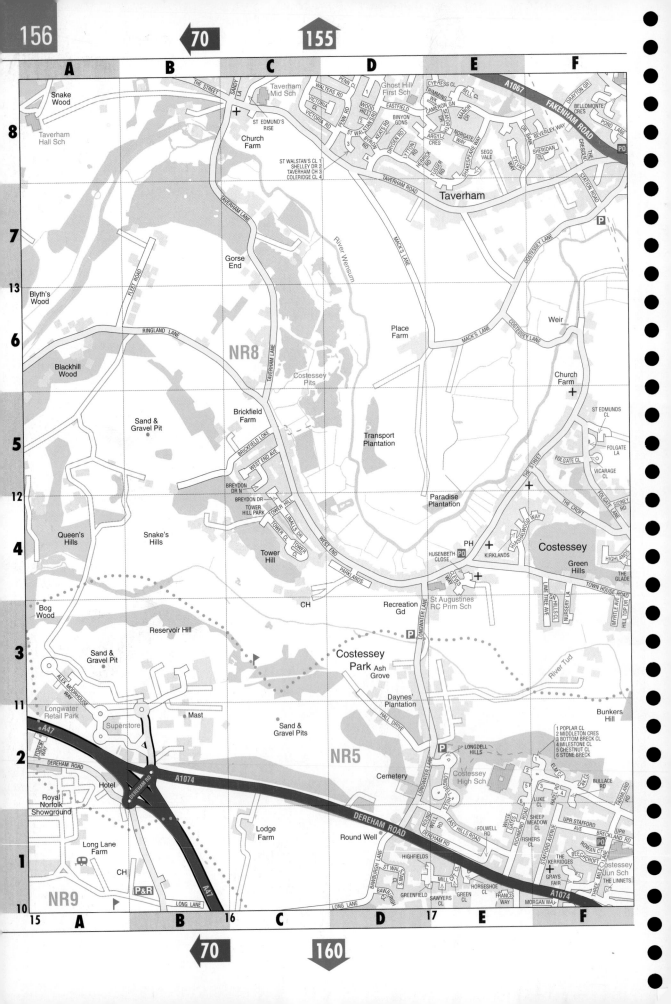

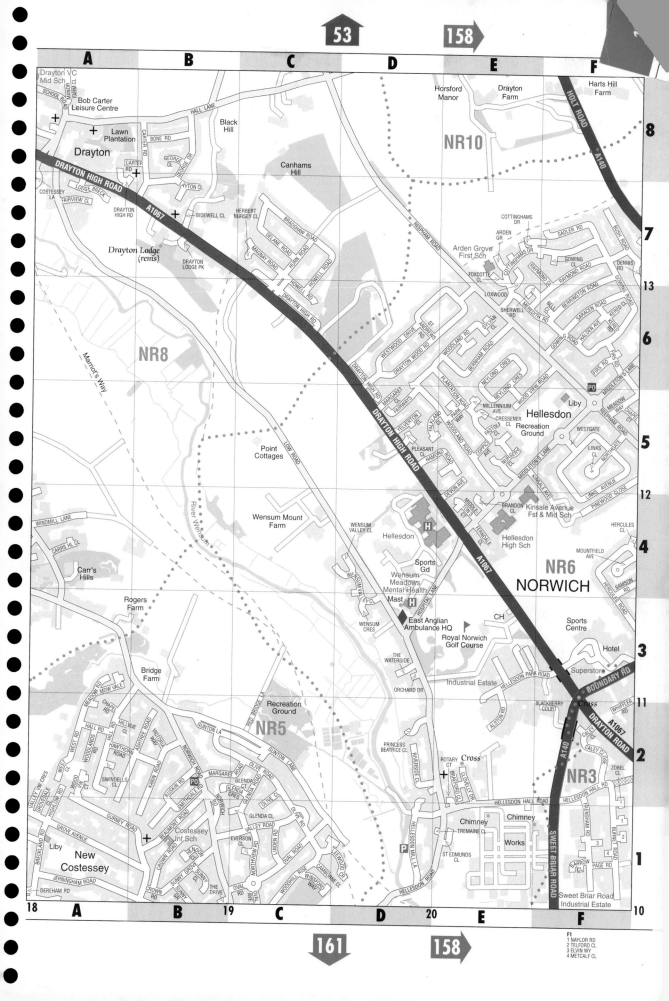

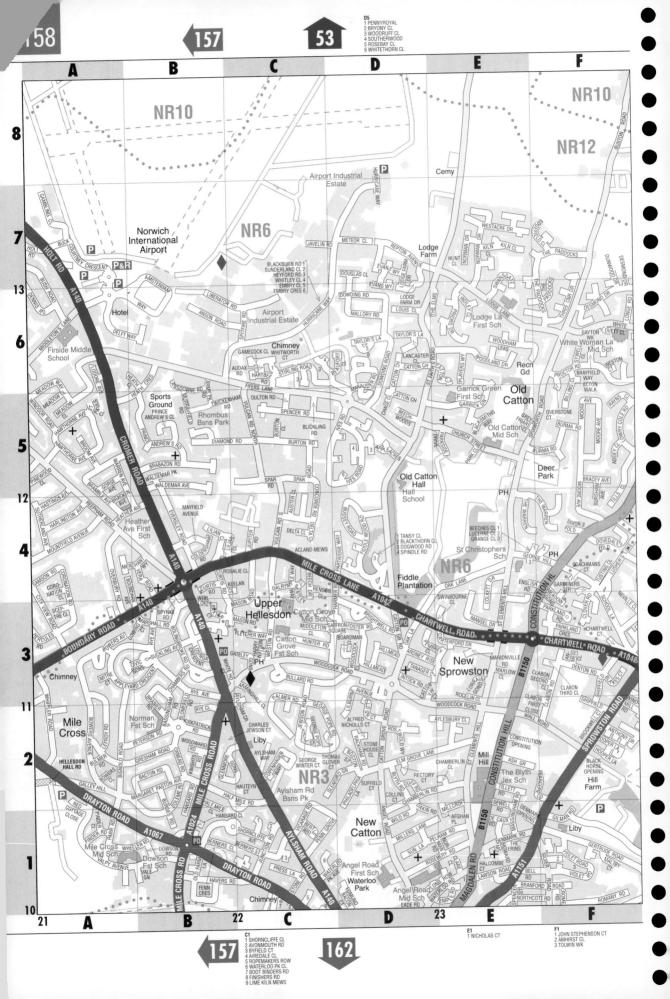

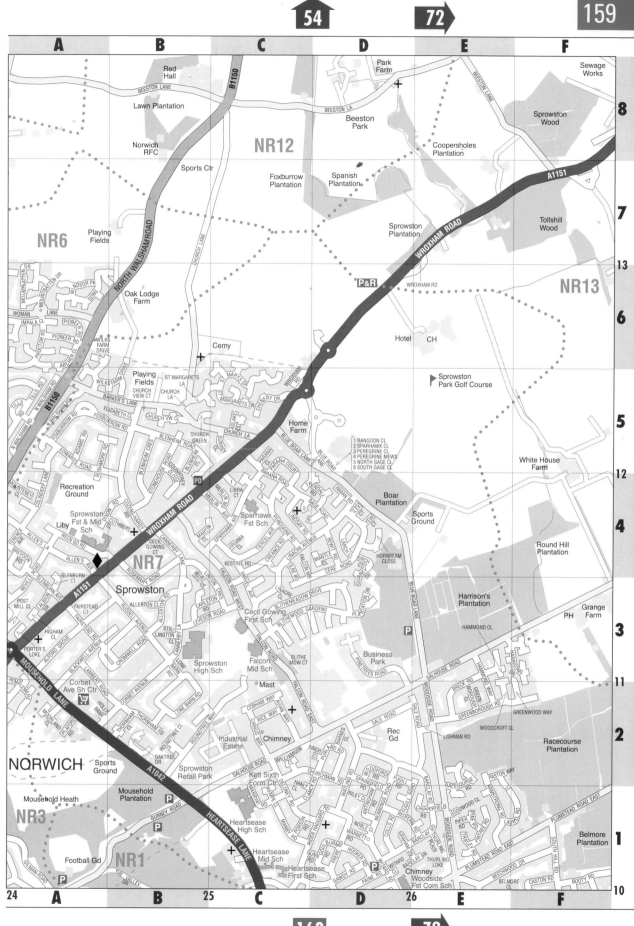

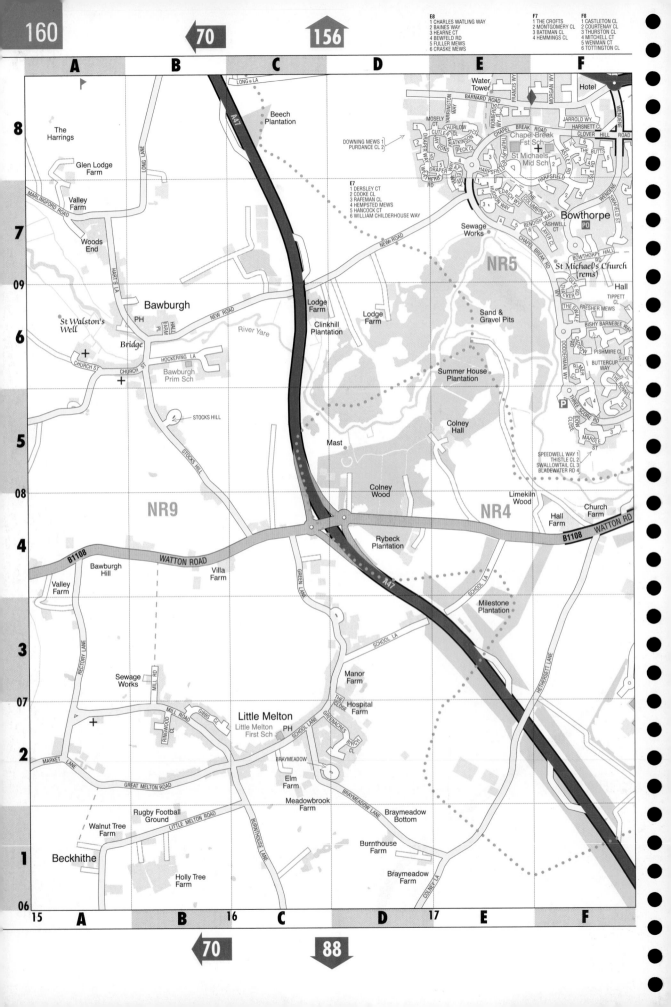

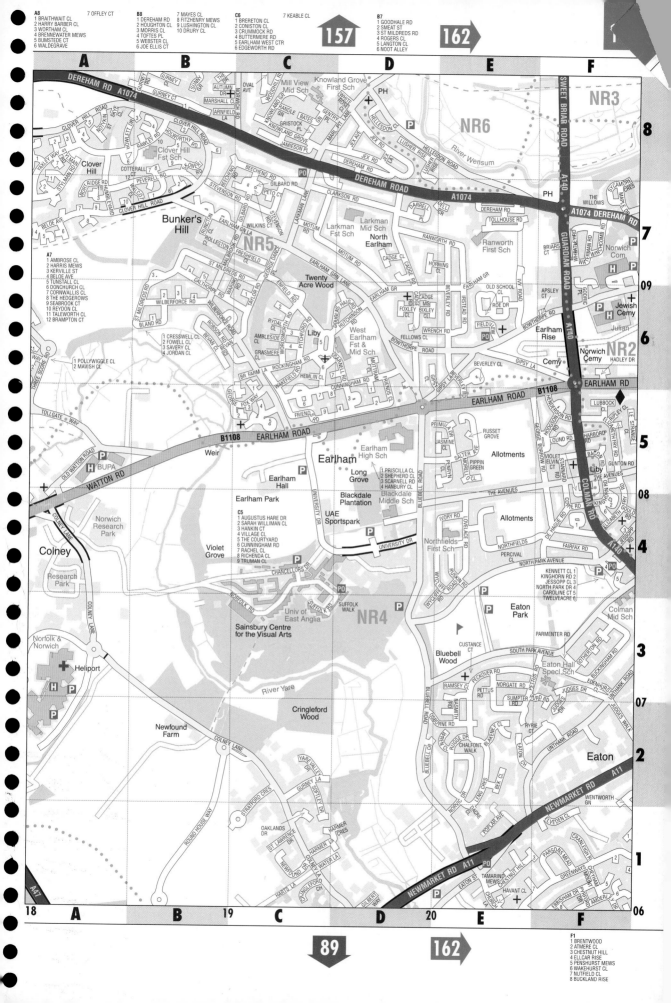

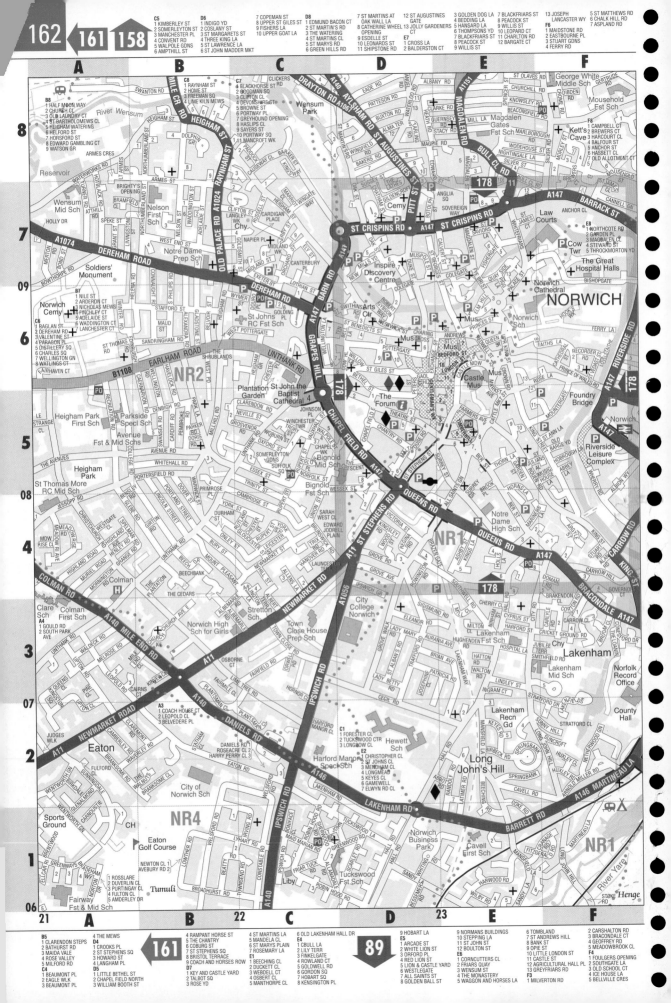

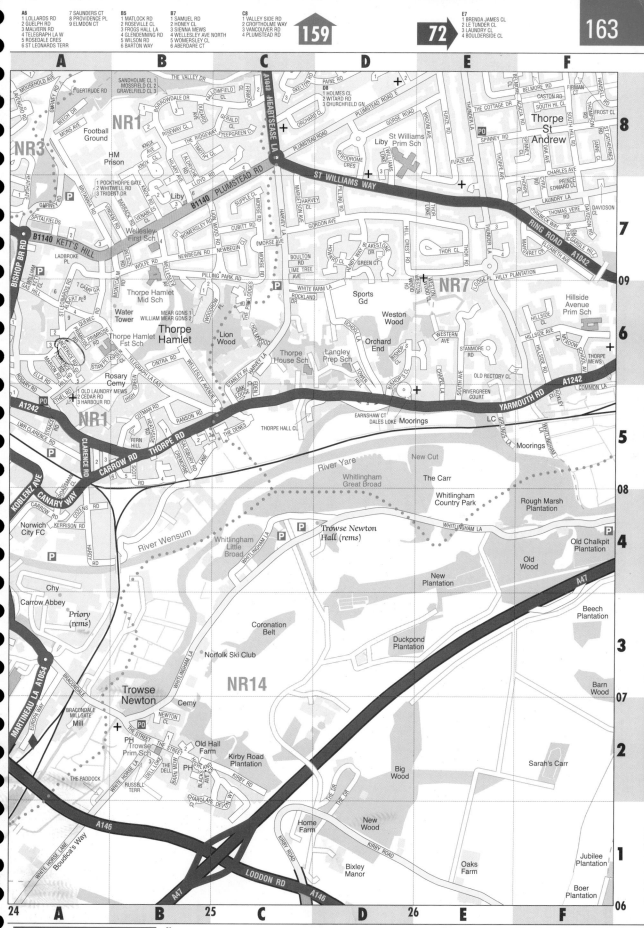

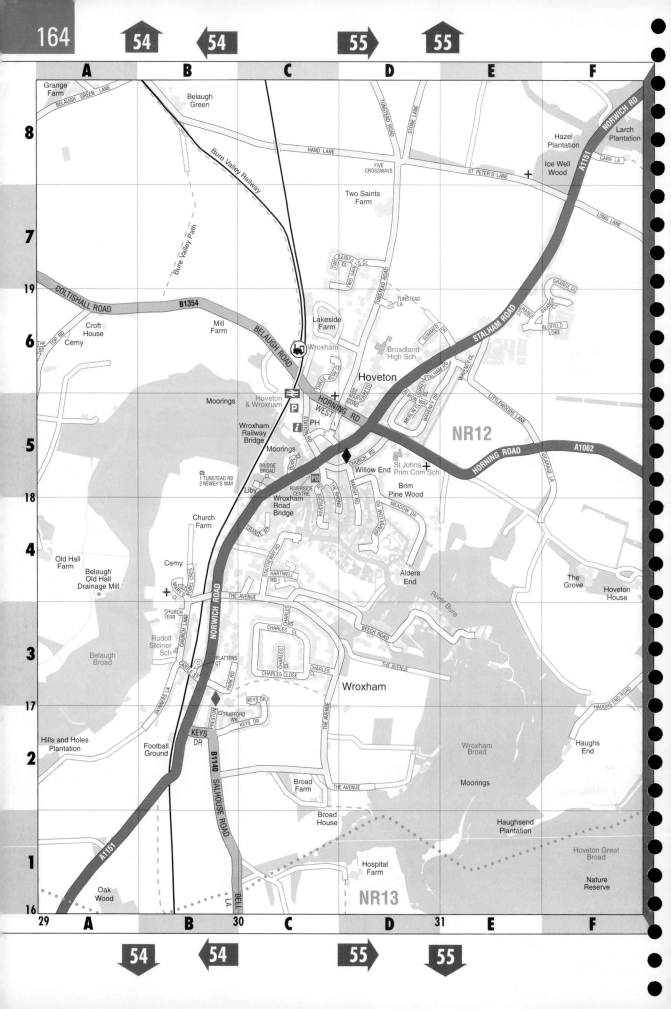

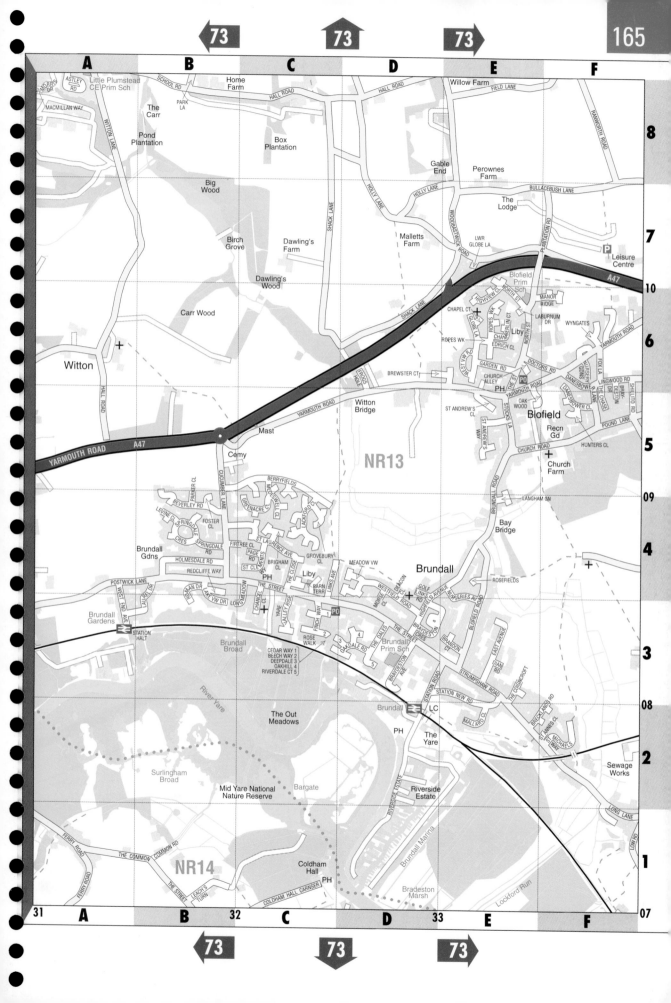

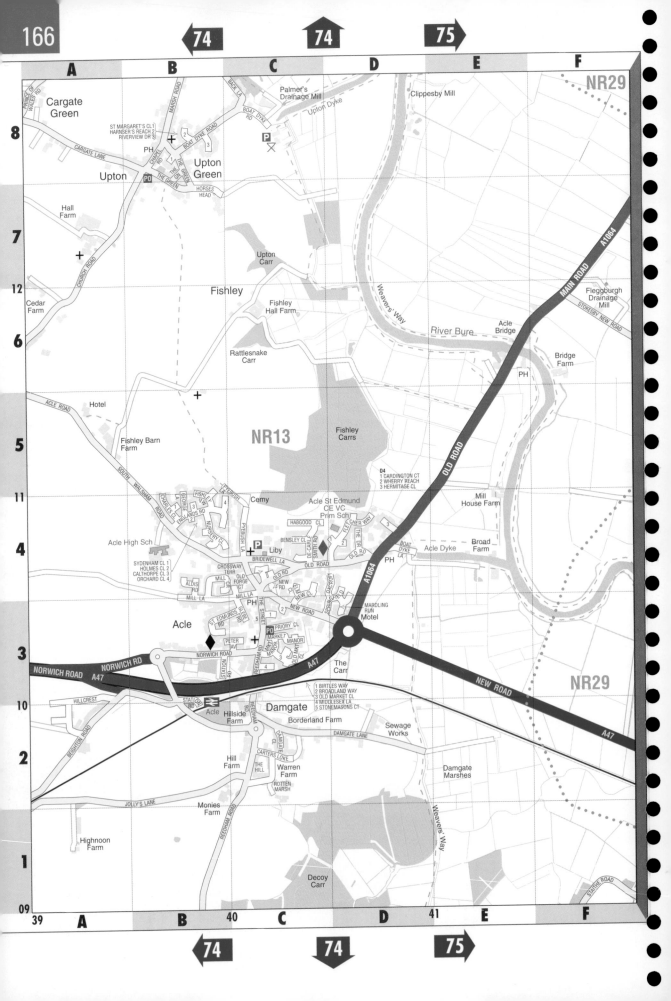

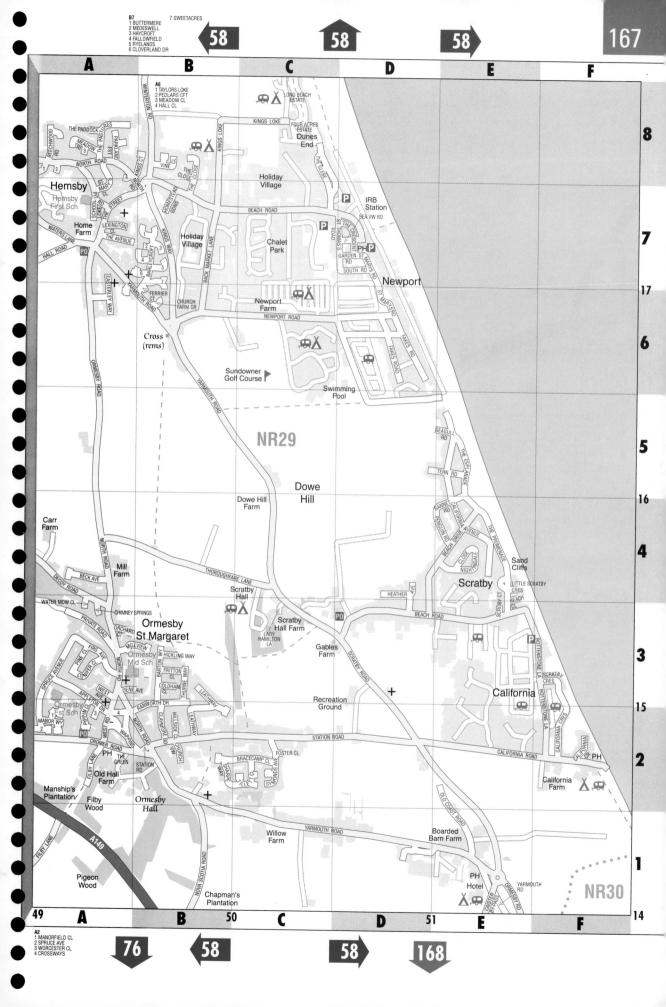

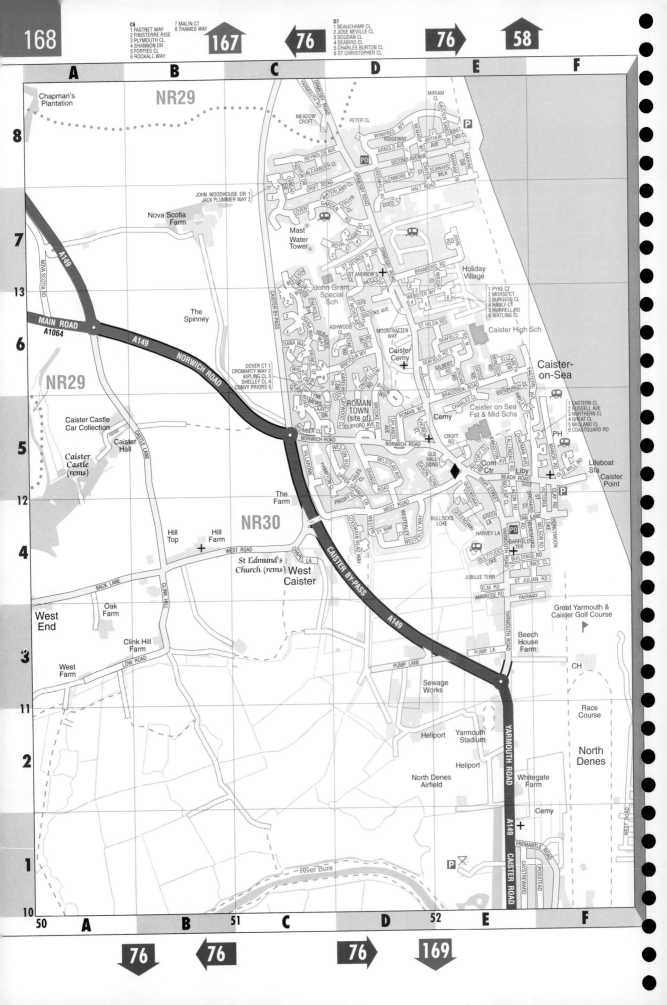

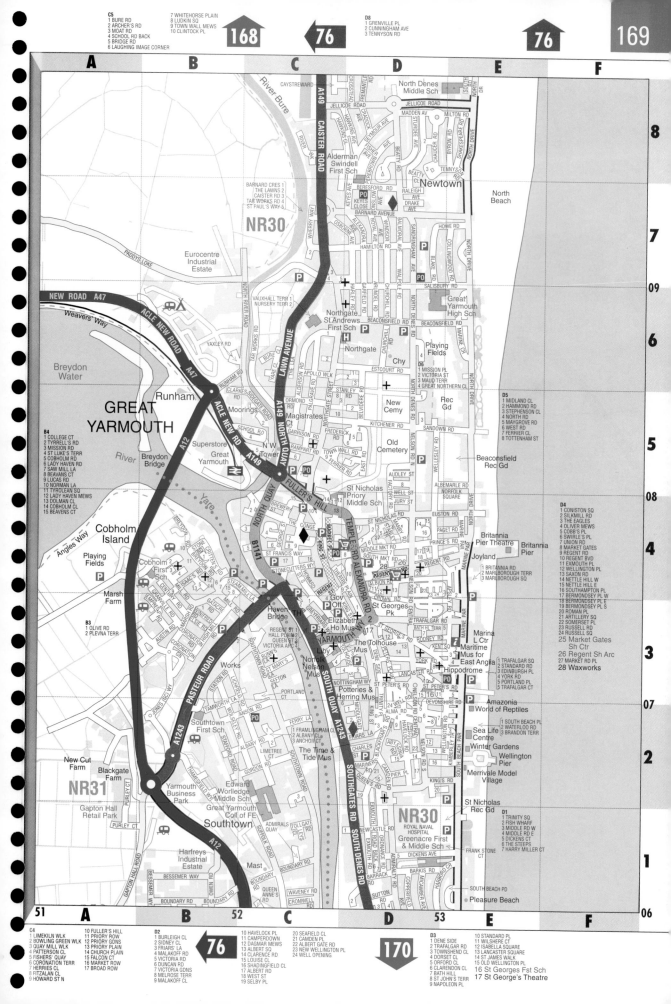

C5
1 BURE RD
2 ARCHER'S RD
3 MOAT RD
4 SCHOOL RD BACK
5 BRIDGE RD
6 LAUGHING IMAGE CORNER

7 WHITEHORSE PLAIN
8 LUDKIN SQ
9 TOWN WALL MEWS
10 CLINTOCK PL

168

76

D8
1 GRENVILLE PL
2 CUNNINGHAM AVE
3 TENNYSON RD

76

169

C4
1 LIMEKILN WLK
2 BOWLING GREEN WLK
3 QUAY MILL WLK
4 PATTERSON CL
5 FISHERS' QUAY
6 CORONATION TERR
7 HERRIES CL
8 FITZALAN CL
9 HOWARD ST N

10 FULLER'S HILL
11 PRIORY ROW
12 PRIORY GDNS
13 PRIORY PLAIN
14 CHURCH PLAIN
15 FALCON CT
16 MARKET ROW
17 BROAD ROW

D2
1 BURLEIGH CL
2 SIDNEY CL
3 FRIARS' LA
4 MALAKOFF RD
5 VICTORIA RD
6 DUNCAN RD
7 VICTORIA GDNS
8 MELROSE TERR
9 MALAKOFF CL

10 HAVELOCK PL
11 CAMPERDOWN
12 DAGMAR CL
13 ALBERT SQ
14 CLARENCE PL
15 LOUISE CL
16 SHADINGFIELD CL
17 ALBERT RD
18 WEST ST
19 SELBY PL

20 SEAFIELD CL
21 CAMDEN PL
22 ALBERT GATE RD
23 NEW WELLINGTON PL
24 WELL OPENING

76

170

D3
1 DENE SIDE
2 TRAFALGAR RD
3 TOWNSHEND CL
4 DORSET CL
5 ORFORD CL
6 CLARENDON CL
7 BATH HILL
8 ST JOHN'S RD
9 NAPOLEON PL

10 STANDARD PL
11 WILSHERE CT
12 ISABELLA SQUARE
13 LANCASTER SQUARE
14 ST JAMES WALK
15 OLD WELLINGTON PL
16 St Georges Fst Sch
17 St George's Theatre

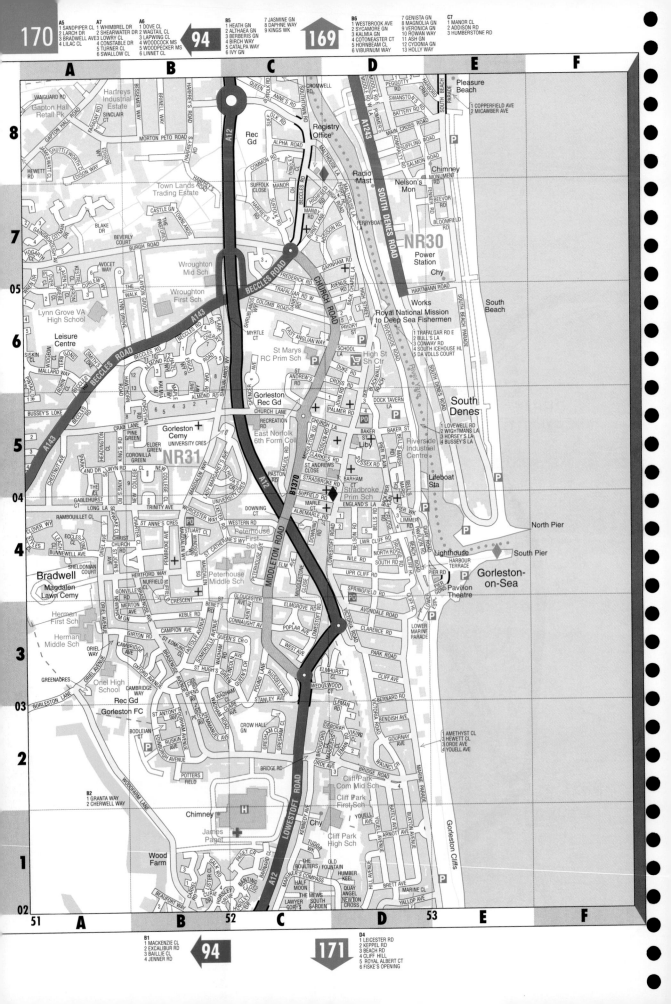

A B C D E F

8

7

01

6

5

00

4

3

99

2

1

98

Suffolk STREET ATLAS

HORSLEY DR
Hobland Plantation
Mast
The Bungalow
Hobland Farm
HOBLAND ROAD
CAMELOT ROAD
BEAUFORT WAY
SIDEGATE ROAD
Oakland Farm
A12 LOWESTOFT ROAD
QUAY OSTEND
MARINER'S COMPASS
MARINER'S CL
MEADOW CT
THE FAIRWAY
LINKS ROAD
MARINE CL
VALLEY
LINKS RD
CLIFF LA
MARINE PARADE
JOSHUA CT
CH
WARREN ROAD
KENNEL LANE
Kennel Farm
Gorleston Golf Course
Masons Farm
Long Belt
Corton Cliffs
Sidegate Farm
NR31
Valley Farm

D5
1 RANDALL CL
2 ST MARGARET'S WAY
3 ANGLIAN WAY
4 GROOMES CL
5 BISHOPS WK
6 ST CLARE CT
7 ST CLEMENT MEWS

Hopton on Sea
HALL ROAD
Sawmill
White House Farm
Reservoir
LOWESTOFT ROAD
RACKHAM CL
IVES CL
FLOWERDAY CL
ROGER'S CL
ANGLIAN WAY
WALTERS CL
THE LAURELS
HOPTON GDNS
MARINERS PARK CL
POTTERS DR
ST VINCENT WK
JULIAN WAY
WARREN ROAD
Holiday Village
1 ST ANDREW CL
2 BARN CL
PO
HALL RD
PH
A12
STATION ROAD
PH
WARREN RD
WATSONS CL
Hopton First Sch
CADIZ WAY
GENEVA WY
NAPLES
MISBY CL
TURIN WY
GONST
ZURICH
PEBBLE VW WK
Bloodman's Corner
Homeclose Shrubbery
IMPERIAL MEWS
YARMOUTH ROAD
SEAFIELDS DR
SEAFIELDS DRIVE
IVES WAY
St Margaret's Church (rems)
OLD CHURCH RD
COAST RD
MANOR RD
MANOR GDNS
SEA VIEW RISE
BEACH ROAD
Holiday & Leisure Centre
League Hole
BACK LANE
Cuckoo Green
Cuckoo Green Farm
Elder Farm
DORKING ROAD
Home Farm
Home Farm
Oak View Farm
LONGFULANS LANE
COAST ROAD
JAY LANE
CHURCH LANE
Hall Farm
Elm Farm
Beehive Farm
Lothingland Middle Sch
NR32
Fourways Farm
Corton Cliffs
Rector's Wood
Great Wood
Brickhill Wood
Red House Farm
MARKET LANE
A12 YARMOUTH ROAD
Mast
Woburn Farm
CHURCH LA
STIRRUPS LANE
COAST ROAD

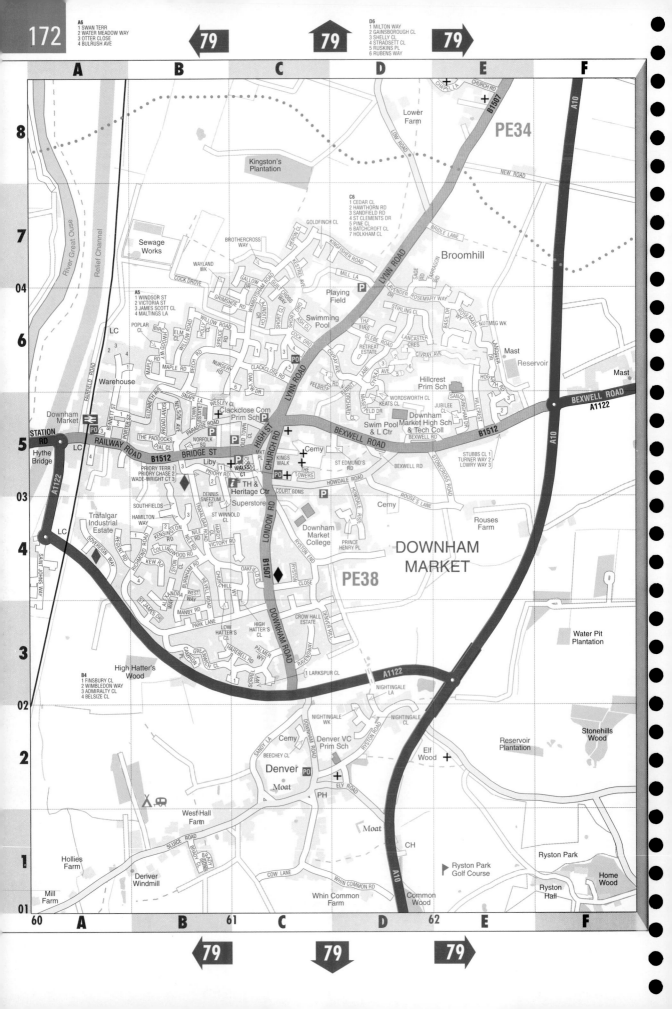

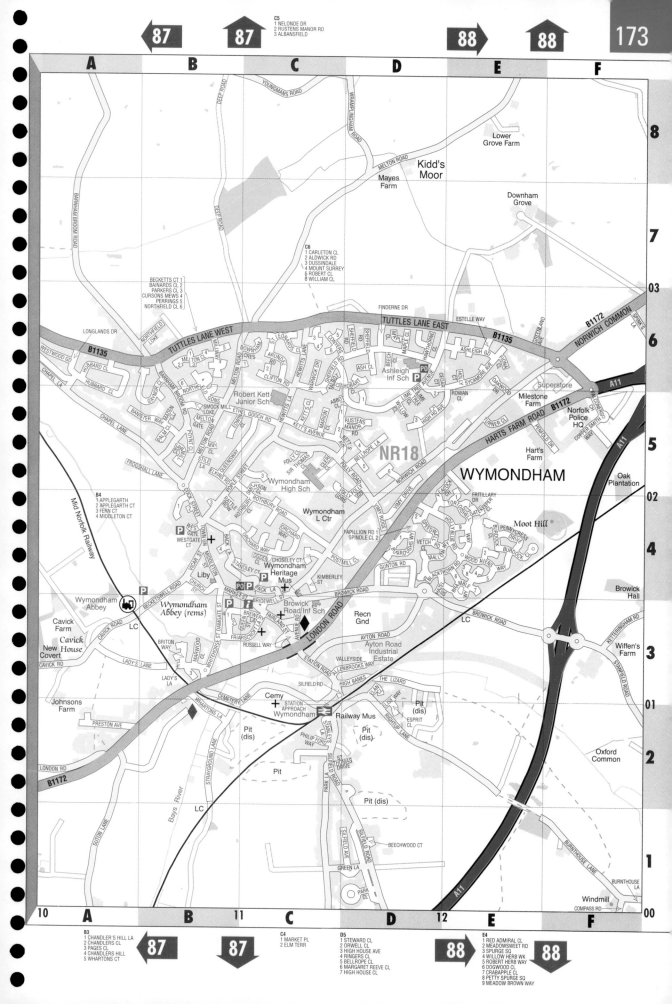

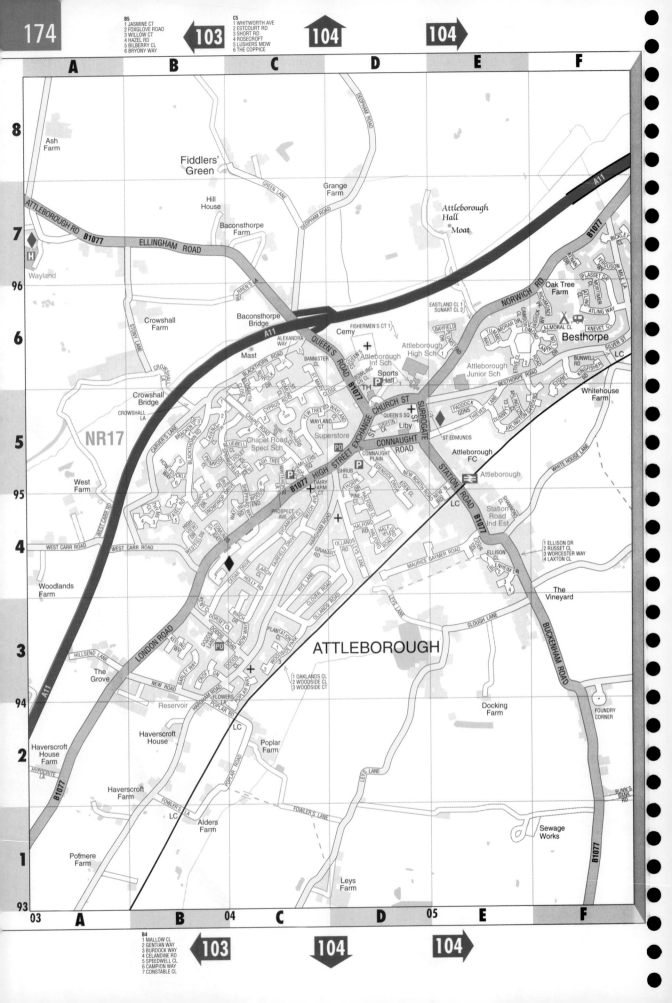

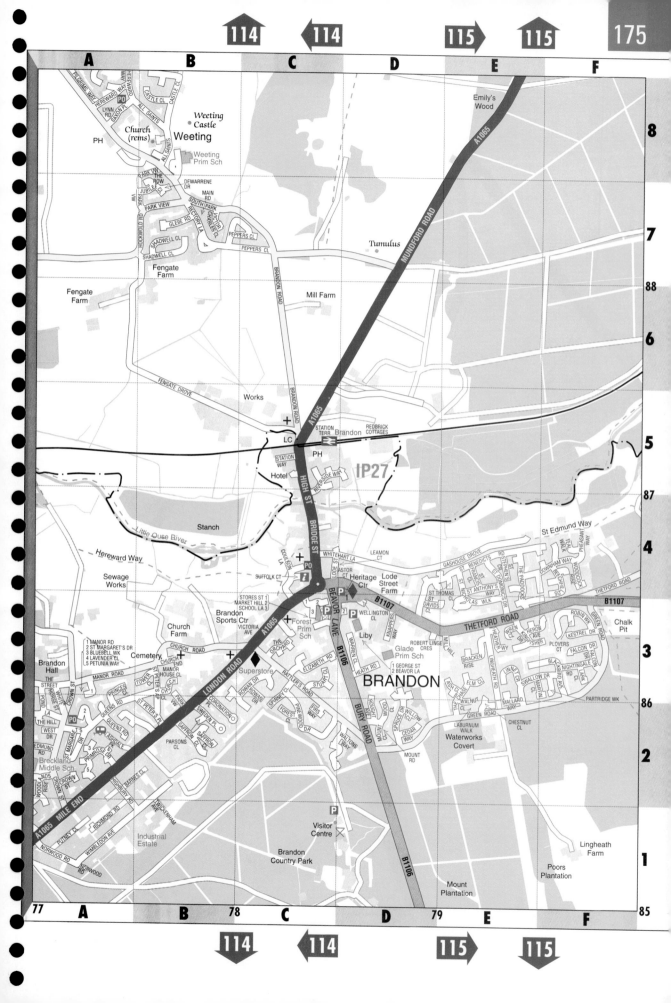

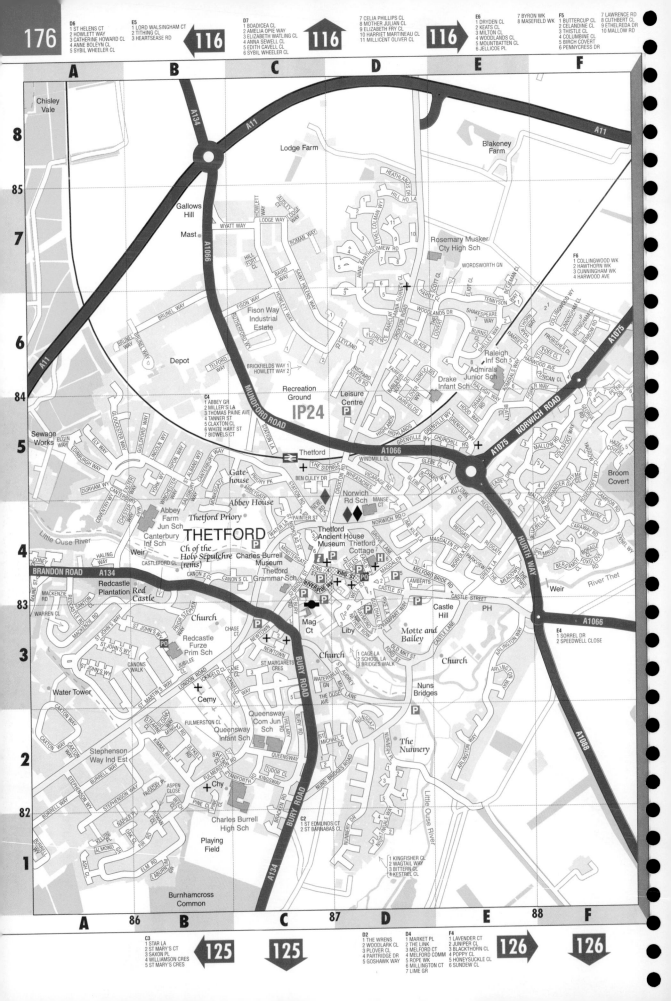

D6
1 ST HELENS CT
2 HOWLETT WAY
3 CATHERINE HOWARD CL
4 ANNE BOLEYN CL
5 SYBIL WHEELER CL

E5
1 LORD WALSINGHAM CT
2 TITHING CL
3 HEARTSEASE RD

D7
1 BOADICEA CL
2 AMELIA OPIE WAY
3 ELIZABETH WATLING CL
4 ANNA SEWELL CL
5 EDITH CAVELL CL
6 SYBIL WHEELER CL

7 CELIA PHILLIPS CL
8 MOTHER JULIAN CL
9 ELIZABETH FRY CL
10 HARRIET MARTINEAU CL
11 MILLICENT OLIVER CL

E6
1 DRYDEN CL
2 KEATS CL
3 MILTON CL
4 WOODLANDS CL
5 MOUNTBATTEN CL
6 JELLICOE PL

7 BYRON WK
8 MASEFIELD WK

F5
1 BUTTERCUP CL
2 CELANDINE CL
3 THISTLE CL
4 COLUMBINE CL
5 BIRCH COVERT
6 PENNYCRESS DR

7 LAWRENCE RD
8 CUTHBERT CL
9 ETHELREDA DR
10 MALLOW RD

← 116   ↑ 116   ↑ 116   → 116

Chisley Vale

Lodge Farm

Blakeney Farm

Gallows Hill
Mast

Rosemary Musker Cty High Sch

F6
1 COLLINGWOOD WK
2 HAWTHORN WK
3 CUNNINGHAM WK
4 HARWOOD AVE

Fison Way Industrial Estate

Depot

Brickfields Way 1
Howlett Way 2 →

Recreation Ground

IP24

Leisure Centre

Raleigh Inf Sch

Sewage Works

C4
1 ABBEY GR
2 MILLER'S LA
3 THOMAS PAINE AVE
4 TANNER ST
5 CLAXTON CL
6 WHITE HART ST
7 BIDWELLS CT

Thetford

Admirals Junior Sch
Drake Infant Sch

Broom Covert

Gate-house

Abbey House

Ben Culey Dr

Norwich Rd Sch

Abbey Farm Jun Sch

THETFORD

Thetford Priory

Canterbury Inf Sch

Thetford Ancient House Museum
Thetford Cottage

Weir

Little Ouse River

Ch of the Holy Sepulchre (rems)

Charles Burrell Museum

Thetford Grammar Sch

Weir

River Thet

Redcastle Plantation
Red Castle

Church

Castle Hill

Motte and Bailey

PH

E4
1 SORREL DR
2 SPEEDWELL CLOSE

Redcastle Furze Prim Sch

Church
Nuns Bridges

Water Tower

Cemy

Newtown

Church

1 CAGE LA
2 SCHOOL LA
3 BRIDGES WALK

Nuns Bridges

Queensway Com Jun Sch
Queensway Infant Sch

The Nunnery

Chy

Stephenson Way Ind Est

Charles Burrell High Sch

C2
1 ST EDMUNDS CT
2 ST BARNABAS CL

Playing Field

Little Ouse River

1 KINGFISHER CL
2 WAGTAIL WAY
3 BITTERN CL
4 KESTREL CL

Burnhamcross Common

C3
1 STAR LA
2 ST MARY'S CT
3 SAXON PL
4 WILLIAMSON CRES
5 ST MARY'S CRES

D2
1 THE WRENS
2 WOODLARK CL
3 PLOVER CL
4 PARTRIDGE DR
5 GOSHAWK WAY

D4
1 MARKET PL
2 THE LINK
3 MELFORD CT
4 MELFORD COMM
5 ROPE WK
6 MILLINGTON CT
7 LIME GR

F4
1 LAVENDER CT
2 JUNIPER CL
3 BLACKTHORN CL
4 POPPY CL
5 HONEYSUCKLE CL
6 SUNDEW CL

← 125   125   → 126   → 126

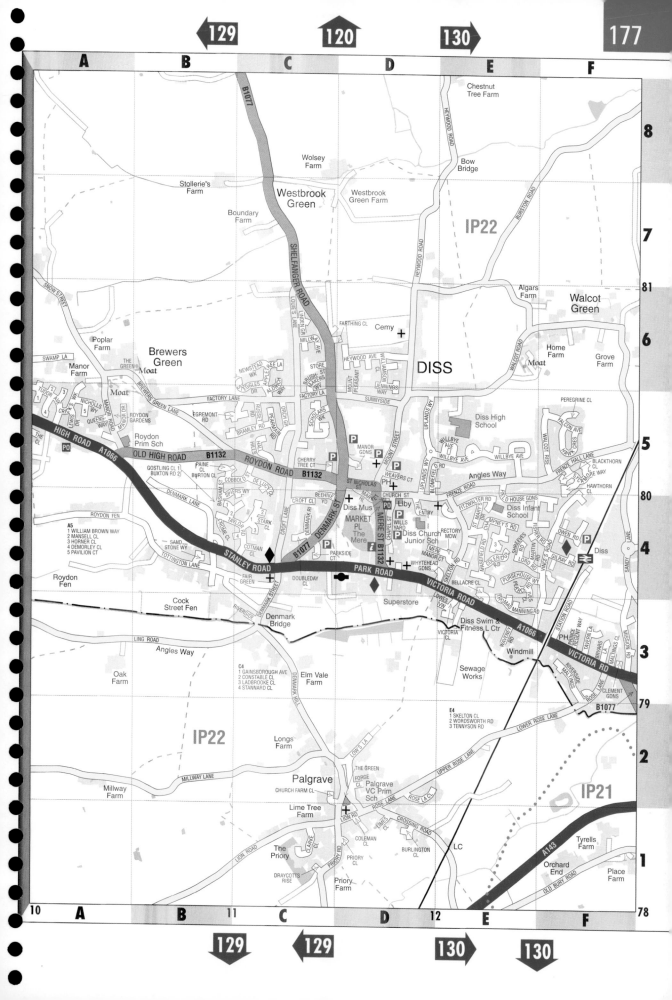

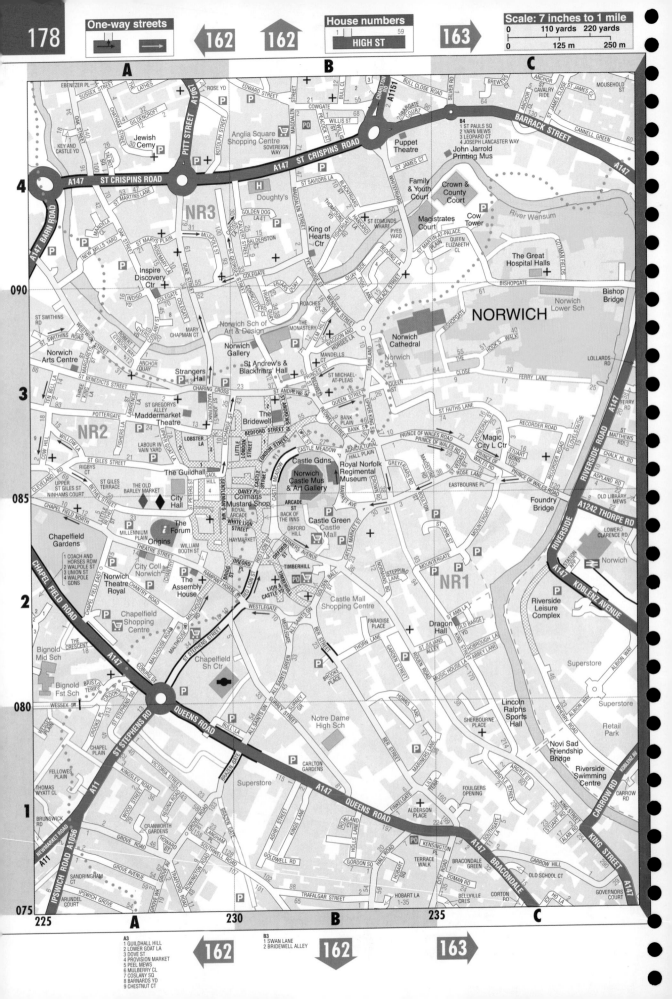

Index

Place name May be abbreviated on the map

Location number Present when a number indicates the place's position in a crowded area of mapping

Locality, town or village Shown when more than one place has the same name

Postcode district District for the indexed place

Page and grid square Page number and grid reference for the standard mapping

Church Rd **6** Beckenham BR2..........**53** C6

Public and commercial buildings are highlighted in magenta **Places of interest** are highlighted in blue with a star★

Abbreviations used in the index

Acad	Academy	Comm	Common	Gd	Ground	L	Leisure	Prom	Promenade
App	Approach	Cott	Cottage	Gdn	Garden	La	Lane	Rd	Road
Arc	Arcade	Cres	Crescent	Gn	Green	Liby	Library	Recn	Recreation
Ave	Avenue	Cswy	Causeway	Gr	Grove	Mdw	Meadow	Ret	Retail
Bglw	Bungalow	Ct	Court	H	Hall	Meml	Memorial	Sh	Shopping
Bldg	Building	Ctr	Centre	Ho	House	Mkt	Market	Sq	Square
Bsns, Bus	Business	Ctry	Country	Hospl	Hospital	Mus	Museum	St	Street
Bvd	Boulevard	Cty	County	HQ	Headquarters	Orch	Orchard	Sta	Station
Cath	Cathedral	Dr	Drive	Hts	Heights	Pal	Palace	Terr	Terrace
Cir	Circus	Dro	Drove	Ind	Industrial	Par	Parade	TH	Town Hall
Cl	Close	Ed	Education	Inst	Institute	Pas	Passage	Univ	University
Cnr	Corner	Emb	Embankment	Int	International	Pk	Park	Wk, Wlk	Walk
Coll	College	Est	Estate	Intc	Interchange	Pl	Place	Wr	Water
Com	Community	Ex	Exhibition	Junc	Junction	Prec	Precinct	Yd	Yard

Index of localities, towns and villages

A

Acle 166 B3
Alburgh 122 F6
Alby Hill 21 B5
Aldborough 21 A5
Aldeby 110 F4
Alderford 52 A5
All Saints South
  Elmham 124 B1
Alpington 90 E4
Anchor Corner 86 A1
Anchor Street 38 B3
Anmer 28 E8
Annis Hill 124 C8
Antingham 22 B4
Arminghall 90 B7
Ashby St Mary 91 C5
Ashill 84 A7
Ashmanhaugh 55 B8
Ashwellthorpe 105 F8
Ashwicken 45 A6
Aslacton 106 A2
Attleborough 174 D3
Attlebridge 52 B3
Aylmerton 10 A2
Aylsham 150 B5

B

Babingley 27 D5
Baconsthorpe 20 A8
Bacton 23 E5
Bacton Green 23 D5
Bagthorpe 14 D3
Bale 18 B7
Banham 119 D7
Banningham 36 D8
Barford 69 F2
Barmer 14 F4
Barney 17 F3
Barnham 125 F6
Barnham Broom 69 C2
Barningham 127 C3
Barningham Green . . . 20 A4
Barton Bendish 81 A8
Barton Turf 38 F1
Bastwick 57 A4
Battlesea Green . . . 131 E2
Bawburgh 160 B6
Bawdeswell 50 E8
Bawsey 44 D6
Beachamwell 81 F8
Beccles 110 D2
Beckett End 82 B1

Beckhithe 160 A1
Bedingham Green . . . 108 B3
Beeston 48 C2
Beeston Regis 138 F5
Beeston St Lawrence . . 55 C8
Beetley 49 D4
Beighton 74 C2
Belaugh 54 E5
Bellmount 144 A7
Belton 93 F6
Bengate 38 A6
Bergh Apton 91 A4
Bessingham 20 E7
Besthorpe 174 B5
Bexwell 79 F6
Billingford
  Bawdeswell 50 B7
  Diss 130 E5
Billockby 75 A7
Binham 6 E2
Bintree 33 B2
Bircham Newton 14 A4
Bircham Tofts 14 B3
Bittering 48 F4
Blackborough End . . . 44 C1
Black Carr 105 A6
Blackwater 51 D6
Blakeney 7 C6
Bleach Green 131 F4
Blenheim Park 15 C3
Blickling 35 F7
Blofield 165 F5
Blofield Corner 73 C6
Blofield Heath 73 D6
Blo' Norton 128 B6
Bloodman's Corner . . 171 A4
Bobby Hill 128 A1
Bodham 9 A3
Bodney 83 B1
Booton 149 E4
Botesdale 128 F2
Boughton 81 A5
Bowbeck 127 A2
Bowthorpe 160 F7
Bracon Ash 89 A2
Bradenham 66 E4
Bradfield 22 C4
Bradwell 94 C7
Brakefield Green . . . 68 D4
Bramerton 90 F7
Brampton 36 E3
Brancaster 3 B6
Brancaster Staithe . . . 3 D7
Brandiston 52 B8
Brandon 175 D3
Brandon Bank 112 B7
Brandon Creek 97 A2

Brandon Parva 69 B2
Breckles 102 E5
Bressingham 129 C8
Bressingham Common . . 119 F1
Brettenham 117 B2
Brewers Green 177 B6
Bridge Green 120 F2
Bridgham 117 F5
Briggate 38 B6
Briningham 18 D4
Brinton 18 D6
Brisley 49 A8
Briston 142 E4
Brockdish 131 C6
Brome 130 B3
Brome Street 130 D3
Brooke 90 E2
Brookville 99 A6
Broome 109 C2
Broom Green 32 E2
Broomhill 172 E7
Broomholm 23 E4
Broomsthorpe 30 C7
Browston Green 94 C4
Brundall 165 D4
Brundish 110 A6
Buckenham 91 F8
Bull's Green 110 C5
Bumwell Hill 105 E2
Bungay 124 A8
Bunker's Hill
  Lowestoft 94 C3
  Norwich 161 B7
Bunwell 105 D4
Bunwell Bottom 105 C6
Burgate 129 C2
Burgh Castle 94 A7
Burgh Common 104 D5
Burgh next Aylsham . . 36 D4
Burgh St Margaret
  (Fleggburgh) 57 C1
Burgh St Peter 111 C4
Burgh Stubbs 142 B8
Burlingham Green . . . 74 A5
Burnham Deepdale . . . 3 E6
Burnham Market . . . 135 C5
Burnham Norton . . . 135 B6
Burnham Overy Staithe . 135 E6
Burnham Overy Town . . 135 E4
Burnham Thorpe 4 D1
Burnham Westgate . . . 135 B3
Burston 120 F2
Bush Green 122 A6
Bushy Common 67 B8
Bustard's Green 106 C3
Buxton 36 E1

C

Caister-on-Sea 168 F6
Caistor St Edmund . . . 89 F6
California 167 E3
Calthorpe 21 A2
Calthorpe Street 39 D4
Candle Street 128 D1
Cangate 55 C6
Cantley 92 B7
Carbrooke 85 B5
Cargate Common . . . 105 E1
Cargate Green 166 A8
Carleton Forehoe . . . 87 C8
Carleton Rode 105 C3
Carleton St Peter . . . 91 E5
Castle Acre 46 F2
Castle Rising 27 C3
Caston 102 E8
Catfield 56 C8
Caudlesprings 85 A4
Cawston 35 B2
Cess 57 C5
Chalkhill 83 C4
Chapel Field 39 A3
Chedgrave 92 A2
Chickering 131 D3
Christchurch 95 A7
Church End 41 F2
Claxton 91 D6
Clenchwarton 145 E5
Cley next the Sea 7 E6
Cliftonville 143 B7
Clint Green 68 C6
Clippesby 57 A1
Clippings Green 68 E7
Cobbler's Green 108 B2
Cobholm Island 169 A4
Cockley Cley 82 D7
Cockthorpe 6 E5
Colby 21 E2
Colegate End 121 E6
Colkirk 31 D5
Colney 161 A4
Coltishall 54 C6
Colton 69 E4
Coney Weston 127 B5
Congham 28 B2
Copy's Green 6 A2
Cordwell 105 E4
Corpusty 19 E1
Costessey 156 F4
Costessey Park 156 D3
Coston 69 A1
Coxford 30 C8
Crabgate 34 D6

Crackthorn Corner . . . 128 D5
Cranwich 99 F6
Cranworth 85 E7
Craymere Beck 18 F1
Crimplesham 80 B6
Cringleford 89 B8
Cromer 139 C7
Crossdale Street . . . 139 D1
Cross Street 131 A3
Cross Ways 94 B4
Crostwick 54 B3
Crostwight 38 D8
Crowgate Street 55 A8
Crownthorpe 87 C6
Crowshill 67 A1
Croxton
  Fakenham 17 E2
  Thetford 116 C5
Cuckoo Green 171 A4
Culfordheath 125 D1

D

Daffy Green 67 C4
Damgate
  Acle 166 C2
  Martham 57 E5
Dam Green 119 C4
Danemoor Green . . . 86 F8
Darrow Green 122 C4
Denham 131 B1
Denton 123 A7
Denver 172 C2
Deopham 86 F3
Deopham Green 86 E2
Deopham Stalland . . . 86 D2
Dereham 154 F4
Dersingham 140 D5
Dickleburgh 121 C1
Dickleburgh Moor . . . 121 C2
Didlington 99 E8
Dilham 38 D4
Diss 177 D6
Ditchingham 109 A2
Dockeney 109 F2
Docking 134 C5
Doddshill 140 F3
Dowe Hill 167 C5
Downham Market . . . 176 D4
Drabblegate 150 D8
Drayton 157 A8
Drurylane 85 A4
Drymere 64 C1
Dumpling Green 154 F3
Dunkirk 150 E8
Dunston 89 E5

Dunton 15 F1
Dussindale Park 72 E4

E

Earlham 161 E1
Earsham 123 E8
Earsham Street 131 F5
East Barsham 16 D4
East Bilney 49 B6
East Carleton 88 F4
Eastgate 35 C2
East Harling 118 C5
Easthaugh 51 C4
East Lexham 47 D3
Easton 70 B5
East Raynham 31 A4
East Rudham 30 A7
East Runton 10 B5
East Ruston 38 E6
East Somerton 58 A6
East Tuddenham 69 C6
East Walton 45 E3
East Winch 44 F3
East Wretham 102 A1
Eaton 161 F2
Eau Brink 43 A3
Eccles on Sea 24 E4
Eccles Road 103 F1
Edgefield 19 D5
Edgefield Street 19 D4
Edge Green 119 B4
Edingthorpe 23 C3
Edingthorpe Green 23 A2
Ellingham 109 D3
Elm 59 B1
Elsing 50 F3
Elveden 125 A7
Emneth 59 D2
Emneth Hungate 59 F2
Emorsgate 42 B7
Erpingham 21 B2
Etling Green 68 B8
Euston 126 B5
Eye 130 C1

F

Fair Green 44 B4
Fairstead 147 D4
Fakenham 141 D6
Fakenham Magna 126 C3
Felbrigg 10 C2
Felmingham 37 A8
Felthorpe 155 C8
Feltwell 98 D1
Fengate 150 C1
Fenside 56 B8
Fen Street
  Hopton 127 E6
  Redgrave 128 F6
Fersfield 119 D2
Fiddlers' Green 174 B8
Field Dalling 7 B1
Filby 75 F8
Filby Heath 76 B8
Fincham 62 F1
Fishley 166 C6
Flaxlands 105 C4
Flitcham 28 C5
Flixton 123 D5
Flordon 106 D8
Fodderstone Gap 62 C4
Fordham 79 D2
Forncett End 105 E4
Forncett St Mary 106 B4
Forncett St Peter 106 B4
Foul Anchor 41 A4
Foulden 82 A2
Foulsham 33 D3
Foxhole 107 A7
Foxley 50 D8
Framingham Earl 90 D4
Framingham Pigot 90 C6
Frankfort 38 A3
Frans Green 51 D1
Freethorpe 92 E8
Frenze 130 B7
Frettenham 54 A4
Friday Bridge 77 A7
Fring 13 D5
Fritton
  Great Yarmouth 93 E3
  Long Stratton 107 B3
  Ludham 56 E5
Frogshall 11 B1
Frost Row 86 B4
Fulmodeston 17 F1
Fundenhall 106 A7

G

Garboldisham 128 A8
Garlic Street 122 A2
Garvestone 68 C2
Gasthorpe 127 D7
Gateley 32 C3
Gayton 45 C5
Gayton Thorpe 45 E5
Gaywood 147 B6
Geldeston 109 F3
Gillingham 110 C2
Gimingham 22 E7
Gissing 120 F4
Glandford 7 E4

Gooderstone 82 A4
Goose Green 120 C6
Gorleston-on-Sea 170 A4
Great Barwick 14 E6
Great Bircham 14 B3
Great Common 124 D6
Great Cressingham 83 D4
Great Dunham 47 E1
Great Ellingham 103 E7
Great Fransham 66 B8
Great Green
  Diss 130 A4
  Wortham 129 B3
Great Hautbois 54 C7
Great Hockham 102 E3
Great Massingham 29 D2
Great Melton 70 B1
Great Moulton 106 B1
Great Plumstead 72 F5
Great Ryburgh 32 B6
Great Snoring 17 A5
Great Walsingham 17 A5
Great Witchingham 51 E7
Great Yarmouth 169 A5
Greengate 50 B3
Greensgate 51 E2
Gresham 9 E1
Gressenhall 49 B3
Grimston 28 B1
Griston 85 A2
Guestwick 34 A6
Guestwick Green 33 F5
Guist 32 F4
Gunthorpe 18 B5

H

Hackford 87 A5
Haddiscoe 110 F8
Hainford 53 E5
Hales 109 F8
Hales Green 109 E7
Hales Street 121 A6
Halvergate 74 F1
Hamrow 31 D3
Hanworth 21 B6
Happisburgh 24 C6
Happisburgh Common . . 24 B4
Hapton 106 C7
Hardingham 86 E6
Hardley Street 92 C4
Hardwick
  King's Lynn 147 B1
  Long Stratton 122 B8
Hargate 105 D2
Harleston 122 E4
Harling Road 118 A7
Harper's Green 32 A1
Harpley 29 D4
Hassingham 92 B8
Hawes' Green 89 F2
Hay Green 144 A1
Heacham 133 E4
Heckfield Green 131 B2
Heckingham 92 C1
Hedenham 108 E4
Helhoughton 30 E5
Hellesdon 157 F5
Hellington 91 B6
Hemblington 73 E6
Hemblington Corner 73 D6
Hempnall 107 D5
Hempnall Green 107 D4
Hempstead
  Holt 19 E8
  Stalham 24 E3
Hempton 141 D4
Hemsby 167 A4
Hengrave 52 A6
Hepworth 127 E1
Herringfleet 111 D8
Hethel 88 F3
Hethersett 88 C8
Hevingham 53 B7
Heydon 34 F6
Hickling 39 E2
Hickling Green 39 F2
Hickling Heath 39 E1
High Common 85 F8
High Green
  Beeston 48 E1
  Bradenham 66 E2
  Hethersett 88 B8
High Kelling 8 E3
Highoak 87 B4
High Street 124 D3
Hilborough 83 A3
Hilgay 79 E1
Hill Common 39 F1
Hillington 28 B4
Hinderclay 128 C3
Hindolveston 33 D8
Hindringham 17 E7
Hingham 86 C5
Hockering 69 B8
Hockering Heath 51 C1
Hockwold cum Wilton . . 114 A7
Hoe 49 F3
Holkham 5 B6
Holly End 59 D1
Holme Hale 66 B2
Holme next the Sea 2 A6
Holt 137 D6
Homersfield 123 B4
Honing 38 C6
Honingham 69 E7
Honington 126 D1

Hopton 127 F6
Hopton on Sea 171 D6
Horning 55 E4
Horningtoft 31 F1
Horsey 40 D2
Horsey Corner 40 D2
Horsford 53 B3
Horsham St Faith 53 D1
Horstead 54 C6
Houghton St Giles 16 E6
Hoveton 164 D6
Howe 90 D3
How Hill 56 B6
Hoxne 131 A4
Humbletoft 154 C7
Hunstanton 132 D5
Hunt's Corner 119 C7
Hunworth 19 A6
Hyltons Crossways 36 F8

I

Ickburgh 100 B6
Ilketshall St Andrew . . . 124 E6
Ilketshall St Lawrence . . 124 F2
Ilketshall St Margaret . . 124 B4
Illington 117 D8
Ingham 39 D4
Ingham Corner 24 D2
Ingleborough 41 B1
Ingoldisthorpe 140 D8
Ingworth 36 B8
Intwood 89 B7
Irstead 56 A7
Irstead Street 55 F6
Itteringham 20 C1
Itteringham Common . . . 35 D8
Ivy Todd 66 B4

J

Johnson Street 56 B4
Jordan Green 51 A8

K

Kelling 8 D5
Kenninghall 119 B5
Kerdiston 34 C3
Keswick
  North Walsham 23 F4
  Norwich 89 C7
Ketteringham 88 E6
Kettlestone 17 C2
Kidd's Moor 173 D8
Kimberley 87 B6
King's Lynn 147 A5
Kirby Bedon 90 E8
Kirby Cane 109 E4
Kirby Green 109 F5
Kirby Row 109 E3
Kirstead Green 108 C8
Knapton 143 B1
Knapton Green 22 F5
Knettishall 127 C7

L

Lakenham 162 F3
Lakenheath 113 E2
Lakes End 95 C7
Lamas 37 A2
Langham 7 B3
Langley Street 92 B4
Langton Green 130 C1
Larling 118 B8
Lenwade 51 D5
Lessingham 24 D3
Letheringsett 8 A1
Letton Green 67 E1
Leziate 44 D6
Limpenhoe 92 D6
Lingwood 73 F3
Litcham 48 A4
Little Barningham 20 C4
Little Barwick 14 E6
Little Cressingham 83 E2
Little Dunham 65 E8
Little Ellingham 86 A2
Little Fransham 66 B7
Little Green 129 B1
Little Hale 67 A1
Little Hautbois 54 B8
Little London
  Aldborough 36 A2
  Corpusty 19 E1
  North Walsham 151 B1
  Northwold 99 D7
Little Marsh 7 A1
Little Massingham 29 C3
Little Melton 160 C2
Little Ouse 112 A8
Little Plumstead 73 B6
Little Ryburgh 32 C7
Little Snoring 17 B3
Little Thornage 7 A1
Little Walsingham 16 F7
Loddon 92 A1
Loddon Ingloss 109 B7
Long Green 129 B4
Longham 49 A2
Long John's Hill 162 E2
Long Stratton 106 E3
Lordsbridge 60 E7

Lound 94 C1
Low Common 105 F3
Lower Bodham 9 A2
Lower East Carleton 89 B6
Lower Gresham 9 F1
Lower Stow Bedon 102 F5
Lower Street
  Southrepps 22 C6
  Wickmere 20 E5
Lower Tasburgh 106 E7
Lower Thurlton 93 A2
Low Street 86 E8
Low Tharston 106 D6
Ludham 56 D5
Lundy Green 107 D3
Lynford 100 D2
Lyng 51 A4
Lyngate
  North Walsham 151 A8
  Worstead 38 A5

M

Magpie Green 129 B5
Manor House 46 E2
Manson Green 86 C6
Marham 63 B4
Market Weston 127 C6
Marlingford 70 A4
Marsham 150 D1
Marshland St James 60 A4
Marsh Side 3 C7
Martham 57 D5
Matlaske 20 D5
Mattishall 68 E5
Mattishall Burgh 68 F7
Mautby 75 F7
Maypole Green 110 C6
Meeting House Hill 38 B7
Mellis 129 E1
Melton Constable 142 B5
Mendham 123 A1
Merton 84 C1
Methwold 99 A5
Methwold Hythe 98 E5
Mettingham 124 E8
Metton 21 C8
Middle Harling 118 B4
Middleton 44 C3
Mile Cross 158 A2
Mileham 48 D6
Mill Common 91 C4
Millgate 150 D7
Mill Green 120 E3
Mill Street 50 E4
Misery Corner 122 F8
Moorgate 154 D3
Morley St Botolph 87 B2
Morningthorpe 107 A3
Morston 7 B6
Morton 52 A4
Moulton St Mary 74 D2
Mount Pleasant 103 C5
Muckleton 3 F2
Mulbarton 89 B3
Mundesley 143 B5
Mundford 100 B4
Mundham 91 C1
Mustard Hyrn 57 C5

N

Narborough 63 E7
Narrowgate Corner 57 C2
Neatishead 55 E2
Neaton 84 E4
Necton 65 F4
Needham 131 D8
New Buckenham 104 F8
New Catton 158 D1
New Costessey 157 A1
Newgate 7 E5
Newgate Corner 75 C8
New Hainford 53 D5
New Holkham 5 A2
New Houghton 29 D6
New Rackheath 72 E7
New Sprowston 158 E3
Newton 47 B2
Newton Flotman 89 C1
Newton Greenways 89 D2
Newton St Faith 53 E4
Newtown 169 D7
Nogdam End 92 D3
Nordelph 78 D3
Nordelph Corner 86 D6
Northacre 85 B1
Northall Green 154 F8
North Barsham 16 D6
North Burlingham 74 A5
North Common 127 D2
North Court 114 C3
North Creake 4 D1
North Denes 168 F2
North Elmham 49 E8
North End 103 C3
North Green
  Harleston 122 A7
  Reymerston 68 C1
North Lopham 119 A2
North Lynn 146 F1
North Pickenham 65 E1
North Runcton 44 A2
North Tuddenham 50 D1
North Walsham 151 E6

Northwold 99 C8
North Wootton 148 C5
Norton Corner 34 C7
Norton Subcourse 92 E1
Norwich 178 A3

O

Oakley 130 E5
Old Beetley 49 D5
Old Buckenham 104 D2
Old Catton 158 E5
Old Hall Street 23 A4
Old Hunstanton 132 E8
Orange Row 144 A6
Ormesby St Margaret . . 167 B3
Ormesby St Michael . . . 58 A1
Ostend 24 A7
Oulton 35 B7
Oulton Street 35 D6
Outwell 77 F6
Overstrand 11 A4
Ovington 84 C5
Oxborough 81 D4
Oxnead 36 E2
Oxwick 31 D4

P

Palgrave 177 C2
Panxworth 73 E7
Paston 143 D2
Paston Green 143 B5
Peaseland Green 50 F3
Pedham 73 D7
Pennygate 38 E2
Pentney 63 C8
Pettywell 34 C7
Pilson Green 74 B8
Plumstead Green
  Great and Little
    Plumstead 73 B6
  Holt 20 B6
Pockthorpe
  Lyng 51 B5
  Watton 102 A7
  West Rudham 29 F6
Podmore 67 B7
Pollard Street 23 D3
Pooley Street 129 A8
Poringland 90 C5
Postwick 72 F2
Pottergate Street 106 B2
Potter Heigham 56 F6
Potthorpe 49 A8
Primrose Corner 55 C1
Primrose Green 51 A3
Pristow Green 120 E8
Pudding Norton 141 B1
Puddledock 104 C3
Pulham Market 121 E5
Pulham St Mary 121 F4

Q

Quidenham 118 F6

R

Rackheath 72 E8
Ragmere 104 D1
Ranworth 55 F1
Ratten Row 59 F8
Raveningham 110 A7
Reading Green 131 C5
Redenhall 122 F3
Redgrave 128 E4
Red Pits 34 D7
Reedham 92 E5
Reepham 149 B5
Repps 56 F4
Reymerston 68 C1
Rickinghall 128 E2
Ridlington 23 E1
Ridlington Street 23 E1
Ringland 70 B8
Ringstead 2 A3
Road Green 107 E4
Rockland All Saints 103 B7
Rockland St Mary 91 B7
Rockland St Peter 103 B8
Rollesby 57 D2
Rougham 47 B7
Roughton 21 E8
Roydon
  Diss 129 D7
  King's Lynn 28 A2
Runcton Holme 61 D3
Runhall 68 F2
Runham
  Filby 75 E6
  Great Yarmouth 169 B6
Rushall 121 F1
Rushford 126 E8
Rush Green 69 B1

S

Saham Hills 84 C6
Saham Toney 84 C5
St Cross South Elmham 123 D2
St James 54 E7
St John's Fen End 60 B6

St John's Highway 42 B1
St Margaret South
  Elmham. 123 E2
St Michael South
  Elmham. 124 A2
St Nicholas South
  Elmham. 123 E2
St Olaves 93 D2
St Peter South Elmham. 124 A3
Salhouse 55 B1
Salle 149 E8
Salters Lode 79 A4
Salthouse 8 B7
Sandringham 27 F7
Santon Downham 115 C6
Sapiston 126 D2
Saxlingham. 7 C2
Saxlingham Green 107 D7
Saxlingham Nethergate 107 C8
Saxlingham Thorpe . . . 107 A8
Saxthorpe 19 F1
Scarning 67 B7
Scole. 130 D6
Scole Common 130 C7
Sco Ruston 54 E8
Scottow 37 D2
Scoulton 85 E3
Scratby. 167 E4
Sculthorpe 16 B2
Sea Palling 40 A6
Sedgeford 13 B7
Seething 108 F8
Setchey 61 E8
Shadwell 117 C2
Sharp Street 56 C7
Sharrington 18 D7
Shelfanger 120 C2
Shelton. 107 B1
Shepherd's Gate 42 D4
Shepherd's Port 12 B4
Shereford 31 A8
Sheringham 138 C7
Sheringwood 138 C5
Shernborne 13 B3
Shimpling 121 A2
Shingham 82 A8
Shipdham 67 B2
Shipmeadow 124 F8
Short Green 120 A5
Shotesham 90 A2
Shouldham 62 D4
Shouldham Thorpe 62 C3
Shropham 103 B4
Sidestrand. 11 C2
Silfield 88 A2
Silvergate 35 F6
Silver Green 107 E3
Sisland 91 E1
Skeyton 37 A4
Skeyton Corner 37 B6
Sloley 37 F4
Smallburgh 38 D3
Smallworth 128 A7
Sneath Common 121 A8
Snetterton 103 C2
Snettisham 12 E5
Snow Street 129 D8
South Acre 46 F1
Southburgh 85 F7
South Burlingham. 74 B2
South Creake 15 D6
South Denes 170 E5
South End 103 C1
Southery 97 B5
Southgate
  Cawston. 35 B3
  South Creake. 15 E5
South Green
  Aylsham. 154 E3

Hoxne 130 F1
  Mattishall. 68 F5
  Pulham St Mary 121 F2
  Terrington St Clement . . . 42 B6
South Lopham 128 D8
South Lynn 146 E2
South Pickenham 83 D6
South Raynham 30 F3
Southrepps 22 B7
South Runcton 61 F3
Southtown. 169 B1
South Walsham 74 A7
Southwood 92 D8
South Wootton 148 D2
Spa Common 23 A1
Sparham 51 B6
Sparhamhill 51 C5
Spixworth 54 A2
Spooner Row 105 A8
Sporle. 65 C6
Sprowston 159 B3
Stacksford 104 C1
Stalham 39 B4
Stalham Green 39 C3
Stalland Common 86 C1
Stanfield 48 F7
Stanford 101 A5
Stanhoe 14 E8
Stanton Chare 127 B1
Starston 122 C3
Stibbard 32 E7
Stiffkey 6 D5
Stockton 109 F4
Stody. 18 F6
Stoke Ferry 80 F3
Stoke Holy Cross 89 F4
Stokesby 75 A5
Stonebridge 102 B1
Stone Street 124 F1
Stow Bardolph 79 E8
Stow Bedon 102 E7
Stowbridge 61 B2
Stradbroke 131 E1
Stradsett 80 D8
Stratton St Michael . . 106 F4
Stratton Strawless . . . 53 F7
Strumpshaw 73 F2
Stubb 39 F1
Stubbing's Green 129 A1
Stubbs Green 109 C8
Stuston 130 B5
Suffield 21 F3
Summerfield. 2 E1
Summerhill 133 C3
Surlingham 73 B1
Sustead 21 A7
Suton 87 D2
Sutton. 39 C3
Sutton Bridge 41 B7
Swaffham 153 D4
Swafield 22 E3
Swainsthorpe 89 D3
Swannington 52 B6
Swanton Abbott 37 C4
Swanton Hill 37 C5
Swanton Morley 50 B3
Swanton Novers 18 B3
Swardeston 89 C5
Syderstone 15 B3
Syleham 131 D5

Tacolneston 105 F5
Tasburgh 106 F7
Tatterford 30 E7
Tattersett. 15 C1
Taverham 155 C1

Ten Mile Bank 96 E7
Terrington St Clement . 144 B4
Terrington St John . . . 42 C2
Tharston 106 E5
The Arms 83 F1
The Brook 129 C3
The Grange 35 C1
The Green 87 B4
The Heath
  Fakenham 141 A1
  Hevingham 53 A8
  Stratton Strawless . . . 53 F8
The Limes 59 C5
The Ling 91 A1
Thelnetham 128 B5
Thelveton 130 D8
The Marsh
  Thrandeston 129 F3
  Wortham 129 C4
Themelthorpe 33 F2
The Smeeth 60 A5
Thetford 176 B4
Thompson 102 A8
Thornage 18 F7
Thornham 2 D6
Thorpe 93 B1
Thorpe Abbotts 131 B6
Thorpe End 72 D6
Thorpe Hamlet. 163 B6
Thorpe Market. 22 A6
Thorpe Marriott. 155 F2
Thorpe Row 67 C4
Thorpe St Andrew . . . 163 F8
Thorpland 61 D3
Thrandeston 129 F3
Three Cocked Hat . . . 110 D7
Threehammer Common . 55 E6
Three Holes 77 E3
Thrigby 75 D7
Thurgarton 20 F5
Thurlton 92 F1
Thurne 56 E3
Thurning 34 C7
Thursford 17 E4
Thursford Green 17 D5
Thurton 91 D4
Thuxton 68 D2
Thwaite St Mary 109 A5
Tibenham 120 E8
Tilney All Saints. . . . 144 F1
Tilney cum Islington . . 60 F8
Tilney Fen End 60 C6
Tilney High End 42 D4
Tilney St Lawrence . . 60 D8
Tipps End 95 C6
Titchwell 2 F7
Tittleshall 48 B8
Tivetshall St Margaret . 121 B5
Tivetshall St Mary . . 121 B5
Toft Monks 110 D5
Toftrees 31 B6
Toftwood 154 E2
Topcroft 107 F3
Topcroft Street 107 F2
Toprow 88 E1
Tottenhill. 62 E8
Tottenhill Row 61 E7
Tottington 101 E6
Tower End 44 C4
Town Green
  Aldborough 21 C4
  South Walsham 74 A7
Town Street 39 F3
Trimingham 11 D2
Trowse Newton 163 B3
Trunch 22 E5
Tungate 37 C8
Tunstall 74 F3
Tunstead 37 F1

Tuttington 36 E6
Twyford 33 B3
Tyby. 34 B6

Upgate 52 C5
Upgate Street
  New Buckenham 105 A3
  Woodton 108 B2
Upper Brandon Parva . . 33 A5
Upper Guist 33 A5
Upper Hellesdon 158 C3
Upper Sheringham . . . 138 A5
Upper Stoke 90 B5
Upper Street
  Horning 55 F4
  Hoveton 55 C5
  Scole 130 F6
  Southrepps 22 B7
  Worstead 38 A3
Upper Weybread 131 E6
Upton 166 A8
Upton Green 166 B8
Upwell 77 F5

Wacton. 106 C2
Wainford 109 B1
Walcot Green 177 E6
Walcott. 24 A7
Walpole Cross Keys . . 41 F7
Walpole Highway . . . 59 F8
Walpole Marsh. 41 C4
Walpole St Andrew. . . 41 D4
Walpole St Peter 41 E3
Walsoken. 152 F6
Walton Highway 59 D8
Walton Warren 45 E2
Wangford 114 C2
Warham 6 A4
Waterheath 110 E5
Waterloo
  Beccles 110 E4
  Coltishall 53 E6
  Diss 130 C6
Watlington 61 E5
Wattisfield 128 B1
Wattlefield 105 C7
Watton 84 E3
Watton Green 84 E4
Waxham 40 C5
Weasenham All Saints. . 47 C8
Weasenham St Peter . . 30 D1
Weeting 175 B8
Welborne 69 A4
Welbourne Common . . 68 F4
Wellingham 30 F1
Wells-Next-The-Sea . 136 C5
Welney 95 D4
Wendling 66 F8
Wereham 80 E4
West Acre 46 B2
West Barsham 16 C4
West Beckham 9 C2
West Bilney 45 B2
Westbrook Green . . . 177 C7
West Caister 168 C4
West Dereham 80 B4
West End
  Necton 66 C4
  West Caister 76 B6
Westfield 67 F4
Westgate 6 D3
Westgate Street 53 B8
West Harling 118 A3

West Head. 78 F8
West Lexham 47 C4
West Lynn 146 C5
West Newton 27 F6
Weston Green 51 E1
Weston Longville 51 E3
West Poringland 90 B4
West Raynham 30 E4
West Rudham 29 F7
West Runton 10 A5
West Somerton 57 E6
West Tofts 100 F4
West Walton 59 B8
Westwick 37 D6
West Winch 43 E3
Weybourne 8 F5
Wheatacre 111 B5
Whimpwell Green 24 C4
Whinburgh 68 A3
Whissonsett 31 D2
Whittington 81 B2
Whitwell Street 149 C3
Wicken Green Village . . 15 D2
Wickhampton 93 A8
Wicklewood 87 B5
Wickmere 20 F4
Wiggenhall St Germans . 43 C1
Wiggenhall St Mary
  Magdalen 61 B6
Wiggenhall St Mary the
  Virgin 61 A8
Wighton. 6 A2
Wilby 119 A8
Wilney Green 129 A8
Wimbotsham 79 D8
Winfarthing 120 B4
Wingfield 131 E4
Wingfield Green 131 D4
Winterton-on-Sea 58 C6
Wisbech 152 A6
Withergate 38 A6
Witton 165 A6
Witton Bridge. 23 E2
Wiveton 7 E6
Wolferd Green 90 B2
Wolferton 27 B7
Wolterton 20 E2
Woodbastwick 55 D2
Wood Dalling 34 D6
Woodgate 50 C3
Wood Green 106 F2
Wood Norton 33 A7
Woodrising 85 E6
Woodton 108 C4
Wormegay 62 C7
Worstead 38 A5
Wortham 129 B4
Worthing 49 F6
Wortwell 123 B4
Wramplingham 69 E1
Wreningham. 88 D1
Wretton 80 E3
Wroxham 164 D3
Wymondham 173 E5

Yaxham 68 A5
Yaxley. 130 A1
Yelverton 90 E5

A

Abbey Cl
Horsham St Faith & Newton St Faith NR10 ... 53 D1
Sheringham NR26 ... 138 D6
Wendling NR19 ... 66 F7
Abbey Farm Mid Sch IP24 ... 176 B4
Abbey Gn 1 IP24 ... 176 C4
Abbey Hill IP21 ... 131 A3
Abbey La
Haveringland NR10 ... 52 D6
Norwich NR1 ... 178 C2
Abbey Pk NR26 ... 138 F5
Abbey Rd
Flitcham with Appleton PE31 ... 28 D5
Flixton NR35 ... 123 F4
Great Massingham PE32 ... 29 D1
Horsham St Faith NR10 ... 53 D1
Old Buckenham NR17 ... 104 D3
Pentney PE32 ... 63 B8
Sheringham NR26 ... 138 C6
10 Watton IP25 ... 84 E3
Abbey St NR12 ... 23 E4
Abbeyfields PE32 ... 29 D1
Abbeygate IP24 ... 176 C5
Abbot Cl NR18 ... 173 C5
Abbot Rd Horning NR12 ... 55 E4
Norwich NR1 ... 162 D2
Abbot's Cl NR11 ... 150 D7
Abbot's La NR14 ... 90 B3
Abbots Way NR12 ... 24 E4
Abbottsinch Rd 5 IP31 126 B1
Aberdare Ct 6 NR1 ... 163 B7
Aberdeen St PE30 ... 146 F4
Abinger Way NR4 ... 89 D8
Abington Gr 4 PE14 ... 59 A1
Abyssinia Rd NR30 ... 169 D2
Acacia Ave Ashill IP25 ... 84 A7
East Dereham NR19 ... 154 E1
22 Martham NR29 ... 57 D4
Wisbech PE13 ... 152 C8
Acacia Gr NR26 ... 138 D4
Acacia Rd NR7 ... 163 E8
Access Rd NR21 ... 15 D2
Acer Rd PE34 ... 43 D4
Ackland Cl 7 NR29 ... 58 B6
Acland Mews NR6 ... 158 C4
Acle High Sch NR13 ... 166 B4
Acle New Rd NR30 ... 169 B5
Acle Rd Beighton NR13 ... 74 E2
South Walsham NR13 ... 74 C7
Upton with Fishley NR13 ... 166 A5
Acle St Edmund CE VC Prim Sch NR13 ... 166 D4
Acle Sta NR13 ... 166 B2
Aconite Rd PE30 ... 147 B7
Acorn Dr PE32 ... 45 B6
Acorn Rd NR28 ... 151 D6
Acorn Way NR19 ... 154 D7
Acres Way NR8 ... 155 E2
Ada Cole Ave NR16 ... 103 D1
Ada Coxon Cl PE30 ... 146 F8
Adam Cl PE30 ... 147 C5
Adams La 4 NR11 ... 19 F1
Adams Rd NR7 ... 159 A5
Adastral Pl PE37 ... 153 C5
Addey Cl NR6 ... 158 F5
Addison Cl
2 Coltishall NR12 ... 54 C7
Feltwell IP26 ... 98 F1
Addison Rd 2 NR31 ... 170 C7
Adeane Mdw IP26 ... 100 A4
Adelaide Ave PE30 ... 147 B7
Adelaide St 5 NR2 ... 162 B7
Adey Cl NR11 ... 150 B5
Admiral's Dr PE35 ... 140 F1
Admirals Cl PE30 ... 147 D3
Admirals Ct PE37 ... 153 D3
Admirals Dr PE13 ... 152 D8
Admirals Jun Sch IP24 ... 176 E6
Admirals Quay NR31 ... 169 C1
Admirals Way
Hethersett NR9 ... 88 D8
Thetford IP24 ... 176 E5
Admirals Wlk 7 NR9 ... 86 C5
Admiralty Cl 3 PE38 ... 172 B4
Admiralty Rd NR30 ... 169 D1
Adventurers' Dro PE33 ... 81 B1
Aerodrome Cres NR7 ... 163 D8
Afghan Pl NR3 ... 158 E1
Agricultural Hall Plain NR1 ... 178 B3
Ailmar Cl PE30 ... 147 A4
Ainsworth Cl 7 NR20 ... 50 B3
Airedale Cl 4 NR3 ... 158 C1
Airfield Rd PE33 ... 63 C4
Airport Ind Est NR6 ... 158 C6
Airstation La IP21 ... 121 E2
Akrotiri Sq IP25 ... 84 F3
Alan Ave NR15 ... 89 D1
Alan Jarvis Way PE34 ... 144 D6
Alan Rd NR1 ... 178 C1
Alban Rd PE30 ... 148 C5
Albansfield 3 NR18 ... 173 C5
Albany Cl NR31 ... 169 C2
Albany Ct NR27 ... 139 B7
Albany Rd
Great Yarmouth NR31 ... 169 C2
Norwich NR3 ... 162 D8
Albany Rd *continued*
Wisbech PE13 ... 152 C6
Albemarle Rd
Great Yarmouth NR30 ... 169 D5
Norwich NR2 ... 162 B3
Albert Ct 18 PE13 ... 152 C4
Albert Gate Rd 22 NR30 169 D2
Albert Myhill Cl 5 NR20 ... 154 E6
Albert Pl NR1 ... 163 A6
Albert Rd 17 NR30 ... 169 D2
Albert Sq 13 NR30 ... 169 D2
Albert St Holt NR25 ... 137 B6
King's Lynn PE30 ... 146 D5
Albert Terr NR2 ... 162 C4
Albion Dr NR7 ... 159 A3
Albion Rd Bungay NR35 ... 124 B8
Great Yarmouth NR30 ... 169 D4
Mundesley NR11 ... 143 A7
Trunch NR28 ... 22 E5
Albion St PE30 ... 146 E5
Albion Way
Norwich NR1 ... 178 C1
Wroxham/Hoveton NR12 ... 164 D6
Alborough Loke 6 NR9 ... 88 C7
Alburgh Rd NR15 ... 107 D4
Alburgh with Denton Fst Sch IP20 ... 123 A5
Alby Craft Ctr★ NR11 ... 21 C3
Aldborough Prim Sch NR11 ... 21 B5
Aldborough Rd NR11 ... 21 A3
Aldeby Rd NR34 ... 110 F6
Alder Cl
Great Yarmouth NR31 ... 94 C7
10 Mulbarton NR14 ... 89 B3
North Walsham NR28 ... 151 D7
Poringland NR14 ... 90 D4
Alder Covert IP24 ... 116 D2
Alder Way NR8 ... 155 E1
Alderman Jackson Specl Sch PO30 ... 147 B8
Alderman Peel High Sch NR23 ... 136 D4
Alderman Swindell Fst Sch NR30 ... 169 D8
Alderson Pl NR1 ... 178 B1
Alderson Rd NR30 ... 169 D5
Aldis Ct NR19 ... 154 D5
Aldis Rd NR13 ... 166 B4
Aldiss Ave NR19 ... 154 D3
Aldiss Cl PE37 ... 153 D3
Aldiss Ct PE13 ... 154 D6
Aldrich Way IP22 ... 177 C5
Aldryche Rd NR1 ... 163 B8
Aldwick Rd 2 NR18 ... 173 C6
Alex Moorhouse Way NR5 ... 156 A3
Alexander Cl
Caister-on-Sea NR30 ... 168 C8
18 Long Stratton NR15 ... 106 E3
Alexander Rise NR11 ... 22 F8
Alexander Way 1 NR19 154 C6
Alexandra Ave NR30 ... 169 D7
Alexandra Cl PE31 ... 140 C4
Alexandra Rd
Cromer NR27 ... 139 B4
Great Yarmouth NR30 ... 169 D4
Hunstanton PE36 ... 132 C3
Mundesley NR11 ... 143 A8
Norwich NR2 ... 162 B6
Sheringham NR26 ... 138 D6
Wisbech PE13 ... 152 C5
Alexandra Way
Attleborough NR17 ... 174 C6
Downham Market PE38 ... 172 B3
Alford Gr NR7 ... 159 A3
Alfred Nicholls Ct NR3 ... 158 D2
Alfred Rd NR27 ... 139 A7
Alfric Cl 11 NR14 ... 91 F1
Algores Way PE13 ... 152 B2
Alice Fisher Cres PE30 ... 146 F7
Alison Cl NR13 ... 73 F3
All Hallows' Hospl NR35 ... 109 B2
All Saints IP27 ... 175 B8
All Saints Ave PE13 ... 152 F7
All Saints CE VA Prim Sch
Ryburgh NR21 ... 32 C6
Winfarthing IP22 ... 120 B4
All Saints Cl
Briston NR24 ... 142 D4
Runhall NR20 ... 69 A5
2 Weybourne NR25 ... 8 F5
Wicklewood NR18 ... 87 B5
1 Wisbech PE14 ... 59 A1
All Saints Dr PE30 ... 148 C4
All Saints Gn NR1 ... 178 B1
All Saints Rd 6 NR14 ... 90 D5
All Saints Sch NR12 ... 24 D3
All Saints' St 15 PE30 ... 146 D4
All Saints Way
Beachamwell PE37 ... 81 F8
Mundesley NR11 ... 143 C6
All Saints Wlk 7 NR20 ... 68 F6
Allanadale Rd NR4 ... 162 C1
Allen Cl PE34 ... 61 B8
Allen Meale Way 5 NR12 ... 39 B4
Allen's Ave NR7 ... 159 A4
Allen's La NR7 ... 159 A4
Allenbrooks Way NR18 ... 173 C3
Allenby's Chase 10 PE12 ... 41 B8
Allendale Rd NR30 ... 168 E5
Allens Cl 1 NR13 ... 73 D6
Allens La NR2 ... 162 C4
Allerton Cl NR7 ... 159 B3
Allerton Rd NR7 ... 159 B3
Alley The PE32 ... 44 C1
Allison St NR10 ... 36 A2
Allotment La NR25 ... 9 B3
Allthorpe Rd 12 IP20 ... 122 D2
Allwood Ave NR19 ... 154 C5
Alma Ave PE34 ... 144 D6
Alma Chase PE34 ... 144 D6
Alma Rd
Great Yarmouth NR30 ... 169 D2
Snettisham PE31 ... 12 E5
Alma Terr NR3 ... 162 D8
Almond Cl 21 NR29 ... 57 D4
Almond Gr IP24 ... 176 A1
Almond Rd NR31 ... 170 B6
Alpha Rd NR31 ... 170 C8
Alpington & Bergh Apton Prim Sch NR14 ... 90 F4
Alston Cl 3 NR14 ... 90 D5
Alston Rd NR6 ... 157 E2
Althaea Gn 2 NR31 ... 170 B5
Altongate 1 NR13 ... 72 D6
Amazonia World of Reptiles★ NR30 ... 169 E2
Ambassador Way NR20 ... 154 F4
Ambleside
16 Hethersett NR9 ... 88 D8
5 Sculthorpe Airfield NR21 15 C2
Ambleside Cl NR5 ... 161 C6
Ambrose Cl 1 NR5 ... 161 A7
Ambrose Rd NR30 ... 168 E3
Amderley Dr 6 NR4 ... 89 C8
Amelia Opie Way 2 IP24 ... 176 D7
Ames Ct NR10 ... 35 B2
Amethyst Cl NR31 ... 170 D2
Amherst Cl 7 PE37 ... 153 C3
Amhirst Cl 2 NR6 ... 158 F1
Amhurst Gdns NR31 ... 94 A5
Amsterdam NR6 ... 158 B6
Amsterdam Way PE13 ... 154 C2
Amys Cl IP25 ... 84 C4
Anchor Cl Norwich NR3 ... 178 C4
Sheringham NR26 ... 138 E6
Anchor Ct NR31 ... 169 C2
Anchor Dro PE38 ... 112 B8
Anchor Quay NR2 ... 178 A3
Anchor Rd
North Walsham NR28 ... 151 F5
Sutton Bridge PE34 ... 41 F8
Anchor St
Coltishall NR12 ... 54 D6
5 Norwich NR3 ... 162 F8
Norwich NR3 ... 178 C4
Tunstead NR12 ... 38 B2
Anchor Way 7 NR33 ... 111 F1
Anchorage View PE31 ... 3 B6
Anderson Cl
King's Lynn PE30 ... 146 E7
Wisbech PE13 ... 152 A7
Andrew Goodall Cl NR19 ... 154 C1
Andrew's Furlong NR16 ... 119 E7
Andrews Pl PE36 ... 132 D2
Angel Dr NR28 ... 151 B4
Angel Rd NR3 ... 158 D1
Angel Rd Fst Sch NR3 ... 158 D1
Angel Rd Mid Sch NR3 ... 158 D1
Angela Cl 2 NR10 ... 53 B3
Angela Cres 3 NR10 ... 53 B3
Angela Rd NR10 ... 53 B3
Angerstein Cl IP27 ... 114 E8
Angle Rd PE14 ... 78 A7
Anglia Sq NR3 ... 178 B4
Anglia Way PE13 ... 152 B2
Anglian Way 3 NR31 ... 171 D5
Anglo-Saxon Cath & Bishops Pal (remains of)★ NR20 ... 49 F8
Anmer Cl NR3 ... 158 F3
Anmer Rd PE31 ... 28 C5
Anna Gurney Cl IP24 ... 176 D6
Anna Sewell Cl 4 IP24 176 D7
Anne Bartholomew Rd IP24 ... 176 D7
Anne Boleyn Cl 4 IP24 176 D6
Anne Cl NR7 ... 163 F8
Anne Rd PE12 ... 41 B8
Anne Stannard Way NR12 ... 23 F4
Annes Cl PE30 ... 148 D1
Annes Dr PE36 ... 132 D1
Annis Hill NR35 ... 124 C8
Anson Cl
5 Hethersett NR9 ... 88 E8
Mundesley NR11 ... 143 A7
Anson Rd
Great Yarmouth NR31 ... 169 C2
Norwich NR6 ... 158 B6
Anson's La NR15 ... 122 A8
Ant Broads & Marshes National Nature Reserve★ NR12 ... 55 F8
Anthony Curton Prim Sch PE14 ... 41 E4
Anthony Dr NR3 ... 158 F2
Anthony Nolan Rd PE30 ... 147 D3
Antingham & Southrepps Com Prim Sch NR11 ... 22 B5
Antingham Dr NR28 ... 151 D6
Antingham Hill NR28 ... 22 B3
Antingham Rd NR7 ... 159 D1
Apeldoorn Wlk PE13 ... 152 D7
Apollo Wlk NR30 ... 169 C6
Apple Yd NR25 ... 137 B6
Appleacres NR6 ... 158 D5
Appledore Cl PE30 ... 148 C2
Appledore La 4 NR21 ... 15 C2
Applegarth 1 NR18 ... 173 B4
Applegarth Ct 2 NR18 ... 173 B4
Appleton Dr NR29 ... 167 A3
Appleton Dro PE31 ... 27 F5
Appletree Cl PE31 ... 133 C6
Appletree La IP22 ... 177 C5
Appleyard Cres NR3 ... 158 A3
Apsley Ct NR5 ... 161 F6
Apsley Rd NR30 ... 169 E3
Arbor Ct NR27 ... 139 B6
Arbor Rd NR27 ... 139 B6
Arcade St NR1 ... 178 B2
Archbishop Sancroft High Sch IP20 ... 122 D2
Archdale Cl PE33 ... 43 F3
Archdale St 3 PE30 ... 146 E5
Archer Cl NR6 ... 159 A5
Archer La PE32 ... 46 F2
Archer's Rd 2 NR30 ... 169 C5
Archers' Ave 3 IP26 ... 98 D1
Archibald Rd NR12 ... 24 A7
Arden Cl NR27 ... 11 A3
Arden Gr NR10 ... 157 E7
Arden Gr Fst Sch NR10 ... 157 E7
Arderon Ct 2 NR2 ... 162 B7
Ardleigh Cl 3 PE13 ... 152 E5
Ardney Rise NR3 ... 158 D3
Argyle St
King's Lynn PE30 ... 146 E3
Norwich NR1 ... 178 C1
Argyll Cres NR8 ... 156 E8
Arles Ave PE13 ... 152 E3
Arlington Cl NR17 ... 174 E5
Arlington Gdns NR17 ... 174 E5
Arlington La NR2 ... 162 C4
Arlington Pk Rd PE32 ... 44 C3
Arlington Way IP24 ... 176 E3
Armada Cl PE13 ... 152 D8
Armes Cres NR2 ... 162 A8
Armes St NR2 ... 162 B7
Arminghall Cl NR3 ... 158 C3
Arminghall La NR14 ... 89 F8
Armitage Cl NR4 ... 89 B8
Arms Pk Rd NR6 ... 158 B6
Armstrong Dr NR19 ... 154 E7
Armstrong Rd NR7 ... 159 E2
Army Rd NR21 ... 15 C2
Arnfield La NR5 ... 161 B8
Arnold Ave NR30 ... 168 D8
Arnold Miller Rd NR1 ... 162 F2
Arnott Ave NR31 ... 170 D1
Arnott Rd NR25 ... 137 D5
Arnside Cl 22 NR9 ... 88 D8
Arthur Ave NR30 ... 168 E8
Arthur Rd NR21 ... 141 A6
Arthurton Rd NR10 ... 54 A1
Artillery Sq 21 NR30 ... 169 D4
Artillery St 12 PE13 ... 152 C4
Arundel Cl NR20 ... 49 C4
Arundel Ct NR2 ... 178 A1
Arundel Dr PE30 ... 148 C1
Arundel Rd
Great Yarmouth NR30 ... 169 D7
Wymondham NR18 ... 173 C6
Ascot Gdns NR19 ... 154 D3
Ash Cl Brandon IP27 ... 175 E3
Downham Market PE38 ... 172 C6
10 Hethersett NR9 ... 88 D8
Swaffham PE37 ... 153 B5
Thetford IP24 ... 176 A1
Wymondham NR18 ... 173 D6
Ash Dr IP23 ... 130 C1
Ash Gn 11 NR31 ... 170 B6
Ash Gr King's Lynn PE30 ... 148 D2
Norwich NR3 ... 158 E2
Sheringham NR26 ... 138 E5
4 West Winch PE33 ... 43 E2
Ash La NR16 ... 105 C2
Ash Rd PE33 ... 63 B4
Ash Tree Cl NR17 ... 174 C5
Ash Tree Rd NR13 ... 74 D1
Ash Yd NR24 ... 18 D8
Ashbey Rd PE30 ... 147 E8
Ashburton Rd IP26 ... 100 C5
Ashby Rd
Ashby St Mary NR14 ... 91 C5
Repps with Bastwick NR29 ... 57 A3
Thurton NR14 ... 91 C4
Ashby St NR1 ... 178 B1
Ashdale Pk
Old Hunstanton PE36 ... 132 F8
Wisbech PE13 ... 152 A5
Ashdown NR8 ... 155 E1
Ashdown Ct NR27 ... 139 C6
Ashfield Ct PE34 ... 144 D6
Ashfield Hill PE30 ... 147 C4
Ashfield Rd NR28 ... 151 E6
Ashford Cl NR34 ... 110 C2
Ashgrove 5 NR8 ... 155 E2
Ashill VC Prim Sch IP25 ... 84 A7
Ashleigh Gdns NR18 ... 173 E6
Ashleigh Inf Sch NR18 ... 173 D6
Ashley Rd NR20 ... 49 D4
Ashley Wlk PE13 ... 154 D4
Ashtree Rd
Norwich NR5 ... 157 B2
12 Watton IP25 ... 84 E3
Ashwell Ct NR5 ... 160 F7
Ashwellthorpe Rd NR16 ... 88 D1
Ashwicken CE Fst Sch PE32 ... 44 F6
Ashwicken Rd PE32 ... 45 A8
Ashwood Cl NR30 ... 168 D6
Aslack Way PE36 ... 2 A6
Aslacton Prim Sch NR15 ... 106 A1
Aslacton Rd NR16 ... 106 B3
Aslake Cl NR7 ... 159 C5
Aspen Cl IP24 ... 176 B2
Aspen Way NR4 ... 89 B8
Aspland Rd NR1 ... 178 C3
Assembly House The NR2 ... 178 A2
Association Way 2 NR7 ... 72 D4
Astell Rd NR1 ... 89 F8
Astley Cooper Pl NR15 ... 90 E1
Astley Cres NR26 ... 132 D6
Astley Prim Sch NR24 ... 142 C4
Astley Rd
Great & Little Plumstead NR13 ... 73 B6
Little Plumstead NR13 ... 165 A8
Norwich NR5 ... 160 F8
Astor Ct IP27 ... 175 D4
Atbara Terr PE30 ... 146 E2
Atcherley Sq PE31 ... 30 B3
Atkinson Cl NR5 ... 160 E8
Atling Cl NR17 ... 174 F6
Atling Way NR17 ... 174 F6
Atmere Cl 2 NR4 ... 161 F1
Attelsey Way NR5 ... 160 E8
Atthill Rd NR2 ... 162 A7
Attleborough High Sch NR17 ... 174 D6
Attleborough Inf Sch NR17 ... 174 D6
Attleborough Jun Sch NR17 ... 174 E6
Attleborough Rd
Attleborough NR17 ... 174 A7
Caston NR17 ... 102 F8
Deopham NR18 ... 86 E1
Great Ellingham NR17 ... 103 F8
Little Ellingham NR17 ... 86 A2
Morley NR18 ... 87 A1
Attleborough Sta NR17 ... 174 E5
Attlee Way 4 NR19 ... 154 C6
Audax Rd NR6 ... 158 C6
Audley Ct PE34 ... 176 C7
Audley End IP21 ... 120 F1
Audley St NR30 ... 169 D5
Augusta St NR26 ... 138 D7
Augustus Hare Dr 1 NR4 ... 161 C5
Aurania Ave NR1 ... 162 D3
Auster Cl NR6 ... 158 C4
Austin Fields PE30 ... 146 E5
Austin Fields Ind Est PE30 ... 146 E5
Austin Rd NR31 ... 169 B3
Austin St
Hunstanton PE36 ... 132 C5
King's Lynn PE30 ... 146 D5
Autumn Cl IP24 ... 176 E4
Autumn Dr NR5 ... 161 B8
Avenue The NR23 ... 5 A2
Avebury Rd NR4 ... 162 B1
Aveling Way 6 NR33 ... 111 F1
Avenue Cl PE38 ... 79 E1
Avenue Fst & Mid Schs NR2 ... 162 B5
Avenue Rd
Great Yarmouth NR31 ... 170 D6
High Kelling NR25 ... 8 E2
Hunstanton PE36 ... 132 C4
King's Lynn PE30 ... 146 F4
North Walsham NR28 ... 151 C4
Norwich NR2 ... 162 B5
Wymondham NR18 ... 173 C3
Avenue S NR26 ... 138 E7
Avenue The
Brome & Oakley IP23 ... 130 D3
Brookville IP26 ... 99 A7
Brumstead NR12 ... 24 A1
Dersingham PE35 ... 140 E1
Hemsby NR29 ... 167 A7
Holkham NR23 ... 5 A4
Horning NR12 ... 55 E4
4 Necton PE37 ... 65 F4
Northrepps NR27 ... 139 D3
Sheringham NR26 ... 138 E7
Snettisham PE31 ... 12 D4
Wiggenhall St Germans PE34 ... 61 A8
Wroxham/Hoveton NR12 ... 164 B4
Wymondham NR18 ... 87 D7
Avenues The
Langley with Hardley NR14 ... 91 F4
Norwich NR4 ... 161 E4
Thurton NR14 ... 91 D3
Avian Way NR7 ... 159 C2
Avocet House Sch NR14 ... 92 C1
Avon Rd PE30 ... 148 C2
Avondale Cl NR13 ... 74 A2
Avondale Rd NR31 ... 170 D3
Avonmouth Rd 2 NR3 ... 158 C1
Aylesbury Cl NR3 ... 158 D2
Aylmer Dr PE34 ... 60 C8
Aylsham Cres NR3 ... 158 C3

Aylsham High Sch
  NR11 . . . . .150 D7
Aylsham Ind Est NR11 .150 E8
Aylsham Rd
  Burgh & Tuttington NR11 . .36 E6
  Cawston NR10 . . . . .35 B2
  Felmingham NR28 . . . . . . .37 A8
  North Walsham NR28 . . . . .22 C1
  Norwich NR3 . . . . .158 C1
  Oulton NR11 . . . . .35 E6
  Swanton Abbott NR10 . . . . .37 C4
Aylsham Rd Bsns Pk
  NR6 . . . . .158 C2
Aylsham Sta NR11 . . . . . .150 D5
Ayre Way PE30 . . . . .147 D8
Ayton Rd NR18 . . . . .173 D3
Ayton Rd Ind Est
  NR18 . . . . .173 D3

B

Babingley Cl 5 PE33 . . . .61 D6
Bachelor's La NR28 . . . . .23 E2
Back Chapel La NR31 . . .170 D6
Back Dro Upwell PE14 . . . .77 D4
  Welney PE14 . . . . .95 D4
Back Hills IP22 . . . . .128 E3
Back La Barford NR9 . . . . .69 F2
  Beeston with Bittering
    PE32 . . . . .48 C2
  Bircham PE31 . . . . .14 B3
  Blakeney NR25 . . . . .7 C7
  Burgh Castle NR31 . . . . . .94 A8
  Burnham Market PE31 . . . .135 D2
  Burnham Thorpe PE31 . . . . .4 D4
  Buxton with Lammas
    NR10 . . . . .53 E8
  Castle Acre PE32 . . . . . . .46 F2
  Catfield NR29 . . . . .56 C8
  Cawston NR10 . . . . .35 B2
  Dereham NR20 . . . . .68 A8
  Diss IP22 . . . . .120 D3
  East Rudham PE31 . . . . . .30 B7
  East Ruston NR12 . . . . . . .24 A3
  Elsing NR20 . . . . .50 F3
  Happisburgh NR12 . . . . . .23 F2
  Hempstead NR25 . . . . . . .19 E7
  Hethersett NR9 . . . . .88 E8
  Kenninghall NR16 . . . . . .119 A5
  Litcham PE32 . . . . .48 A4
  Lound NR32 . . . . .94 C2
  Lyng NR9 . . . . .51 A4
  Marthan NR29 . . . . .57 D5
  Mattishall NR20 . . . . .68 E6
  Mileham PE32 . . . . .48 C6
  North Elmham NR20 . . . . . .49 E7
  Outwell PE14 . . . . .77 E2
  Potter Heigham NR29 . . . . .56 E7
  Quidenham NR16 . . . . . . .119 A8
  Rackheath NR13 . . . . .54 D1
  Ringland NR8 . . . . .52 C1
  Rollesby NR29 . . . . .57 D3
  Roughton NR11 . . . . .21 D8
  Roydon PE32 . . . . .28 A1
  St Mary, South Elmham
    otherwise Homersfield
    IP20 . . . . .123 B4
  Scole IP21 . . . . .121 A1
  Scoulton NR9 . . . . .85 E3
  South Creake NR21 . . . . . .15 E6
  Stanfield NR20 . . . . .48 F8
  Upton with Fishley NR13 . .166 C8
  Walsingham NR22 . . . . . . .16 F7
  Wereham PE33 . . . . .80 E4
  West Beckham NR25 . . . . . .9 B3
  West Caister NR30 . . . . . .168 A4
  West Winch PE33 . . . . . . .43 E2
  Wymondham NR18 . . . . . .173 C4
Back Mkt La NR29 . . . . .167 B7
Back Mundesley Rd
  NR11 . . . . .22 F8
Back of the Inns NR1 . . .178 B2
Back Path 1 NR29 . . . . . .58 B6
Back Pier Plain NR31 . . .170 D4
Back Rd Brockdish IP21 . .131 B8
  East Ruston NR12 . . . . . . .38 F6
  Elm PE14 . . . . .77 A8
  Pentney PE32 . . . . .63 C8
  Somerton NR29 . . . . .57 F6
  Wisbech PE14 . . . . .77 A7
  Wood Dalling NR11 . . . . . .34 D6
  Yelverton NR14 . . . . .90 F5
Back St Binham NR21 . . . . .6 E2
  Fakenham NR21 . . . . . . .141 B3
  Garboldisham IP22 . . . . . .128 A8
  Gayton PE32 . . . . .45 C5
  Harpley PE31 . . . . .29 D5
  Horsham St Faith NR10 . . . .53 D1
  Lakenheath IP27 . . . . . . .113 E1
  Litcham PE32 . . . . .48 A4
  Mundesley NR11 . . . . . . .143 C5
  Reepham NR10 . . . . .149 B4
  South Creake NR21 . . . . . .15 D6
  Tittleshall PE32 . . . . .48 B7
  Trunch NR28 . . . . .22 E5
Back Terr PE37 . . . . .153 B6
Backwood La
  Howe NR15 . . . . .90 C2
  Shotesham NR15 . . . . . . .107 F8
Bacon Rd NR4 . . . . .161 F5
Baconsthorpe Castle★
  NR25 . . . . .9 A1
Bacton Cl PE30 . . . . . . .148 D3
Bacton Rd Bacton NR12 . .23 D5
  North Walsham NR28 . . . . .151 D6
  Norwich NR3 . . . . .158 B2
  Paston NR28 . . . . .143 E2

Bacton Rd continued
  Witton NR28 . . . . .23 C1
Bacton-on-Sea Fst Sch
  NR12 . . . . .23 E4
Bader Cl 7 PE30 . . . . . .147 D4
Badger Cl NR14 . . . . .89 A2
Badgers Brook Rd
  NR8 . . . . .155 F2
Bagge Rd PE30 . . . . . . .147 A5
Bagthorpe Rd PE31 . . . . .30 A7
Bailey Cl
  4 Hethersett NR9 . . . . . .88 D7
  6 Marthan NR29 . . . . . . .57 D5
Bailey La PE34 . . . . . . .145 E7
Bailey Rd NR27 . . . . . . .139 E5
Bailey St PE32 . . . . .46 F2
Bailiwick The 3 NR16 . . .118 C5
Baillie Cl 3 NR31 . . . . . .170 B1
Bainard Rise NR15 . . . . .107 C6
Bainards Rd NR3 . . . . . .173 B6
Baines Rd 4 PE30 . . . . . .146 D1
Baines Way 2 NR5 . . . . . .160 E8
Baird Way IP24 . . . . . . .176 C7

Baker Cl
  King's Lynn PE30 . . . . . . .146 D1
  North Walsham NR28 . . . . .151 D3
Baker La 3 PE30 . . . . . .146 D4
Baker St
  Great Yarmouth NR31 . . . . .170 D5
  14 Stalham NR12 . . . . . . .39 B4
Baker's Rd PE13 . . . . . . .75 A1
Bakers La NR35 . . . . . . .109 A3
Bakers Rd NR3 . . . . .162 D8
Bakers Yd NR23 . . . . . . .136 C6
Bakery Cl NR24 . . . . . . .142 E3
Bakery La NR9 . . . . .51 A5
Balderston Ct NR3 . . . . .178 B4
Baldock Cl 1 NR16 . . . . .105 F5
Baldock Dr PE30 . . . . . .147 B8
Baldric Rd NR8 . . . . . . .155 C1
Baldwin Cl 5 PE13 . . . . .152 D5
Baldwin Rd PE30 . . . . . .147 C6
Baldwins Cl NR24 . . . . . .142 D4
Baldwins Dro 4 PE14 . . . .77 F6
Bale Rd Brinton NR24 . . . .18 C7
  Hindringham NR21 . . . . . .17 E7
Balfour 4 NR27 . . . . .10 A5
Balfour St 4 NR3 . . . . . .162 F8
Baliol Rd NR31 . . . . . . .170 C5
Ball's La NR21 . . . . .17 A5
Ballygate NR34 . . . . . . .110 C1
Balmoral Ave NR30 . . . .169 D7
Balmoral Cl
  Attleborough NR17 . . . . . .174 F6
  Dersingham PE31 . . . . . . .140 D3
Balmoral Cres PE31 . . . .133 C5
Balmoral Rd PE30 . . . . . .147 C7
Balmoral W PE31 . . . . . .140 D3
Bambers La PE14 . . . . . . .59 C2
Bancroft Cl 7 NR14 . . . . .89 F4
Banham Barn Craft★
  NR16 . . . . .119 C6
Banham Dr NR29 . . . . . . .50 B2
Banham Prim Sch
  NR16 . . . . .119 D6
Banham Rd NR16 . . . . . .119 D5
Banham Zoo★ NR16 . . . .119 C6
Banham's La NR35 . . . . .108 B2
Banister Way NR18 . . . . .173 A5
Bank Dr PE13 . . . . .152 A7
Bank Loke 6 NR28 . . . . .151 C5
Bank Plain NR3 . . . . . . .178 B3
Bank Rd PE31 . . . . .140 C4
Bank Side PE34 . . . . . . .146 C5
Bank St Norwich NR2 . . .178 B3
  Pulham Market IP21 . . . . .121 E5
Bankside PE31 . . . . .133 B6
Banning Ct NR28 . . . . . .151 A4
Banningham Rd NR11 . . .150 D8
Bannister Cl NR17 . . . . .174 C6
Bannister's Row PE13 . . .152 B7
Banters La NR34 . . . . . .124 F6
Banting Cl NR31 . . . . . .170 C1
Banyard Cl PE13 . . . . . .154 E5
Banyard Pl 6 NR19 . . . . .154 D4
Banyards Pl PE33 . . . . . . .61 D4
Baptist Rd PE14 . . . . . . .77 D4
Bar Dro PE14 . . . . .77 B8
Barber's La
  Bedingham NR35 . . . . . . .108 B2
  Fakenham NR21 . . . . . . .141 E4
Barberry Cl 5 NR8 . . . . .155 B2
Barbers Yd 1 NR17 . . . . .104 D2
Barchams Yd 16 NR26 . . .138 D7
Barclay Gn NR7 . . . . . . .159 D1
Barclay Rd NR7 . . . . . . .159 E1
Bard Hill NR25 . . . . .8 B6
Bardolph Pl PE34 . . . . . . .61 D1
Bardolph's Way PE33 . . . .62 C6
Bardolphs Ct 1 NR8 . . . .155 B2
Bardwell Rd
  Barningham IP31 . . . . . . .127 C3
  Fakenham Magna IP24 . . . .126 D3
  Stanton IP31 . . . . .127 B1
Bardyke Bank PE14 . . . . .77 F4
Barford Cty Prim Sch
  NR9 . . . . .69 F2
Barford Rd
  Marlingford NR9 . . . . .69 E3
  Sheringham NR26 . . . . . . .138 D7
  Topcroft NR35 . . . . .107 E2
Bargate Ct NR3 . . . . . . .178 B4
Barham Ct NR31 . . . . . . .170 D5
Barham's La NR16 . . . . . .105 D4
Barker St NR2 . . . . .162 C8
Barker Way 5 NR13 . . . . .72 D6
Barker's Dro PE33 . . . . . .81 A3

Barker's La
  Norwich NR7 . . . . .159 A5
  Old Buckenham NR17 . . . . .104 B2
Barkers Herne NR27 . . . .139 A6
Barkis Rd NR30 . . . . . . .169 D1
Barley Way
  Attleborough NR17 . . . . . .174 B3
  Thetford IP24 . . . . .176 B6
Barleycroft NR29 . . . . . .167 B7
Barleyfield Rd 8 NR10 . . . .53 A3
Barn Cl
  1 Hopton on Sea NR31 . . .171 C5
  1 Lingwood NR13 . . . . . .74 A3
Barn Hill NR11 . . . . .73 E2
Barn La
  Gressenhall NR19 . . . . . . .49 B2
  Mautby NR29 . . . . .75 E6
Barn Mdw NR14 . . . . . . .163 B2
Barn Rd Docking PE31 . . .134 F4
  Norwich NR2 . . . . .178 A4
Barn Terr NR15 . . . . . . .165 C4
Barnaby Cl 5 NR19 . . . . .154 C3
Barnard Ave NR30 . . . . .169 D7
Barnard Cl
  Great Yarmouth NR31 . . . . .170 C1
  5 Stoke Holy Cross NR14 . .89 F4
Barnard Cres NR17 . . . . .169 C7
Barnard Rd NR5 . . . . . . .160 E8
Barnards La PE33 . . . . . . .61 D6
Barnards Rd NR28 . . . . . .38 A5
Barnards Yd 8 NR3 . . . . .178 A3
Barnby Rd NR10 . . . . . . .37 B2
Barnes Cl
  Brandon IP27 . . . . .175 A2
  Norwich NR7 . . . . .159 D2
Barnes' Rd IP21 . . . . . . .121 E5
Barnesdale Rd 5 NR4 . . . .89 E8
Barney Rd 17 F2
Barnfield Cl NR12 . . . . . . .39 E2
Barnham Broom Prim Sch
  NR9 . . . . .69 C2
Barnham Broom Rd
  East Tuddenham NR20 . . . . .69 D5
  Wymondham NR18 . . . . . .173 A7
Barnham CE Prim Sch
  IP24 . . . . .125 E5
Barnham Rd IP24 . . . . . .126 B6
Barningham CE VC Prim Sch
  IP31 . . . . .127 C3
Barningham Pl NR11 . . . . .20 C5
Barningham Rd
  Gresham NR11 . . . . .20 D8
  Stanton IP31 . . . . .127 C1
Barns The NR16 . . . . . . .105 C4
Barnwell Rd PE30 . . . . . .147 B6
Baron's Cl NR21 . . . . . . .141 C4
Baron's Hall La NR21 . . .141 D4
Barondole La
  Alburgh IP20 . . . . .122 E8
  Topcroft NR35 . . . . .107 E2
Barr Dr IP27 . . . . .113 E2
Barrack Rd
  Great Yarmouth NR30 . . . . .169 D1
  Norwich NR1 . . . . .163 B7
Barrack St NR3 . . . . . . .178 C4
Barrett Cl PE30 . . . . . . .147 E5
Barrett Rd Holt NR25 . . . .137 D7
  Norwich NR1 . . . . .162 E1
Barrett-Lennard Rd
  NR10 . . . . .53 A4
Barri Cl NR14 . . . . .90 C3
Barrow Cl NR3 . . . . .157 F1
Barrow's Cnr IP24 . . . . .125 A4
Barroway Dro PE38 . . . . .78 E6
Barrows Hole La PE32 . . . .65 E7
Barsham Rd PE30 . . . . . .148 E1
Barsham Rd NR21 . . . . . .17 A5
Bartle Ct NR10 . . . . . . .149 C5
Barton Broad Nature
  Reserve★ NR12 . . . . . . .55 F7
Barton Cl
  North Walsham NR28 . . . . .151 A4
  Swaffham PE37 . . . . .153 C2
Barton Ct PE30 . . . . . . .147 D5
Barton Rd
  Ashmanhaugh NR12 . . . . . .38 D1
  Coltishall NR10 . . . . .37 B2
  Wisbech PE13 . . . . .152 A4
Barton Way
  6 Norwich NR1 . . . . . . .163 B5
  Ormesby St Margaret
    NR29 . . . . .167 B3
Barton's La PE32 . . . . . . .48 A8
Barwick Rd NR23 . . . . . . .14 E6
Bases La NR23 . . . . .136 C6
Basey Rd NR13 . . . . .72 E8
Basham St IP22 . . . . . . .177 B4
Basil Dr PE38 . . . . .172 E6
Basil Rd PE33 . . . . .80 A3
Bassingham Rd NR19 . . .158 B2
Batchcroft Cl 6 PE38 . . . .172 C6
Batchelor Dr NR21 . . . . . .15 C2
Bately Ave 5 NR31 . . . . .170 D1
Bateman Cl 3 NR5 . . . . .160 F7
Bates Cl NR5 . . . . .161 C8
Bates La IP22 . . . . .119 D2
Bates's Dro CB6 . . . . .95 D1
Bath Ave NR20 . . . . . . .154 F5
Bath Hill 7 NR30 . . . . . .169 D3
Bath Hill Terr NR30 . . . .169 D3
Bath Hills Rd NR35 . . . . .123 E8
Bath Rd
  West Dereham PE33 . . . . . .80 D5
  Wisbech PE13 . . . . .152 C7
Bathurst Rd 2 NR2 . . . . .162 B5
Battery Gn
  Fakenham NR21 . . . . . . .141 A3
  Hempton NR21 . . . . .31 C8

Battery Rd NR30 . . . . . .170 D8
Battlesea Hill IP21 . . . . .131 D8
Bawburgh Cl NR5 . . . . . .156 C1
Bawburgh La NR5 . . . . . .156 D1
Bawburgh Prim Sch
  NR9 . . . . .160 B6
Bawburgh Rd NR9 . . . . . .70 B5
Bawdeswell Prim Sch
  NR20 . . . . .50 E7
Bawdeswell Rd 1 NR20 . . .50 C7
Bawsey Ctry Pk★ PE32 . .44 D6
Baxter Cl 2 Hingham NR9 . .86 C5
  3 Wisbech PE13 . . . . . .152 E6
Baxter Ct NR3 . . . . .158 B3
Baxter Rd NR9 . . . . .86 C5
Baxter Row NR14 . . . . . .154 D4
Baxter's La NR16 . . . . . .106 C6
Baxter's La NR15 . . . . . .107 F8
Bayes La NR16 . . . . .106 C6
Bayfield NR17 . . . . .174 E6
Bayfield Ave 3 NR19 . . . .154 C3
Bayfield Cl
  1 Ixworth NR9 . . . . . . .69 F2
  King's Lynn PE30 . . . . . . .147 D4
Baynard's La IP22 . . . . . .129 D7
Bayse's La 18 C5
Bayspole Rd 5 NR15 . . . .106 E3
Beach Cl Hemsby NR29 . . .167 E3
  Mundesley NR11 . . . . . . .143 C6
  Overstrand NR27 . . . . .11 A4
Beach Dr NR29 . . . . .167 E4
Beach La NR25 . . . . .8 E6
Beach Rd Bacton NR12 . . . .23 E5
  Caister-on-Sea NR30 . . . . .168 E5
  Cley next the Sea NR25 . . . .7 F4
  Cromer NR27 . . . . .139 B7
  3 Great Yarmouth NR31 . . .170 D4
  Happisburgh NR12 . . . . . .24 C5
  Hemsby NR29 . . . . .167 C7
  Holme next the Sea PE36 . . .1 F6
  Hopton on Sea NR31 . . . . .171 E4
  Lessingham NR12 . . . . . . .24 E3
  Mundesley NR11 . . . . . . .143 C6
  Runton NR27 . . . . .10 C5
  Salthouse NR25 . . . . .8 C6
  Sea Palling NR12 . . . . . . .40 A6
  Sheringham NR26 . . . . . . .138 E7
  Snettisham PE31 . . . . .12 A4
  Wells-next-the-Sea
    NR23 . . . . .136 C7
  Winterton-on-Sea NR29 . . . .58 B6
Beach Terr Rd PE36 . . . .132 C4
Beachamwell Rd
  PE13 . . . . .153 A3
Beacon Hill PE31 . . . . . .135 C2
Beacon Hill La PE34 . . . .144 A6
Beacon Hill Rd PE31 . . . .135 C1
Beacon Rd NR11 . . . . . . .11 F1
Beaconsfield Rd
  Great Yarmouth NR30 . . . . .169 D6
  Norwich NR3 . . . . .162 E8
Bear's Cl PE37 . . . . .153 B5
Bears Cl 7 NR9 . . . . .86 C4
Bears La NR9 . . . . .86 C5
Bears Rd NR28 . . . . .143 D2
Beatrice Ave NR19 . . . . .154 D4
Beatrice Cl 6 NR28 . . . . .151 C6
Beatrice Rd
  Norwich NR1 . . . . .163 A6
  Wisbech PE13 . . . . .152 D7
Beatty Cl
  Great Yarmouth NR30 . . . . .169 D8
  Thetford IP24 . . . . .176 E5
Beatty Rd
  Great Yarmouth NR30 . . . . .169 D8
  Norwich NR4 . . . . .162 B1
Beauchamp Cl
  1 Caister-on-Sea NR30 . . .168 D7
  Chedgrave NR14 . . . . .92 A2
Beauchamp Rd 2 NR14 . . .92 A2
Beaufort Cl NR1 . . . . . . .158 D6
Beaufort Way
  Great Yarmouth NR30 . . . . .170 B1
  Hopton on Sea NR31 . . . . .171 B8
Beaumont Pl 1 NR2 . . . .162 C4
Beaumont Rd NR5 . . . . . .157 B1
Beaumont Way PE30 . . . .147 C5
Beaupre Ave PE14 . . . . . .77 F7
Beavans Ct 8 NR31 . . . . .169 B4
Beavens Ct 15 NR31 . . . .169 B4
Beavor La IP27 . . . . .175 C4
Beccles Mus★ NR34 . . . .110 C1
Beccles Rd
  Aldeby NR34 . . . . .110 F4
  Aldeby, Wheatacre,
    Burgh St Peter NR34 . . .111 B4
  Belton with Browston
    NR31 . . . . .94 A5
  Bungay NR35 . . . . .124 B8
  Carlton Colville NR33 . . . . .111 F1
  Fritton & St Olaves NR31 . . .93 E3
  Great Yarmouth NR31 . . . . .170 A5
  Haddiscoe NR14 . . . . . . .110 E7
  Hales NR14 . . . . .109 E7
  Loddon NR14 . . . . .92 A1
  Raveningham NR14 . . . . . .110 A7
  Thurlton NR14 . . . . .92 F1
Beccles Sta NR34 . . . . . .110 D1
Becclesgate NR19 . . . . . .154 D6
Beck Ave NR29 . . . . .167 A4
Beck Cl 5 NR25 . . . . .8 F5
Beck La
  Burgh & Tuttington NR11 . . .36 E6
  Horsham St Faith &
    Newton St Faith NR10 . . .53 D2
Beck St IP27 . . . . .127 E3
Beck The Feltwell IP26 . . . .98 E1

Ayl - Bel 183

Beck The continued
  Kenninghall NR16 . . . . . . .119 A5
Beck View 3 IP20 . . . . . .122 D2
Beck Way NR14 . . . . .91 F1
Becketswell Rd NR18 . . . .173 B3
Beckett Cl 6 PE30 . . . . . .148 C4
Becketts Ct NR18 . . . . . .173 B6
Beckmeadow Way
  NR11 . . . . .143 C5
Becks Fur 2 NR8 . . . . . .155 C4
Becks Gn La NR34 . . . . . .124 F4
Beckside 53 A2
Bedding La NR3 . . . . . . .178 A3
Bede Cl PE30 . . . . .148 C4
Bedford Dr PE30 . . . . . .148 B1
Bedford Mews NR26 . . . .138 D6
Bedford Row PE14 . . . . . .41 A4
Bedford St
  Norwich NR2 . . . . .178 B3
  Wisbech PE13 . . . . .152 C6
Bedingfield Rd 6 NR20 . . .50 B3
Beech Ave
  Attleborough NR17 . . . . . .174 C4
  King's Lynn PE30 . . . . . . .148 D2
  7 Marham PE33 . . . . . . .63 B4
  Sheringham NR26 . . . . . . .138 D5
  Taverham NR8 . . . . .155 B1
Beech Cl 1 Gresham NR11 . .9 E1
  High Kelling NR25 . . . . . . .8 E2
  6 Loddon NR14 . . . . . . .92 A1
  Scole IP21 . . . . .130 C3
  Swaffham PE37 . . . . .153 C4
  Thetford IP24 . . . . .176 B2
  Wymondham NR18 . . . . . .173 D6
Beech Cres 6 PE33 . . . . . .43 E2
Beech Ct
  24 Long Stratton NR15 . . .106 E3
  Swaffham PE13 . . . . .154 D5
Beech Dr
  East Dereham NR19 . . . . . .154 E1
  North Walsham NR28 . . . . .151 B6
  Norwich NR6 . . . . .158 C4
  Norwich NR2 . . . . .162 B4
  Norwich NR1 . . . . .163 A8
  Strumpshaw NR13 . . . . . . .73 F3
Beech Drift PE31 . . . . . .140 D3
Beech La NR29 . . . . .75 C8
Beech Rd Beetley NR20 . . .49 D4
  Downham Market PE38 . . . .172 B6
  King's Lynn PE30 . . . . . . .146 E3
  Wroxham/Hoveton
    NR12 . . . . .164 D3
Beech Rise 23 NR31 . . . .94 C7
Beech Way
  Brundall NR13 . . . . .165 C3
  Dickleburgh IP21 . . . . . . .121 C1
Beech Wlk NR14 . . . . . . .90 D5
Beechamwell Rd PE33 . . . .81 B8
Beechbank NR2 . . . . . . .162 B4
Beechbank Dr 6 NR13 . . .72 D6
Beechcroft NR5 . . . . . . .156 F1
Beecheno Rd NR5 . . . . . .161 C8
Beeches Cl NR6 . . . . . . .158 E4
Beeches The 1 NR20 . . . .68 E6
Beechey Cl PE38 . . . . . .172 C2
Beechfields IP27 . . . . . . .175 F4
Beeching Cl 1 NR1 . . . . .162 E1
Beeching Rd NR1 . . . . . .162 E2
Beechlands NR8 . . . . . . .155 B1
Beechlands Pk NR11 . . . . .22 B7
Beechwood Ave
  Aylmerton NR11 . . . . .10 A3
  18 Watton IP25 . . . . .84 D3
Beechwood Cl
  North Walsham NR28 . . . . .151 D6
  Watlington PE33 . . . . .61 E5
Beechwood Ct NR18 . . . .173 C1
Beechwood Dr NR7 . . . . .159 E1
Beechwood Rd
  Hemsby NR29 . . . . .167 A8
  Wisbech PE13 . . . . .152 D7
Beechwoods NR6 . . . . . .158 D5
Beehive Yd PE32 . . . . . .177 C4
Beeleigh Way NR30 . . . .168 C2
Bee-Orchid Way NR14 . . .91 C7
Beerlick's Loke NR14 . . . .73 B1
Beeston Comm NR26 . . .138 E6
Beeston Hall Sch NR27 . . .9 F5
Beeston La
  Barton Turf NR12 . . . . . . .38 D1
  Beeston St Andrew
    NR12 . . . . .159 B8
  Fransham NR19 . . . . .66 B8
Beeston Prim Sch
  PE32 . . . . .48 C2
Beeston Rd
  Beeston with Bittering
    PE32 . . . . .48 D1
  Great Dunham PE32 . . . . . .66 A8
  Mileham PE32 . . . . .48 D5
  Sheringham NR26 . . . . . . .138 E7
Beetley Grange 1 NR20 . . .49 D4
Beetley Mdws 9 NR20 . . .49 D4
Beevor Rd NR30 . . . . . . .170 E2
Begdale Rd PE14 . . . . . . .59 A1
Beighton Rd NR13 . . . . .166 A2
Bek Cl NR4 . . . . .161 E2
Belaugh Gn La NR12 . . . .164 A8
Belaugh La NR12 . . . . . . .55 A7
Belaugh Rd NR12 . . . . . .164 C6
Belgrave Gdns NR19 . . . .154 E3
Bell Cl
  13 Bawdeswell NR20 . . . . .50 E7

Bell Cl continued
East Dereham NR19 ......154 C5
Little Snoring NR21 ....17 B3
Norwich NR6 ....157 F6
Taverham NR8 ....156 E8
Bell La Rocklands NR17 ..103 B8
Saham Toney IP25 ....84 C4
Salhouse NR13 ....164 B1
Bell Mdw 1 Hingham NR9 86 C5
9 Martham NR29 ....57 C5
Bell Rd
Barnham Broom NR9 ......69 B2
Grimston PE32 ....28 C1
Norwich NR3 ....158 E1
Rocklands NR17 ....103 B8
Bell St IP26 ....98 E1
Bellacre Cl IP22 ....177 E4
Bellamy Way NR14 ....90 C4
Bellamy's La
Burnham Norton PE31 ....135 C5
West Walton PE14 ....59 A8
Bellands Way 4 IP23 ..130 C1
Bell's Dro Littleport CB6 ..95 E2
Runcton Holme PE33 ......61 C5
Bell's Marsh Rd NR31 ..170 D5
Bell's Rd 2 PE37 ....66 A4
Bellmere Way IP25 ....84 C4
Bellomonte Cres NR8 ..156 F8
Bellrope Cl 5 NR18 ....173 D5
Bellrope La
Roydon IP22 ....129 D7
Wymondham NR18 ....173 D5
Bells La IP22 ....128 C4
Bells Rd NR31 ....170 D4
Bellview Cl NR24 ....142 B4
Bellville Cres NR1 ......178 C1
Belmore Cl NR7 ....159 E1
Belmore Rd NR7 ....163 F8
Beloe Ave 4 NR5 ....161 A7
Beloe Cres PE30 ....158 A2
Belseybridge Rd NR35 ..108 F3
Belsize Cl 4 PE38 ......172 B4
Belsize Rd NR1 ....163 B7
Belstead Rd NR30 ......168 D5
Belt Rd NR13 ....73 C7
Belvedere Pl 3 NR4 .....162 A3
Belvidere Rd NR30 ......169 D5
Belvoir St NR2 ....162 B6
Ben Culey Dr IP24 ......176 C5
Ben's La PE33 ....80 E4
Benbow Cl 6 NR9 ....88 E8
Benbow Rd NR31 ....176 F6
Bendish Ave NR31 ......170 D2
Bendish Way NR5 ....160 E7
Benedict Cl PE34 ....145 F5
Benedict Rd 10 NR12 ....55 E4
Benets View 3 NR28 ....151 E5
Bengey's Rd 7 PE37 .....65 F4
Benjamin Ct NR27 ......139 B5
Benn's La PE34 ....144 C5
Bennett Cl
Hunstanton PE36 ....132 D2
3 Watlington PE33 ....61 D5
Bennett Rd NR20 ....50 B2
Bennett St NR3 ....172 A5
Bennington's La
Aylmerton NR11 ....138 F1
East Beckham NR11 ....9 D2
Bensley Rd NR13 ....166 C4
Bensley Rd
1 Martham NR29 ....57 D5
Norwich NR4 ....162 A4
Bentinck Way 2 PE34 ..146 C5
Bentley Rd NR16 ....105 F4
Bentley Way NR3 ......158 C4
Bentons Way NR10 ......53 B8
Ber St NR1 ....178 B1
Berberis Gn 3 NR31 ....170 B5
Beresford Rd
Caister-on-Sea NR30 ....168 E4
Great Yarmouth NR30 ..169 D7
Holt NR25 ....137 C5
Bergamot Cl IP24 ......176 F4
Bergen Way PE30 ......146 F8
Bergh Apton Rd
Alpington NR14 ....90 F4
Mundham NR14 ....91 D1
Bermondsey Pl E 19
NR30 ....169 D4
Bermondsey Pl S 18
NR30 ....169 D4
Bermondsey Pl W 17
NR30 ....169 D4
Bernard Cl
High Kelling NR25 ....8 E2
11 New Rackheath NR13 ..72 E7
Bernard Cres PE36 .....132 D6
Bernard Rd
Cromer NR27 ....139 A7
Great Yarmouth NR30 ..170 D2
Berners Cl NR3 ....158 B1
Berners St NR3 ....158 B1
Berney Arms Sta NR30 ..93 D8
Berney Arms Windmill★
NR30 ....93 E7
Bernham Rd NR6 ....157 E6
Berrington Rd NR6 .....157 F6
Berry Cl NR31 ....93 F6
Berry Hall Rd NR12 .....38 E1
Berry's La NR5 ....69 D6
Berryfields NR13 ......165 C5
Bertie Rd NR3 ....158 C1
Bertie Ward Way
NR19 ....154 F2
Bessemer Rd NR4 ......162 D1

Bessemer Way NR31 ...169 B1
Besthorpe Carr NR17 ..105 A6
Besthorpe Rd NR17 ....174 E5
Bestthorpe Rd NR16 ...105 A5
Bethel St NR2 ....178 A3
Betjeman Cl IP24 ......176 E6
Beulah St PE30 ....147 B6
Bevan Cl
Carleton Rode NR16 ....105 C4
Norwich NR5 ....161 B6
Beveridge Way PE33 ....43 E4
Beverley Cl NR5 ....161 E6
Beverley Rd
Brundall NR13 ....165 B4
Norwich NR5 ....161 E6
Beverley Way
Clenchwarton PE34 .....145 E5
Taverham NR8 ....156 F8
Beverly Cl NR5 ....170 A7
Bevis Way PE30 ....147 B7
Bewfield Rd 4 NR5 ....160 E8
Bewick Cl
11 Great Yarmouth NR31 ..94 C8
5 Snettisham PE31 ....12 E5
Bewit Rd NR7 ....159 D4
Bexfield Rd NR20 ....33 C4
Bexwell Rd Bexwell PE38 79 F6
Downham Market PE38 ..172 D5
Bickley Cl NR17 ....174 F7
Bickley Cl NR8 ....157 B7
Bidewell Cl NR8 ....157 B7
Bidwell Rd NR13 ....72 E8
Bidwels ct IP24 ....176 C4
Bidwells PE12 ....128 F5
Big Back La 1 NR14 .....92 A2
Big Row NR34 ....109 F2
Big Yard PE36 ....2 A3
Big Yard The PE36 .....132 E7
Biggin Hill Way IP25 ....85 A3
Biggotts La NR15 ......108 E7
Biggs Rd PE14 ....59 D4
Bignold Fst Sch NR2 ...178 A2
Bignold Mid Sch NR2 ..178 A2
Bignold Rd NR5 ....158 A2
Bilberry Cl 5 NR17 ....174 B5
Bilbys NR14 ....110 B6
Bill Todd Way NR8 .....155 C2
Billing Cl NR6 ....158 F5
Billingford Rd
1 Bawdeswell NR20 ......50 E7
Bintree NR20 ....33 B1
Bilney La NR10 ....155 E8
Bilney Rd Beetley NR20 ..49 B4
East Winch PE32 ....45 B1
Pentney PE33 ....63 C8
Bingles Turn NR10 ......53 B7
Binham Rd
Field Dalling NR25 ....7 A1
Hindringham NR21 ......17 E8
4 King's Lynn PE30 .....148 C3
Langham NR25 ....7 A4
Warham NR23 ....6 A4
Bintree Rd NR20 ....50 B8
Binyon Gdns NR8 ......156 D8
Birbeck Rd NR1 ....162 E2
Birch Ave 8 NR20 ....49 D4
Birch Cl
East Dereham NR19 ....154 C4
Little Melton NR9 ....160 D2
North Walsham NR28 ...151 D6
6 Snettisham PE31 ....12 E4
Birch Covert 5 IP24 ...176 F5
Birch Ct Erpingham NR11 .21 B2
Norwich NR7 ....159 D4
Birch Dr
Attleborough NR17 .....174 C3
Roydon PE32 ....28 A2
Birch Gr
Sheringham NR26 ......138 D4
West Winch PE33 ....43 E2
Wisbech PE14 ....59 B1
Birch Rd Gayton PE32 ....45 C6
11 Hethersett NR9 ....88 D8
Birch Tree Cl PE30 ....146 E4
Birch Way
4 Great Yarmouth NR31 .170 B5
Mundham NR14 ....108 F6
Bircham Rd
Docking PE31 ....134 C4
Reepham NR10 ....149 C5
Snettisham PE31 ....13 A4
Stanhoe PE31 ....14 E7
Bircham Windmill★
PE31 ....14 A3
Birches The PE30 ......148 D4
Birchfield Gdns NR14 ..89 B3
Birchfield La NR14 ......89 B3
Birchfield Rd PE38 ......78 E3
Birchgrove Rd NR14 ...147 C4
Birchwood 4 NR7 ....72 D3
Birchwood St 5 PE30 ..146 E6
Birchwood Way PE38 ..172 B6
Bird View Sq 1 IP26 ....98 E1
Birdcage Wlk PE30 ....146 D3
Birds Cnr IP25 ....67 E4
Birds Rd NR28 ....151 B3
Birkbeck Cl
King's Lynn PE30 ....148 B2
Stoke Holy Cross NR14 ..90 B5
Birkbeck Way NR7 .....163 F7
Birkdale NR4 ....162 A2
Birkin Cl 3 NR16 ......105 F5
Birtles Way NR13 ......166 C3
Biscay Gdns NR30 .....168 C6
Bishop Bonner's Cottage
Mus★ NR19 ....154 D5
Bishop Bridge Rd
NR1 ....163 A6

Bishop Herbert Cl
NR20 ....69 B8
Bishop Rise 3 NR8 ....155 E2
Bishop's Cl NR7 ....163 D5
Bishop's Rd
Hunstanton PE36 ......132 C2
King's Lynn PE30 ......147 B4
Bishopgate NR1 ....178 C3
Bishops Wlk NR31 .....171 D5
Bishoptyne Ave 1 NR19 154 F3
Bishy Barnebee Way
NR5 ....160 F6
Bittering St
4 Beetley NR20 ....49 C4
4 Gressenhall NR20 ....49 C3
Bittern Cl Necton PE37 ..66 A3
Thetford IP24 ....176 D1
Bittern Cres NR12 ......38 F1
Bittern Rd NR29 ....57 D3
Bixley Cl NR5 ....161 D6
Black Bear La PE13 ....152 F7
Black Drif PE37 ....66 A4
Black Dro
Downham West PE38 ....79 B6
Feltwell PE38 ....97 F2
Fincham PE33 ....80 D7
Marshland St James
PE14 ....60 D4
Stow Bardolph PE34 .....78 E8
Black Dyke Rd IP26 ...113 E7
Black Horse La NR15 ...67 B7
Black Horse Dro CB6 ...96 C7
Black Horse Opening
NR6 ....158 F2
Black Horse Rd
Clenchwarton PE34 ....145 C4
Runhall NR9 ....68 F1
Black Mill La NR15 ....121 A7
Black Moor Rd IP25 ....67 D2
Black St Hemsby NR29 ..58 B6
Marthan NR29 ....57 D5
Blackbarn Rd NR16 ....120 D8
Blackberry Ct NR6 ....157 F2
Blackberry Gr NR27 ....10 C4
Blackberry Hall La
NR11 ....11 D1
Blackbird Ave PE37 ....175 F3
Blackbird Cl 17 NR31 ...94 C8
Blackburn Rd NR6 ....158 C6
Blackdale Mid Sch
NR4 ....161 D4
Blackdike Dro IP27 ....112 F5
Blackdyke Cl 8 IP26 ....98 D1
Blackford PE30 ....147 D8
Blackfriar's Rd NR30 ..169 D2
Blackfriars Rd
King's Lynn PE30 ......146 E5
8 Wisbech PE13 ....152 C5
Blackfriars St
King's Lynn PE30 ......146 D4
Norwich NR3 ....178 B4
Blackhills Cnr NR13 .....73 C7
Blackhorse Mdw 10
NR20 ....50 E7
Blackhorse St 1 NR2 ..162 C7
Blackhorse Yd NR23 ...136 C6
Blackmoor Row IP25 ....67 D1
Blacks Ave NR14 ......163 B2
Blackslough La NR16 ..119 D7
Blacksmith La IP24 ....125 E6
Blacksmith's La
Barton Bendish PE33 ....81 B8
Morning Thorpe NR15 ..107 A2
Blacksmith's Loke
NR32 ....94 C2
Blacksmith's Row 1
PE32 ....45 C6
Blacksmiths Cl NR20 ....33 B6
Blacksmiths La
Ashwellthorpe NR16 ....106 B8
Happisburgh NR12 ......24 B6
Hindringham NR21 ....17 E7
Blacksmiths Way NR8 .158 E5
Blackthorn Ave NR25 ..137 C7
Blackthorn Cl
Diss IP22 ....177 F5
Norwich NR6 ....158 D4
3 Thetford IP24 ....176 F4
Blackthorn Dr 3 NR19 ..154 C4
Blackthorn Rd
Attleborough NR17 .....174 B5
King's Lynn PE30 ....148 C3
Wymondham NR18 .....173 D4
Blackthorn Way 16 NR14 90 C5
Blackwall Reach
NR31 ....170 D5
Blackwater Cnr NR11 ...36 F5
Blackwater La
Great Witchingham NR9 .51 C6
Heydon NR11 ....34 D8
Blackwell Ave NR7 ....159 A3
Bladewater Rd NR5 ....160 F5
Blake Cl PE32 ....28 A1
Blake Ct PE13 ....153 C2
Blake Dr NR31 ....170 A4
Blake Rd NR30 ....169 D7
Blakeney CE Prim Sch
NR25 ....7 D6
Blakeney Cl NR4 ......161 E2
Blakeney Long La NR25 ..7 C4
Blakeney Point National
Nature Reserve★ NR25 ..7 C8
Blakeney Rd
Binham NR21 ....6 D1
Letheringsett with Glandford
NR25 ....7 F2
Morston NR25 ....7 B6

Blakeney Short La NR25 ..7 C3
Blakes Cl NR3 ....158 F3
Blakestone Dr NR7 ....163 D7
Bland Rd NR5 ....161 B6
Blatchford Way PE31 ..133 B5
Blencowe Terr 28 PE13 152 C5
Blenheim Ave 4 NR29 ...57 D4
Blenheim Cl
12 Long Stratton NR15 ..106 E3
Norwich NR7 ....159 B5
Blenheim Cres
Beeston with Bittering
PE32 ....48 D2
Griston IP25 ....85 A2
Norwich NR7 ....159 B5
Tittleshall PE32 ....48 A7
Blenheim Dr NR17 ....174 E4
Blenheim Pk Sch NR2 ..15 C3
Blenheim Rd
King's Lynn PE30 ......147 C8
Norwich NR7 ....159 B5
Sculthorpe Airfield NR21 .15 C3
Blenheim Way
Emneth PE14 ....152 E2
2 Roydon IP22 ....129 D7
5 Watton IP25 ....84 E3
Blick Cl 5 PE33 ....43 F2
Blickling Cl 1 PE30 ....148 F1
Blickling Hall★ NR11 ....35 F7
Blickling Rd
Blickling NR11 ....150 A8
Norwich NR6 ....158 C5
Bligh Cl NR14 ....90 D5
Blind Dick's La NR22 ...16 C7
Blind La
Castle Acre PE32 ....46 F1
Hockering NR9 ....51 A2
Honingham NR9 ....69 F5
Horsham St Faith NR10 ..53 D1
Mattishall NR20 ....69 A7
Blithe Mdw Ct NR7 ....159 C3
Blithemeadow Dr
NR7 ....159 C3
Blithewood Gdns NR7 .159 C3
Blo' Norton Rd IP22 ...128 C7
Blocka Rd NR32 ....93 F2
Blofield Cnr Rd NR13 ...73 B6
Blofield Loke NR12 ....164 E6
Blofield Prim Sch
NR13 ....165 E7
Blofield Rd
Brundall NR13 ....165 B3
Lingwood & Burlingham
NR13 ....73 F3
Blofields Loke NR11 ..150 C6
Blomefield Rd
Diss IP22 ....177 D4
Norwich NR3 ....158 B2
Bloodgate Hill NR21 ....15 D6
Bloodhills Rd NR29 .....57 F5
Bloodslat La NR12 .....23 D4
Bloomfield Rd NR30 ...170 E7
Blooms Turn NR28 ......22 E5
Bloomstile La NR25 .....8 B6
Bloomstiles NR25 ....8 B6
Blowlands La NR26 ....138 C5
Blue Boar La NR7 .....159 D3
Blue Doors Loke NR14 ..94 C3
Blue Sky Cl NR31 ....94 C8
Bluebell Cl
Attleborough NR17 .....174 B5
4 East Dereham NR19 ..154 C4
Thetford IP24 ....176 F4
Bluebell Cres NR4 ....161 D2
Bluebell Dr NR26 ......138 B6
Bluebell Gdns NR23 ..136 B6
Bluebell Rd
Mulbarton NR14 ....89 B3
North Walsham NR28 ...151 D6
Norwich NR4 ....161 D3
Bluebell Way 19 NR31 ...94 C6
Bluebell Wlk IP27 .....175 A2
Bluestone Cres NR21 ...15 D6
Bluestone La NR21 .....15 D6
Bluestone Rd NR21 .....15 D6
Blundeston Rd NR32 ..111 F8
Blundeville Manor 6
NR15 ....89 C1
Blunt's Cnr NR23 ....5 B2
Blyth Cres NR26 ......138 D6
Blyth Jex Sch The
NR3 ....158 E2
Blyth Rd NR3 ....158 D2
Boadicea Cl 1 IP24 ....176 D7
Boal Quay PE30 ....146 D4
Boal St PE30 ....146 D4
Boardman Cl NR6 .....158 D3
Boat Dyke La NR13 ....166 D4
Boat Dyke Rd NR13 ...166 B8
Boathouse La NR32 ....111 F3
Boatmans Row NR13 ..136 C6
Bob Carter Leisure Ctr
NR8 ....157 A8
Bodleian Ct NR31 .....170 B2
Boileau Ave 6 NR16 ...105 F5
Boileau Cl 1 NR4 ....89 E8
Boleness Rd PE13 .....152 C2
Bolingbroke Rd NR3 ..158 B3
Boltons The PE30 .....148 C1
Bolts Cl NR23 ....136 D6
Bond Cl IP21 ....121 F4
Bond St 3 Cromer NR27 139 B7
5 Hingham NR9 ....86 C5
Norwich NR2 ....162 A7
Bond's Rd NR15 ....121 C4
Bonds Rd NR13 ....73 C7
Bone Rd NR8 ....157 B8
Bone's Dro NR23 ....4 F7

Boniface Cl NR4 ......162 C1
Bonnetts La PE30 ....60 B5
Boosey's Wlk 6 NR16 ..104 F1
Boot Binders Rd 7
NR6 ....158 C1
Boot La IP22 ....120 D6
Booton Comm Nature
Reserve★ NR10 ....149 E5
Booton Rd NR10 ....35 B2
Booty Rd NR7 ....159 F1
Borage Cl IP24 ....176 F4
Border La NR32 ....94 B2
Border Rd PE33 ....81 A2
Borough Cl PE13 ......152 D3
Borrowdale Dr NR1 ....163 B8
Borton Rd 4 NR13 ......73 C6
Boscombe Rd IP25 .....85 A3
Bosgate Rise 8 NR29 ...57 C4
Boston Cl 4 NR19 .....154 C4
Boston End 6 IP24 ....116 A1
Boston Sq PE36 ....132 C5
Boston Sq Sensory Pk
PE36 ....132 C5
Boston St NR3 ....158 D2
Botolph St NR3 ....178 A4
Boton Dr NR19 ....154 D7
Bottom Breck Cl NR5 ..156 F2
Botwright Dr 5 PE37 ..153 C3
Boudica's Way NR14 ..163 A1
Boughey Cl PE31 ....3 B6
Boughton Long Rd
PE33 ....81 B7
Boughton Rd
Fincham PE33 ....62 E1
Stoke Ferry PE33 ....81 A3
Boulderside Cl 4 NR7 ..163 E7
Boulevard Rd 2 NR27 ..10 A5
Boulevard The
Sheringham NR26 ......138 C7
Thorpe End NR13 ....72 E6
Boulters The NR31 ....170 C1
Boulton Rd NR7 ......163 C7
Boulton St NR1 ....178 B2
Boundary Ave NR6 ....158 A4
Boundary Cl IP26 .....113 C2
Boundary La
Norwich NR7 ....72 E3
Paston NR28 ....23 B3
Boundary Rd
Ashby with Oby NR29 ...56 E2
Great Yarmouth NR31 ..169 B1
1 Hockwold cum Wilton
IP26 ....114 A7
Marham PE33 ....63 C3
Norton Subcourse NR14 ..92 D1
Norwich NR6 ....157 F3
Raveningham NR14 ....110 B8
Boundary Way 1 NR14 ..90 C5
Bourne Cl
King's Lynn PE30 ......148 C2
Long Stratton NR15 ....106 E3
Bow Hill NR9 ....70 A3
Bow St NR9 ....86 B1
Bowers Ave NR3 ......158 A2
Bowers Cl NR3 ....158 A2
Bowlers Cl NR13 ....92 C4
Bowling Gn Cl
Attleborough NR17 .....174 D6
Crostwick NR12 ....54 B2
Bowling Gn The
Raynham NR21 ....30 F4
Wells-next-the-Sea
NR23 ....136 D5
Bowling Gn Wlk 2
NR30 ....169 C4
Bowman Rd 4 NR4 ......89 E8
Bowthorpe Hall Gdns★
PE13 ....152 D5
Bowthorpe Hall Rd
NR5 ....160 F7
Bowthorpe Rd
Norwich NR5 ....161 D6
Wisbech PE13 ....152 D5
Box's La PE37 ....153 D5
Boyces Rd PE13 ......152 E5
Boyd Ave 9 NR19 .....154 D1
Boylandhall La NR15 ..107 B4
Brabazon Rd NR6 .....158 B5
Bracecamp Cl NR29 ...167 C2
Braces La NR35 ....109 E3
Bracey Ave NR6 ......158 F5
Bracken Ave
3 Beetley NR20 ....49 D4
Norwich NR6 ....158 A4
Overstrand NR27 ....11 A3
Bracken Cl
Fakenham NR21 ....141 F4
Horsford NR10 ....53 B2
Stratton Strawless NR10 .53 A6
Bracken Dr NR17 ......174 B5
Bracken Rd
King's Lynn PE30 ......148 C2
Thetford IP24 ....176 C1
Bracken Rise
Brandon IP27 ....175 E3
Mundford IP26 ....100 A4
Bracken Way PE32 ......28 B1
Brackenwoods PE37 ....66 A4
Bracon Rd NR31 ....93 F5
Bracondale NR1 ....178 C1
Bracondale Ct 3 NR1 ..162 F3
Bracondale Gn NR1 ...178 C1
Bracondale Millgate
NR14 ....163 A2
Bradcar Rd NR17 ......103 B3
Braddock Rd NR30 ....168 E5
Bradenham Way NR4 ..162 A1

Bradenham Hall Gdn & Arboretum* IP25 ...66 E4
Bradenham La NR19 ...66 F6
Bradenham Rd IP25 ...67 A2
Bradfield Cl NR28 ...151 A6
Bradfield Pl 3 PE33 ...81 A3
Bradfield Rd
Antingham NR11 ...22 C5
North Walsham NR28 ...151 A6
Swafield NR28 ...22 C5
Bradman's La NR18 ...87 D3
Bradmere La PE31 ...134 E5
Bradshaw Rd NR8 ...157 C7
Bradwell Ave 3 NR31 ...170 A5
Brady Cl PE38 ...172 B1
Brady Gdns PE38 ...172 B1
Braeburn Ave PE13 ...152 C8
Braeford Cl NR28 ...157 E2
Brailsford Cl NR20 ...68 A7
Braithwait Cl 1 NR5 ...161 A8
Brake La NR16 ...16 C4
Bramble Ave NR6 ...158 A5
Bramble Cl
Mundesley NR11 ...143 D5
Sculthorpe Airfield NR21 ...15 C2
4 Taverham NR8 ...155 E2
Bramble Ct NR21 ...141 E4
Bramble Dr PE30 ...148 C2
Bramble Gdns NR31 ...93 F5
Bramble La
Outwell PE14 ...77 D7
Swaffham PE37 ...153 F5
Bramble Way
11 Poringland NR14 ...90 D5
Wymondham NR18 ...173 E4
Brambles Cl 2 NR10 ...54 A1
Bramerton La
Framingham Pigot NR14 ...90 E7
Rockland St Mary NR14 ...91 A7
Bramerton Rd NR14 ...91 A8
Bramfield Cl NR2 ...162 A7
Bramley Cl NR23 ...136 D6
Bramley Dr NR21 ...31 E5
Bramley Rd
Dereham NR20 ...68 A8
Diss IP22 ...177 C5
Wisbech PE13 ...152 C7
Brampton Cl PE13 ...152 A4
Brampton Ct 12 NR5 ...161 A7
Brampton Sta NR10 ...36 E3
Brancaster Cl
King's Lynn PE30 ...147 C8
1 Taverham NR8 ...155 F3
Brancaster Rd PE31 ...134 E7
Brancaster Way PE37 ...153 B2
Branch Rd NR13 ...75 B2
Brand's La
Felthorpe NR10 ...155 D6
Tharston & Hapton NR15 ...106 C5
Brandiston Rd NR10 ...35 B2
Brandon Cl
Norwich NR6 ...157 E4
3 Swaffham PE37 ...153 C3
Brandon Ct NR13 ...165 C3
Brandon Her Ctr* IP27 ...175 D4
Brandon Rd
Cockley Cley PE37 ...83 A4
Methwold IP26 ...99 B4
Saham Toney IP25 ...84 B3
Swaffham PE37 ...65 A1
Thetford IP24 ...176 A4
Wangford IP27 ...114 C1
Watton IP25 ...84 C3
Weeting-with-Broomhill IP27 ...175 C5
Brandon Sports Ctr IP27 ...175 B3
Brandon Sta IP27 ...175 C5
Brandon Terr NR30 ...169 C2
Brandvnvm (Roman Fort) (Branodunum)* PE31 ...3 C6
Branford Rd
Caister-on-Sea NR30 ...168 D7
Norwich NR3 ...158 E1
Branksome Cl NR4 ...162 B2
Branksome Rd NR4 ...162 A2
Branodunum PE31 ...3 B7
Bransby Rd PE30 ...146 F4
Brasenose Ave NR31 ...170 B3
Brasier Rd NR3 ...158 B2
Brawdy Rd 7 IP31 ...126 B1
Bray's La
Guestwick NR20 ...34 A6
Rocklands NR17 ...103 A7
Braydeston Ave NR13 ...165 D3
Braydeston Cres NR13 ...165 D3
Braydeston Dr NR13 ...165 F6
Braydeston Hall La NR13 ...73 E4
Brayfield Way NR6 ...158 F6
Braymeadow NR9 ...160 C2
Braymeadow La NR9 ...160 D2
Brazen Gate NR1 ...178 A1
Breck Farm Cl NR8 ...155 C2
Breck Farm La NR8 ...155 C2
Breck Rd Norwich NR7 ...159 E2
Weston Longville NR9 ...51 E1
Breckland Bsns Pk IP25 ...84 F3
Breckland Leisure Ctr & Waterworld IP24 ...176 D5
Breckland Mid Sch IP27 ...175 A2
Breckland Rd NR5 ...157 A1

Brecklands
Mundford IP26 ...100 B4
11 Stalham NR12 ...39 B4
Brecklands Rd NR13 ...165 E2
Brecon Rd NR15 ...90 E2
Breeze Ave NR11 ...150 B5
Brellows Hill PE34 ...144 A5
Brenda Collison Cl PE31 ...140 C4
Brenda James Cl 1 NR7 ...163 E7
Brennewater Mews 4 NR5 ...161 A8
Brent Ave 5 NR15 ...12 E5
Brentwood 1 NR4 ...161 F1
Brereton Cl 1 NR5 ...161 C6
Bressingham Prim Sch IP22 ...129 B8
Bressingham Rd
5 Gresham NR11 ...9 E1
Roydon IP22 ...129 C8
Sustead NR11 ...20 E8
Bressingham Steam Mus & Gdns* IP22 ...129 C7
Breton Cl 10 NR19 ...154 D2
Brett Ave NR31 ...170 D1
Brett Way PE30 ...147 B8
Brettingham Ave NR4 ...89 B8
Brewers Ct NR3 ...178 C4
Brewers Gn La IP22 ...177 B6
Brewery La NR18 ...173 C3
Brewery Rd NR28 ...22 D5
Brewery St NR30 ...169 C4
Brewster Ct NR13 ...165 D6
Brewsters 8 NR16 ...118 C5
Breydon Dr NR8 ...156 C4
Breydon Dr N NR8 ...156 C5
Breydon Junc NR30 ...76 C3
Breydon Mid Sch NR31 ...94 A5
Breydon Rd
Great Yarmouth NR31 ...169 B4
King's Lynn PE30 ...147 D5
Norwich NR7 ...159 A4
Breydon Way NR30 ...168 D6
Brian Ave NR1 ...162 D3
Briar Ave NR31 ...94 C7
Briar Cl Dereham NR20 ...68 A4
Grimston PE32 ...28 B1
King's Lynn PE30 ...148 C3
14 Lingwood NR13 ...74 A3
9 Necton PE37 ...65 F4
Briar La
Heckingham NR14 ...109 F8
Rickinghall Inferior IP22 ...128 D1
Swainsthorpe NR14 ...89 D3
Briar Rd 39 IP20 ...122 D2
Briars Ct NR5 ...161 F7
Brick Kiln La
Bunwell NR16 ...105 D2
Gillingham NR34 ...110 C5
Long Stratton NR15 ...107 A5
Shipdham IP25 ...67 C2
Brick Kiln Rd
Ellingham NR35 ...109 C4
Hevingham NR10 ...53 A7
North Walsham NR28 ...151 E5
Thursford NR21 ...17 F4
Brick Kilns Rd NR13 ...73 B7
Brick La NR27 ...10 B5
Brickfield Loke NR8 ...156 C5
Brickfields NR13 ...73 F2
Brickfields Way IP24 ...176 C6
Brickkiln La
Ashwellthorpe NR16 ...105 F7
Mulbarton NR14 ...89 C2
South Lopham IP22 ...128 F7
Brickle Loke NR14 ...90 B5
Brickle Rd NR14 ...90 B4
Brickley La PE31 ...140 D7
Brickyard La PE31 ...29 C4
Brickyard Rd NR28 ...22 A2
Bridewell Alley 2 NR2 ...178 B3
Bridewell La
Acle NR13 ...166 C4
Botesdale IP22 ...128 E2
Bridewell Mus The* NR2 ...178 B3
Bridewell St
1 Little Walsingham NR22 ...16 F7
Wymondham NR18 ...173 C3
Bridge Broad Cl NR12 ...164 C5
Bridge Cl
16 Harleston IP20 ...122 D2
Heacham PE31 ...133 E5
Melton Constable NR24 ...142 B4
Bridge Farm La NR4 ...161 C6
Bridge Gdns NR19 ...154 F1
Bridge La IP25 ...84 C3
Bridge Mdw NR29 ...58 A4
Bridge Rd
Brome & Oakley IP21 ...130 C5
Bunwell NR16 ...105 F2
Burston & Shimpling IP22 ...120 E3
Colby NR11 ...36 D8
Downham West PE38 ...79 B5
Great Ryburgh NR21 ...32 C6
5 Great Yarmouth NR30 ...169 C5
High Kelling NR25 ...137 F8
North Elmham NR20 ...32 F3
Potter Heigham NR29 ...56 F5
Stoke Ferry PE33 ...81 A2
Sutton Bridge PE12 ...41 A8
Wymondham NR18 ...88 B2
Bridge St Brandon IP27 ...175 C4
Carbrooke IP25 ...85 A4
Downham Market PE38 ...172 B5

Bridge St continued
Fakenham NR21 ...141 B3
Gressenhall NR20 ...49 C3
Hilgay PE38 ...79 E1
14 King's Lynn PE30 ...146 D4
Loddon NR14 ...92 A2
Stiffkey NR23 ...6 D5
Thetford IP24 ...176 C4
14 Wisbech PE13 ...152 C5
Bridgecourt NR29 ...58 A4
Bridgefoot La NR25 ...7 F3
Bridges Wlk
Fakenham NR21 ...141 A3
Thetford IP24 ...176 D3
Bridgford Cl NR31 ...170 C2
Bridgham La NR16 ...117 F4
Bridle La
Downham Market PE38 ...172 D7
Keswick NR4 ...89 C7
Bridle Rd PE25 ...84 C3
Brig Sq NR23 ...136 C6
Brigg St NR1 ...178 A2
Briggs Loke NR11 ...36 D8
Brigham Cl NR13 ...165 C4
Brighton Rd 1 NR15 ...89 C1
Brightwell Rd NR3 ...158 D3
Brighty's Opening NR2 ...162 B7
Brigstock Rd PE13 ...152 B7
Brimbelow Rd NR12 ...164 D4
Brindle Dr 6 NR14 ...89 B3
Brinell Way NR31 ...170 B8
Brinton Rd NR24 ...142 D8
Briscoe Way IP27 ...113 E2
Brisley CE Prim Sch NR20 ...32 A1
Bristol Terr NR2 ...178 A2
Briston Rd
Briston NR24 ...142 A5
Corpusty NR11 ...19 F1
Edgefield NR24 ...19 C5
Wood Dalling NR11 ...34 C6
Britannia Pier Theatre NR30 ...169 E4
Britannia Rd
Great Yarmouth NR30 ...169 E4
Norwich NR1 ...162 D3
Britannia Way PE13 ...152 C2
Britch La PE34 ...42 B4
Briton Way NR18 ...173 B3
Briton's La
Beeston Regis NR26 ...138 C4
Sheringham NR26 ...9 F5
Briton's La Cl
2 Beeston Regis NR27 ...9 F5
Sheringham NR26 ...138 F5
Britton Cl 9 PE33 ...61 D6
Broad Dro Emneth PE14 ...59 C1
Grimston PE32 ...45 C8
Methwold IP26 ...97 F6
Upwell PE14 ...77 D4
Broad End La PE13 ...152 E4
Broad End Rd PE14 ...152 F4
Broad Fen La NR28 ...38 C4
Broad La Brancaster PE31 ...3 A7
Great & Little Plumstead NR13 ...72 F6
South Walsham NR13 ...74 B8
Swannington NR9 ...52 B5
Broad Rd Alburgh IP20 ...122 E8
Fleggburgh NR29 ...75 C8
Broad Reaches NR29 ...56 C5
Broad Row 17 NR30 ...169 C4
Broad St Bungay NR35 ...124 A8
20 Harleston IP20 ...122 D2
King's Lynn PE30 ...146 D5
Broad View 4 NR13 ...72 D6
Broad Way
Dickleburgh & Rushall IP21 ...130 D8
Rocklands NR17 ...103 A8
Broadacres NR13 ...74 B8
Broadcote Cl NR15 ...90 E1
Broaden La NR15 ...107 C6
Broadfen Dro IP26 ...98 B5
Broadfields Way NR1 ...91 C7
Broadgate NR8 ...155 B2
Broadgate Cl NR27 ...11 A2
Broadgate La
Great Moulton NR15 ...121 B8
Roydon NR21 ...28 A2
Broadhurst Rd NR4 ...162 B1
Broadland Cl NR13 ...93 A4
Broadland Dr NR13 ...72 D6
Broadland High Sch NR12 ...164 D6
Broadland Sports Club NR29 ...75 D8
Broadland Way
Acle NR13 ...166 C3
Postwick with Witton NR7 ...72 E3
Broadlands PE38 ...172 B5
Broadlands Cl PE31 ...140 C4
Broadlands Rd NR12 ...39 E1
Broadmead Gn NR13 ...72 D6
Broadmoor Rd IP25 ...85 B4
Broadsman Rd NR1 ...163 A4
Broadwater La PE32 ...45 B4
Broadwater Rd PE36 ...1 F7
Broadwater Way 1 NR12 ...55 E4
Broadway Cl 5 NR15 ...107 C5
Broadway The
Heacham PE31 ...133 D5
Honingham NR9 ...69 E8
Scarning NR19 ...154 B2
Broadwood Cl NR11 ...11 E1
Brockdish Prim Sch IP21 ...131 D6

Brockley Gn 7 PE30 ...147 C4
Brocks Rd PE37 ...153 B6
Brockwell Ct NR3 ...158 F2
Brome Ave IP23 ...130 C4
Brome Hall La IP23 ...130 D3
Bromedale Ave 19 NR14 ...89 B3
Brook Gr 8 NR19 ...154 D3
Brook La Brookville IP26 ...99 A7
Burgate IP22 ...129 C3
Needham IP20 ...131 E8
St Margaret, Ilketshall NR35 ...124 C3
Brook Pl NR1 ...178 B2
Brook Rd
Dersingham PE31 ...140 D2
Sheringham NR26 ...138 E6
Brook St
Buxton with Lammas NR10 ...36 E1
Cromer NR27 ...139 C7
Lamas NR10 ...53 E8
Brooke Ave NR30 ...168 D5
Brooke Prim Sch NR15 ...90 E1
Brooke Rd
Kirstead NR15 ...91 A1
Mundham NR14 ...108 F8
Seething NR15 ...91 C1
Shotesham NR15 ...107 F8
Brookes Dr NR28 ...151 A4
Brookfield Cl NR15 ...106 F4
Brooks Dr NR19 ...154 B4
Brooks Mdw NR14 ...90 D5
Brookside NR20 ...49 E8
Brookwell Springs 1 PE32 ...44 B3
Broom Ave
Norwich NR6 ...158 A5
Norwich NR7 ...163 E8
Broom Cl
15 Marthan NR29 ...57 D4
Norwich NR1 ...162 F3
Taverham NR8 ...155 C3
Broom Gn Dr NR20 ...32 E4
Broom Gn Rd NR20 ...32 E2
Broom Hill La IP24 ...126 C3
Broom La Easton NR9 ...70 B5
Witton NR28 ...38 C5
Broom Rd
Lakenheath IP27 ...113 F1
Wymondham NR18 ...105 C6
Broome Gdns 2 NR31 ...94 A5
Broomhill 1 NR27 ...10 B5
Broomhill La NR15 ...149 B3
Broomsthorpe Rd PE31 ...30 A7
Brotherscross Way PE38 ...172 C7
Brow of the Hill PE32 ...44 E6
Browick Rd NR18 ...173 C4
Browick Rd Inf Sch NR18 ...173 C3
Brown's La
Holme Hale IP25 ...65 F2
Mautby NR29 ...76 B7
Necton PE37 ...65 F3
Saxlingham Nethergate NR15 ...107 B8
Browne St 5 NR2 ...162 C7
Browning Pl PE30 ...147 A8
Brownsfield NR11 ...21 D8
Brownshill NR27 ...139 B4
Browston Hall Leisure Ctr NR31 ...94 C4
Browston La NR32 ...94 B3
Brummel 1 PE30 ...147 C5
Brumstead Rd
Brumstead NR12 ...24 A1
Stalham NR12 ...39 A4
Brundall Gdns Sta NR13 ...165 A3
Brundall Low Rd NR13 ...72 F3
Brundall Prim Sch NR13 ...165 D3
Brundall Rd NR13 ...165 E4
Brundall Sta NR13 ...165 E4
Brundish Rd NR14 ...110 A4
Brunel Way IP24 ...176 B6
Brunswick Cl
Dereham NR19 ...154 C2
North Walsham NR28 ...151 D6
Brunswick Rd NR3 ...178 A1
Brunswick Terr NR27 ...139 C7
Brush Hill NR20 ...33 A6
Brush Mdw La PE34 ...42 B7
Brushmakers Way IP22 ...177 C6
Brussels Cl NR19 ...154 C2
Bryars La IP22 ...177 F3
Bryden La IP22 ...177 F3
Bryon Cl 2 NR6 ...158 C3
Bryony Cour NR25 ...137 B7
Bryony Ct PE30 ...148 C3
Bryony Way 8 NR31 ...88 D8
Buccaneer Way 8 NR9 ...88 D8
Buck Courtney Cres NR6 ...158 A7
Buck La IP21 ...130 C4
Buck's Heath La NR11 ...11 D1
Buck's La NR18 ...87 B3
Buckenham Cl
1 Fakenham NR21 ...141 C5
Swaffham PE37 ...153 B2
Buckenham Dr PE33 ...81 A2
Buckenham La NR13 ...73 F2
Buckenham Rd
Attleborough NR17 ...174 D1
Lingwood & Burlingham NR13 ...74 A2

Buckenham Rd continued
Strumpshaw NR13 ...73 F2
Buckenham Sta NR13 ...91 F8
Bucket Rd NR21 ...15 D2
Buckingham Cl PE30 ...148 C5
Buckingham Ct PE36 ...132 C5
Buckingham Dr 1 NR9 ...88 C7
Buckingham Rd 4 NR1 ...161 F3
Buckingham Wlk PE13 ...152 D8
Buckland Rise 8 NR4 ...161 F1
Buckholt Rd PE14 ...59 B7
Buckthorn Cl 3 NR8 ...155 B2
Buddell's La NR23 ...5 F2
Bugg's Rd IP22 ...129 B2
Buggs Hole La IP22 ...128 A6
Buildings Rd NR30 ...168 E4
Bull Cl
East Tuddenham NR20 ...69 C6
4 Holt NR25 ...137 B6
Norwich NR3 ...178 B4
Bull Cl La NR21 ...17 B3
Bull Cl Rd NR3 ...178 B4
Bull La NR1 ...178 A1
Bull St NR25 ...137 B6
Bullace Rd NR5 ...156 F2
Bullacebush La NR13 ...165 E7
Bullard Rd NR3 ...158 C3
Bull's La NR31 ...170 D6
Bull's Row NR27 ...11 A2
Bullemer Cl 3 NR12 ...39 B4
Bullfinch Way 4 PE14 ...77 A8
Bullies Way 3 NR13 ...73 D6
Bullman's Cross La NR20 ...69 A6
Bullock Fair Cl 14 IP20 ...122 D2
Bullock Hill NR10 ...53 E1
Bullock Rd PE34 ...144 B1
Bullocks Loke NR30 ...168 E4
Bullockshed La NR14 ...91 A7
Bulmer La NR29 ...58 B6
Bulmer Rd NR3 ...158 A2
Bulrush Ave 4 PE38 ...172 A6
Bulrush Cl
1 East Dereham NR19 ...154 C4
4 Horsford NR10 ...53 A4
Bulstrode Ave 4 NR19 ...154 D2
Bultitudes Loke NR30 ...168 E4
Bulwer Rd
East Dereham NR19 ...154 E7
Lamas NR10 ...36 E1
Bumstede Ct 5 NR5 ...161 A8
Bungalow La NR7 ...72 D3
Bungay High Sch NR35 ...124 A7
Bungay Rd Bixley NR14 ...90 B8
Dickleburgh & Rushall IP21 ...130 E5
Ellingham NR35 ...109 C4
Hempnall NR15 ...107 D5
Loddon NR14 ...109 C7
Poringland NR14 ...90 D4
Scole IP21 ...130 D5
Stockton NR34 ...109 F4
Thwaite NR35 ...109 A5
Bungaygrave La IP20 ...122 D6
Bunkel Rd NR13 ...72 E8
Bunn's Bank Rd
Attleborough NR17 ...174 F1
Old Buckenham NR17 ...104 D4
Bunn's La
Great Yarmouth NR31 ...169 C3
Starston IP20 ...122 C2
Bunnett Ave PE30 ...146 D2
Bunnewell Ave NR31 ...170 A4
Bunting's La IP26 ...98 F5
Buntings The 15 NR31 ...94 C8
Bunwell Hill NR20 ...105 D2
Bunwell Prim Sch NR16 ...105 D3
Bunwell Rd
Aslacton NR16 ...106 A2
Attleborough NR17 ...174 F6
Besthorpe NR17 ...104 F6
Bunwell St NR16 ...105 D5
Bunyan Cl 3 NR13 ...72 E4
Burch Cl NR18 ...147 E4
Burcroft Rd PE13 ...152 B6
Burdett Rd PE13 ...152 B4
Burdock Cl NR18 ...173 E4
Burdock La
Hockwold cum Wilton IP26 ...113 C7
8 Wramplingham NR9 ...69 F2
Burdock Way 3 NR17 ...174 B4
Bure Cl 9 Belton NR31 ...94 A6
Caister-on-Sea NR30 ...168 C5
Great Yarmouth NR30 ...169 C6
4 King's Lynn PE30 ...147 C5
1 Watlington PE33 ...61 D6
Wroxham/Hoveton NR12 ...164 C5
Bure Marshes National Nature Reserve* NR13 ...55 E3
Bure Rd Briston NR24 ...142 C4
1 Great Yarmouth NR30 ...169 C6
Bure Valley La NR11 ...150 E5
Bure Valley Sch NR11 ...150 C5
Bure Way NR11 ...150 C7
Burgate La NR14 ...90 E5
Burgess Cl NR30 ...168 D6
Burgess Rd NR3 ...158 B2

Burgess Way NR15 .....90 E2
Burgh Beck Rd NR24 ..142 B5
Burgh Hall Leisure Ctr
NR31 ....94 B7
Burgh La NR20 ......68 F6
Burgh Rd
Aylsham NR11 ....150 D6
Burgh St Peter NR34 ...111 C5
Great Yarmouth NR31 ...170 B7
Burgh Wood Rd NR29 ...57 E1
Burghley Rd PE30 ...148 E1
Burghwood Dr PE32 ..48 D6
Burhill Cl 3 NR4 ......89 D8
Burkitt St PE30 .....146 E6
Burleigh Cl 1 NR30 ..169 D2
Burley Rd NR12 ....38 A3
Burlingham Dr 2 NR33 ..111 F1
Burlingham Rd NR13 ...73 F6
Burlington Cl IP22 ...177 D1
Burma Cl PE31 ......140 C4
Burma Rd NR6 ......158 E5
Burnet Rd
Great Yarmouth NR31 ...94 C6
Norwich NR3 ....157 F1
Burney Rd PE30 .....146 D2
Burnham Ave PE30 ..147 C8
Burnham Mkt Prim Sch
PE31 ....135 D4
Burnham Rd
Docking PE31 ....134 C6
Downham Market PE38 ..172 B4
North Creake NR21 .....4 D2
Ringstead PE36 ....2 C3
South Creake NR21 ...15 D7
Burns Cl
East Dereham NR19 ...154 C7
Thetford IP24 ......176 E6
Yaxley IP23 ....129 F1
Burnside 3 PE37 ....66 A4
Burnt Fen Turnpike
IP28 ....112 D2
Burnt Hill La NR33 ...111 F3
Burnt Hills NR27 ....139 B4
Burnt House Rd NR13 ..92 B6
Burnt La
Great Yarmouth NR31 ...170 C7
Wiggenhall St Mary Magdalen
PE34 ....61 A4
Burnt St NR23 ......136 D5
Burnthouse Cres PE33 ..63 B4
Burnthouse Dro PE33 ..63 C5
Burnthouse La
Hethersett NR9 ......160 C1
Runhall NR20 ....69 A4
Scole IP20 ....122 A1
Toft Monks NR34 .....110 D5
Wymondham NR18 .....173 F1
Burntoak La IP20 ....122 E4
Burntwood La NR12 ...54 C4
Burr Cl 14 IP25 .....84 E3
Burrell Cl NR25 .....137 D7
Burrell Way IP24 ....176 A1
Burrett Gdns PE13 ...59 C5
Burrett Rd PE13 .....59 C5
Burrettgate Rd PE13 ..152 F5
Burroughs Way NR18 ..173 D4
Burrow Dr IP27 .....113 E2
Burrows Gn NR34 ....110 F5
Burston Rd NR24 ....142 B5
Burston Com Prim Sch
IP22 ....120 E2
Burston Rd
Dickleburgh & Rushall
IP21 ....130 C8
Diss IP22 ....177 E7
Gissing IP22 ....120 F3
Burston Strike Sch*
IP22 ....120 E2
Burton Ave NR28 ....151 B4
Burton Cl
North Walsham NR28 ...151 B4
Norwich NR6 ......158 C5
Roydon IP22 ....177 B5
Burton Dr 9 NR13 ...72 E7
Burton Rd NR6 ......158 C5
Burtontyne Ave NR8 ..68 A7
Bury Bottom IP27 ...115 A1
Bury Rd Botesdale IP22 ..128 F3
Brandon IP27 ....175 D2
Hepworth IP22 ......127 F1
Market Weston IP22 ...127 C4
Rickinghall Inferior
IP22 ....128 D1
Thetford IP24 ......176 C1
Wortham IP22 ......129 C4
Bury St NR2 ....162 B4
Bush Cl PE31 ......140 E3
Bush Dr NR12 ......24 E4
Bush Est NR12 .....24 D4
Bush La Dereham NR20 ..68 B8
Wisbech PE13 ......152 E5
Bush Rd Hemsby NR29 ..58 B5
Norwich NR1 ....157 F7
Bussey Rd NR6 .....158 D4
Bussey's La NR31 ...170 D5
Bussey's Loke
Great Yarmouth NR31 ...170 A5
Hempnall NR15 ......107 D5
Bustards' La PE14 ...41 F3
Butcher's La NR21 ...141 E4
Butchers La PE31 ....3 B7
Butt La Belton NR31 ...94 A6
Litcham PE32 ......48 A4
Butter La NR14 .....92 D1
Butter's Hall La IP24 ..102 C7

Buttercup Cl 1 IP24 ..176 F5
Buttercup Dr 14 NR31 ..94 C6
Buttercup Way NR5 ..160 F6
Buttermere 1 NR29 ..167 B7
Buttermere Rd 4 NR5 ..161 C6
Butterwick 3 PE30 ...147 C5
Buttland's La PE33 ...81 B8
Buttlands Cl NR21 ....6 E2
Buttlands The
Great Cressingham IP25 ..83 D4
Wells-next-the-Sea
NR23 ....136 D5
Buttle's La NR15 ....106 D3
Butts La NR26 ......138 B5
Butts The NR5 .....160 F8
Buxton Ave NR31 ...170 D1
Buxton Cl 4 Cromer NR27 ..10 B5
Easton NR9 ....70 B5
Buxton Prim Sch NR10 ..36 F1
Buxton Rd
Aylsham NR11 ....150 D5
Cawston NR10 ......35 D2
Diss IP22 ....177 B4
Frettenham NR12 .....53 F3
Hainford NR10 ......53 F5
Horstead with Stanninghall
NR12 ....54 B6
North Walsham NR28 ...151 B4
Norwich NR3 ....162 D8
Spixworth NR10 .....158 F8
Buxton Sta NR10 ....36 F2
Byfield Ct 3 NR3 ...158 C1
Byron Ave PE13 ....154 E2
Byron Rd
Great Yarmouth NR30 ...169 C8
Taverham NR8 ......156 D8
Byron Way NR8 ....168 D6
Byron Wlk 7 IP24 ...176 E6

C

Cabbell Rd NR27 ....139 B7
Cabin Cl 11 NR33 ...111 F1
Cadamys Yd NR23 ...136 D5
Cadge Cl NR5 ......161 D7
Cadge Rd NR5 ......161 D6
Cadge's La NR5 .....86 B3
Cadiz Way NR31 ....171 E4
Cadman Way IP25 ...84 D3
Cadogan Rd NR27 ...139 B7
Caernarvon Rd NR2 ..162 B6
Cage La IP24 ......176 D3
Cains The NR8 .....155 C2
Cairns Ct NR4 .....162 A3
Caister By-pass NR30 ..168 C4
Caister Castle Car
Collection* NR30 ....168 A5
Caister High Sch
NR30 ....168 E6
Caister on Sea Fst & Mid
Schs NR30 ....168 E5
Caister Rd NR30 ....169 C7
Caister Sands Ave
NR29 ....168 E8
Caistor La
Caistor St Edmund NR14 ..89 F6
Poringland NR14 .....90 B6
Caistor Roman Town*
NR14 ....89 F6
Caithness Crystal Visitor
Ctr* PE30 ....146 F2
Caius Ct 7 NR31 ....133 C5
Calamint Rd PE30 ...147 A8
Caledonian Way 1 NR31 ..94 A5
Caley Cl NR3 ......157 F2
Caley St PE31 ......133 D5
Calf La NR10 ......53 E2
California Ave NR29 ..167 E4
California Cotts NR23 ..136 E5
California Cres NR29 ..167 F2
California Rd NR29 ...167 E2
Calkewood La IP22 ...128 C1
Calthorpe Cl
Acle NR13 ....166 B4
2 Stalham NR12 .....39 B4
Calthorpe Rd
Ingham NR12 ......39 D4
Norwich NR5 ......161 B6
Calvert St NR3 .....178 B4
Calves Well La
Beeston Regis NR26 ...138 F4
Sheringham NR27 ....10 A5
Camargue Pl 4 PE13 ..152 E3
Cambell Dr NR20 ....50 B5
Camberley Rd NR4 ...162 A2
Cambers La PE31 ...135 D2
Camborne Cl NR5 ...157 C1
Cambridge Ave NR31 ..170 A3
Cambridge Dr PE13 ..152 A6
Cambridge Rd PE30 ..148 D5
Cambridge St
Cromer NR27 ......139 C4
Norwich NR2 ......162 C4
Cambridge Way NR31 ..170 B3
Camden Pl 21 NR30 ..169 D2
Camden Rd NR30 ...169 D2
Camelot Rd NR31 ....171 B8
Cameron Cl NR31 ...133 C4
Cameron Cres 4 PE31 ..12 D4
Cameron Gn NR8 ....156 E8
Camfrey 6 PE30 ....147 B7
Camp Cl 2 IP26 ....98 D1
Camp Gr NR1 ......163 A6
Camp La NR7 ......10 A4
Camp Rd NR8 ......155 C4
Campbell Cl PE36 ...132 D4
Campbell Ct 1 NR3 ..162 F4

Camperdown 11 NR30 ..169 D2
Camping Cl 8 NR20 ...68 F6
Camping Field La PE13 ..39 B4
Campingland PE13 ...153 C4
Campion Ave NR31 ...170 B3
Campion Cl 4 NR28 ..151 E5
Campion Pl PE38 ....172 B3
Campion Rd
1 Dereham NR20 .....68 A8
Thetford IP24 ......176 F4
Campion Way
6 Attleborough NR17 ..174 B4
3 Sheringham NR26 ...138 B6
Campsey Rd PE38 ...97 B6
Canada Cl 6 PE31 ...12 E5
Canada Rd NR27 ....139 B7
Canal Farm La NR28 ..38 C6
Canal St 6 PE13 ....152 C5
Canary Way NR1 ....163 A4
Canberra Rd IP25 ...84 F3
Candle Stick NR9 ....69 A3
Candlemaker Workshop*
NR29 ....75 A5
Candler's La 18 IP20 ..122 D2
Candlestick La PE32 ..45 C8
Canfor Rd NR13 ....72 E7
Cangate Rd NR12 ...55 C6
Cann's La NR14 ....88 D7
Cannell Gn NR3 .....178 C4
Cannell Rd 11 NR14 ..92 A1
Cannerby La NR7 ...159 B3
Cannon St PE13 ....152 C4
Cannon Terr 9 PE13 ..152 C4
Canon Cl 6 IP25 ....84 E3
Canon Hoare Rd NR12 ..54 C6
Canon Pickering VC Jun Sch
IP20 ....122 D2
Canon Pott Ct NR3 ..133 D6
Canon Wake Ct 4 NR29 ..56 C8
Canon's Cl IP24 ....176 B4
Canons Cl 2 NR19 ...154 C2
Canons Wlk IP24 ...176 B4
Canterbury Inf Sch
IP24 ....176 B4
Canterbury Pl NR2 ..162 C7
Canterbury Way IP24 ..176 B5
Cantley Cnr NR13 ...74 B1
Cantley Fst Sch NR13 ..92 B7
Cantley La
Cringleford NR4 .....89 A8
Ketteringham NR18 ...88 F6
Cantley Rd NR13 ....92 D7
Cantley Sta NR13 ...92 B6
Cants Cl 4 NR9 ....69 F2
Capgrave Ave PE30 ..146 F8
Capps La IP19 .....123 F1
Capstan Way 9 NR31 ..133 F1
Captains Cl PE13 ...153 D4
Caraway Ct 22 NR31 ..94 C6
Caraway Rd IP24 ...176 F4
Carbrooke Rd
Caston NR17 ......85 C1
Griston NR17 ......85 A2
Cardiff Rd NR2 .....162 B5
Cardigan Pl NR2 ....162 C7
Cardinal Cl NR9 ....70 B5
Cardington Ct 1 NR13 ..166 D4
Cardington Rd IP25 ..85 A3
Cardun Cl 3 NR13 ...73 C6
Carey House Con Ctr
PE37 ....65 D1
Cargate Comm Rd
NR16 ....105 E1
Cargate La
Saxlingham Nethergate
NR15 ....107 A8
Upton with Fishley NR13 ..166 A8
Carl Cl 5 NR4 .....154 E1
Carl Cres NR28 ....22 E5
Carleton Cl 1 NR18 ..173 C6
Carleton Rd NR7 ...159 B3
Carleton Rode CE Prim Sch
NR16 ....105 C3
Carlton Cl NR19 ....154 D4
Carlton Dr PE30 ....148 D5
Carlton Gdns NR1 ...178 B1
Carlton Marshes Nature
Reserve* NR33 ....111 F3
Carlyle Rd NR1 ....162 F3
Carmelite Terr 16 PE30 ..146 D4
Carmen's La NR28 ...38 B3
Carn Cl NR13 ......74 B2
Carnoustie Ave NR4 ..162 A1
Carnoustie Ct PE31 ..41 C8
Carol Cl NR14 .....90 B5
Carola Sutton Ct
NR25 ....137 B5
Caroline Ct NR4 ....161 F4
Carpenter's Wlk NR15 ..121 D7
Carpenters Cotts
NR25 ....137 B6
Carr La
Great Moulton NR15 ..106 B1
Hoveton NR12 ......164 F8
Northrepps NR27 ....139 C1
Overstrand NR27 ....11 A3
Poringland NR14 ....90 C4
Wendling NR19 .....66 F7
Carr Terr PE31 .....134 E5
Carrell Rd NR1 ....154 F1
Carrington Rd NR27 ..139 D5
Carrow Abbey NR1 ..163 A3
Carrow Cl NR1 .....162 F3
Carrow Hill NR1 ....178 C1
Carrow Rd NR1 ....178 C1
Carrs Hill Cl NR8 ...157 A4
Carrs Rd NR8 .....92 A8
Carshalton Rd 2 NR1 ..162 F3

Cart Gap Rd NR12 ...24 C4
Carter Cl
Caister-on-Sea NR30 ..168 D8
Swaffham PE37 .....153 C2
Carter Rd NR8 .....157 A8
Carter's Cl PE30 ...148 B1
Carters Loke NR13 ..166 C2
Cartledge Cl 1 NR19 ..154 D3
Cartmel 17 NR9 ....88 D8
Carver's La NR17 ...174 B5
Casaubon Cl 6 NR19 ..154 D3
Caslon Cl 3 NR21 ...141 C5
Castelins Way 20 NR14 ..89 B3
Castell Rd NR19 ....154 D7
Castle Acre Castle*
PE32 ....47 A2
Castle Acre CE VC Fst Sch
PE32 ....46 F1
Castle Acre Cl 2 PE30 ..148 C3
Castle Acre Rd PE32 ..47 C3
Castle Cl 3 Gresham NR11 ..9 E1
King's Lynn PE30 ....147 C8
Weeting IP27 ......175 B8
Castle Drift PE32 ...48 D6
Castle Gn NR31 ....170 B3
Castle La Bungay NR35 ..124 A8
Thetford IP24 ......176 B3
West Caister NR30 ...168 B5
Castle Mdw NR1 ....178 B2
Castle Mkt St NR1 ..178 B2
Castle Rd
Mettingham NR35 ...124 D7
Wormegay PE33 ....62 C6
Castle Rise NR8 ....155 F3
Castle Rising Castle*
PE31 ....27 C3
Castle Rising Rd PE30 ..148 C3
Castle Sq 16 NR31 ..152 C5
Castle St Norwich NR2 ..178 B3
Thetford IP24 ......176 D4
Wroxham/Hoveton
NR12 ....164 B3
Castleacre Rd
Great Massingham PE32 ..29 C1
Swaffham PE37 .....153 B6
Castleford Cl IP24 ...176 B4
Castleton Ave NR3 ..111 C1
Castleton Cl 1 NR5 ..160 F8
Castleton Way IP23 ..130 C1
Caston CE VA Prim Sch
NR17 ....85 B1
Caston Cl 5 NR25 ...137 B6
Caston Rd NR7 .....163 F8
Catalpa Way 5 NR31 ..170 B5
Catbridge La NR14 ...89 A4
Catchpole Wlk IP21 ..121 C1
Catfield CE Fst Sch
NR29 ....56 C8
Catfield Rd NR29 ...56 D6
Cathedral Dr NR20 ..49 E8
Cathedral St NR1 ...178 C3
Catherine Howard Cl 3
IP24 ....176 D6
Catherine Wheel Opening 8
NR3 ....162 D8
Catling's La PE13 ...41 A4
Catmere Herne NR14 ..89 A3
Cator Rd NR8 .....155 F1
Catriona Ct NR25 ...8 B6
Cats Cnr NR10 .....37 B7
Cattle Mkt St 4 NR21 ..141 C4
Catton Chase NR6 ..158 D5
Catton Gr Fst Sch
NR3 ....158 C3
Catton Gr Mid Sch
NR3 ....158 C3
Catton Gr Rd NR3 ...158 D2
Catton View Ct NR3 ..158 D3
Caudle Hill IP25 ....83 E5
Caudwell Cl 2 NR14 ..89 F4
Causeway
Brockdish IP21 .....131 C6
Norwich NR6 ......162 C8
Causeway Dr 4 NR12 ..54 C6
Causeway The
Heigham Bridge NR29 ..57 A5
Hickling NR12 .....39 F2
Stow Bardolph PE34 ..61 D1
Cavalier Cl 30 NR7 ..72 E4
Cave's Cl PE34 .....144 B5
Cavell Cl NR14 .....89 C5
Cavell Fst Sch NR1 ..162 E1
Cavell Rd NR1 .....162 E2
Cavendish Cl PE32 ..44 C3
Cavenham Rd PE33 ..80 E4
Cavick Rd NR18 ....173 B3
Cawdor Rd NR17 ...174 C4
Cawston La
Great Witchingham NR9 ..51 E7
Little Witchingham NR9 ..149 E1
Cawston Rd
Aylsham NR11 ......150 A5
Reepham NR10 .....149 D6
Cawston VC Prim Sch
NR10 ....35 B2
Cawstons Mdw 8 NR14 ..90 C5
Caxton Cl NR26 ....138 F5
Caxton Pk NR26 ....138 F5
Caxton Rd NR34 ...110 D1
Caxton Way IP24 ...176 A2
Caystreward NR30 ..168 E1
Cecil Cl 7 PE33 ....61 D6
Cecil Gowing Ct NR7 ..159 B4

Cecil Gowing Fst Sch
NR7 ....159 C3
Cecil Rd
East Dereham NR20 ..154 F5
Norwich NR1 ......162 D3
Cedar Ave 4 NR10 ...54 A2
Cedar Cl
1 Downham Market
PE38 ....172 C6
12 Great Yarmouth NR31 ..94 C7
19 Martham NR29 ....57 D4
12 Mattishall NR20 ...68 E6
North Elmham NR20 ...49 E7
Cedar Ct
North Walsham NR28 ..151 C5
Wymondham NR18 ...173 D6
Cedar Dr
Attleborough NR17 ..174 C4
10 Loddon NR14 .....92 A1
Cedar Gr
North Runcton PE33 ..44 A3
Sheringham NR26 ...138 E5
Cedar Rd
Hethersett NR9 ....88 C8
Marham PE33 ......63 B4
Norwich NR1 ......163 A5
Cedar Rise NR20 ...68 E6
Cedar Row NR25 ....147 B7
Cedar Springs PE31 ..133 B6
Cedar Way
Brandon IP27 ......175 D2
Brundall NR13 .....165 C3
4 Gayton PE32 .....45 C6
King's Lynn PE34 ...146 C4
Cedars The Keswick N12 ..23 F3
Norwich NR2 ......162 B4
Shepherd's Port PE31 ..12 B4
Celandine Cl 2 IP24 ..176 F5
Celandine La 6 NR26 ..138 B6
Celandine Rd 4 NR17 ..174 B4
Celia Phillips Cl 7
IP24 ....176 D7
Cemetery La NR18 ..173 B3
Cemetery Rd
East Dereham NR19 ..154 E7
Lakenheath IP27 ....113 E1
Outwell PE14 ......78 A6
Centenary Way PE12 ..41 C6
Central Ave NR7 ....72 C3
Central Cl 1 NR9 ...88 D7
Central Cres 2 NR9 ..88 D7
Central Dr NR20 ....50 A5
Central Rd
Cromer NR27 ......139 A7
King's Lynn PE30 ...146 D6
Centre Cres NR13 ...140 D3
Centre Point 6 PE30 ..147 D5
Centre Vale NR11 ...140 D3
Centre Vale Rd PE31 ..140 D3
Century Rd 6 Eye IP23 ..130 C1
Great Yarmouth NR31 ..169 B3
Century Way NR8 ...155 F3
Cere Rd NR7 ......159 C4
Cess Rd NR29 .....57 C5
Chadwick Sq 2 PE30 ..147 A7
Chalfont Wlk NR4 ...161 E2
Chalk Hill Rd NR1 ...178 C3
Chalk La Culford IP31 ..125 C1
Narborough PE32 ....63 E5
North End NR16 ....106 D2
Sutton Bridge PE12 ..41 C7
Chalk Pit Rd PE31 ...140 E7
Chalk Rd Brandon IP27 ..114 D3
5 Walpole St Andrew PE14 ..41 E4
Chalkpit Rd PE31 ...3 A6
Chalkrow La PE33 ...81 F4
Chamberlin Cl NR3 ..158 E2
Chamberlin Rd NR13 ..165 E6
Chamberlin Rd NR3 ..158 D1
Chambers Rd NR3 ..158 D4
Chameryhall La NR13 ..73 F7
Champney's Rd IP22 ..177 E4
Chancel Cl NR13 ...165 C3
Chancellors Dr NR4 ..161 C4
Chandler Rd NR14 ...89 F5
Chandler's Hill La 1
NR18 ....173 B3
Chandlers Ct 2 NR18 ..173 B3
Chandlers Cl 8 NR4 ..89 C8
Chandlers Hill NR18 ..173 B3
Changi Rd 5 IP25 ...84 F3
Chantry Ct 8 PE37 ..65 F4
Chantry La PE37 ....66 A4
Chantry Rd NR2 ....178 A2
Chantry The NR2 ...178 A2
Chapel Ave NR15 ...106 E3
Chapel Bank PE36 ..132 E4
Chapel Break Fst Sch
NR5 ....160 F8
Chapel Break Rd NR5 ..160 F8
Chapel Cl
Barnham Broom NR9 ..69 C2
Pulham Market IP21 ..121 E5
Reepham NR10 .....149 B5
Tacolneston NR16 ...105 F4
Winfarthing IP22 ...120 B5
Chapel Cnr NR12 ...55 D6
Chapel Ct
Blofield NR13 .....165 E6
Norwich NR6 ......157 F5
Chapel Field NR13 ..93 A4
Chapel Field E NR2 ..178 A2
Chapel Field N NR2 ..178 A2
Chapel Field Rd
Norwich NR2 ......178 A2
Stalham NR12 .....39 A3
Chapel La
Aldborough NR11 ...21 A5

Chapel La continued
Ashby St Mary NR14 .....**91** D5
Barton Bendish PE33 ...**81** B8
Beeston with Bittering
  PE32 ....**48** C2
Beetley NR20 ....**49** C4
Botesdale IP22 ....**128** E2
Burgate IP22 ....**129** C3
Coltishall NR12 ......**54** D7
East Dereham NR19 ...**154** C2
Emneth PE14 ....**59** B2
Felthorpe NR10 ......**155** C8
Fincham PE33 ....**62** E1
Foulsham NR20 ....**33** D3
3 Great Yarmouth NR31 ..**94** C6
Hempstead NR25 ....**19** E8
Hockering NR20 ....**69** B8
Hunstanton PE36 .....**132** C4
Kirby Row NR35 ......**109** E3
Methwold IP26 ....**99** A5
Necton PE37 ....**66** A4
Norwich NR7 ....**163** E6
Potter Heigham NR29 ..**56** F7
Ringstead PE36 ....**2** A3
Scarning NR19 ....**67** B7
Sculthorpe NR21 ......**16** B1
Shelton NR15 ....**107** B1
Shotesham NR15 ....**90** B2
Skeyton NR10 ....**37** B6
West Caister NR30 ...**168** C4
West Winch PE33 ......**43** E3
Wimbotsham PE34 .....**172** E8
Wiveton NR25 ....**7** E6
Wymondham NR18 ......**173** A5
Chapel Loke
Lessingham NR12 ......**24** C2
Salhouse NR13 ....**55** B1
4 Stoke Holy Cross NR14 ..**89** F4
Surlingham NR14 ......**73** B1
Wymondham NR18 ......**105** A8
Chapel Mdw NR35 .....**109** E3
Chapel Rd
Alby with Thwaite NR11 ..**21** B3
Ashby St Mary NR14 ...**91** D5
Attleborough NR17 ...**174** C5
Beighton NR13 ....**74** C2
Boughton PE33 ....**81** A4
Carleton Rode NR16 ..**105** C3
Dersingham PE31 .....**140** D4
Dilham NR28 ....**38** B3
East Ruston NR12 .....**38** E6
Foxley NR20 ....**50** D8
Grimston PE32 ....**28** A1
Guestwick NR20 ....**33** F6
Hainford NR10 ....**53** E5
Halvergate NR13 ......**75** A2
Lingwood NR13 ....**73** F3
Longham NR19 ....**49** A2
Lowestoft NR33 ......**111** F1
Morley NR18 ....**87** B2
Neatishead NR12 ......**55** E6
Necton PE37 ....**66** B4
Norwich NR5 ....**157** A2
Paston NR28 ....**143** D1
Roughton NR11 ....**21** D8
Roydon PE32 ....**45** A8
St Andrew, Ilketshall
  NR34 ....**124** F6
Scole IP21 ....**121** B1
Sea Palling NR12 .....**40** A6
Southrepps NR11 ......**22** B6
Swafield NR28 ....**22** D3
Terrington St Clement
  PE34 ....**144** B5
Upton with Fishley NR13 ..**166** B8
Wisbech PE13 ....**152** B5
Woodton NR35 ....**108** C4
Wymondham NR18 ......**105** A8
Chapel Rd Specl Sch
  NR17 ....**174** C5
Chapel Rise PE33 .....**63** B4
Chapel St Barford NR9 ..**70** A3
Cawston NR10 ....**35** B3
3 Cromer NR27 ....**139** B7
Diss IP22 ....**177** D4
6 Hingham NR9 ....**86** C5
Ixworth NR9 ....**69** F2
King's Lynn PE30 ....**146** D5
3 Old Buckenham NR16 ..**104** F1
Rocklands NR17 ......**103** B8
Shipdham IP25 ....**67** C2
Warham NR23 ....**6** A4
14 Wisbech PE13 .....**152** C4
Chapel Terr PE30 ....**148** B1
Chapel Wlk 4 NR19 ..**154** C5
Chapel Yd Ashill IP25 ..**84** A7
Wells-next-the-Sea
  NR23 ....**136** C6
Chapelfield Cl 1 NR29 ..**56** C8
Chapman Ave NR30 ...**168** E5
Chapmans Cl 17 NR26 ..**138** D7
Chapnall Cl PE13 ....**152** F6
Chapnall Rd PE13 ....**152** F6
Chappshill Way 22 NR14 ..**89** B3
Chare Rd IP31 ....**127** B1
Charing Cross NR2 ..**178** A3
Charles Ave
Norwich NR7 ....**163** F8
Watton IP25 ....**84** D3
Charles Burrell High Sch
  IP24 ....**176** C1
Charles Burrell Mus★
  IP24 ....**176** C1
Charles Burton Cl 5
  NR30 ....**168** D7
Charles Cl Acle NR13 ..**166** B4
Caister-on-Sea NR30 ..**168** E5
Cromer NR27 ....**10** C4

Charles Cl continued
Dereham NR19 ....**154** C1
Wroxham/Hoveton
  NR12 ....**164** C3
Charles Ewing Cl
  NR11 ....**150** B5
Charles Jewson Ct
  NR6 ....**158** B2
Charles Rash Cl NR28 ..**37** B8
Charles Rd
Fakenham NR21 ......**141** C6
Holt NR25 ....**137** C5
Hunstanton PE36 ....**132** C2
9 Sutton Bridge PE12 ..**41** B8
Charles Sq 6 NR2 ...**162** C6
Charles St
Great Yarmouth NR30 ..**169** D2
King's Lynn PE30 ....**146** E3
11 Wisbech PE13 .....**152** C4
Charles Watling Way 1
  NR5 ....**160** E8
Charles Wood Rd
  NR19 ....**154** F2
Charlock PE30 ......**147** A8
Charlock Dr 8 NR26 ..**138** B6
Charlotte's Cl 1 NR27 ..**9** F5
Charlton Rd NR3 ....**178** B4
Charmbeck Pk NR10 ..**52** D8
Charolais Cl NR14 ..**163** B2
Charter Cl NR31 ....**170** B4
Chartwell Ct NR7 ...**158** F3
Chartwell Rd NR6 ...**158** D3
Chase Ave NR30 .....**146** E3
Chase Cl NR6 ....**158** D5
Chase Ct
East Dereham NR19 ..**154** D6
Thetford IP24 ......**176** B3
Chase St PE13 ......**152** C6
Chase The
Brandon IP27 ....**175** E2
Brundall NR13 ......**165** F6
Stow Bardolph PE34 ..**78** E7
Upwell PE14 ....**77** D3
Walpole St Andrew PE14 ..**41** E4
Wisbech PE13 ....**152** A7
Chatham Cl 1 IP31 ..**126** B1
Chatham St NR3 ....**178** A4
Chatsworth Rd PE36 ..**132** C3
Chaucer Cl 14 NR30 ..**50** F7
Chaucer Rd NR30 ...**169** D8
Checker St PE30 ....**146** E3
Cheese Hill 9 NR16 ..**118** C5
Chenery Dr NR7 ....**159** C5
Cheney Cres NR13 ...**133** D4
Cheney Hill PE31 ...**133** D4
Cheney's La NR16 ...**105** F5
Chepore La NR18 ....**87** C1
Chequer's La NR15 ..**107** D8
Chequers Cl
Briston NR24 ....**142** E3
2 Long Stratton NR15 ..**106** D3
1 Roydon PE32 ....**28** A1
Chequers La
Bressingham IP22 ...**129** B7
Burston & Shimpling
  IP22 ....**120** E4
Great Ellingham NR17 ..**103** E8
Gressenhall NR20 ....**49** B4
North Runcton PE33 ..**44** A2
Saham Toney IP25 ....**84** C5
West Winch PE33 .....**43** F2
Chequers Rd
Roydon PE32 ....**28** A1
Tharston & Hapton
  NR15 ....**106** D3
Wretton PE33 ....**80** C3
Chequers St
Docking PE31 ....**134** D4
East Ruston NR12 ....**38** F5
Gresham NR11 ....**9** E1
Cherry Cl
11 Great Yarmouth NR31 ..**94** C7
Marham PE33 ....**63** A4
Norwich NR1 ....**162** E4
Cherry Dr NR19 .....**154** F5
Cherry Drift NR19 ..**154** E6
Cherry La
Belton with Browston
  NR31 ....**94** A4
Dereham NR20 ....**68** B7
Cherry Orch NR20 ...**154** F5
Cherry Rd
Great Yarmouth NR31 ..**170** B6
Wisbech PE13 ....**152** C8
Cherry Tree Ave 25 NR29 ..**57** D4
Cherry Tree Cl
Holt NR25 ....**137** B7
Mundford IP26 ......**100** A4
North Lopham IP22 ..**119** A2
Wretham IP24 ....**102** B1
Cherry Tree Ct IP22 ..**177** C5
Cherry Tree Dr NR26 ..**146** C4
Cherry Tree La NR28 ..**151** B5
Cherry Tree Rd
Carleton Rode NR16 ..**105** A1
Plumstead NR11 ......**20** A6
Snettisham PE31 .....**12** E5
Tibenham NR16 ......**120** B7
Cherrytree Cl PE13 ..**133** D6
Cherrywood
Alpington NR14 ......**90** F4
10 Redenhall with Harleston
  IP20 ....**122** D1
Cherrywood Ave NR21 ..**15** C2
Chervil Wlk IP24 ...**116** D2
Cherwell Way 2 NR31 ..**170** B2
Chester Pl NR2 .....**162** C4
Chester St NR2 .....**162** C4

Chester Way IP24 ...**176** A4
Chesterfield Cotts 11
  NR27 ....**139** B7
Chestnut Ave
Great Yarmouth NR31 ..**170** A5
North Walsham NR28 ..**151** E4
Sculthorpe Airfield NR21 ..**15** C2
1 Spixworth NR10 ....**54** A2
Welney PE14 ....**95** D5
West Winch PE33 .....**43** E1
Chestnut Cl
Brandon IP27 ....**175** E2
Dersingham PE31 ....**140** D4
East Dereham NR19 ..**154** E1
Norwich NR5 ....**156** E2
5 Watlington PE33 ...**61** D5
Chestnut Ct 9 NR2 ..**178** A3
Chestnut Gr NR26 ...**138** D4
Chestnut Hill 3 NR4 ..**161** F1
Chestnut Loke NR15 ..**107** A6
Chestnut Rd
Dickleburgh IP21 ...**121** C1
East Dereham NR19 ..**154** C5
Pulham St Mary IP21 ..**121** F4
5 Snettisham PE31 ...**12** E4
13 Tasburgh NR15 ...**106** F6
8 Watton IP25 ....**84** E3
8 Wisbech PE13 .....**152** C4
Chestnut Terr PE12 ..**41** B8
Chestnut Wlk PE37 ...**81** F8
Chestnuts The IP22 ..**128** E2
Chew Cl PE30 ....**147** E8
Cheyham Mount NR4 ..**161** F1
Cheyney Ave 1 NR13 ..**55** A1
Chickering Rd IP21 ..**131** B2
Childs Rd NR9 ....**88** C8
Childs Way NR26 ....**138** C5
Chiltern Cres PE36 ..**132** C3
Chilver House La PE32 ..**44** E7
Chilvers Pl PE31 ...**133** D5
Chimes Way NR10 ...**149** B4
Chimney Springs
  NR29 ....**167** A3
Chimney St IP21 .....**46** F1
Chipperfield Rd NR7 ..**159** E1
Chittock Cl 5 NR10 ..**54** A1
Cholmondeley Way 3
  PE33 ....**43** F2
Choseley Ct NR18 ..**173** C4
Choseley Rd
Docking PE31 ....**134** C7
Thornham PE36 ....**2** D6
Christ Church Rd
  NR31 ....**170** A4
Christchurch Rd NR2 ..**162** A4
Christie Cl 6 NR19 ..**154** D1
Christine Ave NR13 ..**74** C4
Christine Rd 1 NR10 ..**54** A1
Christopher Cl
3 Newton Flotman NR15 ..**89** D1
1 Norwich NR1 ......**162** E2
Christopher Dr PE13 ..**152** A7
Church Alley NR13 ..**165** E6
Church Ave
Croxton NR16 ....**116** C5
Halvergate NR13 .....**74** F1
Little Ellingham NR17 ..**86** A1
Norwich NR4 ....**162** B3
Church Ave E NR2 ..**162** B3
Church Bank
Marshland St James PE14 ..**60** C2
Terrington St Clement
  PE34 ....**144** B6
Church Cl
Antingham NR28 .....**22** B3
3 Bawdeswell NR20 ..**50** E7
Beeston Regis NR27 ..**9** F5
Bixley NR14 ....**90** B7
Brandon IP27 ....**175** B3
Caister-on-Sea NR30 ..**168** D5
Cantley NR13 ....**92** C7
Colby NR11 ....**36** D8
9 Coltishall NR12 ...**54** C6
Grimston PE32 ....**45** B8
Hepworth IP22 .....**127** E1
1 Horstead with Stanninghall
  NR12 ....**54** C6
King's Lynn PE34 ...**146** C4
Lamas NR10 ....**36** F1
13 Loddon NR14 ......**92** A2
2 Norwich NR2 ......**162** B8
Overstrand NR27 .....**11** A3
Pentney PE32 ....**63** C8
Poringland NR14 .....**90** C4
Pulham St Mary IP21 ..**122** A4
1 Roydon IP22 ......**129** D7
Sea Palling NR12 ....**40** B5
Shipdham IP25 ....**67** B2
South Walsham NR13 ..**74** A8
Upper Sheringham
  NR26 ....**138** A4
Walpole St Andrew PE14 ..**41** E4
Whissonsett NR20 ....**31** D2
Wiggenhall St Mary Magdalen
  PE34 ....**61** B6
Wortwell IP20 ......**122** F3
Church Cotts NR19 ...**48** E3
Church Crofts PE31 ..**27** C3
Church Dam NR3 .....**93** A5
Church Dro PE14 .....**77** F6
Church End IP27 ....**175** B3
Church Farm Cl
Palgrave IP22 ......**177** C2
4 Weybourne NR25 ....**8** F5
Church Farm Cres
  NR29 ....**167** B6
Church Farm La NR19 ..**154** C5

Church Farm Rare Breeds
  Ctr★ **79** F8
Church Farm Rd PE31 ..**133** F4
Church Field 4 NR4 ..**89** B8
Church Gate 16 PE12 ..**41** B8
Church Gdns IP31 ...**127** C3
Church Gn
Norwich NR7 ....**159** B5
West Acre PE32 ......**46** B2
Church Hill
Banham NR16 ....**119** D7
Beighton NR13 ....**74** C3
Hoxne IP21 ....**131** A4
Reepham NR10 ......**149** C4
Saxlingham Nethergate
  NR15 ....**107** B8
Starston IP20 ......**122** C3
Church Hill Fst Sch
  PE32 ....**45** C8
Church Hill Sch NR16 ..**119** D7
Church La Aldeby NR34 ..**110** F5
Aldeby, Wheatacre,
  Burgh St Peter NR34 ..**111** B5
Antingham NR28 .....**22** B3
Ashwellthorpe NR16 ..**106** A7
Baconsthorpe NR25 ..**19** F7
Bacton NR28 ....**23** C3
Banham NR16 ....**119** D7
Barnham IP24 ....**125** F6
Barton Bendish PE33 ..**81** B8
Belaugh NR12 ....**54** E5
Belton with Browston
  NR31 ....**94** A5
Billingford NR20 ....**50** B7
Bintree NR20 ....**33** B2
Bircham PE31 ....**14** B3
Blo' Norton IP22 ...**128** B6
Boughton PE33 ......**80** B5
Bracon Ash NR14 ....**88** F3
Bradenham IP25 .....**66** D4
Bressingham IP22 ..**129** B7
Briningham NR24 ....**18** D5
Briston NR24 ....**142** E4
Brockdish IP21 .....**131** C6
Broome NR35 ....**109** B3
Bunwell NR16 ......**105** D3
Burgh & Tuttington NR11 ..**36** D4
Claxton NR14 ....**91** C5
Cley next the Sea NR25 ..**7** D1
Corton NR32 ....**171** F1
Cranworth IP25 ......**85** F7
Deopham NR18 ....**86** F4
Dersingham PE31 ...**140** E3
Ditchingham NR35 ..**108** F3
East Tuddenham NR20 ..**69** C6
East Walton PE32 ....**45** E3
East Winch PE32 .....**44** F2
Easton NR9 ....**70** B6
Felthorpe NR10 ....**155** D7
Filby NR29 ....**75** E8
Fleggburgh NR29 ....**57** A1
Frettenham NR12 ....**54** A5
Fritton & St Olaves NR31 ..**93** F3
Great Massingham PE32 ..**29** D1
Great Yarmouth NR31 ..**170** C5
Gresham NR11 ....**9** E1
Gressenhall NR19 ...**49** C2
Guestwick NR20 .....**33** F6
Haddiscoe NR14 ....**110** E7
Hales NR14 ....**109** F7
Harpley PE31 ....**29** C5
Heacham PE31 ......**133** E6
Heckingham NR14 ...**92** C1
Hemblington NR13 ...**73** F6
Hepworth IP22 .....**127** E1
Hevingham NR10 .....**36** B1
Hindolveston NR20 ..**33** C8
Hockwold cum Wilton
  IP26 ....**114** A6
Holme Hale PE37 ....**65** F2
Ixworth NR9 ....**69** E2
Ketteringham NR18 ..**88** E5
King's Lynn PE30 ...**146** E4
Langley with Hardley
  NR14 ....**92** C3
Lessingham NR12 ....**24** E3
Leziate PE32 ....**44** F4
Little Ellingham NR17 ..**86** A1
Little Massingham PE32 ..**29** C2
Long Stratton NR15 ..**106** F4
Lound NR32 ....**171** A3
Marham PE33 ....**63** A4
Marlingford NR9 ....**69** E4
Marsham NR10 ....**36** B2
Mattishall NR20 ....**68** F6
Mautby NR29 ....**75** D5
Morley NR18 ....**87** A3
Mundesley NR11 ....**143** C6
Mundford IP26 .....**100** B4
Neatishead NR12 ....**55** E6
North Elmham NR20 ..**49** E8
Northwold PE33 .....**81** B2
Norwich NR7 ....**159** C5
Norwich NR4 ....**161** E1
Old Buckenham NR17 ..**104** D2
Oulton NR11 ....**35** C7
Potter Heigham NR29 ..**56** F7
Redenhall with Harleston
  IP20 ....**122** D2
Rickinghall Superior
  IP22 ....**128** E1
Roydon PE32 ....**27** F2
Runcton Holme PE33 ..**61** D4
Runhall NR20 ....**69** A6
Runhall NR9 ....**87** A8
St Mary, South Elmham
  otherwise Homersfield
  IP20 ....**123** B4

Church La continued
Sheringham NR26 ...**138** F6
Shipdham IP25 ....**67** B2
Shouldham Thorpe PE33 ..**62** B3
South Creake NR21 ..**14** D7
4 Southery PE38 .....**97** B5
Sparham NR9 ....**51** B6
Spixworth NR10 .....**53** F2
Sprowston NR7 .....**159** B5
Stanfield NR20 ......**48** F8
Stanhoe PE31 ....**14** E7
Stuston IP21 ....**130** B4
Surlingham NR14 ....**73** A1
Sustead NR11 ....**21** B8
Swannington NR9 ....**52** B6
Swanton Abbott NR10 ..**37** C5
Terrington St John PE14 ..**42** B2
Thelnetham IP22 ...**128** B5
Thompson IP24 .....**102** C7
Thwaite NR35 ......**109** A6
Tibenham NR16 .....**120** C8
Tilney All Saints PE34 ..**42** E4
Tittleshall PE32 ....**48** B8
Tivetshall St Mary NR15 ..**121** B4
Tunstead NR12 ......**37** F1
Watlington PE33 ....**61** C6
Weasenham All Saints
  PE32 ....**47** C8
Wicklewood NR18 ...**87** B5
Winfarthing IP22 ..**120** B4
Wood Dalling NR11 ..**34** B5
Wormegay PE33 ......**62** D6
Wroxham/Hoveton
  NR12 ....**164** B3
Yaxham NR19 ....**68** A5
Church Lanes NR21 ..**141** B5
Church Loke NR11 ...**21** D7
Church Marsh Nature
  Reserve★ NR14 ......**73** A1
Church Mdw
Rickinghall Inferior
  IP22 ....**128** D2
Yelverton NR14 ......**90** E5
Church Mdw La NR14 ..**90** F4
Church Mews PE13 ..**152** C5
Church of the Holy Sepulchre
  (rems)★ IP24 ......**176** B4
Church Path PE33 ...**80** C2
Church Pl NR34 ....**134** D5
Church Plain
14 Great Yarmouth NR30 ..**169** C4
Wells-next-the-Sea
  NR23 ....**136** D5
Church Rd
Alburgh IP20 ....**122** F6
Alpington NR14 ......**90** F4
Aslacton NR15 .....**106** A2
Aylmerton NR11 .....**10** A3
Bacton NR12 ....**23** D4
Barningham IP31 ...**127** C3
Barton Bendish PE33 ..**81** B8
Barton Turf NR12 ....**55** E8
Beeston with Bittering
  PE32 ....**48** B2
Beetley NR20 ....**49** B6
Bergh Apton NR15 ...**91** A3
Bintree NR20 ....**33** B2
Brandon IP27 ....**175** B3
Bridgham NR16 .....**118** B5
Brockdish IP21 .....**131** C6
Brundall NR13 .....**165** E6
Burgh Castle NR31 ..**93** F8
Cantley NR13 ....**92** D7
Carleton Rode NR16 ..**105** C2
Catfield NR29 ....**56** C8
Christchurch PE14 ...**95** A7
Clenchwarton PE34 ..**145** D5
Colby NR11 ....**36** D8
Colkirk NR21 ....**31** D5
Crimplesham PE33 ...**80** B6
Denham IP21 ....**131** A1
Deopham NR18 ....**86** F3
Dickleburgh & Rushall
  IP21 ....**130** D8
Dilham NR28 ....**38** C4
Downham Market PE38 ..**172** C5
Earsham NR35 ......**123** F7
Ellingham NR35 ....**109** D3
Elm PE14 ....**77** B7
Elsing NR20 ....**50** F3
Felmingham NR28 ...**37** B7
Flitcham PE31 ....**28** C5
Flixton NR35 ....**123** E5
Fordham PE38 ....**79** B1
Freethorpe NR13 ....**92** F8
Frettenham NR10 ....**53** F4
Gillingham NR34 ...**110** C3
Great & Little Plumstead
  NR13 ....**73** A4
Great Yarmouth NR31 ..**170** C7
Griston IP25 ....**85** A1
Haddiscoe NR14 ....**110** E6
Hardingham NR9 .....**86** D7
Hedenham NR35 ....**108** E4
Hilgay PE38 ....**79** E1
Hoe NR20 ....**49** F6
Holme Hale IP25 ....**66** A2
Honington IP31 ....**126** D1
Horning NR12 ....**55** F3
Hunstanton PE36 ...**132** F7
Itteringham NR11 ...**20** C2
Ketteringham NR18 ..**88** D5
Kirby Cane NR35 ...**109** E4
Kirstead NR15 ....**90** F1

Church Rd *continued*
Leverington PE13 152 F7
Lingwood & Burlingham NR13 73 F3
Little Barningham NR11 20 C4
Market Weston IP22 127 E4
Marlingford NR9 70 A3
Neatishead NR12 55 E6
Newton Flotman NR15 89 C1
North Lopham IP22 119 A1
Norton Subcourse NR14 92 E1
Ovington IP25 84 E5
Postwick with Witton NR13 72 F3
Potter Heigham NR29 56 F6
Quidenham NR16 118 F8
Reedham NR13 93 A5
Repps with Bastwick NR29 57 A4
Runhall NR9 69 A1
Sea Palling NR12 40 A5
Shelfanger IP22 120 B2
Shouldham PE33 62 E3
Shropham NR17 103 B3
Sisland NR14 91 D1
Snettisham PE31 12 E5
Somerton NR29 57 F6
South Lopham IP22 128 D8
Stockton NR34 109 F5
Stoke Ferry PE33 80 E2
Strumpshaw NR13 91 F8
Sutton NR12 39 C3
Swafield NR28 22 C4
Swainsthorpe NR14 89 D4
Tasburgh NR15 106 F6
Terrington St John PE14 42 B1
Tharston & Hapton NR15 106 D5
Thompson IP24 102 B7
Thurlton NR14 92 F1
Thurne NR29 56 E2
Tibenham NR16 120 E8
Tilney All Saints PE34 144 F1
Tilney St Lawrence PE34 42 D2
Toft Monks NR34 110 D6
Topcroft NR35 107 F3
Tunstead NR12 55 B8
Upton with Fishley NR13 166 A6
Wacton NR15 106 C2
Walpole St Andrew PE14 41 E3
Walsingham NR22 16 F8
Watlington PE34 61 C6
Watton IP25 84 E3
Wellingham PE32 30 E1
Wereham PE33 80 E4
West Beckham NR25 9 C2
West Dereham PE33 80 B4
Wheatacre NR34 111 A5
Whinburgh & Westfield NR19 68 A3
Wiggenhall St Germans PE34 61 A8
Wimbotsham PE34 172 E8
Wingfield IP21 131 E3
Woodton NR35 108 B5
Wortham IP22 129 C5
Wreningham NR16 88 E1
Wroxham/Hoveton NR12 164 D5
Yelverton NR14 90 F5
Church Rd N IP21 131 C7
Church St Ashill IP25 84 A7
Attleborough NR17 174 D5
Bawburgh NR9 160 A6
Bradenham IP25 66 E3
Brisley NR20 49 A8
Briston NR24 142 E4
Carbrooke IP25 85 A5
Coltishall NR12 54 C6
Cromer NR27 139 C6
Diss IP22 177 D4
East Dereham NR19 154 D5
Elsing NR20 50 F3
Gimingham NR11 22 E7
Great Ellingham NR17 103 E7
23 Harleston IP20 122 D2
Hingham NR9 86 C5
Holt NR25 137 C6
Horsford NR10 53 B2
Hunstanton PE36 132 C4
Kenninghall NR16 119 B4
King's Lynn PE30 146 D4
Litcham PE32 48 A4
Little Walsingham NR22 16 F7
New Buckenham NR16 104 F1
North Creake NR21 15 D8
11 North Walsham NR28 151 D5
Northrepps NR27 11 A2
Norwich NR6 158 E5
Plumstead NR11 20 A5
Reepham NR10 149 C4
Sheringham NR26 138 D7
Southrepps NR11 22 B7
Stiffkey NR23 6 D6
15 Sutton Bridge PE12 41 B8
Thornham PE36 2 D6
Trimingham NR11 11 D1
Wells-next-the-Sea NR23 136 D5
Wymondham NR18 173 B4
Church Terr
5 Outwell PE14 77 F6
21 Wisbech PE13 152 C5
Wroxham NR12 164 B3
Church View
Harleston IP20 122 E2
Marham PE33 63 B4
Ormesby St Margaret NR29 167 B2
Pentney PE32 63 C8
Church View Cl
Norwich NR7 159 B5
Reedham NR13 93 A5
Church View Ct NR7 159 B5
Church Wlk
Burnham Market PE31 135 B2
Great Yarmouth NR31 94 C6
Shelfanger IP22 120 B2
Churchfarm Wlk PE33 62 E1
Churchfield Gn 3 NR7 163 D8
Churchfield Rd 3 PE14 77 F6
Churchfields NR9 88 D8
Churchfields Rd NR15 106 F4
Churchgate St 2 PE38 97 B5
Churchgate Way PE34 144 C5
Churchill Cl
Hevingham NR10 53 B8
1 Watton IP25 84 D3
Churchill Cres
Fincham PE33 62 E1
Sheringham NR26 138 B5
Churchill Ct NR19 154 D4
Churchill Pl NR15 90 F2
Churchill Rd
Great Yarmouth NR30 169 D6
Norwich NR3 162 E8
Thetford IP24 176 E5
Wisbech PE13 152 D4
Churchill Way PE38 172 B4
Churchman Rd NR7 159 C2
Churchway IP22 128 F5
Cider Cl NR17 174 E4
Cinder La NR34 111 B4
Cintra Rd NR1 163 B6
Cirrus Way NR7 159 C2
City Coll Norwich NR2 178 A2
City of Norwich Aviation Mus★ NR6 53 D1
City of Norwich Sch NR4 162 B2
City Rd NR1 178 C1
City View Rd NR6 158 A4
Civic Gdns NR3 158 B3
Civray Ave PE38 172 C6
Clabburn Cl 1 NR15 89 C1
Clabon Fst Cl NR3 158 F2
Clabon Rd NR3 158 F2
Clabon Second Cl NR3 158 F3
Clabon Third Cl NR3 158 F3
Clackclose Com Prim Sch PE38 172 B5
Clackclose Rd PE38 172 C6
Clancy Rd NR7 159 C1
Clapper La PE34 145 E5
Clare Ave NR31 170 B2
Clare Cl NR3 158 E1
Clare Rd Cromer NR27 139 D5
King's Lynn PE30 148 C3
Clare Sch NR4 162 A3
Claremont Rd
Norwich NR4 162 A2
Wisbech PE13 152 E5
Clarence Ct
Hunstanton PE36 132 C6
17 Watton IP25 84 D3
Clarence Rd
14 Great Yarmouth NR30 169 D2
Hunstanton PE36 132 D6
Norwich NR1 163 A5
Wisbech PE13 152 D6
Clarendon Cl 6 NR30 169 D2
Clarendon Dr 10 NR29 57 D4
Clarendon Rd
Norwich NR2 162 C5
Sculthorpe NR21 141 A5
Clarendon Stps 1 NR2 162 B5
Clark Rd NR35 109 B2
Clark's La NR21 17 E5
Clark's Loke 7 NR13 73 D6
Clarke Cl IP22 177 C1
Clarke Rd NR3 162 D8
Clarke's Cl 2 NR9 69 F2
Clarke's La
Barsham NR34 124 F7
Gooderstone PE33 82 A5
Clarke's Rd NR31 170 C5
Clarkes Rd NR30 169 B5
Clarkson Ave PE13 152 D5
Clarkson Ct PE13 152 D6
Clarkson Inf Sch The PE13 152 E6
Clarkson Rd
10 Lingwood NR13 74 A3
Norwich NR5 161 C7
Claxton Cl Mileham PE32 48 D6
5 Thetford IP24 176 C4
Claxton Cnr NR14 91 C6
Clay Hill PE32 48 B7
Clay La Bacton NR28 23 B3
Bradwell NR31 94 C5
Hepworth IP22 127 F1
Saxlingham Nethergate NR15 107 A7
Swannington NR9 52 C7
Clay Rd NR30 168 F5
Claydon Gr NR31 170 B7
Claymore Gdns NR29 167 B2
Claypit La NR21 141 C5
Claypit Rd NR20 33 D3
Clayton Cl
Dersingham PE31 140 D4
Wisbech PE13 152 F6
Clearview Dr NR14 90 C5
Cleaves Dr NR22 16 F8
Clement Gdns IP22 177 F3
Clement Scott Mews NR27 139 D5
Clements Cl IP21 130 C5
Clements Ct PE34 144 B5
Clenchwarton Prim Sch PE34 145 E5
Clenchwarton Rd PE34 146 B4
Clere Cl NR18 173 C5
Cleveland Rd NR2 178 A3
Cleves Way NR8 156 E4
Cley La IP25 84 C4
Cley Marshes Nature Reserve★ NR25 7 F7
Cley Rd Blakeney NR25 7 D6
Bradwell NR31 94 C7
Cockley Cley PE37 82 E8
Holt NR25 137 B8
Swaffham PE37 153 B2
Clickers Rd NR3 162 C8
Cliff Ave Cromer NR27 139 C6
Great Yarmouth NR31 170 D3
Cliff Cl NR13 92 F4
Cliff Ct PE36 132 C6
Cliff Dr NR27 139 C7
Cliff Hill 4 NR31 170 D4
Cliff La Cromer NR27 139 C6
Great Yarmouth NR31 171 D8
Cliff Par PE36 132 C5
Cliff Pk Com Mid Sch NR31 170 D2
Cliff Pk Fst Sch NR31 170 D2
Cliff Pk High Sch NR31 170 D1
Cliff Rd Cromer NR27 139 D5
Overstrand NR27 11 A3
Sheringham NR26 138 E7
Cliff Terr PE36 132 C5
Cliffe-en-Howe Rd PE32 44 F8
Clifford Ave NR30 168 D5
Clifford Burman Cl PE30 148 A1
Clifford Pye Cl NR10 35 B2
Clifton Cl 3 NR2 162 C7
Clifton Pk NR27 10 C5
Clifton Rd
King's Lynn PE30 148 B1
Wymondham NR18 173 C6
Clifton St NR2 162 B7
Clifton Way NR27 11 B3
Clink Hill NR30 168 B4
Clink Rd NR12 40 A6
Clint Hill IP31 126 D2
Clint St NR29 56 B5
Clintergate Rd IP20 122 C6
Clintock Pl 10 NR30 169 C5
Clipbush La
Banham NR16 119 C7
Fakenham NR21 141 E5
Scoulton NR9 85 C4
Clipped Hedge La NR11 22 B7
Clipstreet La NR21 18 B8
Close The
Brancaster PE31 3 D7
Brundall NR13 165 C4
Docking PE31 134 E4
Great Yarmouth NR31 170 A5
Hemsby NR29 167 B7
Holt NR25 137 C5
Little Melton NR9 160 D2
North Lopham IP22 119 A2
North Walsham NR28 151 D4
Norwich NR1 178 C3
Rackheath NR13 72 D8
Roydon IP22 177 A5
Sheringham NR26 138 D8
Stow Bedon NR17 102 D7
Clough Dr 9 IP26 98 E1
Clough La PE30 146 D4
Clovelly Dr NR6 157 E2
Clover Dr 7 NR26 138 B6
Clover Hill Fst Sch NR5 161 B8
Clover Hill Rd NR5 160 F8
Clover Rd
Attleborough NR17 174 C3
Aylsham NR11 150 D5
Norwich NR7 158 F3
Clover Way
Fakenham NR21 141 E4
Great Yarmouth NR31 170 A4
Thetford IP24 176 D5
Clover Wlk PE34 61 B8
Cloverland Dr 6 NR29 167 B7
Clowes Ct NR34 110 D1
Clubbs La NR23 136 D6
Clydesdale Rise NR31 94 C8
Coach & Horses Row NR2 178 A2
Coach House Ct 1 NR4 162 A3
Coach La NR19 67 C6
Coachmans Ct NR7 158 F4
Coalwharf Rd PE13 152 B4
Coast Rd Bacton NR12 23 F4
Cley next the Sea NR25 7 F7
Corton NR32 171 F1
Happisburgh NR12 23 F3
Hopton on Sea NR31 171 D4
Overstrand NR27 11 B3
Salthouse NR25 8 A7
Wiveton NR25 7 D6
Coastguard Rd NR30 168 F5
Coates Ct 5 PE14 59 D2
Cob Cl 7 NR31 94 C8
Cobb's Pl 5 NR30 169 D4
Cobblers La PE14 41 F2
Cobbleways The 9 NR29 58 B6
Cobbold St IP22 177 B5
Cobbs Hill PE34 144 B5
Cobham Way NR7 159 C2
Cobholm Cl 14 NR31 169 B4
Cobholm Fst Sch NR31 169 B4
Cobholm Rd 5 NR31 169 B4
Coburg Cl 10 IP25 84 D3
Coburg La IP25 84 B6
Coburg St
9 King's Lynn PE30 146 E5
Norwich NR2 178 A2
Cochrane Cl IP25 85 A3
Cock Dro PE38 172 B7
Cock Fen Rd PE14 95 D7
Cock Rd NR14 92 A3
Cock St Ixworth NR9 69 F2
Wymondham NR18 173 B5
Cocketts Dr PE13 152 E5
Cocklehole Rd PE34 41 F8
Codling's La NR11 150 A6
Coigncroft The NR13 165 E3
Coke Rd NR1 162 E1
Coker's Hill NR22 16 F7
Colby Prim Sch NR11 36 E8
Cold Harbour Rd NR29 56 D4
Coldershaw Rd NR6 158 B4
Coldham Cl NR29 167 B3
Coldham Hall Carnser NR14 165 C1
Coldham Rd NR21 17 D7
Coldham's La PE33 80 A5
Coldhorn Cres PE13 152 D7
Coleburn Rd NR1 89 E8
Colegate NR3 178 A3
Colegate End Rd IP21 121 E6
Coleman Cl
Palgrave IP22 177 D1
Taverham NR8 155 F2
Coleridge Cl NR8 156 D8
Coleridge Rd IP22 177 E4
Coles Way NR10 149 C5
Colin Mclean Rd NR19 154 C7
Colindeep La NR7 159 A4
Colkett Dr NR6 158 E3
Colkirk CE VA Prim Sch NR21 31 D5
Coll of W Anglia (Fakenham Learning Ctr) The NR21 141 B4
Coll of W Anglia (Hunstanton Learning Ctr) The PE36 132 D4
Coll of W Anglia (Isle Campus) The PE13 152 E2
Coll of W Anglia (King's Lynn Ctr) The PE30 146 F5
Coll of W Anglia (Sheringham Centre) The NR26 138 C7
Coll of W Anglia (Wispech Campus) The PE13 152 E2
Collectors World of Eric St John Foti★ PE38 79 B6
Colleen Cl
Dereham NR19 67 E5
East Dereham NR19 154 D1
College Cl NR12 54 D7
College Ct 1 NR31 169 B4
College Dr PE31 133 C4
College La Keswick NR4 89 C7
9 King's Lynn PE30 146 D4
Runcton Holme PE33 61 F3
College Rd
Hockwold cum Wilton IP26 113 F7
Norwich NR2 162 A5
Thompson IP24 102 C7
Thurlton NR14 110 C8
Wereham PE33 97 F8
Collen's Gn NR9 51 B3
Collers Way NR10 149 C6
Collett's Bridge La PE14 59 C1
Colley Hill Drift PE32 48 D4
Collin's La PE33 63 C5
Collingwood Cl
Heacham PE31 133 D3
25 Hethersett NR9 88 D7
Collingwood Dr NR11 22 F8
Collingwood Rd
Downham Market PE38 172 B4
Great Yarmouth NR30 169 E7
Hunstanton PE36 132 D3
Collingwood Way IP24 176 F6
Collingwood Wlk 1 IP24 176 F6
Collins Ct NR6 158 D2
Collins La PE31 133 D5
Collis La NR29 57 F5
Colls Rd NR7 159 D1
Colman Ave 1 NR14 89 F4
Colman Fst Sch NR4 162 A3
Colman Hospl NR2 162 A4
Colman Mid Sch NR4 161 F3
Colman Rd NR4 161 F5
Colmans Mustard Shop★ NR1 178 B2
Colne Pl NR27 139 B6
Colne Rd NR27 139 B6
Colney La Colney NR4 161 A3
Hethersett NR9 160 D1
Colney Rd PE30 147 D5
Colomb Rd NR31 170 C6
Coltishall Airfield NR10 54 B8
Coltishall La NR10 53 E2
Coltishall Prim Sch NR12 54 D7
Coltishall Rd
Belaugh NR12 164 A6
Buxton with Lammas NR10 53 F8
Coltishall Sta NR12 54 C7
Colton Rd NR9 69 E6
Coltsfoot Rd NR10 53 A7
Coltsfoot Way IP24 176 F5
Columbia Way PE30 146 F6
Columbine Cl 4 IP24 176 F5
Columbine Rd NR10 53 B2
Columbine The NR5 160 E7
Colvile Rd PE13 152 E5
Colville Rd NR24 142 B5
Comber Cl IP21 130 D6
Comet Rd 7 IP25 84 F3
Comfrey Way IP24 116 D2
Commercial Rd NR19 154 E5
Common Drift NR20 49 C4
Common Dro
Flitcham with Appleton PE31 27 F5
Southery PE38 97 B5
Common End PE32 47 D8
Common La
Beccles NR34 110 D1
Beetley NR20 49 E5
Brancaster PE31 3 D6
Brockdish IP21 131 D6
Burgh & Tuttington NR11 36 E6
East Walton PE32 45 E3
Field Dalling NR25 7 B1
Filby NR29 75 E8
Gayton PE32 45 C4
Great Witchingham NR9 51 D4
King's Lynn PE30 148 C2
North Runcton PE33 44 A2
Norwich NR7 163 F5
Sheringham NR26 138 E6
6 Southery PE38 97 B5
Thorpe Market NR11 22 A6
Common La N NR34 110 D1
Common Loke NR14 92 A2
Common Pl 3 NR22 16 F7
Common Rd
Aldeby NR34 111 B3
Ashwellthorpe NR16 105 E7
Barton Turf NR12 38 F1
Botesdale IP22 128 F1
Bressingham IP22 129 C8
Brumstead NR12 24 A1
Burston & Shimpling IP22 120 E2
Castle Acre PE32 46 E1
East Tuddenham NR20 69 B5
Forncett NR16 105 E5
Foxley NR20 33 D1
Gissing NR15 120 F5
Great Yarmouth NR31 170 C8
Hemsby NR29 57 F4
Hopton IP22 127 F6
Lessingham NR12 24 E2
Martham NR29 57 B4
Mundham NR14 91 C1
Neatishead NR12 55 E6
Pulham Market IP21 121 E7
Runcton Holme PE33 61 D4
Runhall NR20 68 F4
Scole IP21 130 F8
Shelfanger IP22 119 F3
Shelton NR15 107 B1
Skeyton NR10 37 A6
Snettisham PE31 12 D4
Somerton NR29 57 E6
Surlingham NR14 165 B1
Swafield NR28 22 D4
Thurne NR29 56 E3
Wacton NR15 106 D2
West Walton PE14 59 D7
Wiggenhall St Germans PE34 60 F7
Common The
Freethorpe NR13 92 E7
1 Harleston IP20 122 D1
Lyng NR9 51 A4
Surlingham NR14 165 A1
Swardeston NR14 89 B6
Commonside NR10 35 A2
Commonwealth Way 12 NR7 72 D4
Compass Rd NR18 173 F1
Compit Hills NR27 139 B3
Concorde Rd NR6 158 C5
Conesford Dr NR1 162 F3
Coney Weston Rd
Barningham IP31 127 C4
Sapiston IP31 126 D2
Conference Way
Colkirk NR21 31 E5
Wisbech PE13 152 C8
Conge The NR30 169 C4
Congham Rd PE32 28 B1
Conifer Cl NR29 167 A3
Coniston Cl
2 Hethersett NR9 88 E8
King's Lynn PE30 148 F1
2 Norwich NR5 161 C6
Coniston Rd NR15 90 E1
Coniston Sq 1 NR30 169 D4
Connaught Ave NR31 170 C3

Connaught Plain
NR17 . . . . .174 D5
Connaught Rd
Attleborough NR17 . . .174 B4
Cromer NR27 . . . . . . .139 D5
Norwich NR2 . . . . . . .162 B7
Constable Cl
7 Attleborough NR17 . .174 B4
2 Diss IP22 . . . . .177 C4
Constable Ct 15 IP20 . .122 D2
Constable Dr 4 NR31 . .170 A7
Constable Rd NR4 . . . .162 C1
Constitution Hill
Fakenham NR21 . . . . .141 B4
North Runcton PE33 . . .43 F4
Norwich NR6 . . . . . . .158 E3
Constitution Opening
NR3 . . . . .158 E2
Convent Rd 4 NR2 . . .162 C5
Convy Priors NR30 . . .168 C6
Conway Rd
Great Yarmouth NR31 . .170 D6
Sheringham NR26 . . . .138 C5
Conyers NR18 . . . . . . .173 C6
Cook Rd IP25 . . . . .66 A3
Cooke Cl NR5 . . . . . . .160 E7
Cooke's Rd NR15 . . . . .91 B4
Cookley La IP23 . . . . . .130 F1
Cooper La NR1 . . . . . . .89 F8
Cooper Rd
North Walsham NR28 . .151 D6
8 Sheringham NR26 . . .138 C5
Co-operative St NR26 . .138 C5
Coopers Cl NR8 . . . . . .155 E3
Coopers La PE33 . . . . . .62 B2
Copeman Rd
Aylsham NR11 . . . . . .150 D5
Great & Little Plumstead
NR13 . . . . .73 A6
3 Roydon IP22 . . . . . .129 D7
Copenhagen Way
NR6 . . . . .158 C2
Copince's La NR16 . . . .119 C7
Copper Beech Cl
NR21 . . . . .141 D6
Copper Hall PE37 . . . . .153 B3
Copper La NR9 . . . . . . .86 C5
Copper Smith Way
NR18 . . . . .173 F5
Copperfield 4 PE30 . . .147 C5
Copperfield Ave 1
NR30 . . . . .170 D8
Coppice Ave NR6 . . . . .157 E5
Coppice The 6 NR7 . . .174 C5
Coppins Ct PE14 . . . . .152 E2
Corbet Ave NR7 . . . . . .159 B2
Corbett Rd 2 NR28 . . .151 C6
Corbyn Shaw Rd PE30 .147 E4
Cordon St PE13 . . . . . .152 C4
Coriander Dr IP24 . . . .176 F4
Corie Rd NR4 . . . . . . .161 F4
Corkway Dro PE38 . . . . .97 E1
Cormorant Way 10 NR31 .94 C8
Corncutters Cl NR3 . . .178 B3
Corner Comm Rd NR28 .38 B7
Corner La NR10 . . . . . . .53 B3
Corner St 2 NR27 . . . .139 B7
Cornfield The NR25 . . . . .7 A3
Cornfields IP21 . . . . . .121 B1
Cornish Ave NR28 . . . . .22 E5
Cornish Way NR28 . . . .151 C7
Cornwallis Cl 7 NR5 . . .161 A7
Coronation Ave
2 Marthan NR29 . . . . .57 D4
Nordelph PE38 . . . . . .78 D3
1 Rollesby NR29 . . . . .57 D2
West Winch PE33 . . . . .43 F3
Coronation Cl NR6 . . . .158 A4
Coronation Cotts PE32 . .47 F4
Coronation Cres
NR15 . . . . .107 D5
Coronation Gn NR31 . . .169 B3
Coronation Gr PE37 . . .153 B5
Coronation La
Blakeney NR25 . . . . . . .7 D7
Somerton NR29 . . . . . .57 F5
Coronation Pl IP27 . . . .175 B2
Coronation Rd
Clenchwarton PE34 . . .146 A5
Great Yarmouth NR31 . .169 B3
Holt NR25 . . . . .137 C5
Norwich NR6 . . . . . . .158 A4
Coronation Terr
Caston NR17 . . . . . . .102 F8
6 Great Yarmouth NR30 .169 C4
Coronation Wlk NR15 . .91 A5
Coronilla Gn NR31 . . . .170 B5
Corporation Rd PE13 . . .152 D3
Corpusty Prim Sch
NR11 . . . . .19 F1
Corpusty Rd
Briston NR24 . . . . . . .142 F1
Thurning NR24 . . . . . . .19 B2
Wood Dalling NR11 . . . .34 D7
Corton Rd NR1 . . . . . .178 C1
Coslany Sq NR3 . . . . . .178 C4
Coslany St NR3 . . . . . .178 A3
Costessey High Sch
NR5 . . . . .156 E2
Costessey Inf Sch
NR5 . . . . .157 B1
Costessey Jun Sch
NR5 . . . . .156 F1
Costessey
Drayton NR8 . . . . . . .156 E6
Ringland NR8 . . . . . . .70 B8
Taverham NR8 . . . . . .157 A7

Coston La NR18 . . . . . . .87 A8
Cosy Cnr NR28 . . . . . . .151 B4
Cotman Cl IP22 . . . . . .177 C4
Cotman Dr NR31 . . . . .170 A7
Cotman Fields NR1 . . . .178 C4
Cotman Rd NR1 . . . . . .163 B5
Cotoneaster Ct 4 NR31 .170 B6
Cottage Dr The NR7 . . .163 E8
Cottage Farm Abbey
PE32 . . . . .46 C2
Cottage Rd NR29 . . . . . .57 E6
Cotterall Ct NR5 . . . . .161 A8
Cottinghams Dr NR10 . .157 E7
Cotton Rd NR9 . . . . . . .70 A4
Cotton's Cnr PE14 . . . . .77 D2
Cottons Head PE14 . . . .77 E7
Cotts La PE34 . . . . .144 F1
Coughtrey Cl NR7 . . . . .159 B5
Coulson La IP27 . . . . . .175 C4
Coulton Cl PE30 . . . . . .146 E4
Council Rd 4 PE13 . . . .152 E6
County Ct Rd 3 PE30 . .146 E4
Court Cl 6 NR29 . . . . . .57 D2
Court Dr NR27 . . . . . . .139 B6
Court Gdns PE38 . . . . .172 C5
Court Hill NR12 . . . . . . .54 A4
Court Rd
Great Snoring NR21 . . . .17 B5
Rollesby NR29 . . . . . . .57 D2
Courtenay Cl
4 East Dereham NR19 . .154 D5
2 Norwich NR5 . . . . .160 F8
Courtfields PE37 . . . . . .153 B3
Courtnell Pl PE30 . . . . .147 D5
Courtney Cl 7 NR19 . . .154 D5
Courtyard The 5 NR4 . .161 C5
Covent Gdn Rd NR30 . . .168 C7
Coventry St 2 NR21 . . . .15 C2
Coventry Way IP24 . . . .176 A4
Covert Sycamore
IP24 . . . . .176 A3
Covert The IP24 . . . . . .176 E6
Covey Cl
Surlingham NR14 . . . . .91 C8
Taverham NR8 . . . . . .155 D2
Covey Way IP27 . . . . . .113 F1
Cow Hill NR2 . . . . .178 A3
Cow Lake Dro PE14 . . . .59 D5
Cow Mdw Rd NR13 . . . .92 C8
Cow Tro NR29 . . . . .57 D3
Cow Twr★ NR3 . . . . . .178 C4
Cowdewell Mews 7
NR8 . . . . .155 D1
Cowgate NR3 . . . . .178 B4
Cowle's Dro IP26 . . . . .113 D5
Cowper Cl NR11 . . . . . .143 C5
Cowper Rd NR19 . . . . . .154 E5
Cowslip Cl 14 NR14 . . . .89 B3
Cowslip La NR26 . . . . . .138 B6
Cowslip Wlk PE34 . . . . .61 B8
Cox's La PE13 . . . . .152 A3
Coxswain Read Way
NR30 . . . . .168 E4
Cozens Rd NR1 . . . . . .163 A4
Cozens-Hardy Rd NR7 . .159 B4
Crab Apple La NR14 . . .110 E8
Crab La Boughton PE33 . .81 A5
Great Yarmouth NR31 . .170 A5
Crab Marsh PE13 . . . . .152 B8
Crabapple Cl 7 NR18 . . .173 E4
Crabapple La NR9 . . . . .68 D1
Crabb La PE34 . . . . .42 E1
Crabb's Abbey PE34 . . . .61 B2
Crabbe's Cl 7 IP26 . . . . .98 E1
Crabgate La N NR11 . . . .34 D6
Crabgate La S NR11 . . . .34 D5
Crabtree La NR34 . . . . .110 D1
Crabtree Rise IP21 . . . .131 C6
Cradle Wood Rd NR18 . .151 E3
Cradock Ave NR30 . . . .169 D8
Craft La NR27 . . . . .11 A1
Craft The
Raveningham NR14 . . .110 B8
Winterton-on-Sea NR29 . .58 B6
Cramp Cnr NR14 . . . . . .91 F6
Cranage Rd NR1 . . . . . .162 E1
Crane Cl NR19 . . . . . . .154 C3
Crane's La NR10 . . . . . .150 C1
Cranes Mdw 31 IP20 . . .122 D2
Cranes Rd NR14 . . . . . . .88 F3
Cranfield Rd NR26 . . . .138 A4
Cranleigh Rise NR4 . . . .161 F1
Cranley Rd NR7 . . . . . . .72 E4
Cranmer Ave PE30 . . . .148 C4
Cranmer Ct NR11 . . . . .141 C5
Cranny Field Chase
PE14 . . . . .41 E3
Cranwell Rd 10 IP25 . . . .84 F3
Cranworth Gdns NR1 . . .178 A1
Craske Cl 3 NR26 . . . . .138 C5
Craske Dr NR13 . . . . . . .72 C5
Craske La PE34 . . . . . . .42 A4
Craske Mews 6 NR5 . . .160 E8
Craven La PE33 . . . . . . .62 B6
Crawford Rd NR27 . . . .139 D5
Craymere Beck Rd
Briston NR24 . . . . . . .142 E1
Hindolveston NR24 . . . .18 F1
Craymere Rd NR24 . . . .142 E2
Creake Rd
Burnham Market PE31 . .135 D2
Sculthorpe NR21 . . . . .141 A6
Sculthorpe Airfield PE31 . .15 B3
Creance Rd NR7 . . . . . .159 C4

Crecen La PE36 . . . . . .132 C4
Creek The NR31 . . . . . .135 C7
Cremer Cl 14 PE31 . . . .12 E4
Cremer St NR26 . . . . . .138 D7
Cremorne La NR1 . . . . .163 B5
Crescent Pas PE13 . . . .152 C3
Crescent Rd PE36 . . . . .132 C3
Crescent The
Ashwellthorpe NR16 . . .105 F8
Bacton/Walcott NR12 . . .24 A7
East Dereham NR19 . . .154 C1
East Harling NR16 . . . .118 C4
Hemsby NR29 . . . . . . .167 D7
Hethersett NR9 . . . . . . .88 C7
4 Newton Flotman NR15 . .89 D1
Norwich NR2 . . . . . . .178 A2
Taverham NR8 . . . . . .156 F8
Thurton NR14 . . . . . . .91 C4
Wisbech PE13 . . . . . . .152 C4
Cressener Cl NR6 . . . . .157 E5
Cressingham Rd IP25 . . .83 F6
Cresswell Cl NR5 . . . . .161 B6
Cresswell St PE30 . . . . .146 E6
Crest Rd PE31 . . . . .140 C4
Crick's Wlk IP22 . . . . . .177 A5
Cricket Cl NR8 . . . . . . .155 E3
Cricket Gd Rd NR1 . . . .162 E5
Cricket Pasture The
PE31 . . . . .3 E7
Cricketer's Wlk NR13 . . .92 F3
Cricketers Way PE13 . . .152 A6
Crimp Cramp La NR34 . .111 B4
Cringleford CE Fst & Mid Sch
NR4 . . . . .89 B8
Cringleford Chase
NR4 . . . . .161 C1
Crinoline La NR20 . . . . .69 C1
Crisp Cl PE31 . . . . .140 C3
Crisp Rd NR35 . . . . . . .109 E3
Critten's Rd NR31 . . . . .169 B4
Croft Cl Diss IP22 . . . . .177 C4
10 Harleston IP20 . . . . .122 D2
Croft Gn NR17 . . . . . . .174 B3
Croft Hill NR29 . . . . . . .75 B5
Croft La Corpusty NR11 . .19 F2
Diss IP22 . . . . .177 C4
Marsham NR10 . . . . . .150 C1
Croft Rd
Caister-on-Sea NR30 . . .168 E5
Norton Subcourse NR14 . .92 E1
Upwell PE14 . . . . .77 D3
Croft The
Costessey NR8 . . . . . .156 F4
Cromer NR27 . . . . . . .139 B6
Little Snoring NR21 . . . .17 C3
Swanton Novers NR24 . .18 B3
Croft Yd NR3 . . . . .136 D6
Croftholme Way 2 NR7 .163 D4
Crofts Cl PE31 . . . . . . .135 C1
Crofts The 1 NR5 . . . . .160 F7
Cromarty Way NR30 . . .168 D5
Crome Cl IP22 . . . . . . .177 B4
Crome Rd NR3 . . . . . . .162 F8
Cromer High Sch Language
Coll 139 C5
Cromer Hospl NR27 . . .139 D6
Cromer Jun Sch NR27 . .139 C5
Cromer La PE33 . . . . . . .80 F3
Cromer Mus★ NR27 . . .139 C7
Cromer Rd
Aylsham NR11 . . . . . .150 C8
Blickling NR11 . . . . . . .36 B7
Hevingham NR10 . . . . .36 B1
Holt NR25 . . . . .137 D5
Hunstanton PE36 . . . . .132 D5
Mundesley NR11 . . . . .143 B5
North Walsham NR28 . .151 A6
Norwich NR6 . . . . . . .158 A5
Ormesby St Margaret
with Scratby NR29 . . . .167 A2
Overstrand NR27 . . . . .139 F4
Runton NR27 . . . . .10 A5
Sheringham NR26 . . . .138 E6
Southrepps NR11 . . . . .22 C8
Trimingham NR11 . . . . .11 C2
Cromer Sta NR27 . . . . .139 A7
Cromes Oak Cl NR14 . . .90 C4
Cromes Pl NR10 . . . . . .37 B2
Crompton Rd NR11 . . . .150 C4
Cromwell Cl
6 Cromer NR27 . . . . .139 C6
3 Hethersett NR9 . . . . .88 D8
7 Marthan NR29 . . . . .57 D4
Swaffham PE37 . . . . . .153 D3
Cromwell Rd
Cromer NR27 . . . . . . .139 C6
Great Yarmouth NR31 . .169 C1
Norwich NR7 . . . . . . .159 B3
Weeting-with-Broomhill
IP27 . . . . .114 E8
Wisbech PE13 . . . . . . .152 A2
Cromwell Terr 6 PE30 . .146 E4
Crooks Pl NR1 . . . . . . .178 A1
Crosby Row PE12 . . . . . .41 A8
Cross Bank Rd PE30 . . .146 C6
Cross Dro Hilgay PE38 . . .96 D7
Southery PE38 . . . . . . .97 B3
Cross Keys Cl 2 NR10 . . .53 D2
Cross La Brancaster PE31 . .3 B7
Lessingham NR12 . . . . .24 E4
Northwold IP26 . . . . . .99 C7
Norwich NR3 . . . . . . .178 A4
Runton NR27 . . . . .10 A5
Stanhoe PE31 . . . . . . .14 E7
Swanton Novers NR24 . .18 A3
Wisbech NR14 . . . . . . .91 A8
Cross Rd
Ashby with Oby NR29 . . .56 F1

Cross Rd continued
Great Yarmouth NR31 . .170 D6
Starston IP20 . . . . . . .122 C4
Cross St 6 Cromer NR27 .139 B6
Harpley PE31 . . . . .29 C5
2 Holt NR25 . . . . . . .137 B6
Hoxne IP21 . . . . .131 A3
Salthouse NR25 . . . . . . .8 B6
Cross Stone Rd NR14 . . .92 B3
Cross Way PE31 . . . . . .133 C5
Cross's Grave PE31 . . . . .29 E4
Crossing Rd
Great Green IP21 . . . . .130 A5
Palgrave IP22 . . . . . . .177 D1
Crosskeys Way 3 NR20 . .68 F6
Crossroad NR10 . . . . . . .37 C4
Crosstead NR30 . . . . . .169 D8
Crossway Terr
Acle NR13 . . . . .166 B4
5 Loddon NR14 . . . . . .91 F1
Crossways 4 NR29 . . . . .167 A2
Crostwick La NR10 . . . . .54 A2
Crostwight Rd NR28 . . . .38 D7
Croughton La PE31 . . . . .30 B8
Crow Hall Est PE38 . . . .172 C3
Crow Hall Gn NR31 . . . .170 C3
Crow Hill NR11 . . . . . . .34 C7
Crow La Bircham PE31 . . .14 A2
Elsing NR20 . . . . .50 F4
Great Dunham PE32 . . . .47 E1
Crow Rd NR28 . . . . . . .151 D6
Crow St IP31 . . . . .127 B4
Crow's La IP25 . . . . .84 C1
Crowden Rd NR12 . . . . .24 D4
Crowes Loke NR13 . . . . .73 B7
Crown Ave PE14 . . . . . . .95 A7
Crown Cres IP25 . . . . . .84 E5
Crown Ctyd NR16 . . . . .119 A4
Crown Gdns PE33 . . . . . .80 E4
Crown Gn IP22 . . . . . . .120 E2
Crown La
Coney Weston IP31 . . . .127 B4
Fransham NR19 . . . . . .66 D6
Crown Mdw NR10 . . . . .149 C5
Crown Pl 9 NR19 . . . . .154 D5
Crown Rd
Christchurch PE14 . . . . .95 A7
Colkirk NR21 . . . . .31 C5
East Dereham NR20 . . .154 F5
Great Yarmouth NR30 . .169 D3
Horsham St Faith NR10 . .53 D2
Lamas NR10 . . . . .36 E1
Mundford IP26 . . . . . .100 B4
Norwich NR1 . . . . . . .178 B3
2 Old Buckenham NR17 .104 C2
Crown Sq PE30 . . . . . .147 A7
Crown St
Banham NR16 . . . . . . .119 D7
Brandon IP27 . . . . . . .175 A2
Methwold IP26 . . . . . . .99 A5
Crown Way NR16 . . . . .119 D6
Northwold IP26 . . . . . . .99 C7
Crownthorpe Rd NR18 . .87 C6
Crowshall La NR17 . . . .174 B5
Croxton Rd
Fulmodeston NR21 . . . .17 C3
Thetford IP24 . . . . . . .176 D4
Crummock Rd 3 NR5 . . .161 C6
Cubitt Rd NR1 . . . . . . .163 C7
Cubitts Cl NR20 . . . . . . .33 B2
Cuck Stool La 5 PE33 . . .46 F2
Cuckoo Hill Rd PE31 . . .14 B3
Cuckoo La
Brundall NR13 . . . . . . .73 E3
Carbrooke IP25 . . . . . . .85 B4
Redenhall with Harleston
IP20 . . . . .122 F2
Cuckoo Rd PE34 . . . . . . .79 A8
Cuckoofield La NR14 . . .89 A3
Cucumber La NR13 . . . .165 B5
Cuddle Dike Bank PE14 . .78 A3
Cuffer La NR16 . . . . . . .104 F2
Culey Cl PE30 . . . . .146 F7
Culley's Pit Rd NR12 . . .38 A2
Culling's Hill NR13 . . . . .72 F2
Cullum Cl NR20 . . . . . . .50 B3
Culverin Cl 9 NR7 . . . . . .72 D4
Cummings Bvd NR15 . . .15 C2
Cunningham Ave 2
NR30 . . . . .169 D8
Cunningham Cl 1 NR30 .169 D8
Cunningham Rd 6 NR5 .161 C5
Cunningham Wlk 3
IP24 . . . . .176 C5
Curd's Hall NR19 . . . . . .66 A7
Curie Dr NR31 . . . . .170 B1
Curlew Cl 7 IP25 . . . . . .84 C3
Curlew Way NR31 . . . . .170 A6
Curson Cl 11 NR9 . . . . . .88 C7
Curson Rd 8 NR15 . . . .106 F6
Cursons Mews NR18 . . .173 B6
Curtis Dr 1 IP26 . . . . . . .98 D1
Curtis La PE30 . . . . . . .138 E2
Curtis Rd NR3 . . . . .158 A4
Cushing Cl 1 IP25 . . . . .67 B2
Cushing Dr 3 NR21 . . . .17 B3
Custance Ct NR4 . . . . . .161 C6
Customhouse St PE12 . . .41 C8
Cut Loke NR14 . . . . .73 C1
Cuthbert Cl
4 King's Lynn PE30 . . .148 C5
Norwich NR7 . . . . . . .159 B4
8 Thetford IP24 . . . . .176 F5
Cutler Way
Bowthorpe NR5 . . . . . .160 F6
Norwich NR5 . . . . . . .160 E6
Cutthroat La NR19 . . . . .68 A6
Cutting's Rd IP21 . . . . .131 C8
Cuttons Cnr NR13 . . . . .73 D6

Cydonia Gn 12 NR31 . . .170 F6
Cygnet Cl NR17 . . . . . .174 F6
Cygnet Rd NR19 . . . . . .154 E4
Cygnet Wlk PE13 . . . . .153 C2
Cypress Cl NR8 . . . . . . .156 E8
Cypress Cres NR26 . . . .138 D5
Cypress Pl PE36 . . . . . .132 D4
Cyprus Rd NR17 . . . . . .174 C5
Cyprus St NR1 . . . . . . .162 E3
Cyril Rd NR7 . . . . .163 F7

D

Da Volls Ct NR31 . . . . . .170 D6
Dacre Cl NR4 . . . . .161 E1
Dades La PE14 . . . . .60 B6
Daffodil Way NR20 . . . . .68 E6
Dagmar Mews 12 NR30 .169 D2
Dairy Cl PE32 . . . . .48 C2
Dairy Dro CB6 . . . . .95 F2
Dairy Farm Cl NR21 . . . .141 C6
Dairy Farm Rd NR17 . . .174 C5
Dairy La NR11 . . . . .9 E1
Dakenham Cl NR13 . . . . .72 F8
Dakin Rd NR3 . . . . .158 D1
Dalbier Cl 2 NR13 . . . . .72 E4
Dale End PE31 . . . . .3 D7
Dale La NR29 . . . . .56 C8
Dale Rd
East Dereham NR19 . . .154 C6
Scarning NR19 . . . . . . .67 A7
Stanton IP31 . . . . .127 C1
Dales Cl 6 NR31 . . . . . . .94 C8
Dales Loke NR14 . . . . . .163 D5
Dales The NR13 . . . . . . .165 D3
Dalrymple Way NR3 . . .158 C4
Dam La IP22 . . . . .129 D3
Damgate Back La NR29 . .57 D6
Damgate Cl NR13 . . . . .166 C2
Damgate La Acle NR13 . .166 D2
Marthan NR29 . . . . . . .57 D6
Damgate St NR18 . . . . .173 B3
Danby Cl 6 NR4 . . . . . . .89 D8
Danby Rd NR31 . . . . . . .170 C6
Dane Cl NR24 . . . . .176 B3
Danemoor La NR9 . . . . . .86 F2
Danesbower Cl NR13 . . .165 F6
Danesbower La NR13 . . .165 F6
Danesfort Dr 1 NR19 . . .154 E6
Daniels Rd NR4 . . . . . . .162 B2
Danish House Gdns
NR31 . . . . .11 A4
Daphne Way 8 NR31 . . .170 B5
Dark La
Ashmanhaugh NR12 . . .38 C1
Dickleburgh & Rushall
IP21 . . . . .130 B6
Erpingham NR11 . . . . .21 A1
Kimberley NR18 . . . . . .87 B7
Smallburgh NR12 . . . . .38 D3
Somerton NR29 . . . . . .57 F6
Wretham IP24 . . . . . . .101 F2
Darrell Pl NR5 . . . . . . .161 D7
Darrow Gn Rd IP20 . . . .122 F8
Darrow Wood★ IP20 . . .122 F8
Darrow Wood La IP22 . .120 A1
Darwin Cl 5 PE12 . . . . .41 B8
Darwin Wlk NR14 . . . . .154 D4
Daseley's Cl PE30 . . . . .148 A1
Dashwood Cl NR31 . . . . .93 F6
Dauber's La NR13 . . . . . .74 C2
Davey Cl NR35 . . . . . . .124 C8
Davey Pl NR2 . . . . .178 B3
Davidson Cl NR7 . . . . . .163 F7
Davidson Rd NR7 . . . . .163 F7
Davy Pl Heacham PE31 . .133 C5
7 Loddon NR14 . . . . . .92 A1
Dawber Cl PE30 . . . . . .147 B4
Dawes La 2 PE31 . . . . . .12 E4
Dawnay Ave NR30 . . . . .148 B1
Dawsons La NR20 . . . . .33 C3
Day's La IP31 . . . . .127 C4
Day's Lode Rd PE14 . . . .95 C4
De Caux Rd NR3 . . . . . .158 E1
De Grey Rd PE30 . . . . .147 B5
De Hague Rd NR4 . . . . .161 F4
De Havilland Rd
Dereham NR19 . . . . . .154 C6
Wisbech PE13 . . . . . . .152 C6
De Lucy Cl IP22 . . . . . .177 C5
De Morley Cl 4 IP22 . . .177 A5
De Morley Garth
NR26 . . . . .138 D6
De Warrenne Pl PE32 . . .47 A2
Deacon Cl NR13 . . . . . .165 D4
Deacon Dr 14 NR9 . . . . .88 D8
Deben Dr 14 NR31 . . . . .94 A3
Debenne Rd NR28 . . . . .151 C6
Debnam Cl 10 NR31 . . . .94 A5
Deborah Rd NR31 . . . . .170 C2
De-Carle Smith Rd
NR13 . . . . .166 C4
Decoy Rd
Lakenheath IP27 . . . . .112 F4
Ormesby St Margaret
with Scratby NR29 . . . .167 A4
Ormesby St Michael NR29 .57 F2
Potter Heigham NR29 . . .56 F7
Deep Rd NR18 . . . . . . .173 B8
Deepdale NR13 . . . . . . .165 D3
Deepdale Ave 1 NR29 . .57 C4
Deer Row NR35 . . . . . .109 D1
Delane Rd NR8 . . . . . . .157 D7
Delft Way NR6 . . . . . . .158 A6

Delgate La PE31 ....3 E7
Dell Cl NR15 ......106 F8
Dell Cnr La NR13 ....73 F5
Dell Cres NR5 ......161 D7
Dell Loke NR14 ......163 B2
Dell The Bodham NR25 ....9 A3
  Hingham NR9 ......86 B5
  Mundesley NR11 ....143 D5
  Trowse Newton NR14 .163 B2
Deloney Rd NR7 .....159 C2
Delta Cl NR6 ....158 C4
De-Narde Rd NR19 ...154 D7
Denbigh Rd NR2 .....162 B5
Dene Ave NR29 .....167 A3
Dene Side **1** NR30 ...169 D3
Denes The NR11 .....163 C5
Denham Low Rd IP21 .131 A1
Denham Rd IP21 .....131 B2
Denmark Hill IP22 ...177 C3
Denmark La IP22 ....177 B4
Denmark Opening
  NR3 ....158 E1
Denmark Rd
  Beccles NR34 .....110 D1
  2 King's Lynn PE30 .147 B6
  Norwich NR3 ......158 E1
Denmark Rise IP22 ...177 C4
Denmark St IP22 ....177 C3
Denmead Cl **4** NR4 ..89 D8
Dennis Rd NR6 .....157 F7
Dennis Sneezum Ct
  PE38 ....172 B4
Denny Rd PE30 .....147 A4
Denny's Hill IP22 ....123 A2
Denny's Wlk PE32 ...63 E7
Denton Rd
  Denton IP20 ......123 C6
  Norwich NR3 ......158 F3
Denver Hill PE38 ....172 C3
Denver VC Prim Sch
  PE38 ....172 D2
Denver Windmill*
  PE38 ....172 B1
Deopham Rd
  Attleborough NR17 ..174 C7
  Hingham NR9 ....86 C4
  Morley NR18 ....87 A2
Derby St NR2 ....162 C7
Dereham 6th Form Coll
  NR20 ....154 F5
Dereham Church Inf Sch
  NR19 ....154 D5
Dereham Hospl NR19 .154 E7
Dereham La NR19 ....66 C8
Dereham Rd
  5 Bawdeswell NR20 ...50 E6
  Beeston with Bittering
  PE32 ....48 D2
  Brinningham NR24 ..18 D5
  Bylaugh NR20 ......50 C5
  Colkirk NR21 ....31 E5
  Costessey NR5 .....156 D1
  Dereham NR20 .....50 B2
  East Dereham NR19 .154 B5
  Easton NR9 ....70 C4
  Garvestone NR9 ....68 C1
  Gressenhall NR19 ...49 C2
  Hempton NR21 .....141 B2
  Hingham NR9 ......86 B5
  Honingham NR9 ....69 D7
  Kimberley NR18 ....87 A7
  Litcham PE32 ......48 A4
  Mattishall NR20 ....68 D6
  North Elmham NR20 ..49 E6
  1 Norwich NR5 ....161 B8
  Ovington IP25 ......84 E6
  Pudding Norton NR21 .141 B1
  Reepham NR10 ....149 A4
  Scarning NR19 .....154 A4
  Shipdham IP25 .....67 A1
  25 Watton IP25 .....84 D3
  Whinburgh & Westfield
  NR19 ....67 F5
  Whissonsett NR20 ...31 E2
  Yaxham NR19 ......68 A5
Dereham St Nicholas Jun Sch
  NR19 ....154 D4
Dersingham Bog National
  Nature Reserve*
  PE31 ....27 D7
Dersingham Inf Sch
  PE31 ....140 D4
Dersley Ct NR5 .....160 E7
Derwent Ave PE30 ...148 F2
Desborough Way NR13 .72 D4
Desmond Dr NR6 ....158 F6
Devlin Dr **13** NR14 ...90 C5
Devon Ave NR6 .....157 E4
Devon Cres PE30 ....148 D5
Devon Way NR14 ....163 C1
Devonshire Ct **1** PE30 .147 A7
Devonshire Rd NR30 .169 D2
Devonshire St **4** NR2 .162 C7
Dewarrene Dr IP27 ...175 B7
Dewdrop Cl PE31 ....133 D6
Dewing Rd NR13 ....72 E8
Dexter Rd PE34 .....79 A7
Dial Cl PE38 ....172 B5
Diamond Cl IP22 ....120 B5
Diamond Rd NR6 ....158 B5
Diamond St NR6 ....158 D7
Diamond Terr PE30 ...146 D2
Dian Rd NR13 ......165 E3
Diana Cl NR19 .....154 C1
Diana Way NR30 ....168 C6

Dianas Dro PE36 .....132 C2
Dibden Rd NR3 .....162 F8
Dickens Ave NR3 ....169 D1
Dickens Ct **5** NR30 ...169 D1
Dickfool's La NR19 ...66 F8
Dickleburgh Prim Sch
  IP21 ....121 B1
Dickleburgh Rd IP21 .121 A1
Dicks Mount NR34 ...111 D3
Dicky Hill IP20 ......122 D3
Digby Dr NR11 .....141 B6
Dilham Arts Ctr* NR28 .38 C4
Dilham Rd Honing NR28 .38 C6
  Worstead NR28 ......38 A4
Dilldash La NR21 ....17 A5
Dinosaur Adventure Pk*
  ....51 E4
Dirty La
  North Tuddenham NR20 .50 E1
  Pulham St Mary IP21 .121 F3
Diss Church Jun Sch
  IP22 ....177 D4
Diss High Sch IP22 ...177 E5
Diss Inf Sch IP22 ...177 E4
Diss Mus* IP22 .....177 D4
Diss Rd
  Burston & Shimpling
  IP22 ....120 E1
  Garboldisham IP22 ..128 A8
  Scole IP21 ....130 C5
  South Lopham IP22 ..128 E8
  Tibenham NR16 .....120 C8
  Wattisfield IP22 ....128 B1
Diss Sta IP22 ......177 F4
Diss Swimming & Fitness Ctr
  IP22 ....177 E3
Distillery Sq **5** NR2 ..162 C6
Ditchingham Dam
  NR35 ....109 A1
Dix Cl PE31 ....133 E5
Dixon Rd Cromer NR27 .139 B5
  North Walsham NR28 ..151 D5
  Norwich NR7 ......159 A4
Dixon's Dro PE14 ...59 C8
Dixon's Fold NR6 ...158 F4
Dobbs' La NR13 .....54 D2
Dobby Dr PE30 .....146 D6
Dobson Way NR34 ...110 D1
Dock Tavern La NR20 .170 D5
Docking Prim Sch
  PE31 ....134 D4
Docking Rd
  Burnham Westgate
  PE31 ....135 B2
  Ringstead PE36 .....2 B2
  Sedgeford PE36 .....13 B7
  Stanhoe PE31 ......14 D7
  Syderstone PE31 ....15 A3
Doctor's La IP21 ....122 A2
Doctors Mdw **1** NR10 .53 D2
Doctors Rd NR15 ...165 E6
Dodd Cl NR30 .....168 D7
Dodd's La PE32 ....45 B2
Dodderman Way NR5 .160 F6
Dodds Cl NR17 .....174 B3
Dodds La NR17 .....174 A3
Dodds Rd NR17 .....174 B3
Doddshill Rd PE31 ...140 F3
Dodgers La NR15 ...91 A3
Dodma Rd PE32 ....47 C8
Dodman's La NR20 ...31 F2
Dodmans Cl PE30 ...146 E5
Dodmans The NR19 ..154 D4
Dodson Dr
  7 Beetley NR19 ....49 C3
  7 Gressenhall NR20 ..49 C3
Doe La Banham NR16 ..119 E8
  Old Buckenham NR17 .104 E1
Dog Cnr NR11 ......35 A5
Dog La Easton NR9 ..70 B6
  Horsford NR10 .....155 F4
  Shelfanger IP22 ....120 A4
Dogger La NR23 ....136 C6
Doggetts La NR12 ...24 D4
Dogs La NR34 ......110 C3
Dogwood Cl **6** NR18 .173 E4
Dogwood Rd NR6 ...158 D4
Dohamero La **1** PE33 .43 F2
Doit La IP22 ....129 D7
Doit The IP22 ......129 C6
Dolman Rd **13** NR31 ..169 B4
Dolphin Gr NR2 ....162 B8
Doman Rd NR1 .....178 C1
Donchurch Cl **6** NR5 .161 A7
Doris Barnes Ct **1**
  NR19 ....154 E5
Doris Rd NR2 ......162 B5
Dorking Rd NR3 ....171 B4
Dorothea Dr **7** NR19 .154 D3
Dorothy Ave NR31 ...94 C7
Dorrs Dr IP25 ......84 E4
Dorset Cl
  Attleborough NR17 ..174 B3
  4 Great Yarmouth NR30 .169 D3
Doubleday Cl NR12 ...177 C4
Doughty's Hospl NR3 .178 B4
Douglas Bader Cl
  NR28 ....151 C7
Douglas Bader Sch The
  NR10 ....37 B2
Douglas Cl
  Croxton IP24 ......116 C5
  Norwich NR6 ......158 D7
Douglas Haig Rd NR5 .161 D6
Doune Way **9** IP20 ..122 D2
Douro PE14 ....162 C6
Dove Cl
  1 Great Yarmouth NR31 .170 A6

Dove Cl continued
  9 Harleston IP20 ....122 D1
Dove House La **4** NR29 .56 F6
Dove La NR15 ......90 C3
Dove St **3** NR2 ....178 A3
Dovecote Cl NR15 ...90 F2
Dovecote Rd PE14 ...77 D3
Dovedale Rd NR16 ...105 F5
Dovedales Fold NR7 .158 F4
Dovehouse La NR11 ..21 B4
Dover Cl NR30 .....168 C5
Dover St NR2 ......162 B5
Dow Cl NR5 ....160 F5
Dow La NR12 ......54 C3
Dowding Rd
  Norwich NR6 ......158 D6
  3 Watton IP25 .....84 F3
Downham Cres NR18 .173 B6
Downham Dro PE32 ..63 F7
Downham Mkt Coll
  PE38 ....172 C4
Downham Mkt High Sch &
  Tech Coll PE38 ...172 D5
Downham Mkt Sta
  PE38 ....172 A5
Downham Prep Sch
  PE34 ....79 E8
Downham Rd
  Crimplesham PE33 ..80 B7
  Denver PE38 ......172 C2
  Fincham PE33 .....62 E1
  Nordelph PE38 .....78 D3
  Outwell PE14 ......77 F6
  Runcton Holme PE33 .61 D4
  Stradsett PE33 ....80 D8
Downham Way IP27 ..175 F4
Downing Cl NR31 ...170 C4
Downing Mews NR5 ..160 D8
Downing Rd NR31 ...170 C4
Downs Cl PE36 .....132 C4
Downs Farm La IP20 ..123 B3
Downs Rd PE36 ....132 C4
Dowsing Ct **5** NR13 ..72 D5
Dowson Fst Sch NR3 .158 A1
Dowson Rd NR3 ....158 B1
Drabblegate NR11 ...150 D8
Drabbs La NR12 ....38 E6
Dragon Hall* NR1 ...178 C2
Dragoon Cl **27** NR30 ..72 D4
Drake Ave NR30 ....169 D7
Drake Cl **24** NR30 ...88 D8
Drake Inf Sch IP24 ..176 E6
Drake Rd IP24 .....176 E5
Drakes Cl **5** NR16 ...118 C5
Drakes Loke NR10 ...36 F1
Draper Way NR5 ....160 D8
Drapers La NR35 ....109 A3
Draycote Cl NR30 ...147 D8
Draycotts Rise IP22 .177 C1
Drayton Com Fst Sch
  NR8 ....155 F1
Drayton Gr NR8 ....156 F8
Drayton High Rd NR8 .157 A8
Drayton La NR10 ...53 B1
Drayton Lodge Pk
  NR8 ....157 B7
Drayton Rd NR3 ....157 F2
Drayton Wood Rd
  NR6 ....157 D6
Draytonhall La NR19 .154 B3
Dreibholz Ct NR20 ...154 F5
Drewray Dr NR8 ....155 E3
Dried Flower Ctr*
  NR12 ....55 C7
Drift La NR20 ......49 C3
Drift Rd
  Caister-on-Sea NR30 .168 C7
  Lakenheath IP27 ...113 C1
Drift The
  Bawdeswell NR20 ...50 E6
  Beetley NR20 ......49 A6
  Botesdale IP22 ....128 E3
  Fakenham NR21 ....141 D4
  Fulmodeston NR21 ..17 F3
  Heacham PE31 ....133 D6
  Ingoldisthorpe PE31 .140 C8
  Swardeston NR14 ...89 B5
Driftlands NR21 ....141 D5
Driftway PE30 .....148 C1
Driftway The
  1 Holt NR25 ......137 C5
  Sheringham NR26 ...138 D8
Drill St NR11 ......15 C3
Drinkwater Cl **9** NR9 .86 C5
Drive The Acle NR13 ..166 D4
  East Winch PE32 ...45 A2
  Norwich NR5 .....161 B4
  Trowse with Newton
  NR14 ....163 D1
Drout's La IP31 ....127 C3
Drove The
  Brandon IP27 .....114 D4
  Raynham NR21 ....30 E4
  Taverham NR8 .....155 C2
Drovers Rest NR15 ..108 C8
Drudge Rd NR31 ...170 D4
Druids La Litcham NR32 .48 A4
  Shelfanger IP22 ....120 B2
Druids' La IP22 ....120 A3
Drunken Dro PE32 ...46 C8
Drury Cl **12** NR5 ....161 B8
Drury La
  3 Castle Acre PE32 ..46 F2
  6 Loddon NR14 ....91 F1
Dryden Cl **1** IP24 ...176 E6
Dryden Rd NR8 ....156 D8
Duck Decoy Cl PE31 .140 C3
Duck Dro CB7 .....112 A2

Duck's Foot Rd IP21 .121 F6
Duckett Cl **2** NR1 ...162 E1
Duff Rd NR3 ......158 D2
Duffield Cres NR9 ...51 A4
Dugard Ave NR1 ....163 B8
Duke Rd NR31 .....170 D6
Duke St Norwich NR3 .178 A4
  Wisbech PE13 .....152 D4
Duke's La NR17 ....102 E8
Dukesway **1** NR35 ..123 F8
Dulgate La PE37 ...153 D2
Dulgate Rd NR35 ...108 B3
Dull's Rd NR5 .....109 C5
Dumbs La NR10 ....53 E5
Dumpling Gn
  Dereham NR19 ....68 A6
  East Dereham NR19 .154 F2
Dun Cow Gdns PE34 .144 E7
Dun Cow Rd NR34 ..111 B4
Dunburgh Rd NR34 ..110 A2
Duncan Cl IP24 ....176 F6
Duncan Rd **6** NR30 ..169 D2
Dunford La IP24 ....102 A2
Dunham Rd
  Litcham PE32 ......48 A4
  Necton PE37 ......65 F6
Dunhill La IP22 ....127 F1
Dunkirk NR11 .....150 E8
Dunlop Rd NR19 ...154 B6
Dunnett Cl IP25 ....84 F3
Dunnetts Cl IP25 ...84 F3
Dunning's La IP21 ..121 E6
Dunns La NR21 ....4 C1
Dunston Dro PE31 ..133 B1
Dunwood Dr NR6 ...158 F7
Durbidge's Hill IP22 .120 E1
Durham Ave NR31 ...170 B2
Durham Rd NR31 ...170 B2
Durham Way IP24 ...176 A5
Durham St NR2 ....162 B4
Dussindale **3** NR18 .173 C6
Dussindale Dr **15** NR7 .72 C4
Duverlin Cl **2** NR4 ..162 A1
Dyball's La NR12 ...38 F8
Dye's Rd NR13 .....73 C7
Dyers Yd NR3 .....178 A3
Dyes The NR20 ....33 E8

E

Eade Rd NR3 ......162 D8
Eagle Cl NR11 .....21 B2
Eagle House Sch
  NR16 ....119 E7
Eagle Rd NR11 .....21 B2
Eagle Wlk **2** NR2 ...162 C4
Eagles Ct NR23 ....136 E6
Eagles The **3** NR30 ..169 D4
Earl Cl NR7 ....140 C3
Earl of Brandon Ave
  PE31 ....30 B3
Earl Rd NR13 ......72 E8
Earl Warren IP24 ...116 C5
Earlham Gn La NR5 ..161 B7
Earlham Gr NR5 ....161 D6
Earlham High Sch
  NR4 ....161 C5
Earlham Rd NR4 ....161 C5
Earlham W Ctr **5** NR5 .161 C6
Earls' St NR2 ......176 C4
Earlsford Rd IP23 ...129 D1
Earnshaw Ct NR1 ...163 D5
Earsham CE VA Fst Sch
  NR35 ....123 F8
Earsham Dam NR35 .123 F8
Earsham Dr PE38 ...147 D8
Earsham Rd NR35 ...108 C2
Earth La NR32 .....94 C1
East Anglia Transport Mus*
  NR33 ....111 F1
East Anglian Way
  NR31 ....170 C6
East Ave NR13 .....165 E3
East Bank PE12 ....41 C8
East Bilney Rd NR20 ..49 A6
East Carleton Rd NR14 .89 A4
East Cres NR20 ....50 B5
East Dereham Sta
  NR20 ....154 E5
East End PE38 .....79 E1
East End Cl NR30 ...168 E8
East Farm La NR10 ..53 E3
East Gn NR9 ......68 F2
East Gr NR27 ......139 C5
East Harbour Way
  PE31 ....135 D4
East Harling Prim Sch
  NR16 ....118 C4
East Harling Rd NR16 .118 F4
East Hills Rd NR5 ...156 E1
East La PE31 ......134 C1
East Norfolk 6th Form Coll
  NR31 ....170 C5
East Rd
  Great Yarmouth NR30 .169 D5
  Watton IP25 ......84 D3
East Ruston Area Com Sch
  NR12 ....38 F7
East Ruston Old Vicarage
  Gdn* NR12 ......24 A3
East Ruston Rd NR28 .38 D6
East Winch CE Prim Sch
  PE32 ....44 F3
East Winch Rd
  Leziate PE32 ......44 F1
  Middleton PE32 ....44 C2

East Winchcommon (Nature
  Reserve)* PE32 ....45 A2
Eastbourne Pl NR1 ..178 C3
Easterley Way NR29 .167 A7
Eastern Ave
  Caister-on-Sea NR30 .168 E6
  Norwich NR7 .....72 D4
Eastern Cl
  Caister-on-Sea NR30 .168 E5
  32 Norwich NR7 ....72 D4
Eastern Cres NR7 ..72 D4
Eastern Fen NR7 ...72 D4
Eastfen Dro IP26 ...114 B6
Eastfield NR8 ......156 D8
Eastfield Cl PE30 ...147 A6
Eastfield Rd
  Hickling NR12 .....39 F2
  Long Stratton NR15 .106 F4
  1 Wisbech PE13 ....152 E7
Eastfield Way PE13 .152 C6
Eastfields
  King's Lynn PE30 ...147 C4
  Narborough PE32 ...63 D7
Eastgate IP25 .....67 D3
Eastgate Dro
  Congham PE31 ....28 D2
  Grimston PE32 ....45 D8
  Hillington PE31 ....28 C3
Eastgate Prim Sch
  PE30 ....146 E5
Eastgate Rd PE36 ...2 A6
Eastgate St
  2 King's Lynn PE30 ..146 E5
  North Elmham NR20 ..49 E7
  Shouldham PE33 ...62 D4
Easthaugh Rd NR9 ..51 D4
Easthill La NR14 ...90 E8
Eastland Cl NR17 ..174 E6
Eastlands Bank PE14 .41 E5
Eastleigh Gdns **6** NR9 .69 C8
Eastmans La PE32 ..28 C1
Eastmoor Cl PE33 ...81 E4
Eastmoor Rd PE33 ...81 C7
Easton Coll NR9 ...70 C4
Easton Way NR10 ...35 C1
Eastwood PE31 ....134 F3
Eaton Chase NR4 ...161 E2
Eaton Dro
  Sedgeford PE36 ....13 A7
  Snettisham PE31 ...12 F5
Eaton Gdns NR19 ..154 E3
Eaton Hall Specl Sch
  NR4 ....161 F3
Eaton Rd NR4 .....162 B2
Eaton St Cringleford NR4 .89 B8
  Norwich NR4 .....161 E1
Eau Brink Rd PE34 ..43 A2
Ebbisham Dr
  Norwich NR4 .....161 F1
Ebble Cl PE30 .....148 C2
Ebenezer Pl NR3 ...178 A4
Eccles CE Prim Sch
  NR16 ....118 F8
Eccles Rd NR25 ....137 C2
Eccles Rd Sta NR16 .103 E1
Ecclestone Cl NR31 .170 A4
Eckersley Dr NR21 ..141 A6
Ecotech Ctr* PE37 ..153 B6
Ecton Gr **6** PE14 ..59 A1
Ecton Wlk NR6 ....158 F5
Eddington Way NR9 .70 B5
Eden Cl
  Bacton/Walcott NR12 .23 E4
  Norwich NR7 .....163 C6
Eden La NR17 .....174 D5
Edenhurst Cl NR4 ...161 F3
Edenside Dr NR17 ..174 D5
Edge Bank PE14 ...77 F8
Edge's La NR15 ....107 A3
Edgebrook NR26 ...138 D6
Edgefield Cl NR6 ...158 F7
Edgefield Hill NR25 .137 C2
Edgefield Rd NR24 ..142 E5
Edgehill **4** NR7 ...72 E4
Edges La **3** NR15 ..106 E3
Edgeworth Rd **6** NR5 .161 C4
Edinburgh Ave
  Great Yarmouth NR31 .170 B2
  King's Lynn PE30 ...147 C7
Edinburgh Cl
  6 Barnham IP24 ....125 F6
  Caister-on-Sea NR30 .168 E5
  13 Watton IP25 .....84 D3
Edinburgh Ct **7** PE30 .146 E5
Edinburgh Dr
  Fakenham NR21 ....141 C6
  Wisbech PE13 .....152 C8
Edinburgh Pl
  Great Yarmouth NR30 .169 E3
  1 Wiggenhall St Germans
  PE34 ....43 B1
Edinburgh Rd
  Holt NR25 ....137 C5
  Norwich NR2 .....162 A6
Edinburgh Way
  Dersingham PE31 ...140 D3
  Thetford IP24 .....176 A8
Edison Way NR31 ...170 A8
Edith Cavell Cl **5** IP24 .176 D7
Edma St PE30 .....146 E6
Edmondson Wlk NR11 .141 D4
Edmund Bacon Ct **1**
  NR3 ....162 D8
Edmund Moundford Rd **10**
  IP26 ....98 E1
Edmund Rd IP27 ...175 A4
Edrich Cl NR13 ....165 E6
Edrich Way NR5 ...160 E7

Edward Benefer Way
King's Lynn PE30 . . . . . . .146 D6
North Wootton PE30 . . . . .26 E1
Edward Gambling Ct 8
NR2 . . . . .162 B8
Edward Rd NR29 . . . . . . .58 B5
Edward Seago Pl NR15 .90 E2
Edward St
10 King's Lynn PE30 . . . . .146 E3
Norwich NR3 . . . . .178 A4
Edward Worlledge Mid Sch
NR31 . . . . .169 C2
Edwards Cl NR20 . . . . . .50 B5
Edwards Rd NR7 . . . . . .159 A5
Edwin Cl NR18 . . . . .57 E1
Eels Foot Rd NR31 . . . . .57 E1
Egmere Medieval Village of ★
NR22 . . . . .16 B8
Egmere Rd NR22 . . . . . . .16 F8
Egremont Rd IP22 . . . . .177 B5
Eighth Ave PE13 . . . . . .152 E4
El Alamein Way NR31 . .94 C8
Elan Cl NR18 . . . . .173 D3
Elden's La IP26 . . . . . . .98 F5
Elder Gn NR31 . . . . .170 B5
Elder La PE32 . . . . .45 C8
Elderberry Dr 5 NR20 . .68 A8
Elderbush La NR29 . . . . .56 C7
Elders The IP27 . . . . . . .113 F1
Elderton La NR28 . . . . . .22 B5
Eleanor Rd NR1 . . . . . . .162 D3
Eleven Mile Rd NR18 . . .87 C1
Elgin IP24 . . . . .176 A5
Elgood's Brewery & Gdn ★
PE13 . . . . .152 A4
Eliot Cl IP24 . . . . .176 E6
Elise Way NR18 . . . . . . .173 D2
Elizabeth Ave
Downham Market PE38 . . .172 B5
Fakenham NR21 . . . . . . .141 C6
Norwich NR7 . . . . .163 F7
Elizabeth Cl
Attleborough NR17 . . . . .174 C6
East Dereham NR19 . . . . .154 D1
Hunstanton PE36 . . . . . . .132 C3
Norwich NR7 . . . . .159 A5
Reepham NR10 . . . . .149 B4
Elizabeth Cres
Caister-on-Sea NR30 . . . .168 E6
4 Holt NR25 . . . . .137 C5
Elizabeth Dr PE37 . . . . .65 F3
Elizabeth Fry Cl 9
IP24 . . . . .176 D7
Elizabeth Fry Rd NR2 . .161 D4
Elizabeth Rd
Brandon IP27 . . . . .175 C3
10 Poringland NR14 . . . . .90 D5
Elizabeth Terr PE13 . . . .152 D4
Elizabeth Watling Cl 3
IP24 . . . . .176 D7
Elizabeth Way 5 IP23 . .130 C1
Elizabeth Wlk 27 IP20 . .122 D2
Elizabethan House Mus ★
NR30 . . . . .169 C3
Elkins Rd NR18 . . . . . . .173 D5
Ella Rd NR1 . . . . .163 A6
Ellcar Rise 4 NR4 . . . . .161 F1
Ellenhill NR27 . . . . .139 D5
Eller Dr PE33 . . . . .43 E2
Ellingham Prim Sch
NR35 . . . . .109 D3
Ellingham Rd
Attleborough NR17 . . . . .174 B7
Scoulton NR9 . . . . .85 E3
Ellington Rd
2 Barnham IP24 . . . . . . .125 F6
Watton IP25 . . . . .85 A3
Ellinor Rd NR28 . . . . . . .151 D3
Ellis Cl 4 NR12 . . . . .39 B4
Ellison Cl NR17 . . . . .174 E4
Ellison Dr NR17 . . . . . . .174 E4
Elm Ave NR31 . . . . .170 C4
Elm CE Jun Sch PE14 . .59 B1
Elm Cl Acle NR13 . . . . . .166 C4
Brandon IP27 . . . . .175 E3
Downham Market PE38 . . .172 B6
King's Lynn PE30 . . . . . . .148 D2
5 Lingwood NR13 . . . . . . .74 A3
7 Loddon NR14 . . . . .91 F1
Mulbarton NR14 . . . . .89 B3
North Elmham NR20 . . . . .49 E8
Norwich NR5 . . . . .156 F2
Yaxham NR19 . . . . .68 A5
Elm Gr
Garboldisham IP22 . . . . . .128 A8
Sheringham NR26 . . . . . .138 E5
Elm Gr La NR8 . . . . .158 D2
Elm High Rd PE14 . . . . .152 E1
Elm Hill NR3 . . . . .178 B3
Elm La PE31 . . . . .30 D8
Elm Low Rd PE14 . . . . .152 D2
Elm Pk NR19 . . . . .154 E1
Elm Rd
Caister-on-Sea NR30 . . . .168 E4
Lingwood NR13 . . . . .74 A3
Marham PE33 . . . . .63 B4
Thetford IP24 . . . . .176 B1
Wisbech PE13 . . . . .152 D3
Elm Rd Prim Sch
PE13 . . . . .152 D4
Elm Terr 2 NR18 . . . . . .173 C4
Elmdon Ct 9 NR1 . . . . .163 A6
Elmer's La NR15 . . . . . . .107 A8
Elmfield Dr PE14 . . . . . .152 E1
Elmgrove Rd NR31 . . . . .170 C3
Elmham Rd
Beetley NR20 . . . . .49 D4
North Elmham NR20 . . . . .50 A7

Elmhurst Ave NR12 . . . . .39 C2
Elmhurst Dr NR31 . . . . .170 C3
Elmhurst Dr PE30 . . . . .148 C2
Elms Cl 6 NR35 . . . . . . .123 F8
Elms Rd NR34 . . . . .110 E5
Elms The
Hindringham NR21 . . . . . . .17 E6
Norwich NR6 . . . . .158 E6
Elmside PE14 . . . . .59 D1
Elmstead Rd PE30 . . . . .147 C4
Elmtree Gr NR25 . . . . . . .43 E1
Elsden Cl 2 NR25 . . . . .137 C5
Elsie Rd NR31 . . . . .169 B3
Elsing Dr NR3 . . . . .157 F1
Elsing Dr PE30 . . . . .147 D8
Elsing Rd
Bawdeswell NR20 . . . . . . .50 E6
Dereham NR20 . . . . .50 C4
Elsing Rd Lyng NR9 . . . .51 A5
North Tuddenham NR20 . . .50 E2
Swanton Morley NR20 . . . .50 C4
Elstead Cl 11 NR4 . . . . . .89 C8
Elveden Cl NR4 . . . . . . .161 F1
Elveden Rd IP24 . . . . . .125 D6
Elvin Rd NR19 . . . . .154 D6
Elvin Way 3 NR3 . . . . .157 F1
Elvina Rd NR10 . . . . .54 A2
Elvington PE30 . . . . .147 D5
Elworthy Cl IP25 . . . . . . .84 F3
Elwyn Rd 7 NR1 . . . . . .162 E3
Ely Pl 19 PE13 . . . . .152 C5
Ely Rd Denver PE38 . . . .172 D2
Hilgay PE38 . . . . .97 B8
Ely Row PE14 . . . . .42 B1
Ely St NR2 . . . . .162 C7
Ely Way IP24 . . . . .176 A5
Embry Cl NR6 . . . . .158 D6
Embry Cres NR16 . . . . . .158 C6
Emelson Cl NR19 . . . . . .154 D6
Emery Cl 5 NR26 . . . . . .138 C5
Emery's La NR11 . . . . . . .21 B6
Emmanuel Ave NR1 . . . .170 B2
Emmas Way NR13 . . . . . .73 B6
Emmerich Ct 6 PE30 . . .146 E5
Emms's La NR21 . . . . . . .17 E7
Emneth Prim Sch PE14 .59 D1
Emorsgate PE34 . . . . . . .42 B7
Empire Ave PE30 . . . . . .147 B8
Empress Rd NR3 . . . . . . .169 B3
Empsons Loke NR29 . . . .58 B6
End Lodge PE31 . . . . . . .133 C5
Enfield Rd NR5 . . . . . . .161 C6
Engine Rd Hilgay PE38 . .96 F7
Sculthorpe Airfield NR21 . .15 D2
England's La NR31 . . . . .170 D4
Englands Rd NR13 . . . . .166 B4
English Rd NR6 . . . . . . .158 E4
Ennerdale Dr PE30 . . . .148 F2
Enterprise Way
Fakenham NR21 . . . . . . .141 E5
King's Lynn PE33 . . . . .43 E4
Wisbech PE13 . . . . .152 A2
Entrance La NR15 . . . . . .90 E2
Entry The IP22 . . . . .177 D4
Enue 18 PE33 . . . . .63 B4
Eppingham Cl IP24 . . . .176 F6
Epsom Gdns NR19 . . . . .154 E3
Erica Way NR31 . . . . . . .170 B6
Erins The 1 NR6 . . . . . .158 E1
Eriswell Dr IP27 . . . . . . .113 E1
Erpingham Rd NR7 . . . . .159 A3
Erpingham Ct PE36 . . . .132 E7
Erpingham Prim Sch
NR11 . . . . .21 B2
Esdelle St 9 NR3 . . . . . .162 D8
Esplanade NR27 . . . . . . .139 B7
Esplanade The
Hemsby NR29 . . . . .167 E5
Sheringham NR26 . . . . . .138 C7
Esprit Cl NR18 . . . . .173 D2
Essex St NR2 . . . . .162 C5
Estcourt Rd
2 Attleborough NR17 . . .174 C5
Great Yarmouth NR30 . . .169 D6
Estelle Way NR18 . . . . .173 E6
Estuary Cl PE30 . . . . . . .146 E7
Estuary Rd PE30 . . . . . .146 D7
Ethel Colman Way
IP24 . . . . .176 D7
Ethel Gooch Rd NR18 . .173 B5
Ethel Rd NR1 . . . . .163 A5
Ethel Terr NR30 . . . . . . .146 E3
Ethel Tipple Cl NR11 . . .150 C4
Ethel Tipple Dr NR11 . . .150 C4
Ethel Tipple Specl Sch
PO30 . . . . .147 C4
Eurocentre Ind Est
NR30 . . . . .169 B7
Europa Way
Norwich NR1 . . . . .163 A2
Wisbech PE13 . . . . .152 B2
Euston Hall ★ IP24 . . . .126 B5
Euston Rd NR30 . . . . . . .169 D4
Euston Way PE30 . . . . . .148 D1
Euximoor Dro PE14 . . . . .77 B1
Eva Cl 4 IP25 . . . . .67 B2
Eva Rd NR13 . . . . .72 E7
Evans Gdns PE36 . . . . . .132 D3
Evans Lombe Cl NR29 . . .57 A4
Evans Way NR6 . . . . . . .158 D6
Evelyn Cl IP21 . . . . .131 A3
Evelyn Way 4 PE30 . . . .147 A8
Eversley Rd NR6 . . . . . .158 B4
Everson Cl
Norwich NR5 . . . . .157 C1
11 Tasburgh NR15 . . . . .106 F6
Ewing Cl NR10 . . . . .149 B4
Excalibur Rd 2 NR31 . . .170 B1
Exchange Rd 7 NR15 . . .89 D1
Exchange Sq PE13 . . . . .152 B5

Exchange St
Attleborough NR17 . . . . .174 D5
32 Harleston IP20 . . . . . .122 D2
Norwich NR2 . . . . .178 A3
Exeter Cres PE13 . . . . . .148 D5
Exeter Rd NR31 . . . . . . .170 B4
Exeter St NR2 . . . . .162 C7
Exeter Way 9 IP24 . . . .176 F5
Exmouth Cl 11 NR9 . . . . .88 D8
Exmouth Pl 11 NR30 . . .169 D4
Exmouth Rd NR30 . . . . .169 D1
Exton's Gdns PE30 . . . .146 F3
Exton's Rd PE30 . . . . . . .147 A3
Eye Airfield Ind Est
IP23 . . . . .130 B2
Eye La PE31 . . . . .30 B7
Eye Rd IP23 . . . . .130 A1

F

Factory La IP22 . . . . . . .177 B1
Factory Rd NR30 . . . . . .169 D6
Faeroes Dr NR30 . . . . . .168 C6
Fair Cl Beccles NR34 . . .110 D1
4 Feltwell IP26 . . . . .98 E1
Fair Gn NR13 . . . . .177 C4
Fairfax Dr 6 Norwich NR7 72 D4
3 Weeting IP27 . . . . . . .114 E1
Fairfax Rd NR4 . . . . .161 F4
Fairfield Cl
Great & Little Plumstead
NR13 . . . . .73 B7
Mundesley NR11 . . . . . . .143 C6
Fairfield Dr NR17 . . . . . .174 C4
Fairfield La 10 PE33 . . . .61 D6
Fairfield Rd
Downham Market PE38 . . .172 A5
5 Middleton PE32 . . . . . . .44 B3
Norwich NR2 . . . . .162 C3
4 Stoke Ferry PE33 . . . . .81 A3
Fairfield Way 11 IP26 . . .98 E1
Fairfields Cawston NR10 .35 B2
Thetford IP24 . . . . .176 D5
Fairfields Way NR11 . . . . .36 D4
Fairhaven CE VA Prim Sch
NR13 . . . . .74 B8
Fairhaven Rd NR2 . . . . . .162 A6
**Fairhaven Woodland & Water
Gdn** ★ NR13 . . . . .74 A8
Fairhill Dro PE33 . . . . . . .80 C2
Fairholme Cl IP25 . . . . . .84 A8
Fairholme Rd NR10 . . . . .53 E4
Fairisle Dr NR30 . . . . . . .168 C5
Fairland St NR18 . . . . . .173 C3
Fairmile Cl NR2 . . . . .162 B3
Fairstead Cl
North Walsham NR28 . . . .151 A3
Pulham Market NR21 . . . .121 C6
Fairstead Ct NR7 . . . . . . .159 A3
Fairstead Dro PE33 . . . . .62 D4
Fairstead La
Hempnall NR15 . . . . .107 A5
Little Cressingham PE33 . .83 D3
Fairstead Prim Sch
PE30 . . . . .147 D4
Fairstead Rd NR7 . . . . . .159 A3
Fairstead The
Botesdale IP22 . . . . .128 E3
2 Cley next the Sea NR25 . .7 E6
1 Holt NR25 . . . . .137 B6
Scottow NR10 . . . . .37 C5
Fairview Cl NR8 . . . . . . .157 A7
Fairview Dr NR31 . . . . . . .31 C5
Fairview Rd NR28 . . . . . .151 E4
Fairway NR30 . . . . .168 C3
Fairway Fst Sch NR4 . . .162 A1
Fairway Mid Sch NR4 . . .162 A1
Fairway The NR31 . . . . . .171 D4
Fairways Norwich NR6 . .157 D5
Stuston IP21 . . . . .130 B5
Fakenham Coll NR21 . . . .141 B5
Fakenham High Sch
NR21 . . . . .141 B6
Fakenham Hill IP31 . . . .126 C2
Fakenham Jun Sch
NR21 . . . . .141 C4
Fakenham Mus ★
NR21 . . . . .141 B3
Fakenham Race Course
NR21 . . . . .141 D2
Fakenham Rd
Attlebridge NR9 . . . . .52 C2
Beetley NR20 . . . . .49 C5
Briston NR24 . . . . .142 C5
Docking PE31 . . . . .134 E4
East Rudham PE31 . . . . . .30 A7
Foxley NR20 . . . . .33 C1
Great Snoring NR21 . . . . .17 A5
Ryburgh NR21 . . . . .32 A6
Sculthorpe NR21 . . . . . . .141 A5
South Creake NR21 . . . . . .15 E6
Sparham NR9 . . . . .51 A6
Taverham NR8 . . . . .155 B2
Tittleshall PE32 . . . . .48 A7
Fakenham View NR21 . . .31 E5
Fakes Rd NR29 . . . . .167 D6
Falcon Cl Bungay NR35 .109 A1
24 Wisbech PE13 . . . . . .152 C5
Falcon Ct 15 NR30 . . . . .169 C4
Falcon Dr IP27 . . . . .175 F3
Falcon La NR13 . . . . .73 B6
Falcon Mews NR7 . . . . . .159 C3
Falcon Mid Sch NR7 . . . .159 C3
Falcon Rd 14 Feltwell IP26 98 E1
Norwich NR7 . . . . .159 C3
Pulham Market IP21 . . . . .121 E5

Falcon Rd continued
7 Wisbech PE13 . . . . . . .152 C5
Falcon Rd E NR7 . . . . . .159 C5
Falcon Rd W NR7 . . . . . .159 C4
Falconers Chase NR18 . .173 F5
Falgate NR10 . . . . .35 C2
Falkland Cl NR19 . . . . . .157 D5
Falkland Way 13 NR31 . . .94 C8
Falklands Cl PE13 . . . . . .152 E3
Falklands Rd PE12 . . . . . .41 A8
Fall Gn NR14 . . . . .90 D4
Fallow Pipe Rd PE34 . . . .43 B2
Fallowfield
4 Hemsby NR29 . . . . . . .167 B7
8 Poringland NR14 . . . . . .90 D5
Fallowfield Cl NR1 . . . . .163 B8
Fallows The 3 NR8 . . . . .155 E7
Faraday Pl IP24 . . . . . . .176 B2
Faraday Rd NR31 . . . . . .170 A8
Fardell Rd 7 PE13 . . . . .152 C4
Farebrother Way 2
NR19 . . . . .154 C3
Farm Cl Lingwood NR13 . .74 A2
11 Loddon NR14 . . . . .92 A2
Farm Ct St IP20 . . . . . . .123 A1
Farm La NR13 . . . . .56 A1
Farm Rd
Heckingham NR14 . . . . . . .92 D1
Worstead NR28 . . . . .38 A7
Farm View NR28 . . . . . . .151 E5
Farm Wlk Marham PE33 . .63 C5
6 Necton PE37 . . . . .65 F4
Farman Ave NR28 . . . . . .151 D5
Farman Cl 5 Belton NR31 94 A6
Lyng NR9 . . . . .51 A5
7 Salhouse NR13 . . . . . . .55 A1
Farmers Ave NR1 . . . . . .178 B2
Farmland Rd NR5 . . . . . .156 F1
Farmway 7 NR31 . . . . . .154 D2
Farnborough Rd 9 IP25 .84 F3
Farrow Cl
2 Great Moulton NR15 . .106 B1
7 Mattishall NR20 . . . . . . .68 E6
2 Swanton Morley NR20 . .50 B3
Farthing Cl Diss IP22 . . .177 D6
Loddon NR14 . . . . .109 D8
Farthing Dro
Beck Row, Holywell
Row & Kenny Hill IP27 . .112 C2
Lakenheath IP27 . . . . . . .113 A2
Southery PE38 . . . . .97 A2
Farthing Rd PE38 . . . . . . .79 B5
Fastnet Way 1 NR30 . . .168 C6
Fastolf Cl NR6 . . . . .157 E5
Fastolff Ave NR31 . . . . . .170 B3
Fayers Terr PE30 . . . . . .147 A4
Fayregreen NR21 . . . . . .141 D4
Feale Abbey PE34 . . . . . .144 A1
Fearn's Rd NR14 . . . . . . .139 D5
Featherstone Ct 5
NR19 . . . . .154 D2
Felbrigg Cl PE30 . . . . . . .148 F1
**Felbrigg Hall Garden &
Park** ★ NR11 . . . . .10 B2
Felbrigg Rd
Downham Market PE38 . . .172 C6
Roughton NR11 . . . . .21 D8
Fell Way 3 NR31 . . . . . . .94 C8
Fellowes Dr 2 NR31 . . . .94 C6
Fellowes Rd NR9 . . . . . . .69 E6
Fellows Cl NR5 . . . . .161 D6
Felmingham Rd NR28 . . .37 C7
Felsham Way NR8 . . . . . .155 E6
Felsted Ave PE13 . . . . . .152 E5
Felthorpe Rd NR9 . . . . . .52 B3
Feltwell Elementary Sch
IP26 . . . . .98 D1
Feltwell Prim Sch IP26 .98 E2
Feltwell Rd
Hockwold cum Wilton
IP26 . . . . .113 F7
Methwold IP26 . . . . .98 E5
Southery PE38 . . . . .97 D5
Fen Cl PE13 . . . . .152 E6
Fen Dro PE33 . . . . .81 F3
Fen Folgate 6 PE13 . . . . .67 B2
Fen La Banham NR16 . . .119 B6
Beccles NR34 . . . . .110 D2
Ditchingham NR35 . . . . . .108 E3
Garboldisham IP22 . . . . . .128 A7
Grimston PE32 . . . . .45 A7
Harling NR16 . . . . .118 C6
Leziate PE32 . . . . .45 A6
Marham PE33 . . . . .63 A5
Rickinghall Inferior IP22 . .128 C2
Roydon IP22 . . . . .129 C7
Thelnetham IP22 . . . . . . .128 B5
Fen Rd Blo' Norton IP22 .128 C6
Carleton Rode NR16 . . . .105 C2
Hinderclay IP22 . . . . .128 C5
Marham PE33 . . . . .63 B4
Scarning NR19 . . . . .154 B3
Watlington PE33 . . . . .61 D5
Fen St
Attleborough NR17 . . . . .103 F3
Old Buckenham NR17 . . .104 C2
Redgrave IP22 . . . . .128 F6
Rocklands NR17 . . . . . . .103 B6
Fen View
Christchurch PE14 . . . . . . .95 A7
East Dereham NR19 . . . . .154 C2
Fen Way 2 PE14 . . . . .59 A1
Fence Bank PE14 . . . . . . .42 A1
Fences Farm Rd PE34 . . .78 E8
Fendyke Rd PE14 . . . . . . .59 E1
Fengate Heacham PE31 .133 C4
Marsham NR10 . . . . .150 D1
Fengate Dro IP27 . . . . . .175 B6

Fengate Rd PE14 . . . . . . .59 C5
**Fenland & W Norfolk
Aviation Mus** ★ PE14 . . .59 C7
Fenland Rd
King's Lynn PE30 . . . . . . .147 C8
Wisbech PE13 . . . . .152 E6
Fenn Cres NR3 . . . . .158 B1
Fennel Way IP24 . . . . . . .176 F4
Fenner Rd NR30 . . . . . . .170 C2
Fenside PE31 . . . . .133 C4
Fenway PE31 . . . . .133 B3
Ferguson Way NR17 . . . .174 F7
Fermoy Ave PE30 . . . . . .146 E6
Fern Ct 3 NR18 . . . . . . .173 B4
Fern Dr NR28 . . . . .151 E5
Fern Gdns NR31 . . . . . . .93 F5
Fern Hill
Dersingham PE31 . . . . . .140 E4
Norwich NR1 . . . . .163 B5
Ferndale Cl NR6 . . . . . . .157 E4
Fernlea Rd PE30 . . . . . . .147 C4
Ferrier Cl 7 NR30 . . . . . .169 D5
Ferrier Ct NR29 . . . . . . .167 B6
Ferrier Rd NR30 . . . . . . .169 C5
Ferry Bank PE38 . . . . .97 A4
Ferry Cl NR29 . . . . .75 C4
Ferry Hill NR31 . . . . .170 D7
Ferry La
Great Yarmouth NR31 . . .169 C2
Norwich NR1 . . . . .178 C3
Postwick with Witton
NR13 . . . . .73 A2
Stokesby with Herringby
NR29 . . . . .75 B5
Ferry Rd
Carleton St Peter NR14 . . .91 E5
Clenchwarton PE34 . . . . .145 F5
Horning NR12 . . . . .55 E3
King's Lynn PE34 . . . . . . .146 B6
Norton Subcourse NR14 . .92 C6
Norwich NR1 . . . . .178 C3
Oxborough PE33 . . . . .81 D3
Reedham NR13 . . . . .92 E4
Surlingham NR14 . . . . . . .165 A1
Woodbastwick NR13 . . . . .55 D2
Ferry Sq PE34 . . . . .146 C5
Ferry St PE30 . . . . .146 D5
Ferry View Rd NR12 . . . .55 C3
Ferryboat La NR31 . . . . .170 D7
Ferrygate La NR29 . . . . . .57 D5
Fersfield Rd
Bressingham IP22 . . . . . .129 B8
Kenninghall NR16 . . . . . .119 C4
South Lopham IP22 . . . . .128 F8
Festival Cl PE30 . . . . . . .148 B1
Festival Rd NR20 . . . . . . .50 B7
Festival Way CB6 . . . . . . .96 E2
Ffolkes Dr
King's Lynn PE30 . . . . . . .148 C1
Terrington St Clement
PE34 . . . . .144 B5
Ffolkes Pl 1 PE33 . . . . . .61 D3
Fiddle Wood Rd NR6 . . . .158 D4
Field Acre Way NR15 . . .106 E4
Field Barn Cotts PE32 . . .46 E3
Field Barn La PE33 . . . . . .61 F3
Field Dalling Rd
Field Dalling NR25 . . . . . . .7 A3
Gunthorpe NR21 . . . . .18 B8
Field End Cl PE30 . . . . . .147 B6
Field House Gdns
IP22 . . . . .177 E5
Field La Beetley NR20 . . .49 C5
10 Blofield NR13 . . . . . . .73 D6
Blofield NR13 . . . . .165 E8
Fakenham NR21 . . . . . . .141 B6
Hempnall NR15 . . . . .107 C4
King's Lynn PE30 . . . . . . .147 B6
Marsham NR10 . . . . .36 B2
North Walsham NR28 . . . .151 A4
Stody NR24 . . . . .142 F8
Whinburgh & Westfield
NR19 . . . . .67 F4
Wretton PE33 . . . . .80 D3
Field Rd Brandon IP27 . .114 D4
King's Lynn PE30 . . . . . . .147 B5
Ringland NR8 . . . . .70 B8
South Walsham NR13 . . . .74 B8
Stalham NR12 . . . . .39 C3
Fieldbarn Dro PE33 . . . . .82 A4
Fieldbarn Rd PE33 . . . . . .81 B8
Fieldfare Cl 6 NR12 . . . . .54 A1
Fields Rd NR34 . . . . .110 E6
Fields The
Forncett NR16 . . . . .105 E5
Hingham NR9 . . . . .86 C5
Fieldview NR5 . . . . .161 E6
Fiennes Rd 4 NR7 . . . . . .72 D5
Fifers La NR6 . . . . .158 C6
Fifth Ave PE13 . . . . .152 E4
Fifty Dro CB6 . . . . .95 F3
Fifty Rd PE14 . . . . .95 A3
Filbert Rd NR14 . . . . .91 F1
Filberts PE30 . . . . .147 D5
Filby Cl NR29 . . . . .75 F8
Filby Fst Sch NR29 . . . . .75 E8
Filby La NR29 . . . . .167 A1
Filby Rd Coltishall NR10 . .37 C8
Stokesby with Herringby
NR29 . . . . .75 C6
Swaffham PE37 . . . . .153 B2
Finch Cl Cromer NR27 . . .139 C4
Norwich NR1 . . . . .159 D2
Finch Way NR13 . . . . . . .165 C3
Fincham Dro PE32 . . . . . .64 B5

Fincham Rd
Barton Bendish PE33 .....**81** A8
Crimplesham PE33 .....**80** A8
Fincham PE33 .....**63** A1
Shouldham Thorpe PE33 .....**62** C2
Stow Bardolph PE34 .....**79** F8
Wereham PE33 .....**80** F6
Finchdale Cl 5 PE30 ....**148** C4
Finchley Ct 4 NR2 .....**162** B7
Finderne Dr NR18 .....**173** D6
Finishers Rd 8 NR6 .....**158** C1
Finisterre Rise 2 NR30 .**168** C6
Finkelgate NR1 .....**178** B1
Finningham Rd IP22 .....**128** E1
Finsbury Cl 1 PE38 .....**172** B4
Fiona Cl NR18 .....**173** E6
Fir Cl Heacham PE31 .....**133** C6
Mundford IP26 .....**100** B4
Fir Covert Rd
Carleton Rode NR16 .....**105** A1
Taverham NR10 .....**155** D5
Fir Gr NR26 .....**138** D4
Fir La NR10 .....**34** A1
Fir Pk IP25 .....**84** A7
Fir Rd IP24 .....**176** B1
Fir Tree Dr 7 PE33 .....**43** E2
Firethorn Cl NR8 .....**155** B2
Firman Ct NR7 .....**163** F8
Firs Ave NR29 .....**167** A3
Firs La NR12 .....**39** C2
Firs Rd Hethersett NR9 ...**88** D7
Norwich NR6 .....**157** F6
Firs The
Downham Market PE38 ..**172** D6
Lakenheath IP27 .....**113** F1
Firs Way IP27 .....**175** C2
Firside Mid Sch NR6 ..**158** A6
First Ave PE13 .....**152** D5
First Dro IP27 .....**113** C3
First Marsh Rd PE13 .....**59** A6
Firtree Cl NR13 .....**165** B4
Firtree Rd NR7 .....**159** E1
Firwood Cl NR1 .....**163** C8
Fish Wharf 2 NR30 .....**169** D1
Fisher Ave NR30 .....**169** D8
Fisher Rd Diss IP22 .....**177** E4
Fakenham NR21 .....**141** B5
Fisher Row NR12 .....**111** F4
Fisher Way IP24 .....**176** E5
Fisher's La IP21 .....**131** A4
Fishergate NR3 .....**178** B4
Fisherman's Her Ctr★
NR26 .....**138** D8
Fishermen's Ct NR17 ..**174** D6
Fishers Cl NR5 .....**156** E1
Fishers La Beetley NR20 ..**49** D6
Norwich NR2 .....**178** A3
Fishers' Quay 5 NR30 ..**169** C4
Fishley View NR13 .....**166** B4
Fiske's Opening 6
NR31 .....**170** D4
Fiskes Ct NR14 .....**89** F5
Fison Way IP24 .....**176** C6
Fison Way Ind Est
IP24 .....**176** C6
Fitton Rd PE34 .....**61** B8
Fitzalan Cl 8 NR30 .....**169** C4
Fitzgerald Rd
Norwich NR1 .....**162** E1
7 Poringland NR14 .....**90** C5
Fitzhenry Mews 8 NR5 .**161** B8
Fitzwalter Rd IP22 .....**177** E4
Five Acre La NR35 .....**123** E7
Five Acres NR14 .....**89** F4
Five Alls Rd PE14 .....**41** F1
Five Crossways NR12 ..**164** D8
Five Elms 4 PE30 .....**147** C4
Flag St NR21 .....**15** C2
Flaxlands NR16 .....**105** B4
Flaxlands Rd NR16 .....**105** C3
Fleet La NR13 .....**56** B1
Fleet Rd NR8 .....**156** B6
Fleetwood Dr 4 NR13 ...**72** D4
Flegg Gn PE33 .....**80** D4
Flegg High Sch NR29 ....**57** E6
Fleggburgh Prim Sch
NR29 .....**75** C8
Fleggburgh Rd NR29 ....**57** C2
Fleming Ct 8 IP25 .....**84** D3
Fletcher Cl NR12 .....**55** C1
Fletcher Way
Acle NR13 .....**166** D4
Cromer NR27 .....**139** B5
Norwich NR3 .....**158** C3
Flint Dr NR13 .....**136** D5
Flint Gate 17 PE12 .....**41** B8
Flint House Gdns 13 NR9 **88** C7
Flint House Rd PE14 .....**77** F1
Flint Way 2 PE14 .....**77** A8
Flitcham Abbey PE31 ....**28** D5
Flitcham CE Prim Sch
PE31 .....**28** C5
Flixton Marsh La
NR32 .....**111** F6
Flixton Rd
Bungay NR35 .....**124** A7
Flixton NR35 .....**123** E6
Lound NR32 .....**94** C1
St Margaret, South Elmham
IP20 .....**123** E3
Somerleyton, Ashby &
Herringfleet NR32 .....**111** F8
Flordon Rd
Bracon Ash NR14 .....**88** F1
Flordon NR15 .....**106** D8

Florence Barclay Cl
IP24 .....**176** D6
Florence Rd NR1 .....**163** A6
Florence Wlk NR19 .....**154** C2
Florida Bvd NR21 .....**15** C2
Flowerday Cl NR31 .....**171** D5
Flowerdew Cl 12 NR9 ....**88** C7
Flowerdew's La NR13 ....**74** B7
Flowerpot La NR15 .....**106** D3
Flowers La NR17 .....**174** B3
Fludge's La NR20 .....**49** B6
Flymore La NR17 .....**103** A8
Fodderfen Dro PE38 .....**113** A7
Foldgate La PE34 .....**61** A5
Folgate NR16 .....**88** D3
Folgate Cl
Costessey NR8 .....**156** F5
Thornham PE36 .....**2** D6
Folgate La
Costessey NR8 .....**156** F4
Walpole PE14 .....**41** D3
Folgate Rd
Heacham PE31 .....**133** C4
North Walsham NR28 ..**151** B6
Folland Ct 8 NR20 .....**50** E7
Follies The PE37 .....**65** F4
Folly Cl NR18 .....**173** C5
Folly Ct
Fakenham NR21 .....**141** D4
King's Lynn PE30 .....**147** B7
Mattishall NR20 .....**68** F6
Folly Gdns NR18 .....**173** C5
Folly Gr PE30 .....**147** B7
Folly La Beetley NR20 .....**49** B6
Bressingham IP22 .....**129** C8
Claxton NR14 .....**91** D5
3 Hingham NR9 .....**86** C5
Old Buckenham NR17 ...**104** F2
Folly Rd NR18 .....**173** C5
Folly View 5 PE37 .....**65** F4
Folwell Rd NR5 .....**156** E1
Footpath The 11 NR14 ...**90** C5
Ford Ave PE30 .....**148** D5
Ford St IP24 .....**176** D3
Foregate Cl 2 NR8 .....**155** D2
Forest Cl IP27 .....**175** C2
Forest Dr PE31 .....**133** C6
Forest Mount NR1 .....**93** E3
Forest Prim Sch IP27 ...**175** C4
Forest Ret Pk IP24 .....**125** D8
Forester Cl 1 NR4 .....**162** C1
Forester's Ave PE38 .....**97** A8
Forge Cl
Old Buckenham NR17 ...**104** D2
Palgrave IP22 .....**177** D2
Poringland NR14 .....**90** D4
Forge Gr NR14 .....**110** C2
Forge Orchards 1 NR14 ..**89** B3
Forge Rd NR14 .....**91** F3
Forge Way IP22 .....**128** A8
Forget-Me-Not Rd 3
PE31 .....**12** D4
Forncett CE Prim Sch
NR16 .....**106** B3
Forncett Ind Steam Mus★
NR16 .....**106** B5
Forncett Rd
Bunwell NR16 .....**105** F3
Tharston & Hapton
NR15 .....**106** D4
Forster Cl 2 NR11 .....**150** D6
Forster Way NR11 .....**150** D6
Forsythia Rd NR31 .....**170** B5
Forth Cl NR30 .....**168** C5
Forties Cl 5 NR30 .....**168** C6
Fortune Gn NR14 .....**90** E4
Forum The★ NR2 .....**178** A2
Forwater Rd NR10 .....**34** B3
Foster Cl Brundall NR13 ..**165** B4
Ormesby St Margaret
NR29 .....**167** C2
Foster Rd NR3 .....**158** D3
Foulgers Opening
NR1 .....**178** C1
Foulsham Prim Sch
NR20 .....**33** D3
Foulsham Rd
Bintree NR20 .....**33** C2
Guestwick NR20 .....**33** F4
Guist NR20 .....**33** A4
Hindolveston NR20 .....**33** D7
Wood Norton NR20 .....**33** B6
Foundry Cl
Foulsham NR20 .....**33** D3
Northrepps NR27 .....**11** A2
Sculthorpe NR21 .....**16** C2
Foundry Cnr NR17 .....**174** F2
Foundry La PE36 .....**2** A3
Foundry Sq NR19 .....**154** D4
Fountaine Gr PE30 .....**148** C4
Fountains Rd NR4 .....**89** E8
Four Acres Est NR27 ...**167** C8
Fourth Ave PE13 .....**152** E4
Fowell Ct NR5 .....**161** B6
Fowler's La NR17 .....**174** B2
Fox Covert 5 NR19 .....**154** C4
Fox Gr 7 NR16 .....**118** C5
Fox Hill IP20 .....**123** C3
Fox Hill Rd NR12 .....**38** E7
Fox La Brundall NR13 ...**165** F6
Framingham Pigot NR14 ..**90** D6
North Tuddenham NR20 ..**68** F8
Fox Rd Dereham NR19 ..**154** D4
Framingham Pigot NR14 ..**90** D7
Fox's La PE34 .....**146** C6
Foxburrow Rd NR7 .....**159** A5
Foxcotte Cl NR6 .....**157** E7

Foxes Loke 12 NR14 .....**92** A1
Foxes Mdw 2 PE32 .....**46** F2
Foxglove Cl
Fakenham NR21 .....**141** F4
North Walsham NR28 ..**151** E5
Thurton NR14 .....**91** C4
Foxglove Dr 21 NR31 ....**94** C6
Foxglove La NR26 .....**138** B6
Foxglove Rd
2 Attleborough NR17 ...**174** B5
Thetford IP24 .....**176** F4
Foxglove Wlk PE34 .....**61** B8
Foxley Cl NR5 .....**161** D6
Foxley Rd
Bawdeswell NR20 .....**50** D8
Foulsham NR20 .....**33** C2
Foxley Wood National Nature
Reserve★ NR10 .....**33** F1
Foxs Loke NR11 .....**150** B6
Foxwood 9 NR13 .....**73** D6
Foxwood Cl NR8 .....**155** B2
Framingham Earl High Sch
NR14 .....**90** C6
Framingham Earl La
NR14 .....**90** E5
Framingham La NR14 .....**90** F7
Framingham Rd NR14 ....**90** F7
Framlingham Cl NR31 ...**169** C2
Francis Cl NR27 .....**139** C5
Francis La NR13 .....**73** C6
Francis Rd NR15 .....**106** E3
Francis Stone Ct NR7 ....**72** D3
Francis Way NR5 .....**160** E8
Frank Stone Ct NR30 ...**169** E1
Franklin Cl PE34 .....**145** E6
Fransham Forge★
NR19 .....**66** D8
Fransham Rd PE32 .....**48** B1
Frazer Cres NR11 .....**143** F4
Fred Nicholson Specl Sch
NR19 .....**154** E2
Frederick Cl PE30 .....**148** D6
Frederick Rd NR30 .....**169** C5
Free La NR35 .....**108** F2
Freebridge Haven PE33 .**43** F3
Freedom Bridge PE13 ..**152** B6
Freeland Cl NR18 .....**155** C3
Freeland Cnr NR10 .....**155** C6
Freeman Cl NR14 .....**109** D8
Freeman Sq NR2 .....**162** C8
Freeman St NR30 .....**169** E3
Freestone Ct 7 PE30 ...**146** E4
Freethorpe Com Prim Sch
NR13 .....**92** F7
Freethorpe Rd
Cantley NR13 .....**92** D6
Freethorpe NR13 .....**74** F1
Freiston 2 PE30 .....**147** C5
Fremantle Rd NR30 .....**168** E1
French's Rd PE14 .....**41** C4
Frensham Rd NR3 .....**157** F2
Frenze Hall La IP22 .....**177** F5
Frenze Rd IP22 .....**177** E4
Frere Cnr 6 IP22 .....**129** D7
Frere Rd
30 Harleston IP20 .....**122** D2
Norwich NR7 .....**159** D1
Fresher Mews NR5 .....**160** F6
Freshfield Cl NR5 .....**161** C7
Freshgap La NR20 .....**33** B6
Freshwater Way NR8 ...**155** F3
Frettenham Fst Sch
NR12 .....**54** A4
Frettenham Rd
Hainford NR10 .....**53** F5
Horstead with Stanninghall
NR12 .....**54** B5
Freyden Way NR12 .....**54** A4
Friar Tuck Rd NR4 .....**162** C1
Friar's La PE31 .....**135** D4
Friars' La 3 NR30 .....**169** D2
Friars Quay NR3 .....**178** B3
Friars St PE30 .....**146** E3
Friars The 17 PE30 .....**146** D4
Friarscroft La NR18 .....**173** B3
Friday Bridge Prim Sch
PE14 .....**77** A7
Friday Mkt 4 NR22 .....**16** F7
Fridaybridge Rd
Elm PE14 .....**77** A8
Wisbech PE14 .....**59** A1
Friends Cl NR5 .....**161** D6
Friends Rd NR4 .....**161** E5
Fring Rd Bircham PE31 ...**14** A3
Snettisham PE31 .....**13** A5
Frinton Way 4 PE13 .....**152** E5
Frith Way NR15 .....**106** B1
Fritillary Dr NR18 .....**173** E4
Fritton Cl NR29 .....**167** B3
Fritton La NR29 .....**56** E6
Fritton Lake Ctry World★
NR31 .....**93** F2
Fritton Rd NR29 .....**56** E6
Frobisher Cl IP24 .....**176** F6
Frobisher Cres PE36 ....**132** F7
Frog's Hall La NR20 .....**50** C2
Frogge La
Coltishall NR12 .....**54** C8
Scottow NR12 .....**37** C1
Frogs Hall La 3 NR1 .....**163** B5
Frogs Hole
Blofield NR13 .....**165** D6
Somerleyton, Ashby &
Herringfleet NR32 .....**93** F1
Frogshall La NR18 .....**173** A5
Front Rd
Tydd St Giles PE13 .....**41** A4
Wood Dalling NR11 .....**34** D6

Front St Binham NR21 .....**6** E2
Burnham Market PE31 ..**135** C3
Trunch NR28 .....**22** E5
Front Way PE30 .....**147** A7
Frost Cl Norwich NR7 ...**163** F8
20 Watton IP25 .....**84** D3
Frost's La NR15 .....**106** B1
Fugill Rd NR7 .....**159** D1
Fulcher Ave NR27 .....**139** A7
Fulford Cl NR4 .....**162** A2
Fuller Cl
2 Rackheath NR13 .....**72** E7
9 West Winch PE33 .....**43** F2
Fuller Mews 5 NR5 .....**160** F8
Fuller Rd
North Walsham NR28 ..**151** B4
Redenhall with Harleston
IP20 .....**122** D1
Fuller's Cl NR34 .....**110** C5
Fuller's Hill 10 NR30 ...**169** C4
Fulmar Cl 9 NR31 .....**94** C7
Fulmer La PE32 .....**46** E2
Fulmerston Cl IP24 .....**176** B2
Fulmerston Rd IP24 .....**176** B2
Fulmodeston Rd
Fulmodeston NR21 .....**18** B1
Hindolveston NR20 .....**33** C8
Stibbard NR21 .....**32** E7
Fulton Cl 4 NR4 .....**162** A1
Fundenhall Rd NR15 ....**106** B7
Fundrey Rd PE13 .....**152** F6
Furlong Dro PE33 .....**81** A3
Furlong Rd 1 PE33 .....**81** A3
Furness Cl PE30 .....**148** F1
Furthest Dro PE27 .....**113** C4
Furze Ave NR7 .....**163** E8
Furze Hill NR27 .....**139** C5
Furze Hill Dr NR28 .....**151** E3
Furze La
Great Witchingham NR9 .**149** C2
Guist NR20 .....**33** A6
Furze Rd NR7 .....**163** E8
Furze Way IP22 .....**129** B1
Fye Bridge St NR3 .....**178** B3

G

Gablehurst Ct NR31 .....**170** A4
Gables Ave NR11 .....**22** B7
Gage Rd NR7 .....**159** C4
Gagman's La NR19 .....**68** A5
Gainsborough Ave
1 Diss IP22 .....**177** C4
Great Yarmouth NR31 ...**170** A7
Gainsborough Cl 2
PE38 .....**172** D6
Gale Cl NR14 .....**109** F8
Gales Ct NR23 .....**136** C5
Gales Rd NR23 .....**136** C6
Gallant's La NR16 .....**118** C5
Galley Cl 8 NR33 .....**111** F1
Galley Hill NR3 .....**158** A2
Gallow Dr PE38 .....**172** C7
Gallow Hill (Tumulus)★
NR25 .....**8** B5
Gallow La PE33 .....**62** D2
Galloway Cl 6 PE30 .....**68** A8
Gallowhill La NR24 .....**18** C3
Gallows La NR16 .....**103** E1
Galyon Rd PE30 .....**147** B8
Gambling Cl NR6 .....**158** A7
Gamecock Cl NR6 .....**158** C6
Gamewell Cl 6 NR1 .....**162** E2
Gangway The NR27 .....**139** C7
Ganners Hill NR8 .....**155** E3
Gannet Rd NR29 .....**167** E4
Gant Cl 9 NR20 .....**68** F6
Gaol Hill NR2 .....**178** A3
Gaol St 13 PE13 .....**152** C4
Gapton Hall Ind Est
NR31 .....**170** A8
Gapton Hall Rd NR31 ...**170** A8
Gapton Hall Ret Pk
NR31 .....**169** A1
Garboldisham Rd
Harling NR16 .....**118** C3
Kenninghall NR16 .....**118** F5
Garboldisham VC Prim Sch
IP22 .....**128** A8
Garden Cl Briston NR24 .**142** B4
Bungay NR35 .....**124** B8
North Walsham NR28 ..**151** C6
4 Watton IP25 .....**84** E3
Garden Ct
King's Lynn PE30 .....**147** A4
1 Loddon NR14 .....**92** A1
Garden La NR25 .....**8** A1
Garden Pl 2 NR3 .....**162** E8
Garden Rd
Brundall NR13 .....**165** E6
Hemsby NR29 .....**167** D7
Sheringham NR26 .....**138** D6
3 Wiggenhall St Germans
PE34 .....**43** B1
Garden Row PE30 .....**146** E3
Garden St
Cromer NR27 .....**139** B7
Norwich NR1 .....**178** B2
Gardeners Terr NR7 .....**158** F4
Gardenhouse La IP22 ..**128** C3
Gardyn Croft 5 NR8 .....**155** D2
Garfield Rd NR30 .....**169** D7
Garfield Terr NR30 .....**168** E4
Gargle Hill NR7 .....**163** F7
Garianonum (Roman Fort)★
NR31 .....**93** F2
Garlic St IP21 .....**122** A2

Garlondes 6 NR16 .....**118** C5
Garner's La PE34 .....**41** D8
Garnham Rd NR20 .....**170** C7
Garrett Cl NR3 .....**158** F1
Garrick Cl NR30 .....**169** C5
Garrick Gn NR6 .....**158** E5
Garrick Gn Fst Sch
NR6 .....**158** E5
Garrison Rd NR30 .....**169** C5
Garrood Dr NR21 .....**141** E5
Garvestone Prim Sch
NR9 .....**68** C2
Garvestone Rd NR9 .....**68** E4
Garwood Cl PE30 .....**147** E4
Gas Hill NR1 .....**163** A6
Gas House La PE12 .....**41** B8
Gashouse Dro PE27 .....**175** E4
Gashouse Hill NR11 .....**150** D6
Gaskell Way NR30 .....**148** C1
Gatacre Rd NR31 .....**169** B3
Gatehouse La PE30 .....**148** C6
Gatekeeper Cl NR18 ....**173** E4
Gateley Gdns NR3 .....**158** B3
Gateley Rd NR20 .....**49** B8
Gaultree Sq PE14 .....**59** D2
Gavell St IP19 .....**124** D1
Gawdy Cl 2 IP20 .....**122** D2
Gawdy Rd NR7 .....**159** D1
Gaye Cres 1 IP23 .....**130** C1
Gayford Rd NR10 .....**35** B2
Gaymer Cl NR16 .....**119** D7
Gaymer's Way NR28 ....**151** B6
Gaynor Cl NR18 .....**173** B5
Gayton Fst Sch PE32 ...**45** C6
Gayton Rd
East Winch PE32 .....**45** A4
Grimston PE32 .....**45** C8
King's Lynn PE30 .....**147** C5
Gayton Wlk NR6 .....**158** E5
Gaywood Cl NR30 .....**168** D5
Gaywood Com Prim Sch
PE30 .....**147** C7
Gaywood Hall Dr
PE30 .....**147** B5
Gaywood Rd PE30 .....**146** F5
Geddes Way 5 NR20 ....**68** F6
Gedge Rd NR30 .....**168** E6
Geldeston Hill NR34 ....**109** F2
Geldeston Rd
Ellingham NR35 .....**109** D3
Geldeston NR34 .....**110** B2
Gelham Manor NR1 .....**140** C3
Generals Wlk 5 PE30 ...**147** C5
Geneva Gdns NR31 .....**171** E4
Genista Gn 7 NR31 .....**170** B6
Gentian Way 2 NR17 ....**174** B4
Gentleman's Wlk NR2 ..**178** A3
Gentlemans Wlk NR14 ..**92** A3
Gentry Pl NR5 .....**161** C8
Geoffrey Rd 4 NR1 .....**162** F3
George Beck Rd 8 NR29 .**58** B6
George Borrow Rd
2 East Dereham NR19 ..**154** F3
Norwich NR4 .....**161** E5
George Cl NR8 .....**157** B8
George Dance Pl NR5 ..**161** C7
George Dr NR7 .....**157** B7
George Edwards Rd
NR21 .....**141** D5
George Elliot Way 6
NR19 .....**154** D2
George Fox Way NR5 ...**161** B5
George Hill
Norwich NR6 .....**158** E4
Stanton IP31 .....**127** C1
George La Acle NR13 ...**166** B4
2 Loddon NR14 .....**92** A1
George Pope Cl NR3 ....**158** C2
George Pope Rd NR3 ...**158** C2
George Rd IP24 .....**176** F5
George St
Brandon IP27 .....**175** D3
Great Yarmouth NR30 ..**169** C4
6 King's Lynn PE30 .....**146** E6
Sheringham NR26 .....**138** D7
George Trollope Rd 15
IP25 .....**84** D3
George Westwood Way
NR34 .....**110** D2
George White Mid Sch
NR3 .....**162** F8
George Winter Ct
NR3 .....**158** C2
Georges Rd NR19 .....**154** D5
Georgia Rd NR21 .....**15** C2
Gerald Cl NR1 .....**163** C8
German's La PE34 .....**42** A4
Germander Ct 8 NR31 ...**94** C6
Gertrude Rd NR3 .....**158** F1
Ghost Hill Fst Sch
NR8 .....**156** C8
Gibbet La
East Beckham NR11 .....**138** D2
Wereham PE33 .....**80** B2
Gibbs Cl NR9 .....**160** B2
Gibson Rd 5 IP25 .....**67** B2
Gidney Dr PE31 .....**133** C5
Gigli Cl NR28 .....**151** B3
Gilbard Rd NR5 .....**161** C1
Gilbert Cl NR14 .....**90** F4
Gilbert Rd NR30 .....**168** E6
Gilbert Way NR4 .....**161** D1
Gilchrist Cl 8 NR4 .....**89** E8
Gildencroft NR3 .....**178** A4
Gilderswood NR16 .....**105** F3
Giles Rd NR10 .....**54** A1
Gillingham Rd NR34 ....**110** A2
Gillingham Dam NR34 ..**110** C2
Gilman Rd NR3 .....**158** F1

Gilpin's Ride NR19 .....154 D4
Gilray Rd IP22 ....177 F4
Gimingham Rd
  Mundesley NR11 ....143 A6
  Southrepps NR11 ....22 C7
Gipsies' La NR25 ....9 A3
Gipsies La NR29 ....56 C6
Gipsy Cl NR5 ....161 E6
Gipsy La Norwich NR5 ...161 E5
  Watlington PE33 ....61 D5
Girling Rd NR19 ....154 C6
Girlings La NR7 ....163 E5
Girton Rd
  Great Yarmouth NR31 ...170 A3
  Norwich NR2 ....162 B4
Gissing Rd IP22 ....120 F2
Glade Prim Sch IP27 ...175 D3
Glade The
  Costessey NR8 ....156 F4
  Overstrand NR27 ....11 A3
  Thetford IP24 ....176 D6
Gladstone Rd
  Fakenham NR21 ....141 B4
  4 King's Lynn PE30 ...146 E3
Gladstone St NR2 ....162 B6
Glamis Ct 26 IP20 ......122 D2
Glandford Rd NR25 ....7 E5
Glasbury Wlk PE13 .....153 C3
Glaven PE30 ....147 C5
Glaven Cl NR28 ....151 D5
Glaven Hale Cl NR25 ...137 C6
Glaven Rd NR25 ....137 D5
Glebe Ave
  Hunstanton PE36 ......132 C5
  Watlington PE33 ....61 E5
Glebe Cl Fransham NR19 .66 C7
  Hingham NR9 ....86 B5
  19 Long Stratton NR15 .106 E3
  Northwold IP26 ....99 C8
  2 Potter Heigham NR29 .56 F6
  Taverham NR8 ....155 F1
  Thetford IP24 ....176 D5
Glebe Ct NR28 ....151 D6
Glebe Est PE34 ....144 C7
Glebe House Sch
  PE36 ....132 D5
Glebe La PE31 ....135 F6
Glebe Mdw NR17 ....103 E7
Glebe Rd Acle NR13 ....166 C3
  Dersingham PE31 ......135 F6
  Downham Market PE38 ..172 D6
  Gissing IP21 ....121 A4
  Norwich NR2 ....162 A4
  7 Watton IP25 ....84 E3
  Weeting IP27 ....175 B7
Glebe The
  2 Harling NR16 ....118 C5
  Hemsby NR29 ....167 C8
  Honing NR28 ....38 C6
  Stibbard NR21 ....32 E7
  Wells-next-the-Sea
  NR23 ....136 D6
Glebe Way 5 NR12 ......54 C6
Glebes The 18 NR13 .....94 A5
Glenalmond NR4 ....162 A1
Glenburn Ave NR7 ......159 A3
Glenburn Cl NR7 ....159 A3
Glenda Cl NR5 ....157 C1
Glenda Cres NR5 ....157 B2
Glenda Ct NR5 ....157 B1
Glenda Rd NR5 ....157 C1
Glendenning Rd 4 NR1 .163 B5
Glenfield Cl NR14 ......78 A5
Glengarry Cl NR9 ....88 C8
Glenham Ct PE31 ....140 C4
Glenmore Ave NR30 .....168 D7
Glenmore Gdns NR3 ....158 B2
Glenn Rd NR14 ....90 C4
Globe La NR13 ....165 E6
Globe Pl NR2 ....162 C5
Globe St IP26 ....99 B5
Glosthorpe Manor
  PE32 ....44 F5
Gloucester Ave NR31 ...170 C4
Gloucester Ct PE13 ....152 D7
Gloucester Pl NR24 ....142 D4
Gloucester Rd PE30 ....147 B6
Gloucester St NR2 .....162 C4
Gloucester Way IP24 ...176 A5
Gobbett's Rd IP22 .....152 D7
Goddard Cres 1 PE13 ..152 D7
Goddards Ct 1 IP25 .....84 D3
Godfrey Rd 5 NR10 .....54 A2
Godric Pl NR2 ....161 F6
Godwick Medieval Village
  of* PE32 ....31 C1
Godwin Rd PE13 ....152 D7
Goffe Cl IP25 ....84 D4
Goffins La NR29 ....56 C6
Gogg's Mill Rd NR21 ...141 A3
Goggles La NR19 ....66 C6
Gogle Cl 8 NR20 ....68 E6
Golden Ball St NR1 ....178 B2
Golden Dog La NR3 .....178 B4
Golden Fleece Heritage
  Mus* NR28 ....38 A4
Golden Gates NR23 .....136 B2
Golden Gates Dr
  NR23 ....136 A2
Golden Pightle 7 NR9 ...69 F2
Golden Sq 10 NR2 ......139 B7
Goldfinch Cl PE38 .....172 C7
Goldfinch Way 13 IP25 ..84 C3
Golding Pl
  Norwich NR2 ....162 C6
  16 Wisbech PE13 ......152 C4
Golds Pightle PE36 ......2 B3
Goldsmith St NR2 ......162 C7

Goldsmith Way IP21 ...121 F4
Goldwell Rd NR1 ....162 E3
Golf Cl King's Lynn PE30 .148 D1
  Runton NR27 ....10 A5
Golf Course Rd PE36 ...132 E8
Golf La NR19 ....154 D7
Golf Links Rd
  Brundall NR13 ....165 D4
  Wymondham College
  NR18 ....104 E8
Gong La NR13 ....135 F6
Gonville Cl PE31 ......133 C5
Gonville Rd NR31 ......170 A4
Gooch Cl NR28 ....151 C6
Gooderstone CE Prim Sch
  PE33 ....82 A5
Gooderstone Rd PE33 ...81 F5
Gooderstone Water Gdns*
  PE33 ....82 A5
Goodhale Rd 1 NR5 ....161 B7
Goodman Sq 3 NR2 .....162 C7
Goodminns PE36 ....13 A7
Goodrick Pl PE13 ......153 C4
Goodwin Rd NR11 ......143 C6
Goodwins Rd PE30 .....146 E3
Goodwood Cl NR7 ......159 E1
Goosander Cl 4 PE31 ...12 C5
Goose Gn
  8 Sutton Bridge PE12 ..41 B8
  Winfarthing NR21 .....120 C6
Goose Gn La IP22 ......120 B6
Goose Gn Rd PE31 ......12 E4
Goose La
  Alby with Thwaite NR11 .21 B3
  Stalham NR12 ....39 C4
Gooseacre La IP25 .....67 D3
Goose's La PE14 ....41 D5
Gooseberry Hill NR20 ..50 B3
Gordon Ave NR7 ....163 C7
Gordon Cl PE13 ....152 C3
Gordon Fendick Sch
  PE13 ....152 D8
Gordon Godfrey Way
  NR10 ....53 A3
Gordon Rd
  Briston NR24 ....142 A4
  3 East Dereham NR20 ..154 E5
  Great Yarmouth NR31 ..169 C2
Gordon Sq NR1 ....178 B1
Gordon Terr NR11 .....143 B4
Gore La NR15 ....121 C5
Gorgate Rd NR20 ......49 E3
Gorleston La NR31 ....170 A2
Gormans La NR21 ......31 D5
Gorse Ave NR6 ....158 A5
Gorse Cl 4 Belton NR31 .94 A5
  2 East Dereham NR19 .154 C4
  Fakenham NR21 ....141 F4
  Mundesley NR11 ......143 B5
Gorse Ind Est IP24 ....125 C6
Gorse Rd NR7 ....163 D8
Gorse View 4 NR20 ....49 D4
Gorse Vw 4 NR20 .....49 D4
Goshawk Way 5 IP24 ..176 D2
Gosmoor La PE14 ......59 B1
Gostling Cl IP22 ......177 B4
Gothic Cl IP20 ....122 D1
Goulburn Rd NR7 .....159 D1
Gould Rd 1 NR2 ......162 A4
Gournay Ave NR31 ....170 D2
Governors Ct NR1 ....178 C1
Gowing Cl NR6 ....157 F7
Gowing Ct NR3 ....158 B3
Gowing Rd
  11 Mulbarton NR14 ...89 B3
  Norwich NR6 ....157 F6
Gowing Way NR15 ....107 B5
Grace Edwards Cl
  NR8 ....155 F2
Grafton Cl PE30 ......147 C8
Grafton Rd PE30 .....147 C8
Graham Dr 2 PE32 .....44 B3
Graham Sq NR7 ......159 D1
Graham St PE30 .....146 E3
Grammar Sch Rd
  NR28 ....151 C4
Granary Cl
  Briston NR24 ....142 F3
  Freethorpe NR13 ......92 E7
  9 Lingwood NR13 .....74 A3
Granary Cl PE30 ......146 D4
Granary Loke NR10 ..149 C4
Granary Rd NR17 ....174 C4
Grand Cl NR19 ......154 C4
Grange Ave NR11 .....11 B3
Grange Cl Briston NR24 .142 E3
  Ludham NR29 ....56 D5
  Norwich NR6 ....158 E4
  10 Snettisham PE31 ...12 E4
  Wroxham/Hoveton
  NR12 ....164 E6
Grange Cres PE33 ....63 C5
Grange Ct NR28 .....151 C5
Grange La
  Honingham NR9 ......69 F8
  West Winch PE33 ....61 E8
Grange Rd
  Caister-on-Sea NR30 .168 D5
  Cantley NR13 ....92 C6
  Flixton NR35 ....123 E4
  Hainford NR10 ....53 F5
  Ludham NR29 ....56 D5
  Mundham NR14 ......108 F7
  Norwich NR2 ....162 A4
  Scarning NR19 ......154 A4
  Sutton Bridge PE34 ..41 E8
  Wendling NR19 ......66 F8
  Wisbech PE13 ....152 A7

Grange Wlk NR12 .....164 C4
Granny Bard's La NR12 .54 C3
Grant Rd NR10 ....54 A2
Grant St NR2 ....162 A7
Granta Way 1 NR31 ...170 B2
Grantly Ct NR19 .....154 D5
Granville Cl 8 NR30 ..169 B4
Granville Rd NR31 ...169 B4
Granville Terr PE12 ...41 A8
Grapes Hill NR2 ......162 C6
Grasmere 19 NR9 .....88 D8
Grasmere Cl NR5 ....161 C6
Grassgate La PE14 ...59 B7
Gravel Bank PE14 ....60 D6
Gravel Dam NR32 ....111 D4
Gravel Hill NR14 .....89 F4
Gravel Pit La NR25 ..137 C5
Gravelfield Cl NR1 ..163 B8
Gravelhill La PE33 ...43 F1
Gravelpit Hill NR12 ..102 F6
Gray Dr NR20 ....50 B4
Gray's La Barsham NR22 .16 E6
  Pulham Market IP21 ..121 D5
Grays Fair NR5 ......156 F1
Grays La PE14 ....59 C2
Grays Rd NR34 ......111 C3
Great Barn Rd NR23 ...5 A4
Great Barwick Medieval
  Village of* PE31 .....14 E6
Great Cl NR30 ....168 F5
Great Comm La NR34 .124 C5
Great Dunham Prim Sch
  PE32 ....47 F1
Great Eastern Rd
  PE13 ....152 B4
Great Eastern Way
  Fakenham NR21 ......141 A4
  Wells-next-the-Sea
  NR23 ....136 E5
Great Ellingham Prim Sch
  NR17 ....103 E4
Great Hautbois Rd
  NR12 ....54 C7
Great Hockham Prim Sch
  IP24 ....102 E4
Great Hospl NR1 .....178 C4
Great Man's Way NR33 .81 A2
Great Massingham VC Prim
  Sch PE32 ....29 E1
Great Melton Rd
  Hethersett NR9 ....88 C8
  Little Melton NR9 ...160 A2
Great Northern Cl
  NR30 ....169 D6
Great Palgrave Medieval
  Village of* PE32 .....65 B6
Great Snoring Rd NR21 .17 C3
Great Witchingham Prim Sch
  NR9 ....51 D3
Great Yarmouth Coll
  NR31 ....169 C1
Great Yarmouth High Sch
  NR30 ....169 E6
Great Yarmouth Race Course
  NR30 ....168 F2
Great Yarmouth Sea Life
  Ctr* NR30 ....169 E2
Great Yarmouth Sta
  NR30 ....169 B5
Greatheath Rd NR20 ..32 D1
Grebe Cl
  Great Yarmouth NR31 .170 A7
  7 Rollesby NR29 .....57 D2
Green Bank PE36 ......2 A5
Green Cl
  Hempton NR21 ......141 A2
  Norwich NR5 ....156 E1
Green Comm La PE31 ..3 C6
Green Ct
  Fakenham NR21 .....141 E4
  Norwich NR6 ....163 D7
Green Dragon La
  NR23 ....136 D5
Green Dro PE14 ......77 D6
Green Gr PE33 ....81 D8
Green Hill La PE31 ...14 B3
Green Hills Cl NR8 ..156 F3
Green Hills Rd 6 NR3 .162 D8
Green House La PE37 .153 E5
Green La Alpington NR14 .90 F3
  Attleborough NR17 ...174 C7
  Aylsham NR11 ....150 A6
  Bawburgh NR9 ....160 C4
  Beetley NR20 ....49 D4
  Billingford NR20 ....49 F8
  Burgh St Peter NR34 .111 C4
  Burnham Thorpe PE31 ..4 D3
  Caister-on-Sea NR30 .168 E4
  Christchurch PE14 ...95 A7
  Coltishall PE14 .....54 C6
  Dereham NR19 ......154 E6
  Ditchingham NR35 ..109 B2
  Earsham NR35 ......108 C2
  5 Feltwell IP26 ......98 E1
  Filby NR29 ....75 F8
  Foulsham NR20 ......33 E3
  Great & Little Plumstead
  NR13 ....72 E5
  Great Ellingham NR17 .103 E8
  Great Moulton NR15 .106 B1
  Great Yarmouth NR31 ..69 A8
  Guist NR20 ....33 A5
  Hales NR14 ....109 E8
  Haveringland NR10 ..52 F7
  Horsford NR10 ......53 B4
  King's Lynn PE30 ...148 E2
  Little Ellingham NR17 .86 A1
  Methwold IP26 ....99 A7

Green La continued
  Mundford IP26 ....100 B5
  Postwick with Witton NR7 .72 C4
  Potter Heigham NR29 ..56 F6
  Pudding Norton NR21 .141 A1
  Redenhall with Harleston
  IP20 ....122 C2
  Rocklands NR17 ......103 C7
  Saxlingham Nethergate
  NR15 ....107 B7
  Shipdham IP25 ....67 D4
  Shipmeadow NR34 ...109 F1
  Somerleyton, Ashby &
  Herringfleet NR32 ....111 E8
  South Walsham NR13 ..74 B6
  Starston NR20 ......122 D4
  Stow Bedon NR17 ...103 B8
  Syleham IP21 ......131 C1
  Thelnetham IP22 ...128 A2
  Thetford IP24 ......176 E4
  Thornham PE36 ......2 D6
  Thrandeston IP21 ..129 F2
  Tivetshall St Margaret
  NR15 ....121 B5
  Toft Monks NR34 ...110 C6
  Tottenhill PE33 .....61 F5
  Troston IP31 ....126 A1
  Upwell PE14 ....95 B6
  Walsoken PE14 .....152 F4
  Wicklewood NR18 ...87 C5
  Wramplingham NR18 .87 F7
  Wymondham NR18 ...173 D1
  Yaxham NR19 ....68 B6
Green La E NR13 ......72 E7
Green La N NR13 .....72 D5
Green La W
  Horsham St Faith NR13 .53 D1
  Rackheath NR13 ....72 D8
Green Man La NR13 ..53 D1
Green Oak Rd 2 IP25 ..84 D3
Green Pk 42 IP20 .....122 D2
Green Pk Rd NR10 ...53 B3
Green Quay The*
  PE30 ....146 D4
Green Rd Brandon IP27 .175 D7
  Hales NR14 ....109 E8
  Upwell PE14 ....77 E4
Green St NR21 ....141 A4
Green The Ashill IP25 .84 A7
  Belton with Browston
  NR31 ....94 A5
  Boughton PE33 ......80 F4
  Brisley NR20 ....49 B8
  Burnham Market PE31 .135 C3
  Deopham NR18 .....86 E2
  Dersingham PE31 ...140 D4
  Diss IP22 ....177 A6
  8 Earsham NR35 ...123 F8
  Fakenham NR21 ....141 A3
  Freethorpe NR13 ...92 E8
  Hickling NR12 .....39 E2
  Hockham NR12 ....102 E3
  Hunstanton PE36 ..132 C4
  Lound NR32 ....94 C2
  North Lopham IP22 .119 A2
  North Wootton PE30 .148 C5
  Norwich NR2 ......178 D2
  Ormesby St Margaret
  NR29 ....167 A2
  Runhall NR9 ....68 F2
  Saxlingham Nethergate
  NR15 ....107 D7
  South Wootton PE30 .149 C2
  Surlingham NR14 ...73 B1
  Thornham PE36 ......2 D6
  Upton with Fishley NR13 .166 B8
  Wicklewood NR18 ...87 B4
Green Way
  Barsham NR22 ......16 C6
  Stiffkey NR23 ......6 C6
  Swaffham PE37 .....153 B6
Green Wood Dr NR19 .154 C5
Greenacre Cl
  Brundall NR13 .....165 C4
  King's Lynn PE30 ..148 B2
Greenacre Fst & Mid Sch
  NR30 ....169 D1
Greenacre Rd NR9 ...86 B5
Greenacres
  Bradwell NR31 .....170 A3
  Little Melton NR9 ..160 C2
Greenacres Dr NR5 ...90 C5
Green's La NR27 .....10 C4
Greenborough Cl NR7 .159 E2
Greenborough Rd
  NR7 ....159 E2
Greencourts 10 NR29 .58 B6
Greenfield NR5 .....156 D1
Greenfield Cl NR27 .139 C5
Greenfields NR18 ...118 B5
Greenfields Rd NR14 .154 F4
Greengate NR20 ....50 B2
Greengate La
  Bircham PE31 ......13 F4
  Great Massingham PE32 .29 C1
Greenhill Ave NR30 .168 D8
Greenhill Rd PE32 ...46 B2
Greenhoe Pl PE37 ...153 B3
Greenland Ave
  King's Lynn PE30 ..146 E8
  Wymondham NR18 .173 D1
Greenlands Way NR26 .138 C6
Greenlands Way W 2
  NR26 ....138 B6
Greenpark Ave PE30 .146 E6
Greens Rd
  East Dereham NR20 .154 F3

Gil - Gro 193

Greens Rd continued
  North Walsham NR28 ..151 A5
Greenway Cl
  Fakenham NR21 .....141 C5
  2 North Walsham NR28 .151 C5
Greenway La
  Fakenham NR21 .....141 C5
  Tharston & Hapton
  NR15 ....106 D6
Greenway Pk NR21 ..141 C6
Greenways
  Bunwell NR16 ......105 D4
  Flordon NR15 ......106 E8
  Holt NR25 ....137 C7
  Newton Flotman NR15 .89 C1
  Norwich NR4 ....161 F1
Greenways Cl NR15 .106 E8
Greenways La
  Bunwell NR16 ......105 D4
  Carleton Rode NR16 .105 A5
Greenwich Cl
  Dersingham PE31 ...140 E3
  Downham Market PE38 .172 B3
Greenwood Cl NR16 .105 D4
Greenwood Rd NR4 .162 C1
Greenwood Way
  5 Shipdham IP25 ....67 C2
  Thorpe St Andrew NR7 .159 C4
Greevegate PE36 ....132 C4
Gregor Shanks Way 27
  IP25 ....84 D3
Gregory Cl 1 PE30 ..148 C5
Gregs Cl NR20 ....68 F5
Grenville Cl 3 NR9 ...88 E8
Grenville Pl 1 NR30 .169 D8
Grenville Way IP24 .176 D5
Gresham Cl
  Great Yarmouth NR31 .170 C2
  King's Lynn PE30 ..147 C8
Gresham Rd
  Baconsthorpe NR25 ..20 B8
  Norwich NR3 ....158 B2
Gresham Village Sch
  NR11 ....9 E1
Greshams Prep Sch
  NR25 ....137 D7
Greshams Sch NR25 .137 D7
Gresley Cl NR20 .....49 C4
Gressenhall Farm &
  Workhouse* NR20 ...49 D4
Gressenhall Rd NR20 .49 D4
Grey Sedge PE30 ...147 A7
Greyfriars Cl NR6 ...158 A5
Greyfriars Cty Prim Sch
  PE30 ....146 E4
Greyfriars Rd NR1 ..178 B3
Greyfriars Way NR30 .169 C3
Greyhound La
  Banham NR16 ......119 D7
  Hopton IP22 ....127 E5
Greyhound Opening 7
  NR2 ....162 C7
Greylag Cl 8 NR13 ..55 A1
Greys Manor NR16 ..119 D6
Grice Cl 4 NR26 ....138 C5
Griffin La
  Attleborough NR17 ..174 D5
  Thorpe St Andrew NR7 .72 D3
Grigsons Wood 1
  NR16 ....118 C5
Grime's Graves* IP27 .115 C8
Grimmer La NR13 ...92 B7
Grimmer's Rd 6 PE13 .152 B4
Grimshoe Rd PE38 ..172 B6
Grimston Jun Sch PE32 .28 D3
Grimston Pott Row Fst Sch
  PE32 ....45 A3
Grimston Rd
  Gayton PE32 ....45 C6
  King's Lynn PE30 ..148 E1
Gristock Pl NR5 .....161 C8
Griston Rd
  Thompson IP24 .....102 B8
  Watton IP25 ....84 E3
Groomes Cl 4 NR31 .171 D5
Grosvenor Rd
  Norwich NR2 ....162 B5
  Wisbech PE13 ......152 D7
Grouts La NR25 ......8 B6
Grove Ave
  Norwich NR5 ......157 A1
  Norwich NR1 ......178 A1
Grove Cl
  8 East Dereham NR19 .154 C4
  Holt NR25 ....137 D6
  2 Newton Flotman NR15 .89 C1
Grove Dale 3 NR15 ..89 C1
Grove End IP21 .....131 F1
Grove Gdns 7 PE32 ..45 C6
Grove House Inf Sch
  NR19 ....154 D4
Grove La Booton NR10 .52 A8
  Fakenham NR21 ....141 C6
  Forncett NR16 .....106 A3
  Holt NR25 ....137 D6
  Sparham NR9 ......51 B6
  Tasburgh NR15 ....106 F2
  Thetford IP24 .....176 D4
Grove Rd
  Banham NR16 ......119 C6
  Barsham NR21 .....16 C4
  Brockdish IP21 ....131 C6
  Cantley NR13 ......92 D8
  Cromer NR27 ......139 D5
  Gissing IP21 ......121 A4

Grove Rd continued
Hethersett NR9 ....88 D8
Ingham NR12 ....24 C1
4 Marthan NR29 ....57 D5
Melton Constable NR24 .142 A4
North Walsham NR28 ...151 D5
Norwich NR1 ....178 A1
Repps with Bastwick
NR29 ....57 A4
Starston IP20 ....122 C2
Wells-next-the-Sea
NR23 ....136 E4
Grove The
Coltishall NR12 ....54 D6
East Dereham NR19 ...154 D4
Fleggburgh NR29 ....57 A1
2 Necton PE37 ....65 F4
Roydon PE32 ....28 A1
Shotesham NR15 ....90 B1
Grove Way NR15 ....89 C1
Grove Wlk NR1 ....178 A1
Grovebury Cl NR13 ...165 C4
Grovedale Cl NR5 .....157 A1
Grovelands PE31 .....140 D8
Groveside PE31 ....30 A7
Growle Abbey NR24 ...19 B2
Grub La IP19 ....124 E1
Grub St
Happisburgh NR12 .....24 B4
Shotesham NR15 ....90 B2
Grubb's La NR12 .....24 C1
Guanock Pl **12** PE30 .146 E3
Guanock Terr PE30 ...146 E3
Guardian NR5 ....161 F7
Guelph Rd **2** NR1 ...163 A6
Guernsey Rd NR3 .....162 E8
Guestwick Rd
Foulsham NR20 ....33 A3
Hindolveston NR20 .....33 F7
Wood Norton NR20 .....33 C6
Guild Rd PE13 ....152 E6
Guild St NR22 ....16 F8
Guildford Way IP24 ..176 B5
Guildhall Hill **2** NR2 .178 A3
Guildhall La IP21 ....121 E5
Guildhall St IP24 ....176 D3
Guiler's La NR18 ....105 B8
Guilt Cross Way PE38 .172 C6
Guist Bottom Rd NR21 .32 E6
Guist Rd NR20 ....33 C4
Gulgate La NR11 ....21 A1
Gull La NR14 ....90 E6
Gullpit Dro PE34 ......61 D1
Gun St **7** NR26 .....138 D7
Gunn Rd NR7 ....159 D1
Gunn St NR20 ....33 C3
Gunn's Cnr NR12 ......38 D2
Gunner Cl **3** NR7 ....72 D5
Gunthorpe Rd PE14 ....41 B5
Gunton La NR5 ....157 B2
Gunton Rd
Loddon NR14 ....109 C8
Norwich NR2 ....161 F5
Wymondham NR18 .....173 D4
Gunton Sta NR11 ......22 B6
Gurney Cl NR5 ....161 B8
Gurney Ct NR5 ....161 B8
Gurney Dr NR7 ....159 D3
Gurney La NR4 ....161 C2
Gurney Rd
Norwich NR5 ....157 A1
Norwich NR1 ....163 A7
Gwyn Cres NR21 .....141 F5
Gymkhana Way PE31 ..133 B5

H

Habgood Cl NR13 ....166 C4
Hackford Rd
Hardingham NR9 ....86 E6
Wicklewood NR18 ......87 A5
Haconsdale **3** NR9 ...88 D7
Haddiscoe Dam NR14 .110 F4
Haddiscoe Rd NR34 ..110 F6
Haddiscoe Sta NR31 ...93 D1
Hadfield Rd NR28 ....151 B6
Hadley Cres PE31 ....133 C5
Hadley Dr NR2 ....161 F6
Hadley Rd NR28 .....151 C6
Hagbech Hall Cl **2** PE14 59 D2
Haggard's Cl IP25 ....66 E3
Haig Cl NR19 ....154 D3
Hainford Fst Sch NR10 .53 E6
Hainford Rd NR10 .....53 E7
Halcombe Ct NR3 ....158 E1
Halden Ave NR6 .....157 F6
Hale Ct NR13 ....73 A4
Hale Dro Littleport CB6 .96 B2
Welney PE14 ....95 C6
Hale Fen Rd CB6 ......96 B1
Hale Rd Ashill IP25 ....84 A7
Bradenham IP25 ....66 D3
Necton PE37 ....65 F4
Hales Rd NR30 ....168 D5
Hales Ct NR25 ....137 B6
Hales Hall & Gdns★
NR14 ....109 D6
Hales St NR15 ....121 A6
Halesworth Rd NR34 ..124 E4
Haley Cl **4** PE13 ....152 C8
Half Acre Cl NR27 .....10 B4
Half Mile Cl NR3 ....158 B2
Half Mile Rd NR3 ....158 B2
Half Moon NR31 .....170 C1

Half Moon La IP22 ...128 E4
Half Moon Way **1** NR2 .162 B8
Half Year Cl **7** NR1 ...10 B5
Halfar Rd **8** IP31 ...126 B1
Halffield La NR18 .....86 D2
Halford Cl NR17 .....174 D4
Halford La IP22 ......129 A7
Halford Pl NR17 .....174 D4
Halford Rd NR17 .....174 D4
Halfpenny La
Beetley NR20 ....49 C5
Elm PE14 ....59 A2
Wisbech PE14 ....152 D1
Halfpenny Toll Rd PE14 .95 B8
Halifax Cres NR21 .....15 C3
Haling Way IP24 .....176 A4
Hall Bridge Rd PE14 ...77 D5
Hall Cl Fakenham NR21 .141 D4
Heacham PE31 ....133 D7
4 Hemsby NR29 ......167 A7
5 Hethersett NR9 .....88 D7
3 Hingham NR9 ....86 C4
3 Southery PE38 ......97 B5
Hall Comm Rd NR29 ...56 C4
Hall Cres PE33 ....63 C5
Hall Dike PE14 ....77 F7
Hall Dr Costessey NR5 .156 D2
16 Feltwell IP26 ......98 E1
Honingham NR9 ....69 E6
North Runcton PE33 ...44 A3
Santon Downham IP27 .115 C6
Hall Farm Gdns PE32 ..44 F3
Hall Farm Pl NR9 ....160 B6
Hall Hills IP22 ......177 C5
Hall La
Baconsthorpe NR25 .....19 F8
Bressingham IP22 ....119 D1
Burston & Shimpling
IP21 ....121 A2
Colkirk NR21 ....31 E5
Deopham NR18 ....86 F4
East Carleton NR14 ....88 E4
East Dereham NR20 ...154 F4
East Ruston NR12 .....24 A4
East Tuddenham NR20 .69 B6
Felthorpe NR10 ....52 E5
Frettenham NR12 ......54 B3
Gunthorpe NR24 ....18 A5
Hingham NR9 ....86 C5
Horsford NR10 ....53 B1
King's Lynn PE30 .....148 B1
Knapton NR28 ....143 B1
Long Stratton NR15 ..106 F3
Morley NR18 ....87 B2
North Tuddenham NR20 .68 F8
North Walsham NR28 ..151 D5
Northwold IP26 ....99 C7
Postwick with Witton
NR13 ....72 F2
Redgrave IP22 ....128 E4
Ringstead PE36 ....2 A3
Roydon IP22 ....129 D7
Saxlingham Nethergate
NR15 ....107 C7
Scole IP21 ....130 E8
Shelfanger IP22 ......120 B2
Shelton NR15 ....122 A8
Taverham NR8 ....157 B8
Tharston & Hapton
NR15 ....106 D5
Thompson IP24 ......102 B7
Thornham PE36 ....2 D6
Thursford NR21 ....17 F5
Wacton NR15 ....106 C1
West Winch PE33 ......43 E2
Whissonsett NR20 .....31 D2
Wiveton NR25 ....7 D6
Wood Norton NR20 ....33 B6
Hall Loke NR28 ....38 C8
Hall Moor Rd NR9 .....86 C4
Hall Orchards PE32 ....44 C3
Hall Plain NR30 .....169 C3
Hall Rd Alderford NR9 ...52 A5
Barsham NR34 ....124 F7
Barton Turf NR12 .....55 E8
12 Bawdeswell NR20 ..50 E7
Bedingham NR35 ......107 A3
Beetley NR20 ....49 D5
Blofield NR13 ....165 C8
Bracon Ash NR14 ......88 E4
Brockdish IP21 ......131 D7
Bunwell NR16 ....105 E2
Burston & Shimpling
IP22 ....120 E3
Cantley NR13 ....92 C8
Carleton Rode NR16 ..105 B4
Catfield NR29 ....56 B8
Clenchwarton PE34 ...145 D6
Cromer NR27 ....139 B5
Earsham NR35 ....123 E8
Easton NR9 ....70 B5
Ellingham NR35 ......109 C3
Elsing NR20 ....50 D2
Felbrigg NR27 ....139 A4
Fleggburgh NR29 ......57 A1
Framingham Earl NR14 .90 D5
Gimingham NR11 ......22 D7
Great Melton NR9 .....88 B8
Great Witchingham NR9 .51 F5
Hainford NR10 ....53 E5
Hemsby NR29 ....167 A7
Hoe NR20 ....49 F3
Honing NR28 ....38 D8
Hopton on Sea NR31 ..171 B6
King's Lynn PE30 .....148 C1
Ludham NR29 ....56 B4
Marthan NR29 ....57 D4

Hall Rd continued
Mautby NR29 ....76 A6
Northrepps NR27 .....139 D2
Norwich NR5 ....157 A2
Norwich NR1 ....178 B1
Oulton NR11 ....35 B7
Outwell PE14 ....77 F7
Postwick with Witton
NR13 ....165 A5
Pulham St Mary IP21 .122 A4
Reedham NR13 ....92 F6
Roudham IP24 ....117 E6
Runhall NR20 ....69 A4
Smallburgh NR12 ......38 D2
9 Snettisham PE31 ....12 C5
Sutton NR12 ....39 D3
Swafield NR28 ....22 C5
Tacolneston NR16 ....105 E6
Tharston & Hapton
NR15 ....106 E5
Thurton NR14 ....91 C3
Tivetshall St Margaret
NR15 ....121 B6
Toft Monks NR14 ....110 D7
Walpole Highway PE14 .59 F8
Winfarthing IP22 .....120 C5
Wood Dalling NR11 ....34 C6
Hall Sch NR6 ....158 D5
Hall St NR24 ....142 E3
Hall Staithe NR21 ...141 B4
Hall View Rd PE30 ...147 B4
Hall Wlk NR9 ....51 D5
Hall's Dr NR20 ....49 C4
Hallback La NR14 .....90 A7
Hallfield Rd IP24 ....102 A7
Hallfields PE33 ....62 D4
Hallgate PE33 ....72 D6
Hallowing Cres **3** NR15 106 B1
Hallowing La NR15 ...121 B8
Halls Cnr NR10 ....53 B8
Halls Cnr Rd NR10 ....53 B8
Hallwong La IP20 ....122 D3
Halstead Cl **2** PE13 .152 E5
Halt Rd NR30 ....168 D7
Halton Rd **8** IP25 ....84 F3
Halvergate Rd
Beighton NR13 ....74 E1
Reedham NR13 ....93 A6
Hambling's Piece
NR16 ....118 C4
Hamburg Way PE30 ..147 A8
Hamilton Cl
North Walsham NR28 ..151 C5
South Walsham NR13 ..74 A4
Hamilton Ct **1** NR21 .141 B4
Hamilton Dr PE37 ....153 D3
Hamilton Rd
3 Cromer NR27 .....139 B7
Great Yarmouth NR30 .169 D7
Old Hunstanton PE36 .132 E7
Hamilton Rd W PE36 .132 E7
Hamilton Way PE38 ..172 B5
Hamilton Wlk NR29 ...57 D4
Hamlet Cl NR28 .....151 D7
Hamlin Way PE30 ....146 F1
Hammond Cl NR7 ....159 E3
Hammond Rd **2** NR30 .169 D5
Hammond Way NR7 ..159 E3
Hamon Cl PE36 ....132 E7
Hamond Rd NR6 .....157 D5
Hamonds High Sch
PE37 ....153 C3
Hampden Dr **19** NR7 ...72 D4
Hampden Rd **2** PE13 .152 D5
Hampton Ave **3** NR4 ...92 F1
Hampton Cl NR30 ....168 C5
Hanbury Cl **4** NR5 ...161 D5
Hancock Cl **3** NR12 ...54 C7
Hancock Cn NR5 .....160 E7
Hand La Barsham NR34 ..16 C5
Hoveton NR12 ....164 C8
Handel Dr NR19 .....154 F3
Handford Dr NR26 ...138 E6
Hanginghill NR19 .....74 C6
Hankin Ct **3** NR4 ....161 C5
Hankinson's Est PE34 ..42 A5
Hanly Cl NR7 ....159 C2
Hanly Ct NR30 ....168 D6
Hannah Cl NR26 .....138 C5
Hannah Rd NR20 ......50 B4
Hannant Rd NR28 ....151 D6
Hanover Ct
Dersingham PE31 .....140 E3
King's Lynn PE30 .....147 D5
Hanover Gdns PE36 ..132 D3
Hanover Rd NR2 .....162 C4
Hanrae Ct NR26 .....138 F6
Hans Pl **4** NR27 ....139 B7
Hansa Rd PE30 ......146 F2
Hansard Cl NR3 .....158 B1
Hansard La NR3 .....178 B4
Hansard Rd NR3 .....158 B1
Hansell Rd NR7 .....163 F8
Hantons Loke NR13 ...74 B2
Hanworth Cross NR11 ..21 D5
Happisburgh Fst Sch
NR12 ....24 C5
Happisburgh Rd
East Ruston NR12 .....24 A3
Lessingham NR12 .....24 D4
North Walsham NR28 .151 D4
Witton NR28 ....24 C5
Hapton Prim Sch
NR15 ....106 C7
Harbord Cl **4** NR28 ..151 C7
Harbord Cres NR30 ..170 D8
Harbord Rd
Cromer NR27 ....139 C5

Harbord Rd continued
Norwich NR4 ....161 F5
Overstrand NR27 ......11 A3
Harbour La IP22 .....128 A7
Harbour Rd
1 Frettenham NR12 ...54 A4
Norwich NR1 ....163 A5
Harbour Terr NR31 ..170 E4
Harcourt Cl **3** NR3 ..158 A4
Hardesty Cl **9** NR14 ...90 D5
Hardingham Dr **6**
NR26 ....138 C5
Hardingham Rd NR9 ...86 D5
Hardingham St **4** NR9 .86 C4
Hardley Cross★ NR14 ..92 E4
Hardley Hall La NR14 ..92 C3
Hardley Rd NR14 .....92 A2
Hardley St NR14 .....92 B3
Hardwick Cl **1** NR4 ...89 D8
Hardwick Ind Est
PE30 ....147 B2
Hardwick Rd
King's Lynn PE30 .....146 E2
Pulham Market IP21 ..121 F7
Shelton NR15 ....122 C8
Hardy Cl
Downham Market PE38 .172 B4
1 North Walsham NR28 .151 C5
Thetford IP24 ....176 D5
Hardy Rd NR1 ....163 A4
Hardy's La PE32 ......46 C2
Hare Cl **2** NR14 ......89 B2
Hare Rd NR13 ....72 F5
Harebell Rd PE38 ....172 B3
Harecroft Gdns PE30 .146 E6
Harecroft Par **7** PE30 .146 E6
Harecroft Rd PE13 ...152 B5
Harecroft Terr PE30 ..146 E6
Harefen La NR13 ......74 B7
Harefield Rd IP24 ....116 C5
Hares Cl IP21 ....17 C3
Harewood PE31 ......134 F4
Harewood Dr
9 King's Lynn PE30 ..146 E6
Taverham NR8 ....155 E3
Harewood Par **8** PE30 .146 E6
Harford Manor Cl
NR2 ....162 C2
Harford Manor Specl Sch
NR4 ....162 C2
Harford St NR1 ......162 E3
Harfrey's Rd NR31 ...170 B4
Harfreys Ind Est
Gorleston-on-Sea NR31 .170 A8
Great Yarmouth NR31 .169 B1
Hargate Cl PE34 ......42 B7
Hargham Cl **5** NR17 .104 C3
Hargham Rd
Attleborough NR17 ...174 B2
Old Buckenham NR17 .104 B2
Shropham NR17 ......103 C3
Harker Way **6** NR13 ...73 D6
Harleston Mus★ IP20 .122 D2
Harleston Prim Sch
IP20 ....122 E2
Harleston Rd
Pulham Market IP21 ..121 E4
Scole IP21 ....121 D1
Harley Rd NR3 ....169 D6
Harling Dro IP27 ....115 E7
Harling Rd
Garboldisham IP22 ...118 C2
Hockham IP24 ....102 A3
North Lopham IP22 ..119 A2
Harling Rd Sta NR16 .118 A6
Harlington Ave NR6 ..158 A4
Harlingwood La NR17 .104 C1
Harman Cl **12** NR9 ....88 D8
Harman's La IP20 ....122 C1
Harmer Cl NR28 .....151 C1
Harmer Cres NR1 ....161 C1
Harmer La NR4 ......161 C1
Harmer Rd NR3 .....158 D3
Harmer's La NR11 ....21 A5
Harnser's Reach NR13 .166 B8
Harp Cl NR21 ....141 B5
Harp's Hall Rd PE14 ..59 E5
Harper's La NR22 ......32 A1
Harpley CE VC Prim Sch
PE31 ....29 C4
Harpsfield NR5 ......160 E8
Harrier Cl **26** NR9 ....88 D8
Harriet Cl PE12 ....41 A8
Harriet Martineau Cl **10**
IP24 ....176 D7
Harriott's Way NR11 .150 B5
Harris Mews **2** NR5 ..161 A7
Harris Rd
11 Swanton Morley NR20 .50 B3
12 Watton IP25 ....84 F3
Harrisons Dr NR7 ....159 E3
Harrold Cl
1 South Walsham NR13 .74 A4
Taverham NR8 ....155 E2
Harrolds Cl PE13 ......59 C5
Harrow Cl PE34 .....146 C5
Harry Barber Cl **2** NR5 161 A8
Harry Blunt Way **10**
NR19 ....154 C4
Harry Miller Ct **7** NR30 169 D1
Harry Perry Cl NR4 ..162 C2
Harry Watson Ct NR3 .158 C4
Harry's La IP21 ......121 D1
Harrys Way
Hunstanton PE36 .....132 D1
Wisbech PE13 ....152 C2
Harsnett Cl NR5 .....160 F8
Hart La NR25 ....9 A2

Hart's La NR9 ....160 A7
Hartbee Rd NR26 ....158 C6
Hartington Rd NR9 ..139 D4
Hartley Cl PE36 .....132 D4
Hartmann Rd NR30 ..170 E6
Harts Farm Rd NR18 .173 E5
Harts La NR4 ....161 C1
Hartwell Rd NR12 ...164 C4
Harvard Rd **6** IP26 ...98 D1
Harvest Cl **1** NR10 ...53 E5
Harvest La NR21 ......17 D6
Harvey Cl
2 Hethersett NR9 .....88 C7
Norwich NR7 ....163 C7
Tasburgh NR15 ......106 E7
Harvey Dr NR28 .....151 C7
Harvey Est NR11 ......22 E7
Harvey Gn **10** NR14 ...91 F1
Harvey La
Caister-on-Sea NR30 ..168 E4
Dickleburgh IP21 ....121 C1
Norwich NR7 ....163 C6
Harvey St **21** IP25 ....84 D3
Harvey's La NR15 ....108 D6
Harwood Ave **4** IP24 .176 E6
Harwood Rd NR1 ....162 E1
Hase's La NR9 ....51 C4
Haslips Cl **8** NR1 ....162 C7
Haspalls Rd PE37 ....153 B3
Hassett Cl **6** NR3 ...162 F8
Hastings Ave NR6 ...158 A4
Hastings Cl
Briston NR24 ....142 A5
6 Tasburgh NR15 ....106 F6
Hastings Ct NR24 ...142 E4
Hastings Dr PE36 ...132 D6
Hastings La
15 Sheringham NR26 .138 D7
Wiggenhall St Germans
PE34 ....61 C8
Hastings Rd **6** IP25 ...84 F3
Hastings Way NR12 ...39 C3
Hatherley Gdns PE33 ..81 B8
Hatton Rd NR1 ......162 E3
Haugh Cnr NR16 ....119 F7
Haugh Rd NR16 .....119 F8
Haughs End Rd NR12 .164 F2
Hautbois Rd NR10 ....37 B2
Hauteyn Ct NR6 .....158 C2
Havaker The NR13 ....92 F5
Havant Cl NR4 ......161 B1
Havelock Pl **10** NR30 .169 D2
Havelock Rd
Great Yarmouth NR30 .169 D2
Norwich NR2 ....162 B6
Sheringham NR26 ....138 E5
Havergate **7** NR12 ....54 C6
Haveringland Rd NR10 .52 E6
Havers Rd NR3 ......158 B1
Haverscroft Cl NR18 .155 C2
Hawk Cres IP22 .....177 F5
Hawkes La NR14 ......89 A2
Hawkins Cl NR30 ....169 C8
Hawkins Cl NR30 ....169 C8
Hawkins Dr **1** PE13 ..152 E5
Hawthorn Ave **6** PE33 .63 B4
Hawthorn Cl Diss IP22 .177 F5
3 Spixworth NR10 ...54 A1
6 Watlington PE33 ...61 D5
Hawthorn Cotts PE31 .140 D4
Hawthorn Cres NR31 ..94 C6
Hawthorn Dr
Dersingham PE31 .....140 D5
East Dereham NR19 ..154 B3
Hawthorn Rd
2 Downham Market
PE38 ....172 C6
Emneth PE14 ....59 D1
6 Gayton PE32 ......45 C5
Great Yarmouth NR31 .170 B6
Norwich NR5 ....157 A2
Hawthorn Rise NR11 .143 B5
Hawthorn Way IP24 ..176 E6
Hawthorn Wlk **2** IP24 .176 F6
Hawthorne Ave
Grimston PE32 ....28 B1
Hellesdon NR6 ....158 A5
Wisbech PE13 ....152 C8
Hawthorne Cl
2 Loddon NR14 ......91 F1
Wymondham NR18 ...173 D6
Hawthorns PE30 .....147 C4
Hay Gn Rd PE34 .....144 A3
Hay Gn Rd N PE34 ....42 B6
Hay Gn Rd S PE34 ....42 A5
Haycroft **3** NR29 ....167 B2
Hayes La NR21 ......141 A5
Hayfield Rd PE30 ....148 C4
Haygate **2** IP23 .....130 C1
Haylett Cl NR30 .....168 E5
Haymarket NR2 .....178 B2
Haythill La IP26 ......98 D2
Hayward Cl **3** NR25 ...7 C1
Haywood End IP22 ..120 D6
Hazel Ave NR26 .....138 C4
Hazel Cl Grimston PE32 .28 B1
5 King's Lynn PE30 ..148 C3
Taverham NR8 ....155 D3
West Winch PE33 ......43 E1
Wymondham NR18 ...173 D4
Hazel Covert IP24 ...176 F5
Hazel Cres **4** PE33 ...63 B4
Hazel Gdns **1** PE13 ..152 D4
Hazel Gr NR19 ......154 F4
Hazel Rd
4 Attleborough NR17 .174 A3
Norwich NR5 ....156 F1
Hazel Way NR31 .....170 B6

Hazell Rd NR28 ....151 C7
Heacham Fst Sch PE31 ....133 D5
Heacham Jun Sch PE31 ....133 C4
Heacham Rd PE36 ....13 A7
Headington Cl NR31 ....170 A5
Headland Dro IP26 ....113 A5
Headley Dr NR28 ....151 C4
Hearne Ct **3** NR6 ....160 E8
Heartsease Fst & Mid Sch NR7 ....159 C1
Heartsease High Sch NR7 ....159 C1
Heartsease La NR7 ....159 B1
Heartsease Mid Sch NR7 ....159 C1
Heartsease Rd **3** IP24 ....176 E5
Heartwell Rd NR27 ....139 C5
Heater La NR13 ....73 F4
Heath Cl **16** Horsford NR10 53 A3
  Lenwade NR9 ....51 D5
  Norwich NR6 ....158 A6
Heath Cres NR6 ....158 B5
Heath Dr NR25 ....137 D5
Heath Farm La NR11 ....36 E6
Heath Gn **1** NR31 ....170 B5
Heath La
  Fakenham NR21 ....141 F4
  Gimingham NR11 ....22 D8
  Great Witchingham NR9 ..51 E6
  Gunthorpe NR24 ....18 B5
  Lenwade NR9 ....51 D5
  Mundesley NR11 ....143 B5
  Roughton NR11 ....21 E8
  Thursford NR21 ....17 E4
  Tittleshall NR32 ....47 F7
Heath Rd
  Ashby with Oby NR29 ....57 B2
  Banham NR16 ....119 E7
  Brandon IP27 ....175 D3
  Catfield NR29 ....56 D8
  Corpusty NR11 ....19 D1
  Dersingham PE31 ....140 D2
  East Dereham NR19 ....154 C7
  Felmingham NR28 ....37 B8
  Fritton & St Olaves NR31 ..93 E1
  Geldeston NR34 ....110 A3
  Gunthorpe NR24 ....18 B5
  Heydon NR11 ....34 D8
  Hickling NR12 ....39 E1
  Hockering NR20 ....69 B8
  Honing NR28 ....23 E1
  Kenninghall NR16 ....119 A3
  Lessingham NR12 ....24 F2
  Lyng NR9 ....51 A4
  Norwich NR3 ....162 D8
  Quidenham NR16 ....118 E8
  Rollesby NR29 ....57 B2
  Sapiston IP31 ....126 E3
  Sheringham NR26 ....138 D6
  Shotesham NR15 ....107 F8
  9 Thorpe End NR13 ....72 D6
  Troston IP31 ....126 B1
  Winfarthing IP22 ....120 A7
Heath Rise
  Fakenham NR21 ....141 E4
  Sculthorpe Airfield PE31 ..15 B3
Heath The NR10 ....52 F8
Heath Way Blofield NR13 ..73 C6
  Fakenham NR21 ....141 F4
Heather Ave
  Hemsby NR29 ....167 D4
  Norwich NR6 ....158 A4
Heather Ave Fst Sch NR6 ....158 B4
Heather Barrow Ct NR21 ....141 D4
Heather Cl PE30 ....148 D5
Heather Dr NR25 ....137 B7
Heather Gdns NR31 ....93 F6
Heather Rd **12** NR31 ....94 A6
Heather Way
  Brandon IP27 ....175 E3
  Great Moulton NR15 ....121 B8
Heatherwood Pk **7** NR13 72 D6
Heathfield Cl **8** 3 E3
Heathfield Rd NR25 ....8 E3
Heathgate NR3 ....163 A8
Heathlands PE37 ....153 D2
Heathlands Dr IP24 ....176 D8
Heathside Rd NR1 ....163 B5
Hebrides Way NR30 ....168 C4
Heckingham Holes NR14 ....92 B1
Hedgehog Wlk NR12 ..24 E4
Hedgelands **1** PE13 ....152 C8
Hedgemere **1** NR31 ....155 D2
Hedgerows The **8** NR5 .161 A7
Hedley La NR33 ....111 F1
Heffer Cl NR19 ....154 D3
Heggatt Rd NR12 ....54 C5
Heidi Cl **7** NR19 ....154 D1
Heigham Gr NR2 ....162 C6
Heigham Pk Fst Sch NR2 ....162 A5
Heigham Rd NR2 ....162 B6
Heigham St NR2 ....162 B8
Heigham Watering **5** NR2 ....162 B8
Helen Ave **7** NR29 ....57 C4
Helena Rd
  Norwich NR2 ....162 B6
  Witton NR12 ....23 F3
Helford St **6** NR2 ....162 B8
Hellesdon Cl NR5 ....161 D8
Hellesdon Hall Rd NR6 ....157 E1

Hellesdon High Sch NR6 ....157 E4
Hellesdon Hospl NR6 .157 E4
Hellesdon Mill La NR6 ....157 D1
Hellesdon Pk Rd NR6 .157 E5
Hellesdon Rd NR6 ....161 D8
Hellgate La NR11 ....20 F8
Hellington Cnr NR14 ....91 B5
Hellington Hill NR14 ....91 B6
Hellpit La NR24 ....19 B2
Helsinki Way NR1 ....154 C2
Helska Leisure Ctr NR12 ....55 E3
Hemblington Hall Rd NR13 ....73 E6
Hemblington Prim Sch NR13 ....73 E4
Hemington Cl PE30 ....147 D8
Hemlin Cl NR5 ....161 C6
Hemmant Way NR34 ....110 B3
Hemmings Cl **4** NR5 ....160 F7
Hempnall Rd NR35 ....108 A4
Hempnall Sch NR15 ....107 C5
Hempstead Rd
  Holt NR25 ....137 D5
  Lessingham NR12 ....24 D3
Hempsted Mews NR5 .160 E7
Hempton Rd NR21 ....141 B3
Hemsby Fst Sch NR29 .167 A7
Hemsby Rd
  13 Martham NR29 ....57 D4
  Winterton-on-Sea NR29 ..58 B5
Henby Way NR7 ....163 D7
Henderson Rd NR4 ....161 F5
Hendon Ave **18** IP25 ....84 F3
Hendon Cl NR25 ....157 B1
Hendrie Rd NR25 ....137 C7
Henley Rd NR2 ....162 A4
Hennessey's Loke NR28 .23 A3
Henry Bell Cl PE30 ....147 A5
Henry Blogg Rd NR27 .139 B5
Henry Cross Cl **1** IP25 ..67 C2
Henry Page Rd **1** 150 B5
Henry Preston Rd **1** NR15 ....106 F6
Henry St PE13 ....152 C5
Henry Warby Ave **7** PE14 ....59 A1
Henry Ward Rd **1** IP20 122 D2
Henry's Ct **1** IP25 ....84 F3
Henson Cl **3** PE13 ....152 C8
Henstead Rd NR9 ....88 D8
Hepworth Rd IP31 ....127 D3
Herbert Colman Cl NR13 ....73 D7
Herbert Dr IP26 ....98 F5
Herbert Nursey Cl NR8 ....157 C7
Herbert Ward Way PE34 ....144 D6
Hercules Cl NR6 ....157 F4
Hercules Rd NR6 ....157 F4
Hereford Way PE33 ....43 E4
Hereward Cl **1** PE13 ..152 D5
Hereward Way
  5 Feltwell IP26 ....98 D1
  Weeting IP27 ....175 A8
  Weeting-with-Broomhill IP27 ....114 E8
Herman Fst Sch NR31 .170 A3
Herman Mid Sch NR31 ....170 A3
Hermanus Leisure Ctr NR29 ....58 B6
Hermitage Cl **3** NR13 .166 D4
Herne Cotts NR19 ....67 D5
Herne Dro PE14 ....95 D5
Herne La
  Beeston with Bittering PE32 ....48 C1
  Shipdham NR19 ....67 D5
Herolf Way **11** IP20 ....122 D2
Heron Ave IP27 ....175 E3
Heron Cl
  Downham Market PE38 .172 C7
  6 Fakenham NR21 ....141 E4
  Great Yarmouth NR31 ..170 A7
  Salhouse NR13 ....55 B1
Heron Gdns NR12 ....39 B3
Heron Rd PE13 ....152 D2
Heron Way
  Hickling NR12 ....39 E1
  12 Watton IP25 ....84 C3
Herrick Rd NR8 ....156 E8
Herries Cl **7** NR30 ....169 C4
Herring La NR9 ....69 A1
Herring's La PE31 ....135 C4
Herringfleet Rd NR31 ..93 E2
Hertford Way NR31 ....170 B4
Hethel Old Thorn Nature Reserve★ NR14 ....88 E3
Hethel Rd NR16 ....88 D7
Hethersett High Sch NR9 ....88 D7
Hethersett La NR4 ....160 F3
Hethersett Old Hall Sch NR9 ....88 D7
Hethersett Rd
  East Carleton NR14 ....88 B5
  Great Melton NR9 ....88 B8
Hevingham Prim Sch NR10 ....53 B8
Hewett Cl NR31 ....170 D2
Hewett Rd NR31 ....170 A8
Hewett Sch NR1 ....162 D2
Hewitts Cl NR24 ....142 E4

Hewitts La NR18 ....173 C5
Hextable Rd PE30 ....146 E6
Heydon Hall★ NR11 ....34 E7
Heydon Rd NR11 ....34 E7
Heydon Rd
  Aylsham NR11 ....150 A7
  Corpusty NR11 ....34 F8
  Wood Dalling NR11 ....34 D6
Heyford Rd NR6 ....158 C6
Heywood Ave IP22 ....177 D6
Heywood Rd Diss IP22 .177 E8
  Shelfanger IP22 ....120 C2
  Tibenham NR16 ....120 D6
  Winfarthing IP22 ....120 C4
Heywood The IP22 ....120 E5
Hickathrift Field PE14 ..61 A4
Hickling Broad National Nature Reserve★ NR12 ....57 A8
Hickling Broad Visitor Ctr★ NR12 ....40 A1
Hickling Cl PE37 ....153 C2
Hickling Fst Sch NR12 ..39 F2
Hickling La NR14 ....89 D4
Hickling Rd
  Sea Palling NR12 ....24 F1
  Sutton NR12 ....39 C2
Hickling Way NR12 ....167 B3
Hickory Gdns **13** NR31 ..94 C7
Hickory Rd PE30 ....147 C5
High Ash Rd NR18 ....88 C5
High Banks NR18 ....173 C3
High Bridgham Rd NR16 ....117 C5
High Bungay Rd NR14 .109 D8
High Comm NR18 ....87 D2
High Comm Rd IP22 ..128 C8
High Cross NR20 ....33 A2
High Ct IP20 ....122 E2
High Fen Dro IP26 ....98 B8
High Gn Brooke NR15 ....90 D1
  Great Melton NR9 ....88 B8
  5 Great Moulton NR15 ..106 B1
  Great Moulton NR15 ..121 B8
  Norwich NR1 ....163 B5
High Gn Gdns NR15 ....90 D1
High Hatter's Cl PE38 .172 C3
High Hill Rd NR12 ....38 F6
High House Ave
  7 Wymondham NR18 ..173 D5
  3 Wymondham NR18 ..173 D5
High House Cotts PE32 .47 E5
High House La **8** NR13 ..73 D6
High House Rd NR14 ....73 D6
High Lodge Forest Ctr★ IP27 ....115 C3
High London La IP22 ..120 A4
High Mill Rd NR31 ....169 B3
High Noon La NR13 ....73 E6
High Noon Rd NR11 ....21 D2
High Oak La NR18 ....87 B4
High Oak Rd NR18 ....87 B3
High Rd Beighton NR13 ..74 B1
  Bressingham IP22 ....129 C4
  Burgh Castle NR31 ....94 B8
  Cantley NR13 ....92 B8
  Forncett NR16 ....106 B6
  Great Yarmouth NR31 ..170 D7
  Lessingham NR12 ....24 C2
  Needham IP20 ....131 E7
  Repps with Bastwick NR29 ....57 A4
  Roydon IP22 ....177 A5
  Tilney St Lawrence PE34 ..60 F8
  Wiggenhall St Germans PE34 ....42 F1
  Wortwell IP20 ....123 A3
High St
  Attleborough NR17 ....174 D5
  Blakeney NR25 ....7 C5
  Brandon IP27 ....175 C5
  Caister-on-Sea NR30 ..168 E5
  Castle Acre PE32 ....46 F2
  Cawston NR10 ....35 B3
  Cley next the Sea NR25 ..7 E6
  Coltishall NR12 ....54 C7
  Cromer NR27 ....139 B7
  Docking PE31 ....134 E4
  Downham Market PE38 .172 C5
  East Dereham NR19 ....154 D5
  Feltwell IP26 ....98 E1
  Fincham PE33 ....62 E1
  Foulsham NR20 ....33 D3
  Great Yarmouth NR31 ..170 D6
  Heacham PE31 ....133 D5
  Hilgay PE38 ....79 E1
  Holt NR25 ....137 B6
  Hopton IP22 ....127 F6
  Hunstanton PE36 ....132 C4
  Ketteringham NR18 ....88 D5
  King's Lynn PE30 ....146 D5
  Lakenheath IP27 ....113 E1
  Loddon NR14 ....92 A1
  Ludham NR29 ....56 C5
  Marsham NR10 ....150 C1
  Methwold IP26 ....99 A5
  Mundesley NR11 ....143 C5
  North Elmham NR20 ....49 E8
  Northwold IP26 ....99 C7
  Overstrand NR27 ....11 A3
  Ringstead PE36 ....2 A3
  St Margaret, Ilketshall NR35 ....124 D3
  5 Sheringham NR26 ..138 D7
  Shipdham IP25 ....67 B2
  Southrepps NR11 ....22 B7
  Stalham NR12 ....39 B4
  Stoke Ferry PE33 ....81 A2

High St continued
  Sutton Bridge PE12 ....41 C8
  Thelnetham IP22 ....128 B4
  Thornham PE36 ....2 D6
  Thursford NR21 ....17 D5
  Tittleshall PE32 ....48 B8
  Walsingham NR22 ....16 F7
  Watton IP25 ....84 D3
  Wells-next-the-Sea NR23 ....136 D5
  Whissonsett NR20 ....31 D3
  Wicklewood NR18 ....87 B5
  Wighton NR23 ....5 F2
  Wisbech PE13 ....152 C5
High View Dr NR17 ....174 B4
High Way **15** NR13 ....74 A3
High Wrong Cnr IP24 .115 C1
Higham Cl NR7 ....159 A3
Higham Gn **3** PE30 ....147 C4
Highbridge Gravel Dro IP27 ....113 D2
Highbridge Rd PE34 ....78 F8
Highbury Rd IP27 ....175 A2
Higher Gn Cl **7** NR15 ..89 D1
Highfield **3** Eye IP23 ..130 C1
  Field Dalling NR25 ....7 B2
  Great & Little Plumstead NR13 ....73 B7
  King's Lynn PE30 ....147 C5
Highfield Ave NR13 ....165 D3
Highfield Cl
  1 Norwich NR7 ....72 D3
  Ryburgh NR21 ....32 A5
Highfield La NR21 ....32 A6
Highfield Rd
  East Dereham NR19 ....154 D8
  Fakenham NR21 ....141 B5
  Great Yarmouth NR31 ..170 C7
  Taverham NR8 ....155 F1
Highfield Way **4** NR12 ..54 C7
Highfields
  Felmingham NR28 ....37 A8
  Lakenheath IP27 ....113 F1
  Norwich NR5 ....156 D1
Highgate PE30 ....146 E5
Highgate Inf Sch PO30 ....146 F6
Highgrove Ct NR14 ....90 C6
Highland Ave NR2 ....162 A4
Highland Cl NR2 ....162 C6
Highland Cres NR14 ....163 B2
Highland Rd
  Norwich NR2 ....162 A4
  Taverham NR8 ....155 D1
Highlands
  Costessey NR8 ....156 F4
  Thetford IP24 ....176 D5
Highlow Rd NR5 ....157 A1
Highmoor Dro IP26 ....99 D8
Highview Cl NR13 ....165 C6
Highview Pk NR27 ....139 C4
Hilary Ave NR1 ....163 B8
Hilary Cl **6** NR3 ....74 A3
Hilda Rd NR11 ....143 C6
Hilgay Rd Ryston PE38 ..79 F3
  West Dereham PE33 ....80 A4
Hilgay Village Prim Sch PE38 ....79 E1
Hill Ave NR31 ....170 D1
Hill Cl NR27 ....139 C4
Hill Comm NR12 ....39 F1
Hill Crest Rd NR7 ....163 D7
Hill Est The PE33 ....62 B6
Hill Farm Rd NR15 ....106 F3
Hill Fields NR19 ....154 C1
Hill Fort Cl IP24 ....176 C7
Hill House La IP24 ....176 C7
Hill House Rd
  Bramerton NR14 ....90 F8
  Norwich NR1 ....163 A5
Hill La Runhall NR20 ....69 A4
  Sculthorpe Airfield NR21 ..15 C2
Hill Rd
  Ingoldisthorpe PE31 ....140 C8
  King's Lynn PE30 ....147 B8
  Middleton PE33 ....44 B3
  Morley NR18 ....104 D8
  Norwich NR5 ....157 A2
  Tibenham NR16 ....120 F8
  Wymondham NR18 ....105 A3
Hill Side Cl **3** NR32 ....44 B3
Hill St **19** Feltwell IP26 ..98 E1
  5 Wisbech PE13 ....152 C5
Hill The Brandon IP27 ..175 A2
  Coltishall NR12 ....54 D7
  Damgate NR13 ....166 C2
  Horsham St Faith NR10 ..53 D1
  Little Snoring NR21 ....17 B3
  Shipmeadow NR34 ....124 F8
  Westwick NR10 ....37 D5
  Woodbastwick NR13 ....55 F1
Hill Top
  Cley next the Sea NR25 ..7 E7
  Stanton IP31 ....127 C1
Hill Top Dr NR8 ....156 F3
Hill View Rd NR26 ....138 E7
Hillary Rd IP24 ....176 C2
Hill's Cl **8** Corpusty NR11 ..19 F1
  Sporle PE32 ....65 C6
Hill's Ct PE38 ....79 E1
Hillburn Rd PE13 ....152 B4
Hillcrest Acle NR13 ....166 A3
  Downham Market PE38 .172 C5
  Great Ryburgh NR21 ....32 B6

Hillcrest continued
  7 Loddon NR14 ....92 A2
Hillcrest Ave NR19 ....154 C1
Hillcrest Prim Sch PE38 ....172 E6
Hillen Rd PE30 ....146 D2
Hillfield NR12 ....38 D3
Hillgate St PE34 ....144 A4
Hillingdon Pk NR27 ....11 A4
Hillings Way PE32 ....28 A1
Hillington Sq PE30 ....146 E4
Hillmead NR3 ....158 D3
Hills Rd IP25 ....84 C5
Hills The NR2 ....162 A3
Hillsend La NR17 ....174 A3
Hillside
  Barnham Broom NR9 ....69 B2
  Barsham NR21 ....16 D5
  Brandon IP27 ....114 D4
  Briston NR24 ....142 B4
  Cromer NR27 ....139 C4
  Loddon NR14 ....92 A2
  Marham PE33 ....63 B5
  Mundesley NR11 ....143 D5
  North Pickenham PE37 ..65 E2
  Poringland NR14 ....90 C5
  Roughton NR11 ....10 D1
  Sheringham NR26 ....138 F7
  Swaffham PE37 ....153 D4
Hillside Animal Sanctuary★ NR12 ....54 B4
Hillside Ave NR13 ....163 F6
Hillside Ave Prim Sch NR7 ....163 F6
Hillside Cl
  Norwich NR7 ....163 F6
  Ormesby St Margaret NR29 ....167 B2
  Swardeston NR14 ....89 C5
Hillside Cres NR18 ....87 B5
Hillside Fst Sch NR31 ..94 C7
Hillside Rd
  Horning NR12 ....55 E3
  Norwich NR7 ....163 F6
  Sheringham NR26 ....138 F5
Hillside Rd E NR35 ....124 B7
Hillside Rd W NR35 ....124 A7
Hilltop Way IP31 ....127 C1
Hillview PE37 ....65 E2
Hillview Dr NR29 ....58 B6
Hillvue Cl NR5 ....157 A2
Hilly Cl IP31 ....126 D1
Hilly Plantation NR7 ..163 E7
Hilton Cl PE37 ....153 C4
Hilton Ct PE13 ....153 D4
Hiltons La **5** PE34 ....43 B1
Hinchingbrook Cl PE30 ....148 E1
Hinderclay La IP22 ....128 B5
Hinderclay Rd
  Redgrave IP22 ....128 D5
  Rickinghall Inferior IP22 ....128 B3
  Wattisfield IP22 ....128 B1
Hindolveston Rd
  Foulsham NR20 ....33 D4
  Fulmodeston NR21 ....17 F1
  Guestwick NR20 ....33 F6
  Thurning NR20 ....34 A8
Hindringham Prim Sch NR21 ....17 D7
Hindringham Rd
  Binham NR21 ....6 C4
  Gunthorpe NR21 ....18 A7
  Hindringham NR21 ....17 F7
  Walsingham NR22 ....17 A8
Hingham Prim Sch NR9 ....86 C5
Hingham Rd
  Deopham NR18 ....86 F5
  Garvestone NR9 ....86 C8
  Great Ellingham NR17 ..103 E8
  Hardingham NR9 ....86 E6
  Little Ellingham NR17 ..86 A8
Hingley Cl NR31 ....170 C8
Hinks Cl NR10 ....155 C3
Hinshalwood Way NR8 ....156 E4
Hipkin Rd PE31 ....140 C3
Hipperson Cl **2** NR28 .151 C7
Hippodrome★ NR30 ..169 E3
Hobart Cl NR18 ....173 C6
Hobart High Sch NR14 ..92 A1
Hobart La NR1 ....178 B1
Hobart Sq NR1 ....178 B1
Hobb's La NR13 ....92 B7
Hobbies Mus of Fretwork & Craft Ctr★ NR19 ....154 D5
Hobbs's La NR15 ....108 D7
Hobland Rd
  Belton with Browston NR31 ....94 C4
  Bradwell NR31 ....171 A7
Hobrough La NR1 ....178 C2
Hockering La NR9 ....160 B6
Hockering Prim Sch NR20 ....69 B8
Hockham St PE30 ....146 D2
Hockwold Prim Sch IP26 ....114 A6
Hockwold Rd IP27 ....175 B7
Hodgson Rd NR4 ....161 F5
Hoe Hall NR20 ....49 F3
Hoe Rd Hoe NR20 ....49 F5
  Longham NR19 ....49 A3

Hoe Rd E NR20 ....50 A4
Hoe Rd N NR20 ....50 A3
Hoe Rd S NR20 ....50 A2
Hoe Rough Nature Reserve★
 NR20 ....49 E4
Hog Bog La NR10 .....53 F3
Hog La NR34 ....124 F2
Hogarth Cl 13 NR31 ....94 C8
Hogarth Rd PE38 ....172 E6
Hogg La NR35 ....108 C1
Hogg's Dro PE33 ......63 B5
Hogherd's La 9 PE13 .152 C5
Hogsty La IP21 ......122 A1
Holbrigg La NR21 ......17 C1
Holcombe Ave PE30 ..146 F3
Holders La IP26 ....99 A7
Holgate Hill NR25 ....8 D4
Holgate La 5 NR27 ....10 B5
Holgate Rd
 North Walsham NR28 ...151 F1
 South Creake NR21 ......15 C7
Holkham Ave PE37 ...153 B2
Holkham Cl 7 PE38 ...172 C6
Holkham Hall & Bygones
 Mus★ NR23 ....5 A5
Holkham National Nature
 Reserve★ NR23 ......5 B8
Holkham Rd NR23 ....136 B6
 Garvestone NR9 ....68 B1
Holl La Billingford NR20 ..50 B7
Holl Rd NR11 ....21 B4
Holland Ct 8 NR19 ...154 D1
Holland's La NR35 ....108 C3
Holley Wlk NR11 .....150 C4
Hollies The
 Clenchwarton PE34 ....145 D5
 5 North Walsham NR28 .151 C5
Hollow Hill Rd NR35 ..109 A2
Hollow La
 Barningham IP31 ......127 D4
 4 Langham NR25 ......7 A4
 Raynham NR21 ....30 F3
 Shotesham NR15 ....89 F2
Hollow Way Hill NR34 .110 D4
Holloway Rd NR14 .....91 B8
Holls La NR1 ....178 B1
Hollway La NR20 ......33 A4
Holly Ave NR31 ....94 C7
Holly Bank NR7 ......159 A2
Holly Blue Rd NR18 ...173 E4
Holly Cl Dereham NR19 .154 F4
 Downham Market PE38 ..172 B6
 Holt NR25 ....137 D7
 King's Lynn PE30 ......148 D2
 14 Marthan NR29 ......57 D4
 Mattishall NR20 ....68 E6
 Rougham PE32 ....47 B7
 1 West Winch PE33 ....43 E2
Holly Ct
 34 Harleston IP20 ....122 C2
 Swaffham PE13 ....153 C4
 Wymondham NR18 ....173 E6
Holly Dr NR2 ....162 A7
Holly Farm Rd NR13 ...93 A4
Holly Gr NR26 ....138 D5
Holly La Blofield NR13 .165 D7
 Lackenheath IP27 ......113 E1
 9 Tharston & Hapton
 NR15 ....106 D3
 Wood Dalling NR11 .....34 D5
Holly Rd NR17 ....174 C4
Holly Way 13 NR31 ....170 B6
Hollybush Rd NR28 ...151 F5
Hollycroft Cl PE13 .....59 D1
Hollycroft Rd PE14 .....77 D8
Hollywell Gdns PE13 ..153 B4
Holman Cl NR11 .....150 B7
Holman Rd NR11 .....150 B6
Holman's Chase PE38 ..97 B6
Holme Cl Hopton IP22 .127 F6
 Runcton Holme PE33 ....61 D4
Holme Dunes National
 Nature Reserve★ PE36 .2 A8
Holme Rd PE36 ....2 A4
 Norwich NR7 ....163 D8
Holmes Cl Acle NR13 ..166 B4
 Norwich NR7 ....163 D8
Holmes Dr PE13 ......152 E5
Holmes Rd
 East Ruston NR12 ....38 F5
 Somerton NR29 ....57 F7
Holmesdale Rd NR13 ..165 B4
Holmwood Rise NR7 ...163 C6
Holt Ct PE14 ....41 E3
Holt Ctry Pk★ NR25 ..137 C4
Holt House La PE34 ....44 D5
Holt Prim Sch NR25 ...137 B5
Holt Rd Aylmerton NR11 .10 B3
 Briston NR24 ....142 E5
 Cawston NR10 ....35 D2
 Cley next the Sea NR25 ....7 E6
 Cromer NR27 ....139 A6
 Fakenham NR21 ....141 C4
 Felthorpe NR10 ....52 F6
 Field Dalling NR25 ....7 B2
 Gresham NR11 ....9 E1
 Guist NR20 ....32 F4
 Hoe NR19 ....154 C8
 Langham NR25 ....7 A4
 Letheringsett with Glandford
 NR25 ....8 A1
 Little Snoring NR21 .....17 C3
 North Elmham NR20 .....49 E7
 Norwich NR10 ....157 F8
 Sheringham NR26 ......138 B5
 Thornage NR25 ....18 F7
Holt Rd continued
 Upper Sheringham
 NR26 ....138 C3
 Walsingham NR22 ......16 F7
 Weybourne NR25 ....8 E5
Holt Sta NR25 ....137 E8
Holt's La PE38 ....79 D1
Holway Cl NR27 ......139 B3
Holway Rd NR26 .....138 D5
Holway The NR29 .....58 B6
Holworthy Rd NR5 ....161 B8
Holy Rd NR24 ....18 D5
Holyrood Dr NR31 ....140 D3
Home Cl
 Great Ellingham NR17 ..103 E8
 Lyng NR9 ....51 A4
 6 Sheringham NR26 ...10 A5
Home Farm La NR18 ..104 E8
Home Farm Rd NR35 ..109 C3
Home Farm Rise NR25 ..8 E5
Home La
 Hilborough IP25 ....83 B4
 Hindringham NR21 ......17 E7
Home Piece IP22 .....127 E4
Home St NR2 ....162 C8
Homebred La 1 NR14 ..91 F1
Homefield Ave NR31 ...94 C7
Homefield Fst Sch
 NR31 ....94 C7
Homefields La PE36 ..132 D4
Homeland Rd 10 PE30 .146 E6
Homelea Cres 13 NR13 .74 A3
Homestead Cl 7 NR13 ..74 A3
Homestead Gdns
 NR29 ....167 B7
Honey Cl 2 NR1 ......163 B7
Honey Dro PE33 ....80 B1
Honey Hill PE34 ....79 D8
Honey Hills PE31 ......14 A5
Honeycombe Rd NR13 ..73 B8
Honeymoon Loke
 NR30 ....168 F4
Honeymoon Row
 NR23 ....136 D5
Honeypot Dro PE32 ....46 C5
Honeypot La
 Kirby Cane NR35 ......109 C5
 Longham NR19 ....48 F2
 Seething NR15 ....108 E8
Honeysuckle Cl
 North Walsham NR28 ...151 E4
 5 Thetford IP24 .....176 F4
Honeysuckle Dr NR20 .154 F4
Honeysuckle Way
 NR17 ....174 B5
Honing Long La NR28 ..38 C7
Honing Rd NR28 ....38 D5
Honing Row NR28 ......38 A5
Honingham La NR8 .....70 A8
Honingham Rd NR9 .....69 C3
Honington Airfield
 IP31 ....126 A2
Honington Rise IP31 ..126 C1
Honington VC Prim Sch
 IP31 ....126 D1
Hood Way NR24 ......176 E5
Hook's Wlk NR1 ......178 C3
Hooker Rd NR7 ......159 D1
Hooks Hill Rd NR26 ..138 C6
Hookwood La NR18 ...104 C8
Hooper La NR3 ....158 F2
Hooton's Row PE38 ....78 F6
Hope Ct PE30 ....147 A8
Hope La PE14 ....60 A4
Hopton CE VC Prim Sch
 IP22 ....127 F5
Hopton Cl 6 NR7 ......72 D4
Hopton Fst Sch NR31 ..171 E4
Hopton Gdns NR31 ...171 D5
Hopton Rd
 Barningham IP31 ......127 D4
 Garboldisham IP22 ....128 A8
 Thelnetham IP22 ......128 A5
Horizon Views NR12 ...24 A7
Hornbeam Cl
 5 Great Yarmouth NR31 .170 B6
 Norwich NR7 ....159 D4
Hornbeam Dr 15 NR14 ..90 C5
Horner Cl 3 IP22 .....177 A5
Horning Cl NR5 ......161 D7
Horning Fst Sch NR12 ..55 F3
Horning Rd
 Hoveton NR12 ....164 E5
 Neatishead NR12 ....55 D6
 Woodbastwick NR13 ....55 D2
Horning Rd W NR12 ..164 C5
Hornor Cl NR2 ....162 C3
Horns La NR1 ....178 B2
Horns Row NR21 .....141 A3
Horsbeck Way NR10 ...53 A3
Horse Fair 2 PE13 ...152 C5
Horse Rescue Ctr★
 NR16 ....103 C2
Horse Shoe Rd NR20 ...69 A4
Horsefen Rd NR29 .....56 D4
Horsehead Dro PE14 ...95 C8
Horses Head NR13 ....166 B7
Horseshoe Cl NR5 ....156 E1
Horse-Shoe Cnr PE13 .152 B7
Horseshoe La NR24 ...142 F4
Horseshoe Terr PE13 .152 B7
Horsey Rd NR29 ....57 E7
Horsey Windpump★
 NR29 ....40 D1
Horsey's La NR31 ....170 D5
Horsford All Saints Mid Sch
 NR10 ....53 B4
Horsford St 7 NR2 ...162 B8
Horsford VC Fst Sch
 NR10 ....53 B3
Horsham St Faith VC Fst Sch
 NR10 ....53 C2
Horsley Dr
 Great Yarmouth NR31 ..170 B1
 Hopton on Sea NR31 ...171 D4
Horsley's Chase PE30 .146 E3
Horsley's Ct 7 PE30 ..146 E3
Horsley's Field PE30 ..146 E2
Horton Rd PE30 ......147 D6
Hospital La
 Hellesdon NR6 ....157 D3
 Norwich NR1 ....162 E3
Hospital Rd
 Great & Little Plumstead
 NR13 ....73 A5
 Sutton Bridge PE12 .....41 E8
 Wicklewood NR18 ....87 C4
Hospital Wlk PE30 ....146 E4
Hotblack Rd NR2 .....162 A8
Hotch PE14 ....60 B8
Hotson Cl 5 NR15 ....106 D3
Houghton Ave PE30 ..148 D1
Houghton Cl 2 NR5 ...161 B8
Houghton Hall★ PE31 ..29 C7
Houghton La PE37 .....65 E1
House Gdns NR10 ......53 E5
Hovell's La IP26 ....99 C7
Hoveton & Wroxham Sta
 NR12 ....164 C5
Hoveton Cl PE30 .....147 D5
Hoveton Dr PE37 ....153 C1
Hoveton Hall Gdns★
 NR12 ....55 B7
Hoveton Pl NR10 ......37 B2
How Hill Nature Reserve★
 NR29 ....56 A6
How Hill Rd NR29 .....56 B6
Howard Cl
 Harleston IP20 ....122 E2
 Norwich NR7 ....163 D7
 4 Swanton Morley NR20 .50 B3
 Terrington St Clement
 PE34 ....144 B4
Howard Cres NR19 ...154 D4
Howard Inf Sch PE30 ..147 B4
Howard Jun Sch PE30 .147 B4
Howard Mews NR3 ...158 C1
Howard St NR1 ....178 A1
Howard St N 9 NR30 ..169 C4
Howard St S NR30 ...169 C4
Howard Way NR11 ...150 C5
Howard's Hill NR27 ....29 A6
Howard's Way NR10 ...35 B2
Howard's Hill Rd NR28 ..38 C7
Howards Cl PE36 .....132 E7
Howards Hill Cl NR27 ..10 C5
Howards Hill W 1
 NR27 ....139 A7
Howards The PE30 ...148 D4
Howdale Rd PE38 ....172 C5
Howdale Rise PE38 ...172 D5
Howe Gn NR15 ....90 D2
Howe La NR15 ....90 D3
Howe Rd NR30 ....169 D7
Howell Rd NR8 ......157 C6
Howes Cl 10 NR9 ......88 D7
Howes La NR20 ....68 D6
Howes Yd 1 NR25 ......7 E6
Howland Ct NR21 ....141 B5
Howlett Cl
 4 East Dereham NR19 ..154 D3
 North Walsham NR28 ..151 A5
Howlett Dr NR5 ......161 A8
Howlett Way 2 IP24 ..176 D6
Howletts Hill PE13 ....154 E5
Hoxne Rd Denham IP21 .131 B1
 Eye IP23 ....130 E1
 Syleham IP21 ....131 C4
 Upper Weybread IP21 ..131 E6
Hubbard Cl
 11 Long Stratton NR15 ..106 E3
 Wymondham NR18 .....173 A6
Hubbard's Dro PE38 ...79 E1
Hudson Leisure Ctr
 PE13 ....152 A5
Hudson Way NR5 ....160 E7
Hugh Cl PE30 ....148 C5
Hughenden Rd NR1 ...162 E3
Hughes Ct 13 NR9 .....88 D8
Hulton Rd PE30 ......147 A5
Hulver Rd NR13 ....73 E8
Hulver St NR19 ....66 F6
Humber Cl NR30 .....168 C5
Humber Keel NR31 ...170 D1
Humberstone Rd 3
 NR31 ....170 C7
Humbletoft Rd NR19 ..154 C7
Humbleyard NR5 .....161 A7
Hungate La NR11 ....150 C4
Hungate Rd PE14 ......59 E2
Hungate St NR11 ....150 C5
Hungry Hill NR27 ......11 B2
Hunstanton Commercial Pk
 PE36 ....132 D3
Hunstanton Inf Sch
 PE36 ....132 D4
Hunstanton Rd
 Dersingham PE31 ......140 D5
 Heacham PE31 ....132 D1
Hunstanton Sea Life
 Sanctuary★ PE36 ...132 B3
Hunstead La NR15 .....90 F2
Hunt Cl Old Catton NR6 .158 E7
 5 Redenhall with Harleston
 IP20 ....122 D2
Hunter Ave NR20 ......68 F5
Hunter Dr 4 NR31 .....94 C8
Hunter Rd
 Norwich NR3 ....158 C3
 Troston IP31 ....126 B1
Hunter's Dro PE14 .....60 B6
Hunters Cl
 Brundall NR13 ....165 F5
 Terrington St Clement
 PE34 ....144 F6
Hunters Oak 2 IP25 ....84 E3
Huntley Cres NR26 ...138 E6
Hunts Gn NR16 ......105 B4
Hunwurth Rd NR24 ...142 D8
Hurd Rd NR4 ....161 E3
Hurdle La NR25 ....7 E4
Hurn La NR16 ....106 A6
Hurn Rd Dereham NR20 ..68 A7
 Taverham NR8 ....157 C7
Hurrell Rd NR20 ....68 D6
Hurricane Way NR6 ..158 C6
Hurst Rd 8 NR14 ......92 A2
Hurth Way IP24 ......176 E4
Husenbeth Cl NR8 ....156 E4
Hutchinson Rd NR5 ..161 D6
Huxley Cl NR1 ....162 F2
Huxley Rd NR1 ....162 F2
Hyde Cl PE31 ....14 D4
Hyde Ct NR13 ....72 E5
Hyde Rd NR19 ....154 D3
Hypocrite La NR17 ...174 A2
Hyrn Cl NR29 ....57 D4
Hythe Rd Feltwell IP26 ..98 E3
 Foulden IP26 ....82 A1
 Methwold IP26 ....98 F5

I

Ice House Ct 17 NR15 ..106 E3
Ice House La NR1 ....178 C1
Iceni Dr PE37 ....153 D2
Icknield Cl IP24 .....176 B3
Icknield Way IP24 ...176 B3
Ickworth Cl PE30 ....148 E1
Ilex Ct NR7 ....159 D4
Illington Rd IP24 ....117 C8
ILPH Hall Farm★
 NR16 ....118 B7
Impala Cl NR6 ....159 A6
Imperial Mews NR31 .171 C4
Impson Way IP26 ....100 A4
Incleborough Cl 2 NR27 .10 B5
Independent Way 14
 NR7 ....72 D4
Indigo Yd NR3 ....178 A3
Ingham Cnr NR12 .....24 D1
Ingham Rd
 Lessingham NR12 ......24 D2
 Stalham NR12 ....39 B4
Ingle Rd PE14 ....59 B1
Ingleby Cl
 Heacham NR31 ....133 E6
 King's Lynn PE30 .....147 B4
Ingloss La NR14 .....109 B3
Ingoldale PE31 ......140 C8
Ingoldisthorpe Fst Sch
 PE31 ....140 E8
Ingoldsby Ave PE31 ..140 C6
Ingolside PE31 ....12 D4
Ingram Ct NR1 ......162 E3
Ingram's Rd IP21 ....131 C7
Inman Rd NR7 ....159 D4
Inspire Discovery Ctr★
 NR3 ....178 A4
Intwood La
 East Carleton NR14 .....89 A5
 Swardeston NR14 ....89 C6
Intwood Rd NR4 ....89 B8
Invaders Ct NR23 ....136 D6
Ipswich Gr NR2 ......178 A1
Ipswich Rd
 2 Norwich NR4 ....89 E8
 Norwich NR2 ....178 A1
 Pulham Market NR15 ..121 E8
 Saxlingham Nethergate
 NR15 ....107 A7
 Scole IP21 ....130 D5
 Yaxley IP23 ....130 A1
Ireton Cl 25 NR7 ......72 D4
Iris Cl NR1 ....174 B5
Irmingland Rd NR11 ...34 F8
Ironside Way NR9 .....86 D5
Irstead Rd
 Barton Turf NR12 ......55 F7
 Norwich NR5 ....161 E6
Irving Rd NR4 ....162 C1
Irwin Cl NR10 ....149 C5
Isaac's Rd NR31 .....169 B4
Isabella Cl PE30 .....147 D5
Isabella Sq 12 NR30 ..169 D3
Isbets Dale NR8 .....155 D2
Isis Cl NR31 ....170 B3
Isle Bridge Rd PE14 ...77 E6
Isle Rd PE14 ....77 F7
Iveagh Cl PE31 ......140 E2
Ives Cl IP22 ....177 E4
Ives Rd NR6 ....158 D5
Ivory Rd NR4 ....161 E4
Ivy Gn 6 NR31 ......170 B5
Ivy Rd Earlham NR5 ...161 E7
 3 Spixworth NR10 .....54 A2
Ivy Todd Rd PE37 .....66 B4
Ivy Way NR20 ....68 E6
Ixworth Rd IP31 ....126 D1

J

Jack Plummer Way
 NR30 ....168 C7
Jaguar Rd 9 NR9 ......88 D8
James Bradfield Prim Sch
 PE33 ....81 A2
James Cl PE30 ....148 B1
James Gn Cl 14 NR10 ..54 A2
James Jackson Rd
 PE31 ....140 C3
James Paget Hospl
 NR31 ....170 B1
James Rd 7 NR12 .....55 E4
James Scott Cl 3 PE38 172 A5
James St PE36 ....132 D4
James Watt Cl NR31 ..170 A8
Jamieson Pl NR5 .....161 C8
Jane Forby Cl PE33 ....80 E2
Jankin La PE34 ......144 A1
Jannys Cl NR11 ......150 B6
Jarrold Cl IP31 ......127 D3
Jarrold Way NR5 .....160 F8
Jarvie Cl PE36 ....13 A7
Jarvis Dr NR21 ....31 E5
Jarvis Rd PE30 ......146 E8
Jasmin Cl PE13 ......152 F7
Jasmine Cl
 Earlham NR4 ....161 E5
 Thetford IP24 ....176 F4
Jasmine Gn 1 NR17 ..174 B5
Jasmine Gdns 7 NR31 ..94 C7
Jasmine Gn 7 NR31 ...170 B5
Javelin Rd NR6 ......158 C7
Jay Gdns NR5 ....160 E8
Jay La NR32 ....171 C3
Jay's Gn IP20 ....122 E2
Jefferey Ave 4 PE13 ..152 E7
Jeffery Cl PE30 ......146 E8
Jegon Cl NR11 ......150 D5
Jellicoe Pl 6 IP24 ....176 E5
Jellicoe Rd NR30 ....169 C8
Jenkinsons Pightle
 NR35 ....108 B4
Jenner Rd 4 NR31 ...170 B1
Jennings Cl PE31 ....133 C5
Jennings Way IP22 ..177 D5
Jenny Rd 8 NR10 ......54 A2
Jermyn Rd PE30 .....147 C6
Jermyn Way 1 NR15 ..106 D3
Jerningham Rd NR5 ..157 A1
Jessopp Cl
 Norwich NR2 ....161 F4
 Scarning NR19 ....67 B7
Jessopp Rd NR4 .....161 F4
Jetty Cl NR27 ....139 B7
Jetty Cliff NR27 .....139 C7
Jetty St 2 NR27 .....139 B7
Jewel Cl NR24 ......142 B4
Jews' La 10 NR31 .....94 C6
Jewson Rd NR3 .....158 C2
Jex Ave NR5 ....161 D8
Jex La NR5 ....161 D8
Jex Rd NR5 ....161 D8
Jickling Yd NR23 ....136 D6
Joan Short's La PE31 .135 D3
Jocelyn Cl IP21 .....121 E5
Joe Ellis Ct 6 NR5 ...161 B8
John Bates Cl 2 NR14 .154 E5
John Chapman Cl 5
 NR21 ....141 E4
John Davis Way PE33 ..61 D5
John Drewry Cl 2 NR14 .90 D5
John F Kennedy Ct 2
 PE13 ....152 A2
John Gale Ct NR8 ....155 E3
John Goshawk Rd
 NR19 ....154 E3
John Grant Specl Sch
 NR30 ....168 D6
John Hill Cl 5 NR15 ..106 E3
John Jarrod Printing Mus★
 NR1 ....178 C4
John Kennedy Rd
 PE30 ....146 D6
John of Gaunt Fst Sch
 NR11 ....150 C5
John O'Gaunt Cl NR11 .150 B6
John Rd
 Caister-on-Sea NR30 ...168 E7
 Great Yarmouth NR31 ..170 D5
John St 3 PE30 ......146 E3
John Stephenson Ct 1
 NR6 ....158 F1
John Thompson Rd 3
 PE13 ....152 D4
John Woodhouse Dr
 NR30 ....168 C7
Johnson Cl 7 NR19 ..154 C3
Johnson Cres PE31 ...133 C4
Johnson Pl NR2 .....162 C5
Jolly Gardeners Ct 13
 NR3 ....162 B4
Jolly Sailor Yd NR23 .136 D6
Jolly's La NR13 ......166 A2
Jones (GC) Way NR31 .169 B2
Jones's Dro PE14 .....95 E8
Jordan Cl Norwich NR5 .161 B6
 Taverham NR8 ....155 E4
Jordan La NR10 ....51 A8
Jordan Rd NR30 .....168 D7
Jose Neville Cl 2 NR30 168 D7
Joseph Lancaster Way 4
 NR1 ....178 B4
Josephine Cl NR1 ...162 D3
Joshua Ct 3 NR31 ...171 D8
Joy Ave 1 NR15 .....107 A8

Joyce La
Heacham PE31 . . . . .133 D5
Walpole PE14 . . . . .41 F3
Joyce Rd NR35 . . . . .124 B8
Joyce Way 9 NR7 . . . . . . .72 D5
Joyland ✶ NR30 . . . . . . .169 E4
Jubilee Ave
  4 East Dereham NR20 . . . .154 E6
East Harling NR16 . . . . . . .118 C5
Fakenham NR21 . . . . .141 C4
Heacham PE31 . . . . .133 B5
Jubilee Bank Rd PE34 .146 A5
Jubilee Cl Cawston NR10 . .35 B2
Downham Market PE38 . . .172 E6
Erpingham NR11 . . . . .21 B2
Hunstanton PE36 . . . . .132 C3
Repps with Bastwick
  NR29 . . . . .57 A4
Thetford IP24 . . . . .176 B3
Weeting IP27 . . . . .175 B7
Jubilee Ct 7 PE30 . . . . .146 D4
Jubilee Dr
Dersingham PE31 . . . . .140 C5
Sheringham NR26 . . . . .138 E6
Jubilee Gdns 7 PE31 . . .12 E4
Jubilee Hall La 2 PE32 . .45 C6
Jubilee La NR27 . . . . . . .139 C4
Jubilee Rd
Heacham PE31 . . . . .133 A5
Holt NR25 . . . . .137 B6
Lackenheath IP27 . . . . .113 E2
Watton IP25 . . . . .84 D3
Jubilee Rise PE33 . . . . . . .61 D3
Jubilee Terr
Caister-on-Sea NR30 . . . . . .168 E4
Cromer NR27 . . . . .139 D4
Norwich NR1 . . . . .162 F3
Jubilee Way 11 PE37 . . . .65 F4
Jubilee Wlk PE13 . . . . . .152 D8
Judas La IP23 . . . . .129 F1
Judges Dr NR4 . . . . .161 F2
Judges Gdns NR8 . . . . . .155 E2
Judges Wlk NR4 . . . . . . .161 F2
Juler Cl NR28 . . . . .151 C6
Julian Hospl NR1 . . . . . .161 F6
Julian Rd
King's Lynn PE30 . . . . .148 C5
  6 Spixworth NR10 . . . . . .54 A2
Julian Way NR31 . . . . . .171 D5
Julians Way IP21 . . . . . .121 E5
Junction Rd NR3 . . . . . . .158 C1
Juniper Cl 2 IP24 . . . . . .176 F4
Juniper Gr NR26 . . . . . . .138 C5
Juniper Way NR8 . . . . . .155 B2
Jupiter Rd NR6 . . . . .158 C4
Jury St NR30 . . . . .169 D4

K

Kabin Rd NR5 . . . . .157 B2
Kalmia Gn 3 NR31 . . . . .170 B6
Karen Cl
  15 Hethersett NR9 . . . . . . .88 C7
Scole IP21 . . . . .130 C5
Keable Cl 7 NR5 . . . . . . .161 C6
Keats Cl
Downham Market PE38 . . .172 D5
East Dereham NR19 . . . . . .154 C7
  2 Thetford IP24 . . . . .176 E6
Keats Rd NR8 . . . . .156 D8
Keble Cl PE30 . . . . .148 B4
Keble Rd NR31 . . . . .170 B3
Kedleston Dr 10 NR4 . . . .89 B8
Keel Cl 12 NR33 . . . . .111 F1
Keelan Cl NR6 . . . . .158 B4
Keeling Hall La NR20 . . . .33 E3
Keeling Way NR17 . . . . . .174 B3
Keene Rd PE30 . . . . .146 D1
Keepers Rd NR15 . . . . . . .89 F1
Keepham Rd NR20 . . . . . .33 F2
Keillers Cl PE13 . . . . .152 A7
Keith Rd 9 NR20 . . . . . . .50 B3
Kell's Acres NR34 . . . . . .109 F3
Kell's Way NR34 . . . . . . .109 F2
Kelling Cl NR25 . . . . .137 C7
Kelling Heath Pk Sta
  NR25 . . . . .8 E4
Kelling Hospl NR25 . . . . .137 F8
Kelling Rd NR25 . . . . . . .137 C7
Kelsey Cl PE36 . . . . .132 D7
Kelvin Pl IP24 . . . . .176 A1
Kemp Dr NR19 . . . . .154 C5
Kemp's Cl PE38 . . . . .79 A4
Kemp's Rd IP21 . . . . .122 A5
Kempe Cl NR7 . . . . .159 C1
Kempe Rd PE34 . . . . .146 C5
Kenan Dr NR17 . . . . .174 F7
Kendal Cl 15 NR9 . . . . . . .88 D8
Kendall Cl NR28 . . . . . . .151 B6
Kendle Way PE30 . . . . . .147 E8
Kenhill Cl 2 PE31 . . . . . . .12 E5
Kenlan Rd PE13 . . . . .152 D6
Kennedy Ave NR31 . . . . .170 C1
Kennedy Cl
East Dereham NR19 . . . . . .154 D1
Easton NR9 . . . . .70 B5
Kennel Loke NR31 . . . . . .171 D8
Kennett Cl NR4 . . . . .161 F4
Kenninghall Prim Sch
  NR16 . . . . .119 A4
Kenninghall Rd
Banham NR16 . . . . .119 B5
Harling NR16 . . . . .118 E4
Kenninghall NR16 . . . . . . .119 A3
Kenside Rd 1 PE31 . . . . .12 E5
Kensington Cl NR15 . . . .107 C8

Kensington Pl NR1 . . . .178 B1
Kensington Rd
Downham Market PE38 . . .172 B4
King's Lynn PE30 . . . . .147 B6
Kent Ave NR31 . . . . .170 C3
Kent Cl
Attleborough NR17 . . . . . .174 B3
  2 Sutton Bridge PE12 . . . .41 B8
Kent Rd PE30 . . . . .147 B6
Kent Sq NR30 . . . . .169 D3
Kenwood Rd PE31 . . . . . .133 D5
Kenwood Rd S PE31 . . . .133 D5
Kenwyn Cl NR25 . . . . . . .137 C7
Kenyon Row NR34 . . . . .110 C2
Keppel Cl PE32 . . . . .48 A5
Keppel Rd 2 NR31 . . . . .170 C2
Kerdiston Rd
Reepham NR10 . . . . .149 A6
Themelthorpe NR20 . . . . . . .33 F2
Kered Cl NR6 . . . . .157 F6
Kered Rd NR6 . . . . .157 F6
Kerridge Ct NR25 . . . . . .137 D5
Kerridge Way
  29 Harleston IP20 . . . . . .122 D2
Holt NR25 . . . . .137 B6
Kerridges NR16 . . . . .118 C4
Kerridges The NR5 . . . . .156 F1
Kerrison Rd NR1 . . . . . . .163 A4
Kerville St 3 NR5 . . . . . .161 A7
Kestrel Ave PE38 . . . . . . .172 C7
Kestrel Cl
Burnham Market PE31 . . . .135 D1
Great Yarmouth NR31 . . . .170 A7
Mulbarton NR14 . . . . .89 A3
Swaffham PE37 . . . . .153 C2
Thetford IP24 . . . . .176 D1
Kestrel Dr
Brandon IP27 . . . . .175 F3
  2 Wisbech PE14 . . . . . . .152 C2
Kestrel Rd NR7 . . . . .159 C4
Keswick NR25 . . . . .147 D5
Keswick Cl NR4 . . . . .89 B8
Keswick Rd Bacton NR12 . .23 C4
Cringleford NR4 . . . . .89 B8
Kett Sixth Form Ctr
  NR7 . . . . .159 C2
Kett's Ave NR18 . . . . . . .173 C5
Kett's Cl
  3 Hethersett NR9 . . . . . . .88 D7
Wymondham NR18 . . . . . .173 C5
Kett's Hill NR1 . . . . .163 A7
Kett's La NR9 . . . . .52 A6
Kett's Oak NR9 . . . . .88 C6
Ketteringham La NR9 . . . .88 D6
Ketteringham Pk NR9 . . . .88 E6
Ketteringham Rd
  NR18 . . . . .173 F3
Kettlestone Rd NR21 . . . .17 D5
Kettlewell La 1 PE30 . . .146 E5
Ketts Hill PE37 . . . . .66 A4
Ketts Rd NR28 . . . . .151 B4
Kevill Davis Dr NR13 . . . .73 A5
Kevin Wlk NR19 . . . . . . .154 D2
Kew Rd NR31 . . . . .172 B4
Key & Castle Yd NR3 . . .178 A4
Keyes Ave NR30 . . . . . . .169 D7
Keyes Cl 5 NR1 . . . . .162 E2
Keyes Rd NR1 . . . . .162 E2
Keys Dr NR12 . . . . .164 B2
Keys Farm 4 NR20 . . . . . .68 F6
Keys The NR15 . . . . .90 F2
Kilderkin Cl PE14 . . . . . . .77 A7
Kilham's Way
King's Lynn PE30 . . . . .146 E7
North Wootton PE30 . . . . . .26 E1
Kiln Cl NR6 . . . . .158 E2
Kiln Farm La IP22 . . . . . .128 E1
Kiln La
Dickleburgh & Rushall
  IP21 . . . . .130 F4
Needham IP20 . . . . .131 D8
Kiln Rd 5 NR10 . . . . .53 A3
Kilverstone Rd IP24 . . . . .117 A2
Kimberley Pk Sta NR18 . .87 A6
Kimberley Rd NR28 . . . . .151 D5
Kimberley St
  1 Norwich NR2 . . . . .162 C5
Wymondham NR18 . . . . . .173 C4
Kimberley Terr NR30 . . . .169 E2
Kimms Belt IP24 . . . . . . .176 B2
Kinderley Rd PE13 . . . . . .152 C8
King Edward VII Sch
  PE30 . . . . .147 A5
King George Cl 3 NR31 . .57 D2
King George Rd NR21 . . . .31 C7
King George V Ave
  PE30 . . . . .146 F5
King George VI Sch
  PE31 . . . . .14 A3
King George's Ave 2
  NR29 . . . . .57 D2
King John Ave PE30 . . . .147 A5
King John Bank PE14 . . . .41 C5
King of Hearts Ctr ✶
  NR1 . . . . .178 B4
King St
East Harling NR16 . . . . . . .118 C5
Great Yarmouth NR30 . . . .169 C4
King's Lynn PE30 . . . . .146 D5
Neatishead NR12 . . . . .55 E7
Norwich NR1 . . . . .178 C1
  13 Sutton Bridge PE12 . . . .41 B8
Swaffham PE37 . . . . .153 B4
Thetford IP24 . . . . .176 C4
Winterton-on-Sea NR29 . . .58 B6
Wisbech PE13 . . . . .152 C5
King William Cl PE34 . . .144 C5

Kingcup PE30 . . . . .148 A1
Kingfisher Cl
  8 Fakenham NR21 . . . . . .141 E4
  7 Fakenham NR21 . . . . . .141 E4
Great Yarmouth NR31 . . . . .94 C7
Thetford IP24 . . . . .176 D1
Kingfisher Dr
Brandon IP27 . . . . .175 E3
Necton NR37 . . . . .66 A3
  6 Wisbech PE14 . . . . . . .152 D2
Kingfisher Rd
Attleborough NR17 . . . . . .174 F6
Downham Market PE38 . . .172 C6
Kingfisher Way 11 IP25 . .84 C3
Kinghorn Rd NR2 . . . . . .161 E4
King's Arms St NR28 . . . .151 C5
King's Ave Anmer PE31 . . .28 C8
King's Lynn PE30 . . . . .147 A3
Kings Croft PE31 . . . . . . .140 E4
Kings Ct NR29 . . . . .167 A8
King's Dam NR34 . . . . . . .110 B2
Kings Gn 6 PE30 . . . . . . .147 C4
Kings Head La
Deopham NR18 . . . . .87 A4
North Lopham IP22 . . . . . . .119 A2
Kings La NR1 . . . . .178 B1
Kings Loke NR29 . . . . . . .167 B8
King's Lynn Arts Ctr
  (Guildhall) ✶ PE30 . . .146 D5
King's Lynn Rd PE36 . . . .132 D4
King's Lynn Sports Ctr
  PE30 . . . . .146 F5
King's Lynn Sta PE30 . . .146 E5
King's Pk NR19 . . . . .154 E6
Kings Pk Fst Sch
  NR19 . . . . .154 E6
East Dereham NR19 . . . . . .154 E6
Fakenham NR21 . . . . .141 A5
King's Rd
Great Yarmouth NR30 . . . .169 D2
Holt NR25 . . . . .137 C5
Kings Rd PE36 . . . . .132 D6
King's Rd NR35 . . . . .108 A4
Kings Rd PE13 . . . . .152 C4
King St NR24 . . . . .19 A6
King's Staithe La 2
  PE30 . . . . .146 D4
King's Staithe Sq 1
  PE30 . . . . .146 D4
Kings Way NR29 . . . . . . .167 B2
King's Wk 4 PE13 . . . . . .152 C4
Kings Wlk
Downham Market PE38 . . .172 C5
  9 Great Yarmouth NR31 . .170 B5
Kingsdale 16 NR31 . . . . . .74 A3
Kingsleigh Cl NR28 . . . . . .22 E5
Kingsley Ave PE13 . . . . . .152 B4
Kingsley Rd NR1 . . . . . . .178 A1
Kingston Ave NR30 . . . . .168 E5
Kingston Rd NR19 . . . . . .154 F3
Kingston Sq NR4 . . . . . . .162 A3
Kingsway 7 Blakeney NR25 .7 C6
  4 Earsham NR35 . . . . . .123 F8
King's Lynn PE30 . . . . .146 E8
Leverington PE13 . . . . .152 F7
  3 Newton Flotman NR15 .107 A8
North Walsham NR28 . . . . .151 A6
Norwich NR2 . . . . .162 A3
Thetford IP24 . . . . .176 C2
Kingswood Ave NR8 . . . .155 C2
Kingswood Cl
Brooke NR15 . . . . .90 E1
  9 Norwich NR4 . . . . .89 C8
Kingswood Pk PE13 . . . . .152 D3
Kinsale Ave NR6 . . . . . . .157 E5
Kinsale Ave Fst & Mid Sch
  NR6 . . . . .157 E4
Kinver Cl NR4 . . . . .162 B3
Kipling Cl NR4 . . . . .168 D6
Kirby Cl 5 NR29 . . . . .57 D5
Kirby Rd Bixley NR14 . . . .90 C8
Norwich NR14 . . . . .163 C2
Kirby St PE30 . . . . .146 E5
Kirk Rd 2 PE14 . . . . .41 D4
Kirkgate La NR23 . . . . .6 A2
Kirkgate St
Holme next the Sea PE36 . . .2 A6
Wisbech PE13 . . . . .152 E7
Kirkham's La PE14 . . . . . .77 C8
Kirkhams Mdw NR19 . . . .66 C7
Kirklands NR8 . . . . .156 E4
Kirklees 6 NR4 . . . . .89 E8
Kirkpatrick Rd NR3 . . . . .158 B2
Kirkstone Gr 2 PE30 . . . .148 F1
Kirstead PE30 . . . . .147 D5
Kirstead Gn NR15 . . . . . .108 C8
Kirstead Ling NR15 . . . . . .91 A1
Kirtons Cl 3 PE14 . . . . . . .41 E4
Kitchener Rd
Great Yarmouth NR30 . . . .169 D5
Melton Constable NR24 . . .142 B5
Kitchener St PE30 . . . . . .146 B2
Kitlings Beck Rd NR28 . . .38 A7
Kittel Cl 24 IP25 . . . . . . .84 D3
Kittens La NR14 . . . . .91 F1
Kittiwake Cl 12 NR31 . . . .94 C8
Kittles La NR10 . . . . .150 A1
Kittles Rd NR15 . . . . .74 D1
Knappers Way IP27 . . . . .175 D3
Knapton Rd
Knapton NR28 . . . . .22 F3
Mundesley NR11 . . . . .22 F5
Trunch NR28 . . . . .22 E5
Knevet St NR17 . . . . .174 F6
Knight St NR22 . . . . .16 F7
Knight's La NR15 . . . . . . .89 E2

Knights Gn NR26 . . . . . .138 C5
Knights Rd NR3 . . . . .158 B2
Knipe Cl 2 NR16 . . . . . . .105 F5
Knitting Needle La
  NR26 . . . . .138 E6
Knowland Gr NR5 . . . . . .161 C8
Knowland Gr Fst Sch
  NR5 . . . . .161 C8
Knowle Cres NR26 . . . . . .138 C5
Knowle Rd NR26 . . . . . . .138 C6
Knowles' La NR12 . . . . . . .38 C2
Knowsley Rd NR3 . . . . . .162 E8
Knox Ave NR1 . . . . .163 B8
Knox Cl NR1 . . . . .163 B8
Knox Rd NR1 . . . . .163 B7
Knudsen Cl 4 NR15 . . . . .107 C5
Knyvett Gn NR16 . . . . . . .105 F8
Koblenz Ave NR1 . . . . . .178 C1
Kooreman Ave PE13 . . . .152 D7
Krons The NR15 . . . . .107 C5

L

Laburnham Rd NR28 . . . .151 B4
Laburnum Ave
  2 Marham PE33 . . . . . . .63 B4
Taverham NR8 . . . . .155 B1
Laburnum Cl
  8 Great Yarmouth NR31 . .94 C7
  2 Horsford NR10 . . . . . . .53 A3
  5 Wisbech PE13 . . . . . . .152 E7
Laburnum Cres NR19 . . .154 C7
Laburnum Dr NR13 . . . . .165 F6
Laburnum Gr
Reepham NR10 . . . . .149 C6
Sheringham NR26 . . . . .138 D4
Thetford IP24 . . . . .176 B1
Laburnum Wlk IP27 . . . .175 E2
Lacey Cl 6 PE33 . . . . .61 D6
Lacey Rd NR8 . . . . .155 D1
Lackford Cl NR13 . . . . . .165 C4
Lacon Rd NR30 . . . . .168 E5
Ladbroke Rd NR13 . . . . .163 A7
Ladbrooke Cl 3 IP22 . . . .177 C4
Laddus Bank PE14 . . . . . .77 A6
Laddus Dro PE14 . . . . . . .77 B6
Ladislaw Way 1 NR19 . . .154 C3
Lady Ann's Rd NR23 . . . . . .5 B7
Lady Betty Rd NR1 . . . . .162 D3
Lady Dro PE38 . . . . .79 A6
Lady Hamilton La
  NR29 . . . . .167 C6
Lady Haven Mews 12
  NR31 . . . . .169 C5
Lady Haven Rd 8 NR31 . .169 B4
Lady Jane Grey Rd
  PE30 . . . . .146 F7
Lady La NR10 . . . . .53 E5
Lady Margaret's Ave
  NR31 . . . . .170 B4
Lady Mary Rd NR1 . . . . .162 D3
Lady's Dro 1 PE14 . . . . . .59 C2
Lady's La
Bressingham IP22 . . . . .119 F1
Wymondham NR18 . . . . . .173 A3
Ladywood Cl 9 PE33 . . . . .63 B4
Ladywood Rd PE33 . . . . . .63 B4
Lake Ave PE14 . . . . .95 C7
Lake Ct PE13 . . . . .152 D4
Lake Dro PE34 . . . . .61 C1
Lake View Cl NR9 . . . . . . .51 D5
Lake View Dr NR13 . . . . .165 B4
Lakeland 3 IP26 . . . . . . .114 A7
Lakeland Way 1 NR9 . . . .88 E8
Lakenfields NR1 . . . . .162 F2
Lakenham Fst Sch
  NR1 . . . . .162 E3
Lakenham Mid Sch
  NR1 . . . . .162 F3
Lakenham Rd NR4 . . . . . .162 C2
Lakenham Way NR1 . . . .162 E3
Lakenheath Airfield
  IP27 . . . . .114 B1
Lakenheath Prim Sch
  IP27 . . . . .113 E1
Lakenheath Sta IP27 . . . .113 F5
Lakes Ave NR14 . . . . .89 B3
Lamb La NR1 . . . . .31 C7
Lambert Cl 1 IP27 . . . . . .114 E1
Lambert Rd NR7 . . . . . . .159 A3
Lambert's La PE32 . . . . . .30 D1
Lamberts Cl 20 PE30 . . . .98 E1
Lammas NR15 . . . . .106 F6
Lammas The IP26 . . . . . .100 A4
Lamport Ct 3 PE30 . . . . .147 D6
Lamsey La PE31 . . . . .133 D3
Lancaster Ave NR21 . . . .141 C4
Lancaster Cl
Fakenham NR21 . . . . .141 C5
Methwold IP26 . . . . .99 A5
Norwich NR6 . . . . .158 D6
  7 Stalham NR12 . . . . . . .39 B4
Lancaster Cres PE38 . . . .172 C6
Lancaster Gdns NR15 . . .150 D5
Lancaster Pl 11 PE31 . . . .12 E5
Lancaster Rd
  4 Feltwell IP26 . . . . .98 E1
Great Yarmouth NR30 . . . .169 D3
King's Lynn PE30 . . . . .147 B4
Sculthorpe Airfield NR21 . . .15 C3
Lancaster Rise NR11 . . . . .22 F8
Lancaster Sq 13 NR30 . . .169 D3
Lancaster Way PE30 . . . . .14 F4
Lanchester Ct 7 NR2 . . . .162 B7
Landlow La NR9 . . . . .70 B1
Lane The Briston NR24 . . .142 D4
Carleton St Peter NR14 . . . .91 E5

Lane The continued
Little Barningham NR11 . . .20 C4
Winterton-on-Sea NR29 . . .58 B6
Lang Gate Way NR35 . .108 D2
Langham Ct
Fakenham NR21 . . . . .141 D4
Sheringham NR26 . . . . .138 C7
Langham Glass & Rural
  Crafts ✶ NR25 . . . . .7 A4
Langham Gn NR13 . . . . . .165 E4
Langham La NR25 . . . . .7 C3
Langham Pl NR1 . . . . . . .178 A1
Langham Rd
Binham NR21 . . . . .6 E2
Blakeney NR25 . . . . .7 C6
Field Dalling NR25 . . . . .7 A2
Morston NR25 . . . . .7 A6
Langham St PE30 . . . . .146 D2
Langhorn's La PE14 . . . . . .78 A7
Langland PE30 . . . . .147 D6
Langley Abbey NR14 . . . .92 A6
Langley Cl 6 NR4 . . . . . . .89 B8
Langley Gn NR14 . . . . . . .91 F6
Langley Prep Sch
  NR7 . . . . .163 D6
Langley Rd
Cantley NR13 . . . . .92 C6
Chedgrave NR14 . . . . .91 F3
King's Lynn PE30 . . . . .147 E8
Loddon NR14 . . . . .92 A2
Langley Sch NR14 . . . . . .91 F3
Langley St NR14 . . . . .92 A4
Langley Wlk NR2 . . . . . . .162 C7
Langmere Rd
Scole IP21 . . . . .130 F8
  1 Watton IP25 . . . . .84 C3
Langton Cl 5 NR5 . . . . . .161 B7
Lansdowne Cl 10 PE32 . . .45 C6
Lansdowne Rd NR6 . . . . .158 B6
Lansdowne St 4 PE30 . . .146 E6
Lantern La NR12 . . . . .24 B5
Lapwing Cl 3 NR31 . . . . .170 A6
Larch Cl
Attleborough NR17 . . . . . .174 C4
King's Lynn PE30 . . . . .148 D2
Norwich NR7 . . . . .159 D4
Larch Cres NR25 . . . . . . .137 C7
Larch Dr
  18 Great Yarmouth NR31 . .94 C7
  2 Great Yarmouth NR31 . .170 A5
Larch Gr NR20 . . . . .49 E7
Larch Rd PE34 . . . . .43 D4
Larch Cl IP27 . . . . .175 F3
Lark Rd 2 PE33 . . . . .61 D6
Lark Rise NR14 . . . . .89 A3
Lark Way NR1 . . . . .94 C7
Larkey's La NR12 . . . . . . .38 F7
Larkman Fst Sch NR5 . . .161 D7
Larkman La NR5 . . . . . . .161 C7
Larkman Mid Sch
  NR5 . . . . .161 D7
Larksfield PE13 . . . . .152 C3
Larkspur Cl PE38 . . . . . . .172 C3
Larkspur Ct 8 NR19 . . . .154 D2
Larner's Drift NR19 . . . . .154 D1
Larners Rd NR19 . . . . . . .154 D2
Larwood Cl 1 PE37 . . . . . .66 A4
Larwood Way 6 IP25 . . . .67 C2
Latchmoor La NR29 . . . . .56 D5
Latchmoor Pk NR29 . . . . .56 D5
Lathes The NR3 . . . . .178 A4
Latimer Rd NR1 . . . . .162 E1
Latimer Way PE37 . . . . . . .65 E1
Laud Cl 24 NR7 . . . . .72 C4
Laughing Image Cnr 6
  NR30 . . . . .169 C5
Launditch Cres PE38 . . . .172 C6
Laundry Cl 3 NR7 . . . . . .163 C8
Laundry La
Blofield NR13 . . . . .73 B6
Norwich NR7 . . . . .163 F7
Laundry Loke NR28 . . . . .151 B6
Laurel Dr
Brundall NR13 . . . . .165 B3
Great Yarmouth NR31 . . . . .94 C7
Laurel Gr 3 PE33 . . . . . . .43 E2
Laurel Rd NR15 . . . . .159 E1
Laurels Cres 1 NR29 . . . .56 C5
Laurels The NR31 . . . . . . .171 D5
Lavender Cl
Attleborough NR17 . . . . . .174 B5
Brandon IP27 . . . . .175 A2
Heacham PE31 . . . . .133 E5
Horsford NR10 . . . . .53 A4
Lavender Ct
  12 Hemsby NR29 . . . . . . .58 B6
  5 King's Lynn PE30 . . . . .147 B6
  1 Thetford IP24 . . . . . . .176 F4
Lavender Dr PE38 . . . . . .172 D6
Lavender Gr NR19 . . . . . .154 D2
Lavender Rd PE30 . . . . . .147 B6
Lavengro Rd NR3 . . . . . . .163 B8
Lawn Ave NR30 . . . . .169 C6
Lawn Cl 11 Horsford NR10 .53 B4
Knapton NR28 . . . . .143 B1
Lawn Cres 6 NR13 . . . . . .72 E6
Lawn's La
Belton with Browston
  NR31 . . . . .94 A5
Fleggburgh NR29 . . . . .57 B2
Lawns The
Fakenham NR21 . . . . .141 C4
Great Yarmouth NR30 . . . .169 C7
Wisbech PE13 . . . . .152 B6

Lawnswood Dr NR30 ..168 D6
Lawrence Cl
  Fakenham NR21 ....141 B5
  Harpley PE31 ....29 D4
Lawrence Pl NR20 ....50 D8
Lawrence Rd
  King's Lynn PE30 ....146 E7
  7 Thetford IP24 ....176 F5
Lawrence Way PE37 ..153 A5
Lawrence's La PE38 ....79 E1
Lawson Rd
  Croxton IP24 ....116 C5
  Norwich NR3 ....158 E1
Lawson Way NR26 ....138 F7
Laxfield Rd NR12 ....39 C3
Laxton Cl NR17 ....174 E4
Layer Cl
  5 Aylsham NR11 ....150 D6
  Norwich NR5 ....160 F7
Laylands Yd NR23 ....136 C6
Layton Cl NR8 ....157 F7
Le Neve Rd NR10 ....150 D1
Le Strange Ave PE30 ..146 E7
Le Strange Cl NR21 ..161 F5
Le Tunder Cl **2** NR7 ..163 E7
Lea Rd **2** NR29 ....56 C8
Lea The NR26 ....169 C6
Lea Way PE30 ....147 B8
Leach Cl
  Great Yarmouth NR31 ...170 A4
  Wisbech PE13 ....152 C2
Leach's Turn NR14 ..165 B1
Leafield Rd PE30 ....147 C3
Leafyoak La NR14 ....90 C3
Leamon Ct IP27 ......175 D4
Leaside PE31 ....133 B6
Leatherpool La NR25 ...7 E6
Leathway NR29 ......167 B2
Lebanon Dr PE13 ....152 F7
Lee Warner Ave NR21 ..141 D6
Lee Warner Rd **10** PE13 ..153 C3
Leeder Hill NR13 ....72 F2
Leeds Way **5** NR12 ..55 E4
Lees Yd NR25 ....137 B6
Leete Way PE33 ......43 E2
Leewood Cres NR5 ..157 C1
Lefevre Way NR31 ..94 C8
Lefroy Rd NR3 ....158 A2
Legge Pl **7** PE34 ....43 B1
Legge-Bourke Ct
  PE13 ....152 F6
Legrice Cres NR28 ..151 C3
Leicester Ave PE30 ..147 B5
Leicester Rd **1** NR31 ..170 D4
Leicester St NR2 ....162 C4
Leigh Cl NR17 ....174 C5
Leman Cl **8** NR14 ....92 A1
Leman Gr **9** NR14 ....91 F1
Leman Rd NR31 ......170 D2
Leng Cres NR4 ......161 E2
Lenthall Cl **18** NR7 ..72 D4
Leonard Cl **4** PE30 ..147 B6
Leonard Medler Way
  NR10 ....53 B8
Leonard's La IP26 ....98 D1
Leonards St **10** NR13 ..162 D8
Leopard Cl **3** NR3 ..178 B4
Leopold Cl **2** NR4 ....162 A3
Leopold Rd NR4 ....162 A3
Lerowe Rd PE13 ....152 E7
Les Baux Pl **5** PE13 ..152 E3
Lesley Wlk NR19 ....154 D2
Lestrange PE36 ......132 C4
Letheringsett La NR25 ..18 F7
Letherington's La NR12 ..55 D5
Letton Rd IP25 ......67 C2
Leven Cl **8** NR7 ......72 D5
Leverington Rd PE13 ..152 A6
Levers Cl PE30 ......147 D8
Leveson Rd NR7 ....159 B3
Levine Cl NR13 ......165 B4
Levishaw Cl NR10 ..36 E1
Lewis Cl Ashill IP25 ..84 A7
  Hopton IP22 ....127 F6
Lewis Dr Roydon IP22 ..177 A5
Wiggenhall St Germans
  PE34 ....61 A8
Lexham Rd
  Great Dunham PE32 ..47 E2
  King's Lynn PE30 ....147 E8
  Litcham PE32 ....47 F4
Lexington Cl NR29 ..167 A7
Ley's La IP25 ....51 C1
Leyland Cl IP24 ......176 D6
Leys Cl NR31 ....169 C1
Leys La
  Attleborough NR17 ..174 D2
  Old Buckenham NR17 ..104 B3
  Yaxley IP23 ....129 F1
Leziate Dro
  Grimston NR20 ....45 A8
  Leziate PE32 ....44 F6
Leziate Heath Nature
  Reserve* PE32 ....44 E6
Liberator Cl NR13 ..72 E8
Liberator Rd NR6 ..158 B6
Libra Ct NR7 ....159 C4
Lichfield Rd NR19 ..169 B3
Lichfield St NR21 ..141 B4
Licking's Dro PE13 ..152 A6
Lifeboat Plain **6** NR26 ..138 D7
Light La PE14 ....59 D6
Lighthouse Cl
  Happisburgh NR12 ....24 C5

Lighthouse Cl continued
  Hunstanton PE36 ......132 D7
Lighthouse La PE36 ..132 D6
Lilac Cl Brandon IP27 ..114 D4
  9 East Dereham NR19 ..154 D2
  20 Great Yarmouth NR31 ..94 C7
  4 Great Yarmouth NR31 ..170 A5
  1 Horsford NR10 ......53 A3
  Wisbech PE13 ....152 F7
Lilac Dr IP27 ....113 E1
Lilac Gr NR26 ......138 C6
Lilac Wood PE30 ....147 B8
Lilburne Ave NR3 ..158 D2
Lilian Cl NR6 ....158 B4
Lilian Rd NR10 ......54 A2
Lily Ave NR20 ......69 B8
Lily La NR34 ....111 A3
Lily Terr NR1 ....178 B1
Limassol Rd NR19 ..154 C2
Lime Ave Stradsett PE33 ..80 C8
  Wisbech PE13 ....152 C7
Lime Cl
  7 Harleston IP20 ....122 D1
  Marham PE33 ....63 A4
Lime Dr NR19 ....154 D2
Lime Gr Gayton PE32 ..45 C6
  Sheringham NR26 ....138 C4
  7 Thetford IP24 ......176 D4
Lime Kiln Cl
  5 Cley next the Sea NR25 ...7 E6
  6 Newton Flotman NR15 ..89 D1
Lime Kiln La
  2 Stoke Ferry PE33 ..81 A3
  Thetford IP24 ....176 D4
Lime Kiln Mews
  9 New Catton NR3 ..158 C1
  Norwich NR3 ....162 C8
Lime Kiln Rd
  Gayton PE32 ....45 C6
  Sparham NR9 ....50 F5
  West Dereham PE33 ..80 C5
Lime St PE12 ....41 C8
Lime Tree Ave
  Costessey NR8 ......156 F4
  Long Stratton NR15 ..106 C2
  Norwich NR7 ....163 C4
  Wymondham NR18 ..173 D6
Lime Tree Cl
  2 East Dereham NR19 ..154 E6
  9 Mattishall NR20 ..68 C8
  Wymondham NR18 ..173 D5
Lime Tree Cres NR19 ..66 C7
Lime Tree Rd
  North Walsham NR28 ..151 D5
  Norwich NR2 ....162 B3
Lime Tree Wlk IP25 ..84 D3
Lime Way NR31 ......170 B5
Limekiln La
  Houghton PE31 ......29 D6
  South End NR16 ....106 C1
Upper Sheringham
  NR26 ....138 A4
Limekiln Wlk **1** NR30 ..169 C4
Limes Ave PE14 ......59 A1
Limes Cl IP22 ....177 D1
Limes Rd **3** NR29 ..56 C8
Limes The IP25 ......84 A6
Limetree Cl **10** NR10 ..53 B3
Limetree Ct
  Great Yarmouth NR31 ..169 C2
  Taverham NR8 ......155 B2
Limmer Ave IP21 ....121 C1
Limmer Rd NR10 ....170 D4
Limpenhoe Rd
  Cantley NR13 ....92 C7
  Reedham NR13 ......92 A6
Linacre Ave NR7 ....159 C4
Linacre Cl NR7 ......159 C3
Linalls Dr NR8 ......156 C4
Lincoln Ave
  Great Yarmouth NR31 ..170 C3
  Hingham NR9 ....86 D5
Lincoln Cl **12** NR20 ..50 B3
Lincoln Ralphs Sports Hall
  NR1 ....178 C1
Lincoln Rd IP25 ......84 F3
Lincoln Sq N PE36 ..132 C5
Lincoln Sq S PE36 ..132 C5
Lincoln St
  Hunstanton PE36 ....132 D5
  Norwich NR2 ....162 B5
Lincoln Way IP24 ..176 B5
Linden Cl NR18 ......86 E3
Linden Dr **5** NR9 ....88 C7
Linden Gr Diss IP22 ..177 C6
  Sheringham NR26 ....138 D4
Linden Rd
  Clenchwarton PE34 ..145 E6
  Norwich NR5 ....157 C1
Linden Tree Gdns **15**
  NR31 ....94 C7
Lindford Dr NR4 ....89 C8
Lindley Cl NR6 ......158 E6
Lindley Rd **9** NR9 ..88 C7
Lindley St NR1 ......162 E3
Lindsay Rd NR7 ....159 C4
Linford PE34 ....145 D6
Linford Clapper La
  PE34 ....145 E6
Linford Est PE34 ..145 E5
Ling Cl **1** NR12 ......54 C7
Ling Comm Rd PE30 ..148 D6
Ling House Rd PE31 ..13 B1
Ling Rd IP22 ....177 B3
Ling Way NR31 ......54 C7
Lingheath Rd IP27 ..175 E3
Lings Cl **5** NR10 ....53 B3
Lings The NR6 ......86 D8

Lingwood Fst Sch NR13 ..73 F3
Lingwood Gdns **2** NR13 ..74 A3
Lingwood Jun Sch
  NR13 ....74 A3
Lingwood Rd
  Blofield NR13 ....73 E4
  Brundall NR13 ......165 F6
Lingwood Sta NR13 ..74 A3
Link The **2** IP24 ....176 D4
Links Ave
  Brundall NR13 ......165 C4
  Cromer NR27 ....139 D4
  Norwich NR6 ....157 F4
Links Cl
  Caister-on-Sea NR30 ..168 E4
  Norwich NR6 ....157 F5
  6 Thurlton NR14 ....92 F1
Links Cres NR26 ....138 C7
Links Rd
  Great Yarmouth NR31 ..171 D8
  Mundesley NR11 ....143 B6
  Sheringham NR26 ..138 C7
Links Way
  Sheringham NR27 ..10 A5
  4 Thurlton NR14 ....92 F1
Linmore Cres **3** IP25 ..84 E3
Linmore Ct IP25 ....84 C3
Linn Chilvers Dr PE31 ..133 B5
Linnet Cl **6** NR31 ..170 A6
Linnet Cres IP27 ..175 E3
Linnets The NR5 ..156 F1
Lintock Rd NR3 ....158 D3
Linton Cl NR7 ......159 B3
Linton Cres NR7 ..159 B4
Lion & Castle Yd NR1 ..178 B2
Lion La NR14 ....91 C3
Lion Rd
  Buxton with Lammas
    NR10 ....36 E1
  Palgrave IP22 ......177 C1
Lion Wood Rd NR1 ..163 B7
Lion's Mouth NR11 ..10 A3
Lisbon Rd NR19 ....154 C2
Lishman Rd NR7 ..159 E2
Lisle Rd NR5 ....160 F7
Lister Cl NR31 ......170 B1
Lister's Rd PE14 ....77 E5
Litcham Hall PE32 ..48 A4
Litcham High Sch PE32 ..48 A4
Litcham Prim Sch PE32 ..48 A5
Litcham Rd
  Beeston with Bittering
    PE32 ....48 D4
  Great Dunham PE32 ..47 F2
  Gressenhall NR20 ..49 C3
  Little Dunham PE32 ..65 F8
  Mileham PE32 ......48 C5
  Tittleshall PE32 ....48 A6
Litcham Village Mus*
  PE32 ....48 A4
Litchmere Rd NR13 ..109 D6
Litester Cl NR28 ....151 D4
Little Armes St NR2 ..162 A8
Little Barney La NR21 ..17 F3
Little Bethel St NR2 ..178 A2
Little Bittering Medieval
  Village of* NR19 ..48 F4
Little Carr Rd PE30 ..148 D5
Little Church St PE13 ..152 C5
Little Dowgate PE13 ..152 A7
Little Ellingham Rd
  NR17 ....86 A3
Little Fendike La PE14 ..77 E8
Little Hockham La
  IP24 ....102 E2
Little Holme Rd PE34 ..41 F6
Little John Rd NR4 ..162 C1
Little La
  1 Castle Acre PE32 ..46 F2
  Docking PE31 ......134 E4
  9 Horsford NR10 ....53 B3
  Roydon IP22 ....28 A1
  Stoke Ferry PE33 ..80 F3
Little London Rd
  North Walsham NR28 ..151 D8
  Northwold IP26 ....99 C7
Little London St NR2 ..178 B3
Little Man's Way PE33 ..81 A3
Little Melton Fst Sch
  NR9 ....160 C2
Little Melton Rd NR9 ..160 B1
Little Money Rd NR14 ..109 D8
Little Oulsham Dro
  IP26 ....98 B2
Little Plumstead CE Prim Sch
  NR13 ....165 A8
Little Scratby Cres
  NR29 ....167 C4
Little Snoring Prim Sch
  NR21 ....17 B3
Little Snoring Rd NR21 ..17 A5
Little Walsingham Cl
  PE30 ....148 C3
Littlebeck La NR15 ..108 B8
Littlefields NR19 ..154 D5
Littleport St PE30 ..146 E5
Littleport Terr **8** PE30 ..146 E5
Littlewoods La IP22 ..164 E5
Livingstone Rise NR11 ..22 F8
Livingstone St NR2 ..162 A7
Lizard The NR18 ..173 D3
Lloyd Ct NR25 ......137 E8
Lloyd Rd Norwich NR1 ..163 B7
  Taverham NR8 ......155 B2
Loanin The NR1 ....162 F3
Lobster La NR2 ......178 A3
Loch La IP25 ....84 D4
Lock Rd NR28 ......38 D6

Lock's La NR34 ......109 F1
Lockerbie Flats **18** NR26 ....138 D7
Lockhart Rd NR35 ..109 D3
Locksley Rd NR4 ..89 E8
Loddon Cl NR15 ....108 C2
Loddon Cnr NR15 ..108 C2
Loddon Fst Sch **18** NR14 ..92 A1
Loddon Mid Sch NR14 ..91 F1
Loddon Rd
  Ditchingham NR35 ..109 B2
  Gillingham NR34 ..110 C2
  Haddiscoe NR14 ..110 D8
  Heckingham NR14 ..92 D1
  Holverston NR14 ..91 A5
  Kirby Cane NR35 ..109 E4
  Norton Subcourse NR14 ..92 E1
  Toft Monks NR34 ..110 D7
  Trowse with Newton
    NR14 ....163 A1
  Yelverton NR14 ......90 E6
Lode Ave PE14 ......77 F5
Lode St IP27 ....175 C4
Lodge Breck NR8 ..157 A7
Lodge Cl NR25 ......137 B5
Lodge Dr IP22 ......120 B5
Lodge Farm Dr NR6 ..158 D6
Lodge Farm Mdws
  NR20 ....49 C4
Lodge Hill NR26 ..138 A3
Lodge La Norwich NR6 ..158 E6
  Riddlesworth IP22 ..127 D7
  Shelfanger IP22 ..120 B1
  18 Snettisham PE31 ..12 E4
Lodge La Fst Sch NR6 ..158 E6
Lodge Pl NR7 ......163 E6
Lodge Rd Catfield NR29 ..56 B8
  Feltwell IP26 ....98 F2
  Heacham PE31 ....133 C5
Lingwood & Burlingham
  NR13 ....74 A3
  St John, Ilketshall
    NR34 ....124 C6
  Tivetshall St Margaret
    NR15 ....121 C6
Lodge Way IP24 ....176 C7
Lodore Ave NR6 ....158 A6
Loggers La IP22 ..128 C5
Loke Rd PE30 ......146 E6
Loke The
  Belton with Browston
    NR31 ....93 F6
  Briston NR24 ......142 D4
  Brumstead NR12 ..24 A2
  Cringleford NR4 ..89 C8
  Cromer NR27 ....139 B6
  East Beckham NR11 ..9 D2
  Felmingham NR28 ..37 B8
  Filby NR29 ....75 E8
  Freethorpe NR13 ....92 E7
  2 Gresham NR11 ....9 E1
  Haddiscoe NR14 ..110 D8
  4 Hemsby NR29 ..58 B6
  Salhouse NR13 ......55 B2
  Strumpshaw NR13 ..73 F2
Loke Wiffens **2** NR9 ..88 D8
Lollards Rd
  1 Norwich NR1 ....163 A6
  Norwich NR1 ......178 C3
Lolly Moor Nature Reserve*
  NR19 ....67 E5
Lomond Rd NR17 ..174 C4
London La
  Mundford IP26 ......100 B4
  South Creake NR21 ..15 C5
London Rd
  Attleborough NR17 ..174 B3
  Brandon IP27 ......175 B3
  Downham Market PE38 ..172 C4
  East Dereham NR19 ..154 E4
  Elveden IP24 ......125 D4
  Harleston IP20 ....122 D1
  King's Lynn PE30 ..146 E4
  Snetterton NR16 ..103 D1
  Thetford IP24 ......176 B3
  Wymondham NR18 ..173 A4
London St
  Brancaster PE31 ......3 B7
  Norwich NR2 ......178 B3
  Swaffham PE37 ....153 C4
  Whissonsett NR20 ..31 C2
Londs The NR27 ....11 A3
Lone Barn Rd NR7 ..159 E4
Lonely Rd
  Pulham St Mary IP21 ..122 B6
  Scole IP21 ....121 C2
Long Barrow Dr NR28 ..151 D3
Long Beach Est NR29 ..167 C8
Long Comm La NR10 ..37 C4
Long Dale NR18 ....155 E2
Long Dro PE38 ......97 D2
Long John Hill NR1 ..162 E2
Long La
  Baconsthorpe NR25 ..20 A7
  Bawburgh NR9 ....160 B8
Burston & Shimpling
  IP22 ....120 E4
  Catfield NR29 ......56 D7
  Feltwell IP26 ......98 D1
  Flordon NR15 ....106 E8
  Great Yarmouth NR31 ..170 A4
  Hoveton NR12 ....164 F7
  Mulbarton NR14 ..89 B2
  Saxlingham Nethergate
    NR15 ....107 B8
  Southrepps NR11 ..22 B7
  Stoke Holy Cross NR14 ..89 F4
  Strumpshaw NR13 ..165 F2

Long La continued
  Swaffham PE37 ....153 E5
  Tharston & Hapton
    NR15 ....106 D6
  West Winch PE33 ..43 E2
  Winfarthing IP22 ..119 F7
Long Lots PE14 ......59 F3
Long Rd
  Barton Turf NR12 ..55 F7
  Poringland NR14 ..90 C5
  Saham Toney IP25 ..84 F8
  Terrington St Clement
    PE34 ....144 A8
  Thurlton NR14 ......93 A1
  Wymondham NR18 ..88 A1
Long Row Norwich NR3 ..158 D1
  Tibenham NR16 ..120 D6
Long St NR17 ......103 E6
Long Straton Mill*
  NR15 ....106 F3
Long Stratton High Sch
  NR15 ....106 E3
Long Stratton Ind Est
  NR15 ....106 D3
Long Stratton Leisure Ctr
  NR15 ....106 E4
Long Stratton Rd
  NR15 ....105 F4
Long's Cres NR13 ..72 D7
Longbow Cl **3** NR4 ..162 C1
Longbrooke Cl NR5 ..89 C4
Longdell Hills NR5 ..156 E2
Longdon Cl **4** PE12 ..41 B8
Longe Rd NR6 ......158 F6
Longfellow Rd NR30 ..168 D5
Longfield Cl **4** NR1 ..91 F1
Longfields PE37 ..153 C3
Longfields Rd NR7 ..72 D5
Longfulans La NR31 ..171 D3
Longham La NR20 ..49 B3
Longham Rd NR19 ..49 A2
Longhead La PE14 ..59 A6
Longlands Dr NR18 ..173 A6
Longmead **4** NR1 ..162 E2
Longmeadow NR13 ..165 B3
Longmeadow Cl IP25 ..85 A1
Longs Cl **4** NR15 ..89 C1
Longview **1** NR9 ..88 D8
Longview Cl **4** PE31 ..12 E4
Longwater La NR8 ..156 C3
Longwater Ret Pk
  NR5 ....156 A3
Lonsdale Cres NR9 ..86 B5
Lonsdale Rd NR13 ..72 E7
Lonsdale Terr PE13 ..152 C3
Loombe Cl **3** NR20 ..50 B3
Loop Rd NR11 ......11 D1
Lopham Rd NR16 ..118 D4
Lord Cres NR20 ....50 B5
Lord Rd IP22 ....177 E4
Lord Walsingham Ct **1**
  IP24 ....176 E5
Lord's La NR31 ......94 B7
Lords La PE31 ......133 D5
Lorraine Gdns NR3 ..158 E3
Losinga Cres NR3 ..158 B3
Losinga Rd PE30 ..146 E2
Lossiemouth Rd **6**
  IP31 ....126 B1
Lothian St NR2 ......162 C6
Lothingland Mid Sch
  NR32 ....171 A3
Louden Rd NR27 ..139 B7
Louie's La IP22 ....177 D5
Louis Cl NR6 ....158 D6
Louis Dahl Rd **3** NR31 ..94 A6
Louise Cl **15** NR30 ..169 D2
Lound Dam NR14 ..111 A3
Lound Rd
  Belton with Browston
    NR31 ....94 B4
  Norwich NR4 ......161 F5
Somerleyton, Ashby &
  Herringfleet NR32 ..111 F8
Lovat Cl IP20 ......122 E2
Love La Fransham NR19 ..66 D7
  Sporle with Palgrave
    PE32 ....65 C6
  Wisbech PE13 ......152 C4
Lovelace Rd NR4 ..161 E4
Lovell Gdns IP25 ..84 E3
Lovell Way PE34 ..144 B4
Lovells The **6** PE14 ..59 D2
Lovelstaithe NR1 ..178 C3
Lovers' La NR29 ..56 C4
Lovett Cl NR6 ......158 F6
Lovewell Rd NR31 ..170 C5
Low Bungay Rd NR14 ..92 A1
Low Comm
  Aslacton NR16 ....106 A2
  Bunwell NR16 ....105 E2
  Deopham NR18 ....86 A3
  Hellington NR14 ..91 B6
  Reedham NR13 ....93 A5
  South Lopham IP22 ..128 F7
  Swardeston NR14 ..89 B6
Low Comm La NR34 ..111 A5
Low Comm Rd
  South Lopham IP22 ..128 E7
  Thurton NR14 ......91 D3
Low Ditch Rd IP20 ..122 F4
Low Farm Rd NR13 ..75 A3
Low Hatter's Cl PE38 ..172 B3
Low La Hevingham NR10 ..53 B8
  Rocklands NR17 ....103 B6
  Terrington St Clement
    PE34 ....144 A5
Low Rd Alburgh IP20 ..122 F6

Low Rd continued
Bunwell NR16 ....105 E1
Denton IP20 ....123 B5
Dickleburgh & Rushall
　IP21 ....130 E5
Forncett NR16 ....106 B5
Freethorpe NR13 ......92 F7
Great & Little Plumstead
　NR13 ....72 E5
Grimston PE32 ....28 B1
Haddiscoe NR14 ....110 F7
Hedenham NR35 ....108 D4
Hellesdon NR6 ....157 C5
Hingham NR9 ....86 B4
Keswick NR4 ....89 C7
Kimberley NR9 ....87 D8
King's Lynn PE30 .....148 C1
Mautby NR29 ....75 E5
Mettingham NR35 .....109 D1
Narborough PE32 ......63 F7
North Tuddenham NR20 .68 E8
Norton Subcourse NR14 .92 E2
Pentney PE32 ....63 C8
Redenhall with Harleston
　IP20 ....122 F1
Repps with Bastwick
　NR29 ....57 A4
Rollesby NR29 ....57 D2
Roydon PE32 ....28 A1
St John, Ilketshall
　NR34 ....124 D6
St John's Fen End PE14 .60 B6
Scole IP21 ....130 C5
Shelton NR15 ....107 B1
Shropham NR17 ....103 B3
Skeyton Corner NR10 ..37 B6
South Walsham NR13 ..74 B8
Starston IP20 ....122 C3
Stoke Ferry PE33 ......80 F2
Stow Bardolph PE34 ...61 C2
Stow Bedon NR17 .....102 E5
Strumpshaw NR13 .....165 F1
Swaffham PE37 ....153 A5
Tasburgh NR15 ....106 E7
1 Thurlton NR14 .....92 F1
Thurlton NR14 ....93 B2
Tibenham NR16 ....120 B8
Walpole Cross Keys PE34 .42 A7
West Acre PE32 ....46 C2
West Caister NR30 ....168 A3
Wicklewood NR18 .....87 C3
Wiggenhall St Germans
　PE34 ....43 D3
Wimbotsham PE34 ....172 D8
Winterton-on-Sea NR29 .58 B6
Wisbech PE14 ....152 E1
Woodbastwick NR13 ...55 C1
Wortham IP22 ....129 A6
Wortwell IP20 ....123 A3
Low Side Dereham
　NR19 ....77 F6
Low St Hardingham NR9 .86 E8
Hoxne IP21 ....131 A4
Ketteringham NR18 ....88 D6
St Margaret, Ilketshall
　NR35 ....124 B4
Sloley NR12 ....37 E3
Smallburgh NR12 .....38 E3
Weasenham St Peter
　PE32 ....30 D2
Wicklewood NR18 .....87 A5
Low Wr La IP22 ......129 D5
Low's La IP22 ....177 D2
Lowe's La PE31 ....4 D4
Lower Clarence Rd
　NR1 ....178 C2
Lower Cliff Rd NR31 ...170 D4
Lower Drag Way IP22 .128 D8
Lower Espl NR31 ......170 D3
Lower Globe La NR13 ..165 E7
Lower Gn NR13 ....92 E8
Lower Goat La 2 NR2 ..178 A3
Lower Hall La NR24 ...18 D7
Lower Hardley Rd
　NR14 ....92 A2
Lower Kiln La NR15 ...90 F3
Lower Lincoln St
　PE36 ....132 C5
Lower Marine Par
　NR31 ....170 D3
Lower Oakley IP21 ...130 D4
Lower Rd
Holme Hale PE37 .....66 B3
Rockland St Mary NR14 .91 C7
Lower Rose La IP21 ..177 E2
Lower Spink's La NR8 .88 B4
Lower St Horning NR12 .55 E4
Salhouse NR13 ....55 A1
**Lower Wood Nature
Reserve★** NR16 ......105 E8
Lowes Ave NR25 ......137 D5
Lowes View IP22 ......177 E3
Lowestoft Rd NR31 ...170 C1
Lowfield PE30 ....147 C4
Lowick Cl 9 NR19 ....154 D3
Lowry Cl 3 NR31 .....170 A7
Lowry Cole Rd NR5 ...158 F5
Lowry Way PE38 .....172 E5
Lowther Rd NR4 .....162 B1
Loxwood NR6 ....157 E6
Lubbock Cl NR2 ......161 F5
Lucas Ct 2 NR7 ......72 D5
Lucas La PE31 ....135 E6
Lucas Rd 9 NR31 ....169 B4
Lucerne Cl NR6 ......158 F4
Lucerne Rd 9 NR31 ...94 C6
Lucombe Dr 9 PE13 ..152 F7
Luddenham Rd NR20 ..50 B2
Ludham Airstrip NR29 .56 D6

Ludham Fst Sch NR29 ..56 C5
Ludham Rd
Catfield NR29 ....56 C6
Potter Heigham NR29 ..56 F5
Ludkin Sq 8 NR30 ...169 C5
Lug's La NR35 ....109 B5
Lugger Yd NR23 .....136 D6
Luke Cl NR5 ....156 F2
Luscombe Way 6 NR13 .72 E7
Lusher Cl 1 NR26 ....138 C5
Lusher Rise NR5 .....161 D8
Lusher's Loke NR7 ...158 F4
Lushers Mdw 5 NR7 ...51 A4
Lushington Cl 9 NR5 .161 B8
Luxembourg Way
　NR19 ....154 C2
Lydgate Cl NR19 .....154 D3
Lyhart Rd NR4 ....162 B1
Lynch Gn 6 NR9 ......88 D8
Lyndford Rd NR12 .....39 B4
Lyndhurst Ct PE36 ...132 C5
Lynewood Cl NR27 ...139 D4
Lynewood Rd NR27 ...139 D4
Lynfield Rd NR28 ....151 C6
Lynford Rd IP26 .....100 B5
Lyng Hall La NR20 ....33 A7
Lyng Hall Rd NR20 ....33 A7
Lyng La IP22 ....118 F1
Lyng Prim Sch NR9 ...51 A4
Lyng Rd NR20 ....51 B5
Lyngate Cl 8 NR9 .....88 C7
Lyngate Rd NR28 ....151 B8
Lynn Cl 7 NR7 ....72 D5
Lynn Ct NR19 ....154 E4
Lynn Gr NR31 ....170 A6
Lynn Gr High Sch
　NR31 ....170 A6
Lynn La PE32 ....29 D1
Lynn Mus★ PE30 ....146 E5
Lynn Rd
Castle Rising PE30 ...148 F5
Clenchwarton PE34 ...144 E4
Dersingham PE31 .....140 C2
Downham Market PE38 .172 C6
East Rudham PE31 .....30 A7
Gayton PE32 ....45 C6
Grimston PE32 ....28 B1
Heacham PE31 ....133 E3
Ingoldisthorpe PE31 ..140 C7
King's Lynn PE30 .....147 A5
Littleport CB7 ....96 E1
Middleton PE32 ....44 D2
Roydon PE32 ....28 A1
Runcton Holme PE33 ..61 F4
Shouldham PE33 ......62 D3
Shouldham Thorpe PE33 .62 B2
Southery PE38 ....97 A6
Stow Bardolph PE34 ...79 E8
Stradsett PE33 ....80 C8
Swaffham PE37 ....153 A5
Terrington St Clement
　PE34 ....42 A6
Tilney St Lawrence PE34 .42 D2
Walpole Cross Keys PE34 .41 F6
Walsoken PE14 ....59 B6
Watlington PE33 ......61 E6
Weeting IP27 ....175 A4
Wereham PE33 ....80 D5
West Rudham PE31 ....29 F6
West Walton PE14 ....59 B4
West Winch PE33 .....61 F8
Wiggenhall St Mary Magdalen
　PE34 ....61 B6
Wisbech PE13 ....152 C6
Wretton PE33 ....80 F3
Lynn Rd Terr PE14 ....59 D8
Lynn St PE37 ....153 B4
Lynton Rd NR24 ......24 A7
Lynwood Terr 13 PE30 .146 E3
Lytton Rd NR8 ....156 D8

M
MacArthur Dr 3 NR19 .154 C6
MacDonald Rd NR27 ..139 A7
Mack's La NR8 ....156 D7
MacKenzie Cl 1 NR31 .170 B1
MacKenzie Rd IP24 ...176 A3
Mackintosh Rd NR13 ..72 E8
Macks Loke NR24 ....142 F2
Macmillan Way NR13 .165 A8
Mad Dog La PE32 ....29 C2
Madden Ave NR30 ...169 D8
Maddermarket Theatre★
　NR2 ....178 A3
Maden Cl NR18 ......173 B6
Magazine Cl PE13 ....152 A4
Magazine La PE13 ....152 A4
Magdalen Cl 3 NR3 ...162 E8
Magdalen Gates Fst Sch
　NR3 ....162 E8
Magdalen High Rd
　PE34 ....61 A6
Magdalen Rd
Norwich NR3 ....162 E8
Tilney St Lawrence PE34 .60 D8
Wiggenhall St Germans
　PE34 ....61 C7
Magdalen Sq NR31 ...170 A6
Magdalen St
Norwich NR3 ....178 B4
Thetford IP24 ....176 D4
Magdalen Way NR31 .170 B4
Magic City Leisure Ctr★
　NR1 ....178 C3
Magnay Rd NR8 .....157 C7
Magnolia Cl NR10 .....53 A4

Magnolia Gn 8 NR31 .170 B6
Magpie Ct 33 IP20 ...122 D2
Magpie Hill IP22 .....129 B5
Magpie La NR17 .....103 B7
Magpie Rd NR3 ......162 D8
Maid Marian Rd NR4 .162 C1
Maida Vale 3 NR2 ...162 B6
Maidens Cl 1 NR13 ...72 E4
Maids Cross Hill IP27 .113 F1
Maidstone Rd NR1 ...178 B3
Main Cross Rd NR30 .170 D8
Main Dereham Rd
　NR21 ....31 F4
Main Dr NR20 ....32 E4
Main Rd
Clenchwarton PE34 ...145 B5
Crimplesham PE33 ....80 B6
Filby NR29 ....76 A8
Fleggburgh NR13 .....166 F6
Holme next the Sea PE36 .2 C1
Lingwood & Burlingham
　NR13 ....74 A5
Methwold IP26 ....99 A7
Narborough PE32 .....63 E8
Ormesby St Michael NR29 .58 A1
Rollesby NR29 ....57 D2
Swardeston NR14 .....89 C5
Tilney All Saints PE34 ..42 A4
Upwell PE14 ....77 E3
Walpole Highway PE14 ..59 E8
Weeting IP27 ....175 B7
West Caister NR30 ....168 A6
West Winch PE33 .....61 F8
Wisbech PE14 ....77 A7
Main St
Hockwold cum Wilton
　IP26 ....113 F7
Honing NR28 ....38 D5
Welney PE14 ....95 D4
Maine St
4 Thetford IP24 .....116 A1
Thetford IP24 ....176 A4
Malakoff Cl 9 NR30 ..169 D2
Malakoff Rd 4 NR30 ..169 D2
Malborough Gn Cres
　NR29 ....57 D4
Malbrook Rd NR5 ....161 B1
Maldon Rd PE13 ....152 E5
Malin Ct 7 NR30 ....168 C6
Mallard Cl
Brundall NR13 ....165 E2
Chedgrave NR14 ......91 D7
9 Loddon NR14 .....92 A2
4 Salhouse NR13 ....55 A1
1 Snettisham PE31 ..12 E5
Mallard Rd 10 IP25 ..84 C3
Mallard Way
Brandon IP27 ....175 E2
Great Yarmouth NR31 .170 A6
Hickling NR12 ....39 F1
Mallory Rd NR6 .....158 D6
Mallow Cl 1 NR17 ...174 B4
Mallow Rd 10 IP24 ..176 F5
Mallow Way NR13 ...173 D4
Malsters Cl IP26 ....100 B5
Malt Dr PE13 ....152 B3
Malt's La IP26 ......113 F7
Malthouse Cl 9 IP25 ..84 D2
Malthouse Cres PE31 .133 D5
Malthouse Ct
East Dereham NR20 ..154 E5
24 Redenhall with Harleston
　IP20 ....122 D2
8 Snettisham PE31 ...12 E5
Thornham PE36 ....2 D6
Malthouse La
Cantley NR13 ....92 B6
Gissing IP22 ....120 F4
Great Yarmouth NR31 .170 C8
Guist NR20 ....32 F4
Ludham NR29 ....56 D5
Malthouse Pl NR23 ..136 D6
Malthouse Rd
4 Hethersett NR9 ....88 C7
Norwich NR2 ....178 A2
Malthouse Yd NR10 ..149 C4
Malting Row IP31 ....126 D1
Maltings Cl IP22 .....177 F3
Maltings Dr 6 IP20 ..122 D2
Maltings La 4 PE38 ..172 A5
Maltings Way NR16 ..119 B6
Maltmas Dro PE14 ...77 A7
Malvern Cl PE30 ....148 A3
Malvern Rd 8 NR1 ...163 A6
Manby Rd
Downham Market PE38 .172 B3
Great Yarmouth NR30 .169 D4
Norwich NR7 ....159 C1
Manchester Pl 3 NR2 .162 C5
Mancroft Wlk 11 NR2 .162 C7
Mandela Cl 3 NR3 ...178 A4
Mandells Ct NR3 ....178 B3
Mangate St PE37 ....153 C5
Mangreen NR14 ......89 D6
Mangreen La NR14 ..89 C5
Mann's La NR20 .....50 B4
Manning's La IP22 ...128 B1
Mannington Hall★
　NR11 ....20 C3
Mannington Pl PE30 ..148 E1
Manor Chase NR8 ...156 E8
Manor Cl
3 Aylsham NR11 .....150 D6
1 Great Yarmouth NR31 .170 C7
Hockering NR20 ......69 B8
Horsham St Faith &
　Newton St Faith NR10 .53 D2

Manor Cl continued
Ingoldisthorpe PE31 ..140 D8
Lamas NR10 ....36 C1
4 Little Snoring NR21 ..17 B3
Tunstead NR12 ....37 F1
Manor Ct
Aylsham NR11 ....150 C6
North Walsham NR28 .151 E5
Manor Dr Litcham PE32 ..48 A4
Roydon IP22 ....177 A3
Terrington St John PE14 .42 B1
Manor Farm Cl NR8 ..157 A8
Manor Farm Rd
Denton IP20 ....122 F8
St John, Ilketshall
　NR34 ....124 D7
Somerton NR29 ......58 A6
Manor Field Fst Sch
　NR15 ....106 E3
Manor Gdns Diss IP22 .177 D5
Hopton on Sea NR31 .171 E4
3 Lingwood NR13 ...74 A3
Wisbech PE13 ....152 A4
Manor House Cl
Brandon IP27 ....175 B3
Mautby NR29 ....75 E6
Manor La NR11 ......12 E5
Manor Pk Gdns 18
　NR15 ....106 E3
Manor Rd
Brandon IP27 ....175 A3
Caister-on-Sea NR30 ..168 F5
Cantley NR13 ....92 B8
Dersingham PE31 .....140 D2
Great Yarmouth NR31 .170 C7
Griston IP25 ....85 A2
Heacham PE31 ....133 D8
Hilgay PE38 ....79 D1
Hopton on Sea NR31 .171 D4
Horsham St Faith &
　Newton St Faith NR10 .53 D3
Hunstanton PE36 ....132 C5
King's Lynn PE30 ....148 C5
Long Stratton NR15 ..106 E3
Mundesley NR11 .....143 C6
Newton St Faith NR10 ..53 D4
North Walsham NR28 .151 E5
Roydon IP22 ....177 A5
Scarning NR19 ....154 A3
Stoke Ferry PE33 .....80 F2
Terrington St Clement
　PE34 ....144 B5
Manor Ridge NR13 ..165 E6
Manor Way
Ormesby St Margaret
　NR29 ....167 A2
Swaffham PE37 ....153 C5
Manor Wlk NR29 .....57 D4
Manorfield Cl 1 NR29 .167 A2
Manorside PE31 .....140 D2
Manse Ct IP24 ......176 D4
Mansel Dr NR31 .....158 E3
Mansell Cl 2 IP22 ....177 A5
Mansell Rd PE13 ....152 D3
Mansfield La 1 NR1 ..162 E1
Manthorpe Cl 5 NR1 .162 E1
Mantle Cl NR7 ......159 D4
Maple Ave PE13 .....152 C7
Maple Cl 10 Beetley NR20 .49 D4
10 Beetley NR20 .....49 D4
5 Gayton PE32 ......45 C6
20 Martham NR29 ....57 D4
Wymondham NR18 ...173 D6
Yaxley IP23 ....129 F1
Maple Dr
King's Lynn PE30 ....148 D3
Norwich NR2 ....161 F7
Sculthorpe Airfield NR21 .15 C3
Taverham NR8 ....155 B1
Maple Gdns 17 NR31 ..94 C7
Maple Rd
Downham Market PE38 .172 B6
King's Lynn PE30 ....148 D3
Maple Way 7 Eye IP23 .130 C1
Great Yarmouth NR31 .170 B6
Mapplebeck Cl NR30 .147 E4
Marauder Rd NR6 ...158 D6
March La PE14 ......59 E8
March Rd Elm PE14 ..77 A7
Welney PE14 ....95 C5
March Riverside PE14 .77 B4
Mardle Rd NR34 ....110 D5
Mardle St NR5 ......160 F5
Mardling Run NR13 ..166 D3
Marea Mdws PE31 ...133 C5
Margaret Cl
3 East Dereham NR19 .154 D1
Norwich NR6 ....157 D1
Margaret Cres NR7 ...163 F7
Margaret English Cl
　NR26 ....138 C5
Margaret Lilly Way 1
　NR11 ....21 A5
Margaret Paston Ave
　NR3 ....158 A2
Margaret Rd NR5 ....157 B7
Margaret Reeve Cl 6
　NR18 ....173 D5
Margaret Rose Cl
　PE30 ....147 E4
Margarets Cl PE34 ...132 D2
Margaretta Cl PE34 ..145 F5
Margetson Ave NR7 ..163 C7
Marguerite Cl 11 NR4 .94 C6
Marham Airfield PE33 .63 C3
Marham Airfield Fst Sch
　PE33 ....63 B4
Marham Cl PE34 ....146 B5

Low - Mar　199

Marham Mid Sch PE33 .63 B5
Marham Rd PE33 ....62 B2
Marie Cl PE33 ....92 B6
Marigold Cl 6 NR10 ..53 A3
Marina Leisure Ctr★
　NR30 ....169 E3
Marina Rd NR11 ....143 C6
Marine Cl NR31 .....170 D1
Marine Cres
Great Yarmouth NR30 .169 E6
5 Hemsby NR29 .....58 E6
Marine Dr NR30 ....168 E8
Marine Par NR31 ...170 D2
Mariner's Cl NR31 ...171 D8
Mariner's Compass
　NR31 ....171 C8
Mariners La NR1 ....178 B1
Mariners Pk Cl NR31 .171 C5
Mariners' Rd NR30 ..169 D2
Mariners Way PE30 ..146 F8
Marion Cl NR18 .....173 C5
Marion Rd NR1 ......163 A6
Marion Wlk 1 NR19 .154 C4
Marionville Rd NR3 ..158 E4
Maritime Mus for E Anglia★
　NR30 ....169 E3
Marjoram Cl NR18 ...151 E4
Marjoram Rd 24 NR31 ..94 C6
Mark La PE27 ....115 C6
Mark Lemmon Cl 2 NR4 .89 C8
Mark's Cl La NR9 ....52 A7
Market Ave NR1 .....178 B3
Market Gates 8 NR30 .169 D4
Market Hill
Brandon IP27 ....175 C3
Colkirk NR21 ....31 D5
Diss IP22 ....177 D4
Market La
Blundeston NR32 ....171 D1
Brancaster PE31 ......3 B6
Burston & Shimpling
　IP22 ....120 E1
Crimplesham PE33 ....80 A6
Filby NR29 ....76 B7
Great Melton NR9 .....70 C1
Great Moulton NR15 ..106 C1
King's Lynn PE30 .....146 D5
Little Melton NR9 .....160 A2
Salthouse NR25 ......8 B6
Shotesham NR15 .....107 E8
Somerleyton, Ashby &
　Herringfleet NR32 ...94 A1
Terrington St Clement
　PE34 ....42 B6
Walpole Cross Keys PE34 .41 F5
Wells-next-the-Sea
　NR23 ....136 D4
Market Manor NR13 ..166 C3
Market Mews PE13 ..152 C5
Market Pl
Aylsham NR11 ....150 C6
Burnham Westgate
　PE31 ....135 C3
Diss IP22 ....177 D4
Downham Market PE38 .172 C6
2 East Dereham NR19 .154 D5
Fakenham NR21 ......141 B4
Great Yarmouth NR30 .169 C4
22 Harleston IP20 ....122 D2
Holt NR25 ....137 B6
4 Loddon NR14 .....92 A1
North Walsham NR28 .151 C5
Reepham NR10 ......149 B4
Swaffham PE13 ......153 C4
1 Thetford IP24 .....176 D4
14 Winterton-on-Sea NR39 .58 B6
Wisbech PE13 ....152 C5
1 Wymondham NR18 .173 C4
Market Rd
Burgh Castle NR31 ....94 B8
Potter Heigham NR29 .56 E6
Market Rd Pl 27 NR30 .169 D4
Market Row 16 NR30 .169 C4
Market St
East Harling NR16 ...118 C5
15 King's Lynn PE30 ..146 E5
North Walsham NR28 .151 C5
Shipdham IP25 ....67 C2
Tunstead NR12 ....37 F1
18 Wisbech PE13 ....152 C5
Wymondham NR18 ...173 C4
Market Weston Rd
　IP22 ....127 E3
Marketfield La NR10 .53 C2
Markshall Farm Rd
　NR14 ....89 E7
Markshall La NR14 ..89 F7
Marl Hill Rd NR9 ....51 F3
Marl Pit La NR5 .....161 C8
Marland Rd 4 NR8 ..155 D2
Marlborough Ct PE13 .152 A4
Marlborough Rd NR3 .162 E8
Marlborough Sq NR30 .169 E4
Marlborough Terr
　NR30 ....169 E4
Marle Cl NR31 ......170 C6
Marle Pit Cl NR16 ...119 C8
Marlinge Pl NR26 ...138 F5
Marlingford Rd
Easton NR9 ....160 A7
Marlingford NR9 ......70 B5
Marlingford Sports Club
　NR9 ....70 B4
Marlingford Way NR9 .70 B5
Marlow Cl NR3 ......158 E3

Marlpit La NR15 ......**106** F6
Marlpit Rd
Hempstead NR25 ....**19** E7
Thompson IP24 ......**102** A7
Marram Dr NR30 ....**168** E8
Marram Way PE31 ....**133** B6
Marrams Ave NR27 ..**139** E4
Marriot Cl NR2 ......**162** C7
Marriott Chase NR8 ..**155** E1
Marriott Way NR24 ..**142** A5
Marriotts Way ❸ NR26 .**138** D7
Marryat Rd NR7 .....**159** C1
Marryats Loke ❸ NR25 ..**7** A4
Marsh Cl ❼ NR29 ....**57** D5
Marsh La Aldeby NR34 .**111** A6
Bracon Ash NR14 ......**89** A2
Burgh Castle NR31 ....**94** A8
Carlton Colville NR33 ..**111** F2
❸ Earsham NR35 ...**123** F8
King's Lynn PE30 .....**148** A1
❺ New Buckenham NR16 .**104** F1
North Cove NR34 ....**111** B1
Somerleyton, Ashby &
Herringfleet NR32 ....**111** C8
Tharston & Hapton
NR15 ....**106** C8
Wells-next-the-Sea
NR23 ....**136** D5
Wiveton NR25 ....**7** E6
Worlingham NR34 ....**110** F1
Wortham IP22 ......**129** D4
Marsh Loke NR28 ....**23** D1
Marsh Rd Cantley NR13 ..**92** D6
Fleggburgh NR29 .....**75** C8
Fritton & St Olaves NR31 .**93** E3
Great Yarmouth NR31 ..**169** B3
Halvergate NR13 .....**75** A1
North Wootton PE30 ..**148** A4
Outwell PE14 ....**77** F8
Potter Heigham NR29 ..**57** A6
Repps with Bastwick
NR29 ....**56** F4
South Walsham NR13 ..**74** B8
Thurne NR29 ....**56** E3
Upton with Fishley NR13 .**166** B8
Walpole PE14 ....**41** C4
Wroxham/Hoveton
NR12 ....**164** D5
Marsh Side PE31 ......**3** B7
Marsh The PE14 ......**41** C4
Marsh Wlk PE13 ....**152** D5
Marshall Cl
Norwich NR5 ....**161** B8
❸ Spixworth NR10 ....**54** A2
Marshall Rd NR3 ....**158** B3
Marshall St ❺ PE30 ..**146** E5
Marsham Prim Sch
NR10 ....**150** C1
Marshgate NR28 ....**151** E6
Marshland High Sch
PE14 ....**59** B8
Marshland Smeeth & Fen
Mus ★ PE14 ....**60** C6
Marshland St PE34 ...**144** B5
Marshland St James VC Prim
Sch PE14 ....**60** A4
Marston La ❿ NR4 ....**89** C8
Marston Moor ❼ NR7 ..**72** D4
Martham Broad National
Nature Resrve ★ NR29 .**57** D7
Martham Fst Sch NR29 .**57** D5
Martham Rd
Martham NR29 ....**57** F4
Rollesby NR29 ......**57** D3
Somerton NR29 .....**57** E6
Martin Cl Brandon IP27 .**175** E3
❺ Great Yarmouth NR31 .**94** C7
Norwich NR7 ....**159** B4
❸ Weybourne NR25 ....**8** F5
Martin Rd Diss IP22 ...**177** E4
Harleston IP20 .....**122** E2
Martineau La NR1 ....**162** F1
Marvell Gn ❿ NR7 ....**72** D5
Marwood Cl NR18 ....**173** B3
Mary Chapman Cl ❸❶
NR7 ....**72** D4
Mary Chapman Ct
NR3 ....**178** A3
Maryland NR23 ......**136** D5
Masefield Dr PE38 ...**172** D5
Masefield Mews NR14 .**154** C7
Masefield Rd IP22 ...**177** E4
Masefield Wlk ❽ IP24 .**176** E6
Mashs Row NR11 ....**150** D8
Mason Gdns ❶❶ PE33 ..**43** F2
Mason Rd Norwich NR6 .**158** B3
❺ Swanton Morley NR20 .**50** B3
Masons Dr PE37 .....**65** F4
Masquers Cl NR31 ...**170** C2
Massey Ct ❷ NR21 ...**141** C4
Massingham Rd
Castle Acre PE32 .....**46** F2
Grimston PE32 ......**28** C1
Norwich NR3 ....**158** E1
Weasenham All Saints
PE32 ....**30** B1
Mast Cl ❶❸ NR33 ....**111** F1
Masters Ct NR28 ....**151** D5
Mather La IP20 ......**122** B1
Matlock Rd ❶ NR1 ...**163** B5
Matsell Way NR19 ...**154** E5
Matthews Cl ❹ NR15 ..**106** F6
Mattishall La
Hockering NR20 ....**69** A7

Mattishall La continued
Mattishall NR20 ......**68** F7
Mattishall Prim Sch
NR20 ....**68** F5
Mattishall Rd
Dereham NR20 ....**68** B8
East Tuddenham NR20 ..**69** B6
Garvestone NR9 ......**68** D2
Honingham NR9 ......**69** D6
Runhall NR9 ....**69** A3
Maud St NR2 ......**162** B6
Maud Terr NR30 ....**169** D6
Maurice Gaymer Rd
NR17 ....**174** D3
Mautby La NR29 .....**75** F6
Mavish Cl NR5 ......**161** A6
Max Carter Cl NR28 ..**38** A4
May Cl NR18 ....**173** B5
Maybank NR28 .....**151** D7
Mayes Cl ❼ NR5 ....**161** B8
Mayfield Ave NR28 ..**158** B4
Mayfield Dr NR27 ...**139** B5
Mayfield Way NR28 ..**151** D7
Mayflower Ave PE30 .**146** F7
Mayflower Rd ❶ PE13 .**152** E3
Mayflower Way ❶❹ IP20 .**122** D1
Maygrove Rd ❺ NR30 ..**169** D5
Mayton Ave NR12 ...**54** A4
Mdws The ❷ PE31 ...**12** D4
Mead Cl NR10 ......**36** E1
Meadon Way PE34 ...**146** B4
Meadow Brown Way ❾
NR18 ....**173** E4
Meadow Cl
❷ Beetley NR20 .....**49** C3
Cromer NR27 ....**139** A6
❸ Hemsby NR29 .....**167** A8
Hethersett NR9 ......**88** C7
Holt NR25 ....**137** D6
❸ King's Lynn PE30 ..**148** C5
Mundesley NR11 ....**143** C5
Narborough PE32 ....**63** E7
❷ Norwich NR14 ....**163** B2
Shipdham IP25 ......**67** D2
❺ Thurlton NR14 ....**92** F1
Meadow Cotts PE32 ..**48** B6
Meadow Ct
Fakenham NR21 .....**141** E4
Great Yarmouth NR31 .**171** C8
Meadow Dr
❶ Beetley NR19 .....**49** C3
❻ East Dereham NR19 .**154** C4
❶ Gressenhall NR20 ..**49** C3
Lackenheath IP27 ....**113** E2
Mundesley NR11 ....**143** C5
Wroxham/Hoveton
NR12 ....**164** D4
Meadow Farm Dr NR4 .**89** B4
Meadow Farm La NR10 .**53** E2
Meadow Gdns NR6 ...**158** A4
Meadow Gr
North Runcton PE33 ...**44** A2
❷❻ Watton IP25 ....**84** D3
Meadow La
Briston NR24 ....**142** B5
Carbrooke IP25 .....**85** A5
Kelling NR25 ....**8** C5
Norwich NR7 ....**163** F6
❺ Rollesby NR29 ....**57** D2
Meadow Loke ❷ NR20 .**50** E7
Meadow Patch NR28 .**151** C6
Meadow Rd
Bungay NR35 ....**124** B8
Cromer NR27 ....**139** B6
Heacham NR12 .....**133** D5
King's Lynn PE30 ....**148** C2
Narborough PE32 ....**63** E7
Norwich NR5 ....**157** A2
Meadow Rise NR29 ..**167** A8
Meadow Rise Ave
NR2 ....**162** A4
Meadow Rise Cl NR2 ..**162** A4
Meadow Rise Rd NR2 ..**162** A4
Meadow Vale NR5 ...**157** A3
Meadow View NR13 ..**165** D4
Meadow View Terr
NR11 ....**150** B5
Meadow Way
Attleborough NR17 ...**174** C3
East Carleton NR14 ...**88** D5
Horsford NR10 ......**53** B3
Norwich NR6 ....**157** F5
Poringland NR14 ....**90** C4
Sheringham NR26 ...**138** B6
Meadowbrook Cl ❺
NR1 ....**162** F3
Meadowcroft NR29 ..**168** C8
Meadowgate La PE14 .**152** E2
Meadowgate Sch
PE13 ....**152** E3
Meadowland Dr ❶❼ NR16 .**94** C6
Meadowrise NR21 ...**15** E4
Meadows The
Aylsham NR11 ......**150** C7
❻ Hingham NR9 .....**86** C4
South Wootton PE30 ..**148** B2
Thetford IP24 ......**176** A4
Thurton NR14 ......**91** D4
Meadowside IP22 ...**128** B6
Meadowsweet ❶❸ NR10 .**53** A3
Meadowsweet Dr
NR26 ....**138** B6
Meadowsweet Rd ❷
NR18 ....**173** E4
Meadowvale Gdns
PE30 ....**147** B7
Meadway ❶❸ NR4 ....**89** B8

Mear Gdns NR1 ....**163** B6
Mears Cnr NR16 ....**105** B5
Medeswell ❷ NR29 ..**167** B7
Medeswell Cl NR13 ..**165** C5
Medway Cl PE13 ....**152** E4
Meer Dyke La PE14 ...**59** D5
Meeting Hill Rd NR28 .**38** A7
Meeting House Hill Rd
NR28 ....**38** B6
Melbourne Rd
North Walsham NR28 ..**151** D6
❹ Sheringham NR26 ..**138** D7
Melford Bride Rd
IP24 ....**176** A4
Melford Cl PE30 ....**148** E1
Melford Comm ❹ IP24 .**176** D4
Melford Ct ❸ IP24 ..**176** D4
Mellis Rd
Thrandeston IP21 ....**129** F2
Wortham IP22 ......**129** C3
Yaxley IP23 ....**130** A1
Mellisash Rd IP23 ...**129** D1
Melrose Dr NR11 ....**10** A2
Melrose Rd NR4 .....**162** A3
Melrose Terr ❽ NR30 .**169** D2
Melton Cl NR8 ......**173** B6
Melton Constable Hall ★
NR24 ....**18** D2
Melton Ct NR9 ......**88** C8
Melton Dr
Hunstanton PE36 ....**132** C3
Taverham NR8 ......**155** C1
Melton Gate NR18 ...**173** B5
Melton Rd
Hindolveston NR20 ...**33** D8
Wymondham NR18 ..**173** B5
Melton St NR24 .....**142** A5
Melville Rd IP24 ....**116** C5
Memorial Way
Thorpe St Andrew NR7 .**72** E4
Watton IP25 ....**84** D4
Mendham Cl
❸❻ Harleston IP20 ..**122** D2
❸ Norwich NR1 .....**162** E2
Mendham La
❸❽ Harleston IP20 ..**122** D2
St Mary, South Elmham
otherwise Homersfield
IP20 ....**123** B3
Mendham Prim Sch
IP20 ....**123** A2
Mercedes Ave PE36 ..**132** D2
Merchant Way NR6 ..**158** A4
Merchants Ct NR27 ..**139** C7
Mere Cl IP25 ....**84** C4
Mere Manor Ct IP22 .**177** D4
Mere Plot Dro PE33 ..**62** E5
Mere Rd Scoulton NR9 .**85** E4
Stow Bedon NR17 ...**102** E7
Litcham PE32 ......**48** A4
Mere St IP22 ......**177** D4
Meredith Rd NR6 ...**157** E6
Mereside NR15 .....**90** F2
Mergate La NR14 ...**89** A2
Meridian Way NR7 ..**72** E3
Merlewood IP21 ....**121** C1
Merlin Ave NR7 ....**159** B4
Merlin Cl NR12 ....**164** D5
Merlin Mews NR7 ...**159** C4
Merriman Rd ❺ NR29 .**57** C4
Merrivale Model Village ★
NR30 ....**169** E2
Merrow Gdns ❼ NR4 ..**89** C8
Merryweather Cl ❸
NR15 ....**106** E3
Merryweather Rd ❾
PE13 ....**153** C3
Merton Ave NR31 ...**170** A3
Merton Rd
Norwich NR2 ....**162** A7
Watton IP25 ....**84** D2
Metcalf Ave NR3 ....**146** D2
Metcalf Cl ❹ NR3 ...**157** F1
Meteor Cl NR6 .....**158** D7
Methuen Ave PE30 ..**147** A6
Methwold High Sch
IP26 ....**99** A6
Methwold Prim Sch
IP26 ....**99** A5
Methwold Rd
Methwold IP26 .....**98** E5
Northwold IP26 .....**99** C7
Metton Rd
Felbrigg NR11 ......**139** A2
Roughton NR11 .....**21** D8
Mews Ct ❼ IP25 ....**67** C2
Mews The
Great Yarmouth NR31 .**170** C1
❹ Norwich NR2 .....**162** C4
Micawber Ave ❷ NR30 .**170** D8
Michaels Ct NR19 ...**154** C5
Mid Norfolk Rly ★
NR19 ....**154** E5
Mid Yare National Nature
Reserve ★ NR13 ....**165** D1
Midden Sta The NR23 .**136** F4
Middle Dro Denver PE38 .**79** B4
Marshland St James PE14 .**60** C2
Stow Bardolph PE14 ..**78** D8
Middle Gates Dro PE14 .**60** B8
Middle Hill
Alby with Thwaite NR11 ..**21** A5
Reedham NR13 .....**92** F4
Middle La NR34 ....**111** D4
Middle Mkt Rd NR30 .**169** D4
Middle Rd
Blo' Norton IP22 ....**128** C6
Docking PE31 ......**134** D4
Earsham IP20 ......**123** C8

Middle Rd continued
Great & Little Plumstead
NR13 ....**72** F5
Hardingham NR9 ....**86** E8
Morning Thorpe NR15 .**107** B3
Shouldham Thorpe PE33 .**62** C2
Terrington St Clement
PE34 ....**42** B8
Middle Rd E ❹ NR30 ..**169** D1
Middle Rd W ❸ NR30 .**169** D1
Middle St NR11 ....**11** E1
Middle Wall NR29 ...**57** A6
Middlebrook Way
Cromer NR27 ....**139** A6
Runton NR27 ....**10** C4
Middlegate NR30 ...**169** D2
Middlemarch Rd ❺
NR19 ....**154** D3
Middlesex La NR13 ..**166** C3
Middlestone Cl NR31 .**170** C4
Middleton Ave NR20 .**50** B4
Middleton Cl
Norwich NR3 ....**158** C3
❷ Sheringham NR26 ..**138** C5
Middleton Cres NR5 ..**156** E2
Middleton Ct ❹ NR18 .**173** B4
Middleton Gdns NR31 .**170** C4
Middleton Prim Sch
PE32 ....**44** C2
Middleton Rd NR31 ..**170** C4
Middleton St NR18 ..**173** B4
Middleton's Cl NR6 ..**157** E4
Middleton's La NR6 ..**157** F5
Middlewood ❷ PE30 .**147** C4
Midland Cl
Caister-on-Sea NR30 ..**168** F5
❶ Great Yarmouth NR30 .**169** D5
Midland Rd NR28 ...**151** C4
Midland St NR2 ....**162** C7
Midland Wlk NR2 ...**162** C7
Mikanda Cl PE14 ...**152** C2
Mildenhall Rd CB7 ...**112** B3
Mildred Rd NR1 ....**162** E2
Mile Cross La NR6 ...**158** C4
Mile Cross Mid Sch
NR3 ....**158** B1
Mile Cross Rd NR3 ...**162** B8
Mile End IP27 ......**175** A1
Mile End Cl NR4 ....**162** A3
Mile End Rd
Littleport CB7 ......**112** A3
Norwich NR4 ....**162** A3
Mile Rd
Carleton Rode NR16 ..**105** A5
Garvestone NR9 .....**68** A1
Mileham Prim Sch
PE32 ....**48** D6
Mileham Rd
Beeston with Bittering
PE32 ....**48** C3
Litcham PE32 ......**48** A4
Milestone Cl NR5 ...**156** F2
Milestone La NR18 ..**87** A4
Milford Rd ❺ NR2 ..**162** B5
Mill Bank PE14 .....**59** F7
Mill Cl Aylsham NR11 ..**150** A6
❷ Blofield Heath NR13 .**73** D6
Hempton NR21 .....**141** A3
Hethersett NR9 .....**88** C7
Hickling NR12 ......**39** F2
Kirby Row NR35 ....**109** E3
Mattishall NR20 ....**68** F5
❸ Norwich NR1 .....**162** B3
Poringland NR14 ....**90** C5
Pulham Market IP21 ..**121** E5
❻ Salhouse NR13 ....**55** A1
Thurton NR14 ......**91** C4
Wisbech PE13 ......**152** C6
Mill Cnr NR9 ......**86** C4
Mill Comm NR14 ...**91** C4
Mill Comm Rd NR28 ..**23** C4
Mill Cres NR13 ....**166** B4
Mill Croft Cl NR5 ...**156** E1
Mill Ct Fakenham NR21 .**141** B3
Holt NR25 ....**137** B6
Wells-next-the-Sea
NR23 ....**136** D5
Mill Drift
Beeston with Bittering
PE32 ....**48** C3
Hockwold cum Wilton
IP26 ....**114** A7
Mill Dro
Gooderstone PE33 ...**81** F4
Middleton PE32 .....**44** D2
Southery PE38 .....**97** A5
Mill Farm Nurseries
PE37 ....**153** B2
Mill Field Cl PE14 ...**42** C1
Mill Gdns
Bedingham NR35 ....**108** B4
Horsford NR10 .....**53** B3
Mill Gn
Burnham Market PE31 .**135** D3
Stoke Holy Cross NR14 .**89** F4
Mill Hill Bradenham IP25 .**66** E3
Bramerton NR14 ....**90** F8
Brancaster PE31 .....**3** B6
Brandon IP27 ......**175** E3
❷ Horning NR12 .....**55** E4
Mettingham NR35 ...**109** D1
Norwich NR3 ....**158** E2
Roughton NR11 .....**139** A1
Salhouse NR13 .....**55** B1
Strumpshaw NR13 ..**73** F2
Mill Hill Rd
Boughton PE33 .....**80** F5
Norwich NR2 ....**162** B6
Mill Houses PE30 ...**146** F6

Mill La Acle NR13 .....**166** C3
All Saints & St
Nicholas, South Elmham
IP20 ....**123** E1
Aslacton NR15 .....**106** A1
Attleborough NR17 ..**174** F7
Aylsham NR11 .....**150** B6
Bacton/Walcott NR12 ..**23** E4
Barnham PE32 .....**125** E6
Bircham PE31 ......**13** F3
Blackborough End PE32 ..**44** C1
Briston NR24 ......**142** F3
Brooke NR15 ......**108** A8
Burnham Thorpe PE31 ..**4** D4
Carbrooke IP25 .....**85** B4
Catfield NR29 ......**56** C7
Claxton NR14 ......**91** E6
Clenchwarton PE34 ..**145** F6
Crimplesham PE33 ..**80** B7
Cromer NR27 ......**10** B5
Dereham NR19 .....**154** A8
Docking PE31 ......**134** E4
Downham Market PE38 .**172** D7
Ellingham NR35 ....**109** E3
Felthorpe NR10 ....**155** C8
Fleggburgh NR29 ...**57** B1
Foulsham NR20 ....**33** D4
Garboldisham IP22 ..**128** A7
Great Ellingham NR17 .**103** D7
Great Massingham PE32 .**29** D2
Great Yarmouth NR31 .**94** C7
Haddiscoe NR14 ....**110** D8
Hindringham NR21 ..**17** E8
Hockering NR20 ....**69** B3
Hockwold cum Wilton
IP26 ....**114** A7
Hoe NR20 ....**49** D3
Honingham NR9 ....**69** E6
Hopton IP22 ....**127** F7
Horsford NR10 .....**53** B3
Horsham St Faith &
Newton St Faith NR10 ..**53** E2
Keswick NR4 ......**89** D7
King's Lynn PE30 ...**147** B8
Kirby Bedon NR14 ..**90** E7
Long Stratton NR15 ..**106** F3
Morley NR18 ......**87** A3
Newton Flotman NR15 .**89** E2
Norwich NR3 ......**162** E8
Ormesby St Margaret
with Scratby NR29 ...**58** A1
Ovington IP25 .....**84** C4
Postwick with Witton
NR13 ....**73** A3
Pulham Market IP21 ..**121** E5
Redgrave IP22 .....**128** E5
Repps with Bastwick
NR29 ....**57** B3
Rickinghall Inferior
IP22 ....**128** D2
Rocklands NR17 ....**103** C7
St John, Ilketshall
NR34 ....**124** E6
Seething NR15 .....**91** C1
Shelton NR15 ......**122** B8
❶ Southery PE38 ....**97** B5
❶❹ Sutton Bridge PE12 ..**41** B8
Swaffham PE37 ....**153** C3
Syderstone PE31 ...**15** B3
Thetford IP24 ......**176** D4
Tilney St Lawrence PE34 ..**42** C1
Tunstead NR12 .....**38** A3
Walpole Highway PE14 ..**59** F7
Walsingham NR22 ..**16** F8
West Walton PE14 ..**59** C8
Weybread IP21 .....**131** F7
Wreningham NR16 ..**88** D1
Yaxham NR19 ......**68** B5
Mill Loke ❹ NR12 ...**55** E4
Mill Orch IP21 .....**121** E5
Mill Pightle NR11 ..**150** B6
Mill Pool La NR35 ..**109** E3
Mill Rd Alburgh IP20 ..**122** E6
Aldborough NR11 ...**21** A6
All Saints South Elmham
IP19 ....**124** B1
Ashby St Mary NR14 ..**91** C4
Aylsham NR11 .....**150** C6
Bacton NR28 ......**23** A1
Banham NR16 .....**119** D7
Barnham Broom NR9 ..**69** B2
Barningham IP31 ...**127** C3
Barton Turf NR12 ...**38** E1
Bergh Apton NR14 ..**91** A4
Bintree NR20 ......**33** A2
Blofield Heath NR13 ..**73** D6
Botesdale IP22 .....**128** F2
Brancaster PE31 .....**3** B6
Briston NR24 ......**142** F3
Brockdish IP21 .....**131** B7
Burgh Castle NR31 ..**94** A8
Burgh St Peter NR34 .**111** B4
Burnham Market PE31 .**135** B4
Burston & Shimpling
IP22 ....**120** E2
Carleton Rode NR16 ..**105** A4
Colby NR11 ....**36** F7
Coltishall NR12 ....**54** C6
Cromer NR27 ......**139** C5
Dersingham PE31 ...**140** F5
Dilham NR28 ......**38** D4
East Ruston NR12 ...**24** A4
Emneth PE14 ......**59** D2
Forncett NR16 .....**106** B3
Foxley NR20 ......**50** D8
Freethorpe NR13 ...**92** F8
Frettenham NR12 ...**54** A4
Great Yarmouth NR31 .**169** B3

Mill Rd continued
Gresham NR11 ....9 D1
Halvergate NR13 .....74 F1
Hardingham NR9 .....86 E8
Harpley PE31 ....29 D4
Hempnall NR15 ......107 C5
Hemsby NR29 ....58 A4
7 Hethersett NR9 ....88 C7
Honington IP31 ......126 D1
Kirby Row NR35 ....109 D3
Lakenheath IP27 ....113 E1
Little Melton NR9 ...160 B2
Loddon NR14 ....92 A1
Long Stratton NR15 .107 A2
Marlingford NR9 ......70 A3
Marsham NR10 ....36 C2
Mattishall NR20 ......68 E6
Mautby NR29 ....75 E7
North Walsham NR28 .151 D3
Old Buckenham NR17 .104 C1
Potter Heigham NR29 .56 F5
Reedham NR13 ....93 A5
Reepham NR10 ......149 B2
Repps with Bastwick
  NR29 ....57 A4
Ryburgh NR21 ....32 C6
Salhouse NR13 ....55 A1
Shelton NR15 ....122 B8
Shipdham IP25 ....67 C3
Shouldham Thorpe PE33 .62 C3
Stalham NR12 ....39 A3
Stoke Holy Cross NR14 .89 F4
Stokesby with Herringby
  NR29 ....75 A6
Surlingham NR14 .....91 B8
Sutton NR12 ....39 C3
Terrington St John PE14 .42 B1
Thelnetham IP22 ....128 B5
Thompson IP24 ......102 A7
Thurlton NR14 ....110 D8
Tibenham NR16 .....120 D8
Tivetshall St Mary NR15 .121 B5
Topcroft NR35 ....107 F4
Walpole St Andrew PE14 .41 E3
Watlington PE34 ......61 D8
Watton IP25 ....84 D3
Wells-next-the-Sea
  NR23 ....136 B5
West Walton PE14 ....59 B8
Weybread IP21 ......131 F8
Whissonsett NR20 ....31 D2
Wiggenhall St Germans
  PE34 ....43 C1
Wiggenhall St Mary Magdalen
  PE34 ....61 B5
Winfarthing IP22 ....120 B4
Mill Rd S IP22 .....128 F2
Mill Reach NR10 ....36 F1
Mill Row NR11 .....150 D7
Mill St Bradenham IP25 .66 E3
Elsing NR20 ....50 F4
Gimingham NR11 .....22 E7
Holt NR25 ....137 B6
Horsham St Faith NR10 .53 E2
Lamas NR10 ....36 F1
Mattishall NR20 ......68 F5
3 Necton PE37 ......65 F4
Swanton Morley NR20 .50 B4
Mill View
Barnham Broom NR9 .69 B8
Saham Toney IP25 ....84 C5
Sedgeford PE36 ....13 A7
Mill View Cl NR11 ..143 D5
Mill View Mid Sch
  NR5 ....161 C8
Mill Way PE14 ......77 B8
Millard Cl NR28 ....151 A6
Millcroft NR3 ....158 E1
Millennium Plain NR2 .178 A2
Millennium Way PE34 .146 A5
Miller Cl **7** NR19 .154 C4
Miller's Breck NR5 .155 D1
Miller's La
2 Thetford IP24 .....176 C4
Wimbotsham PE34 ...79 E8
Millers Cl NR35 ....124 B8
Millers Dr IP21 ....121 B1
Millers Gn **4** IP20 .122 D2
Millers La Harpley PE31 .29 D4
Norwich NR3 ....158 D1
Millers Sq NR17 ...174 C5
Millers Way **1** NR10 .53 B3
Millers Wlk NR21 ..141 C3
Millfield Ashill IP25 ..84 A8
Eye IP23 ....130 B1
Millfield Cl **5** NR13 .73 D6
Millfield La PE33 ....43 F3
Millfield Prim Sch
  NR28 ....151 B3
Millfield Rd
Barningham IP31 ....127 D3
North Walsham NR28 .151 B4
Millfields **2** NR15 .107 C5
Millfleet **4** PE30 ...146 E4
Millgate NR11 ......150 D7
Millgate St IP26 .....99 A5
Millhill La NR18 .....86 F2
Millicent Oliver Cl **11**
  IP24 ....176 C4
Millington Ct **6** IP24 .176 D4
Millmarsh Dro IP27 .113 D2
Mills Cl NR8 ....155 C1
Millside Hales NR14 .109 F8
Stalham NR12 ....39 B3
Millview NR29 ......167 A3
Millway NR18 ......173 B6
Millway Ave IP22 ...177 C6

Millway La
Palgrave IP22 ....177 B2
Wortham IP22 ....129 D5
Milner Rd PE13 ....152 C4
Milnes Way **3** NR33 .111 F1
Milton Ave PE30 ...146 F5
Milton Cl
East Dereham NR19 .154 C7
Norwich NR1 ....162 E3
3 Thetford IP24 .....176 E6
Milton Rd
Great Yarmouth NR30 .169 D8
8 Swanton Morley NR20 .50 B3
Milton Way **1** PE38 .172 D6
Milverton Cl **1** NR1 .162 F3
Mindhams Yd NR23 .136 C6
Mingay Rd IP24 ....176 B2
Minion Cl **8** NR7 ...72 D4
Minsmere Rd **1** NR31 ..94 A6
Minster Ct PE30 ...147 C5
Minstergate IP24 ...176 C4
Miriam Cl NR29 ...168 E8
Misburgh Way NR31 .171 E4
Mission La
Docking PE31 ....134 E4
Fakenham NR21 ......141 E4
Mission Pl NR30 ...169 D6
Mission Rd Diss IP22 .177 F3
3 Great Yarmouth NR31 .169 B4
Rackheath NR13 ......72 E8
Mitchell Ct **4** NR5 .160 F1
Mitre Ct Cromer NR27 .139 B7
Diss IP22 ....177 D5
King's Lynn PE30 .....146 F4
Mount Surrey NR14 .173 C6
Mount Tumbledown Cl **7**
  PE12 ....41 B8
Mountain's Rd **2** NR11 ..19 F1
Mountbatten Cl **5** IP24 .176 E6
Mountbatten Dr
Bungay NR35 ....124 A7
Dersingham PE31 ....140 C3
Mountbatten Way
  NR30 ....168 D6
Mounteney Cl NR7 ..159 A4
Mountergate NR1 ..178 B2
Mountfield Ave
Hellesdon NR6 ....157 F4
Norwich NR6 ....158 A4
Mousehold Ave NR3 .163 A8
Mousehold Fst Sch
  NR3 ....162 F8
Mousehold La NR7 .159 A3
Mousehold St NR3 .178 C4
Mowles Rd NR20 ...68 C8
Moyse's Bank
Emneth Hungate PE14 .59 F2
Marshland St James PE14 .60 A2
Muck La NR13 ....72 F8
Muckleburgh Collection
  The ★ NR25 ....8 E6
Mud Rd NR21 ....15 D2
Mudd's Dro PE14 ....77 F2
Muir La NR15 ......106 B2
Mulbarton Fst Sch
  NR14 ....89 B3
Mulbarton Mid Sch
  NR14 ....89 B3
Mulberry Cl
17 Feltwell IP26 ......98 E1
6 Norwich NR3 ......178 A3
Mulberry Ct **2** NR8 .155 B2
Mulberry Gr **4** NR31 ..94 C6
Mulberry La NR15 .107 A3
Mulberry Rd PE30 ..147 D4
Mullicourt Rd PE14 ..78 B6
Mumby's Dro PE14 ..77 E1
Mundesley Hospl NR11 ..22 F7
Mundesley Jun & Fst Sch
  NR11 ....143 B5
Mundesley Maritime Mus★
  NR11 ....143 C6
Mundesley Rd
Gimingham NR11 .....22 E7
North Walsham NR28 .151 C6
Overstrand NR27 ......11 A3
Paston NR28 ....143 D3
Trimingham NR11 .....11 E1
Trunch NR28 ....22 F5
Mundford Prim Sch
  IP26 ....100 B4
Mundford Rd
Thetford IP24 ....176 C6
Weeting-with-Broomhill
  IP27 ....175 D7
Mundham La NR14 ..91 D2
Mundham Rd
Loddon NR14 ....91 C1
Mundham NR14 ......109 A8
Mundy's Rd IP20 ...123 A1
Munhaven Cl NR11 .143 C5
Munnings Cl NR14 ..89 D4
Munnings Rd NR7 ..159 D1
Munson's La IP26 ...98 E2
Munson's Pl IP26 ....98 E2
Murgot's La PE33 ....81 D7
Muriel Kenny Ct **10** NR9 .88 C7
Muriel Rd NR2 ......162 A4
Muriel Way IP25 .....85 B4
Murrayfield Rd NR1 .158 B5
Mus of the Broads The★
  NR12 ....39 B3
Museum Sq PE13 ...152 C5
Music House La NR1 .178 B2

Morston Rd continued
Stiffkey NR23 ....6 D6
Mortimer Cl NR17 ..174 F6
Morton Cl **1** NR11 .150 D6
Morton Cres **22** NR31 .94 C7
Morton La NR9 ......51 F3
Morton Peto Cl NR32 .111 D7
Morton Peto Rd NR31 .170 B8
Morton Rd NR11 ...150 D6
Mosely Ct NR5 ......160 E8
Mossfield Cl NR1 ...163 B8
Mother Julian Cl **8**
  NR24 ....176 D7
Mother Quy's NR24 .115 C1
Mottram Cl NR5 ....161 B6
Motum Rd NR5 .....161 C7
Moulton Rd
Halvergate NR13 .....74 F1
Tivetshall St Margaret
  NR15 ....121 A7
Mount Cl Brandon IP27 .175 F4
Swaffham PE37 ......153 A5
Mount Dr PE13 .....152 E4
Mount Pk Cl PE32 ..44 C3
Mount Pleasant
Little Walsingham NR22 .16 F8
Norwich NR2 ....162 B4
Mount Pleasant Rd
  PE13 ....152 C7
Mount Rd IP27 .....175 D2
Mount St Cromer NR27 .139 B7
Diss IP22 ....177 D5

Musketeer Way **29** NR7 ..72 D4
Muspole St NR3 ....178 A4
Musticott Pl PE13 ..152 F6
Myles Way PE13 ...152 C8
Myrtle Ave
Costessey NR8 ......156 F3
East Dereham NR19 .154 E4
Myrtle Ct NR31 ....170 C6
Myrtle Rd NR9 ....88 C8

N

Naber Furlong **1** NR8 .155 E2
Napier Cl PE30 .....147 C5
Napier Pl Norwich NR2 .162 C7
  Thetford IP24 ....176 A1
Naples Cl NR31 ....171 E4
Napoleon Pl **9** NR19 .169 D3
Narborough Hill PE33 .63 E2
Narborough Rd PE33 .63 D8
Narborough VC Fst Sch
  PE32 ....63 E7
Narford La PE32 ....45 F2
Narford Rd PE32 ...63 F7
Narrows Trading Est The
  PE30 ....147 A1
Naseby Way **28** NR7 ..72 D4
Nash Rd NR10 ......155 C8
Nash's La NR28 ......23 E1
Nasmith Rd NR4 ...161 E3
Naylor Rd **1** NR3 ..157 F1
Neale Cl NR11 ......150 B6
Neatherd High Sch
  NR20 ....154 F5
Neatherd Moor NR20 .154 F6
Neatherd Rd NR19 .154 E5
Neatishead Prim Sch
  NR12 ....55 D7
Necton CE Fst Sch
  PE37 ....66 A4
Necton Mid Sch PE37 .66 A4
Necton Rd PE32 ....65 E7
Needham Bank PE14 .77 C8
Needham Rd IP20 ..122 C1
Neil Ave NR25 ......137 B5
Neilsen Cl NR3 .....136 E6
Nelonde Dr **1** NR18 .173 C5
Nelson Ave PE38 ...172 B6
Nelson Cl
Bradenham IP25 ......66 E3
4 Hethersett NR9 ....88 E8
Nelson Cres PE37 ..153 D3
Nelson Ct IP25 ......84 D4
Nelson Dr NR11 ....132 D3
Nelson Fst Sch NR2 .162 B7
Nelson Gdns PE13 .152 D6
Nelson Hts NR27 ..139 A7
Nelson Pl **3** NR19 .154 D5
Nelson Rd
Caister-on-Sea NR30 .168 F4
Fakenham NR21 .....141 B4
Great Yarmouth NR31 .170 D7
North Walsham NR28 .151 D5
Sheringham NR26 ...138 F7
Nelson Rd Central
  NR30 ....169 D3
Nelson Rd N NR30 .169 D5
Nelson Rd S NR30 .169 D2
Nelson St
King's Lynn PE30 ....146 D4
Norwich NR2 ....162 B7
Nelson Way
Hevingham NR10 .....53 B8
Mundesley NR11 ....143 A4
7 North Walsham NR28 .151 C5
Nene Mdws PE12 ...41 C8
Nene Par PE13 ......152 B6
Nene Quay PE13 ...152 C5
Nene Rd
Hunstanton PE36 ...132 C4
4 Watlington PE33 ..61 D4
Nene Sch The PE13 .152 D4
Nenelands PE12 .....41 C8
Nether Row IP24 ...176 D3
Nethergate St
Ditchingham NR35 ..124 A8
Harpley PE31 ....29 C4
Hopton IP22 ....127 C5
Netherwood Gn NR1 .162 F2
Nettle Hill E **15** NR30 .169 D4
Nettle Hill W NR30 .169 D4
Neve's Cl NR13 ......73 F3
Neville Cl
East Dereham NR19 .154 E1
Norwich NR7 ....158 D7
Saham Toney IP25 ....84 B5
Neville La PE31 .....133 C6
Neville Rd
Heacham PE31 ......133 C6
Norwich NR7 ....159 A3
Stalham NR12 ....39 C3
Neville St NR2 ......162 C5
New Bridge La
Elm PE14 ....59 A1
Wisbech PE14 ....152 A1
New Bridge Rd PE14 .77 D5
New Cl NR13 ....166 C3
New Coll NR31 .....170 B5
New Comm Rd IP22 .127 C4
New Conduit St PE30 .146 D5
New Dro **3** PE13 ...152 D2
New Eccles Hall Sch The
  NR16 ....118 F7
New England Way **2**
  IP24 ....116 A4
New Fen Dro PE38 ..97 A5

New Hampshire Way **5**
  IP24 ....116 A1
New Inn Hill NR14 ..91 C7
New Inn La NR19 ..154 B5
New La Banham NR16 .119 B8
Bradenham IP25 ......66 F4
Hoveton NR12 ....55 C4
Mattishall NR20 ......68 F5
New Mills Yd NR3 ..178 A4
New N Rd NR17 ....174 D5
New Par NR27 ......139 C7
New Rd Acle NR13 ..166 C3
Attleborough NR17 ..174 B3
Aylsham NR11 ....150 D7
Baconsthorpe NR25 ..20 A8
Bawburgh NR9 ......160 B6
Belton NR31 ....94 A5
Blakeney NR25 ....7 C6
Bodham NR25 ....9 B1
Brettenham IP24 ....117 B2
Brinton NR24 ....18 D8
Burnham Overy Staithe
  PE31 ....135 E7
Catfield NR29 ....56 C8
Crimplesham PE33 ...80 A6
Dickleburgh & Rushall
  IP21 ....130 D8
Dunton NR21 ....16 A2
Fritton & St Olaves NR31 .93 E3
Gissing IP22 ....120 F4
Great Yarmouth NR30 .169 A6
Haddiscoe NR14 ....110 F7
Halvergate NR13 .....75 B4
Hethersett NR9 ....88 C7
Hingham NR9 ....86 C3
Itteringham NR11 ....35 D8
King's Lynn PE30 ...147 B6
12 Lingwood NR13 ....74 A3
Longham NR19 ....48 F2
Methwold IP26 ....98 A5
Mettingham NR35 ..124 C7
Morley NR18 ....87 A3
North Runcton PE33 ..44 A3
North Walsham NR28 .151 D5
Northrepps NR27 ....139 E1
Norton Subcourse NR14 .92 E1
Oulton NR11 ....35 D7
Outwell PE14 ....77 E5
Palgrave IP22 ....129 F4
Reedham NR13 ....92 F4
Reepham NR10 .....149 C5
St Cross, South Elmham
  IP20 ....123 D1
Saxlingham Nethergate
  NR15 ....107 B8
Sculthorpe NR21 .....16 A3
Sheringham NR26 ..138 D7
Shipdham IP25 ....67 B2
Shouldham PE33 ......62 D4
Skeyton NR10 ....37 A5
South Creake NR21 ..15 C3
Stanfield NR20 ....48 F7
Stokesby with Herringby
  NR29 ....75 A6
Surlingham NR14 .....73 B1
Sutton NR12 ....39 D2
Sutton Bridge PE12 ..41 B8
Tacolneston NR16 ..105 E5
Thelnetham IP22 ....127 F3
Thetford IP24 ....176 B4
Thrandeston IP21 ...130 A4
Tilney St Lawrence PE34 .42 C1
Tivetshall St Mary NR15 .121 B4
Toft Monks NR34 ...110 D6
Welney PE14 ....95 D5
Whissonsett NR20 ....31 D2
Wimbotsham PE34 ..172 E8
Wiveton NR25 ....7 E6
Wormegay PE33 ......62 C8
New Roman Bank
  PE34 ....144 B7
New Row PE31 .....133 D6
New Sporle Rd PE37 .153 C5
New St Cawston NR10 ..35 B2
Cromer NR27 ....139 B7
Holt NR25 ....137 B6
King's Lynn PE30 ...147 B6
Sheringham NR26 ..138 D7
New Wellington Pl **23**
  NR30 ....169 D2
Newall Rd **3** IP24 ..125 F6
Newarch La NR14 ...90 E7
Newark Cl **22** NR17 ..72 D4
Newarp Way NR30 .168 D8
Newbegin Cl NR1 ..163 C7
Newbegin Rd NR1 ..163 B7
Newbury Way **20** NR7 ..72 D4
Newby Rd **2** PE30 .147 D6
Newcastle Cl **3** NR7 ..72 D4
Newcastle Rd NR30 .169 D1
Newcombe Cl PE14 ..42 B1
Newcombe Dr **15** PE26 ..98 E1
Newell Cresent NR27 ..10 A4
Newey's Way **2** NR12 .164 C5
Newfen Gravel Dro
  IP27 ....113 D4
Newfields PE33 ......65 C5
Newfound Dr NR4 ..161 C2
Newgate NR35 .....109 E3
Newgate La
Kirby Cane NR35 ....109 E3
Wells-next-the-Sea
  NR23 ....136 D6
Newhaven Cl NR27 .139 B6
Newhaven Ct NR27 .139 B6

Newlands Ave PE30 ...146 E7
Newlands Cl 40 IP20 ...122 D2
Newman Rd NR13 ....72 D7
Newmarket Rd
  2 Cringleford NR4 ....89 B8
  Norwich NR2 ....178 A1
Newmarket St NR2 ...162 C4
Newnham Gn NR31 ...170 A4
Newport NR29 ....167 D6
Newport Rd
  Hemsby NR29 ....167 C6
  South Walsham NR13 ..74 A6
Newstead Wlk IP22 ..177 C6
Newstead's La NR27 ..10 C4
Newton Cl
  Horsham St Faith &
    Newton St Faith NR10 ..53 D4
  10 Newton Flotman NR15 ..89 D1
  Norwich NR4 ....162 B1
Newton Cross NR31 ..170 D1
Newton Flotman Prim Sch
  NR15 ....89 D1
Newton St NR10 .....53 D4
Newtown IP24 ......176 C3
Neylond Cres NR6 ...157 E6
Nicholas Ave PE34 ..145 E6
Nicholas Hamond Way 4
  PE37 ....153 C3
Nicholas Mews 3 NR2 162 B7
Nicholls Way IP22 ...177 A5
Nick's La IP23 ......130 B2
Nicolson Ave NR20 ...50 B5
Nightingale Cl
  Denver PE38 ....172 D2
  Fakenham NR21 .....141 F4
  Hemsby NR29 ....167 E4
  Mulbarton NR14 .....89 A3
Nightingale Dr NR8 .155 B1
Nightingale Fst Sch
  NR8 ....155 B1
Nightingale La
  Denver PE38 ....172 D2
  8 Feltwell IP26 ......98 E1
  3 Feltwell IP26 ......98 E1
  Norwich NR3 ....162 B8
Nightingale Rd IP27 .175 F3
Nightingale Way IP24 176 D1
Nightingale Wlk PE38 172 C2
Nightmarsh La PE31 ..27 C4
Nile Rd
  Downham Market PE38 172 B4
  Great Yarmouth NR31 170 D4
Nile St 1 NR2 ......162 B7
Nimrod Cl 27 NR9 ....88 D8
Nine Acre La NR24 ...19 C4
Ninham St NR1 .....162 B3
Ninhams Ct NR2 ....178 A3
Nobb's Loke NR12 ...38 F4
Nobbs' Cnr NR35 ...108 A4
Nobel Cres NR12 ....164 B4
Noble Cl NR7 ....159 D1
Noel Cl NR31 ....171 C5
Noot Alley 6 NR5 ...161 B7
Nordelph Cnr NR9 ...86 D6
Norfolk & Norwich Univ
  Hospl NR4 ....161 A3
Norfolk & Suffolk Aviation
  Mus* NR35 ....123 D6
Norfolk Arena PE34 .168 F2
Norfolk Dr NR17 ....174 C4
Norfolk Lavender Visitor
  Ctr* PE31 ....133 E6
Norfolk Motor Cycle Mus*
  NR28 ....151 C4
Norfolk Nelson Mus*
  NR30 ....169 C3
Norfolk Rd
  10 Honington IP31 ...126 B1
  10 Marham PE33 .....63 B4
  Norwich NR4 ....161 B3
  Sheringham NR26 ...138 D6
  Thetford IP24 ....176 E4
Norfolk Record Office
  NR1 ....162 F3
Norfolk Shire Horse Ctr*
  NR27 ....9 F5
Norfolk Sq
  Downham Market PE38 172 B5
  Great Yarmouth NR30 169 E5
Norfolk St
  4 King's Lynn PE30 ..146 E5
  Norwich NR2 ....162 C5
  Wisbech PE13 ......152 C4
Norfolk Wildlife Ctr &
  Country Pk* NR9 ...51 C6
Norfolk Wildlife Hospl
  (RSPCA)* PE32 ....44 F3
Norgate La IP21 .....130 E6
Norgate Rd NR4 ....161 C5
Norgate Way NR8 ...156 E8
Norman CE Prim Sch
  IP26 ....99 C7
Norman Cl
  East Dereham NR19 ..154 C5
  Fakenham NR21 .....141 B6
Norman Dr
  Northwold PE33 ....81 B2
  Norwich NR6 ....158 E7
Norman Fst Sch NR3 158 B2

Norman La 10 NR31 ...169 B4
Norman Rd
  Flitcham with Appleton
    PE31 ....28 E7
  Norwich NR3 ....158 A1
Norman Troller Ct 9
  NR27 ....139 B7
Norman Way PE31 ....15 B3
Norman's Burrow Rd
  NR21 ....31 B3
Normandy Cl IP26 ....99 C7
Normans Bldgs NR1 .178 B2
Normans La NR1 .....4 D1
North Ave NR20 .....50 B5
North Beach PE36 ...132 B1
North Brink PE13 ...152 A4
North Cambridgeshire Hospl
  PE13 ....152 D5
North Denes Airfield
  NR30 ....168 D2
North Denes Mid Sch
  NR30 ....169 D8
North Denes Rd NR30 169 D6
North Dr
  Fakenham NR21 .....141 C5
  Great Yarmouth NR30 169 E4
North Elmham Chapel*
  NR20 ....49 F8
North Elmham Prim Sch
  NR20 ....49 E8
North End
  Haddiscoe NR14 .....93 B1
  Stoke Holy Cross NR14 .89 E5
  Wisbech PE13 ......152 B6
North End La NR16 ..106 D3
North Everard St
  PE30 ....146 E3
North Gage Cl NR7 ..159 C4
North Gn NR9 ....68 B1
North Gn Rd IP21 ...122 A4
North La NR21 ......17 E5
North Lawn PE38 ....97 B6
North Lopham Rd
  NR16 ....119 A3
North Lynn Ind Est
  PE30 ....147 A8
North Mkt Rd
  7 Great Yarmouth NR30 169 D4
  Winterton-on-Sea NR29 .58 B6
North Norfolk Rly*
  NR26 ....9 B6
North Pickenham Rd
  PE37 ....153 D4
North Pk NR21 ......141 B6
North Pk Ave NR4 ...161 C4
North Pk Dr NR4 ....161 F4
North Quay NR30 ...169 C4
North Rd Bunwell NR16 105 C4
  4 Great Yarmouth NR30 169 D5
  Hemsby NR29 ......167 A7
  Ormesby St Margaret
    with Scratby NR29 ..167 A4
  Watton IP25 ....84 D3
North River Rd NR30 169 C6
North St Brundall NR13 165 E6
  6 Castle Acre PE32 ..46 F2
  Great Dunham PE32 ..47 E2
  King's Lynn PE30 ...146 D6
  Langham NR25 ....7 A4
  North Walsham NR28 151 C5
  Sheringham NR26 ...138 C7
  Wisbech PE13 ......152 C5
North View NR21 ....17 F3
North Walsham Cottage
  Hospl NR28 ....151 C4
North Walsham Fst Sch
  NR28 ....151 D5
North Walsham High Sch
  NR28 ....151 D4
North Walsham Jun Sch
  NR28 ....151 D4
North Walsham Rd
  Bacton NR28 ....23 C3
  Coltishall NR12 ......54 D7
  Crostwick NR12 .....54 B2
  Felmingham NR28 ...37 B8
  Happisburgh NR12 ...23 F2
  Northrepps NR27 ....10 E1
  Norwich NR6 ....159 A5
  Paston NR28 ....151 F7
  Sprowston NR6 .....159 B6
  Swafield NR28 ....22 E4
  Thorpe Market NR11 ..22 A7
  Witton NR28 ....38 B8
North Walsham Sta
  NR28 ....151 C4
North Way PE30 ....147 A8
North Wootton Prim Sch
  PE30 ....148 D4
Northcote PE31 .....134 D6
Northcote Rd 1 NR3 ..162 E8
Northern Cl NR30 ...168 F5
Northfield Ave NR23 136 D6
Northfield Cl NR18 ..173 B6
Northfield Cres NR23 136 E5
Northfield Gdns NR18 173 B6
Northfield La
  Plumstead NR11 ....20 B6
  Wells-next-the-Sea
    NR23 ....136 A6
Northfield Loke NR18 173 B6
Northfield Rd
  Forncett NR16 .....106 A4
  Mundesley NR11 ...143 C5
  North Walsham NR28 151 B6
  Swaffham PE37 .....153 C6

Northfield Way NR23 136 E6
Northfields NR4 ....161 E4
Northfields Fst Sch
  NR4 ....161 E4
Northgate
  Beccles NR34 ......110 D1
  Dereham NR19 .....154 C7
  11 Harleston IP20 ...122 D1
  Hunstanton PE36 ...132 C5
  Norwich NR6 ....157 F5
  3 Thorpe End NR13 ..72 D6
Northgate Cty High Sch
  NR19 ....154 D6
Northgate Hospl
  NR30 ....169 D6
Northgate Prec PE36 132 C6
Northgate St NR30 ..169 C5
Northgate St Andrews Fst
  Sch NR30 ....169 C6
Northgate Way PE34 144 D6
Northmead Dr NR28 151 C6
Northolt Rd IP25 .....85 A3
Northrepps Prim Sch
  NR27 ....11 A2
Northrepps Rd NR27 139 E3
Northside NR7 ....72 E3
Northumberland St
  PE37 ....153 C5
North-West Twr*
  NR30 ....169 C5
Northwold Rd IP26 ...99 A6
Norton Dr 2 Norwich NR4 89 D8
  Norwich NR4 ....162 A1
Norton Hill NR13 ....74 A8
Norton Rd NR14 .....92 B1
Nortridge Rd NR5 ...161 A7
Norvic Dr NR4 ......161 E1
Norway Cl PE31 ....133 C6
Norwich Arts Ctr*
  NR2 ....178 A3
Norwich Bsns Pk NR4 162 A1
Norwich Castle Mus & Art
  Gall* NR1 ....178 B3
Norwich Cath* NR1 ..178 B3
Norwich City FC NR1 163 A4
Norwich Com Hospl
  NR2 ....161 F7
Norwich Comm NR18 173 F6
Norwich Dr NR20 ....32 C4
Norwich Gall* NR1 ..178 B3
Norwich Gates NR35 140 E1
Norwich High Sch for Girls
  NR2 ....162 B3
Norwich Int Airport
  NR6 ....158 B7
Norwich La IP31 ....127 A4
Norwich Lower Sch
  NR1 ....178 C3
Norwich Puppet Theatre
  NR1 ....178 B4
Norwich Rd Acle NR13 166 A3
  Ashmanhaugh NR12 ..55 C7
  Attleborough NR17 ..174 C4
  Aylsham NR11 .....150 C6
  Barnham Broom NR9 ..69 D2
  Bawdeswell NR20 ...50 E7
  Bracon Ash NR14 ....88 F2
  Briston NR24 ......142 E5
  Brooke NR15 ....90 E3
  Burgh & Tuttington NR11 36 E6
  Caister-on-Sea NR30 168 C5
  Cantley NR13 ....92 D7
  Carbrooke IP25 .....85 B3
  Cawston NR10 ......35 B2
  Chedgrave NR14 .....91 F2
  Cromer NR27 ....139 C5
  Denton IP20 ....123 B7
  Dickleburgh & Rushall
    IP21 ....130 D6
  Ditchingham NR35 ..109 A2
  Earsham NR35 ......108 E1
  East Dereham NR20 .154 F5
  East Tuddenham NR20 .69 C6
  Edgefield NR24 ......19 D6
  Fakenham NR21 .....141 C4
  Foxley NR20 ....50 D8
  Gillingham NR34 ...110 C2
  Great & Little Plumstead
    NR13 ....73 A7
  Guist NR20 ....33 A4
  Hardingham NR9 ....86 E8
  9 Hethersett NR9 ...88 D7
  Hingham NR9 ......86 D5
  Holt NR25 ....137 B5
  Horning NR12 ......55 E4
  Horsham St Failth NR10 53 D2
  Horstead with Stanninghall
    NR12 ....54 C4
  Ingworth NR11 ......36 B8
  Kimberley NR18 .....87 B7
  Langley with Hardley
    NR14 ....91 F6
  Lingwood & Burlingham
    NR13 ....74 A2
  12 Loddon NR14 .....92 A2
  Long Stratton NR15 .106 F5
  Ludham NR29 ....56 C5
  Marlingford NR9 ....69 F4
  Mattishall NR20 ....68 F6
  Mulbarton NR14 ....89 B4
  Neatishead NR12 ...164 F8
  North Walsham NR28 151 B3
  Norwich NR5 ....157 B2
  Poringland NR14 ....90 B6
  Pulham St Mary IP21 121 F4

Norwich Rd continued
  Rackheath NR13 ....72 F8
  Reepham NR10 .....149 C5
  Roughton NR11 .....21 D8
  Salhouse NR13 ......55 B1
  Saxlingham Nethergate
    NR15 ....107 B8
  Scole IP21 ....121 B1
  Shotesham NR15 ....89 F2
  Shouldham PE33 ....62 F3
  Smallburgh NR12 ....38 D2
  Stockton NR34 .....109 F5
  Strumpshaw NR13 ...73 F2
  Swaffham PE37 .....153 D4
  Swanton Morley NR20 .50 B2
  4 Tacolneston NR16 ..105 F5
  Tacolneston NR16 ..106 A6
  Tharston & Hapton
    NR15 ....106 C7
  Thetford IP24 ......176 D4
  Thurton NR14 ....91 C3
  Tivetshall St Mary NR15 121 C5
  West Caister NR30 ..168 B6
  Weston Longville NR9 ..51 E5
  Wisbech PE13 ......152 E5
  Woodton NR35 .....108 C6
  Wroxham/Hoveton
    NR12 ....164 B3
  Wymondham NR18 ..173 D5
  Yaxham NR19 ....68 B5
Norwich Rd Sch IP24 176 D4
Norwich Research Pk
  NR4 ....161 A4
Norwich Riverside
  NR1 ....178 C2
Norwich Sch NR1 ...178 B3
Norwich Sch of Art & Design
  NR3 ....178 B3
Norwich St
  East Dereham NR19 .154 E5
  Fakenham NR21 .....141 B4
  Hingham NR9 ....86 C5
  Mundesley NR11 ...143 A7
  Norwich Sta NR1 ...178 C2
Norwich Theatre Royal
  NR2 ....178 A2
Norwood Rd IP27 ...175 A1
Notre Dame High Sch
  NR1 ....178 B1
Notre Dame Prep Sch
  NR2 ....162 B7
Nottingham Rd PE30 146 E8
Nottingham Way
  NR30 ....169 C3
Notykin St NR5 .....161 A8
Nourse Dr PE31 ....133 E5
Nova Scotia Rd
  Filby NR29 ....168 A7
Ormesby St Margaret
  with Scratby NR29 ..167 B1
Nowhere La NR33 ...80 D4
Nuffield Cl NR31 ....170 B4
Nuffield Cres NR31 .170 B4
Nunn's Way NR19 ..154 D5
Nunnery Dr NR4 ...176 D1
Nunnery Pl IP24 ....176 D2
Nunnery The* IP24 .176 D2
Nuns' Bridges Rd
  IP24 ....176 D2
Nunsgate IP24 .....176 D2
Nurseries Ave NR13 165 E4
Nursery Cl Acle NR13 166 B4
  2 Beetley NR19 .....49 C3
  7 Belton NR31 ......94 A5
  2 Gressenhall NR20 ..49 C3
  King's Lynn PE30 ...148 C3
  8 Marthan NR29 ....57 D5
  Norwich NR6 ....157 E5
  2 Roydon PE32 .....28 A1
Nursery Dr
  Hunstanton PE36 ...132 C4
  North Walsham NR28 151 B3
  Wisbech PE13 ......152 E8
Nursery Gdns NR13 165 E5
Nursery La
  Brancaster PE31 .....3 E6
  Costessey NR8 .....156 F3
  Hockwold cum Wilton
    IP26 ....114 A6
  King's Lynn PE30 ...148 C3
Nursery Rd NR28 ...172 C6
Nursery Terr NR30 .169 C6
Nursery Way PE32 ...28 A1
Nursey Cl NR35 ....109 D3
Nut La NR27 ....139 F3
Nuthall Cl 7 NR4 ...161 F1
Nuthall Cres PE30 ..147 A8
Nutmeg Wlk PE38 ..172 E6
Nuttele Cl NR15 ....107 C6
Nuttery Vale IP23 ..130 F2
Nutwood Cl NR8 ...155 D2

O

Oak Ave
  14 Great Yarmouth NR31 94 C7
  King's Lynn PE30 ...148 D2
  Marham PE33 ....63 B4
  North Elmham NR20 ..49 E7
  Norwich NR7 ......163 F8
  9 Poringland NR14 ...90 C5
  West Winch PE33 ....43 F7
Oak Cl 4 Hethersett NR9 88 D8
  Norwich NR5 ....156 F6
  1 Tasburgh NR15 ...106 F6
  Thetford IP24 ......176 A1
Oak Cres IP23 .....130 C1

Oak Dr PE14 ....77 F7
Oak Gr 7 Horsford NR10 .53 B3
  Sheringham NR26 ...138 D5
Oak La East Ruston NR12 .38 E7
  2 Hingham NR9 .....86 C4
  Norwich NR3 ....158 D3
Oak Lodge NR7 ....163 C5
Oak Rd Dilham NR28 ..38 D4
  Great Yarmouth NR31 170 B6
  North Walsham NR28 151 B4
  Stoke Ferry PE33 ...81 A2
Oak St Fakenham NR21 141 B4
  Feltwell IP26 ....98 E1
  Norwich NR3 ....178 A4
Oak Tree Bsns Pk NR13 72 E8
Oak Tree Cl 3 NR29 ..57 D5
Oak Tree Way 8 IP20 122 D1
Oak View Dr PE38 ..172 C6
Oak Wood NR13 ....165 E5
Oakapple Dr NR19 ..154 D8
Oak's La IP23 ......72 F2
Oakcroft Dr NR14 ...90 C5
Oakdale Rd NR13 ...165 D3
Oakdene NR21 ......15 C3
Oakfield Cl PE38 ...172 C4
Oakfield Dr 8 NR13 ..74 B8
Oakfield Rd
  Aylsham NR11 .....150 C6
  Long Stratton NR15 106 F3
Oakfields NR14 ......91 F2
Oakfields Cl 1 NR4 ..89 C8
Oakfields Rd NR4 ...89 B8
Oakhill NR13 ....165 D3
Oakland Dr 5 NR20 ..49 C8
Oaklands
  Little Snoring NR21 ..17 C3
  4 Old Buckenham NR17 104 D2
  Poringland NR14 ....90 C6
  6 Taverham NR8 ...155 B2
Oaklands Cl
  Attleborough NR17 ..174 C3
  Halvergate NR13 ....74 F2
Oaklands Dr
  Brandon IP27 ......114 D4
  Cringleford NR4 ....161 C1
  Walsoken PE13 .....152 F7
Oaklands La 2 PE33 ..61 D3
Oaklands Pk NR28 ..151 B6
Oaklands The PE37 .153 C3
Oakleigh Dr PE13 ..153 A5
Oakley Church La
  IP21 ....130 D4
Oakley Cl PE13 ....152 E4
Oakroyd Cres PE13 .152 C6
Oaks Cl PE37 ......153 C3
Oaks Dr Necton PE37 ..65 F4
  Swaffham PE37 ....153 C3
Oaks La NR34 ......111 B5
Oaks The Ashill IP25 ..84 A7
  3 Beetley NR19 .....49 C3
  3 Gressenhall NR20 ..49 C3
  Mattishall NR20 .....68 F5
Oaktree Dr NR7 ....159 B2
Oakwood Dr NR19 ..154 D8
Oakwood Dr NR18 ..173 E6
Oakwood Rd NR19 ..154 D8
Oasis Leisure Ctr
  PE36 ....132 C4
Oasis Sport & Leisure Ctr
  NR7 ....72 C2
Oasis Way PE36 ...132 C2
Oatfield Cl 7 NR10 ..53 A3
Obelisk La NR28 ....37 F5
Obelisk Plain NR25 .137 A6
Occupation Rd 1 NR20 68 F6
Octagon Dr 4 PE13 .152 A6
Octavia Cl PE13 ...152 F6
Octavia Hill Birthplace Mus*
  PE13 ....152 C5
Oddfellows Field 4 NR25 7 C5
Oddfellows Row PE31 134 E4
Offley Ct 7 NR5 ....161 A8
Ogden Cl NR18 ....173 C4
Oil Mill La PE13 ...152 B5
Old Allotment Ct 7
  NR3 ....162 F8
Old Bakery Ct PE31 133 C5
Old Barge Yd NR1 ..178 C2
Old Barley Mkt The
  NR2 ....178 A3
Old Bear Ct NR28 ..151 C5
Old Becclesgate NR19 154 D5
Old Brandon Rd IP26 ..98 F1
Old Brewery Ct 14 PE30 146 E3
Old Brewery La NR10 149 C4
Old Buckenham High Sch
  NR17 ....104 D2
Old Buckenham Prim Sch
  NR17 ....104 D2
Old Buckenham Rd
  NR16 ....105 A4
Old Bungay Rd NR35 109 D4
Old Bury Rd
  Palgrave IP22 .....129 E4
  Stuston IP21 ......177 F1
  Thetford IP24 ......176 C4
  Wortham IP22 .....129 D4
Old Catton Mid Sch
  NR6 ....158 E5
Old Chapel Rd
  Cantley NR13 ....92 E7
  2 Hemsby NR29 ....58 B6
Old Chapel Way NR7 .72 E3
Old Church Cl NR14 ..89 F6
Old Church Rd
  Hainford NR10 ......53 E6
  Hopton on Sea NR31 171 D4
  Snettisham PE31 ....12 E5

Old Coach Rd NR27 ....139 C6
Old Coast Rd NR29 ....167 E2
Old Fakenham Rd
  Attlebridge NR9 ....52 B3
  Foxley NR20 ....50 D8
Old Farm La NR3 ....158 B1
Old Feltwell Rd IP26 ...99 A5
Old Forge Cl IP22 .....129 B4
Old Forge Ct
  Acle NR13 ....166 C4
  Brockdish IP21 ....131 D6
Old Fountain NR31 ....170 C1
Old Friendship La
  NR10 ....35 C2
Old Gr Ct NR3 ....158 D2
Old Hall Cl
  Ashwellthorpe NR16 ...105 F8
  1 Norwich NR14 ....163 B2
  Saham Toney IP25 ......84 B5
Old Hall Dr PE31 ......140 E3
Old Hall Gdns
  Brooke NR15 ....90 F2
  Buxton with Lammas
  NR10 ....37 A2
  Caister-on-Sea NR30 ..168 E5
Old Hall La PE37 ....81 F8
Old Hall Rd
  East Dereham NR19 ....154 D2
  Mattishall NR20 ....68 D5
  Witton NR28 ....38 B8
Old Hall The PE31 ......27 C3
Old Harleston Rd
  NR35 ....123 E7
Old High Rd IP22 ......177 A5
Old Hithe Rd NR26 ....138 A6
Old Hunstanton Rd
  PE36 ....132 E7
Old Kiln 10 PE33 ....43 F2
Old La East Ruston NR12 .24 A5
  Happisburgh NR12 ......23 F1
  Reepham NR10 ....34 B1
  Thelnetham IP22 ......128 A2
Old Lakenham Hall Dr 6
  NR1 ....162 E1
Old Laundry Ct 3 NR2 .162 B8
Old Laundry Mews
  NR1 ....163 A5
Old Liby Mews NR1 ....178 C2
Old Lynn Rd PE13 .....152 E7
Old Maltings The
  PE13 ....153 B4
Old Manor Cl PE30 ....148 C1
Old Methwold Rd
  Feltwell IP26 ....98 E2
  Northwold PE33 ....81 B2
Old Mill Dr IP21 ......121 F4
Old Mill Rd
  Caister-on-Sea NR30 ..168 F5
  3 Poringland NR14 .....90 C5
  Roughton NR11 ....139 B1
Old Mkt PE13 ....152 C5
Old Mkt Cl NR13 ......166 C3
Old Mkt Gn 3 NR14 ....92 A1
Old Mkt Pl 21 IP20 ...122 D2
Old Mkt St
  14 King's Lynn PE30 ..146 E5
  Thetford IP24 ....176 D3
Old Mkt Way NR15 ....107 C5
Old Norwich Rd
  Horsham St Faith &
  Newton St Faith NR10 ..53 D1
  Yaxley IP23 ....130 A1
Old Pal Rd NR2 ....162 B7
Old Pools Dro CB6 .....95 F1
Old Post Office La
  NR35 ....109 E3
Old Post Office St
  2 Fakenham NR21 .....141 B4
  2 Shipdham IP25 ......67 B2
Old Post Rd NR12 .....142 E4
Old Quarry Ct NR19 ...154 E6
Old Rd Acle NR13 .....166 C4
  1 Great Moulton NR15 .106 B1
Old Rectory Cl
  King's Lynn PE30 .....148 D5
  4 Mulbarton NR14 .....89 B3
  Norwich NR7 ....163 E6
  7 Roydon IP22 ....129 D7
  South Wootton PE30 ..148 B1
Old Rectory Rd NR12 ..24 A1
Old Reepham Rd 4
  NR20 ....50 E7
Old Rly Rd IP20 ......123 B5
Old Rly Yd PE13 ......135 C2
Old Roman Bank
  PE34 ....144 A7
Old Sch Cl NR5 ....161 E5
Old Sch Ct NR1 ....178 C1
Old Sch Rd
  East Ruston NR12 ......38 F8
  Guestwick NR20 ....33 F5
Old Severalls Rd IP26 ..98 E6
Old South NR30 ....147 C4
Old Southwood Rd
  NR13 ....74 B2
Old St 2 NR15 ....107 A8
Old Sta La NR35 ......109 D2
Old Sta Way 6 NR25 ..137 C7
Old Stoke Rd NR14 .....89 F8
Old Town Way PE36 ...132 E7
Old Turnpike Rd NR11 ..21 D7
Old Vicarage Pk PE32 ..63 E7
Old Warren NR8 ......155 D2
Old Watton Rd NR4 ...161 A5
Old Wellington Pl 15
  NR30 ....169 D3
Old Wells Rd
  Sculthorpe NR21 ....16 A2

Old Wells Rd continued
  Walsingham NR22 ......16 E8
Old Woman's La NR25 ...7 F6
Old Yarmouth Rd NR12 .39 C2
Oldfield Ave PE14 ......59 B1
Oldfield Ct 3 NR19 ...154 E6
Oldfield La PE13 ......152 B3
Oldhall La NR16 ......118 C5
Oldhall Rd NR4 ....89 E8
Oldmedow Rd PE30 ...147 A2
Oldsunway PE30 ......146 D5
Oldwash La NR16 .....105 D3
Olive Ave NR15 ....89 D1
Olive Cl NR5 ....157 C1
Olive Cres NR10 ....53 A4
Olive Rd
  Great Yarmouth NR31 .169 B3
  Norwich NR5 ....157 C1
Oliver Ct
  5 Cromer NR27 ....139 C6
  2 Weeting IP27 ....114 E1
Oliver Mews 4 NR30 ..169 D4
Olivet Way NR21 .....141 C3
Olivia Cl NR21 ....141 A5
Ollands Rd
  Attleborough NR17 ...174 C3
  Reepham NR10 ....149 C4
Ollard Ave PE13 ......152 D7
Olley Rd 1 NR27 ......10 A5
Olney Rd NR19 ....154 D5
Onedin Cl PE31 ......140 C5
Onley St NR2 ....162 B4
Onslow Ave NR30 ....169 D7
Onyx Ct 10 PE13 .....152 C4
Opie St NR2 ....178 B3
Opportune Rd PE13 ..152 E7
Orange Gr 3 PE13 ...152 C4
Orange Row NR19 ...144 A5
Orange Row Rd PE34 .144 A6
Orchard Bank NR8 ...156 E8
Orchard Cl Acle NR13 .166 B4
  Ashill IP25 ....84 A6
  Attleborough NR17 ...174 C3
  Blofield Heath NR13 ..73 C6
  Brancaster Staithe PE31 ..3 D7
  Briston NR24 ....142 D4
  Caister-on-Sea NR30 .168 E4
  Dersingham PE31 ....140 D4
  Downham Market PE38 172 D5
  Fakenham NR21 ......141 D4
  3 Ixworth NR9 ....69 F2
  Mundesley NR11 .....143 B7
  North Elmham NR20 ...49 E7
  North Walsham NR28 .151 C6
  Norwich NR7 ....163 C8
  Roughton NR11 ....21 D7
  Sheringham NR26 ....138 D7
  Tacolneston NR16 ...105 F4
  Watlington PE33 ......61 E5
  19 Watton IP25 ....84 D3
  8 Wisbech PE14 ......59 A1
Orchard Cres 4 NR15 .106 C1
Orchard Ct
  King's Lynn PE30 ....147 B6
  Ormesby St Margaret
  NR29 ....167 A8
Orchard Dr
  Hellesdon NR6 ......157 D3
  3 Potter Heigham NR29 .56 F6
  West Walton PE14 ....59 C8
  Wisbech PE13 ....152 E4
Orchard Gdns 3 PE30 .147 B6
Orchard Gr Diss IP22 .177 C5
  Kettlestone NR21 .....17 C2
  King's Lynn PE34 ....146 C3
Orchard La
  Aylsham NR11 ....150 C6
  Castle Acre PE32 .....46 F2
  King's Lynn PE30 ....147 B5
  Reepham NR10 ......149 D5
  Shouldham PE33 ......62 D4
Orchard Pl
  Swaffham PE37 ......153 B4
  Thompson IP24 ......102 A7
Orchard Rd
  8 Gayton PE32 ....45 C6
  Lingwood NR13 ....73 F3
  5 Mattishall NR20 ....68 E6
  2 Spixworth NR10 ....54 A2
  4 Wiggenhall St Germans
  PE34 ....43 B1
Orchard St NR2 ......162 A2
Orchard The
  4 Belton NR31 ....94 A4
  Brandon IP27 ....175 C3
Orchard Way
  Banham NR16 ....119 D7
  4 Burgh St Margaret
  (Fleggburgh) NR29 ...57 C1
  5 Hethersett NR9 ....88 D8
  7 Tasburgh NR15 ....106 F6
  Terrington St John PE14 .42 B1
  Thetford IP24 ....176 D5
  Wymondham NR18 ...173 D4
Orchards Prim Ssh
  PE13 ....152 D8
Orchid Ave NR19 .....154 D1
Orde Ave NR31 ....170 C2
Ordnance Rd NR30 ...169 D1
Orford Cl 5 NR30 ....169 C5
Orford Hill NR1 ......178 B2
Orford Pl Norwich NR1 .178 B2
  7 West Winch PE33 ...43 F2
Orford Rd PE37 ......153 C6
Orford St NR1 ....178 B2
Orhard Gr PE33 ....43 E2
Oriel Ho NR30 ....170 A3

Oriel High Sch NR31 ..170 A3
Origins★ NR2 ....178 A2
Ormesby 4 NR30 .....147 D5
Ormesby Fst Sch
  NR29 ....167 A2
Ormesby La NR29 .....76 A8
Ormesby Mid Sch
  NR29 ....167 A3
Ormesby Rd
  Caister-on-Sea NR30 .168 D7
  Hemsby NR29 ....167 A6
  Ormesby St Margaret
  with Scratby NR10 ..168 C8
  Scottow NR10 ....37 B2
Ormond Rd NR30 ....169 C5
Orwell Cl
  King's Lynn PE30 ....147 C4
  2 Wymondham NR18 .173 D5
Orwell Cres NR31 .....94 A6
Orwell Rd NR2 ....162 C3
Osbert Cl NR1 ....162 E1
Osborne Ave NR29 ...169 C7
Osborne Cl 1 NR28 ..151 C7
Osborne Ct NR4 .....162 B3
Osborne Pk PE13 ....152 C8
Osborne Rd
  Norwich NR4 ....161 D2
  Wisbech NR13 ....152 B7
Osier Cl NR19 ....154 B4
Osier La NR25 ....9 C1
Osprey Cl NR12 ......164 D5
Ostend Gap NR12 .....24 A7
Ostend Pl NR12 ......24 A7
Ostend Rd NR12 ......24 A6
Ostrich La NR19 ......49 A3
Otter Cl
  3 Downham Market
  PE38 ....172 A6
  5 Salhouse NR13 .....55 A1
Otter Dr 7 NR14 ......89 B3
Otter Trust The★
  NR35 ....123 E7
Oulton Cl PE37 ......153 C2
Oulton Rd NR6 ......158 C5
Ouse Ave NR30 ......146 D2
Ouse Ave The IP24 ...176 C3
Ouse La NR12 ....39 F1
Out S Gates PE30 ....146 E3
Outney Rd NR35 .....124 A8
Outwell Rd Emneth PE14 .59 B2
  Stow Bardolph PE34 ...78 E8
Oval Ave NR5 ....161 C8
Oval Rd NR5 ....157 C1
Oval The IP25 ....84 B5
Over Cross NR16 ....119 C8
Overbury Rd NR6 ...158 A4
Overstone Ct NR6 ...158 F5
Overstrand Belfry VA Prim
  Sch NR27 ....11 A3
Overstrand Rd NR27 .139 C6
Overstrand Sports Club
  NR27 ....11 A3
Overtons Way 14 NR14 ..90 C5
Overwood La NR16 ..106 A3
Overy Rd PE31 ......135 D3
Ovington Rd PE33 ....84 C4
Owen Rd PE30 ......147 A4
  Great Yarmouth NR31 .169 B1
Owen's Cl 22 NR15 ..106 E3
Owl Dr 3 NR14 ....89 B3
Oxborough Dr PE30 ..148 E1
Oxborough La NR21 .141 C4
Oxborough Rd
  Oxborough PE33 ......81 D3
  Stoke Ferry PE33 .....81 A2
Oxburgh Cl 1 PE13 ..152 A7
Oxburgh Hall Gdns & Estate★
  PE33 ....81 D4
Oxcroft NR13 ....166 C4
Oxford Ave NR30 ....170 B3
Oxford Pl PE34 ......144 F6
Oxford Rd 2 Feltwell IP26 98 E1
  2 Feltwell IP26 ....98 E1
Oxford St NR2 ......162 C5
Oxford Way 11 NR29 .57 C4
Oxnead Dr NR30 ....168 C7
Oxnead La NR35 ....107 F4
Oxnead Rd NR3 .....158 B2

P

Pack La Briston NR24 .142 F3
  East Carleton NR14 ...89 A6
  Strumpshaw NR13 ....73 F3
Packway The IP20 ...123 A3
Paddock Cl Belton NR31 .93 F6
  3 Fakenham NR21 ...141 E4
Paddock Farm IP31 .127 B4
Paddock Farm Dr NR29 .75 F8
Paddock Rd 13 IP20 ..122 D2
Paddock St NR2 .....162 C8
Paddock The
  3 Cromer NR27 ......10 B5
  Hemsby NR29 ....167 A8
  Trowse with Newton
  NR14 ....163 A2
Paddocks The
  Aylsham NR11 ....150 C6
  Bacton/Walcott NR12 .23 E4
  Beetley NR20 ....49 D4
  Brandon IP27 ....175 C4
  Downham Market PE38 172 B5
  Griston IP25 ....85 A1
  Norwich NR6 ....158 A4
  Swaffham PE37 .....153 B3
Paddy's La NR9 ....51 E1

Paddys Loke NR30 ...169 A7
Padgate NR13 ....72 D6
Padgett's Rd PE14 ....95 A6
Page Cl
  3 North Walsham NR28 .151 C6
  Poringland NR14 ......90 C5
Page Rd Brundall NR13 .165 C4
  Norwich NR3 ....157 F1
Page Stair La PE30 ..146 D5
Pages Cl 3 NR18 ....173 B3
Pages La IP25 ....84 B5
Paget Adams Dr 4 NR20 .68 A8
Paget Cres NR31 ....170 C1
Paget Rd NR30 ......169 D4
Paige Cl 1 PE33 ......61 D5
Paine Cl IP22 ....177 B5
Paine Rd NR7 ....163 D8
Painter St IP24 ......176 C4
Pakenham Dr PE31 ..140 C3
Palace St NR3 ......178 B3
Pales Gn 4 PE32 .....46 F2
Palgrave Cl NR8 ....155 B1
Palgrave Rd
  Great Dunham PE32 ..47 E1
  Great Yarmouth NR30 .169 C5
  Little Dunham PE32 ...65 D8
Palgrave VC Prim Sch
  IP22 ....177 D2
Palling Rd NR12 ......24 D1
Palm Cl NR18 ....173 B5
Palmer Rd
  Great Yarmouth NR31 .170 D5
  8 New Rackheath NR13 .72 E7
  Norwich NR8 ....158 C3
Palmer Way PE38 ...172 C3
Palmer's La
  Aylsham NR11 ......150 C6
Palmers La NR13 .....55 C5
Palmers La PE31 .....14 D8
Pandora 1 PE30 ....147 C4
Pansey Dr PE31 ....140 C4
Panton Cl 3 NR20 ..146 D2
Panxworth Church Rd
  NR13 ....73 E8
Panxworth Rd NR13 ..73 F7
Paper St NR19 ....68 C6
Papillon Rd NR18 ...173 D4
Paradise La
  6 Bawdeswell NR20 ..50 E7
  7 King's Lynn PE30 ..146 D5
Paradise Par 10 PE30 .146 D5
Paradise Pl NR1 ....178 B2
Paradise Rd
  7 Bawdeswell NR20 ..50 E7
  Downham Market PE38 172 B5
  9 King's Lynn PE30 ..146 D5
Paragon Pl 4 NR2 ..162 C6
Parana Cl NR7 .....159 C5
Parana Ct NR7 .....159 C5
Parana Rd NR7 .....159 C5
Parish Rd NR10 ......37 B2
Park Ave 5 Barford NR9 .69 F2
  King's Lynn PE30 ....146 F4
  North Walsham NR28 .151 D5
  Scottow NR10 ....37 D2
  Wisbech PE13 ....152 C6
Park Cl Hethersett NR9 .88 D7
  Holt NR25 ....137 D5
  Norwich NR6 ....158 E5
  Thurton NR14 ....91 C4
  Wymondham NR18 ..173 D1
Park Comm La NR16 .119 B5
Park Cres PE34 ......61 B5
Park Cl Harling NR16 .118 C5
  North Walsham NR28 .151 D5
Park Dr NR9 ....88 C7
Park Est 3 IP25 ......67 B2
Park Farm La
  Euston IP24 ....126 C4
  Hoxne IP21 ....131 C2
Park High Sch PE30 .147 A4
Park Highatt Dr 2 IP25 .67 C2
Park Hill PE31 ......140 D5
Park La Blofield NR13 .165 B8
  Cromer NR27 ....139 D4
  Deopham NR18 ......87 A4
  Downham Market PE38 172 B3
  Helhoughton NR21 ...30 E5
  Hockering NR20 ......69 C8
  North Walsham NR28 .151 D5
  Norwich NR2 ....162 B5
  Reepham NR10 ......149 B4
  Scarning NR19 ....67 B6
  Snettisham PE31 .....12 E4
  Wymondham NR18 ..173 C2
Park Rd Cromer NR27 .139 D5
  Diss IP22 ....177 D4
  East Dereham NR19 .154 E6
  Great Yarmouth NR31 .170 D3
  Gressenhall NR20 ....49 C3
  Hunstanton PE36 ...132 C4
  St Cross, South Elmham
  IP20 ....123 C3
  Spixworth NR10 .....54 A1
  Upper Sheringham
  NR26 ....138 A4
  Warham NR23 ....6 A4
  Wells-next-the-Sea
  NR23 ....136 C6
  Wisbech PE13 ....152 D6
  Wroxham/Hoveton
  NR12 ....164 B3
Park St 4 PE13 .....152 D6
Park The NR16 ......118 B5
Park View
  Botesdale IP22 .....128 F3
  Brandon IP27 ....175 B2
  Weeting IP27 ....175 A4

Old - Pec 203

Park View Ave NR29 ..57 D3
Park Way NR6 ......157 E5
Parker Cl NR13 .....165 B4
Parker Dr NR21 ....141 D4
Parker Rd NR2 .....162 B5
Parker's La NR15 ...106 F2
Parker's Rd 10 NR20 .68 F6
Parker's Cl NR9 .....70 C5
Parkers Cl NR18 ...173 B6
Parkers Prim Sch IP25 .84 C5
Parkes La NR15 ....106 D6
Parkhill 4 PE32 ......44 B3
Parkland Cl 8 NR12 .55 E4
Parkland Cres
  9 Horning NR12 .....55 E4
  Norwich NR6 ....158 F3
Parkland Dr NR31 ..170 A5
Parkland Est NR29 .167 A8
Parkland Rd NR6 ...158 F3
Parklands NR8 .....156 D4
Parklands Ave IP25 ..67 B2
Parklands Way 41 IP20 122 D2
Parkside PE36 ....13 A7
Parkside Ct IP22 ...177 D4
Parkside Dr NR6 ...158 E5
Parkside Specl Sch
  NR2 ....162 A5
Parkview IP24 ......176 E4
Parkway PE30 ......147 B4
Parliament Ct 5 NR7 ..72 C4
Parliament La NR2 ..102 E3
Parmenter Rd NR4 .161 F3
Parmeter Cl NR11 ..150 D6
Parr Rd NR3 ....158 A1
Parrow La NR11 .....21 C6
Parsons Cl IP27 ...175 B2
Parsons La PE31 .....14 D8
Parsons Mead NR4 .161 F1
Partridge Dr
  Mulbarton NR14 ......89 A3
  4 Thetford IP24 ....176 D2
Partridge Gr PE37 ..153 D3
Partridge Rd NR11 .150 B6
Partridge Way NR6 .158 D4
Partridge Wlk IP27 .175 F3
Parva Cl NR11 ....20 B4
Pasteur Rd NR31 ...169 B2
Paston Cl 4 NR11 ....9 E1
Paston Coll NR28 ...151 C5
Paston Dr NR30 ....168 C8
Paston Great Barn★
  NR28 ....143 E2
Paston Rd
  Great Yarmouth NR31 .170 D5
  Mundesley NR11 ....143 D5
Paston Way NR7 ...159 E2
Pasture Cl PE31 .....28 B4
Pastures The
  5 Blakeney NR25 .....7 C6
  Great Yarmouth NR31 .170 B7
  Hemsby NR29 ......167 A8
  Little Snoring NR21 ...17 B3
Patricia Ave NR12 ...54 C6
Patricia Rd NR1 ....162 D3
Patrick Rd 4 NR15 .106 D3
Patten La NR15 ....121 B3
Patterson Cl 4 NR30 .169 C4
Patteson Cl 8 NR4 ..89 B8
Patteson Rd NR3 ...162 D8
Paul Dr PE32 ....44 B3
Pauls La NR27 ....11 A3
Pavilion Ct 5 IP22 ..177 A5
Pavilion Rd NR31 ...170 C4
Pavilion Theatre
  NR31 ....170 E4
Paxman Rd PE30 ...146 F2
Paxton Terr PE30 ...146 E5
Payne Ave PE13 ....152 D7
Payne's La IP26 ......98 E1
Paynes Hill IP20 ...122 F4
Peachman Way 5 NR7 .72 E4
Peachtree St 6 NR21 .15 C2
Peacock Chase NR18 173 B2
Peacock Cl Easton NR9 .70 B5
  Hockwold cum Wilton
  IP26 ....113 F6
Peacock La
  Beetley NR20 ....49 E5
  Holt NR25 ....137 B7
Peacock St NR3 ....178 B4
Peacock Way NR4 ..142 A4
Peacocks The NR25 .137 C7
Peakhall Rd PE32 ....48 B8
Peakwell Cl NR8 ...155 C2
Pear Tree Cl NR11 ...68 E6
Pear Tree Cnr NR21 .31 C5
Pearce Rd IP22 ....177 E4
Pearce's Cl 2 IP26 .114 A7
Pearcefield NR3 ....158 E2
Pearmain Rd IP22 ..177 C5
Pearson's Rd NR25 .137 C6
Pearsons Cl
  Freethorpe NR13 ....92 E7
  Holt NR25 ....137 C6
Peartree Ave 2 NR29 .57 C4
Peartree Way 9 PE14 .59 A1
Peatlings La PE13 ..152 A7
Pebble Cl 3 PE12 ....41 B8
Pebble View Wlk
  NR31 ....171 D6
Peck Cl NR5 ....160 E8
Peckover Cty Prim Sch
  PE13 ....152 B6
Peckover Dr PE13 ..152 E4

Peckover House★
PE13 ....152 B5
Peckover Rd
Fakenham NR21 ......141 A6
Norwich NR4 ....161 E3
Peckover Way PE30 ..147 E8
Peddars Cl PE36 ....132 D6
Peddars Dr PE36 ....132 D6
Peddars' La NR34 ...110 C6
Peddars Way NR8 ...155 D2
Peddars Way N PE36 ..2 A4
Peddlars Turnpike
NR20 ....33 F3
Pedham Rd NR13 .....73 E7
Pedlar's Gr PE37 ...153 C5
Pedlar's La NR21 ....17 F1
Pedlars Croft 2 NR29 .167 A8
Pedley La PE13 .....152 A6
Peel Mews 5 NR31 ..178 A3
Peel St PE30 ....146 F4
Pegasus Cl NR30 ....168 D7
Pegg Cl NR9 ....70 B5
Pegg Rd NR26 ....138 C5
Pegg's La NR16 .....105 C6
Peggotty Rd NR30 ...170 D8
Peldon Dr PE13 .....152 E5
Pelham Rd NR3 ......158 D1
Pell Pl 2 PE33 ....43 F2
Pell Rd PE31 ....140 D4
Pellew Pl NR31 .....151 C6
Pemberton Rd 6 IP20 .122 D1
Pembrey Cl NR31 ....158 D3
Pembroke Ave NR31 ..170 B4
Pembroke Rd NR2 ...162 B5
Pendlesham Rise NR8 .155 E2
Pendula Rd PE13 ....152 E7
Penfold Dr NR18 ....173 E5
Penfold St NR11 ....150 C6
Penguin Rd NR29 ....167 D4
Penhill La NR17 ....103 D7
Penn Cl NR8 ....156 D8
Penn Gr NR3 ....158 C1
Penn Rd NR3 ....156 D8
Pennington Way PE31 .140 A1
Penny Croft 3 NR21 ..15 C2
Pennycress Dr
6 Thetford IP24 ......176 F5
Wymondham NR18 ....173 E4
Pennygate La NR12 ...38 F1
Pennyroyal 1 NR6 ...158 D5
Penrose Cl PE30 ....147 B8
Penrose Gdns PE13 ..152 E4
Penryn Cl NR4 ......161 E5
Penshurst Mews 5
NR4 ....161 F1
Pensthorpe Nature Reserve &
Gdns★ NR21 ....32 B8
Pentney Abbey Leisure Ctr
PE32 ....63 A7
Pentney Dro PE33 ....62 E6
Pentney La PE32 .....63 D8
Pepper La PE38 ......97 C8
Pepper's Gn PE30 ...148 B1
Peppers Cl IP27 ....175 B7
Percival Cl NR4 .....161 E4
Perebrown Ave NR30 .169 D7
Pereers Cl NR25 ....137 A4
Peregrine Cl Diss IP22 .177 F5
Norwich NR7 ....159 C4
Peregrine Mews NR7 .159 C4
Peregrine Rd NR7 ...159 C4
Perkin Field PE34 ...144 B4
Perrings NR18 ......173 B6
Perrys La NR10 ......35 C2
Persimmon PE30 ....147 C5
Peter Ave NR13 .....166 B3
Peter Beales Roses★
NR17 ....103 F3
Peter Cl NR29 ....168 D8
Peter Dr IP24 ......176 F5
Peter's Dro PE34 ....61 A7
Peterhouse Ave NR31 .170 C4
Peterhouse Fst Sch
NR31 ....170 C4
Peterhouse Mid Sch
NR31 ....170 B4
Peterkin Rd 3 NR4 ...89 E8
Peters Cl NR19 .....154 C1
Peterscourt PE30 ...147 D6
Petersfield Cl NR15 .106 F4
Peterson Rd NR3 ....158 A2
Peterson's La NR11 ..150 B7
Peterspoint PE12 ....41 A7
Peto Ct NR5 ....161 C7
Peto's Cnr NR32 ....111 F8
Petre Cl 3 NR28 ....151 C7
Petticoat Dro PE32 ..64 E8
Petticoat La PE33 ....62 D6
Pettingales 3 NR14 ..89 F4
Pettits La IP21 .....130 C7
Pettitts Animal Adventure
Pk★ NR13 ....93 A5
Petts Cl 3 PE13 ....152 B1
Pettus Rd NR4 ......161 E3
Petunia Way IP27 ...175 A2
Peverell Rd NR5 ....161 B7
Pheasant Cl NR14 ....89 A3
Pheasant Way IP27 ..175 A4
Pheasant Wlk 2 NR13 .74 B8
Pheasants Wlk NR35 .123 E8
Phelps Rd NR7 ......163 F7
Philadelphia La NR3 .158 D2
Philip Ford Way NR18 .173 C2
Philip Nurse Rd PE31 .140 B3
Philip Pl NR19 .....154 D2

Philip Rudd Ct PE32 ..45 A8
Philips' Chase PE36 .132 D2
Phillippo Cl 4 PE32 ..28 A1
Pickards Way PE13 ..152 A6
Pickford Cl NR28 ...151 E6
Picton Rd NR15 .....106 D4
Pier Gdns NR31 .....170 E4
Pier Pl NR30 ....169 D2
Pier Plain NR31 ....170 D5
Pier Rd NR31 ....170 E4
Pier Wlk NR31 ......170 D4
Pigeon St PE14 ......41 D3
Pigg La NR3 ....178 B4
Pightle Cl 21 NR14 ...89 B3
Pightle The PE37 ...153 C4
Pightle Way Lyng NR9 .51 A4
Reepham NR10 ....149 C5
Pigot La NR14 ....90 C6
Pike La IP24 ....176 D3
Pikeman Pl NR13 ....72 E5
Pikes Nursery NR29 ..56 C5
Pilgrim's Way 7 IP20 .122 D2
Pilgrims Way
Little Cressingham IP25 .83 F3
Weeting IP27 ....175 A8
Pilling Pk Rd NR1 ...163 B7
Pilling Rd NR7 ......163 D7
Pilot St 2 PE30 .....146 D5
Pimpernel Rd NR10 ...53 B2
Pinder Cl NR3 ......158 A1
Pinder Rd NR3 ......158 A1
Pine Ave
Cockley Cley PE37 .....82 D2
Marham PE33 ....63 B4
Pine Cl
5 Downham Market
PE38 ....172 C6
8 Eye IP23 ....130 C1
4 Harleston IP20 .....122 D1
Hunstanton PE36 .....132 D4
17 Marthan NR29 ......57 D4
Norwich NR4 ....162 A3
Ormesby St Margaret
NR29 ....167 A3
3 Snettisham PE31 ....12 E5
Thetford IP24 ....176 B1
Pine Coombe 1 NR21 ..15 C2
Pine Ct NR17 ....174 D4
Pine Gn NR31 ......170 B5
Pine Gr
East Dereham NR19 ...154 D2
Sheringham NR26 ....138 E6
Pine Loke NR14 ......90 B5
Pine Mall PE31 .....133 C6
Pine Rd
King's Lynn PE30 ....148 D2
Norwich NR7 ....159 E1
Pine Tree Chase PE33 .43 F1
Pine Tree Ct IP22 ...127 F5
Pine Trees Bsns Pk
NR7 ....159 D3
Pine Wlk 6 NR25 .....8 F5
Pinecot Ave 7 NR31 ..94 C6
Pineheath Rd NR25 ...8 E3
Pinelodges The NR7 .163 C6
Pinetrees NR31 ......93 E3
Pinetrees Rd NR7 ...159 D3
Pinewood Cl NR6 ...157 F4
Pinewood Dr
Brandon IP27 ....175 C2
6 Horning NR12 ......55 E4
Pinewood Leisure Ctr
NR25 ....9 B3
Pinfold La
Hindolveston NR20 ....33 D8
Northwold IP26 ....99 B8
Pinfold Rd PE14 .....77 E5
Pingle Rd PE14 ......78 A4
Pingles Rd PE30 ....148 C4
Pinkney La NR24 .....19 B5
Pintail Dr 2 Blakeney NR25 .7 C6
Great Yarmouth NR31 .170 A8
Pioneer Rd NR6 .....159 A6
Piper Rd
King's Lynn PE30 ....146 F1
Norwich NR7 ....159 E1
Pipit's Mdw NR11 ....21 A5
Pippin Cl
Dereham NR19 ....154 C3
Ormesby St Margaret
NR29 ....167 A2
Pippin Gdns PE13 ...152 F7
Pippin Gn NR4 ......161 E5
Pippin Pl PE13 .....152 E2
Pirnhow St NR35 ....109 B1
Pishmire Cl NR5 ....160 F6
Pit La PE37 ....153 C4
Pit Rd
Aldeby, Wheatacre,
Burgh St Peter NR34 .111 B4
Hemsby NR29 ....167 A7
Northrepps NR27 ......11 A1
Woodbastwick NR13 ...55 D1
Pit St NR11 ....22 C6
Pitchford Rd NR5 ...161 C6
Pitt Sq NR9 ....86 C4
Pitt St NR3 ....178 A4
Pitt's Hill NR15 ....107 B8
Pitts Hill Cl NR15 ..107 B8
Pius Dro PE14 ....77 E6
Plaford Rd NR7 .....159 A2
Plane Rd NR31 .....170 B6
Plantation Cl NR17 .174 C3
Plantation Dr NR7 ..159 D3
Plantation Gdn The★
NR2 ....162 C5

Plantation Rd
Aslacton NR15 ....121 A7
Blofield NR13 ....165 F7
4 Fakenham NR21 ....141 E4
North Walsham NR28 .151 C5
Norwich NR6 ....157 E6
Plantation The NR2 .162 B4
Plantsman Cl NR2 ...162 B3
Plasset Dr NR17 ....174 F7
Platten's Cl 1 NR11 ..19 F1
Plattens Ct NR12 ...164 B3
Playbarn The★ NR15 ..90 C3
Players Way NR6 ....158 E6
Playing Field La 12 NR29 .57 D4
Pleasance Ct PE30 ..147 A5
Pleasant Cl NR6 ....157 D5
Pleasant Ct 1 PE30 ..146 E3
Pleasant Pl PE31 ...133 D6
Pleasant Row 1 PE37 .153 C3
Pleasure Beach★
NR30 ....169 E1
Plevna Terr NR31 ...169 B3
Plough La
Hardingham NR9 ......86 D6
Watlington PE33 ......61 E5
Ploughboy La IP25 ...84 C6
Ploughman Rd PE30 .147 C4
Ploughman's Dro IP26 .98 B1
Ploughman's La IP21 .17 C6
Ploughman's Piece PE36 .2 E6
Plover Cl
Great Yarmouth NR31 .170 A7
3 Thetford IP24 .....176 D2
Plovers Ct IP27 .....175 F3
Plovers Way IP26 ...113 F7
Plowright Pl PE13 ..153 B4
Plum La NR11 ....20 C8
Plumb's Cl NR24 ....142 E4
Plumbly Cl NR15 ....151 D3
Plummer's La NR15 .107 C7
Plummers Hill NR23 .136 D5
Plump Rd NR15 .....106 D5
Plumsgate Rd NR12 ..39 C1
Plumstead Dr NR17 .174 E6
Plumstead Rd
Baconsthorpe NR25 ...20 A7
Edgefield NR24 ....19 C5
Great & Little Plumstead
NR13 ....72 C6
4 Norwich NR1 ......163 C8
Thorpe End NR13 .....72 E6
Woodbastwick NR13 ...73 D7
Plumstead Rd E NR13 .163 D8
Plymouth Cl 3 NR30 .168 C6
Plymouth Rd 2 IP31 .126 B1
Pocahontas Way PE31 .133 E5
Pockthorpe Gate NR3 .163 A7
Pockthorpe La IP24 .102 A7
Pockthorpe Loke
Barnham Broom NR9 ...69 D2
Hickling NR12 ....39 F2
Pockthorpe Rd NR9 ..88 A8
Podmore La NR19 ....67 C8
Point Dr 2 PE37 ....153 C3
Police Rd PE14 ......41 D4
Polka Rd NR23 .....136 D5
Pollard Rd NR10 .....53 E6
Pollywiggle Cl NR5 .161 A6
Pommer's La NR30 ..170 D8
Pond Cl 14 NR9 ......88 C7
Pond Hills Rd NR15 ..19 E7
Pond La Brandon IP27 .175 A2
Knapton NR28 ....143 B2
Surlingham NR14 .....73 B1
Taverham NR8 ....156 F4
Pond Rd
Antingham NR28 ......22 B4
East Dereham NR19 ...154 C4
3 Horsford NR10 .....53 A3
Swafield NR28 ....22 C3
Ponds End La IP22 ..127 E4
Pooley St IP22 .....128 F7
Poorhouse La NR14 ..89 A2
Pope's La PE34 .....144 A4
Poplar Ave
Great Yarmouth NR31 .170 C3
Heacham PE31 ....133 C6
King's Lynn PE34 .....43 D4
5 Marham PE33 ....63 B4
Norwich NR4 ....161 E1
Poplar Cl
Downham Market PE38 .172 B6
Honington IP31 ......126 B1
12 Horsford NR10 ....53 A3
Long Stratton NR15 ..106 F4
Norwich NR5 ....156 F2
Poplar Dr Filby NR29 .75 F8
Happisburgh NR12 ....23 F3
King's Lynn PE30 ....148 D2
Poplar Gr NR26 .....138 E5
Poplar Rd
Attleborough NR17 ...174 B2
West Winch PE33 .....43 F1
Poplar Way NR17 ...174 C2
Poplars The Hilgay PE38 .96 F8
Spexhall IP19 ....124 F1
Swanton Abbott NR10 ..37 C4
Tacolneston NR16 ....105 F4
Pople St NR18 .....173 B4
Poppy Cl
Chedgrave NR14 ......91 F2
North Walsham NR28 .151 F5
4 Thetford IP24 .....176 F4
Poppy Dr 5 NR26 ...138 B6
Poppy's La IP21 ....121 F5
Poppyfields 14 NR10 ..53 A3
Poringland Prim Sch
NR14 ....90 D5

Poringland Rd NR14 ..90 B5
Porson Rd NR7 .....159 C1
Port Rd NR15 ......122 B8
Port Row NR9 ....51 B4
Portal Ave IP25 .....84 F3
Portal Cl
4 Barnham IP24 .....125 F6
7 Feltwell IP26 ......98 D1
Portalfield 10 NR12 ..39 B4
Porter Rd 8 NR15 ...106 E3
Porter St PE38 .....172 A5
Porter's La NR9 .....51 E5
Porter's Loke
1 Belton NR31 ....94 A6
Burgh Castle NR31 ....93 F6
Norwich NR7 ....159 A3
Porter's Rd
Beighton NR13 ....74 E1
Freethorpe NR13 .....92 E8
Porterbush Rd 18 NR14 .89 B3
Portersfield Rd NR2 .162 B5
Porthole Cl 10 NR22 .111 F1
Portland Ct NR31 ...169 C3
Portland Pl
Great Yarmouth NR30 .169 E3
King's Lynn PE30 ....146 D2
3 Thetford IP24 .....116 A1
Portland St
12 King's Lynn PE30 .146 E5
Norwich NR2 ....162 B5
Portsmouth Rd 3 IP31 .126 B1
Portway Pl 6 NR2 ...162 C7
Portway Sq 10 NR2 ..162 C7
Post Mill PE30 .....147 C5
Post Mill Cl NR7 ...159 A3
Post Office Cl 8 NR13 .74 A3
Post Office La
Corpusty NR11 ....34 F8
Garvestone NR9 ......86 B8
Weston Longville NR9 .51 E2
12 Wisbech PE13 ....152 C5
Post Office Rd
Dersingham PE31 ....140 D3
Frettenham NR12 .....54 A4
Great & Little Plumstead
NR13 ....73 B7
Lingwood NR13 ....74 A3
Lingwood & Burlingham
NR13 ....73 F3
Toft Monks NR34 ....110 E5
Postmill Cl NR18 ...173 C4
Postwick La NR13 ...165 A4
Postwick Sta NR7 ...72 E5
Potash La
Bracon Ash NR16 .....88 D2
Eye IP23 ....130 B2
Potato Dro PE14 .....60 B4
Potspoon Hole
Coltishall NR12 ......54 D8
Tunstead NR12 ....37 D1
Potter Heigham Rd
NR29 ....56 D8
Potter's La
Rickinghall Superior
IP22 ....128 F1
Wymondham NR18 ...105 B6
Pottergate NR2 .....178 A3
Pottergate St NR15 .106 A2
Potters Cres NR15 ..121 C8
Potters Dr NR31 ....171 D5
Potters Vale IP22 ..128 C3
Pottle's Alley 4 NR9 ..86 C5
Pottles La NR13 .....92 F5
Poulter's Dro PE14 ..77 D1
Poultry Rd IP27 ....113 A3
Pound Cl
4 Harleston IP20 ....122 D2
Hevingham NR10 .....53 C8
Pound Gn La IP25 ...67 C2
Pound Hill IP25 .....84 B5
Pound La
Aylsham NR11 ....150 B6
Brundall NR13 ......165 F5
Burgh St Margaret (Fleggburgh)
NR29 ....75 C8
Ditchingham NR35 ...108 E2
Docking PE31 ....134 D5
Filby NR29 ....75 F8
Great Yarmouth NR31 .170 C3
Heacham PE31 ....133 D6
Litcham PE32 ....48 A4
Loddon NR14 ....109 C8
North Tuddenham NR20 .50 D2
Norwich NR7 ....72 C4
Runhall NR20 ....69 A4
Sloley NR12 ....37 F2
Toft Monks NR34 ....110 E5
Pound Rd
East Ruston NR12 ....38 F7
Hevingham NR10 .....53 C8
Ludham NR29 ....56 C5
North Walsham NR28 .151 D5
Powell Ct 5 NR19 ...154 C6
Power's Pl PE38 .....79 D1
Poynt Cl NR18 .....173 B5
Pratts Hill NR14 .....73 A1
Press La NR3 ....158 A2
Preston Ave NR3 ....173 A2
Preston Cl
Freethorpe NR13 .....92 E7
Wroxham/Hoveton
NR12 ....164 B2
Preston La NR14 ....109 F8
Preston Rd NR28 ...151 D6
Preston VC Prim Sch
NR15 ....106 F7
Pretty Dr IP21 .....130 C6
Pride Way NR13 .....72 E5

Primrose Cl
Attleborough NR17 ...174 B5
East Dereham NR19 ..154 B4
15 Mulbarton NR14 ...89 B3
Mundesley NR11 .....143 B5
Thetford IP24 ....176 F4
Trunch NR28 ....22 E5
Primrose Cres 2 NR7 ..72 D3
Primrose Ct 3 NR7 ...72 E5
Primrose Dr IP27 ...175 A2
Primrose Hill NR20 ..50 B4
Primrose La
Crostwick NR12 ....54 C3
Sheringham NR26 ....138 C5
Swanton Morley NR20 ..50 B4
Primrose Pl NR2 ....162 B5
Primrose Rd
Hingham NR9 ....86 B5
Norwich NR1 ....163 A6
Primrose Sq NR20 ...50 B4
Primrose Way
15 Great Yarmouth NR31 .94 C6
10 Horsford NR10 ....53 A3
Primrose Wlk NR28 .151 E4
Primula Dr NR4 .....161 D5
Prince Andrew Dr
PE31 ....140 D3
Prince Andrew's Cl
2 Aldborough NR11 ...21 A5
Norwich NR6 ....158 B5
Prince Andrew's Rd
NR6 ....158 B5
Prince Charles Cl
PE31 ....140 D3
Prince Edward Cl NR7 .163 F7
Prince Henry Pl PE38 .172 D4
Prince of Wales Cl
PE13 ....152 D8
Prince of Wales Rd
Caister-on-Sea NR30 .168 C6
Cromer NR27 ....139 B7
Norwich NR1 ....178 B3
Upton with Fishley NR13 .166 A8
Prince Regent Way
IP22 ....177 F3
Prince Rupert Way
NR13 ....72 D5
Prince St PE13 .....152 D5
Prince William Cl
PE36 ....132 C3
Prince's Rd
Bungay NR35 ....124 A3
Great Yarmouth NR30 .169 D4
Prince's St PE12 .....41 B8
Princes Rd PE13 ....152 C4
Princes St
North Walsham NR28 .151 A5
Norwich NR3 ....178 B3
Swaffham PE37 .....153 B4
Princes Way PE30 ..146 F5
Princess Beatrice Cl
NR6 ....157 D2
Princess Cl 7 IP25 ...84 D3
Princess Ct 5 NR25 .137 C5
Princess Dr PE36 ...132 D2
Princess Theatre
PE36 ....132 C4
Princess Way 5 NR35 .123 B4
Princess's Dr
Dersingham PE35 ....140 C1
Sandringham PE35 ....27 D7
Pringle Way 5 PE38 ..97 B5
Prins Ave PE13 .....152 D7
Prins Ct 3 PE13 ....152 D7
Printing Mus★ NR34 .110 D1
Prior Bank Orch 3
NR27 ....139 C6
Prior Cl 5 NR15 ....106 F6
Prior Rd NR7 ....72 D5
Prior Stephen Way
IP24 ....176 B3
Priors Dr NR6 ......158 E6
Priorswood NR8 ....155 E3
Priory Chase
Downham Market PE38 .172 B5
Wormegay PE33 ......61 F8
Priory Cl Acle NR13 .166 C3
Alpington NR14 ......90 F5
Caister-on-Sea NR30 .168 D4
2 Fritton & St Olaves
NR31 ....93 D2
7 Hethersett NR9 .....88 D7
Palgrave IP22 ....177 D1
Sheringham NR26 ....138 F5
Sporle with Palgrave
PE32 ....65 D6
Priory Cres NR21 .....6 E2
Priory Dro IP25 .....83 D4
Priory Gdns
1 Fritton & St Olaves
NR31 ....93 D2
12 East Dereham NR30 .169 C4
Priory La Ingworth NR11 .21 A1
12 Hethersett NR9 ...146 D4
Shotesham NR15 ......90 A2
Priory Maze & Gdns★
NR26 ....138 F6
Priory Pk IP24 .....176 C5
Priory Pl PE32 ......65 D6
Priory Plain 13 NR30 .169 C4
Priory Rd Bacton NR12 .23 E4
Castle Acre PE32 .....46 F1
Downham Market PE38 .172 B5
Fritton & St Olaves NR31 .93 D2
Great Cressingham IP25 .83 D5
Hethersett NR9 ....88 D7
King's Lynn PE30 ....148 C5

Priory Rd continued
Palgrave IP22 . . . .**177** C1
Sheringham NR26 . . . . . .**138** E7
Watton IP25 . . . .**84** E3
Woodbastwick NR13 . . . . .**55** F1
Priory Row 11 NR30 . . . . . .**169** C4
Priory St NR31 . . . .**170** D6
Priory Terr PE38 . . . .**172** B3
Priscilla Cl 1 NR5 . . . . . .**161** D5
Pristow Gn La NR16 . . . .**120** E7
Private Rd
Earsham NR35 . . . .**123** D8
Ormesby St Margaret
NR29 . . . .**167** A3
Procession La PE32 . . . . .**153** F6
Proctor Ave 3 NR14 . . . . .**92** A2
Proctor Cl 4 NR14 . . . . . .**92** A2
Proctor Rd
Chedgrave NR14 . . . .**91** F2
5 Loddon NR14 . . . .**92** A1
Norwich NR6 . . . .**158** F6
Proctors Cl PE30 . . . . . .**146** C5
Progress Way IP23 . . . . .**130** B1
Prom The NR29 . . . .**167** E4
Promenade
Overstrand NR27 . . . .**11** A4
Sheringham NR26 . . . . . .**138** E7
Prophets Alley PE34 . . . .**61** B6
Prospect Pl PE13 . . . . . .**152** C4
Proudfoot Way NR11 . . . .**150** B5
Provan Cres 8 NR11 . . . . .**94** A5
Provence Pl 2 PE13 . . . . .**152** C4
Providence Pl
Briston NR24 . . . .**142** E5
8 Thorpe Hamlet NR1 . . .**163** A6
Providence St 5 PE30 . . .**146** E4
Providence Terr PE13 . . . .**153** A5
Provision Mkt NR2 . . . . .**178** A3
Provost Rd · IP26 . . . .**98** D1
Pudding Norton Medieval
Village of★ NR21 . . . . .**31** E6
Puddingmoor NR34 . . . . .**110** C1
Pug St IP21 . . . .**121** B2
Pulham CE Prim Sch
IP21 . . . .**121** E5
Pullover Rd PE34 . . . . . .**146** A1
Pump La NR30 . . . .**168** D3
Punsfer Way PE34 . . . .**60** C8
Purbeck Cl PE13 . . . .**152** A4
Purdance Cl NR5 . . . . . .**160** D8
Purdy St NR25 . . . .**8** B6
Purdy Way NR11 . . . .**150** B6
Purfleet PE30 . . . .**146** D5
Purfleet St
11 King's Lynn PE30 . . . . .**146** D5
8 King's Lynn PE30 . . . . .**146** D5
Purland Rd NR7 . . . .**159** D2
Purley Cl NR31 . . . .**169** A1
Pursehouse Way IP22 . . .**177** E4
Purtingay Cl 3 NR4 . . . . .**162** A4
Putney Cl IP27 . . . .**175** A1
Pye La Cranworth IP25 . . . .**86** A6
Deopham NR18 . . . .**86** E2
Pye's La Castle Acre PE32 . .**46** F2
Swanton Morley NR20 . . . .**50** C3
Pyebush La NR13 . . . .**166** B5
Pyecroft Rd PE14 . . . .**41** E3
Pyehurn La NR10 . . . .**53** A3
Pyehurn Mews NR8 . . . . .**155** E3
Pyes Cl 1 NR25 . . . .**7** C6
Pyes Mill Rd NR14 . . . . . .**92** A1
Pyes Yd NR3 . . . .**178** B4
Pyghtle The 4 NR16 . . . . .**118** C5
Pyke Ct NR30 . . . .**168** D7
Pym Cl NR15 . . . .**72** E5
Pymar's La 6 NR15 . . . . .**107** C5
Pyrford Dr NR4 . . . .**161** F1

Q

Quaker La
Fakenham NR21 . . . .**141** B4
Norwich NR6 . . . .**53** E1
8 Spixworth NR12 . . . .**54** A1
Tasburgh NR15 . . . .**106** F6
Wisbech PE13 . . . .**152** A3
Quarry La NR9 . . . .**51** A5
Quay Angel NR31 . . . . . .**170** D1
Quay La NR25 . . . .**7** A7
Quay Mill Wlk 3 NR30 . .**169** C4
Quay Rd NR31 . . . .**170** D4
Quay Side NR3 . . . .**178** B4
Quay The Blakeney NR25 . . .**7** C6
Wells-next-the-Sea
NR23 . . . .**136** D6
Wiveton NR25 . . . .**7** E7
Quebec Cl 14 NR4 . . . .**89** B8
Quebec Rd
Dereham NR19 . . . .**154** D7
Norwich NR1 . . . .**163** A6
Quebec St NR19 . . . .**154** D5
Queen Anne's Rd
NR31 . . . .**170** C8
Queen Elizabeth Ave
PE30 . . . .**147** B7
Queen Elizabeth Cl
NR3 . . . .**178** C4
Queen Elizabeth Dr
Dersingham PE31 . . . .**140** D3
Wisbech PE13 . . . .**152** A3
Queen Elizabeth Hospl
PE30 . . . .**147** E5
Queen Elizabeth Way
Bawsey PE30 . . . .**147** F6
Castle Rising PE30 . . . .**27** C1
Queen Mary Rd PE30 . .**147** A5

Queen St
Great Yarmouth NR30 . . . .**169** C3
King's Lynn PE30 . . . .**146** D5
New Buckenham NR16 . . .**104** F1
Norwich NR1 . . . .**178** B3
Stradbroke IP21 . . . .**131** E1
12 Sutton Bridge PE12 . . . .**41** B8
Swaffham PE37 . . . .**153** B4
Wisbech PE13 . . . .**152** C6
Wymondham NR18 . . . . . .**173** C3
Queen's Cl PE33 . . . .**80** E4
Queen's Cres
Bircham PE31 . . . .**14** A3
Great Yarmouth NR30 . . . .**170** B3
Queen's Ct NR17 . . . .**174** D6
Queen's Dr PE14 . . . .**77** A7
Queen's Pl 2 PE34 . . . . . .**43** B1
Queen's Rd
Attleborough NR17 . . . . . .**174** C6
Clenchwarton PE34 . . . . .**146** A5
Fakenham NR21 . . . .**141** C4
Great Yarmouth NR30 . . . .**169** D2
Hethersett NR9 . . . .**88** D8
Holt NR25 . . . .**137** C5
Queen's Sq NR17 . . . .**174** C6
Queens Ave PE30 . . . . . .**146** D4
Queens Cl
6 Blakeney NR25 . . . .**7** C6
Norwich NR4 . . . .**162** A3
Queens Ct 1 NR15 . . . . . .**106** E3
Queens Dr PE36 . . . .**132** C6
Queens Gdns PE36 . . . . .**132** D6
Queens Rd
Brandon IP27 . . . .**175** A2
Cromer NR27 . . . .**139** D4
Norwich NR1 . . . .**178** A1
Wisbech PE13 . . . .**152** C4
Queens Sch The PE13 . . .**152** C3
Queensway
Caister-on-Sea NR30 . . . .**168** E4
7 Earsham NR35 . . . .**123** F8
King's Lynn PE30 . . . .**147** C6
North Walsham NR28 . . . .**151** A5
Roydon IP22 . . . .**177** A5
Thetford IP24 . . . .**176** C2
Watton IP25 . . . .**84** D3
Wymondham NR18 . . . . . .**173** B5
Queensway Com Jun Sch
IP24 . . . .**176** C2
Queensway Inf Sch
IP24 . . . .**176** C2
Quidenham Rd
Harling NR16 . . . .**118** D5
Kenninghall NR16 . . . .**119** A5
Quidenham NR16 . . . .**118** F8

R

Rabbit La
Downham Market PE38 . . . .**172** D6
Great Witchingham NR9 . . .**51** E6
Raby Ave PE30 . . . .**146** E6
Racecourse Rd NR7 . . . . .**159** E1
Raceys Cl 4 PE14 . . . .**59** D2
Rachel Cl 7 NR5 . . . .**161** C5
Rackham Rd NR31 . . . . . .**171** C5
Rackham Rd NR3 . . . .**158** D2
Rackheath La NR12 . . . . . .**54** B2
Rackheath Prim Sch
NR13 . . . .**54** D1
Radcliffe Rd NR8 . . . .**155** E2
RAF Air Defence Radar Mus★
NR12 . . . .**55** E5
Rafeman Cl NR5 . . . .**160** E7
Raglan St 1 NR2 . . . .**162** C6
Ragmere Rd NR17 . . . . . .**104** D1
Railway App 2 NR26 . . . .**138** D7
Railway Hill IP20 . . . .**122** C2
Railway La PE12 . . . .**41** B7
Railway Mus★ NR18 . . . .**173** D2
Railway Rd
Downham Market PE38 . . . .**172** A5
King's Lynn PE30 . . . .**146** E5
Wisbech PE13 . . . .**152** C3
Rainey Ct 37 IP20 . . . . . .**122** D2
Rainsborough Rise
NR13 . . . .**72** D5
Rainsthorpe PE30 . . . . . .**147** D8
Rainthorpe Hall★
NR15 . . . .**106** F8
Raleigh Ave NR30 . . . . . .**169** D7
Raleigh Inf Sch IP24 . . . .**176** E6
Raleigh Rd PE30 . . . .**147** B4
Raleigh Way IP24 . . . . . .**176** E6
Ram La NR15 . . . .**121** C4
Ramblers The NR14 . . . . . .**90** B6
Rambouillet Dr NR31 . . . .**170** A4
Ramm's La PE37 . . . .**66** A4
Ramms St NR23 . . . .**136** D5
Ramnoth Cty Jun Sch
PE13 . . . .**152** A4
Ramnoth Rd PE13 . . . . . .**152** C4
Rampant Horse St
NR2 . . . .**178** A2
Rampart Rd NR30 . . . . . .**169** C5
Rampart Way IP24 . . . . . .**176** D3
Ramsay Gdns PE36 . . . . .**132** D3
Ramsey Cl
Norwich NR4 . . . .**161** B3
Thetford IP24 . . . .**176** E6
Randall Cl 1 NR31 . . . . . .**171** D5
Randell Rd NR28 . . . .**151** E4
Randle Gn NR5 . . . .**161** C8
Randolf Rd NR1 . . . .**162** E2
Rands Rd PE14 . . . .**60** C5
Rangoon Cl NR7 . . . .**159** C4
Ransome Ave IP21 . . . . . .**130** D6

Ransome's Cl PE14 . . . . . .**77** E5
Ranson Rd NR1 . . . .**163** B5
Ranworth 5 PE30 . . . . . .**147** D5
Ranworth
8 Belton NR31 . . . .**94** A6
Swaffham PE37 . . . .**153** B1
Ranworth Dr NR29 . . . . .**167** B2
Ranworth Fst Sch
NR5 . . . .**161** E7
Ranworth Rd
Blofield NR13 . . . .**165** F8
Norwich NR5 . . . .**161** D7
South Walsham NR13 . . . . .**74** A8
Rash's Cres IP22 . . . .**129** C6
Rash's Gn NR19 . . . .**154** F2
Ratcliffe Rd NR21 . . . . . .**141** C4
Rattle Row
Mileham PE32 . . . .**48** C6
Wymondham NR18 . . . . . .**173** B4
Rattler's Rd IP27 . . . .**175** C3
Rattlerow Hill IP21 . . . . .**131** F2
Raven Cl NR31 . . . .**170** A7
Raven's La PE31 . . . .**29** D5
Raveningham Gdns★
NR14 . . . .**110** A7
Raveningham Rd
Gillingham NR34 . . . .**110** C5
Stockton NR34 . . . .**110** A5
Ravensway PE38 . . . .**172** C3
Ravine Rd NR31 . . . .**93** E1
Rawhall La NR20 . . . .**49** B5
Rawley Rd NR5 . . . .**161** B8
Rawlings Way 21 PE14 . . . .**98** E1
Rawlinsons La NR11 . . . . .**150** C7
Ray Bond Way NR11 . . . .**150** C4
Raymond Cl NR6 . . . .**157** E7
Raymond Rd NR6 . . . .**157** F7
Raymond St
Thetford IP24 . . . .**176** D3
15 Wisbech PE13 . . . .**152** C4
Rayner's Cl 6 NR20 . . . . . .**68** E6
Rayner's La NR35 . . . . . .**109** D4
Rayner's Way NR20 . . . . . .**68** E6
Raynham Cl PE30 . . . . . .**147** B4
Raynham Rd
Dunton NR21 . . . .**31** C4
Hempton NR21 . . . .**141** A4
Whissonsett NR20 . . . .**31** C2
Raynham Ride NR19 . . . .**154** D7
Raynham St NR2 . . . .**162** B7
Rayns Cl NR6 . . . .**158** F5
Read's Cross NR14 . . . . .**109** E8
Readscross La NR14 . . . .**109** E8
Recorder Rd NR1 . . . . . .**178** C3
Recreation Dr PE38 . . . . . .**97** A5
Recreation Gd Rd
NR7 . . . .**159** A4
Recreation Rd
East Dereham NR19 . . . . .**154** C1
Great Yarmouth NR31 . . . .**170** C6
Hethersett NR9 . . . .**88** C7
North Walsham NR28 . . . .**151** B6
Norwich NR2 . . . .**162** A5
Stalham NR12 . . . .**39** A4
Rectory Cl
Caister-on-Sea NR30 . . . .**168** E5
Coltishall NR12 . . . .**54** D7
21 Long Stratton NR15 . . .**106** E3
2 Newton Flotman NR15 . . .**89** D1
Rollesby NR29 . . . .**57** C2
Roydon PE32 . . . .**27** F2
Rectory Ct NR3 . . . .**158** C4
Rectory Dr PE34 . . . .**145** E5
Rectory Gdns
Hingham NR9 . . . .**86** B5
Wisbech PE13 . . . .**152** E6
Rectory Hill IP22 . . . .**128** D2
Rectory La
Bracon Ash NR14 . . . .**88** E3
Bunwell NR16 . . . .**105** C4
Great Ellingham NR17 . . . .**103** E8
Haddiscoe NR14 . . . .**110** F7
Hedenham NR35 . . . .**108** D4
Little Melton NR9 . . . .**160** A3
Loddon NR14 . . . .**92** A2
Mettingham NR35 . . . . . .**124** D8
Mulbarton NR14 . . . .**89** B3
North Runcton PE33 . . . . . .**44** A3
Poringland NR14 . . . .**90** D5
Scole IP21 . . . .**121** C1
Stuston IP21 . . . .**130** B4
Watlington PE33 . . . .**61** D5
Weeting IP27 . . . .**175** B7
West Winch PE33 . . . .**43** F3
Rectory Mdw
Diss IP22 . . . .**177** E4
Litcham PE32 . . . .**48** A4
Rectory Rd
Aldeby, Wheatacre,
Burgh St Peter NR34 . . . .**111** A4
Bacton NR28 . . . .**23** C3
Brome & Oakley IP23 . . . .**130** B4
Broome NR35 . . . .**109** B3
Burston & Shimpling
IP22 . . . .**120** E2
2 Coltishall NR12 . . . .**54** C6
Dickleburgh IP21 . . . .**121** B1
East Carleton NR14 . . . . . .**89** A4
Edgefield NR24 . . . .**19** D5
Elsing NR20 . . . .**50** F4
Gillingham NR34 . . . .**109** F4
Gissing IP22 . . . .**120** F4
Haddiscoe NR14 . . . .**110** F7
Hockering NR20 . . . .**69** B8
Hoveton NR12 . . . .**55** A7
Lyng NR9 . . . .**51** B4
Northrepps NR27 . . . .**11** A1
Outwell PE14 . . . .**77** F6

Rectory Rd continued
Rocklands NR17 . . . .**103** B7
Shelfanger IP22 . . . .**120** B2
Sutton NR12 . . . .**39** C2
Swanton Morley NR20 . . . .**50** B4
Tivetshall St Mary NR15 . .**121** C4
Topcroft NR35 . . . .**107** F4
Weston Longville NR9 . . . .**51** D2
Whissonsett NR20 . . . .**31** E2
Wood Norton NR20 . . . . . .**33** A7
Wortham IP22 . . . .**129** D6
Red Admiral Cl 11 NR18 .**173** E4
Red Barn La NR5 . . . .**9** D1
Red Bridge La NR5 . . . . .**157** C2
Red Cottage Cl NR3 . . . .**158** A2
Red Lion Cl
Holme Hale IP25 . . . .**66** B2
Hoxne IP21 . . . .**131** B4
Red Lion St
3 Aylsham NR11 . . . .**150** C7
Norwich NR1 . . . .**178** B2
Red Lion Yd NR23 . . . . . .**136** D6
Red Robin Cl 9 NR15 . . . .**106** D3
Redbrick Cotts IP27 . . . .**175** D5
Redcastle Furze Prim Sch
IP24 . . . .**176** B3
Redcastle Rd IP24 . . . . . .**176** A4
Redcliffe Way NR13 . . . . .**165** B4
Redell Cl 3 NR13 . . . .**55** A1
Redenhall Rd IP20 . . . . . .**122** C3
Redfern Cl
East Dereham NR19 . . . . .**154** B4
King's Lynn PE30 . . . .**147** E8
Redfern Rd NR7 . . . .**159** D1
Redgate IP24 . . . .**176** E4
Redgate Hill PE36 . . . . . .**132** D2
Redgate Jun Sch
PE36 . . . .**132** D2
Redgate Rd PE13 . . . .**41** A4
Redgrave & Lopham Fen
National Nature Reserve★
IP22 . . . .**128** F6
Redgrave Rd
South Lopham IP22 . . . . .**128** E7
Wortham IP22 . . . .**129** A5
Redman Rd NR28 . . . .**151** D3
Redmere Cl 4 NR12 . . . . . .**54** A4
Redmere Dro CB7 . . . . . .**112** D5
Redwell St NR2 . . . .**178** B3
Redwing Dr
1 Great Yarmouth NR31 . . .**94** C7
5 Wisbech PE13 . . . .**152** D2
Redwing Gdns 7 NR10 . . .**54** A1
Redwings Horse Sanctuary
(Caldecott)★ NR31 . . . . .**93** F4
Reed La NR19 . . . .**48** F3
Reed Way 3 PE14 . . . .**77** A8
Reeder Cl NR19 . . . .**154** D3
Reeder's La NR14 . . . .**90** E4
Reedham Prim Sch
NR13 . . . .**93** A4
Reedham Rd
Acle NR13 . . . .**166** B1
Beighton NR13 . . . .**74** E1
Cantley NR13 . . . .**92** D6
Reedham Sta NR13 . . . . . .**92** F5
Reedham Sta NR13 . . . . . .**92** F5
Reepham High Sch
NR10 . . . .**149** B3
Reepham Prim Sch
NR10 . . . .**149** B4
Reepham Rd
Bawdeswell NR20 . . . .**50** F8
Briston NR24 . . . .**142** E2
Felthorpe NR10 . . . .**155** D5
Foulsham NR20 . . . .**33** D3
Guestwick NR20 . . . .**34** A5
Horsford NR10 . . . .**157** D7
Norwich NR6 . . . .**157** E2
Swannington NR9 . . . .**52** B5
Thurning NR20 . . . .**34** B8
Wood Dalling NR11 . . . . . .**34** D5
Reeve Cl IP21 . . . .**130** D6
Reeve Pl NR27 . . . .**139** D4
Reeves Ave NR30 . . . . . .**147** B8
Reeves Ct NR28 . . . .**151** C5
Reeves La IP26 . . . .**114** A7
Reffley La NR30 . . . .**147** D5
Reffley Prim Sch
PE30 . . . .**147** D8
Reg Houchen Rd
PE31 . . . .**140** C3
Regal Ct 23 IP25 . . . .**84** D3
Regal Rd PE13 . . . .**152** B2
Regency Ave PE30 . . . . . .**147** C5
Regent Bvd 10 NR30 . . . .**169** D4
Regent Cl NR19 . . . .**154** D1
Regent Pl 1 PE30 . . . .**146** E4
Regent Rd
Downham Market PE38 . . . .**172** A4
9 Great Yarmouth NR30 . .**169** D4
Regent St
Great Yarmouth NR30 . . . .**169** C3
Wickmere NR11 . . . .**20** E4
Regent Way 6 PE30 . . . . .**146** D4
Regents Cl NR25 . . . .**137** B5
Regents Ct NR28 . . . .**151** B5
Regents Pk PE30 . . . .**147** C5
Regina Rd NR1 . . . .**178** A1
Regis Ave 4 NR27 . . . .**9** F5
Regis Pl NR26 . . . .**138** E7
Reid Way PE30 . . . .**147** A8
Renowood Cl PE32 . . . . . .**48** B8
Renson Rd NR3 . . . .**158** C4
Renwick Pk E NR27 . . . . .**10** A4
Renwick Pk W NR27 . . . . .**10** A4
Repps Rd
Ashby with Oby NR29 . . . .**57** B3
1 Marthan NR29 . . . .**57** D4

Repps Rd continued
Thurne NR29 . . . .**56** E3
Repton Ave NR6 . . . .**158** D7
Repton Cl NR11 . . . .**150** D5
Retreat PE38 . . . .**172** D6
Reve Cres 5 NR13 . . . . . .**73** C6
Revell Rd PE38 . . . .**172** B4
Reydon Cl 10 NR5 . . . . . .**161** A7
Reynerson Rd NR7 . . . . . .**68** B2
Reynolds Ave NR30 . . . . .**168** C8
Reynolds La NR29 . . . .**56** E7
Reynolds Way PE31 . . . . .**140** C3
Rhombus Bsns Pk
NR6 . . . .**158** B5
Rhond The NR12 . . . .**164** C5
Rhone Pl 3 PE13 . . . .**152** E3
Rhoon Rd PE34 . . . .**144** E8
Rice Way NR7 . . . .**159** C2
Richard Easter Rd
IP24 . . . .**176** D6
Richard Haggard Cl 3
IP25 . . . .**67** C2
Richard Hicks Dr 9
NR19 . . . .**154** C4
Richard Young Cl 2
PE13 . . . .**152** C8
Richards Rd NR21 . . . .**15** D2
Richardson Cres NR8 . . . .**88** C8
Richenda Cl 8 NR5 . . . . .**161** C5
Riches Cl 2 NR15 . . . . . .**106** F6
Richmond Cl
Honingham NR9 . . . .**69** E6
Lyng NR9 . . . .**51** A5
Richmond Ct PE13 . . . . . .**152** A4
Richmond Pk NR17 . . . . .**174** F6
Richmond Pl NR9 . . . .**51** A4
Richmond Rd
Brandon IP27 . . . .**175** A1
Downham Market PE38 . . .**172** B4
4 Long Stratton NR15 . . .**106** E3
Norwich NR5 . . . .**156** E1
Saham Toney IP25 . . . .**84** C4
Richmond Rise NR10 . . . .**149** C5
Rickinghall Inf Sch
IP22 . . . .**128** C3
Riddlesworth Hall Sch
IP22 . . . .**127** C8
Rider Haggard Rd
NR7 . . . .**159** D1
Ridgeway
Caister-on-Sea NR30 . . . .**168** D8
Cromer NR27 . . . .**139** C4
Ridgeway The NR1 . . . . . .**163** B8
Ridings The
5 Cringleford NR4 . . . .**89** B8
Fakenham NR21 . . . .**141** E4
2 Poringland NR14 . . . . . .**90** C5
Ridland's Rd NR24 . . . . . .**142** C1
Rigby Cl 1 NR14 . . . .**90** D5
Rigbys Cl NR2 . . . .**178** A3
Rigg Cl 2 PE13 . . . .**152** E3
Rightup Dro IP27 . . . .**113** E5
Rightup La NR18 . . . .**173** D2
Riley Cl NR7 . . . .**159** D1
Rill Cl PE30 . . . .**148** B4
Rimer Cl NR5 . . . .**160** F6
Ring Rd NR7 . . . .**163** F7
Ringbank La NR11 . . . .**21** A6
Ringers Cl 4 NR18 . . . . . .**173** D5
Ringers La NR9 . . . .**86** C5
Ringland Cl
Costessey NR8 . . . .**156** B6
Easton NR9 . . . .**70** B5
Morton on the Hill NR9 . . . .**52** A2
Weston Longville NR9 . . . .**51** F3
Ringland Rd NR8 . . . .**155** A1
Ringmere Cl 2 IP25 . . . . . .**84** C3
Ringmere Rd 3 IP25 . . . . .**84** C3
Ringmore Rd PE38 . . . . . .**97** B6
Ringsfield Rd NR34 . . . . .**124** C5
Ringstead Downs Nature
Reserve★ PE36 . . . .**1** F2
Ringstead Rd
Burnham Market PE31 . . .**135** A2
Docking PE31 . . . .**134** A6
Heacham PE31 . . . .**133** E6
Ringstead PE31 . . . .**2** A2
Sedgeford PE36 . . . .**13** B8
Thornham PE36 . . . .**2** D6
Ringwood Cl NR9 . . . .**160** B2
Ripley Cl NR2 . . . .**161** F5
Ripon Way IP24 . . . .**176** B5
Rippingall Cl 6 NR11 . . . .**150** D6
Rippingall Rd NR11 . . . . .**150** D6
Rise The 10 Loddon NR14 . .**92** A2
Sheringham NR26 . . . . . .**138** E6
Riseway Cl NR1 . . . .**163** B8
Rising Way 3 NR29 . . . . . .**57** C4
Risley Cl NR16 . . . .**117** C5
River Cl PE32 . . . .**63** E8
River Ct NR21 . . . .**141** A3
River Dro PE33 . . . .**80** C2
River La Cranworth IP25 . . . .**85** F7
King's Lynn PE30 . . . .**147** A6
West Walton PE14 . . . .**59** A8
River Terr PE13 . . . .**152** A8
River View
Beccles NR34 . . . .**110** C2
7 Beetley NR20 . . . .**49** D4
River View Cl NR21 . . . . .**141** E4
River Vw 7 NR20 . . . .**49** D4
River Way NR31 . . . .**93** F6
River Wlk
Great Yarmouth NR30 . . . .**169** C8
King's Lynn PE34 . . . .**146** C6

Riverdale Ct NR13 .....165 D3
Riverdene Mews NR8 ..155 E3
Rivergreen Ct NR1 ....163 E6
Rivermead NR12 ....39 B3
Riverside
Cockley Cley PE37 ....82 D7
Diss IP22 ....177 B3
King's Lynn PE30 ....147 B7
Norwich NR1 ....178 C2
Reedham NR13 ....92 F4
Riverside Cl NR6 ......157 D2
Riverside Ctr NR12 ....164 C5
Riverside Est NR13 ....165 D1
Riverside Ind Ctr
NR31 ....170 D5
Riverside Ind Est
PE30 ....146 D7
Riverside Maltings
IP22 ....177 F3
Riverside Rd
Great Yarmouth NR31 ....170 D6
Holt NR25 ....8 A1
Norwich NR1 ....178 C3
Wroxham/Hoveton
NR12 ....164 C4
Riverside Swimming Ctr
NR1 ....178 C1
Riverside Way
Brandon IP27 ....175 C5
1 Wisbech PE13 ....152 B3
Riverside Wlk IP24 ....176 C4
Riversway PE30 ....146 E7
Riverview Dr NR13 ....166 B8
RNLI Henry Blogg Mus★
NR27 ....139 B7
Roaches Ct NR3 ....178 B3
Robberds Way NR5 ....160 E8
Robert Andrew Cl
NR18 ....87 B2
Robert Balding Rd
PE31 ....140 C3
Robert Cl Trunch NR28 ...22 E5
5 Wymondham NR18 ...173 C6
Robert Gybson Way
NR2 ....178 A3
Robert Herb Way 5
NR18 ....173 E4
Robert Kett Jun Sch
NR18 ....173 C5
Robert Key Dr 2 NR20 ..68 E6
Robert Linge Cres
IP27 ....175 D3
Robert St 8 PE30 ......146 E3
Roberts Cl 3 NR15 ....107 C5
Robertson Cl NR26 ....138 E6
Robin Cl
Great Yarmouth NR31 ....170 A5
Mulbarton NR14 ....89 A3
Robin Hill PE31 ....133 D8
Robin Hood Rd NR4 ...162 C1
Robin Kerkham Way
PE34 ....145 E6
Robin Mews 4 PE14 ....152 D2
Robin Wlk IP27 ....175 F3
Robins La NR10 ....149 B4
Robinson Rd IP21 .....130 C5
Robson Rd NR5 ....161 B6
Robyns Rd
3 Sheringham NR26 ....9 F5
Sheringham NR26 ....138 F5
Rocelin Cl NR3 ....158 E3
Rochford Rd 4 NR29 ....57 C4
Rochford Wlk 5 PE13 ..152 E5
Rockall Way 6 NR30 ...168 C6
Rockingham Rd NR5 ..161 C6
Rockland Cl PE13 .....153 B2
Rockland Dr NR7 ......163 C6
Rockland La NR17 ......85 F1
Rockland Rd NR14 ......90 F7
Rockland St Mary Prim Sch
NR14 ....91 B6
Rocklands Prim Sch
NR17 ....103 B7
Rocklands Rd NR17 ...103 B4
Rode La NR16 ....105 B3
Rodham Rd PE15 ....77 A1
Rodinghead 1 PE30 ...147 D5
Rodney Rd NR30 ......169 D3
Rodwell Cnr NR10 ......35 C1
Roe Dr NR5 ....161 E5
Roedich Dr NR8 ....155 C1
Roger Ride 3 NR19 ....154 D2
Roger's Cl NR31 ......171 D5
Roger's La NR15 ....89 F1
Rogers Cl 4 NR5 ......161 B7
Roland Dr NR15 ....107 D5
Rolfe Cres PE31 ......133 E5
Rollesby Ave PE13 ....153 B2
Rollesby Fst Sch NR29 ..57 D3
Rollesby Gdns 9 NR29 ..57 D2
Rollesby Pl NR10 ....37 B2
Rollesby Rd
Fleggburgh NR29 ....57 C1
King's Lynn PE30 ....147 A3
Martham NR29 ....57 D4
Swaffham PE37 ....153 B2
Rolleston Cl NR5 .....161 B7
Rollingpin La NR19 ...154 D4
Roman Cres PE37 .....153 D2
Roman Dr NR13 ....165 B3
Roman Pl 20 NR30 ....169 D4
Roman Way
Brancaster PE31 ....3 B7
Caister-on-Sea NR30 ....168 D5
Thetford IP24 ....176 C7
Romany Cl 8 NR29 .....57 D2
Romany Rd NR3 ....158 F1
Romany Wlk 6 NR14 ....90 C5
Romer Dro PE33 ....81 B3
Romney Wlk NR19 ....154 D4
Rook Dr NR8 ....155 E2
Rookery Cl PE34 ......145 E5
Rookery Farm Rd NR28 .23 F2
Rookery Hill NR14 ......91 B7
Rookery La NR35 ......107 F3
Rookery Rd PE34 .....145 E4
Rookery The IP27 .....114 D5
Room La NR15 ....122 D8
Rope Wlk 5 IP24 ......176 D4
Ropemakers Row 5
NR3 ....158 C1
Ropes Hill NR12 ....55 D4
Ropes Hill Dyke NR12 ..55 D4
Ropes Wlk NR13 ......165 E6
Rosa Cl NR12 ....54 B1
Rosa Vella Dr 3 NR20 ...68 A8
Rosalie Cl NR6 ....158 B4
Rosary Cl 8 NR14 ....89 B3
Rosary Rd NR1 ....163 A6
Rose Ave IP22 ....129 D7
Rose Cottage's NR19 ...66 D8
Rose Dr NR20 ....68 A8
Rose La Botesdale IP22 .128 E3
Diss IP22 ....177 F3
3 Elm PE14 ....59 A1
Norwich NR1 ....178 C3
Palgrave IP22 ....177 D1
Rose La Cl IP22 ....177 D2
Rose Valley 4 NR2 ....162 B5
Rose Wlk
Brundall NR13 ....165 C3
Sculthorpe Airfield NR21 ...15 C2
1 Wisbech PE13 ....152 A6
Rose Yd NR3 ....178 A4
Roseacre Cl NR2 ......162 C2
Roseacre Est NR25 ......9 A2
Rosebay 1 PE30 ......148 C3
Rosebay Cl 5 NR6 ....158 D5
Roseberry Rd PE14 .....59 B1
Rosebery Ave
King's Lynn PE30 ....147 B6
7 Poringland NR14 ......90 D5
Rosebery Rd
Cromer NR27 ....139 D5
Great & Little Plumstead
NR13 ....73 A4
Norwich NR3 ....158 D1
3 Sheringham NR27 ......10 A5
Rosecroft 4 NR17 .....174 C5
Rosecroft Way IP24 ...176 F4
Rosedale Cres 5 NR1 ..163 A6
Rosedale Gdns NR31 ...94 A5
Rosefields NR13 ......165 E4
Rosemary La
11 Gayton PE32 ....45 C6
2 New Buckenham NR16 .104 F1
Norwich NR3 ....178 A4
Rosemary Musker Cty High
Sch IP24 ....176 E7
Rosemary Rd
Blofield NR13 ....73 C6
Norwich NR7 ....159 B4
Rosemary Terr NR21 ...141 B5
Rosemary Way PE38 ..172 D6
Rosery The NR14 ....89 C3
Roses Ct NR23 ....136 D5
Rosetta Rd NR10 ....54 A2
Roseville Cl 2 NR1 ...163 B5
Rosewood NR28 ......151 E5
Roslyn Rd NR31 ....170 C5
Rosslare 1 NR4 ....162 A1
Rossons Rd NR8 ......155 C1
Rostwold Way NR3 ....158 D2
Rosyth Rd 4 IP31 .....126 B1
Rothbury Cl NR18 .....173 B4
Rothbury Rd NR18 ....173 C4
Rotten Marsh NR13 ....166 C2
Rottenstone La NR29 ..167 F3
Roudham Rd NR16 ....117 F6
Rouen Rd NR1 ....178 B2
Rougham Cnr IP26 ......99 F3
Rougham End PE32 .....47 C8
Rougham Hall PE32 .....47 A7
Rougham Rd PE32 ......29 E1
Roughlands IP27 ......113 E1
Rougholme Cl
6 Beetley NR19 ....49 C3
6 Gressenhall NR20 ......49 C3
Rought Ave IP27 ......175 D2
Roughton Rd
Roughton NR27 ....139 B2
Thorpe Market NR11 ......21 F7
Roughton Rd Sta
NR27 ....139 B4
Round House Way
NR4 ....161 B1
Round Well Rd NR5 ...156 D1
Roundabout La NR14 ..109 B8
Roundham Medieval Village
of★ NR16 ....117 E6
Roundhead Ct 26 NR7 ...72 D4
Roundtree Cl NR7 .....159 B2
Roundtree Way NR7 ...159 B2
Roundway Down 17 NR7 .72 D4
Rouse's La PE38 ......172 D4
Row Hill 6 PE33 ....43 F2
Row The Weeting IP27 ..175 A7
Wereham PE33 ....80 D3
West Dereham PE33 ......80 B4
Rowan Cl
10 Great Yarmouth NR31 ..94 C7
Thetford IP24 ....176 B1
7 Watlington PE33 ....61 D5
Rowan Cl *continued*
Wisbech PE13 ....152 F7
Rowan Ct NR5 ....156 F1
Rowan Dr
Brandon IP27 ....175 C3
Gayton PE32 ....45 C6
Rowan Rd
King's Lynn PE34 ....43 D4
Martham NR29 ....57 D4
Rowan Way
Fakenham NR21 ....141 F4
10 Great Yarmouth NR31 .170 B6
Holt NR25 ....137 B7
Row's Mdw 1 NR15 ....107 C5
Rowington Rd NR1 ....178 A1
Rowland Ct NR1 ......178 B1
Rowley Cnr IP26 ....83 A5
Rowton Heath 16 NR7 ...72 D4
Roxley Cl NR7 ....163 F5
Royal Albert Ct 5 NR31 170 D4
Royal Arcade NR2 .....178 B2
Royal Ave NR30 ......169 D7
Royal Cl 11 PE12 ....41 B8
Royal Norfolk Regimental
Mus★ NR1 ....178 B3
Royal Pl 2 PE13 ......152 C4
Royal Thames Rd
NR30 ....168 D7
Royalist Dr 23 NR7 .....72 D4
Royden Way 3 NR29 ....57 C1
Roydon Comm National
Nature Reserve★
PE32 ....27 F1
Roydon Fen IP22 .....177 A4
Roydon Gdns IP22 ....177 A5
Roydon Prim Sch
IP22 ....177 B5
Roydon Rd IP22 ......177 C5
Royston Gn NR28 .....151 D6
Rubens Way 6 PE38 ..172 D6
Rudd's Drift PE32 ......48 E5
Rudds La NR10 ....149 B3
Rudham CE Prim Sch
PE31 ....30 A6
Rudham Rd
Great Massingham PE32 ...29 D2
Syderstone PE31 ....15 A3
Rudham Stile La NR21 .141 B6
Rudolf Steiner Sch
NR12 ....164 B3
Rugg's La NR29 ....75 C8
Rugge Dr NR4 ....161 E2
Ruin Rd NR28 ....38 A5
Rumburgh La NR35 ...124 D2
Rump Cl 10 NR20 ....50 B3
Run La NR14 ....91 B6
Runcton Cl NR5 ....161 B7
Runcton Holme CE VA Prim
Sch PE33 ....61 E3
Runcton Rd PE33 ....61 F2
Runhall Rd NR9 ....69 A2
Runham Rd
Great Yarmouth NR30 ....169 B5
Stokesby NR29 ....75 B5
Runnel The NR5 ....160 F6
Runton House Cl NR27 ..10 A5
Runton Rd NR27 ......139 A7
Rupert St NR2 ....162 C4
Rushall Rd IP20 ....122 B2
Rushford Rd
Coney Weston IP31 ......127 B5
Euston IP24 ....126 D7
Rushmead Cl PE30 ....148 C3
Rushmeadow Rd
NR19 ....154 A5
Rushmer Way NR26 ...138 C5
Rushmore Rd NR7 .....159 A4
Ruskin Ave NR31 ......170 B2
Ruskin Cl PE31 ....133 E5
Ruskin Pl 5 PE38 .....172 D6
Ruskin Rd NR4 ....161 E4
Russell Ave
Caister-on-Sea NR30 ....168 E5
Great Yarmouth NR31 ....170 C3
Norwich NR7 ....159 B3
9 Spixworth NR10 ....54 A2
Russell Cl NR23 ....136 C6
Russell Ct NR23 ....136 D6
Russell Rd NR30 ......169 D4
Russell Sq 24 NR30 ...169 D4
Russell St
King's Lynn PE30 ....146 F3
Norwich NR2 ....162 C7
Wisbech PE13 ....152 C6
Russell Terr
Mundesley NR11 ....143 C6
Trowse Newton NR14 ....163 B2
Russell Way NR18 ....173 C3
Russet Cl NR17 ....174 E4
Russet Gr NR4 ....161 E5
Russet Rd IP22 ....177 C5
Russet Way NR19 .....154 E3
Russets The PE14 ......77 E6
Russett Cl PE30 ......147 C8
Rustens Manor Rd 2
NR18 ....173 C5
Rustons Rd PE14 ....59 F3
Ruthen Pl 1 NR19 ....154 D5
Rutherford Way IP24 ..176 C6
Rutland St NR2 ....162 C4
Ryalla Drift PE30 .....148 B4
Ryburgh Dr NR20 ....32 D5
Rydal Cl NR5 ....161 C6
Ryders Way IP22 ......128 E2
Rye Ave NR3 ....158 B3
Rye Cl
North Walsham NR28 ....151 E6
Norwich NR3 ....158 B2
Rye La NR17 ....174 C4
Rye's Cl PE33 ....62 D3
Ryeland Rd 2 PE30 ....148 C4
Ryelands 5 NR29 ......167 B7
Ryelands Rd PE30 .....148 D4
Ryley Cl PE30 ....147 E8
Ryrie Ct NR4 ....161 E2
Ryston Cl PE38 ....172 C4
Ryston End PE38 ......172 C4
Ryston Pk PE38 ....172 F1
Ryston Rd Denver PE38 .172 D2
West Dereham PE33 ......80 B4

S

Sackville Cl 4 NR30 ..169 C3
Sacred Heart Convent Sch
PE37 ....153 C5
Saddlebow Ind Est
PE34 ....43 C4
Saddlebow Rd PE30 ...146 D1
Sadler Cl PE30 ....146 F7
Sadler Rd NR6 ....157 F7
Sadlers Ct 11 NR26 ...138 D7
Sadlers Way NR28 ....151 E5
Saffron Cl IP27 ....175 B2
Saffron Sq NR6 ....158 C3
Sage Rd PE38 ....172 D7
Saham Rd IP25 ....84 C4
Sainsbury Ctr for the Visual
Arts★ NR4 ....161 C3
St Alban's Rd NR1 ....162 D3
St Albans Way IP24 ...176 B5
St Andrew Cl 1 NR31 ..171 E5
St Andrew's & Blackfriars
Halls★ NR1 ....178 B3
St Andrew's Cl
Blofield NR13 ....165 E5
Caister-on-Sea NR30 ....168 D7
Holme Hale IP25 ....66 A2
Holt NR25 ....137 C6
Northwold IP26 ....99 C8
3 Old Buckenham NR17 .104 D2
St Andrew's Rd
Great Yarmouth NR31 ....170 C6
Lingwood NR13 ....73 F3
Sheringham NR26 ....138 D6
St Andrew's Way
NR13 ....165 E5
St Andrews Ave 5 NR7 ..72 D3
St Andrews CE VA Prim Sch
IP22 ....119 A1
St Andrews Cl
Barningham IP31 ....127 C3
Buxton with Lammas
NR10 ....36 E1
Framingham Earl NR14 ....90 D5
Great Yarmouth NR31 ....170 C5
1 Hingham NR9 ....86 C4
Long Stratton NR15 .....106 E4
Poringland NR14 ....90 D5
West Dereham PE33 ......80 C4
Worstead NR28 ....38 A4
St Andrews Dr
3 Norwich NR4 ....89 C8
Quidenham NR16 ....103 E1
St Andrews Drift 2 NR25 .7 A4
St Andrews Hill NR2 ...178 B3
St Andrews La
Necton PE37 ....65 F5
Roydon PE32 ....28 A2
St Andrews Rd
North Runcton PE30 .....147 B3
Norwich NR6 ....157 D6
Scole IP21 ....130 D5
St Andrews Sch NR27 ...10 B5
St Andrews St NR2 ....178 B3
St Andrews Way PE37 ...65 F5
St Andrews Wlk PE33 ...80 C5
St Ann La NR1 ....178 C2
St Ann's St PE30 ......146 D5
St Anne's Cres
Clenchwarton PE34 .....145 D6
Great Yarmouth NR31 ....170 B4
St Annes Rd 4 NR14 ....90 D5
St Anns Fort PE30 .....146 D6
St Anthony's Way
IP27 ....175 E4
St Antony's Ave NR31 .170 B2
St Audreys IP24 ......176 D3
St Augustines Gate 12
NR3 ....162 D8
St Augustines RC Prim Sch
NR8 ....156 E3
St Augustines Rd
PE13 ....152 C5
St Augustines St NR3 .162 D8
St Augustines Way 3
PE30 ....148 C4
St Austin's Gr NR26 ..138 E7
St Barnabas Cl 2 IP24 .176 C1
St Bartholomews Cl 4
NR2 ....162 B8
St Benedicts Cl NR34 ..110 D5
St Benedicts Rd IP27 ..175 E4
St Benedicts St NR2 ..178 A3
St Benet's Abbey★
NR12 ....56 C2
St Benet's Cl 9 NR12 ...39 B4
St Benet's Rd
Great Yarmouth NR31 ....170 B3
Stalham NR12 ....39 B4
St Benets Ave NR28 ...151 E4
St Benets Gr PE30 ....148 D3
St Benets Rd NR29 .....56 C3
St Botolph's Cl 3 PE30 148 C3
St Botolphs CE VC Prim Sch
IP22 ....128 F3
St Catherine's Ave 5
NR29 ....56 C8
St Catherine's Way
NR31 ....170 B4
St Catherines Rd NR7 .163 F8
St Christopher Cl
16 Belton NR31 ....94 A6
6 Caister-on-Sea NR30 ..168 D7
St Christophers Cl
NR15 ....108 C7
St Christophers Sch
NR6 ....158 E4
St Clare Ct 6 NR31 ....171 D5
St Clement Cl 2 PE14 ...77 F6
St Clement Mews 7
NR31 ....171 D5
St Clements Dr 4 PE38 172 C6
St Clements High Sch
PE34 ....144 C6
St Clements Hill NR3 ..158 E2
St Clements Way
NR13 ....165 C4
St Crispins Rd NR3 ...178 A4
St Cross Rd IP20 ......123 B4
St David's Cl 17 NR31 ...94 A6
St David's Rd NR9 ......88 C7
St Davids Cl
Brandon IP27 ....175 D3
Long Stratton NR15 .....106 E4
St Davids Dr 8 NR13 ....72 D6
St Dominic Sq 8 PE30 .146 D5
St Domonic's Dr IP27 .175 E4
St Edmund Cl
Attleborough NR17 ......174 C5
Great Yarmouth NR31 ....170 B3
Poringland NR14 ....90 B6
St Edmund Rd IP27 ...114 E8
St Edmund's Ave
PE36 ....132 D5
St Edmund's Rd
Downham Market PE38 ..172 D5
Lingwood NR13 ....73 F3
Taverham NR8 ....155 C1
St Edmund's Rise 2
NR8 ....155 C1
St Edmund's Terr
Hunstanton PE36 ....132 C4
King's Lynn PE30 ....146 C7
St Edmunds NR17 .....174 E5
St Edmunds Cl
Costessey NR8 ....156 F5
Norwich NR6 ....157 E1
St Edmunds Com Sch
PE30 ....146 E8
St Edmunds Ct 1 IP24 .176 C1
St Edmunds Dr PE14 ...59 D1
St Edmunds Gate
Attleborough NR17 ......174 B4
11 Honington IP31 ......126 B1
St Edmunds Prim Sch
IP21 ....131 A2
St Edmunds RC Prim Sch
NR35 ....124 B8
St Edmunds Rd NR13 ..166 B3
St Edmunds Sq 18 IP31 .126 B1
St Edmunds Wharf
NR3 ....178 B4
St Edmundsbury Rd
PE30 ....146 E7
St Ethelberts Cl PE31 ..135 C2
St Faith's Church★
NR9 ....51 F7
St Faith's Cl NR9 ....51 E5
St Faith's Dr PE30 ....147 A6
St Faith's Rd NR6 .....158 D6
St Faiths La NR1 ......178 C3
St Francis Cl IP27 .....175 E4
St Francis Way NR30 ..169 C4
St Furseys' Way 2 NR31 .94 A6
St George's Cl
Saham Toney IP25 ....84 B5
Thurton NR14 ....91 C4
St George's Dr
Caister-on-Sea NR30 ....168 D7
East Dereham NR19 .....154 D1
St George's Rd NR30 ..169 D3
St George's Theatre 16
NR30 ....169 D3
St Georges Fst Sch 16
NR30 ....169 D3
St Georges Mid Sch
PE31 ....13 A1
St Georges Rd NR31 ....94 A6
St Georges St NR3 ....178 A4
St Germans Prim Sch
PE34 ....43 B1
St Giles Gr PE14 ....59 B1
St Giles' La IP24 ......176 D4
St Giles Rd NR24 ....18 B2
St Giles St NR2 ....178 A3
St Giles Terr NR2 .....178 A3
St Gregorys Alley NR2 .178 A3
St Guthlac Cl PE37 ....153 C6
St Helena Way NR10 ....53 A3
St Helens Ct 1 IP24 ..176 D6
St Helens Rd NR12 .....23 F3
St Helens Way IP24 ...176 C7
St Hilda Cl NR19 ......154 C6
St Hilda Rd
Caister-on-Sea NR30 ....168 D6
East Dereham NR19 .....154 C6
St Hilda's Cres NR31 ..170 B5
St Hugh's Gn NR31 ....170 B3
St James Cl NR3 ......178 C4
St James Cres 18 NR31 ..94 A6
St James Ct NR3 ......178 B4

St James Dr PE38 .....172 B4
St James Rd IP19 ....124 A1
St James' Rd PE30 ....146 E4
St James St PE30 ....146 D4
St James Way NR15 ...106 E4
St James Wlk **14** NR30 .169 D3
St James's Rd PE32 ....47 A2
St John Maddermarket
NR2 ....178 A3
St John St NR1 ....178 C2
St John the Baptist Cath★
NR2 ....162 C5
St John's Ave NR31 ...170 A4
St John's Cl
Coltishall NR12 ....54 D7
11 Hethersett NR9 ....88 D7
Oxborough PE33 ....81 E4
St John's Rd
Bungay NR35 ....124 A8
Terrington St John PE34 .60 C8
St John's Terr
8 Great Yarmouth NR30 .169 D3
King's Lynn PE30 ....146 E4
St John's Way **12** IP26 .98 E1
St Johns Cl
2 Norwich NR1 .....162 C6
Swaffham PE37 ......153 C4
St Johns Ct PE13 ....153 C4
St Johns La NR14 ...109 A8
St Johns Prim Sch
NR12 ....164 D5
St Johns RC Fst Sch
NR2 ....162 C6
St Johns Rd Belton NR31 .93 F6
Stalham NR12 ....39 B4
St Johns Way PE38 ...172 A4
St Joseph's Rd NR26 .138 D6
St Julian Rd NR30 ...168 E4
St Julians Alley NR1 .178 B2
St Laurence Ave NR13 .165 C4
St Lawrence Dr 161 C1
St Lawrence La NR1 ..178 A3
St Lawrence Prim Sch
NR34 ....124 F2
St Leger NR15 ....106 E3
St Leonards Cl
Scole IP21 ....130 D5
Wymondham NR18 ....173 A6
St Leonards Rd NR1 ..163 A6
St Leonards St IP26 ..100 B4
St Leonards Terr **6**
NR1 ....163 A6
St Luke's Terr **4** NR31 .169 B4
St Magdalen Way
PE13 ....153 C2
St Margaret's Cl
3 Coltishall NR12 .....54 C6
Upton with Fishley NR13 .166 B8
St Margaret's Cres
IP24 ....176 C3
St Margaret's Dr IP27 .175 A4
St Margaret's La
2 Cromer NR27 ....139 C6
10 King's Lynn PE30 ..146 D4
St Margaret's Pl **11**
PE30 ....146 D4
St Margaret's Rd
Bungay NR35 ....124 A6
1 Cromer NR27 .....139 C6
St Margaret's Way
1 Burgh St Margaret
(Fleggburgh) NR29 ....57 C1
2 Hopton on Sea NR31 .171 D5
St Margarets Ave **8**
PE33 ....63 B4
St Margarets Cl **2**
NR10 ....155 F3
St Margarets Dr NR7 .159 C5
St Margarets Gdns
NR12 ....164 D6
St Margarets La NR7 .159 B5
St Margarets Mdw
PE34 ....145 E5
St Margarets Pl NR12 ..40 A5
St Margarets Rd NR1 .178 A3
St Marthas RC Prim Sch
PE30 ....147 C6
St Martin's Cl NR27 ..139 C5
St Martin's Gdns **1**
NR16 ....104 F1
St Martin's La IP24 ...125 E6
St Martin's Rd
2 Norwich NR3 ....162 D8
Wisbech PE13 ......152 E7
St Martin's Way IP24 .176 B2
St Martin-at-Palace Plain
NR3 ....178 B4
St Martins at Oak Wall La **7**
NR3 ....162 D8
St Martins Cl **4** NR3 .162 D8
St Martins La NR3 ...178 A4
St Mary Cl NR17 .....174 C6
St Mary's **4** NR16 ...104 F1
St Mary's Cl
Alpington NR14 ....90 F5
Flixton NR35 ....123 C4
Harleston IP20 .....122 E2
Heacham PE31 ......133 E6
Hemsby NR29 ....167 A7
Horsham St Faith &
Newton St Faith NR10 .53 E2
King's Lynn PE30 ....148 C2
Newton Flotman NR15 ..89 C1
12 Snettisham PE31 ...12 E4
1 Watton IP25 ....84 E3
Wroxham/Hoveton
NR12 ....164 B4
St Mary's Cres **5** IP24 .176 C3

St Mary's Ct **2** IP24 ...176 C3
St Mary's Dr IP22 ...177 E4
St Mary's La NR31 ...169 C3
St Mary's Rd
Aldeby NR34 ....111 A3
Cromer NR27 ....139 B6
20 Long Stratton NR15 .106 E3
Poringland NR14 ....90 D5
West Walton PE14 .....59 B8
St Mary's Way **3** NR1 .151 C5
St Marys Dr NR13 .....73 A5
St Marys Dr NR16 ...102 A8
St Marys Endowed Prim Sch
NR11 ....21 E8
St Marys Gr NR7 ....159 C5
St Marys La **1** NR25 ....7 A4
St Marys Mid Sch
NR15 ....106 E4
St Marys Plain NR3 ..178 A4
St Marys Prim Sch
NR20 ....49 D4
St Marys RC Prim Sch
NR31 ....170 C6
St Marys Rd
Ashby St Mary NR14 ....91 C4
Hemsby NR29 ....167 D6
5 Norwich NR3 ......162 D8
12 Stalham NR12 ....39 B4
St Marys Wlk **5** NR15 ..89 D1
St Matthews Dr PE12 ..41 B8
St Matthews Rd NR1 .178 A1
St Michael's Ave PE13 .152 C7
St Michael's Cl
Aylsham NR11 ......150 C7
Thetford IP24 ......176 C3
St Michael's Cres IP25 ..83 D4
St Michael's Hospl
NR11 ....150 A6
St Michael's Rd PE30 .146 D1
St Michael-at-Pleas
NR3 ....178 B3
St Michaels NR12 .....39 C2
St Michaels CE Prim Sch
Gillingham NR34 .....110 B2
King's Lynn PE30 ....146 D1
St Michaels Cl NR20 ...69 B7
St Michaels Inf Sch
NR11 ....150 C7
St Michaels Mid Sch
NR5 ....160 F8
St Michaels Way NR15 .165 F2
St Michels Rd NR15 ..106 E4
St Mildreds Rd **3** NR5 .161 B7
St Nicholas Cl
Dersingham PE31 ....140 E3
6 Gayton PE32 ....45 C6
1 King's Lynn PE30 ..146 D5
St Nicholas Ct
1 Great Yarmouth NR31 .94 C6
10 North Walsham NR28 .151 C5
St Nicholas Dr
Caister-on-Sea NR30 ..168 D6
Feltwell IP26 ....98 E2
St Nicholas Gdns **6**
NR31 ....94 C6
St Nicholas House Sch
NR28 ....151 D4
St Nicholas Pl **1** NR26 .138 D7
St Nicholas Priory Mid Sch
NR30 ....169 C5
St Nicholas Rd
Great Yarmouth NR30 .169 D4
North Walsham NR28 .151 D4
St Nicholas St
Diss IP22 ....177 D5
East Dereham NR19 ..154 D6
3 King's Lynn PE30 ..146 D5
Thetford IP24 ......176 C4
St Nicholas Wlk IP27 .175 E4
St Nicholas's NR14 ...88 F3
St Olaves Rd
Herringfleet NR32 ....111 D8
Norwich NR3 ....162 E8
St Omer Cl NR14 .....89 B4
St Paul's Cl
Brockdish IP21 ......131 C6
4 Horsford NR10 .....53 B7
6 Wisbech PE13 .....152 C4
St Paul's Rd S PE14 ...59 D8
St Paul's Way NR30 ..169 C7
St Pauls Cl NR6 .....158 A5
St Pauls Sq **1** NR3 ..178 B4
St Peter & St Paul Prim Sch
IP25 ....85 A5
St Peter's App IP27 ..175 B3
St Peter's Cl
Brockdish IP21 ......131 C6
King's Lynn PE34 ...146 B4
Strumpshaw NR13 .....73 F2
Yaxham NR19 ....68 A5
St Peter's La NR12 ..164 E1
St Peter's Pl IP27 ...175 B2
St Peter's Rd
Brooke NR15 ....90 F2
Fakenham NR21 .....141 B6
Great Yarmouth NR30 .169 D3
King's Lynn PE34 ...146 C5
Lingwood NR13 ....73 F3
9 Sheringham NR26 .138 D7
5 Wisbech PE13 .....152 C4
St Peter's Way **12** NR10 .54 A2
St Peter's Wlk PE13 ..113 F7
St Peters Ave NR31 ..170 B2
St Peters CE Jun Sch
PE13 ....152 E6
St Peters CE VC Prim Sch
NR9 ....70 B6
St Peters Cl **3** NR4 ...89 B8

St Peters Dr NR9 .....70 B5
St Peters Hill NR18 ...87 A2
St Peters' Plain NR30 .169 D3
St Peters Rd
Outwell PE14 ....77 E5
Watlington PE34 ......61 C7
Wiggenhall St Germans
PE34 ....61 B8
St Peters St NR2 ....178 A2
St Peters Terr PE34 ..146 C4
St Philips Rd NR2 ....162 B6
St Roberts Way **15** NR31 .94 A6
St Saviors La NR3 ...178 B4
St Stephen's Cres
IP27 ....175 E4
St Stephens Rd NR1 ..178 A1
St Stephens Sq NR1 ..178 A1
St Stephens St NR1 ..178 A2
St Swithins Rd NR2 ..178 A3
St Thomas Cl IP27 ...175 E4
St Thomas Dr NR18 ..173 C2
St Thomas' La NR18 ...88 C4
St Thomas More RC Mid Sch
NR2 ....162 A5
St Thomas Rd NR2 ...162 A6
St Thomas's La
Ingoldisthorpe NR31 ..140 D8
Snettisham PE31 ......12 F4
St Thomas's Rd NR29 .167 C4
St Valery La PE30 ....146 D2
St Vedast St NR1 ....178 C3
St Vincent Wlk NR31 .171 E5
St Walstan's Cl
Norwich NR5 ....156 D1
Taverham NR8 ......156 D8
St Walstan's Rd NR8 .156 D8
St Williams Prim Sch
NR7 ....163 D8
St Williams Way NR7 .163 C7
St Winnold Cl PE38 ..172 B4
St Withburga La **8**
NR19 ....154 D5
Saker Cl **11** NR7 .....72 C4
Salamanca Rd **7** NR15 .106 D3
Salcott Dr PE13 .....152 E5
Sale Ct **5** NR14 .....92 A1
Sale Rd NR13 ....92 E6
Salhouse Dr PE37 ...153 B2
Salhouse Prim Sch
NR13 ....55 B1
Salhouse Rd
Great & Little Plumstead
NR13 ....73 B6
New Rackheath NR13 ..72 E7
Norwich NR7 ....159 C2
Sprowston NR13 ......72 D6
Woodbastwick NR13 ...55 C1
Wroxham NR12 ......164 B2
Salhouse Sta NR13 ....54 F1
Salisbury Rd
Cromer NR27 ....139 D4
Great Yarmouth NR30 .169 D4
Norwich NR1 ....163 B5
Sheringham NR26 ....138 C7
Salisbury Way IP24 ..176 B4
Sallow La
Framingham Pigot NR14 .90 E7
Snetterton NR16 .....118 B8
Salmon Rd NR30 ....170 D8
Salmon's Way NR21 ..141 F5
Salmond Dr **1** IP24 ..125 C4
Salmond Rd **11** IP25 ...84 F3
Salter Ave NR4 .....161 E5
Salter's La PE32 ......48 C4
Salter's Rd PE30 ....146 E7
Salters Way PE13 ...152 A2
Salthouse Marshes Nature
Reserve★ NR25 ....8 B7
Saltings The PE34 ...144 A5
Salts Rd PE14 ....59 C8
Samphire **5** PE30 ...147 B7
Sampson Rd NR28 ..151 C3
Samson Rd NR6 .....157 F4
Samson's La IP22 ...129 C7
Samuel Rd **1** NR1 ..163 B7
Sancroft Way IP20 ...123 A3
Sand Stone Way IP22 .177 B4
Sandale Rd PE30 ....147 C6
Sandall Rd PE13 ....152 C5
Sandfield Rd **3** PE38 .172 C6
Sandhole La NR13 .....73 A7
Sandhole Rd NR13 ....74 F1
Sandholme Cl NR1 ...163 B8
Sandover Cl **4** PE33 ...43 F2
Sandown Rd
Great Yarmouth NR30 .169 D5
Wisbech PE13 ......152 A2
Sandpiper Cl **1** NR31 .170 A5
Sandpiper Ct **13** NR39 .58 B6
Sandpit La
Gimingham NR11 ......22 E8
Saxlingham Nethergate
NR15 ....107 A8
Thorpe Market NR11 ...21 F7
Sandringham & W Newton
CE Prim Sch PE31 ....27 C6
Sandringham Ave
Great Yarmouth NR30 .169 D7
12 Marham PE33 ......63 C4
Wisbech PE13 ......152 D6
Sandringham Cres
PE30 ....148 D5
Sandringham Ct
Norwich NR2 ....178 A1
6 Watton IP25 ....84 D3
Sandringham Ctry Pk★
PE35 ....27 E7

Sandringham Dr
Downham Market PE38 .172 E5
Heacham PE31 ......133 C4
Sandringham House Mus &
Gdns★ PE35 ....27 F7
Sandringham Private Hospl
PE30 ....147 E6
Sandringham Rd
Dersingham PE31 ....140 E2
Hunstanton PE36 ...132 D4
King's Lynn PE30 ...147 C7
Norwich NR2 ....162 B6
Sandringham Way
PE37 ....153 C2
Sands Cl NR31 ......171 E4
Sandy Cl PE31 ......140 C7
Sandy Cres PE31 ....140 C7
Sandy Hill La NR25 ....8 F4
Sandy La Aylsham NR11 .150 B6
Bacton NR12 ....23 D3
Barningham IP31 ....127 C4
Beighton NR13 ....74 D2
Belton with Browston
NR31 ....93 F5
Blackborough End PE32 .44 C2
Bradwell NR31 ....94 C3
Buxton with Lammas
NR10 ....53 F8
Canadas NR11 ......10 A3
Cantley NR13 ....92 E6
Castle Acre PE32 .....47 A2
Cromer NR27 ....139 A6
Denver PE38 ....172 C2
Dereham NR19 ......154 C8
Diss IP22 ....177 F4
Docking PE31 ....134 D6
East Dereham NR19 ..154 C6
East Tuddenham NR20 .69 D8
Fakenham NR21 .....141 A5
Fleggburgh NR29 .....75 B8
Great Massingham PE32 .46 E8
Grimston PE32 ....44 C8
Hardingham NR9 .....86 D7
Hilgay PE38 ....97 C8
Hoveton NR12 ....55 C4
Ingoldisthorpe PE31 .140 C7
King's Lynn PE30 ...148 F1
Loddon NR14 ....92 B1
Mundham NR14 .....109 A7
Norwich NR4 ....162 D1
Old Hunstanton PE36 .132 E8
Oulton NR11 ....35 B7
Raveningham NR14 ..110 B8
Rocklands NR17 ....103 A6
Runton NR27 ....10 C4
St Mary, South Elmham
otherwise Homersfield
IP20 ....123 B3
Sheringham NR27 .....10 A5
Somerton NR29 ......57 E6
South Wootton PE30 ...27 C1
Southrepps NR11 .....22 B7
Taverham NR8 ......156 C8
Thurning NR20 ....34 C8
West Acre PE32 ......46 B2
Weston Longville NR9 ..51 D4
Wisbech PE13 ......152 F4
Sandy La E NR19 ...154 C6
Sandy Way NR31 ....140 C7
Sandygate La PE34 ..144 F5
Sandyland PE13 .....152 B5
Sankence La NR11 ....35 E5
Santon Cl PE32 .....176 A3
Sapiston Rd IP31 ...126 D1
Sapwell Cl NR11 ....150 A6
Saracen Rd NR6 ....157 F6
Sarah W Cl NR2 ....162 C4
Sarah Williman Cl **2**
NR4 ....161 C5
Sarahs Rd PE36 ....132 C2
Sardis Way NR19 ...154 D4
Saturday Mkt Pl PE30 .146 D4
Saunders Ct **7** NR1 .163 A6
Savery Cl NR5 ......161 B6
Savory Rd PE13 ....152 B7
Saw Mill La
Brancaster PE31 ......3 B6
7 Great Yarmouth NR31 .169 B4
Sawmill Cl NR8 ....173 B5
Sawston **1** PE30 ...147 D6
Sawyer's La NR18 ....87 D2
Sawyers Cl NR5 ....156 E1
Saxlingham La NR15 .106 F7
Saxlingham Prim Sch
NR15 ....107 B7
Saxlingham Rd
Blakeney NR25 ....7 C5
Saxlingham Nethergate
NR15 ....107 C8
Shotesham NR15 .....89 F1
Saxon Cres **9** IP31 ..126 B1
Saxon Ct PE37 .....153 D2
Saxon Field PE31 .....3 B6
Saxon Gdns NR30 ..168 D5
Saxon Pl
3 Thetford IP24 ....176 C3
Weeting IP27 ....175 A8
Saxon Rd NR30 .....169 D4
Saxon Way
Dersingham PE31 ....140 D4
Wormegay PE33 .....62 C6
Saxon Wlk PE36 ....100 A4
Saxonfields NR14 ....90 C4
Sayer Cl **2** NR3 .....9 A2
Sayers St **9** NR2 ...162 C7
Scama La IP22 .....129 A2
Scania Way PE30 ...147 A1
Scarborough Rd NR22 .17 A8

Scarfield La PE14 .....59 C2
Scarlet Rd NR4 .....162 D1
Scarnell Rd NR5 ....161 C6
Scarning Fen NR19 ..154 C2
Scarning VC Prim Sch
NR19 ....154 A4
Scarrow Beck La NR11 .21 A2
Sceptre Cl NR6 .....158 A3
Scholars Wlk IP22 ...177 C5
School Ave NR7 ....163 F6
School Cl
Kenninghall NR16 ...119 A4
Knapton NR28 ......143 A1
3 Ludham NR29 .....56 C5
Northrepps NR27 .....11 A2
4 Rollesby NR29 ....57 D2
School Comm Rd NR12 .24 C3
School Hill
Reedham NR13 ....93 A4
Tasburgh NR15 .....106 E6
School La
Brandon IP27 ....175 C3
Cantley NR13 ....92 B7
Colney NR4 ....160 E3
East Dereham NR19 ..154 E1
East Harling NR16 ..118 C5
Gimingham NR11 .....22 E8
Great Yarmouth NR31 .170 D6
17 Harleston IP20 ...122 D2
Heckingham NR14 ...109 F8
Little Dunham PE32 ...65 E7
Little Melton NR9 ...160 C2
Neatishead NR12 .....55 D7
North Runcton PE33 ..44 A2
Northwold IP26 ....99 C7
Norwich NR7 ....158 F3
Rockland St Mary NR14 .91 B7
Runhall NR9 ....68 F1
Skeyton NR10 ....37 A5
Smallburgh NR12 .....38 D3
Stoke Ferry PE33 .....80 F2
Surlingham NR14 .....73 B1
Thetford IP24 ......176 D3
Walpole St Andrew PE14 .41 E3
Wereham PE33 ....80 E4
1 Wisbech PE13 ....152 C5
Wramplingham NR18 ..69 F1
Wymondham NR18 ..105 B3
School Loke
Bodham NR25 ....9 A2
Hemsby NR29 ......167 A7
School Pastures PE31 ..3 E7
School Plain NR19 ..154 B5
School Rd
Alburgh IP20 ....123 A5
Aldborough NR11 .....21 A5
Ashmanhaugh NR12 ..55 B7
Bacton NR28 ....23 B4
Barton Turf NR12 ....38 E1
Bedingham NR35 ...108 B3
Beetley NR20 ....49 C5
Blofield NR13 ....165 B8
Bracon Ash NR14 ....89 A3
Bradenham IP25 .....66 D3
Bressingham IP22 ..129 B8
Brisley NR20 ....49 A8
Catfield NR29 ....56 C8
Colkirk NR21 ....31 D5
Earsham NR35 .....123 F8
East Ruston NR12 ....38 E7
Erpingham NR11 .....21 B2
Foulden IP26 ....82 A1
Freethorpe NR13 .....92 F7
Frettenham NR12 .....54 A4
Great Massingham PE32 .29 C7
Great Yarmouth NR30 .169 B5
Haveringland NR10 ...52 D7
Heacham PE31 .....133 D5
Hinderclay IP22 ....128 C3
Holme Hale IP25 .....66 A2
Horning NR12 ....55 F3
Kirby Cane NR35 ...109 E4
Lessingham NR12 ....24 D3
Lingwood NR13 ......74 A3
Little Cressingham IP25 .83 F2
Little Plumpstead NR13 .73 B6
Ludham NR29 ....56 B5
Marshland St James PE14 .60 B4
Mautby NR29 ....75 E5
Middleton PE32 ......44 C2
Morning Thorpe NR15 .107 B3
Neatishead NR12 .....55 E7
1 Necton NR37 ....65 F4
Newton Flotman NR15 ..89 D1
Outwell PE14 ....77 D4
Potter Heigham NR29 .56 F6
Reepham NR10 .....149 B4
Runcton Holme PE33 ..61 E3
St Andrew, Ilketshall
NR34 ....124 C4
Sculthorpe Airfield NR21 .15 C3
Seething NR15 ......108 E8
10 Snettisham PE31 ...12 E4
South Walsham NR13 ..74 A8
Strumpshaw NR13 ....73 F1
Swannington NR9 ....52 B5
Taverham NR8 ......155 F1
Terrington St John PE14 .60 B7
Thompson IP24 ....102 B7
Tilney All Saints PE34 ..42 E4
Tilney St Lawrence PE34 .60 C7
Tivetshall St Mary NR15 .121 B5
Walpole Highway PE14 .59 F8
Walton Highway PE14 ..59 C8
Watlington PE33 ......61 D6

School Rd continued
Weasenham All Saints
PE32 ....47 D8
Weasenham St Peter
PE32 ....30 D1
West Rudham PE31 ......29 F6
West Walton PE14 ......59 B8
Whissonsett NR20 ......31 E2
Wiggenhall St Germans
PE34 ....61 B8
Worstead NR28 ....38 A5
School Rd Back 4
NR30 ....169 C5
School Sq IP24 ....102 E3
School Terr 3 NR14 ..163 B2
School View NR34 ....124 F1
Schoolfield NR10 .....155 C8
Schoolhouse La 1
NR11 ....150 C7
Scole Comm IP21 .....130 C6
Scole Comm Rd IP21 ..130 D6
Scole Prim Sch IP21 ..130 D6
Scole Rd IP21 ....131 C6
Scolt Head Island National
Nature Reserve★ PE31 ..3 E8
Sconch Beck Rd IP20 ..123 A2
Scotch Hill Rd NR8 ...155 B1
Scotgate Cl IP24 .....102 E3
Scott Cl IP24 ....176 E6
Scott Rd NR11 ....163 B5
Scott's Cnr NR16 .....105 B4
Scott's Hill NR14 .....89 A4
Scott's La IP26 ....99 A7
Scotter Rise 7 NR26 ..138 C5
Scottow Rd NR10 ......37 B2
Scoulton Rd NR17 .....85 F3
Scratby Cres NR29 ....167 F3
Scratby Rd NR29 ......167 D3
Scroby Ct NR29 ....167 E3
Scrumpy Way NR16 ....119 D7
Sculthorpe Airfield
NR21 ....15 E2
Sculthorpe Ave PE34 .146 B5
Sculthorpe Bvd 7 NR21 .15 C2
Sculthorpe CE VA Prim Sch
NR21 ....16 C2
Sculthorpe Eastgate
NR21 ....141 A5
Sculthorpe Rd NR21 ...141 A5
Sea Cl PE31 ....133 B6
Sea La PE36 ....132 E7
Sea Palling Rd NR12 ...39 F3
Sea View Rd
Hemsby NR29 ....167 D7
Mundesley NR11 ....143 B7
Sea View Rise NR31 ...171 E4
Seabank Rd
Heacham NR23 ....133 B6
Wisbech PE13 ....152 F6
Seabank Way PE30 ....146 E7
Seabird Cl 4 NR30 ....168 D7
Seabrook Ct 9 NR5 ....161 A7
Seacliff NR26 ....138 E7
Seafield Cl 20 NR30 ...169 D2
Seafield Rd N NR30 ....168 E6
Seafield Rd S NR30 ....168 D6
Seafields Dr NR31 .....171 E4
Seaforth Dr NR8 ......156 E8
Seagate PE36 ....132 C3
Seagate Rd PE36 ......132 B3
Seagull Rd NR29 ......167 E5
Seamere Rd NR9 ....86 D4
Searle Cl NR21 ....141 F5
Sears Cl NR11 ....150 C6
Seaside La NR12 ....24 E4
Seates The 6 NR8 .....155 D2
Seathwaite Rd NR30 ...147 D8
Seaview Cres NR26 ....138 D5
Seawake Cl NR31 ......170 A4
Seaward Cres NR11 ....143 B6
Seaward Wlk NR30 ....168 E8
Seckar Dr NR19 ....154 C4
Second Ave
Caister-on-Sea NR30 ...168 D8
Wisbech PE13 ....152 D4
Second Dro IP27 ......113 C3
Second Marsh Rd PE14 .59 A7
Sedge Cl NR21 ....141 E4
Sedge Dro PE38 ....96 C7
Sedge Fen Rd PE38 ....97 B3
Sedge Rd NR19 ....154 B4
Sedgefen Dro PE38 ....112 E2
Sedgefen Rd IP27 .....112 F3
Sedgeford Fst Sch
PE36 ....13 B7
Sedgeford La 5 PE30 ..146 D4
Sedgeford Rd
Docking PE31 ....134 B4
Snettisham PE31 ......12 F5
Seeche Abbey PE34 ....43 D1
Seething & Mumdham Sch
NR15 ....108 E8
Seething Old Hall Pk
NR15 ....91 B1
Seething Rd NR35 .....108 D5
Seething St NR15 .....108 E8
Seeview Cres NR14 ....24 A7
Sefton Ave PE13 ......152 E6
Sefton La NR31 ....169 C3
Sego Vale NR8 ....156 E8
Segrave Rd 6 PE30 ....147 A8
Selby Pl 19 NR30 .....169 D2
Self's La IP22 ....128 C7
Selwyn Dr 9 NR31 .....94 A5
Selwyn Gdns IP21 .....121 E5

Selwyn Rd NR31 ......170 A5
Semere Gn La IP21 ....121 D2
Semere La IP21 ....121 D4
Sendall Rd NR28 ......151 B3
Sennowe Rd NR20 ......32 F4
Senter's Rd PE31 ......140 D2
Seppings Rd NR21 .....141 A6
Seppings Way NR13 ....72 E6
Serpentine La NR10 ....53 C6
Setch Rd Middleton PE33 .44 A1
West Winch PE33 ......43 F1
Seton Rd NR8 ....155 E1
Setons Halt Sta NR23 ..5 F1
Seven Sisters Cl PE30 ..146 D4
Seventh Ave PE13 .....152 E4
Severalls Rd IP26 .....98 D5
Sewell Rd Lamas NR10 ..36 F1
Norwich NR3 ....158 E1
Sewell's La NR15 ......90 D3
Sewells Cl 5 NR15 .....89 C1
Sexton Rd NR35 ....108 D2
Seymour Ave
Brandon IP27 ....114 D4
Great Yarmouth NR30 ..169 D8
Shack La NR13 ....165 D6
Shadingfield Cl 16
NR30 ....169 D2
Shadwell Cl IP27 ......175 B7
Shakers' Rd
Brandon IP27 ....115 A1
Wangford IP27 ....114 F1
Shakespeare Rd NR30 ..169 E8
Shakespeare Way
Taverham NR8 ....156 E8
Thetford IP24 ....176 E6
Shannock Ct 14 NR29 ..138 D7
Shannon Dr 4 NR30 ....168 C6
Shannons Cl NR17 .....174 E4
Sharman Ave IP25 .....84 D4
Sharmans Loke NR31 ...93 F5
Sharon Cl
2 East Dereham NR19 ..154 D1
Felmingham NR28 .....37 A8
Sharp St NR29 ....56 C7
Sharpe Way NR29 ......167 B2
Sharper's Cnr IP27 ....113 D2
Sharrington Rd NR24 ...18 B5
Shaw's Yd PE31 ....30 B7
Shawcross Rd NR27 ....10 A4
Shearwater Dr 2 NR31 ..170 A7
Sheddick Ct NR19 .....154 D6
Sheep Mdw Cl NR5 .....156 E1
Sheffield Rd NR18 .....173 C5
Sheldonian Ct NR31 ....170 A4
Sheldrake Cl NR21 .....141 F5
Sheldrick Pl NR19 .....154 E2
Shelduck Dr 7 NR31 ....12 E5
Shelfanger Rd IP22 ....177 C7
Shelford Dr PE30 ......147 B8
Shell Mus The★ NR25 ..7 E4
Shelley Cl NR30 ....168 D6
Shelley Dr NR8 ....156 D8
Shelley Way NR30 .....176 E6
Shelly Cl 3 PE38 ......172 D6
Shelterhouse Cnr
IP24 ....125 A4
Shelton with Hardwick Sch
NR15 ....107 B2
Shepheard Cl 1 NR28 ..151 E6
Shepheards Cl NR11 ...150 E8
Shepherd Cl
2 Norwich NR4 ....161 D5
Sheringham NR26 .....138 B6
Shepherd Way NR8 ....155 E2
Shepherd's Fold PE37 ..153 D2
Shepherd's La NR10 ...36 A2
Shepherds Cl
Cromer NR27 ....10 B5
11 Horsford NR10 .....53 A3
Runton NR27 ....10 B5
Shepherds La
Burgate IP22 ....129 B3
Oulton NR11 ....35 B6
Shepherds Pightle PE36 .2 D6
Shepherdsgate Rd
PE34 ....144 C1
Shepley Cres 2 PE30 ..147 D5
Sheppard Way NR17 ...174 C5
Sherbourne Pl NR1 .....178 C1
Shereford Rd
Fakenham NR21 ......141 A3
Hempton NR21 ....31 C8
Sheridan Cl NR8 ......156 F8
Sheridan House Sch
IP25 ....86 A7
Sheringham Com Prim Sch
NR26 ....138 C5
Sheringham High Sch
NR26 ....138 C5
Sheringham Little Theatre
NR26 ....138 D7
Sheringham Mus★
NR26 ....138 D7
Sheringham Pk★ NR26 ..9 B6
Sheringham Pk Visitor Ctr★
NR26 ....9 B4
Sheringham Rd
West Beckham NR25 ...9 B3
Weybourne NR25 .....8 F5
Sheringham Sta NR26 ..138 C7
Sheringham Woodfields Spec
Sch NR26 ....138 C5
Sheringwood NR26 .....138 E4
Shernborne Rd PE31 ...140 E7
Sherwell Rd NR6 ......157 E6
Sherwood Ave PE13 ....152 D7
Sherwood Rd NR4 .....162 C1
Sheval Cl NR15 ....121 A8

Shickle Pl IP22 ....127 F6
Shillgate Way NR8 ....155 B2
Shillito Rd NR13 ......165 F6
Shimpling Rd IP21 .....121 B1
Ship La PE36 ....2 C6
Shipden Ave NR27 .....139 A7
Shipden Ct NR27 ......139 A7
Shipdham Airfield IP25 ..67 E2
Shipdham Airfield Ind Est
IP25 ....67 F2
Shipdham Rd
Carbrooke IP25 ....85 A5
East Dereham NR19 ...154 D1
Scarning NR19 ....67 B6
Shipdham NR19 ......67 E5
Shipfield NR3 ....158 F2
Shipgate Rd PE31 .....29 B5
Shippea Hill Sta CB7 ..112 C3
Shipstone Rd 11 NR3 ..162 D8
Shire Ave 5 NR31 .....94 C8
Shiregreen PE30 ......147 C4
Shires The NR8 ....155 F2
Shirley Cl 3 NR12 .....54 A4
Shoe Devil La NR35 ...124 C4
Shoemakers La PE37 ...64 E3
Shooters Cl NR8 ......155 D1
Shop La Hethersett NR9 ..88 E8
Tunstead NR12 ....38 A3
Wells-next-the-Sea
NR23 ....136 D6
Shop St NR19 ....68 A3
Shorncliffe Ave NR3 ...158 C1
Shorncliffe Cl 1 NR3 ..158 C1
Short Beck 18 IP26 ....98 E1
Short Cl PE38 ....172 C6
Short Dro PE38 ....172 C6
Short Gn IP22 ....120 B5
Short La Billingford NR20 ..50 A8
Feltwell IP26 ....98 D1
Happisburgh NR12 ....24 B3
Harpley PE31 ....29 D4
Mautby NR29 ....75 E6
Swardeston NR14 .....89 C5
Short Rd
3 Attleborough NR17 ..174 C5
Belton with Browston
NR31 ....94 A4
Short St 8 NR15 ......89 D1
Short-thorn Rd NR10 ...52 F5
Shotesham La NR15 ....107 C8
Shotesham Rd
Howe NR15 ....90 C2
Poringland NR14 ......90 B3
Woodton NR35 ....108 A6
Shotford Rd IP20 ......122 D1
Shouldham Cl PE31 ....140 C3
Shouldham La PE37 ....153 A4
Shouldham Rd
Marham PE33 ....63 A3
Shouldham Thorpe PE33 ..62 C2
Shreeves Rd IP22 ......177 E4
Shropham Rd IP24 .....102 E3
Shrub Cl NR17 ....174 D5
Shrub Dro PE38 ....112 E6
Shrub Hill PE38 ....112 F7
Shrublands The
Horsford NR10 ....53 B4
Norwich NR2 ....162 B6
Shrublands Way NR31 ..170 A5
Shuttleworth Cl NR31 ..170 A8
Sidegate La
Great Yarmouth NR30 ..169 C5
Hopton on Sea NR31 ...171 B7
Sidell Cl 11 NR4 ......89 B8
Sidestrand Hall Specl Sch
NR27 ....11 B2
Siding Rd NR34 ....111 C1
Sidings The IP24 ......176 C5
Sidney Cl
2 Great Yarmouth NR30 ..169 D2
8 Martham NR29 .....57 C4
Sidney Rd
Costessey NR8 ....156 F4
Ingham NR12 ....39 D4
Sidney St PE30 ....146 F3
Sienna Mews 3 NR1 ....163 B7
Sigismund Rd NR1 .....162 D3
Silfield Ave NR18 .....173 D1
Silfield Gdn PE36 .....132 D4
Silfield Rd NR18 ......173 C2
Silfield St PE30 ....147 C6
Silfield St NR18 ......88 A2
Silkmill Rd 2 NR30 ....169 D4
Silt Rd Nordelph PE38 ..78 B2
Runcton Holme PE33 ...61 C4
Terrington St Clement
PE34 ....25 F3
Upwell PE14 ....77 F1
Silver Cour NR27 ......11 A2
Silver Dr PE31 ....140 C4
Silver Drif PE37 ....64 E5
Silver End NR10 ......149 B5
Silver Gdns 5 NR31 ....94 A5
Silver Hill NR30 ......147 D6
Silver Rd NR3 ....178 C4
Silver St
Attleborough NR17 ....174 F6
Besthorpe NR17 ......104 D7
Fleggburgh NR29 .....75 C8
Garvestone NR9 ......86 C8
Norwich NR3 ....162 E8
South Lopham IP22 ...128 F7
Wisbech PE13 ....152 C6
Silvergate La NR11 ....35 F6
Silvertree's Way PE33 ..43 E1
Simon Scotland Rd
PE30 ....146 F2
Simpson Cl NR28 ......151 B5

Sinclair Ct NR31 ......170 A8
Sir Douglas Bader Espl
PE36 ....132 C4
Sir Edward Stracey Rd
NR13 ....72 D8
Sir Lewis St PE30 .....146 E6
Sir Thomas Cl NR18 ...173 C5
Sir William's Cl NR11 ..150 D7
Sir William's La NR11 ..150 D7
Siskin Cl NR31 ....170 A6
Sitka Cl PE31 ....133 C6
Six Crossways NR14 ...91 D3
Sixteen Foot Bank
PE14 ....77 D1
Sixth Ave PE13 ....152 E4
Skedge Way 6 NR13 ...73 C6
Skelton Cl 1 IP22 .....177 E4
Skelton Rd Diss IP22 ..177 E4
Norwich NR7 ....163 C8
Sketton View NR28 ....151 B3
Skeyton Cnr NR10 .....37 B6
Skeyton New Rd NR28 ..151 B5
Skeyton Rd
Coltishall NR10 ....37 B2
North Walsham NR28 ..151 A4
Skinner's La IP20 .....122 B4
Skinners La NR12 .....164 B2
Skipping Block Row
NR18 ....88 B6
Skippon Way NR13 ....72 D5
Skitfield Rd NR20 .....33 E6
Skoner Rd NR5 ....161 B8
Skoyles' La NR19 .....88 A8
Skye Cl NR5 ....161 A8
Slad La NR20 ....50 C6
Slade La
Framingham Pigot NR14 ..90 E6
Old Buckenham NR17 ..104 B1
Wortham IP22 ....129 B6
Yelverton NR14 ......90 F6
Slade Rd NR21 ....18 B7
Sleaford Gn NR3 ......158 C2
Sleigh La IP25 ....84 E2
Sleights Dr PE14 ......59 C5
Slessor Cl 2 IP25 .....84 F3
Slip Rd NR14 ....93 A1
Slip The PE36 ....2 C3
Slipshoe La NR15 .....122 B7
Sloane Way IP24 ......176 B2
Sloe La NR13 ....72 D8
Sloley Rd NR28 ....38 A3
Slopers Rd NR18 ......87 F7
Slough La
Attleborough NR17 ....174 E3
North Tuddenham NR20 ..68 E8
Slough Rd IP22 ....129 A1
Slugs La NR32 ....111 C8
Sluice Dro IP26 ....113 C2
Sluice Rd Denver PE38 ..172 B1
Wiggenhall St Germans
PE34 ....61 A8
Slutshole La
Besthorpe NR17 ......104 D7
Wymondham NR17 ....105 A7
Small Lode PE14 ......77 F5
Smallburgh Rd
Barton Turf NR12 .....55 E8
Smallburgh NR12 .....38 D2
Smallholdings Rd
PE34 ....145 D4
Smallworth La IP22 ...128 B7
Smea The NR12 ....39 E1
Smeat St 2 NR5 ......161 B7
Smee La NR13 ....72 E4
Smee Rd NR13 ....72 E4
Smeeth Rd Emneth PE14 ..59 F2
St John's Fen End PE14 ..60 A5
Smith Ave NR30 ......146 E6
Smith's Dro PE38 .....112 C8
Smith's Loke NR31 ....170 A6
Smithdale Rd NR5 .....157 B1
Smithdon High Sch
PE36 ....132 D4
Smithfield Rd NR1 .....162 E3
Smiths Dr IP21 ....121 B1
Smiths La NR21 ....141 E5
Smithson Cl NR18 .....173 C4
Smithson Dr NR20 .....68 F5
Smithtyne Ave
Dereham NR19 ....68 A7
3 East Dereham NR19 ..154 F3
Smithy Cl PE31 ....133 D5
Smithy Rd PE31 ......140 D8
Smock Mill Loke
NR18 ....173 B5
Smuggler's La NR10 ...149 B4
Smugglers Cl PE36 ....132 F8
Smugglers' Rd IP26 ...100 F8
Snaefell Pk NR26 .....138 D6
Snake's La Lound NR32 ..94 C2
Topcroft NR35 ....108 A4
Snape Hall Rd 14 NR15 ..106 C3
Snape Hill IP22 ....128 C2
Snape La PE38 ....172 B5
Sneath Rd NR15 ......121 A8
Snetterton Circuit
NR16 ....118 D8
Snettisham Beach
PE31 ....12 A3
Snettisham Nature Reserve★
PE31 ....12 E4
Snettisham Pk★ PE31 ..12 E4
Snettisham Prim Sch
PE31 ....12 E5
Snoring Rd NR21 ......17 C3
Snow St IP22 ....177 A6
Snow's Hill 6 NR14 ...92 A4
Snow's La NR14 ......92 A4

Snowberry Cl 4 NR8 ..155 B2
Snowdrop Cl 20 NR31 ..94 C6
Snowdrop Dr NR17 ....174 B4
Snowhill Drift NR19 ...154 D6
Soame Cl NR11 ....150 D5
Soames Pl NR19 ......67 B7
Soanes Ct NR9 ....51 A5
Softley Dr NR4 ....161 C2
Soken Dr 5 Beetley NR19 ..49 C3
5 Gressenhall NR20 ....49 C3
Solace Cl NR35 ....124 C3
Sole Cl 6 NR10 ....53 B3
Soleme Rd NR3 ....158 B1
Solent Cl NR30 ....168 E5
Somerleyton Gdns
NR2 ....162 C5
Somerleyton Hall & Gdns★
NR32 ....111 E8
Somerleyton Prim Sch
NR32 ....111 D8
Somerleyton St 2 NR2 ..162 C5
Somerleyton Sta
NR32 ....111 C7
Somers Rd NR13 ......152 B4
Somersby Cl 2 PE30 ...147 A8
Somerset Pl 22 NR30 ..169 C4
Somerset Way NR8 ....155 A1
Somerton Rd
Martham NR29 ....57 D5
Somerton NR29 ......58 A6
Somerville Ave NR11 ..170 B3
Somerville Rd 11 PE30 ..146 E3
Sorrel Cl PE30 ....147 C8
Sorrel Dr
Attleborough NR17 ....174 B4
1 Thetford IP24 ......176 E4
Sorrel La NR20 ....49 D5
Sorrel Rd 25 NR31 ....94 C6
Sorrel Way PE38 ......172 C3
Sotherton Rd NR4 .....161 F3
Soudan Cl 3 NR30 .....168 D7
South Acre Hall PE32 ..46 E1
South Acre Rd PE32 ...46 F1
South Ave Norwich NR7 ..163 E5
Swanton Morley Airfield
NR20 ....50 B5
South Beach PE31 .....133 A3
South Beach Par
NR30 ....170 E6
South Beach Pl NR30 ..169 E2
South Beach Rd
Heacham PE31 ....133 A4
Hunstanton PE36 ....132 A3
South Brink PE13 .....152 A3
South Burlingham Rd
NR13 ....74 B3
South Cl NR25 ....7 A6
South Cnr PE31 ....3 B7
South Creake Maize Maze★
NR21 ....15 E6
South Croft NR9 ......88 C7
South Denes Rd NR30 ..169 D1
South Everard St
PE30 ....146 E3
South Gage Cl NR7 ....159 C4
South Gn NR31 ....170 C1
South Gn
East Dereham NR19 ...154 E3
Terrington St Clement
PE34 ....144 B5
South Gn Gdns NR19 ..154 E3
South Harford Mid Sch
NR4 ....89 E8
South Hill Cl NR7 .....163 F8
South Hill Rd NR7 .....163 F8
South Icehouse Hill
NR31 ....170 D6
South Lynn Plain
PE30 ....146 E4
South Mkt Rd NR30 ...169 D4
South Moor Dr PE31 ...133 C6
South Pk IP27 ....175 B7
South Pk Ave 2 NR4 ...162 A4
South Quay
Great Yarmouth NR30 ..169 D4
8 King's Lynn PE30 ...146 D4
South Rd
Great Yarmouth NR30 ..169 E8
Hemsby NR29 ....167 D7
Watton IP25 ....84 D3
South Rise NR28 ......151 B3
South St
Great Dunham PE32 ...47 F1
Hockwold cum Wilton
IP26 ....113 F6
2 King's Lynn PE30 ...146 E4
Sheringham NR26 ....138 C7
South Walsham Rd
Acle NR13 ....166 A5
South Walsham NR13 ..74 B5
South Wlk NR35 ......72 E5
South Wood Dr NR14 ..90 B6
South Wootton Fst Sch
PE30 ....148 C2
South Wootton Jun Sch
PE30 ....148 B3
South Wootton La
PE30 ....148 C1
Southacre Rd PE32 ....65 C7
Southampton Pl 16
NR30 ....169 D4
Southburgh La NR9 ....86 A5
Southburgh Rd NR9 ...86 A7
Southend
Bradenham IP25 ......66 D3
East Dereham NR19 ...154 D4
Southend Rd PE36 ....132 C3
Southern La IP22 .....128 D5

Southern Reach 7 NR14 .89 B3
Southerwood 4 NR6 ..158 D5
Southery Prim Sch
PE38 ....97 A5
Southery Rd
Feltwell IP26 ....98 B2
Methwold IP26 ....97 F3
Southfield PE32 .....65 C5
Southfield Dr 8 PE33 .43 F2
Southfield La NR13 ...55 C1
Southfields
Downham Market PE38 ..172 B4
1 King's Lynn PE30 ...147 B6
Southgate 12 IP20 ...122 D1
Southgate Cl NR23 ..136 C5
Southgate La
Norwich 178 C2
Snettisham PE31 ....12 E4
Southgate St NR30 ..146 E3
Southgates Dr NR21 ..141 B5
Southgates Rd NR30 .169 D2
Southlands PE37 .....153 B2
Southrepps Rd
Antingham NR28 ......22 B4
Gimingham NR11 ......22 E6
Southside NR34 .....79 D8
Southtown Fst Sch
NR31 ....169 B2
Southtown Rd NR31 .169 C2
Southwell Rd
5 Horsham St Faith &
Newton St Faith NR14 ..53 D2
Norwich NR1 ....178 A1
Wisbech PE13 ......152 C7
Southwood Rd
Beighton NR13 ....74 C1
Cantley NR13 ....92 C8
Sovereign Cl 2 PE13 ..152 A6
Sovereign Way PE38 ..172 A4
Sow's La NR12 ......55 E6
Spa La Aylsham NR11 ..150 B3
Oulton NR11 ....35 B8
Spalding's Chair Hill
IP24 ....126 E8
Spar Rd NR6 ....158 C5
Sparhawk Ave NR7 ..159 C4
Sparhawk Cl NR7 ...159 C4
Sparhawk Fst Sch
NR7 ....159 C4
Sparrow Cl 4 NR31 ...94 C7
Sparrowgate Rd PE14 ..59 C5
Speedwell
5 Attleborough NR17 ..174 B4
2 Thetford IP24 ....176 C4
Speedwell Rd NR18 .173 D4
Speedwell Way
Norwich NR5 ......160 F5
13 Redenhall with Harleston
IP20 ....122 D1
Speke St NR2 ......162 A7
Spelman Rd NR2 ....162 A4
Spencer Ave NR31 ..170 C6
Spencer Cl
Great & Little Plumstead
NR13 ....73 B7
11 Lingwood NR13 ....74 A3
West Walton PE14 ...59 B8
Spencer Ct 12 IP25 ...84 D3
Spencer Rd NR6 ....158 C5
Spencer St NR3 ....162 E8
Spencers Cl NR20 ...49 E7
Spens Ave NR31 ....170 B3
Spenser Ave NR28 ..151 D4
Spenser Rd PE30 ...148 B1
Spice Chase NR34 ...60 C7
Spicer's La NR16 ...106 B5
Spiers Way IP22 ....177 B4
Spindle Cl NR18 ....173 D4
Spindle Rd NR6 .....158 D4
Spindrift Cl 11 NR29 ...58 B6
Spink's La NR18 ....173 F6
Spinks' La NR35 ....108 D2
Spinks La NR18 .....88 B4
Spinners Cl PE37 ...153 B5
Spinners La PE37 ...153 B5
Spinney Cl Beetley NR20 .49 D4
Brandon IP27 .....175 C2
King's Lynn PE30 ..148 B4
9 Long Stratton NR15 ..106 E3
Norwich NR7 ......163 F8
Spinney Rd NR7 ....163 E8
Spinney The NR14 ..110 B7
Spirkett's La IP20 ..122 D1
Spitalfields NR1 ....163 A7
Spitfire Rd NR6 ....158 C6
Spixworth Fst Sch
NR10 ....54 A2
Spixworth Rd
Hainford NR10 ....53 F4
Horsham St Faith &
Newton St Faith NR10 ..53 E2
Norwich NR6 ......158 E5
Splash Leisure Complex
NR26 ....138 B7
Splashes The PE37 .153 B7
Spong La
Carleton St Peter NR14 ...91 D5
East Carleton NR14 ....88 F4
Shropham NR17 .....103 C4
Spooner Row Prim Sch
NR18 ....105 A8
Spooner Row Sta
NR18 ....105 A8
Sporle Fst Sch PE32 ..65 D6
Sporle Rd
Little Dunham PE32 ....65 D7
Swaffham PE37 .....153 C5
Spring Cl PE30 .....148 C1

Spring Gr PE34 .....144 B4
Spring La
Forncett NR16 ......106 B5
Hempnall NR15 .....107 E3
King's Lynn PE30 ...147 C7
North Barsham NR22 ...16 A7
Shouldham NR19 ....62 A6
South Creake NR22 ...16 A6
Yaxham NR19 ....68 B6
Spring Rd IP31 .....127 A1
Spring Sedge 4 PE30 ..147 A8
Spring View 1 PE31 ...12 D4
Springbank NR1 ....162 E2
Springdale Cres NR13 .165 B4
Springdale Rd NR13 .165 B4
Springfield NR13 ...166 C3
Springfield Cl
Crimplesham PE33 ....80 B6
Hemsby NR29 ....58 A4
Springfield N NR29 ..58 A4
Springfield Rd
Great Yarmouth NR31 ..170 D4
Hemsby NR29 ....58 A4
Norwich NR7 ......159 D2
Taverham NR8 .....155 C1
Walpole St Andrew PE14 ..41 D4
Springfield Way NR9 ..86 B5
Springfield Wlk IP21 ..121 E5
Springfields
Attleborough NR17 ..174 B5
12 Poringland NR14 ...90 C5
Springfiled Cl 4 NR25 ...8 F5
Springles The 6 NR7 ...10 B5
Springvale 3 PE32 ...45 C6
Springwell La NR9 ...51 F6
Springwell Rd NR20 ...31 C2
Springwood
Taverham NR8 .....155 E1
Woodton NR35 .....108 A6
Springwood High Sch
PE30 ....147 C6
Sprowston Fst & Mid Sch
NR7 ....159 A4
Sprowston High Sch
NR7 ....159 B3
Sprowston Rd NR3 ..158 F2
Sprowston Ret Pk
NR7 ....159 C2
Spruce Ave 2 NR29 ..167 A2
Spruce Cl PE31 ....133 B6
Spruce Cres 4 NR14 ..90 C5
Spruce Dr IP27 ....175 D2
Spruce Rd PE38 ...172 B6
Spur La NR14 ....90 C6
Spur Rd NR9 ....69 C2
Spurdens Cres NR28 .151 D3
Spurge Sq 3 NR14 ..173 E4
Spynke Rd NR3 ....158 B3
Squire's Dr PE14 ....77 E3
Squire's Dro PE14 ...78 A3
Squire's Rd NR13 ...75 A2
Squires Hill PE33 ...63 B4
Stablefields IP26 ...99 C7
Stacy Rd NR13 ....162 E8
Staden Pk NR11 .....11 D1
Stafford Ave NR5 ..156 F1
Stafford Rd NR31 ..169 B2
Stafford St NR2 ....162 B6
Stag Pl PE30 ......147 A7
Stainsby Cl PE31 ..133 D4
Staithe Cl 3 NR12 ...55 E4
Staithe La PE36 ......2 C7
Staithe Rd
Barton Turf NR12 ....38 F1
Burgh St Peter NR34 .111 C3
Catfield NR29 ....56 D8
Halvergate NR13 ...166 F1
Heacham PE31 .....133 C5
Hickling NR12 ....39 E1
Langley with Hardley
NR14 ....91 F4
Ludham NR29 ....56 C5
Martham NR29 ......57 D5
Repps with Bastwick
NR29 ....56 F4
Somerton NR29 .....57 E6
Stalham NR12 ....39 B3
Wisbech PE13 .....152 E5
Staithe Stree NR23 .136 D6
Staithe The NR11 ..150 D8
Staitheway Rd NR12 .164 C4
Stalham Firehouse Mus★
NR12 ....39 B3
Stalham High Sch
NR12 ....39 B3
Stalham Mid Sch NR12 .39 B3
Stalham Rd
Ashmanhaugh NR12 ...55 C8
Hickling NR12 ....39 E2
Sea Palling NR12 ....24 F1
Wroxham/Hoveton
NR12 ....164 D6
Stalland La NR18 ....86 D2
Stalland The NR18 ..86 D2
Stallett Way NR34 ..60 C8
Stan Petersen Cl NR1 .163 A6
Standard Rd
Great Yarmouth NR30 ..169 E3
Wells-next-the-Sea
NR23 ....136 D6
Standley Ct NR18 ..173 B4
Stanfield Rd
Mileham PE32 ....48 E6
Tittleshall PE32 ....48 C7
Wymondham NR18 ..173 F3
Stanford Cres NR13 ..73 B7

Stanford Tuck Rd
NR28 ....151 B7
Stanhoe Rd PE31 ..134 E4
Staniforth Rd IP24 ..176 B2
Stanley Ave
Great Yarmouth NR31 ..170 C3
Neatishead NR12 ....55 E7
Norwich NR7 ......163 C5
Stanley Cl NR13 ....92 B6
Stanley Dr PE12 ....41 A8
Stanley Rd Diss IP22 .177 B4
Great Yarmouth NR30 ..169 C5
North Walsham NR28 .151 D6
Stanley St 10 PE30 .146 E5
Stanley Terr NR18 ..169 D4
Stanleys NR18 .....173 C2
Stanmore Rd NR7 ..163 E6
Stannard Cl 4 IP22 .177 C4
Stannard Rd NR4 ..161 F5
Stanninghall Rd NR12 .54 B4
Stanton Rd
Barningham IP31 ...127 C2
Dersingham PE31 ..140 C3
Star Farm 21 NR31 ..94 C6
Star Hill NR12 ....24 C3
Star La
Long Stratton NR15 .106 E3
1 Thetford IP24 ...176 C3
Tivetshall St Margaret
NR15 ....121 C5
Star Mdw NR21 ....141 B4
Stark Cl IP22 ......177 C4
Starling Cl NR11 ...150 C5
Starling Rd NR3 ...162 D8
Starling Rise NR27 ..11 B2
Starston La IP20 ...122 C1
Statham Cl NR4 ...162 B2
Station App
Norwich NR1 ......178 C2
12 Sheringham NR26 .138 D7
Wymondham NR18 ..173 C2
Station Cl
East Dereham NR19 .154 D6
4 Lingwood NR13 ...74 A3
6 Marthan NR29 ....57 D4
Sheringham NR27 ...10 A5
Swainsthorpe NR14 ..89 D4
Station Dr
Fransham NR19 .....66 A8
Reedham NR13 ......92 F5
Wisbech PE13 .....152 C4
Station Gdns PE13 .153 B5
Station Halt NR13 .165 B3
Station Hill IP20 ...122 D2
Station La
Garvestone NR9 .....68 D1
Hethersett NR9 .....88 E4
Thetford IP24 .....176 C5
Thornham PE36 ......2 C6
Station New Rd NR13 .165 D3
Station Rd Acle NR13 .166 B2
Alburgh NR15 ......123 A5
Aldeby NR34 ....110 F6
Attleborough NR17 ..174 E5
Attlebridge NR9 .....52 A4
Aylsham NR11 .....150 D6
Barnham IP24 .....125 E6
Beccles NR34 ......110 D1
Brundall NR13 .....165 D2
Burnham Market PE31 .135 C3
Burston & Shimpling
IP21 ....120 F2
Cantley NR13 ....92 C6
Clenchwarton PE34 .145 B4
Coltishall NR12 .....54 C7
Congham PE32 ......27 F3
Corpusty NR11 ......19 F1
Cromer NR27 ......139 D5
Dersingham PE31 ..140 B4
Diss IP22 ....177 F3
Ditchingham NR35 .109 B2
Docking PE31 ......134 D5
Downham Market PE38 .172 A6
East Dereham NR19 .154 E4
East Rudham PE31 ...30 B5
East Winch PE32 ....44 F3
Ellingham NR35 ....109 D3
Flordon NR15 ......106 E8
Forncett NR16 .....106 C4
Foulsham NR20 .....33 C3
Fransham NR19 .....66 B7
Fulmodeston NR21 ...17 F4
Geldeston NR34 ....109 F2
Great Moulton NR15 .121 A7
Great Ryburgh NR21 ..32 B6
Great Yarmouth NR31 .169 B3
Guestwick NR20 .....33 F5
Haddiscoe NR31 .....93 D1
Hardingham NR9 ....86 E8
Harleston IP20 .....122 D2
Heacham PE31 .....133 D6
Hilgay PE38 ....96 C6
Hindolveston NR20 ..33 E8
Holme Hale IP25 ....65 F2
Holt NR25 ....137 C6
Honing NR28 ....38 C6
Hopton on Sea NR31 .171 D4
Kimberley NR18 .....87 A6
King's Lynn PE30 ..148 B5
Lakenheath IP27 ...112 C3
Lenwade NR9 ....51 E5
Lingwood & Burlingham
NR13 ....74 A3
Middleton PE32 .....44 C4
Mundesley NR11 ...143 B6
North Elmham NR20 ..49 F7
North Walsham NR28 .151 B4

Station Rd continued
Ormesby St Margaret
with Scratby NR29 ..167 B2
5 Potter Heigham NR29 ..56 F6
Pulham Market IP21 .121 E4
Pulham St Mary IP21 .122 A4
Quidenham NR16 ...118 E8
Rackheath/Salhouse
NR13 ....72 F8
Reedham NR13 .....92 F5
Reepham NR10 ....149 C5
Roydon PE32 ....28 A2
6 Sheringham NR27 ..10 A5
Sheringham NR26 ..138 D7
Snettisham PE31 ....12 D4
Somerleyton, Ashby &
Herringfleet NR32 ..111 C7
South Wootton NR8 .149 C5
Stanhoe PE31 ......14 E8
Strumpshaw NR13 ...91 F8
Taverham NR8 .....156 F8
Terrington St Clement
PE34 ....144 C2
Thetford IP24 .....176 C5
Thorpe Market NR11 ..22 A6
Tilney All Saints PE34 .144 C2
Tivetshall St Margaret
NR15 ....121 B7
Walsingham NR22 ...16 F7
Walsoken PE14 .....59 E4
Watlington PE33 ....61 C6
Wells-next-the-Sea
NR23 ....136 D5
Wendling NR19 .....66 F7
West Beckham PE33 ..80 B3
Weybourne NR25 .....8 F5
Whinburgh & Westfield
NR19 ....68 A5
Worstead NR28 .....37 F3
Wroxham/Hoveton
NR12 ....164 C5
Wymondham NR18 ..173 C3
Station Rd Ind Est
NR17 ....174 E4
Station Rd N
Belton NR31 ....93 F6
Walpole Cross Keys PE14 ..41 F5
Station Rd S
Belton NR31 ....93 F5
Walpole Cross Keys PE14 ..41 F5
Station St PE37 ....153 B5
Station Terr IP27 ...175 C5
Station Way IP27 ..175 C5
Station Yd PE13 ...153 B5
Steam Mill La NR31 .169 B4
Stearne Cl IP24 ....176 B2
Stebbings Cl 3 PE32 ..28 A1
Steel's Dro PE38 ...79 C1
Steepgreen Cl NR1 .163 C8
Steeple Chase NR8 .155 F2
Steeple La NR15 ...106 A2
Steeple View PE13 .153 B4
Steeps The 6 NR30 .169 D1
Steer Rd PE31 ......27 B8
Stegg's La NR19 ....67 F4
Steggles Dr IP22 ..177 C5
Stephen Beaumont Way
NR19 ....154 C4
Stephenson Cl
3 Great Yarmouth NR30 .169 D5
West Raynham Airfield
PE31 ....30 B3
Stephenson Way IP24 .176 A2
Stephenson Way Ind Est
IP24 ....176 A2
Stepping La NR1 ...178 B2
Stepping Stone La
NR12 ....39 A4
Steppings La NR15 .107 C3
Stepshort NR31 .....94 A6
Stermyn St 22 PE13 .152 C5
Steven's La
Ashwellthorpe NR16 .106 B8
2 Wreningham NR16 ..88 E1
Stevens Cl IP25 ....84 D4
Stevens Rd
Cromer NR27 ......139 C4
2 Little Snoring NR21 ..17 B3
Stevenson Rd NR5 .161 B7
Steward Cl 1 NR18 .173 D5
Steward St 4 NR3 ..162 E8
Steward Way NR19 .154 C5
Stewards Cl NR10 .149 C4
Stewks Hall Drift NR9 .51 B6
Stibbard Rd NR21 ...17 F1
Stickfer La NR16 ...106 A6
Stiffkey Cl 8 PE33 ..61 D6
Stiffkey Rd Warham NR23 .5 F5
Wells-next-the-Sea
NR23 ....136 F5
Stigand's Gate NR19 .154 D7
Stile Cl 12 NR14 ....89 B3
Stile La NR18 ......173 B5
Stileman Way 11 PE31 .12 E4
Stillington Cl NR7 ..159 B3
Stilwell Dr NR19 ...154 B6
Stirling Cl
Downham Market PE38 .172 D6
Taverham NR8 .....155 F3
Stirling Rd
Old Catton NR6 ....158 C6
Sculthorpe Airfield NR21 .15 C3
Stirrups La NR32 ...171 E1
Stitch The PE14 .....77 B8
Stock Lea Rd 1 NR30 .148 C4
Stockholm Way NR19 .154 C2
Stocks Hill NR9 ....160 B5
Stocks La NR13 ...165 E5

Stockton Rd NR34 ..110 A3
Stody Dr PE30 .....148 E1
Stody Rd NR24 ......18 D6
Stoke Holy Cross Prim Sch
NR14 ....89 F4
Stoke La NR14 ......89 F5
Stoke Rd
Barton Bendish PE33 ..81 C5
Bixley NR14 ....162 F1
Boughton PE33 .....81 A4
Caistor St Edmund NR14 .89 F7
Methwold IP26 ......99 A6
Poringland NR14 ....90 B5
Wereham PE33 .....80 E4
Wormegay PE33 ....62 A5
Stokes Ave IP25 ....84 C3
Stokesby New Rd
NR13 ....166 F6
Stokesby Rd NR29 ..75 D6
Stone Breck NR5 ..156 E2
Stone Brigg NR18 ...87 A7
Stone Cl 2 PE33 ....61 D5
Stone Hill Rd NR30 .168 D6
Stone House Cl NR6 .158 D2
Stone La Bintree NR20 ..33 B3
Bressingham IP22 .119 F2
5 Hingham NR9 ....86 C4
Hoveton NR12 .....164 D8
Runhall NR9 ....68 F3
Stone Rd 6 Beetley NR20 .49 D4
6 Beetley NR20 ....49 D4
Briston NR24 ......142 E2
East Dereham NR19 .154 C2
Great Yarmouth NR31 .169 B4
Halvergate NR13 ....75 A1
Hockering NR20 .....51 B6
Mattishall NR20 .....68 C6
Norwich NR3 ......158 C1
Strumpshaw NR13 ...73 F1
Yaxham NR19 ....68 B4
Stone St IP19 ......124 F1
Stonebridge Rd NR28 ..23 D2
Stonecross Rd PE38 .172 D5
Stonecutters Way
NR30 ....169 C4
Stonefield Rd NR25 ..20 A8
Stonegate
Aylsham NR11 .....150 A3
Morley NR18 ....87 A3
Stonegate St PE30 .146 E4
Stonehill Way NR27 ..10 C4
Stonehouse Rd
Norwich NR7 ......159 B4
Salhouse NR13 .....54 F2
Upwell PE14 ....77 E5
Stonemasons Ct NR13 .166 C3
Stoney End 2 NR20 ..68 F6
Stoney La Beetley NR20 .49 B4
Reepham NR10 ....149 B6
Stoney Rd PE32 .....27 F2
Stony La
Attleborough NR17 ..174 B6
Pulham Market IP21 .121 E7
Raveningham NR14 .110 B6
Tivetshall St Margaret
NR15 ....121 B5
Wortwell IP20 .....122 F4
Storbeck Rd 2 PE13 .152 D7
Stores St IP27 .....175 C3
Story's La NR16 ...105 E5
Stow Barn Rd PE33 ..80 A7
Stow Bedon Rd IP24 .102 C2
Stow Bridge Rd
Stow Bardolph PE34 ..61 D1
Wimbotsham PE34 ...79 B3
Stow Gdns PE13 ...152 E4
Stow La PE13 .....152 E4
Stow Rd Outwell PE14 ..78 A4
Runcton Holme PE33 ..62 B3
Wiggenhall St Mary Magdalen
PE34 ....61 B5
Wisbech PE13 .....152 F5
Stow Windmill★
NR28 ....143 D4
Stowlay La NR17 ...103 B6
Stracey Rd Lamas NR10 .36 F1
Norwich NR1 ......163 A5
Strachan Cl PE31 ..133 E5
Stradbroke CE Prim Sch
IP21 ....131 E1
Stradbroke Prim Sch
NR31 ....170 D5
Stradbroke Rd NR31 .170 C5
Stradsett Cl 4 PE38 .172 D6
Straight La 19 IP20 .122 D2
Strangers Hall★ NR2 .178 A3
Stranton Ave NR19 ..68 A5
Strasbourg Way NR19 .154 B1
Stratford Cl
Dersingham PE31 ..140 E3
Norwich NR1 ......162 E2
Stratford Cres NR4 .161 C1
Stratford Dr NR1 ...162 E3
Stratton Cl 6 PE37 .153 C3
Stratton Rd
Hainford NR10 ......53 E6
Stratton Strawless NR10 .53 E8
Wacton NR15 ......106 D2
Straw Mus The★ NR11 .21 D3
Strawberry Cl 3 PE13 .152 A6
Strawberry Fields NR12 .39 B3
Strayground La NR18 .173 B2
Street Hill NR12 .....55 C5
Street The Acle NR13 .166 C3
Alburgh IP20 ......122 F6

Street The *continued*
Aldborough NR11 ....**20** F5
Aldeby NR34 ....**110** F4
Ashby St Mary NR14 ....**91** C5
Ashwellthorpe NR16 ...**106** A8
Aslacton NR15 ....**106** A1
Aylmerton NR11 ....**10** A2
Baconsthorpe NR25 .....**19** F8
Bacton NR28 ....**23** B2
Barnham IP24 ....**125** E6
Barton Turf NR12 ......**55** E8
Bawdeswell NR20 ....**50** E7
Beachamwell PE37 ......**81** E8
Beeston with Bittering
  PE32 ....**48** C2
Belaugh NR12 ....**164** A6
Bergh Apton NR15 .....**91** A3
Billingford NR20 ......**50** B7
Bintree NR20 ....**33** B2
Blo' Norton IP22 .....**128** B6
Booton NR10 ....**149** E4
Botesdale IP22 ....**128** E2
Bracon Ash NR14 ......**89** A3
Bramerton NR14 ....**90** F7
Brampton NR10 ....**36** E3
Brandon IP27 ....**175** A3
Bressingham IP22 ....**119** D2
Bridgham NR16 ....**117** E4
Brinton NR24 ....**18** D6
Brockdish IP23 ......**131** D6
Brome & Oakley IP23 .**130** C3
Brooke NR15 ....**90** E2
Brundall NR13 ....**165** C7
Burgh & Tuttington NR11 .**36** E4
Caston NR17 ....**102** E8
Catfield NR29 ....**56** C8
Claxton NR14 ....**91** D6
Coltishall NR12 ......**54** E7
Coney Weston IP31 ...**127** B4
Corpusty NR11 ....**19** F1
Costessey NR8 ....**156** E5
Croxton IP24 ....**116** C6
Dickleburgh IP21 ....**121** B1
Dilham NR28 ....**38** D4
Earsham NR35 ....**123** F8
East Tuddenham NR20 ..**69** C6
Erpingham NR11 ....**21** A2
Felthorpe NR10 ......**155** C8
Flixton NR35 ....**123** E6
Flordon NR15 ....**106** D8
Foxley NR20 ....**50** D8
Framingham Pigot NR14 .**90** D6
Fulmodeston NR21 ....**17** F3
Garvestone NR9 ....**68** B1
Geldeston NR34 ......**109** F2
Gooderstone IP25 .....**81** F5
Great Cressingham IP25 .**83** C4
Great Snoring NR21 ...**17** A5
Great Yarmouth NR30 ..**76** F5
Halvergate NR13 ......**74** F1
Hempnall NR15 ......**107** C5
Hemsby NR29 ....**167** A7
Hevingham NR10 ......**53** C8
Heydon NR11 ....**34** F6
Hickling NR12 ....**39** F2
Hinderclay IP22 .....**128** C3
Hindolveston NR20 ...**33** D8
Hindringham NR21 .....**17** E7
Hockering NR20 ....**69** B8
Honingham NR9 ....**69** E6
Horsey NR29 ....**40** E1
Kelling NR25 ....**8** C5
Ketteringham NR18 ...**88** E6
Kettlestone NR21 .....**17** C2
Knapton NR28 ....**143** B1
Lamas NR10 ....**37** A1
Lenwade NR9 ....**51** D5
Lessingham NR12 .....**24** D3
Little Barningham NR11 ..**20** B4
Little Snoring NR21 ...**17** B3
Long Stratton NR15 ..**106** E3
Lound NR32 ....**94** C2
Marham PE33 ....**63** B5
Market Weston IP22 ..**127** E4
Marlingford NR9 ......**69** E4
Mautby NR29 ....**75** E5
Melton Constable NR24 .**142** A5
Mileham PE32 ....**48** D6
Morning Thorpe NR15 .**107** C4
Morston NR25 ....**7** A6
Morton on the Hill NR9 .**52** A3
North Lopham IP22 ...**119** A2
North Pickenham PE37 .**65** E1
Norwich NR14 ....**163** B2
Ovington IP25 ....**84** E5
Poringland NR14 ......**90** C5
Pulham St Mary IP21 .**122** A3
Redenhall with Harleston
  IP20 ....**122** F1
Redgrave IP22 ......**128** E5
Reepham NR10 ....**149** C3
Riddlesworth IP22 ...**127** D7
Ringland NR8 ....**70** B8
Rockland St Mary NR14 .**91** B7
Rocklands NR17 .....**103** C7
Rougham PE32 ....**47** B7
Ryburgh NR21 ....**32** C7
St Margaret, South Elmham
  IP20 ....**123** E2
St Michael South Elmham
  IP19 ....**124** A2
Salle NR10 ....**149** D8
Saxlingham Nethergate
  NR15 ....**107** B8
Scoulton NR9 ....**85** D3

Street The *continued*
Sculthorpe NR21 ....**16** B1
Sculthorpe Airfield PE31 .**15** B3
Sea Palling NR12 ......**40** A5
Shelton NR15 ....**122** B8
Shotesham NR15 ......**90** A2
Somerleyton, Ashby &
  Herringfleet NR32 ..**111** D8
Somerton NR29 ....**57** F6
South Lopham IP22 ...**128** D8
South Pickenham PE37 ..**83** D7
South Walsham NR13 ..**74** A8
Sparham NR9 ....**51** B4
Sporle with Palgrave
  PE32 ....**65** C7
Starston IP20 ....**122** C3
Surlingham NR14 ....**165** B1
Sustead NR11 ....**20** E7
Swafield NR28 ......**151** D8
Swanton Abbott NR10 .**37** C4
Swanton Novers NR24 .**18** C2
Taverham NR8 ....**156** B8
Tharston & Hapton
  NR15 ....**106** C7
Themelthorpe NR20 ...**33** F2
Thornage NR25 ....**18** E6
Thurlton NR14 ....**92** F1
Thurne NR29 ....**56** E2
Thurton NR14 ....**91** C3
Tibenham NR16 ......**120** E8
Tivetshall St Mary NR15 .**121** B5
Topcroft NR35 ......**107** F3
Warham NR23 ....**6** A4
Waterloo IP21 ......**130** C5
Wattisfield IP22 ....**128** A1
Wellingham NR21 .....**47** F8
West Beckham NR25 ...**9** B2
Weybourne NR25 ......**8** E5
Winfarthing IP22 ...**120** B4
Witton NR28 ....**23** E1
Wiveton NR25 ....**7** E6
Woodton NR35 ....**108** C5
Stretton Sch NR21 ...**162** C3
Strickland Ave **9** PE31 .**12** E4
Strickland Cl **8** PE31 ..**12** E4
Stringside Dro PE33 ...**81** B3
Strumpshaw Rd NR13 .**165** E3
Strumpshaw Steam Mus ★
  NR13 ....**73** E1
Stuart Cl Brandon IP27 ..**175** C3
  Great Yarmouth NR31 ..**170** B4
  7 Hethersett NR9 .....**88** D8
Stuart Gdns NR1 .....**178** C3
Stuart Rd
  Aylsham NR11 ....**150** A1
  Norwich NR1 ....**178** C1
Stubb Rd NR12 ....**39** F2
Stubbs Cl PE38 ......**172** E5
Stubbs Gn La NR14 ...**109** C8
Sturdee Ave NR30 ...**169** D8
Sturdee Cl IP24 ....**176** F6
Sturmy Cl **16** NR15 ..**106** E3
Stuston La IP21 ....**130** B4
Stuston Rd IP21 ....**130** B5
Style Loke NR9 ....**69** F2
Styles Cl NR11 .....**170** A4
Stylman Rd NR5 .....**161** B4
Suckling Ave NR3 ...**158** B3
Suckling Dro PE14 ...**78** C5
Suckling La
  Framingham Pigot NR14 ..**90** D6
  Hickling NR12 ....**39** F3
Suckling Pl NR35 ...**108** C5
Suffield Cl
  7 Cringleford NR4 ...**89** B8
  3 Long Stratton NR15 .**106** D3
  North Walsham NR28 .**151** A6
Suffield Ct **16** NR6 ...**158** D2
Suffield Pk Inf Sch
  NR27 ....**139** C5
Suffield Rd NR31 ...**170** C4
Suffield Way PE30 ..**147** B8
Suffling Rd NR30 ...**170** D8
Suffolk Ave IP31 ...**126** B1
Suffolk Cl NR31 ....**170** C7
Suffolk Ct IP27 ....**175** C4
Suffolk Pl IP19 ....**154** C1
Suffolk Rd
  Great Yarmouth NR31 ..**170** C8
  King's Lynn PE30 ...**147** C6
  Norwich NR4 ....**161** C3
  Sheringham NR26 ...**138** D6
Suffolk Sq NR2 .....**162** C5
Suffolk Wlk NR4 ....**161** D3
Sugar La PE31 .....**140** E4
Sukey Way NR5 .....**160** F6
Summer Cl **4** PE14 ...**41** E4
Summer Dr NR12 ...**164** D6
Summer La IP25 .....**85** A4
Summerfield Cl PE13 .**152** A6
Summerfield Rd NR29 .**58** A4
Summerhouse Cl
  NR27 ....**139** A6
Sumpter Rd NR4 ....**161** E3
Sun Barn Rd NR10 ..**149** B4
Sun Barn Wlk NR10 .**149** B4
Sun La
  Great Yarmouth NR31 ..**94** C6
  Norwich NR3 ......**158** D1
Sun Rd NR35 ....**109** B2
Sunart Cl NR17 ....**174** C6
Sundew Cl **6** IP24 ..**176** F4
Sunk Rd NR22 ....**16** F7
Sunley Cl NR35 ....**109** C2
Sunningdale NR4 ...**162** A2
Sunninghill Cl **14** NR31 .**94** C8

Sunny Cl NR5 ......**157** B1
Sunny Cnr NR28 ...**151** B4
Sunny Gr NR5 .....**161** B8
Sunny Hill NR1 ...**162** D1
Sunnyside
  Bedingham NR35 ...**108** C4
  Diss IP22 ....**177** D5
  Heacham PE31 .....**133** D5
Sunnyside Ave **10** NR14 .**90** C5
Sunnyside Cl PE31 ..**133** D5
Sunnyside Rd PE32 ...**29** D2
Sunsalve Ride NR19 .**154** C1
Sunset Gdns PE13 ..**152** E4
Sunset Wlk NR12 ....**24** E4
Supple Cl NR1 .....**163** C7
Surlingham Dr PE37 .**153** B1
Surlingham La
  Bramerton NR14 .....**90** F8
  Rockland St Mary NR14 ..**91** B8
Surlingham Prim Sch
  NR14 ....**73** B1
Surrey Cl NR7 .....**159** C5
Surrey Gr NR1 .....**178** B1
Surrey St Cromer NR27 .**139** C7
  6 King's Lynn PE30 .**146** D5
  Norwich NR1 ......**178** B2
  9 Wiggenhall St Germans
    PE34 ....**43** B1
Surrogate St NR17 .**174** D5
Sursham Ave NR6 ...**158** F4
Sussex Rd NR31 ....**170** D5
Sussex St NR3 .....**178** A4
Sustead La NR11 ....**20** F8
Sustead Rd NR11 ....**9** F1
Suters Dr NR8 .....**155** E2
Sutherland Ave NR6 .**158** A4
Sutherland Ct Gdns
  NR27 ....**139** C6
Suton La NR18 .....**173** A1
Sutton Cres NR13 ...**92** F8
Sutton Est PE31 ...**135** C2
Sutton Fst Sch NR12 ..**39** C2
Sutton Lea NR31 ...**135** C2
Sutton Mdws PE13 ..**152** A8
Sutton Rd Catfield NR29 .**39** C1
  Great Yarmouth NR30 .**169** D1
  Hickling NR12 ......**39** D1
  Swaffham PE37 ....**153** B1
Sutton Windmill & Broads
  Mus ★ NR12 ....**39** D2
Suttons Cl **1** PE14 ...**77** F6
Swaffham Com Hospl
  PE37 ....**153** C5
Swaffham Gap IP26 ...**82** C1
Swaffham Greenhoe Mid Sch
  PE37 ....**153** B3
Swaffham Leisure Ctr
  PE37 ....**153** C2
Swaffham Mus ★ PE37 .**153** B4
Swaffham Raceway
  PE37 ....**64** C4
Swaffham Rd
  Ashill IP25 ....**84** A7
  Barton Bendish PE33 ..**63** A3
  Cockley Cley PE37 ...**82** D7
  East Dereham NR19 ..**154** D6
  Mundford IP26 ....**100** B4
  Narborough NR32 ....**63** F7
  Oxborough PE33 ....**81** E4
  Raynham NR21 ......**30** F2
  Swaffham PE37 ....**64** A4
  Watton IP25 ....**84** C4
Swaffham VC Fst Sch
  PE37 ....**153** C4
Swafield Rise NR28 .**151** D7
Swafield St NR5 ...**160** F7
Swale The NR5 .....**160** F6
Swallow Cl **6** NR31 .**170** A7
Swallow Dr IP27 ...**175** E3
Swallowfield Rd PE30 .**147** C4
Swallowtail Cl NR5 .**160** F5
Swamp La
  Great Ellingham NR17 .**103** F7
  Roydon IP22 ......**177** A6
Swan Cl Aylsham NR11 .**150** C6
  Swannington NR9 ...**52** B5
Swan Cotts PE32 ....**47** D5
Swan Dr NR20 ....**49** C3
Swan Entry **2** NR22 ..**16** F7
Swan La
  Coney Weston IP31 ..**127** B4
  Fincham PE33 ....**62** E1
  King's Lynn PE30 ..**147** A6
  1 Norwich NR2 ....**178** B3
  Redenhall with Harleston
    IP20 ....**122** D2
  Shipdham IP25 .....**67** C3
  Thurston & Hapton
    NR15 ....**106** A4
Swan Loke NR28 ...**151** C5
Swan Rd NR19 .....**154** E4
Swan St
  Fakenham NR21 ....**141** B3
  Horsham St Faith NR10 .**53** D2
Swan Terr **1** PE38 .**172** A6
Swangey La NR17 ..**103** D4
Swann Gr NR25 ....**137** C6
Swanns Yd NR28 ....**38** A4
Swansea Rd NR2 ...**162** B5
Swansgate NR6 ....**158** D4
Swanston's Rd NR30 .**170** D8
Swanton Abbot Rd
  NR10 ....**37** A5

Swanton Abbott Com Sch
  NR10 ....**37** B5
Swanton Ave NR14 .**154** E7
Swanton Cl NR19 ..**154** E7
Swanton Dr NR20 ..**154** E6
Swanton Gr NR19 ..**154** E6
Swanton Morley Prim Sch
  NR20 ....**50** B4
Swanton Morley Rd
  Hoe NR20 ....**50** A6
  North Elmham NR20 ..**49** F9
Swanton Rd
  Dereham NR20 ......**50** A1
  East Dereham NR19 .**154** E6
  Gunthorpe NR24 ....**18** B5
  Norwich NR3 ......**162** B8
Swardeston La NR14 .**89** B6
Swargate La NR15 ..**108** E8
Swash La NR13 ......**54** D2
Sweden Pl IP27 ...**175** B2
Sweet Briar Rd
  7 Long Stratton NR15 .**106** C3
  Norwich NR6 ......**161** F8
Sweet Briar Rd Ind Est
  NR3 ....**157** F1
Sweetacres **7** NR29 .**167** B6
Sweetbriar Gdns NR20 .**49** C4
Sweetbriar La
  Edgefield NR24 .....**19** D5
  Sheringham NR26 ..**138** C7
Sweyn Cl IP24 .....**176** B2
Swim Rd NR29 ....**75** F6
Swinbourne Cl NR6 .**158** E3
Swindells Cl NR5 ..**157** A2
Swingy La NR18 ....**87** A3
Swirle's Pl **6** NR30 .**169** D4
Swiss Terr PE30 ...**146** F5
Sybil Rd PE13 ....**152** C6
Sybil Wheeler Cl **5**
  IP24 ....**176** D6
Sycamore Ave
  16 Great Yarmouth NR31 .**94** C7
  28 Martham NR29 ....**57** D4
  Wymondham NR18 .**173** E6
Sycamore Cl
  Attleborough NR17 .**174** C4
  King's Lynn PE30 ..**148** D2
  8 Loddon NR14 .....**91** F1
  North Walsham NR28 .**151** D6
  Thompson IP24 ....**102** A7
Sycamore Covert
  IP24 ....**116** D2
Sycamore Cres NR2 .**161** F7
Sycamore Gn **2** NR31 .**170** B6
Sycamore Gr NR26 .**138** D5
Sycamore Way IP22 .**177** E5
Sycamores The NR19 .**154** E3
Sydenham Cl NR13 .**166** B4
Syderstone Comm Nature
  Reserve ★ PE31 ....**15** A3
Syderstone Rd NR15 .**15** B3
Sydney Dye Ct PE32 .**65** C5
Sydney Rd **11** NR10 ..**54** A2
Sydney Terr **2** PE30 .**146** D1
Syers La PE32 ......**48** D2
Syleham Hall La NR21 .**131** F5
Syleham Rd IP21 ..**131** B4
Sylvan Cl NR6 ....**157** C6
Sylvan Way
  2 Blofield Heath NR13 .**73** C6
  Taverham NR8 ....**156** E8
Sylvden Dr PE13 ..**152** F6
Symonds Ave NR29 .**167** C2
Syon Cl PE38 .....**172** B4
Sywell Cl NR6 ....**158** F6
Sywell Gr **5** PE14 ..**59** A1

T

Tabernacle La NR16 .**105** F4
Tacolneston VC Prim Sch
  NR16 ....**105** F6
Tagg Way **3** NR13 ...**72** E7
Talbot Cl IP18 ....**173** C5
Talbot Sq NR3 ....**178** A4
Talbots Mdw IP21 ..**130** B5
Tales of the Old Gaol
  House ★ PE30 .....**146** D4
Taleworth Cl NR5 ..**161** A4
Tallon St IP26 .....**82** A2
Tamarind Mews NR4 .**161** E1
Tamarisk PE30 ....**148** B1
Tamworth La NR31 .**169** B2
Tan La NR30 ......**168** E4
Tanager Cl NR3 ...**158** D3
Tanner St **4** IP24 ..**176** C4
Tanners Gn NR9 ....**68** C3
Tanning La **7** NR16 .**104** F1
Tanns La IP22 ....**119** A2
Tansy Cl NR6 .....**158** D4
Tantallon Dr NR17 .**174** F6
Tar Works Rd NR30 .**169** C6
Target Hill IP20 ..**123** B2
Tarragon Cl **16** NR31 .**94** C6
Tarragon Rd PE38 .**172** D7
Tas Valley Vineyard ★
  NR16 ....**106** A3
Tasburgh Rd NR15 .**106** F8
Tasman Dr NR11 ....**22** F8
Tatterford Dr PE31 ..**30** E7
Tattersett Pk Bsns Ctr
  NR21 ....**15** C1
Tattersett Rd PE31 ..**15** B2
Tattlepot Rd IP21 .**121** E5
Taverham Chase NR8 .**156** D8
Taverham Hall Sch
  NR8 ....**156** A8

Taverham High Sch
  NR8 ....**155** B2
Taverham La NR8 ..**156** C6
Taverham Mid Sch
  NR8 ....**156** C8
Taverham Rd
  Felthorpe NR10 ...**155** C7
  Honingham NR9 ....**69** F6
  Taverham NR8 ....**156** D8
Tavern Cl NR20 ....**49** D4
Tavern La Diss IP22 .**177** F3
  East Dereham NR19 .**154** E3
Tavistock Rd PE13 .**152** D5
Tawny Sedge **3** PE30 .**147** A8
Taylor Ave **9** NR4 ..**89** B8
Taylor Rd Diss IP22 .**177** B4
  Norwich NR5 .....**161** C6
Taylor's La
  Gressenhall NR20 ...**49** C3
  Norwich NR6 .....**158** D6
  Trimingham NR11 ...**11** E1
Taylors Loke
  3 Cley next the Sea NR25 ..**7** E6
  1 Hemsby NR29 ...**167** A8
Taymor Pl PE14 ...**95** D4
Teal Cl **3** PE31 ....**12** E5
Teal Wlk Brandon IP27 .**175** F4
  16 Great Yarmouth NR31 .**94** C8
Teasel Cl NR20 ....**68** A8
Teasel Dr IP24 ...**176** E5
Teasel Rd NR17 ...**174** B4
Teasel Rise **4** NR26 .**138** B6
Tebbutt Ave **6** NR19 .**154** C3
Ted Ellis Nature Reserve ★
  NR14 ....**91** D8
Tedder Cl
  5 Barnham IP24 ...**125** F6
  13 Watton IP25 ....**84** E3
Tee Cl **1** NR14 ....**89** B2
Telegraph La E NR1 .**163** B6
Telegraph La W **4** NR1 .**163** A6
Telford Cl
  King's Lynn PE30 ..**147** D4
  2 Norwich NR3 ...**157** F1
Telford Way IP24 ..**176** B6
Temple Cl NR25 ....**8** F6
Temple Dr NR25 ....**8** F6
Temple Rd
  Great Yarmouth NR30 .**169** D4
  King's Lynn PE30 ..**148** D1
  Norwich NR3 .....**158** D1
Templemere NR3 ...**159** A2
Templewood La NR25 .**137** B8
Ten Bell La NR2 ...**178** A3
Ten Mile Bank
  Hilgay PE38 ....**96** F6
  Littleport CB6 .....**96** E1
Ten Mile Bank Prim Sch
  PE38 ....**96** F7
Tennyson Ave PE30 .**146** E4
Tennyson Rd
  3 Diss IP22 .....**177** E4
  3 Great Yarmouth NR30 .**169** D8
  King's Lynn PE30 ..**146** F4
Tennyson Way IP24 .**176** B6
Tensing St NR35 ..**108** C5
Terence Airey Ct **25**
  IP20 ....**122** D2
Terence Ave NR7 ..**159** A4
Teresa Rd **6** NR12 ..**39** B4
Tern Cl **9** IP25 ....**84** C3
Tern Gdns NR31 ...**170** A6
Tern Rd NR29 .....**167** E5
Terr The **12** NR28 .**151** C5
Terrace Wlk NR1 ..**178** B1
Terrington Cl **3** PE14 .**59** D2
Terrington St Clements Sch
  PE34 ....**144** C4
Terrington St John Prim Sch
  PE14 ....**60** B8
Testerton Cotts NR21 .**32** A6
Texas Ave NR21 ...**15** C2
Texel Way NR11 ...**143** A7
Thacker Way NR5 .**160** B1
Thain's La NR27 ...**10** B5
Thames Way **8** NR30 .**168** C5
Thamesfield Way
  NR31 ....**169** B2
Thatchwood Ave PE14 .**59** C2
Theatre Plain NR30 .**169** C4
Theatre Rd NR23 ..**136** C5
Theatre St
  East Dereham NR19 .**154** D6
  Norwich NR2 .....**178** A2
  Swaffham PE37 ...**153** B4
Thelnetham Rd
  Blo' Norton IP22 ..**128** B8
  Hopton IP22 .....**127** F5
Themelthorpe Rd NR20 .**33** E1
Theobald Rd NR1 ..**89** E8
Thetford Ancient House
  Mus ★ IP24 ......**176** C4
Thetford Cottage Hospl
  IP24 ....**176** D4
Thetford Gram Sch
  IP24 ....**176** C4
Thetford Priory ★
  IP24 ....**176** C4
Thetford Rd
  Brandon IP27 ....**175** C3
  Coney Weston IP31 .**127** B4
  Euston IP24 .....**126** B4
  Garboldisham IP22 .**127** F8
  Northwold IP26 ...**99** B8
  Santon Downham IP27 .**115** B5
  Watton IP25 .....**84** D3
  Wretham IP24 ....**117** A2
Thetford Sta IP24 .**176** C5

Thetford Warren Lodge★ IP24 ... 115 E3
Thetford Way PE30 ... 148 C3
Thicket The 6 NR8 ... 155 E2
Thiefgate La PE34 ... 43 D2
Thieves' Bridge Rd PE33 ... 61 E5
Thieves' La
  Attleborough NR17 ... 174 E5
  Burgh & Tuttington NR11 ... 36 E6
  Little Ellingham NR17 ... 103 C8
Thieves La NR13 ... 55 A1
Third Ave PE13 ... 152 E5
Third Marsh Rd PE14 ... 59 A7
Thirlby Rd NR28 ... 151 D3
Thirlmere 18 NR9 ... 88 D8
Thistle Cl Norwich NR5 ... 160 F5
  3 Thetford IP24 ... 176 F5
Thistledown Rd NR10 ... 53 B2
Thomas Bole Cl IP22 ... 128 A8
Thomas Bullock Prim Sch ... 67 C2
Thomas Cl 4 PE33 ... 61 D5
Thomas Dix Ct NR28 ... 151 D5
Thomas Drew Cl PE31 ... 140 C3
Thomas Glover Ct NR6 ... 158 C2
Thomas Manning Rd IP22 ... 177 E4
Thomas Paine Ave 8 IP24 ... 176 C4
Thomas St NR3 ... 146 E3
Thomas Vere Rd NR7 ... 163 F7
Thomas Way NR30 ... 168 C6
Thomas Wyatt Cl NR2 ... 178 A1
Thompson Ave 7 NR25 ... 137 C5
Thompson Cl ... 50 B4
Thompson Prim Sch IP24 ... 102 B7
Thompson Rd
  Griston IP25 ... 85 A1
  Norwich NR7 ... 163 F8
Thompson's La PE33 ... 81 A2
Thompsons Yd NR3 ... 178 B4
Thor Cl NR7 ... 163 E7
Thor Loke NR7 ... 163 E7
Thor Rd NR7 ... 163 E7
Thoresby Ave PE30 ... 147 B4
Thoresby Coll PE30 ... 146 D4
Thorn La NR1 ... 178 B2
Thorn Rd Catfield NR29 ... 56 C8
  Fakenham NR21 ... 141 D4
Thornage Rd PE32 ... 137 A5
Thornham Cl NR7 ... 159 B2
Thornham Cnr PE36 ... 2 E2
Thornham Rd
  Methwold IP26 ... 99 A6
  Norwich NR7 ... 159 B2
Thornton Cl NR24 ... 142 E4
Thornycroft Gdns 1 NR33 ... 111 F1
Thoroughfare La NR29 ... 167 B4
Thoroughfare The IP20 ... 122 D2
Thorp Ct NR19 ... 154 D4
Thorpe Abbots Rd IP21 ... 131 A8
Thorpe Ave NR7 ... 163 E8
Thorpe Cl NR7 ... 163 F7
Thorpe Dr NR17 ... 174 D4
Thorpe Hall Cl NR7 ... 163 C5
Thorpe Hamlet Fst Sch NR1 ... 163 B6
Thorpe Hamlet Mid Sch NR1 ... 163 B6
Thorpe House Sch NR7 ... 163 C6
Thorpe Mews NR7 ... 163 F6
Thorpe Mkt Rd NR11 ... 21 E7
Thorpe Rd
  Haddiscoe NR14 ... 110 F8
  Norwich NR1 ... 178 C2
  Southrepps NR11 ... 22 A7
Thorpe St Andrew Sch NR7 ... 72 D4
Thorpeland Cl 4 PE33 ... 61 D3
Thorpeland La 3 PE33 ... 61 D3
Thorpland Rd NR21 ... 141 E6
Threadneedle St NR15 ... 91 A4
Three Acre La PE32 ... 164 C6
Three Cnr Dr NR6 ... 158 F6
Three King La NR2 ... 178 A3
Three Mile La NR5 ... 156 F1
Three Oaks PE30 ... 147 C3
Three Post Rd 5 IP25 ... 84 C3
Three Score Rd
  Colney NR5 ... 161 A5
  Norwich NR5 ... 160 F5
Threxton Rd IP25 ... 84 C3
Thrigby Hall Wildlife Gdns★ NR29 ... 75 E7
Thrigby Rd NR29 ... 75 E6
Throckmorton Yd 5 NR3 ... 162 E8
Thrush Cl 2 NR14 ... 89 B3
Thumb La NR20 ... 31 F2
Thunder La NR7 ... 163 E7
Thurgarton Rd NR11 ... 21 A5
Thurland's Dro PE14 ... 77 D5
Thurlby Rd NR5 ... 160 E8
Thurlin Rd PE30 ... 147 B4
Thurloe Pl PE13 ... 152 C2
Thurlow Cl NR5 ... 160 E8
Thurlton Prim Sch NR14 ... 92 F1

Thurlton Rd NR14 ... 110 B7
Thurne Rd NR29 ... 57 A2
Thurne Rise 2 NR29 ... 57 D5
Thurne Way NR29 ... 167 B3
Thurning Rd NR20 ... 33 E8
Thursford Collection★ ... 17 D5
Thursford Rd
  Great Snoring NR21 ... 17 A5
  Hindringham NR21 ... 17 E6
  1 Little Snoring NR21 ... 17 B3
Thursford Wood Nature Reserve★ NR21 ... 17 D4
Thurst Rd NR27 ... 11 A3
Thurston Cl 3 NR5 ... 160 F8
Thurston Prim Sch NR14 ... 91 D6
Thuxton Sta NR9 ... 68 C2
Thwaite Rd NR35 ... 109 A2
Thyme Cl
  Attleborough NR17 ... 174 B4
  Thetford IP24 ... 176 F5
Thynne's La NR20 ... 68 E5
Tibenham Rd NR15 ... 121 A4
Tiercel Ave NR7 ... 159 C4
Tillett Cl NR29 ... 167 C2
Tillett Rd NR3 ... 158 E2
Tills Cl NR6 ... 158 F4
Tills Rd NR6 ... 159 A5
Tilney All Saints Prim Sch PE34 ... 42 A4
Tilney Rd PE30 ... 69 C6
Tilney St Lawrence CP Sch PE34 ... 60 C8
Timber Rd NR11 ... 118 C5
Timberhill NR1 ... 178 B2
Time & Tide Mus★ NR30 ... 169 D2
Timothy Cl NR1 ... 163 B8
Timperley Est NR21 ... 31 B5
Tindall Cl PE13 ... 152 C8
Tinker's Dro PE13 ... 152 D7
Tinker's La NR15 ... 121 C4
Tinkers' La
  Garvestone NR9 ... 68 C1
  Strumpshaw NR13 ... 73 D1
Tintern Gr 4 PE30 ... 148 C4
Tippett Cl NR5 ... 160 F6
Tipton Cl NR9 ... 154 D2
Titchwell Marsh Nature Reserve★ PE31 ... 2 F1
Tithe Barn Cl IP26 ... 100 C5
Tithe Barn La NR24 ... 142 F3
Tithebarn La
  Marham PE33 ... 63 D6
  2 Thurlton NR14 ... 92 F1
Tithing Cl 2 IP24 ... 176 E5
Titlow Rd 28 IP20 ... 122 D2
Tittleshall Rd
  Litcham PE32 ... 48 A5
  Mileham NR20 ... 48 A8
  Tittleshall PE32 ... 48 C6
Tivetshall Cty Prim Sch NR15 ... 121 B5
Tivetshall Rd IP21 ... 121 D5
Toad Hole Cottage Mus★ NR29 ... 56 A6
Toad La
  Ditchingham NR35 ... 108 F5
  Great & Little Plumstead NR13 ... 72 F5
  Thwaite NR35 ... 109 A5
Todhunter Ave NR34 ... 110 C4
Todkill's La PE12 ... 41 C8
Toftes Pl 4 NR5 ... 161 B8
Toftwood Inf Sch NR19 ... 154 E1
Toftwood Jun Sch NR19 ... 154 E2
Tolhouse Mus★ NR30 ... 169 C3
Tolhouse St NR30 ... 169 C3
Toll Bar NR21 ... 141 A6
Tollgate Rd NR31 ... 169 C1
Tollgate Way NR5 ... 161 A5
Tollhouse Rd NR5 ... 161 E7
Tolwin Wlk 3 NR6 ... 158 F1
Tolye Rd NR5 ... 160 F7
Tombland NR3 ... 178 B3
Tooks Comm La NR34 ... 124 F5
Top Driftway IP24 ... 117 C8
Top Rd Belaugh NR12 ... 164 A6
  St Andrew, Ilketshall NR34 ... 124 C5
  Wicklewood NR18 ... 87 B4
  Wingfield IP21 ... 131 E3
Topcliffe Ave 2 NR13 ... 55 A1
Topshill Rd NR11 ... 21 E6
Torrey Cl PE31 ... 133 C5
Tortoishell Way NR18 ... 173 C4
Tottenham St 8 NR3 ... 169 D5
Tottington Cl 6 NR5 ... 160 F8
Tottington La PE22 ... 177 B4
Tottington Rd
  Little Cressingham IP25 ... 101 C8
  Thompson IP24 ... 102 A7
  Tottington IP24 ... 101 F7
Tower Cl Brandon IP27 ... 175 B3
  Costessey NR8 ... 156 C4
Tower Hill
  Costessey NR8 ... 156 C4
  Norwich NR7 ... 163 D6
Tower Hill Pk NR8 ... 156 C4
Tower La
  Middleton PE32 ... 44 D4
  Sidestrand NR27 ... 11 B3
Tower Mdws PE37 ... 153 C5
Tower Mill Rd NR35 ... 124 A8

Tower Pl 13 PE30 ... 146 D4
Tower Rd
  Burgh St Margaret (Fleggburgh) NR29 ... 57 C1
  Burnham Overy PE31 ... 135 E7
  Canadas NR11 ... 10 A4
  Elm PE14 ... 77 A7
  Hilgay PE38 ... 97 A8
  Repps with Bastwick NR29 ... 57 A5
  Terrington St Clement PE34 ... 144 C7
Tower St PE30 ... 146 D4
Town Bridge 25 PE13 ... 152 B5
Town Cl Corpusty NR11 ... 19 E1
  East Winch PE32 ... 44 F3
  Holt NR25 ... 137 B6
Town Cl House Prep Sch NR2 ... 162 C3
Town Cl Rd NR2 ... 162 C3
Town Cnr NR10 ... 53 C8
Town End NR11 ... 143 C6
Town Est PE38 ... 172 B5
Town Gn NR18 ... 173 B4
Town Gn Rd PE32 ... 84 E3
Town House La IP22 ... 128 B2
Town House Mus★ PE30 ... 146 D4
Town House Rd NR8 ... 156 F4
Town La Aylsham NR11 ... 150 C7
  Brancaster Staithe PE31 ... 3 D7
  Castle Acre PE32 ... 46 F2
  Garvestone NR9 ... 68 C2
Town Lands Trading Est NR31 ... 170 B7
Town Rd
  Burgh St Margaret (Fleggburgh) NR29 ... 57 C1
  Ingham NR12 ... 57 A7
Town St Outwell PE14 ... 77 D5
  Swanton Morley NR20 ... 50 B4
Town Wall Mews 9 NR30 ... 169 C5
Town Wall Rd NR30 ... 169 C5
Town Yd 4 NR25 ... 7 E6
Townlands NR9 ... 68 C2
Townley Cl PE14 ... 77 E5
Townley Prim Sch PE14 ... 95 A7
Townsend Gn N NR21 ... 141 F5
Townsend Rd
  Norwich NR4 ... 162 C1
  Upwell PE14 ... 77 A3
Townshend Cl 3 NR30 ... 169 D3
Townshend Gn E NR21 ... 141 F5
Townshend Gn W NR21 ... 141 F5
Townshend Pl 4 IP25 ... 67 C2
Townshend Rd
  Dereham NR19 ... 154 D7
  Wisbech PE13 ... 152 D6
Townshend Terr 2 PE30 ... 146 E6
Tracey La NR7 ... 159 E1
Trafalgar Ct
  Cliftonville NR5 ... 143 B7
  Great Yarmouth NR30 ... 169 D4
Trafalgar Ind Est PE38 ... 172 A4
Trafalgar Rd
  Downham Market PE38 ... 172 B4
  2 Great Yarmouth NR30 ... 169 D3
Trafalgar Rd E NR31 ... 170 D6
Trafalgar Rd W NR31 ... 170 C6
Trafalgar Sq NR30 ... 169 E3
Trafalgar St NR1 ... 178 B1
Trafford Est PE14 ... 59 C8
Trafford Pk 1 PE13 ... 152 E6
Trafford Rd
  Norwich NR1 ... 178 A1
  Wisbech PE13 ... 152 C5
Trafford Wlk NR13 ... 164 B2
Traice Rd NR16 ... 105 D2
Transport La NR14 ... 109 D7
Trap La NR21 ... 141 B6
Trelawny Rd 5 NR29 ... 57 D4
Tremaine Cl NR6 ... 157 E1
Trenchard Cres 4 IP25 ... 84 F3
Trenchard Sq IP26 ... 98 D1
Trendall Rd NR7 ... 159 C4
Trenowaths Pl 13 PE30 ... 146 D5
Trent V C CI IP26 ... 99 A5
Tretts Loke NR29 ... 57 C1
Trident Dr NR1 ... 163 A7
Trimingham Rd
  Gimingham NR11 ... 22 E8
  Trimingham NR11 ... 11 E1
Trimming Wlk NR8 ... 156 E8
Trinity Ave NR31 ... 170 B4
Trinity Cl NR19 ... 154 D4
Trinity Hospl (Bede House)★ PE31 ... 27 C1
Trinity Pl NR30 ... 169 D3
Trinity Rd
  Walpole Highway PE14 ... 59 F8
  Wisbech PE13 ... 152 E6
Trinity Sq 1 NR30 ... 169 D1
Trinity St NR2 ... 162 C5
Triple Plea La NR35 ... 108 B4
Triple Plea Rd NR35 ... 108 B4
Trix Rd NR2 ... 162 C4
Tropical Butterfly World★ NR11 ... 103 F5
Trory St NR2 ... 162 C4
Troston Rd IP31 ... 126 C1
Troutbeck 21 NR9 ... 88 D2

Trowse Prim Sch NR14 ... 163 B2
True's Yd Fishing Heritage Mus★ PE30 ... 146 D6
Truman Cl
  9 Norwich NR4 ... 161 C5
  Rackheath/Salhouse NR13 ... 72 F8
Trumpery La NR14 ... 90 C8
Trunch Hill IP20 ... 123 A7
Trunch Rd Denton IP20 ... 123 B6
  Mundesley NR28 ... 143 B4
  Swafield NR28 ... 22 E4
Tucker St NR27 ... 139 B7
Tucks Rd NR28 ... 38 A5
Tuckswood Ctr 4 NR4 ... 162 C1
Tuckswood Fst Sch NR4 ... 162 D1
Tuckswood La NR4 ... 162 D1
Tud La NR9 ... 69 E6
Tuddenham Rd NR11 ... 150 B6
Tudor Ave IP22 ... 177 A5
Tudor Cl IP24 ... 176 C2
Tudor Cres PE36 ... 132 D2
Tudor Way
  Dersingham PE31 ... 140 D4
  6 Mulbarton NR14 ... 89 B3
Tudor Wlk
  Great Yarmouth NR31 ... 170 C1
  12 Honington IP20 ... 126 B1
Tuesday Mkt Pl 5 PE30 ... 146 D5
Tuffen La IP22 ... 128 B4
Tulip Cl NR17 ... 174 C5
Tulip Tree Dr 5 NR4 ... 90 C5
Tumbler Hill PE37 ... 153 C6
Tumbleyhill Rd PE32 ... 46 C3
Tumbril La IP21 ... 131 D7
Tummel Way NR17 ... 174 C6
Tunbeck Cl IP20 ... 123 A3
Tunbeck Rd IP20 ... 123 A4
Tungate Cres NR4 ... 89 B8
Tungate Rd NR28 ... 151 A5
Tungate Way 6 NR12 ... 54 C6
Tunn St 4 NR21 ... 141 B4
Tunneys La NR35 ... 109 B2
Tunns Yd NR23 ... 136 D6
Tuns Rd PE37 ... 65 F4
Tunstall Cl 5 NR5 ... 161 A2
Tunstall Rd NR13 ... 74 F2
Tunstead La NR12 ... 164 D6
Tunstead Prim Sch NR12 ... 37 F1
Tunstead Rd
  Tunstead NR12 ... 37 E1
  1 Wroxham/Hoveton NR12 ... 164 C5
Turbine Way PE37 ... 153 B6
Turbo Rd NR21 ... 15 D2
Turbus Rd PE30 ... 146 E7
Turf Fen La NR29 ... 56 B5
Turf Lot Dro PE14 ... 95 B5
Turin Way NR31 ... 171 E4
Turkey La NR24 ... 19 D6
Turn The NR10 ... 53 A8
Turner Cl
  Ditchingham NR35 ... 109 B2
  5 Great Yarmouth NR30 ... 170 A4
  Wymondham NR18 ... 173 E5
Turner Rd NR2 ... 162 A7
Turner Way PE38 ... 172 E5
Turner's Cl PE34 ... 79 E8
Turnham Gn 10 NR7 ... 72 D4
Turning The NR26 ... 138 C6
Turnpike Cl Foxley NR20 ... 50 D8
  2 Wisbech PE13 ... 152 E6
Turnpike The
  Ashwellthorpe NR16 ... 106 A7
  Carleton Rode NR16 ... 105 D2
Tusser Rd NR8 ... 156 E8
Tusting Cl NR7 ... 158 F4
Tuttington Rd NR11 ... 150 F8
Tuttles La E NR18 ... 173 D6
Tuttles La W NR18 ... 173 B6
Tuxhill Chase PE34 ... 42 B4
Tuxhill Rd PE34 ... 42 B5
Twelveacre NR4 ... 161 F4
Twickenham Ave IP27 ... 175 B1
Twickenham Rd NR6 ... 158 B5
Twiss Cl 5 IP22 ... 129 D7
Two Acres 6 NR12 ... 54 C6
Two Fields Way 11 NR20 ... 50 E7
Two Furlong Hill NR23 ... 136 C5
Two Saints Cl NR12 ... 164 D7
Two Sisters Cl 6 PE12 ... 41 B8
Twrs The PE38 ... 172 C4
Twyford La NR20 ... 33 C3
Twyford Rd NR20 ... 33 A6
Tyndale PE30 ... 148 C5
Tyne Mews NR31 ... 168 C5
Tyrolean Sq NR31 ... 169 B4
Tyrrell's Rd 2 NR31 ... 169 B4

U

UEA Sportspark NR4 ... 161 D4
Ulfkell Rd IP24 ... 176 B2
Ullswater Ave
  Castle Rising PE30 ... 27 C1
  King's Lynn PE30 ... 148 F1
Ullswater Dr 20 NR9 ... 88 D8
Ulph Pl PE31 ... 135 D3
Uncle's La IP19 ... 124 B2
Unicorn Yd 2 NR11 ... 150 C6
Union Drift NR20 ... 68 A4
Union La
  4 King's Lynn PE30 ... 146 D4

V

Vale Cl 8 NR10 ... 53 B3
Vale Cl 5 IP27 ... 114 E1
Vale Gn NR6 ... 158 B1
Vale Rd High Kelling NR25 ... 8 E2
  Mundesley NR11 ... 143 A8
  Thurton NR14 ... 91 C3
Valentine Ct PE36 ... 132 C5
Valentine Rd PE36 ... 132 D4
Valentine St 3 NR2 ... 162 C6
Valerian Rise IP24 ... 116 D2
Valinger's Pl 6 PE30 ... 146 E4
Valingers Rd PE30 ... 146 E3
Valley Dr The NR1 ... 163 B8
Valley Gdns 1 NR28 ... 151 E5
Valley La NR25 ... 137 B5
Valley Rd Norwich NR5 ... 157 C1
  9 Tasburgh NR15 ... 106 F6
Valley Rise PE31 ... 140 C4
Valley Side Rd 1 NR1 ... 163 C8
Valley View NR19 ... 154 C6
Valley View Cres NR5 ... 157 A1
Valley Way NR21 ... 141 E4
Valleyside NR18 ... 173 C3
Valpy Ave NR3 ... 158 A1
Vancouver Ave PE30 ... 146 E3
Vancouver Rd 3 NR7 ... 163 C8
Vane Cl NR7 ... 72 D4
Vanguard Rd
  2 Great Yarmouth NR31 ... 94 C8
  Great Yarmouth NR31 ... 170 A8
Varsity Rd IP25 ... 84 C3
Varvel Ave NR7 ... 159 C4
Vassar Ct 6 NR20 ... 68 F6
Vaunce's La IP21 ... 131 B8
Vaunces La IP21 ... 131 B8
Vauxhall St NR2 ... 162 C5
Vauxhall Terr NR30 ... 169 C6
Vawdrey Rd NR8 ... 155 F1
Veltshaw Cl NR13 ... 133 B4
Venables Cl NR1 ... 163 B4
Venta Icenorum (Roman Town)★ NR14 ... 89 E6
Ventura Cl IP26 ... 98 F5
Vera Cl 10 NR13 ... 72 E7
Vera Rd
  New Rackheath NR13 ... 72 E1
  Norwich NR6 ... 158 B4
Verdon's La NR18 ... 87 F2

Union La continued
  Wortham IP22 ... 129 D5
Union Pl 17 PE13 ... 152 C5
Union Rd
  7 Great Yarmouth NR30 ... 169 D4
  Smallburgh NR12 ... 38 C3
Union St Norwich NR2 ... 178 A4
  4 Wisbech PE13 ... 152 C5
University Cres NR31 ... 170 B4
University Dr NR4 ... 161 C5
University of E Anglia
  Norwich NR6 ... 157 D4
  Norwich NR4 ... 161 C3
Unthank Rd NR4 ... 161 F2
Upgate NR14 ... 90 D5
Upgate Rd NR15 ... 108 E7
Upgate St
  Carleton Rode NR16 ... 105 A4
  Southery PE38 ... 97 B5
Uphalle PE38 ... 155 D1
Uplands Ave NR30 ... 168 D5
Uplands Pk NR26 ... 138 C6
Uplands Way IP22 ... 177 D5
Upper Breckland Rd NR5 ... 156 F1
Upper Brook La IP20 ... 131 E8
Upper Burnthouse La IP20 ... 131 E8
Upper Cliff Rd NR31 ... 170 D4
Upper Goat La NR2 ... 178 A3
Upper Grange Cres NR30 ... 168 D5
Upper Hall La NR24 ... 18 D8
Upper Harmans La IP20 ... 122 B1
Upper Kiln La NR15 ... 90 F4
Upper King St NR2 ... 178 B3
Upper Mkt 3 NR21 ... 141 B4
Upper Oakley IP21 ... 130 E4
Upper Olland St NR35 ... 124 A8
Upper Rose La IP22 ... 177 E2
Upper St Gissing IP22 ... 120 F4
  Salhouse NR13 ... 55 B2
Upper St Giles St NR2 ... 178 A3
Upper Stafford Ave NR5 ... 156 F1
Upper Staithe Rd 15 NR12 ... 38 B4
Upper Tumbril La
  Brockdish IP20 ... 131 D8
  Needham IP20 ... 122 A1
  Scole IP20 ... 131 D8
Upton Broad Nature Reserve★ NR13 ... 74 C8
Upton Cl NR4 ... 162 A3
Upton Dr PE37 ... 153 D2
Upton Rd Norwich NR4 ... 162 A3
  South Walsham NR13 ... 74 B8
Upton Way NR12 ... 24 C5
Uptons Way IP26 ... 82 A2
Upwell Prim Sch PE14 ... 77 D4
Upwell Rd PE14 ... 95 A7
Utopia Way NR12 ... 39 B3

Verdun Rd PE13 ....152 D5
Veronica Gn 9 NR31 ....170 B6
Vervain Cl 23 NR31 .....94 C6
Vetch Cl NR18 ....173 D4
Viburnum Way 6 NR31 .170 B6
Vicar St NR18 ....173 B4
Vicarage Cl
  Costessey NR8 ....156 F5
  Foulden IP26 ....82 A1
  1 Potter Heigham NR29 ...56 F6
Vicarage La
  Bungay NR35 ....124 C8
  Hoveton NR12 ....164 E5
Vicarage Mdws NR19 ..154 D4
Vicarage Rd
  Cromer NR27 ....139 B6
  Deopham NR18 ....86 D3
  East Ruston NR12 .....24 A3
  Foulden IP26 ....82 A2
  Hockham NR16 ....102 D3
  Norwich NR3 ....158 C1
  Paston NR28 ....143 D2
  Salhouse NR13 ....55 A2
  Sheringham NR26 ....138 C6
  Thetford IP24 ....176 D5
  Wingfield IP21 ....131 E3
  Worstead NR28 ....38 A5
Vicarage St NR28 .....151 C5
Vicarage Wlk 11 IP25 ...84 E3
Viceroy Cl PE31 ......140 C4
Victor Charles Cl IP27 .175 B7
Victoria Arc NR30 ....169 C3
Victoria Ave
  Brandon IP27 ....175 C3
  Hunstanton PE36 .....132 D5
Victoria Cl Diss IP22 ..177 E3
  Heacham NR12 ....133 E6
  Taverham NR8 ....156 C8
Victoria Cotts PE31 ...133 D6
Victoria Ct
  Sheringham NR26 ....138 E7
  22 Watton IP25 ....84 D3
Victoria Gdns 7 NR30 .169 D2
Victoria Hill IP23 .....130 C1
Victoria La
  Deopham NR18 ....86 F3
  Fakenham NR21 ......141 E4
  Victoria Pl 17 PE13 ..152 C4
  5 Great Yarmouth NR30 .169 D2
  Great Yarmouth NR31 .170 D3
  Mundesley NR11 .....143 C6
  3 Taverham NR8 .....155 C1
  Taverham NR8 ....156 C8
  Terrington St John PE14 .42 C2
  Wisbech PE13 ....152 C4
Victoria St
  Caister-on-Sea NR30 ..168 F4
  2 Downham Market
    PE38 ....172 A5
  Great Yarmouth NR30 ..169 D6
  Norwich NR1 ....178 A1
  Sheringham NR26 ....138 D7
Victoria Terr PE34 ....146 C4
Victoria Way NR5 ....157 B2
Victory La PE34 ....60 C8
Victory Rd
  Downham Market PE38 .172 B4
  Wisbech PE13 ....152 B3
Vienna Wlk NR19 ....154 C1
Viking Cl
  Great Yarmouth NR31 ..170 D2
  Swaffham PE37 ....153 D2
Viking Rd 1 NR6 ....94 C8
Village Cl 4 NR4 ......161 C5
Villarome NR30 ....168 C5
Villavon Way 4 NR13 ..73 D6
Villebois Rd PE33 .....63 B4
Vimy Dr NR18 ....173 D4
Vimy Ridge NR18 ....173 D4
Vince's Rd IP22 ......177 F4
Vincent Cl 6 IP26 .....98 E1
Vincent Cl 16 IP25 ....84 D3
Vincent Rd
  Norwich NR1 ....163 A7
  Sheringham NR26 ....138 E7
Vincents Rd NR9 ......69 A4
Vine Cl
  Coney Weston IP31 ...127 B5
  Hemsby NR29 ....167 B8
Vine Ct NR21 ....141 B4
Vine Hill PE34 ....61 C2
Vinery Cl 1 PE34 .....146 C5
Violet Cl
  Attleborough NR17 ...174 C5
  18 Great Yarmouth NR31 .94 C6
Violet Dr NR20 ......138 B6
Violet Elvin Ct NR5 ..161 F5
Violet Rd NR3 ....158 F1
Violet Way NR19 .....154 C4
Virginia Cl NR7 ......159 C4
Vong La Grimston PE32 ..28 B1
  Roydon PE32 ....45 A8
Vulcan Rd N NR6 ....158 C5
Vulcan Rd S NR6 .....158 C4

W

Waddington Ct 6 NR2 .162 B7
Waddington St NR2 ...162 B7
Waddling La NR32 ....111 F7
Wade Cl NR11 ....150 C5
Wadehall La NR34 ....111 B1
Wades Way NR28 ......22 E5

Wadham Cl NR31 .....170 B3
Wadham Rd NR31 ....170 B3
Waggon & Horses La
  NR3 ....178 B3
Wagtail Cl 2 NR31 ...170 A6
Wagtail Way IP24 ....176 D1
Wainford Mills Rd
  Bungay NR35 ....124 C8
  Wainford NR35 ......109 C1
Wainford Rd NR35 ...124 C8
Wakefield Cl NR5 ....161 C5
Wakehurst Cl 6 NR4 ..161 F1
Wakes La NR19 ......154 D5
Walcot Cl NR5 ....161 A7
Walcot Rd IP22 ......177 E6
Walcot Rise IP22 ....177 F5
Walcott Road N12 .....23 E4
Walcup's La PE32 .....29 D2
Waldeck Rd NR4 .....162 A3
Waldegrave 6 NR5 ...161 A8
Waldemar Ave NR6 ..158 B5
Waldemar Pk NR6 ...158 B5
Wales Bank PE14 ......59 A1
Wales Ct PE38 ....172 C5
Walk The
  Great Yarmouth NR31 ..170 B6
  Hickling NR12 ....39 F3
  Oulton NR11 ....35 A8
Walker St 1 PE30 ....146 E6
Walkers Cl PE31 .....135 D2
Walks The NR34 .....111 A4
Walkway The NR12 ...24 A7
Wall La PE31 ....29 C4
Wall Rd Erpingham NR11 .20 F3
  Norwich NR3 ....158 E2
Wallace Cl
  Dereham NR19 ......154 B6
  King's Lynn PE30 ....147 D4
Wallace Twite Way
  PE31 ....140 C3
Waller Cl NR13 ....72 D5
Wallers La NR20 ......33 C3
Wallgate La PE31 .....17 D5
Walnut Ave 5 PE33 ..43 E2
Walnut Ave N 2 PE33 .43 E2
Walnut Cl
  Brandon IP27 ....175 E2
  Foulden IP26 ....82 A2
  Hopton IP22 ....127 F5
  Taverham NR8 ......155 D2
Walnut Gr
  1 Fakenham NR21 ...141 E4
  Watton IP25 ....84 D4
Walnut Hill NR14 ....73 A1
Walnut Pl PE33 ....82 A5
Walnut Rd PE14 ......41 E4
Walnut Tree Ave 24
  NR29 ....57 D4
Walnut Wlk PE33 ....63 B4
Walnuts The
  Grimston PE32 ....28 B1
  Norwich NR4 ....162 A4
Walpole Bank PE14 ...41 C3
Walpole Cross Keys Prim Sch
  PE34 ....42 A6
Walpole Gdns 4 PE14 .178 A2
Walpole Highway Prim Sch
  PE14 ....59 F8
Walpole La PE14 ......41 F4
Walpole Rd
  Great Yarmouth NR30 ..169 D7
  King's Lynn PE30 ....146 E2
Walpole St PE30 .....178 A2
Walpole Way 8 PE33 ..43 E2
Walpole Wr Gdns ★
  PE14 ....41 E3
Walsham Cl 3 PE30 ..147 D5
Walsingham Abbey Grounds
  & Shirehall Mus ★
  NR22 ....16 F7
Walsingham Ct 2 PE13 152 A4
Walsingham Dr NR8 ..155 E3
Walsingham Prim Sch
  NR22 ....16 F8
Walsingham Rd
  Binham NR21 ....6 C1
  Burnham Thorpe PE31 .135 F2
  Grear Balsingham NR22 ..17 B8
Walsoken Rd PE14 ....59 D3
Walter Howes Cres
  PE32 ....44 C3
Walters Cl NR31 .....171 D5
Walters Rd NR8 .....156 C8
Walton Cl PE30 ......148 C4
Walton Rd
  Norwich NR1 ....162 A3
  St John's Fen End PE14 ...60 A5
  West Walton PE14 ...59 F5
  Wisbech PE13 ....152 E7
Waltons Way IP27 ...175 D2
Wangford Rd IP27 ....113 F3
Wansbrough Rd 10
  NR15 ....106 E3
Wanton La PE34 .....144 A5
Waples Way NR19 ...154 D3
Wapping NR29 ......167 A2
Warbler Cl 6 NR31 ...94 C7
Ward Rd NR13 ....55 B1
Ward's Chase PE34 ...79 B8
Wardley Hill Rd NR35 .109 D4
Warham Rd Binham NR21 ..6 D7
  Wells-next-the-Sea
  NR23 ....136 C4
Warham St Mary's Halt Sta
  NR23 ....5 F4
Waring Rd NR5 .....161 B6
Warner Ave NR19 ....154 E7

Warnes Cl 4 NR27 ....139 C6
Warnett Rd NR7 ......159 D1
Warren Ave
  Fakenham NR21 .....141 F4
  Norwich NR6 ....158 A5
Warren Cl
  Brandon IP27 ....175 D3
  High Kelling NR25 .....8 E3
  15 Horsford NR10 ....53 A3
  Thetford IP24 ....176 A3
  Watlington PE33 .....61 D5
Warren Ct 7 NR27 ...139 C6
Warren Dr NR11 .....143 B5
Warren Loke NR31 ....93 E3
Warren Pl 4 NR19 ...154 D1
Warren Rd
  Great Yarmouth NR31 .171 D8
  High Kelling NR25 ....8 E3
  Hopton on Sea NR31 .171 D5
  Shouldham PE33 .....62 D4
  Southrepps NR11 ....22 C6
Warren The
  Cromer NR27 ....139 C6
  Horsham St Faith &
    Newton St Faith NR10 .53 D2
  Little Snoring NR21 ..17 C3
  Norwich NR6 ....158 E4
Warren View NR14 ...109 D8
Warren's La NR17 ...174 C6
Warren's Rd PE34 ...145 D6
Warren's Way 5 NR16 .105 F5
Warrens Yd NR23 ....136 C4
Warstade Way PE37 .153 B4
Warwick Dr NR18 ...173 C5
Warwick St NR2 .....162 B5
Wash La Alburgh IP20 .122 E7
  Aslacton NR15 ....106 A1
  Banham NR16 ....119 D6
  Burgh St Peter NR34 .111 C4
  Clenchwarton PE34 ..145 E6
  Gissing IP22 ....120 E5
  Hales NR14 ....109 E6
  Hinderclay IP22 ....128 C4
  Howe NR15 ....90 C2
  Redgrave IP22 ......129 A5
  St Peter, South Elmham
    NR35 ....123 F3
  Saxlingham Nethergate
    NR15 ....107 D8
  Shelfanger IP22 .....120 B2
  Shotesham NR15 .....89 F1
  Topcroft NR35 ....108 A4
  Wacton NR15 ....106 B2
  Whissonsett NR20 ...31 E2
Wash National Nature
  Reserve The ★ PE30 ..26 B5
Wash Rd PE14 ....95 E4
Washbridge 10 NR19 .154 D5
Washpit Dro
  South Acre PE32 .....64 D8
  Swaffham PE37 .....153 C8
  West Rudham NR21 ...29 F6
Watch House Hill
  NR35 ....107 D8
Watch House La NR12 ..23 E4
Water End La PE32 ...48 D2
Water Gdns The PE13 .152 A5
Water La Barnham IP24 .125 E6
  Barsham NR21 ....16 F4
  Botesdale IP22 .....128 D1
  Cringleford NR4 ....161 D1
  Garboldisham IP22 .128 A8
  Great & Little Plumstead
    NR13 ....73 A5
  Ingham NR12 ....24 D2
  4 King's Lynn PE30 ..146 D5
  Letheringsett with Glandford
    NR25 ....8 A2
  Middleton PE32 ......44 C1
  Mundesley NR11 ....143 C4
  Neatishead NR12 ...55 E7
  Runton NR27 ....10 A5
  Thelnetham IP22 ....128 B5
  Thetford IP24 ....176 C4
Water Mdw Cl NR29 .167 A3
Water Mdw Way 2
  PE38 ....172 A6
Water Mill La IP21 ...131 A4
Water Moor La NR21 .141 C6
Water Sports Ctr PE34 .43 C3
Water Twr Rd NR14 ...88 E4
Waterbank Rd 10 NR26 .138 D7
Watercress La NR20 ...68 E6
Waterden Cl 5 PE30 ..147 A8
Waterfield Ave NR21 .141 D5
Waterfield Cl 2 NR21 .141 C5
Waterfield Mdws
  NR28 ....151 E5
Waterheath Rd NR34 .110 E5
Watering La PE33 .....43 E2
Watering Piece La
  NR29 ....56 C7
Watering Rd IP21 ....131 B1
Watering The 3 NR3 .162 D8
Wateringpit La IP22 ..55 A8
Waterlees Rd
  Walsoken PE13 ......59 A6
  2 Wisbech PE13 ....152 E7
Waterloo Ave 4 IP22 .129 D7
Waterloo Cl 3 NR10 ...53 D2
Waterloo Pk Ave NR3 .158 C1
Waterloo Pk Cl 6 NR3 .158 C1
Waterloo Rd
  Great Yarmouth NR30 .169 C2
  Hainford NR10 ....53 D6
  Horsham St Faith NR10 .53 E2

Waterloo Rd continued
  Norwich NR3 ....162 D8
Waterloo St 13 PE30 .146 E5
Waterlow Rd PE34 ...42 C4
Waterman Rd NR2 ...161 F7
Waterman's La PE38 ..79 D1
Waterman's Way PE38 .79 A4
Watermeadow Cl 3
  NR14 ....91 F1
Watermill Cl NR11 ....9 F1
Watermill Gn IP24 ..176 C3
Watermill La PE37 ...82 A6
Waters La NR29 .....167 A7
Watersfield Way
  NR19 ....154 D2
Waterside PE30 .....146 F7
Waterside The NR6 ..157 D3
Waterworks Rd
  Norwich NR2 ....162 A7
  Old Hunstanton PE36 .132 F7
Watery La
  Beeston with Bittering
    PE32 ....48 B3
  Grimston PE32 ....45 B8
  Guist PE32 ....33 A4
  Matlask NR11 ....20 C5
  Necton PE37 ....66 B4
  Scarning NR19 ......154 A1
  Shipdham IP25 ......67 C2
Wathen Way NR10 ...150 C1
Watkin Rd NR4 ....89 D7
Watling Cl NR30 .....168 E5
Watling Rd
  Attleborough NR17 ..174 F6
  Norwich NR7 ....159 D1
Watlings The NR19 ...67 B6
Watlington Prim Sch
  PE33 ....61 D5
Watlington Rd PE33 ..61 D6
Watlington Sta PE33 .61 D5
Watson Gr 9 NR2 ...162 B8
Watsons Cl NR31 ....171 E4
Watson-Watt Gdns
  NR11 ....143 A7
Wattlefield Rd
  Tacolneston NR16 ...105 C6
  Wymondham NR18 ...88 A1
Watton Jun Sch IP25 .84 D3
Watton Rd Ashill IP25 ..84 A6
  Barford NR9 ....69 C2
  Colney NR4 ....160 F4
  Great Cressingham IP25 .83 D4
  Great Ellingham NR17 .103 D8
  Great Melton NR9 ....70 B2
  Griston IP25 ....85 A2
  Hingham NR9 ....86 B5
  Hockham IP24 ......102 E4
  Larling NR16 ....118 A8
  Little Cressingham IP25 .83 F2
  Little Melton NR9 ...160 B4
  North Pickenham PE37 .83 C8
  Shipdham IP25 ......67 B1
  Shropham NR17 ....103 A4
  Stow Bedon NR17 ..102 D7
  Swaffham PE37 .....153 D2
  Thompson IP25 ....102 A8
Waunci Cres NR31 ..170 D2
Wavell Rd NR19 .....154 C7
Waveney Cl
  Hoveton NR12 ......164 E6
  Hunstanton PE36 ...132 D3
  Wells-next-the-Sea
    NR23 ....136 D4
Waveney Dr
  10 Belton NR31 ......94 A6
  Wroxham/Hoveton
    NR12 ....164 D5
Waveney Fst Sch NR31 .94 A5
Waveney Hill NR32 ..111 F3
Waveney Hts IP21 ...131 C6
Waveney Rd
  Bungay NR35 ....124 B8
  Diss IP22 ....177 E3
  Ditchingham NR35 ..109 B2
  Great Yarmouth NR31 .169 C1
  Hunstanton PE36 ....132 C3
  King's Lynn PE30 ...147 D5
Waveney Valley Swimming
  Pool NR35 ....124 B7
Waverley Rd NR4 ....162 A2
Waxham Cl IP22 .....40 A5
Waxham Rd NR12 ....40 B5
Waxworks 28 NR30 ..169 D4
Wayford Rd NR12 ....38 F4
Wayland Ave 4 IP25 .84 C3
Wayland Cl NR17 ...174 D5
Wayland Com High Sch
  IP25 ....84 D3
Wayland Ct NR17 ...174 C5
Wayland Hospl NR17 .174 A7
Wayland Rd NR17 ...103 C8
Wayland Way NR16 .119 D7
Wayland Wlk PE38 ..172 B2
Weasenham La 1 PE13 152 D2
Weasenham Prim Sch
  PE32 ....47 D8
Weasenham Rd
  Great Massingham PE32 .29 E1
  Litcham PE32 ....47 E7
Weatherby Rd NR5 ..160 D8
Weavers Cl 4 NR10 ..53 D2
Weavers Croft 8 IP20 .122 D2
Weavers Ct IP22 ....177 D5
Weavers View NR12 ..37 F1
Webb Dr 4 NR13 ....72 E7
Webbs Cl 2 NR28 ...151 E5
Webdell Ct 3 NR1 ...162 E1

Webster Cl
  5 Norwich NR5 .....161 B3
  8 Stoke Holy Cross NR14 ..89 F4
Webster Way NR30 ..168 D6
Wedgewood Ct NR31 .170 C3
Wedgwood Dr PE13 .152 D5
Weedon Way PE30 ..147 A8
Weeting Castle ★
  IP27 ....114 E8
Weeting Heath National
  Nature Reserve ★
  IP27 ....114 C7
Weeting VC Prim Sch
  IP27 ....175 B8
Welbeck Ave 8 NR29 ..57 D4
Welbeck Rd PE13 ...152 E4
Welborne Rd NR20 ...68 F5
Welden Rd NR19 ....154 B4
Welgate Cl 11 NR20 ..68 E6
Welgate Rd NR20 ....68 E5
Welholme's Cl 13 NR15 .106 E3
Well Cl NR9 ....51 A6
Well Creek Rd PE14 ..77 F6
Well End PE14 ....77 A7
Well Hall La PE32 ....45 A6
Well Hill NR19 ....68 C5
Well La NR9 ....51 A6
Well Loke NR3 ......158 B3
Well Medieval Village of ★
  PE32 ....45 B7
Well Opening 24 NR30 .169 D2
Well Rd Cantley NR13 ..92 D6
  Great Yarmouth NR30 .169 D2
Well St Docking PE31 .134 C5
  Great Yarmouth NR30 .169 D4
  Thetford IP24 ....176 D3
  Witton NR28 ....23 D3
Wellbeck NR15 ....90 F2
Wellbeck Rd NR15 ....91 A2
Wellesley Ave NR1 ..163 B7
Wellesley Ave N 4 NR1 163 B7
Wellesley Ave S NR1 .163 B6
Wellesley Fst Sch
  NR1 ....163 B7
Wellesley Rd
  Great Yarmouth NR30 .169 D5
  8 Long Stratton NR15 .106 D3
Wellesley St 11 PE30 .146 E5
Wellingham Rd
  Litcham PE32 ....47 F6
  Tittleshall PE32 .....48 A8
Wellington Cl
  Brandon IP27 ....175 D3
  Gimingham NR11 ....22 F4
Wellington Cres NR21 .15 C3
Wellington La NR2 ..162 C6
Wellington Pl 12 NR30 .169 D4
Wellington Rd
  Briston NR24 ....142 B4
  East Dereham NR19 .154 D5
  3 Feltwell IP26 ....98 E1
  Great Yarmouth NR30 .169 E2
  6 Long Stratton NR15 .106 D3
  Norwich NR2 ....162 B6
Wellington Terr 1
  PE13 ....152 C4
Wells Ave NR28 .....151 A3
Wells Cl 2 NR10 ....53 E5
Wells' La IP20 ......122 D1
Wells Maritime Mus ★
  NR23 ....136 D6
Wells next the Sea Prim Sch
  NR23 ....136 E5
Wells next the Sea Sta
  NR23 ....136 F4
Wells Rd
  Burnham Overy Staithe
    PE31 ....135 E2
  Fakenham NR21 .....141 B4
  Hindringham NR21 ..17 D5
  Needham IP20 ......122 C1
  North Creake NR21 ...4 D1
  Stiffkey NR23 ....6 C6
  Walsingham NR22 ..16 F8
  Wighton NR23 ....5 F3
Wellspring Rd NR11 ..22 C8
Welney Wildfowl Refuge ★
  PE14 ....95 F6
Welsford Rd
  5 Norwich NR4 ....89 D8
  Norwich NR4 ....162 B1
Weltons Loke NR9 ...52 A6
Wendene NR5 ....160 F7
Wendling Rd NR19 ...48 F2
Wendover Rd NR13 ...72 D8
Wenman Ct 5 NR5 ..160 F8
Wensom Cl 3 PE33 ..61 D6
Wensum Cres NR6 ..157 D3
Wensum Ct NR21 ....32 C6
Wensum Dr NR20 ....49 F7
Wensum Gdns 1 NR20 .50 B3
Wensum Mdws Mental
  Health Hospl NR6 ..157 D4
Wensum Mid Sch
  NR2 ....162 A7
Wensum Rd NR9 ....51 A4
Wensum St NR3 ....178 B3
Wensum Valley Cl
  NR6 ....157 D4
Wensum Way
  11 Belton NR31 ......94 A6
  2 Fakenham NR21 ..141 E4
Wensum Wlk NR8 ...155 F3
Wentworth Cl NR4 ..114 E1
Wentworth Gn NR4 .161 F2
Wereham Row PE33 ..80 D3
Wesley Ave PE34 ....144 B5

Wesley Cl
  Downham Market PE38 ..172 B5
  4 Mattishall NR20 ....68 E6
  Mundesley NR11 ....143 D5
  Terrington St Clement
    PE34 ....144 B5
Wesley Rd
  King's Lynn PE30 ......148 C5
  Terrington St Clement
    PE34 ....144 B5
Wessex St NR2 ....178 A1
West Acre Gdns★
  PE32 ....46 B4
West Acre Rd PE37 ...153 A6
West Ave
  Great Yarmouth NR31 ..170 C3
  Ormesby St Margaret
    NR29 ....167 A3
West Carr Rd NR17 ...174 A3
West Church St NR16 .119 A5
West Cl NR5 ....157 A5
West Cliff
  Cromer NR27 ....139 B7
  Sheringham NR26 ....138 D7
West Cres NR26 ......50 A5
West Croft NR9 ......88 C7
West Dereham Rd
  PE33 ....80 D3
West Dr Brandon IP27 .175 A2
  1 Friday Bridge PE14 ..77 A8
West Dro N PE14 .....59 D8
West Dro S PE14 .....59 E8
West Earlham Fst Sch
  NR5 ....161 D6
West Earlham Mid Sch
  NR5 ....161 D6
West End Briston NR24 142 F5
  Costessey NR8 ....156 C4
  Hilgay PE38 ....79 D1
  Northwold IP26 ....99 B8
West End Ave
  Brundall NR13 ....165 A4
  Costessey NR8 ....156 C5
West End Ct 6 IP25 ..84 C3
West End St NR2 .....162 B7
West Flegg Mid Sch
  NR29 ....57 D5
West Gate NR18 ......173 B4
West Hall Rd
  Dersingham PE31 ....140 D3
  Mundford IP26 ....100 B4
West Harling Rd NR16 .118 B4
West Head Rd PE34 ...78 F8
West Herne La IP22 ..128 D5
West La NR10 ....53 D1
West Lexham Hall
  PE32 ....47 C4
West Lynn Cty Prim Sch
  PE34 ....146 C5
West Parade
  Norwich NR2 ....162 B6
  Wisbech PE13 ....152 B7
West Pottergate NR2 .162 B6
West Raynham Prim Sch
  NR21 ....30 F4
West Raynham Rd
  NR21 ....30 F4
West Rd
  Caister-on-Sea NR30 ...168 D4
  Dersingham PE31 ....140 D3
  Great Yarmouth NR30 ..168 F1
  Norwich NR5 ....157 A4
  Ormesby St Margaret
    NR29 ....167 A2
  Shouldham Thorpe PE33 .62 C2
  Tacolneston NR16 ......105 F4
  Watton IP25 ....84 D3
  West Caister NR30 .....168 B4
West Runton Sta NR27 .10 A5
West St
  North Creake NR21 .....4 D1
  Wisbech PE13 ....152 C4
West Stree 18 NR19 ..169 D2
West Tofts Rd IP26 ..100 D3
West View
  Dereham NR19 ....154 E1
  South Pickenham PE37 ..83 D7
West View Dr NR12 ...74 A2
West View Rd NR13 ...165 E6
West Way
  Downham Market PE38 ..172 B4
  Stow Bardolph PE34 ....61 D1
  Tacolneston NR16 ......105 E5
  Wimbotsham PE34 ....79 D8
West Winch Prim Sch
  PE33 ....43 E2
West Winch Rd PE33 ..43 F4
West Wood Cotts NR21 .32 B5
Westacre Dr NR6 .....158 E7
Westbourne Rd NR12 ..54 D7
Westbriggs Dro PE33 .62 B5
Westbrook La 1 NR31 .170 B6
Westcliff Ave NR27 ..139 A7
Westerley Cl NR30 ...168 D4
Westerley Way NR30 ..168 D4
Western Ave NR7 .....163 C6
Western Bypass NR11 .150 B5
Western Cl 4 IP26 ..98 D1
Western Rd NR1 ......170 C4
Westfield Ave NR23 ..136 C6
Westfield Cl 7 PE33 .57 C1
Westfield Inf Sch IP25 .84 D3
Westfield La NR19 ...154 F1
Westfield Rd
  Brundall NR13 ....165 D4
  East Dereham NR19 .....154 E2
  Swaffham PE37 ....153 B4
  Wisbech PE13 ....152 E7

Westfields
  Attleborough NR17 .....174 B4
  King's Lynn PE30 ......147 C4
  Narborough PE32 ....63 E7
Westfields Cl
  Terrington St John PE14 .60 C8
  Tilney St Lawrence PE34 .42 C1
Westgate
  Hevingham NR10 ....53 B8
  Hunstanton PE36 ....132 C4
  Norwich NR6 ....157 F5
  Shropham NR17 ....103 B8
  Walsingham NR22 ....16 F8
Westgate Cl NR2 .....162 A4
Westgate Ct NR18 ....173 B4
Westgate Gn NR10 ....53 B8
Westgate Rd PE36 ....1 F6
Westgate St
  Hevingham NR10 ....52 B8
  Hilborough IP26 ....83 A3
  Holme next the Sea PE36 .2 A6
  Shouldham PE33 ....62 D4
  Southery PE38 ....97 A5
Westhall IP21 ....131 F1
Westhorpe Cl 3 PE38 .147 A8
Westland Chase PE33 .43 F1
Westlegate NR1 ......178 B2
Westmark PE30 ....147 C4
Westmead Ave PE13 ..152 E9
Westmead Rd PE13 ...141 C4
Weston Cl 1 NR13 ...73 C6
Weston Ct NR6 ....158 F6
Weston Miller Dr
  PE13 ....152 C7
Weston Rd Easton NR9 .70 A7
  Norwich NR3 ....158 C3
  17 Wisbech PE13 .....152 C4
Weston Rise NR30 ....168 D5
Weston Sq 8 NR25 ...137 B6
Weston Terr NR26 ....138 E7
Weston Wood Cl NR7 .163 E7
Weston Wood Rd NR7 .163 D7
Westry Cl PE13 ......59 C5
Westwick Dr NR28 ...151 A4
Westwick Rd NR28 ...37 F5
Westwick St NR2 ....178 A3
Westwood Dr NR6 ....157 D6
Westwood Gdns NR18 .173 A6
Westwood La NR21 ...32 B5
Weybourne Rd
  Bodham NR25 ....9 A3
  Sheringham NR26 ......138 B7
  Weybourne Sta NR25 ..8 F5
Weynor Gdns NR25 ...8 E5
Wharf St PE12 ......41 B8
Wharton Dr NR28 ....151 E7
Whartons La 5 NR18 .173 B3
Wheat Fields NR8 ...155 F2
Wheatacre Cl 9 NR10 .53 A3
Wheatacres PE14 ....176 D5
Wheatcroft Way NR20 .68 A8
Wheatfield Way NR15 .106 F4
Wheatfields
  Hillington PE31 ......28 B4
  Rickinghall Superior
    IP22 ....128 E2
Wheatley Bank PE14 .59 C5
Wheatley Dr NR30 ...148 B4
Wheatley Rd NR2 ....161 F7
Wheel Rd NR14 ......90 E4
Wheelbarrow La IP20 .123 F1
Wheeler Rd NR3 .....158 A1
Wheelers La NR15 ...108 E8
Wheelwright Rd PE30 .147 C5
Wheelwrights Cl NR13 .92 E8
Wherry Cl NR28 .....151 E7
Wherry Rd
  Bungay NR35 ....124 C8
  Norwich NR1 ....178 C1
Wherry Reach 2 NR13 .166 C4
Wherry Way NR30 ....169 C7
Whiffler Rd NR3 ....157 F2
Whimbrel Dr
  8 Great Yarmouth NR31 .94 C8
  1 Great Yarmouth NR31 .170 A4
Whimpell St NR2 ....24 C4
Whin Comm Rd
  Denver PE38 ....172 D1
  Tottenhill PE33 ......61 F6
Whinburgh Rd NR19 ..67 F3
Whinchat Way 3 NR31 .94 C7
Whinmere Rd NR12 ..39 E3
Whipp's La NR16 ....105 F7
Whisson Cl 1 PE30 ..147 A8
Whissonsett Rd NR20 .48 E8
Whistle Dro IP28 ...112 D1
Whitby St 3 PE13 ...152 C5
White City Rd PE14 ..78 D6
White Clover Rd 26 NR31 94 C6
White Cross
  Burgh & Tuttington NR11 .36 E4
  Hardingham NR9 ....86 E8
White Cross Rd PE37 .153 C4
White Farm La NR7 ..163 C6
White Gate La NR11 .11 D2
White Gates NR5 ....156 E1
White Hall Dr NR34 .146 C4
White Hart St
  2 Aylsham NR11 .....150 C7
  East Harling NR16 ....118 C5
  Foulden IP26 ....82 A2
White Heath Rd NR15 .91 B3
White Horse Dr PE31 .140 C4
White Horse La
  Bixley NR14 ....89 F8
  Trowse with Newton
    NR14 ....163 A1
  Worstead NR28 ....38 B6

White Horse St IP27 .175 A2
White House Ct NR3 .158 B3
White House Dr 23
  NR15 ....106 E3
White House Est
  NR27 ....139 D4
White House Farm La
  IP21 ....122 B2
White House Gdns 12
  NR14 ....90 D5
White House La NR17 .160 D2
White House Rd CB7 ..112 A7
White La PE33 ......63 A3
White Lion Rd
  Coltishall NR12 ......54 D6
  Wheatacre NR34 ......111 B4
White Lion St
  Holt NR25 ....137 B6
  Norwich NR2 ....178 A4
White Lodge Bsns Est
  NR4 ....89 E8
White Oaks PE37 ....65 E2
White Post Rd NR11 .21 D5
White Rd
  Barton Bendish PE33 ..63 D1
  Methwold IP26 ....99 A5
White Rose Cl NR5 ..161 D8
White Sedge PE30 ...147 A8
White St NR29 ......57 D5
White Woman La NR6 .159 A6
White Woman La Mid Sch
  NR6 ....158 F6
Whitecross La PE34 .144 E4
Whitedike Dro IP26 ..113 B8
Whitefriars NR3 ....178 B4
Whitefriars CE Prim Sch
  PE30 ....146 D3
Whitefriars Rd PE30 .146 D3
Whitefriars Terr PE30 .146 D3
Whitegates Cl 6 NR9 .88 D7
Whitegates Rd NR11 .22 B7
Whitehall Rd NR2 ...162 B5
Whitehall Yd 8 NR26 .138 D7
Whitehart La IP27 ..175 C4
Whitehart St 6 IP24 .176 C4
Whitehorse La NR17 .174 C5
Whitehorse Plain 7
  NR30 ....169 C5
Whitehorse St
  1 Fakenham NR21 ...141 C3
  Wymondham NR18 ......173 B3
Whitehouse La
  Earsham NR35 ....108 C1
  Wicklewood NR18 .....87 C4
Whitelands IP21 ....141 D5
Whiteplot Rd IP26 ..98 D5
Whitethorn Cl 6 NR6 .158 D5
Whiteway Rd PE31 ...135 B3
Whiting Rd NR4 .....162 D1
Whiting's La NR17 ..103 A6
Whitley Cl NR6 ....158 C6
Whitlingham La
  Whitlingham Ctry Pk★
    NR7 ....163 E4
  Whitlingham La NR14 .163 C4
Whitsands Rd PE37 ..153 A5
Whittington Hill PE33 .81 B3
Whittome Rd 1 PE38 .79 D1
Whitwell Rd
  Norwich NR1 ....163 A7
  Reepham NR10 ....149 A2
  Sparham NR10 ....51 B6
Whitwell St NR10 ...149 C5
Whitworth Ave 1 NR17 174 C5
Whytehead Gdns
  IP22 ....177 D4
Wick Farm Cl 3 IP25 .84 D3
Wick La NR29 ......57 D2
Wickhampton Rd NR13 .93 A8
Wicklewood Prim Sch
  NR18 ....87 B5
Wicklewood Rd NR18 .87 B6
Wickmere Rd NR11 ..20 C5
Wicks Yd 5 NR19 ...154 D5
Wiclewood Way PE31 .140 C3
Widgeon Cl NR31 ...170 A6
Wier Ave NR20 .....68 F6
Wigg Rd NR21 .....141 B6
Wiggenhall Rd NR4 .44 E2
Wiggenhall St Mary
  Magdalen Prim Sch
    PE34 ....61 B5
Wiggets La 1 NR11 .34 D7
Wiggs Rd NR14 ....110 F3
Wight Dr NR30 ....168 C6
Wightmans La NR10 .170 D5
Wighton Halt Sta NR23 .5 F3
Wigwam Hill IP22 ..129 C5
Wilberforce Rd
  Norwich NR5 ....161 B6
  Wisbech PE13 ....152 D5
Wilby Rd Norwich NR1 .162 E1
  Quidenham NR16 ......118 F8
Wild Flower Ctr★ NR25 .7 E4
Wild Radish Cl 18 NR14 .89 B3
Wild Rd NR3 ....158 D1
Wildbriar Cl PE33 ..43 E1
Wilde Rd 1 NR13 ...72 E7
Wilderness Cl 3 IP20 .122 D1
Wilderness La NR20 .122 D2
Wildfields Cl PE34 .145 C5
Wildfields Rd PE34 .145 C6
Wildflower Way NR35 .109 A2
Wilkins Ct NR5 ....161 C7
Wilkins Rd PE14 ...59 D1
Wilkinson Rd NR13 .72 E7
Wilks Farm Dr NR7 .159 A5
Willbye Ave IP22 ..177 E5

William Booth Rd
  PE30 ....147 D5
William Booth St NR2 .178 A4
William Brown Way 1
  IP22 ....177 A5
William Bush Cl NR10 .35 B2
William Childerhouse Way 6
  NR5 ....160 E2
William Cl 5 Watton IP25 84 D3
  6 Wymondham NR18 ..173 C6
William Cowper Cl
  NR19 ....154 E1
William Kett Cl NR1 .163 A6
William Marriot Mus★
  NR25 ....137 E8
William Marshall CE Prim
  Sch PE14 ....95 D4
William Mear Gdns
  NR1 ....163 B6
William O'Callaghan Pl 1
  NR19 ....154 D5
William Paston Rd
  NR28 ....151 D6
William Peck Rd 7 NR10 54 A2
William Rd
  Fakenham NR21 ....141 F5
  Wisbech PE13 ....152 C5
William St 9 PE30 ..146 E3
William Way NR19 ...154 C1
Williams Loke NR7 ..163 D8
Williams Way
  3 Holt NR25 ....137 C5
  5 North Walsham NR28 151 C6
Williamson Cl
  Diss IP22 ....177 D6
  Norwich NR7 ....159 C3
Williamson Cres 4
  IP24 ....176 C2
Williman Cl IP31 ...133 D6
Willis St NR3 ......178 B4
Willoughby Way 5 NR13 72 E7
Willow Ave NR31 ...94 C7
Willow Cl
  Brandon IP27 ....175 D2
  Lingwood NR13 ....74 A2
  Long Stratton NR15 ..106 E2
  10 Mattishall NR20 .68 E6
  Middleton PE32 ......44 B4
  North Walsham NR28 ..151 D7
  Wortwell IP20 ....123 A4
  Wymondham NR18 .....173 D5
Willow Cres 3 PE13 .63 B4
Willow Ct
  3 Attleborough NR17 .174 B5
  Beetley NR20 ....49 C4
Willow Dr
  Clenchwarton PE34 ...145 E5
  Dersingham PE31 .....140 D3
  King's Lynn PE33 ....43 F4
  Tilney All Saints PE34 .42 E4
  West Winch PE33 .....43 F1
Willow Gr
  East Dereham NR19 ...154 D2
  Sheringham NR26 ....138 E5
Willow Heath Rd PE33 .80 B7
Willow Herb Wlk 4
  NR18 ....173 E4
Willow La
  Bedingham NR35 .....108 B3
  Broome NR35 ....109 C3
  Carbrooke IP25 .....85 B5
  Norwich NR2 ....178 A3
Willow Pk PE30 ....147 C8
Willow Pl PE33 ....43 F4
Willow Rd
  Downham Market PE38 .172 B6
  East Dereham NR19 ...154 B4
  Hunstanton PE36 ....132 C3
  King's Lynn PE30 ....148 D2
Willow Way
  2 Ludham NR29 .....56 C5
  18 Martham NR29 ...57 D4
  Wisbech PE13 ....152 D3
Willow Wlk 5 IP20 ..122 D1
Willowbrook Cl 4 NR33 111 F1
Willows Ct 16 NR29 ..57 D4
Wilshere Ct 11 NR30 .169 D3
Wilson Dr 7 PE32 ..44 F3
Wilson Rd 6 NR1 ...163 B5
Wilson's Dro PE32 ..45 E3
Wilson's Way NR25 .7 D6
Wilton Cres 3 PE30 .146 E3
Wilton Rd Feltwell IP26 .98 E1
  Heacham PE31 ....133 C6
Wilton View NR28 ...151 D5
Wimbledon Ave IP27 .175 A1
Wimbledon Way 2
  PE38 ....172 B4
Wimbotsham Rd PE38 .172 C6
Wimpole Dr PE30 ...148 E1
Winceby Cl 15 NR7 ..72 D4
Winch Rd PE32 ....45 C5
Winchcomb Rd NR2 ..161 F7
Winchester Twr NR2 .178 A2
Winchester Way IP24 .176 B5
Windermere Rd NR15 .90 E2
Windermere Rd PE30 .148 F2
Windle The NR13 ...74 C5
Windmill Ave NR20 .68 A8
Windmill Cl
  7 Poringland NR14 .90 C4
  Thetford IP24 ......176 D5
Windmill Hill PE31 ..14 A3
Windmill La
  Costessey NR8 ......157 A4
  Syleham IP21 ....131 D4
  Wretham IP24 ....102 B1

Windmill Rd
  Gimingham NR11 ......22 F8
  1 Marham PE33 .....63 B4
  Norwich NR3 ....158 F2
  Worstead NR28 ......38 A6
  Wortwell IP20 ......123 A3
Windsor Ave NR30 ...169 D7
Windsor Chase NR28 .155 D1
Windsor Cl 7 IP24 ..125 F6
Windsor Cres PE31 ..133 C5
Windsor Ct 4 IP25 ..84 D3
Windsor Dr
  Dersingham PE31 ....140 D3
  Wisbech PE13 ....152 D8
Windsor Pk
  East Dereham NR19 ..154 D8
  2 King's Lynn PE30 .146 E3
Windsor Pk Gdns NR6 .159 A6
Windsor Rd
  Caister-on-Sea NR30 .168 E6
  Cantley NR13 ....92 C6
  King's Lynn PE30 ...146 E3
  Norwich NR6 ....158 A5
Windsor Rise NR26 ..132 C2
Windsor Rd 1 PE38 ..172 A5
Windsor Terr NR26 ..146 E3
Windsor Way NR31 ..170 B4
Windy Cres PE33 ...63 B3
Windy La NR15 .....107 B8
Windy Ridge PE33 ..63 B3
Winfarthing Ave PE30 .146 D3
Winfarthing Rd
  Banham NR16 ....119 D6
  Shelfanger IP22 ....120 B2
Wing's La NR20 ....33 B7
Wingate Way NR2 ...162 C2
Wingfield PE30 ....147 D5
Wingfield Rd
  Lakenheath IP27 ....113 E2
  Norwich NR3 ....162 D8
  Syleham IP21 ......131 D5
  Weybread IP21 .....131 F6
Wings Rd IP27 ....113 E1
Winifred Ct NR26 ..138 E7
Winifred Rd NR31 ..169 B3
Winifred Way NR30 .168 D8
Winmer Ave 6 NR29 .58 B6
Winn's Cl NR25 ....137 A7
Winners Wlk NR8 ...155 E3
Winsford Way NR5 ..157 C1
Winstanley Rd 21 NR7 .72 D4
Winston Churchill Dr
  PE30 ....147 C4
Winston Dr NR21 ...15 E6
Winter Gdns★ NR30 .169 E2
Winter Rd NR2 .....162 A6
Winterton Dures National
  Nature Reserve★
    NR29 ....58 B7
Winterton Fst Sch
  NR29 ....58 B6
Winterton Rd
  Hemsby NR29 ....167 B8
  Somerton NR29 .....57 F6
Wisbech & Fenland Mus★
  PE13 ....152 C4
Wisbech Castle★
  PE13 ....152 C4
Wisbech Gram Sch
  PE13 ....152 B5
Wisbech Rd
  King's Lynn PE30 ...146 D2
  Manea PE15 ....95 A2
  Nordelph PE38 .....78 A3
  Outwell PE14 ......77 F7
  Walpole PE14 ......41 D4
  Walsoken PE13 .....152 E8
  Welney PE14 ....95 D8
Wissey View IP26 ..100 B3
Wistaria Rd PE13 ..152 F7
Wisteria Cl NR20 ..154 F4
Witard Cl NR7 .....159 D1
Witard Rd NR7 ....163 D8
Withersdale Rd IP20 .123 A4
Withington St 1 PE12 .41 B8
Withy Way NR8 ....155 E1
Witton Cl
  Heacham PE31 .....133 C5
  Reedham NR13 .....92 F5
Witton Gn NR13 ...92 F5
Witton La NR13 ...165 A8
Wittons La IP21 ..131 A3
Wiveton Rd NR25 ..7 D6
Woburn St NR2 ....162 C5
Wodehouse Cl 1 NR12 39 B4
Wodehouse Ct 11 IP25 .84 D3
Wodehouse Rd
  Bacton NR12 ....23 D4
  Old Hunstanton PE36 .132 C4
Wodehouse St NR3 ..162 E1
Wolfe Rd NR1 .....163 B7
Wolferton Dr PE37 .153 B2
Wollaston Ave NR19 .154 D7
Wolseley Rd NR31 ..169 B2
Wolterton Pk★ NR11 .20 E2
Wolterton Rd NR11 .20 C2
Womersley Cl 5 NR1 .163 B4
Womersley Rd NR1 ..163 B7
Wood Avens Way
  NR18 ....173 E4
Wood Cl Brandon IP27 .175 D4
  Kenninghall NR16 ...119 A4
Wood Dalling Rd
  Guestwick NR20 ....34 A6
  Reepham NR10 .....149 C6

Wood Dene Sch NR11 ....9 F3
Wood Dr ⑪ Beetley NR20 .49 D4
⑪ Beetley NR20 ....49 D4
Wood Gn NR13 ....72 F8
Wood Hill NR8 ....156 D8
Wood La Aldeby NR34 ..110 E5
Bedingham NR35 ......108 C2
Bradenham IP25 ....66 D4
Bressingham IP22 .....119 E2
Bunwell NR16 ....105 D3
Burgh & Tuttington NR11 ..36 D5
Dickleburgh & Rushall
IP21 ....130 F6
Great Ellingham NR17 ..103 D8
Hepworth IP22 ....127 E2
Holme Hale IP25 ......66 B1
Honingham NR9 ....69 E8
Kelling NR25 ....8 C5
Little Ellingham NR17 ..86 B1
Long Stratton NR15 ...107 A4
Morley NR18 ....87 A1
Pulham Market IP21 ..121 E8
Scole IP21 ....130 F8
Starston IP20 ....122 C5
Strumpshaw NR13 ....73 F2
Swardeston NR14 .....89 C5
Thelnetham IP22 .....128 A2
Wicklewood NR18 .....87 B4
Wood Norton Rd
Foulsham NR20 ....33 C5
Stibbard NR21 ....32 E7
Wood Rising Rd NR9 ..86 A5
Wood St Norwich NR1 .178 A1
Wisbech PE13 ....152 B6
Wood St Rd NR29 .....56 B8
Wood View NR28 .....151 A4
Wood View Ct NR5 ...157 A2
Wood View Rd NR6 ...157 E5
Wood's La NR20 ....49 B8
Woodbastwick Rd
Blofield NR13 ....165 E7
Blofield Heath NR13 ..73 C6
Woodbastwick NR13 ..55 E1
Woodbine Cl
North Walsham NR28 ..151 F5
Potter Heigham NR29 ..56 F7
Woodbridge Way
PE30 ....147 D4
Woodcock Cl NR3 ....158 D3
Woodcock Cl PE34 ....61 B7
Woodcock Mews ④
NR31 ....170 A6
Woodcock Rd NR3 ....158 C3
Woodcock Rise IP27 ..175 F4
Woodcock's La NR9 ...88 A8
Woodcote Pk PE13 ...152 A4
Woodcroft Cl NR7 ....159 E2
Woodend Rd PE31 ...133 E5
Woodfarm La NR31 ...170 A2
Woodfield
Briston NR24 ....142 C4
① East Dereham NR19 ..154 D1
Woodfield Rd NR25 ..137 C7
Woodforde Rd NR7 ..159 D2
Woodfordes Brewery &
Visitors Ctr★ NR13 ..55 C2
Woodgate ⑫ NR4 ....89 B8
Woodgate La NR20 ...50 B3
Woodgate Rd NR20 ..50 A2

Woodgate Way PE31 ..134 F4
Woodhall Rd PE38 ....97 B8
Woodham Leas NR6 ..158 E6
Woodhill Rise NR5 ...161 C8
Woodhouse Cl ① NR26 .138 B6
Woodland Dr
Bungay NR35 ....124 A7
Ellingham NR35 .....109 E3
Norwich NR6 ....158 E6
Thorpe End NR13 ....72 D5
Woodland Farm Ind Units
NR10 ....53 A6
Woodland Gdns PE30 .148 D5
Woodland La NR24 ...142 F2
Woodland Rd NR6 ...157 E6
Woodland Rise
Sheringham NR26 ...138 E5
⑫ Tasburgh NR15 ...106 F6
Woodland Rise W
NR26 ....138 D4
Woodland View Mid Sch
NR10 ....54 A2
Woodland View Mobile Home
Pk NR10 ....53 D6
Woodlands
㉟ Harleston IP20 ...122 D2
⑦ Thorpe Marriott NR8 .155 B2
Woodlands Cl
Holt NR25 ....137 D7
④ Thetford IP24 ....176 E6
Woodlands Cres ① NR7 .72 D5
Woodlands Ct PE13 ..152 F7
Woodlands Dr IP24 ..176 D6
Woodlands Mid Sch
NR31 ....94 C6
Woodlands Rd NR5 ..157 A2
Woodlands Rise IP27 ..175 A2
Woodlands The IP25 ..84 A7
Woodlands Way Rd
NR12 ....55 D4
Woodlark Cl ② IP24 ..176 D2
Woodpecker Dr ⑧ IP25 .84 C3
Woodpecker Mews ⑤
NR31 ....170 A6
Woodrising Rd NR9 ..85 D4
Woodrow Ave NR25 ..137 B5
Woodrow La NR15 ...121 A8
Woodrow Pl NR1 ....163 B6
Woodruff Cl ③ NR6 ..158 D5
Woods Cl ③ NR9 .....88 C7
Woods End NR17 ....174 C4
Woodside
Burnham Market PE31 .135 A2
⑤ King's Lynn PE30 ..147 C4
North Walsham NR28 ..151 E4
Woodside Ave
Dersingham PE31 ...140 C5
Heacham PE31 .....133 D4
Woodside Cl
Attleborough NR17 ..174 C3
Dersingham PE31 ...140 C5
Woodside Ct NR7 ....174 C3
Woodside Fst Com Sch
NR7 ....159 E1
Woodside Fst Sch NR9 .88 D7
Woodside Pk NR17 ..174 C3
Woodside Rd NR7 ...159 E1
Woodstock La NR15 ..120 F8
Woodstock Way ③ NR29 .57 D4
Woodton Prim Sch
NR35 ....108 C5

Woodton Rd NR35 ....108 A7
Woodview NR28 ......38 A4
Woodview Cl IP25 ....84 C4
Woodview Rd NR9 ....70 B5
Woodward Cl PE33 ...62 D4
Woodward Rd NR3 ..158 B2
Woodwark Ave ③ PE30 .146 E6
Woodyard Cl ⑨ NR14 ..89 B3
Woodyard Sq The
NR35 ....108 C5
Wooll Dr NR28 ....151 D7
Woolner's La NR14 ..90 E7
Woolstencroft Ave
PE30 ....146 F7
Wootton Rd PE30 ...147 B7
Worcester Cl ③ NR29 .167 A2
Worcester Rd PE13 ..152 C7
Worcester Way
Attleborough NR17 ..174 E4
Great Yarmouth NR31 .170 B4
Wordsworth Cl PE38 ..172 D5
Wordsworth Gn IP24 .176 E7
Wordsworth Rd
② Diss IP22 ....177 E4
Norwich NR5 ....161 C6
Workhouse La
Foulsham NR20 ......33 D4
Tilney St Lawrence PE34 .42 C1
Upwell PE14 ....77 D4
Workhouse Rd NR12 ..38 C3
Worlds End NR13 ....74 C1
Wormegay Prim Sch
PE33 ....62 A6
Wormegay Rd
Blackborough End PE32 .44 C1
Wormegay PE32 ....62 D8
Worstead Prim Sch
NR28 ....38 A5
Worstead Rd NR28 ..38 B4
Worstead Sta NR28 ..37 F4
Wortham Cl ③ NR5 ..161 A8
Wortham Prim Sch
IP22 ....129 C4
Worthing Rd
North Elmham NR20 ..49 F7
Swanton Morley NR20 .50 B6
Wramplingham Rd
NR18 ....173 D8
Wren Cl Brandon IP27 .175 E3
Necton PE37 ....66 A3
Norwich NR4 ....161 E2
Wren Dr
② Great Yarmouth NR31 ..94 C7
Great Yarmouth NR31 .170 A6
Wrench Cl ④ NR11 ..150 D6
Wrench Rd NR5 .....161 D6
Wreningham Prim Sch
NR16 ....88 D1
Wrens The ① IP24 ..176 D2
Wretton Fen Dro PE33 .80 D1
Wretton Rd PE33 ....80 F2
Wretton Row PE33 ..80 E3
Wright Ave NR19 ...154 D1
Wright Cl NR30 ....168 E7
Wright Dr NR19 ....154 C4
Wright's Cl Holt NR25 .137 C7
North Walsham NR28 ..151 B4
Wright's La PE12 ....41 B8
Wright's Loke NR28 ..22 E5
Wright's Wlk ⑫ NR19 .154 D5
Wrights Cl NR11 ....150 C7
Wroe The PE14 ......59 C1

Wroo Rd NR17 ......103 F5
Wroughton Fst Sch
NR31 ....170 B6
Wroughton Mid Sch
NR31 ....170 B7
Wroxham Ave PE37 .153 C2
Wroxham Rd
Coltishall NR12 ......54 E6
Rackheath NR13 .....72 D8
Salhouse NR13 ......54 E2
Sprowston NR7 .....159 C5
Wroxham Sta NR12 .164 C6
Wyatt St PE30 ......146 E5
Wyatt Way IP24 ....176 B7
Wycliffe Rd NR4 ....161 D3
Wylde Croft NR8 ...155 D2
Wymans Way NR21 ..141 E5
Wymer Dr NR11 ....150 C4
Wymer St NR2 ......162 B6
Wymers La NR13 ....74 B8
Wymondham Abbey (rems)★
NR18 ....173 B3
Wymondham Abbey Sta
NR18 ....173 A3
Wymondham Coll NR18 .87 B1
Wymondham Heritage Mus★
NR18 ....173 C4
Wymondham High Sch
NR18 ....173 C5
Wymondham Leisure Ctr
NR18 ....173 C4
Wymondham Rd
Bracon Ash NR14 ....88 E2
Bunwell NR16 ......105 B5
East Carleton NR14 ..88 F4
Flordon NR15 ......106 C8
Kimberley NR18 ....87 B6
Morley NR18 ....87 A3
Wreningham NR16 ..88 B2
Wymondham NR18 .105 A8
Wymondham Sta
NR18 ....173 C2
Wyndfields ⑩ PE37 ..65 F4
Wyndham Pk NR27 ..10 C5
Wyndham St NR26 ..138 D7
Wyngates NR13 ....165 F6
Wynne's La PE34 ...145 C4

Y

Yallop Ave NR31 ....171 D8
Yare Cl
Caister-on-Sea NR30 .168 D6
Great Yarmouth NR30 .169 C6
Yare Rd NR31 ....94 A6
Yare Valley Dr NR4 .161 C2
Yare Valley Rise NR13 .165 C3
Yare View Cl NR13 ..92 F4
Yarmouth Bsns Pk
NR31 ....169 B2
Yarmouth Rd
Blofield NR13 ......165 F6
Broome NR35 ......110 C2
Brundall NR13 .....165 C5
Caister-on-Sea NR30 .168 E2
Corton NR32 ....171 D1
Dilham NR28 ....38 C4
Geldeston NR34 ...110 A3
Hales NR14 ....109 F8
Hemsby NR29 .....167 A6
Kirby Cane NR35 ...109 E3

Yarmouth Rd continued
Lound NR32 ....94 B3
Ludham NR29 ......56 C5
North Walsham NR28 .151 C4
Norwich NR7 ......163 E5
Ormesby St Margaret
NR29 ....167 C1
Postwick with Witton
NR13 ....165 A5
Raveningham NR14 ..110 B8
Stalham NR12 ......39 B3
Thurlton NR14 ......93 A1
Toft Monks NR34 ...110 E5
Worstead NR28 ....38 A6
Yarmouth Stadium
NR30 ....168 E2
Yarmouth Way NR30 .169 C3
Yarn Mews ② NR3 ..178 B4
Yarrington Way NR5 .160 E8
Yarrow Cl IP24 .....176 F5
Yarrow Rd Bintree NR20 ..33 D2
② Dereham NR20 ...68 A8
Yaxham CE Prim Sch
NR19 ....68 C6
Yaxham Rd
East Dereham NR19 .154 E4
Mattishall NR20 ....68 C6
Yaxham Sta NR19 ..68 A4
Yaxley Way NR5 ...161 A8
Yaxley's La NR11 ..150 C6
Yaxley's Rd NR30 ..169 B6
Yeats Way NR19 ...154 B6
Yelverton Cl NR6 ..157 D5
Yelverton Rd NR14 ..90 E5
Yesmere ⑯ NR14 ...89 B3
Yew Ct NR7 ....159 D4
Yew Tree Cl ㉔ NR31 ..94 C7
Yew Tree Ct NR20 ..69 B7
Yew Tree Rd NR17 ..174 C5
York Ave PE36 .....132 D5
York Gdns PE13 ...152 D6
York La ⑱ NR12 ....39 B4
York Rd ④ Cromer NR27 .139 D5
Great Yarmouth NR30 .169 D3
King's Lynn PE30 ..146 E3
Wisbech PE13 .....152 D6
York Row PE13 ....152 C5
York St NR2 ....162 B4
York Terr Cromer NR27 .139 D5
Wisbech PE13 .....152 C6
York Villa Cl NR29 ..75 E8
York Way IP24 ....176 B5
Youell Ave NR31 ...170 D1
Young's Cres NR13 ..92 E7
Young's Row PE12 ..41 A8
Youngman's La NR10 .37 C5
Youngmans Cl NR28 .151 D3
Youngmans La NR12 ..38 E6
Youngmans Rd NR18 .173 C8

Z

Zara Way NR19 ....154 C1
Zephyr Cl NR30 ....168 D7
Zig-Zag La NR15 ...108 C8
Zobel Cl NR3 ....157 F2
Zurich Cl NR31 .....171 E4